Lecture Notes in Computer Science 12645

More information about this subseries at http://www.springer.com/series/7409

Katharina Toeppe · Hui Yan ·
Samuel Kai Wah Chu (Eds.)

Diversity, Divergence, Dialogue

16th International Conference, iConference 2021
Beijing, China, March 17–31, 2021
Proceedings, Part I

Editors
Katharina Toeppe
Humboldt University of Berlin
Berlin, Germany

Hui Yan
Renmin University of China
Beijing, China

Samuel Kai Wah Chu
The University of Hong Kong
Hong Kong, Hong Kong

ISSN 0302-9743   ISSN 1611-3349   (electronic)
Lecture Notes in Computer Science
ISBN 978-3-030-71291-4   ISBN 978-3-030-71292-1   (eBook)
https://doi.org/10.1007/978-3-030-71292-1

LNCS Sublibrary: SL3 – Information Systems and Applications, incl. Internet/Web, and HCI

This Springer imprint is published by the registered company Springer Nature Switzerland AG
The registered company address is: Gewerbestrasse 11, 6330 Cham, Switzerland

Preface

Since last year's iConference our globalized world has been in turmoil: The Coronavirus, COVID-19 has changed our lives immensely – economically, ecologically, scientifically, and socially. The information sciences have never before been of so much importance. Increasing interest in scientific research by the majority population was just one outcome, leading to misinformation, fake news, and information overload. Our everyday work and social lives shifted as well: Working in home office became a new standard, video chat apps the new way to see friends, family, and coworkers.

Even though the world grew physically apart, new mental connections were formed. The 16th iConference was the second online conference in this series since 2005, but as the first iConference being planned in an online format from an early stage on, a plethora of new possibilities for scientific advancement and networking emerged. This abundance of new opportunities was mirrored by the conference theme of *Diversity, Divergence, Dialogue.*

Under this banner the 2021 iConference took place in Beijing, China, hosted by the Renmin University School of Information Resource Management.

The conference theme attracted a total of 485 submissions with 103 full research papers, 122 short research papers, and 63 posters. In a double-blind review process with an average number of two reviews per submission and two papers per reviewer 242 entries emerged, including 32 full research papers, 59 short research papers, and 48 posters. This selection was the result of a meticulous review process by 296 internationally renowned experts, with only 31% of the full research papers and 48% of the short research papers being chosen for presentation at the conference. 103 additional submissions were selected in case of the Workshops, the Sessions for Interaction and Engagement, the Virtual Interactive Sessions, the Doctoral Colloquium, the Early Career Colloquium, the Student Symposium, the Chinese papers, and the Archival Education.

The full and short research papers are published for the fourth time in Springer's *Lecture Notes in Computer Science* (LNCS). These proceedings are sorted into the following eleven categories, once again depicting the diversity of the iField: AI & Machine Learning, Data Science, Human-Computer Interaction, Social Media, Digital Humanities, Education & Information Literacy, Information Behavior, Information Governance & Ethics, Archives & Records, Research Methods, and Institutional Management. The conference posters are available at the *Illinois Digital Environment for Access to Learning and Scholarship* (IDEALS).

We would like to thank the reviewers immensely for their expertise and valuable review work and the track chairs for their hard work and vast expert knowledge. This conference would not have been possible without them. We wish to extend our gratitude to the full research paper chairs Daqing He from the University of Pittsburgh and

Maria Gäde from Humboldt-Universität zu Berlin, and the short research paper chairs Toine Bogers from Aalborg University and Dan Wu from Wuhan University.

Once again the iConference broadened the field of information science, forming and strengthening connections between scholars and scientists from all around the world in practicing *Diversity, Divergence, Dialogue*.

February 2021   Katharina Toeppe
                                                                   Hui Yan
                                                       Samuel Kai Wah Chu

Organization

Organizer

Renmin University of China, People's Republic of China

Conference Chairs

Yuenan Liu   Renmin University of China, People's Republic
                              of China
Bin Zhang   Renmin University of China, People's Republic
                              of China

Conference Honorary Co-chair

Sam Oh   Sungkyunkwan University, Korea

Program Chairs

Hui Yan   Renmin University of China, People's Republic
                              of China
Samuel Kai Wah Chu   The University of Hong Kong, People's Republic
                              of China

Local Arrangements Chairs

Jian (Jenny) Wang   Renmin University of China, People's Republic
                              of China
Hui Yan   Renmin University of China, People's Republic
                              of China
Minghui Qian   Renmin University of China, People's Republic
                              of China

Proceedings Chair

Katharina Toeppe   Humboldt-Universität zu Berlin, Germany

Full Research Paper Chairs

Daqing He   University of Pittsburgh, USA
Maria Gäde   Humboldt-Universität zu Berlin, Germany

Short Research Paper Chairs

Toine Bogers   Aalborg University, Denmark
Dan Wu   Wuhan University, People's Republic of China

Chinese Paper Chairs

Xiaobin Lu   Renmin University of China, People's Republic
                             of China
Qinghua Zhu   Nanjing University, People's Republic of China
Zhiying Lian   Shanghai University, People's Republic of China
Gang Li   Wuhan University, People's Republic of China

Poster Chairs

Atsuyuki Morishima   University of Tsukuba, Japan
Leif Azzopardi   University of Strathclyde, UK

Workshops Chairs

Yuxiang (Chris) Zhao   Nanjing University of Science and Technology,
                             People's Republic of China
Jiqun Liu   University of Oklahoma, USA

Sessions for Interaction and Engagement Chairs

Ming Ren   Renmin University of China, People's Republic
                             of China
Pengyi Zhang   Peking University, People's Republic of China

Virtual Interactive Session Chairs

António Lucas Soares   University of Porto, Portugal
Chern Li Liew   Victoria University of Wellington, New Zealand

Archival Education Chairs

Jian (Jenny) Wang   Renmin University of China, People's Republic
                             of China
Patricia Whatley   University of Dundee, UK

Doctoral Colloquium Chairs

Xiaomi An   Renmin University of China, People's Republic
                             of China
Anne Gilliland   University of California at Los Angeles, USA

Early Career Colloquium Chairs

Mega Subramaniam   University of Maryland, USA
Sohaimi Zakaria   Universiti Teknologi MARA, Malaysia

Student Symposium Chairs

Ian Ruthven   University of Strathclyde, UK
Yuelin Li   Nankai University, People's Republic of China
Yao Zhang   Nankai University, People's Republic of China

Doctoral Dissertation Award Chairs

Udo Kruschwitz   Universität Regensburg, Germany
George Buchanan   University of Maryland, USA

Conference Coordinators

Michael Seadle   iSchools Organization, USA
Clark Heideger   iSchools Organization, USA
Slava Sterzer   iSchools Organization, USA
Cynthia Ding   iSchools Organization, USA

Reviewers Full and Short Papers iConference 2021

Jacob Abbott
Amelia Acker
Noa Aharony
Shameem Ahmed
Isola Ajiferuke
Dharma Akmon
Bader Albahlal
Michael Albers
Daniel Alemneh
Hamed Alhoori
Wafaa Ahmed Almotawah
Sharon Amir
Lu An
Muhammad Naveed Anwar
Leif Azzopardi
Cristina Robles Bahm
Alex Ball
Syeda Batool
Edith Beckett
Ofer Bergman

Nanyi Bi
Bradley Wade Bishop
Toine Bogers
Erik Borglund
Christine L. Borgman
Ceilyn Boyd
Sarah Bratt
Jenny Bronstein
Jo Ann M. Brooks
Ricardo Brun
Sarah A. Buchanan
Julia Bullard
Christopher Sean Burns
Yu Cao
Daniel Carter
Vittore Casarosa
Biddy Casselden
Niel Chah
Yung-Sheng Chang
Tiffany Chao

Hsin-liang Chen
Hsuanwei Chen
Jiangping Chen
Chola Chhetri
Shih-Yi Chien
Yunseon Choi
Steven Siu Fung Chong
Barry Chow
Rachel Clarke
Johanna Cohoon
Mónica Colón-Aguirre
Anthony Joseph Corso
Kaitlin Costello
Andrew Martin Cox
Hong Cui
Amber L. Cushing
Mats Dahlstrom
Dharma Dailey
Gabriel David
Rebecca Davis
Shengli Deng
Bridget Disney
Brian Dobreski
Philip Doty
Jennifer Douglas
Helmut Hauptmeier
Kedma Duarte
Patrick Dudas
Emory James Edwards
Lesley Farmer
Yuanyuan Feng
Fred Fonseca
Helena Francke
Henry A. Gabb
Maria Gäde
Chunmei Gan
Daniel Gardner
Rich Gazan
Tali Gazit
Yegin Genc
Patrick Golden
Koraljka Golub
Michael Gowanlock
Elke Greifeneder
Melissa Gross
Michael Robert Gryk

Ayse Gursoy
Stephanie W. Haas
Jutta Haider
Lala Hajibayova
Ruohua Han
Susannah Hanlon
Preben Hansen
Jennifer Hartel
Jiangen He
Zhe He
Alison Hicks
Shuyuan Mary Ho
Kelly M. Hoffman
Chris Holstrom
Liang Hong
Jiming Hu
Kun Huang
Yun Huang
Gregory Hunter
Charles Inskip
Joshua Introne
Isa Jahnke
Hamid R. Jamali
David Jank
Wei Jeng
Tingting Jiang
Jenny Johannisson
Michael Jones
Nicolas Jullien
Jaap Kamps
Jeonghyun Kim
Kyung Sun Kim
Vanessa Kitzie
Emily Knox
Kyungwon Koh
Kolina Sun Koltai
Rebecca Koskela
Ravi Kuber
Jin Ha Lee
Kijung Lee
Lo Lee
Myeong Lee
Noah Lenstra
Aihua Li
Daifeng Li
Kai Li

Sue Yeon Syn
Jian Tang
Rong Tang
Yi Tang
Carol Tenopir
Andrea Karoline Thomer
Kentaro Toyama
Aaron Trammell
Chunhua Tsai
Tien-I Tsai
Yuen-Hsien Tseng
Pertti Vakkari
Frans Van der Sluis
Merce Væzquez
Nitin Verma
Julie Walters
Hui Wang
Jieyu Wang
Lin Wang
Xiangnyu Wang
Xiaoguang Wang
Yanyan Wang
Ian Watson
Jingzhu Wei
Brian Wentz
Michael Majewski Widdersheim
Rachel Williams
R. Jason Winning
Dietmar Wolfram
Maria Klara Wolters
Adam Worrall
Dan Wu
I-Chin Wu
MeiMei Wu
Peng Wu
Qunfang Wu

Lu Xiao
Iris Xie
Juan Xie
Jian Xu
Lifang Xu
Shenmeng Xu
Xiao Xue
Erjia Yan
Hui Yan
Lijun Yang
Qianqian Yang
Seungwon Yang
Siluo Yang
Ying (Fred Ying) Ye
Geoffrey Yeo
Ayoung Yoon
JungWon Yoon
Sarah Young
Liangzhi Yu
Xiaojun Yuan
Marcia L. Zeng
Xianjin Zha
Bin Zhang
Chengzhi Zhang
Chenwei Zhang
Jinchao Zhang
Mei Zhang
Ziming Zhang
Yang Zhao
Yuxiang (Chris) Zhao
Lihong Zhou
Xiaoying Zhou
Qinghua Zhu
Xiaohua Zhu
Zhiya Zuo
林五

Contents – Part I

AI and Machine Learning

Understanding the Evolution of the Concept of Artificial Intelligence
in Different Publication Venues 3
  Lianjie Xiao, Weiwei Jiang, Kai Qin, and Ying Ding

Understanding Team Collaboration in Artificial Intelligence
from the Perspective of Geographic Distance 14
  Xuli Tang, Xin Li, Ying Ding, and Feicheng Ma

Something New Versus Tried and True: Ensuring 'Innovative'
AI is 'Good' AI 24
  *Stephen C. Slota, Kenneth R. Fleischmann, Sherri Greenberg,
  Nitin Verma, Brenna Cummings, Lan Li, and Chris Shenefiel*

Insights from People's Experiences with AI: Privacy
Management Processes 33
  Kristin Walters and Daniela M. Markazi

People's Perceptions of AI Utilization in the Context of COVID-19 39
  Daniela M. Markazi and Kristin Walters

Characterizing Dementia Caregivers' Information Exchange on Social
Media: Exploring an Expert-Machine Co-development Process 47
  *Zhendong Wang, Ning Zou, Bo Xie, Zhimeng Luo, Daqing He,
  Robin C. Hilsabeck, and Alyssa Aguirre*

Bimodal Music Subject Classification via Context-Dependent
Language Models 68
  Kahyun Choi

Spatio-Temporal Deepfake Detection with Deep Neural Networks......... 78
  Andrey Sebyakin, Vladimir Soloviev, and Anatoly Zolotaryuk

Data Science

A Knowledge Representation Model for Studying Knowledge Creation,
Usage, and Evolution 97
  Zhentao Liang, Fei Liu, Jin Mao, and Kun Lu

Biomedical Knowledge Graph Refinement and Completion Using Graph
Representation Learning and Top-K Similarity Measure   112
   Islam Akef Ebeid, Majdi Hassan, Tingyi Wanyan, Jack Roper,
   Abhik Seal, and Ying Ding

Comparison of Data Analytics Software Usage in Biomedical and Health
Sciences Research: A Case Study   124
   Fei Yu and Nandita S. Mani

Semantic Shifts Reveal the Multipurpose Use of Potential
COVID-19 Treatments   137
   Baitong Chen, Qi Yu, Yi Bu, and Ying Ding

Producing Web Content Within Platform/Infrastructure Hybrids   146
   Daniel Carter

Aggregation and Utilization of Metadata for Intangible Folk Cultural
Properties Using Linked Open Data   154
   Itsumi Sato and Masao Takaku

Post-GDPR Usage of Students' Big-Data at UK Universities   165
   Carolyn Fearn and Kushwanth Koya

Understanding Parachuting Collaboration   183
   Ajay Jaiswal, Meijun Liu, and Ying Ding

Characterizing Research Leadership Flow Diffusion: Assortative Mixing,
Preferential Attachment, Triadic Closure and Reciprocity   190
   Chaocheng He, Guiyan Ou, and Jiang Wu

An Author Interest Discovery Model Armed with Authorship Credit
Allocation Scheme   199
   Shuo Xu, Ling Li, Liyuan Hao, Xin An, and Guancan Yang

Human-Computer Interaction

Hybrid Research on Relevance Judgment and Eye Movement for Reverse
Image Search   211
   Dan Wu, Chenyang Zhang, Abidan Ainiwaer, and Siyu Lv

A Comparative Study of Lexical and Semantic Emoji Suggestion Systems . . .   229
   Mingrui "Ray" Zhang, Alex Mariakakis, Jacob Burke,
   and Jacob O. Wobbrock

Smile! Positive Emojis Improve Reception and Intention to Use
Constructive Feedback   248
   Chulakorn Aritajati and Mary Beth Rosson

"They Each Have Their Forte": An Exploratory Diary Study of Temporary
Switching Behavior Between Mobile Messenger Services.   268
   Florian Meier, Amalie Langberg Schmidt, and Toine Bogers

Appealing to the Gut Feeling: How Intermittent Fasters Choose Information
Tab Interfaces for Information Acquisition   287
   Hyeyoung Ryu and Seoyeon Hong

Evaluating an mHealth Application: Findings on Visualizing Transportation
and Air Quality.   301
   Pattiya Mahapasuthanon, Niloofar Kalantari, and Vivian Genaro Motti

Immersive Stories for Health Information: Design Considerations
from Binge Drinking in VR   313
   *Douglas Zytko, Zexin Ma, Jacob Gleason, Nathaniel Lundquist,
   and Medina Taylor*

Engagement and Usability of Conversational Search – A Study
of a Medical Resource Center Chatbot.   328
   Tamás Fergencs and Florian Meier

Hey Alexa, What Should I Read? Comparing the Use of Social
and Algorithmic Recommendations for Different Reading Genres   346
   Huiwen Zhang, George Buchanan, and Dana McKay

The Moderating Effect of Active Engagement on Appreciation
of Popularity in Song Recommendations   364
   Mark P. Graus and Bruce Ferwerda

Social Media

Attracting Attention in Online Health Forums: Studies of r/Alzheimers
and r/dementia   377
   Olivia A. Flynn, Abinav Murugadass, and Lu Xiao

Repurposing Sentiment Analysis for Social Research Scopes: An Inquiry
into Emotion Expression Within Affective Publics on Twitter During
the Covid-19 Emergency   396
   Chamil Rathnayake and Alessandro Caliandro

Fine-Grained Sentiment Analysis of Political Tweets with Entity-Aware
Multimodal Network   411
   Li Yang, Jianfei Yu, Chengzhi Zhang, and Jin-Cheon Na

An Examination of Factors Influencing Government Employees to Adopt
and Use Social Media   421
   Bader Albahlal

Digital Humanities

Digital Humanities Scholarship: A Model for Reimagining Knowledge
Work in the 21st Century   435
   Alasdair Ekpenyong

Understanding the Narrative Functions of Visualization in Digital
Humanities Publications: A Case Study of the *Journal
of Cultural Analytics*   446
   Rongqian Ma, Kai Li, and Daqing He

A Comparative Studies of Automatic Query Formulation in Full-Text
Database Search of Chinese Digital Humanities   457
   Chengxi Yan, Tzu-Yi Ho, and Jun Wang

Improving Measures of Text Reuse in English Poetry: A TF–IDF
Based Method   469
   Wenyi Shang and Ted Underwood

Identifying Creative Content at the Page Level in the HathiTrust Digital
Library Using Machine Learning Methods on Text and Image Features   478
   Nikolaus Nova Parulian and Glen Worthey

Semantics Expression of Peking Opera Painted Faces Based
on Color Metrics.   490
   Guancan Yang, Shuang Gao, Zeyu Feng, Lingling Wang, and Yidan Xu

A Semantic Framework for Chinese Historical Events Based on Linked
Data and Knowledge Graph   502
   Hao Wang, Yueyan Li, and Sanhong Deng

Concept Identification of Directly and Indirectly Related Mentions
Referring to Groups of Persons.   514
   Anastasia Zhukova, Felix Hamborg, Karsten Donnay, and Bela Gipp

Education and Information Literacy

Promoting Diversity, Equity, and Inclusion in Library and Information
Science through Community-Based Learning   529
   Alex H. Poole

Embracing the Diversity: Teaching Recordkeeping Concepts to Students
from Different Cultural and Linguistic Backgrounds   541
   Viviane Frings-Hessami

Exploring Interdisciplinary Data Science Education for Undergraduates:
Preliminary Results   551
   Fanjie Li, Zhiping Xiao, Jeremy Tzi Dong Ng, and Xiao Hu

Pre-service Librarians' Perspective on the Role of Participatory Design
in Libraries with Youth   562
  Kung Jin Lee, Jin Ha Lee, and Jason C. Yip

A Pilot Ethnographic Study of Gamified English Learning Among Primary
Four and Five Students in a Rural Chinese Primary School   575
  Na Meng, Shum Yi Cameron Lee, and Samuel Kai Wah Chu

Multidisciplinary Blockchain Research and Design: A Case Study
in Moving from Theory to Pedagogy to Practice.   587
  Chelsea K. Palmer, Chris Rowell, and Victoria L. Lemieux

How Asian Women's Intersecting Identities Impact Experiences
in Introductory Computing Courses.   603
  Mina Tari, Vivian Hua, Lauren Ng, and Hala Annabi

Societal Information Cultures: Insights from the COVID-19 Pandemic.   618
  Gillian Oliver, Charles Jeurgens, Zhiying Lian,
  Ragna Kemp Haraldsdottir, Fiorella Foscarini, and Ning Wang

Locating Embodied Forms of Urban Wayfinding: An Exploration.   635
  Rebecca Noone

Author Index   645

Contents – Part II

Information Behavior

"We Can Be Our Best Alliance": Resilient Health Information Practices
of LGBTQIA+ Individuals as a Buffering Response to Minority Stress   3
   Valerie Lookingbill, A. Nick Vera, Travis L. Wagner,
   and Vanessa L. Kitzie

Pregnancy-Related Information Seeking in Online Health Communities:
A Qualitative Study.   18
   Yu Lu, Zhan Zhang, Katherine Min, Xiao Luo, and Zhe He

COVID-19 Epidemic Information Needs and Information Seeking Behavior
of Overseas Chinese Students.   37
   Lin Wang, Ziqiao Ma, and Yuwei Jiang

Demographic Factors in the Disaster-Related Information
Seeking Behaviour   48
   Rahmi Rahmi and Hideo Joho

Information Practices of French-Speaking Immigrants to Israel:
An Exploratory Study   66
   Yohanan Ouaknine

How the Intellectually Humble Seek and Use Information   75
   Tim Gorichanaz

Gamification as a Way of Facilitating Emotions During Information-
Seeking Behaviour: A Systematic Review of Previous Research   85
   Amira Ahmed and Frances Johnson

The Dark Side of Personalization Recommendation in Short-Form
Video Applications: An Integrated Model from Information Perspective.   99
   Jing Li, He Zhao, Shah Hussain, Junren Ming, and Jie Wu

Effects of Question Type Presentation on Raised Questions in a Video
Learning Framework 114
   Hinako Izumi, Masaki Matsubara, Chiemi Watanabe,
   and Atsuyuki Morishima

The Impact of Question Type and Topic on Misinformation and Trolling
on Yahoo! Answers. 127
   Pnina Fichman and Rachel Brill

Counteracting Misinformation in Quotidian Settings   141
    Abdul Rohman

Towards Target-Dependent Sentiment Classification in News Articles   156
    Felix Hamborg, Karsten Donnay, and Bela Gipp

What Are Researchers' Concerns: Submitting a Manuscript
to an Unfamiliar Journal   167
    Chang-Huei Lin and Jeong-Yeou Chiu

German Art History Students' Use of Digital Repositories: An Insight.   176
    Cindy Kröber

Information Governance and Ethics

Encouraging Diversity of Dialogue as Part of the iSchools Agenda   195
    Simon Mahony and Yaming Fu

No Longer "Neutral Among Ends" – Liberal Versus Communitarian
Ethics in Library and Information Science   207
    David McMenemy

Identification of Biased Terms in News Articles by Comparison
of Outlet-Specific Word Embeddings.   215
    Timo Spinde, Lada Rudnitckaia, Felix Hamborg, and Bela Gipp

The Model of Influence in Cybersecurity with Frames.   225
    Philip Romero-Masters

Data and Privacy in a Quasi-Public Space: Disney World as a Smart City . . .   235
    Madelyn Rose Sanfilippo and Yan Shvartzshnaider

Research on the Decision-Making Process of Civil Servant Resisting Open
Data Based on Perceived Risks.   251
    Si Li and Yi Chen

Open Government Data Licensing: An Analysis of the U.S. State Open
Government Data Portals   260
    Xiaohua Zhu, Christy Thomas, Jenny C. Moore, and Summer Allen

Information Systems as Mediators of Freedom of Information Requests   274
    Daniel Carter and Caroline Stratton

Archives and Records

Towards a Human Right in Recordkeeping and Archives   285
    Kathy Carbone, Anne J. Gilliland, Antonina Lewis, Sue McKemmish,
    and Gregory Rolan

Is This Too Personal? An Autoethnographic Approach to Researching
Intimate Archives Online   301
  Jennifer Douglas

Assessing Legacy Collections for Scientific Data Rescue   308
  Hilary Szu Yin Shiue, Cooper T. Clarke, Miranda Shaw,
  Kelly M. Hoffman, and Katrina Fenlon

Multi-generational Stories of Urban Renewal: Preliminary Interviews
for Map-Based Storytelling.   319
  Myeong Lee, Mark Edwin Peterson, Tammy Dam, Bezawit Challa,
  and Priscilla Robinson

The Politics of Digitizing Art and Culture in Vietnam: A Case Study
on Matca Space of Photography in Hanoi   327
  Emma Duester

Creating Farmer Worker Records for Facilitating the Provision
of Government Services: A Case from Sichuan Province, China   339
  Linqing Ma and Ruohua Han

Case Study on COVID-19 and Archivists' Information Work   348
  Deborah A. Garwood and Alex H. Poole

Research Methods

A Meta-review of Gamification Research   361
  Ping Zhang, Jian Tang, and Eunmi (Ellie) Jeong

Research Agenda-Setting in Medicine: Shifting from a Research-Centric
to a Patient-Centric Approach   374
  Ania Korsunska

Conducting Quantitative Research with Hard-To-Reach-Online
Populations: Using Prime Panels to Rapidly Survey Older Adults During
a Pandemic   384
  Nitin Verma, Kristina Shiroma, Kate Rich, Kenneth R. Fleischmann,
  Bo Xie, and Min Kyung Lee

Collaborative Research Results Dissemination: Applying Postcolonial
Theory to Indigenous: Community Collaboration in Research
Results Dissemination   394
  Lisa G. Dirks

Studying Subject Ontogeny at Scale in a Polyhierarchical
Indexing Language   404
  Chris Holstrom and Joseph T. Tennis

Characterizing Award-Winning Papers in Library and Information Science
(LIS): A Case Study of LIS Journals Published by Emerald Publishing   413
   Yi Chen, Shengang Wang, and Li Yang

Institutional Management

Becoming Open Knowledge Institutions: Divergence, Dialogue
and Diversity   431
   Katie Wilson, Lucy Montgomery, Cameron Neylon,
   Rebecca N. Handcock, Richard Hosking, Chun-Kai (Karl) Huang,
   Alkim Ozaygen, and Aniek Roelofs

Toward Context-Relevant Library Makerspaces: Understanding the Goals,
Approaches, and Resources of Small-Town and Rural Libraries   441
   Soo Hyeon Kim and Andrea Copeland

The Historical Development of Library Policy in the State of Oregon:
Discussions on Library Management by Special Districts   458
   Issei Suzuki and Masanori Koizumi

Importance of Digital Library Design Guidelines to Support Blind
and Visually Impaired Users: Perceptions of Key Stakeholders   466
   Iris Xie, Rakesh Babu, Shengang Wang, Tae Hee Lee,
   and Hyun Seung Lee

Usage of E-books During the COVID-19 Pandemic: A Case Study
of Kyushu University Library, Japan   475
   Mei Kodama, Emi Ishita, Yukiko Watanabe, and Yoichi Tomiura

Image-Building of Public Library from Readers' Perspective: A Case Study
on the Northern Haidian Library   484
   Tianji Jiang and Linqi Li

Development and Evaluation of a Digital Museum of a National Intangible
Cultural Heritage from China   493
   Xiao Hu, Jeremy Tzi-Dong Ng, and Ruilun Liu

Author Index   503

AI and Machine Learning

Understanding the Evolution of the Concept of Artificial Intelligence in Different Publication Venues

Lianjie Xiao[1,2] (iD), Weiwei Jiang[3]([✉]) (iD), Kai Qin[1] (iD), and Ying Ding[4] (iD)

[1] Nanjing University, Nanjing 210023, China
[2] Jiangsu Key Laboratory of Data Engineering and Knowledge Service, Nanjing 210023, China
[3] Nanjing University of Finance and Economics, Nanjing 210023, China
luckyjww@163.com
[4] The University of Texas at Austin, Austin, TX 78705, USA

Abstract. This study aims to clarify the contours of artificial intelligence (AI) and present how it has evolved in different publication venues in the different stages of its development. Based on the noun phrases extracted from scientific papers of AI, the authors constructed the co-occurrence network of noun phrases to visualize the context of AI. There exists a tension between the original descriptive concept of AI as defined initially in the workshop at Dartmouth College and the relatively recent, vague, and extensible concept of AI. AI is used as a technique or boundary object by different scientific publication venues. This paper creatively applies the boundary object theory to clarify the contours of the concept of AI. Besides, the results will bridge the gap between different stakeholders (e.g., AI researchers, government policy makers, and business entities) in different communities together and promote the efficient and effective discussion and communication about AI.

Keywords: Artificial Intelligence · Publication venues · Boundary object · SpaCy · Noun phrases · Co-occurrence network

1 Introduction

Artificial intelligence (AI) is one of the most booming disciplines in recent years. According to the *AI Index 2019 Annual Report* [1] published by Stanford University in 2019, the proportion of AI papers published in the worldwide has tripled from 1998 to 2018. They accounted for 3% of peer-reviewed journal publications and 9% of published conference papers by 2018. However, with the increasing width of researchers' interests and the broader implementation of AI in our lives, the contours of AI have changed over time, and become more and more vague compared to its original descriptive concept defined by McCarthy, Minsky, and other scientists at a seminal workshop held at Dartmouth College in 1956. They coined the initial concept of AI, which is to simulate human's intelligence by using machines. This workshop promoted the development of AI in later years. Over time, different researchers have been trying to define what is AI. For example, Bellman [2] summarized AI as the automation of machine activities related

© Springer Nature Switzerland AG 2021
K. Toeppe et al. (Eds.): iConference 2021, LNCS 12645, pp. 3–13, 2021.
https://doi.org/10.1007/978-3-030-71292-1_1

to human thinking, such as decision-making, problem solving and learning. Winston [3] outlined AI as a study of computation, which could teach machines to perceive, reason and act. Minsky [4] defined AI as the science that is dedicated to enabling machines to obtain intelligence like human beings when performing tasks.

Based on the definitions of AI proposed by previous researchers, Russel and Norvig [5] described that the definitions of AI could be divided to two binary dimensions. The two dimensions are shown in Table 1.

Table 1. Four categories of the definitions of AI [5]

	Bound rationality	Entire rationality
Thinking	Machines think like humans	Machines think rationally
Behavior	Machines act like humans	Machines act rationally

The line of "Thinking" describes the machines' thinking process and reasoning (mainly focus on methods and techniques), and the line of "Behavior" pays attention to the machines' behavior (mainly focus on tasks and applications). In addition, the column of "Bound Rationality" takes human as a reference to measure the performance of machines, and the column of "Entire Rationality" focuses on one of the characterizes of humans – rationality.

The four categories of the definition of AI inspired us to ask: what is the concept of AI, and how it has evolved over time in different publication venues? Does each publication venue have its preference for AI "Thinking" or "Behavior"?

To address these questions, we first designed experiments to present the concept of AI and its evolution over the time in three publication venues by visualizing the co-occurrence networks of noun phrases. Then, we applied the boundary object theory to help clarify the concept of AI. The results of our study can bridge the gap between different stakeholders (e.g., AI researchers, government policy makers, and business entities) in different publication venues together and promote the effective discussion and communication about AI.

2 Methodology

2.1 Data Set

We selected two top conferences of AI: AAAI Conference on Artificial Intelligence (AAAI, H5-index = 124) and Annual Conference on Neural Information Processing Systems (NeurIPS, H5-index = 192). The former focuses on interdisciplinary data science and the latter on neural information processing. Additionally, we selected one international conference that mainly pays attention to bioinformatics, i.e. the IEEE International Conference on Bioinformatics and Biomedicine (BIBM, H5-index = 8).

As a heterogeneous graph that updates in one week, Microsoft academic graph (MAG)[1] provides metadata sources for the conference papers and data extraction tool named as Azure Data Lake Analytics (DLA)[2] by using U-SQL. Based on MAG, records (e.g., title, authors, abstract, year, references, citations) of a total number of 24,858 papers published in AAAI, NeurIPS, and BIBM were observed. The distribution of the number of papers for each conference in our experiment is shown in Fig. 1 and Table 2.

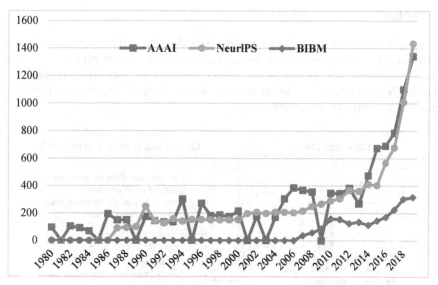

Fig. 1. Distribution of the number of AI papers in different publication venues

Table 2. Statistics of papers in three AI-related conferences

Publication venue	No. of papers	Timeline
AAAI	10,946	1980 to 2019
NeurIPS	9,794	1987 to 2019
BIBM	4,118	2007 to 2019

Since not all the papers in BIBM are related to AI, we had to filter out the papers focus on AI research by using AI research topic keywords in a designed dictionary. The dictionary contains 249 keywords in nine research subfields of AI [6], including natural language processing, knowledge representation and reasoning, planning, and

---

[1] Arnab Sinha, Zhihong Shen, Yang Song, Hao Ma, Darrin Eide, Bo-June (Paul) Hsu, and Kuansan Wang. 2015. An Overview of Microsoft Academic Service (MAS) and Applications. In Proceedings of the 24th International Conference on World Wide Web (WWW'15 Companion). ACM, New York, NY, USA, 243–246. DOI = https://dx.doi.org/10.1145/2740908.2742839.

[2] https://azure.microsoft.com/en-us/services/data-lake-analytics/.

scheduling, information retrieval, robotics, intelligence agents, computer vision, deep learning, and machine learning. If the title or abstract of one paper contains any one of the keywords in the dictionary, then this paper shall be appended to the set of AI papers. After applying this filter rule to all the papers of BIBM, we obtained a total of 2034 papers, which can be treated as AI research papers in the field of bioinformatics and biomedicine.

2.2 Method

As Fig. 2 demonstrates, we first executed the data cleaning and preprocessing by using a designed regular expression. Then, we applied the industrial strength natural language processing python package spaCy[3] to extract the noun phrases from the papers we collected. Next, we used the social network theory to guide the construction of co-occurrence networks of noun phrases.

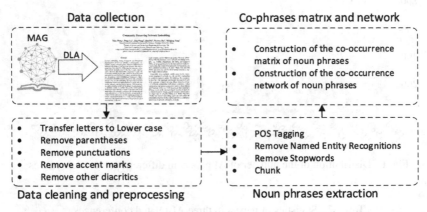

Fig. 2. The methodological framework of our study

Noun Phrases Extraction. Since most of the papers we collected from the three AI conferences do not have keywords, we need to extract the keywords first. In our study, we prefer phrases over single words. Keywords are terms that consists of one word or several consecutive words. To the best of our knowledge, only a single word sometimes will lead to misunderstanding. For instance, when using terms like "decision tree" in a scientific publication, the single word "decision" and "tree" can only express their designated meanings and are easily cause misleading if used separately. Also, they might be too general, e.g. words like "machine" and "learning" are not specific enough to distinguish "machine learning" from "learning machine". Therefore, unlike the prior researches, we apply noun phrases as the nodes of the co-occurrence networks constructed in the subsequent subsection.

---

[3] https://spacy.io/.

Data Cleaning and Preprocessing. To automatically extract the noun phrases, we first clean up and preprocess the title and abstract of papers. Hence, the following list provides the filter rules for the data cleaning and preprocessing, which are:

- Transfer all the letters to lower case.
- Remove the parentheses (e.g., '[]', '{}', '()') and the content inside them (e.g., abbreviation).
- Removing punctuations, accent marks, and other diacritics except for comma and period.
- Removing special characters (e.g., '/', '\', '_', '$', '...', ' > ', ' ≥ ', ' < ', ' ≤ ', ' = ').

Noun Phrases Extraction. We extracted the noun phrases from the sentences based on the open resource of natural language processing package NLTK,[4] spaCy, and scispaCy.[5] NLTK and spaCy are popular and widely used open resource natural language processing python libraries. They provide multiple powerful text processing pipelines for different text analysis tasks. scispaCy is a python library built upon spaCy, which was developed by Allen Institute for Artificial Intelligence (AI2) in 2019. It is trained on biomedical and scientific papers and outperforms the state-of-the-art language models on natural language processing tasks, such as part of speech (POS) tagging, dependency parsing, and named entity recognition. The pipelines in our experiments are shown as below.

- Tokenization (sentence tokenize, and word tokenize)
- Entity extraction
- Lemmatization. We lemmatize every word to its base form according to the dictionary provided by WordNet.
- Remove Stop words.
- Remove the target Named Entity Recognition. (e.g., PERSON, ORG, GPE, LOC, DATE, TIME, PRECENT)

According to Wikipedia [7] and Russell and Norvig's research [5], we divide the history of AI to seven stages, they are the gestation of AI (1952–1956), the first golden years of AI (1957–1974), the first winter of AI (1974–1980), the booming of AI (1980–1987), the second winter of AI (1987–1993), the smooth transition of AI (1993–2011), and the new era of AI (2011-onward).

Since the earliest AAAI conference was held in 1980, we will focus the concept of AI and its revolution in different publication venues in the latter four stages.

Noun Phrase Co-occurrence Matrix and Co-occurrence Network. Let k_{ij} be the number of co-occurrence of two different noun phrases p_i and p_j in the same conference among all AI papers. Specifically, if two different noun phrases p_i and p_j co-occur in one paper, then the value of k_{ij} will add 1, so do the rest of papers. Then, the noun phrase co-occurrence matrix(k_{ij}) could be constructed as soon as the iteration was finished, and

---

[4] https://www.nltk.org/.
[5] https://spacy.io/universe/project/scispacy.

$k_{ij} = k_{ji}$, $k_{ii} = 0$. If a noun phrase appears more than one time in the title or abstract, count them once.

The positive mutual information (PPMI) was considered to calculate the value of k_{ij} in our experiments. The equations were shown as Eq. 1 and Eq. 2.

Pointwise mutual information.

$$PMI(p_i, p_j) = \log_2 \frac{P(p_i, p_j)}{P(p_i)P(p_j)} \tag{1}$$

Positive pointwise mutual information.

$$PPMI(p_i, p_j) = \max(\log_2 \frac{P(p_i, p_j)}{P(p_i)P(p_j)}, 0) \tag{2}$$

where $P(p_i, p_j)$ represents the probability of co-occurrence of noun phrase p_i and noun phrase p_j, $P(p_i)$ indicates the probability of occurrence of noun phrase p_i, and $P(p_j)$ indicates the probability of occurrence of noun phrase p_j. The value of $PPMI(p_i, p_j)$ represents the degree of co-occurrence of noun phrase p_i and noun phrase p_j, and the larger the $PPMI(p_i, p_j)$, the stronger association of co-occurrence between noun phrase p_i and noun phrase p_j will be.

Although the frequency of noun phrase is commonly used to construct the co-occurrence matrix, it may be biased by most high frequent phrases. For instance, assuming there are 10,000 papers, the frequency of noun phrase p_1 is 8,000 and the frequency of noun phrase p_2 is 6,000, their probability of occurrence is 0.80 and 0.60, respectively. The number of co-occurrence of noun phrase p_1 and noun phrase p_2 is 5,000, the probability of their co-occurrence and the PPMI are 0.50 and 0.06, respectively. The frequency of noun phrase p_3 is 3,000 and the frequency of noun phrase p_4 is 3,000, their probability of occurrence is 0.3 and 0.3, respectively. The number of co-occurrence of noun phrase p_3 and noun phrase p_4 is 2,000, the probability of their co-occurrence and the PPMI are 0.2 and 1.15, respectively. Although the number of co-occurrence of noun phrase p_3 and noun phrase p_4 is smaller than that of noun phrase p_1 and noun phrase p_2, their association degree of co-occurrence seems much stronger.

We exported the nodes data and the edges data of the co-occurrence matrix(k_{ij}), and imported them into Gephi 0.9.2[6] to visualize the co-occurrence networks of noun phrases. In the co-occurrence network of noun phrases, the nodes represent the noun phrases and the edges represent their co-occurrence relationship. The scale of nodes indicates how many nodes they connect to, and the width of edge between two nodes indicates the PPMI values between them.

3   Results and Discussion

3.1   Co-occurrence Network of Noun Phrase of AI in Different Stages

As shown in Fig. 3, the concept of AI can mainly be defined by the top 5 frequent noun phrases in the context of AAAI between 1980 and 1987. The top 5 frequent noun

---

[6] https://gephi.org/.

phrases are "knowledge representation", "knowledge acquisition", "logic", "inference", and "reasoning". Also, we can describe the concept of AI from the top 5 frequent noun phrases in the context of AAAI between 1988 and 1993. Figure 4 shows the top 5 frequent noun phrases are "knowledge", "logic", "knowledge representation", "reasoning" and "knowledge base".

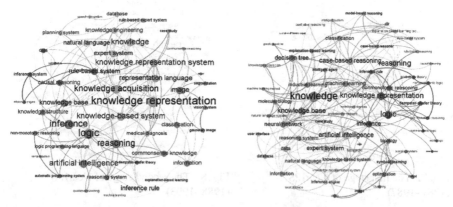

Fig. 3. The first stage of AAAI (1980–1987)   **Fig. 4.** The second stage of AAAI (1988–1993)

As illustrated in Fig. 5, the selected top 5 frequent noun phrases used for defining AI in the context of AAAI between 1994 and 2011 are "machine learning", "datasets", "data mining", "inference" and "knowledge representation". From Fig. 6, we can find that the concept of AI can mainly be defined by the top 5 frequent noun phrases in the context of AAAI between 2012 and 2019. They are "computer vision", "embedding", "deep neural network", "convolutional network" and "deep learning".

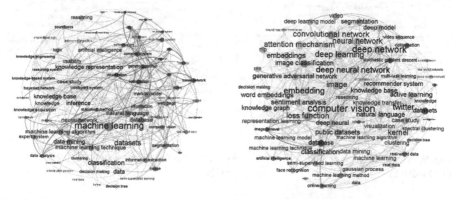

Fig. 5. The third stage of AAAI (1994–2011)   **Fig. 6.** The fourth stage of AAAI (2012–2019)

As shown in Fig. 7, the concept of AI can be defined by the top 5 frequent noun phrases in the context of NeurIPS between 1981 and 1987. The top 5 frequent noun phrases are "data", "associative memory", "computer simulation", "chip" and "information". As shown in Fig. 8, the concept of AI can be defined by the top 5 frequent noun phrases in the context of NeurIPS between 1988 and 1993. The top 5 frequent noun phrases are "speech recognition", "classification", "data", "image" and "error rate".

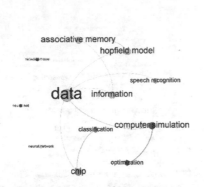

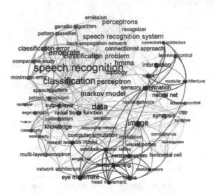

Fig. 7. The first stage of NeurIPS (1981–1987)

Fig. 8. The second stage of NeurIPS (1988–1993)

As shown in Fig. 9, the concept of AI can be defined by the top 5 frequent noun phrases in the context of NeurIPS between 1994 and 2011. The top 5 frequent noun phrases are "Gaussian process", "clustering", "segmentation", "hyperparameters" and "kernel function". As shown in Fig. 10, the concept of AI can be defined by the top 5 frequent noun phrases in the context of NeurIPS between 2012 and 2019. The top 5 frequent noun phrases are "covariance matrix", "learning rate", "machine learning algorithm", "neuroscience" and "estimation error".

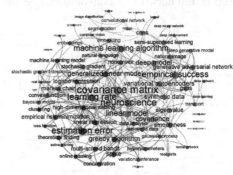

Fig. 9. The third stage of NeurIPS (1994–2011)

Fig. 10. The fourth stage of NeurIPS (2012–2019)

Figure 11 gives the outline of the applications of AI in the field of biomedicine. The top 5 frequent noun phrases in the context of BIBM between 1994 and 2011 are "gene", "cancer", "yeast", "protein" and "knowledge". As shown in Fig. 12, the top 5 frequent noun phrases used for describing AI in the context of BIBM between 2012 and 2019 are "precision medicine", "prognosis", "cancer", "pathway" and "molecular mechanism".

Fig. 11. The first stage of BIBM (1994–2011)

Fig. 12. The second stage of BIBM (2012–2019)

3.2 The Concept of AI Changes over Time

From the analysis presented above, we gained some interesting findings.

Firstly, according to the four categories of definition of AI shown in Table 1, we find that the concept of AI can be categorized to "Thinking" during the first stage of AAAI (1980–1987), the second stage of AAAI (1988–1993), and the third stage of AAAI (1994–2011). That means in these three stages, the research of multiple methods and technique placed the dominant research share of AI. Specifically, in the first stage of AAAI, the top frequent noun phrases are "knowledge representation", "knowledge acquisition", "logic", "inference" and "reasoning". All these methods would enable the machines to have the intelligence of humans. Whereas, in the fourth stage of AAAI (2012–2019), although the research of "Thinking" remained to be the leading share of AI research, the research of "Behavior" began to expand, including "computer vision", "image classification" and "segmentation".

Secondly, for NeurIPS, it is a publication venue that keeps a balance of the research share of "Thinking" and "Behavior" in the last three stages except for the first stage (1981–1987). That means, NeurIPS concerns more about the research of "Thinking" in the first stage. In the last three stages, the hot research topics of AI in NeurIPS are might half belong to the research of "Thinking" and half belong to the research of "Behavior".

Thirdly, as a publication venue that is dedicated to the research of AI application in biomedicine, it not only focusses on the research of "Thinking" but the research of "Behavior" in the first and the second stage of BIBM. Researchers begin to address scientific questions of medicine by using many AI techniques, such as "support vector machine", "machine learning" and "deep learning".

Above all, in the past few decades, although the concepts of AI presented by different communities in different stages have varied, they remain to keep the immutable content. The differences regarding the concept of AI that exist in various communities primarily depend on the use and interpretation of AI. Data-driven AI, as a part of AI is powered by big data, information, and knowledge. This claim can be demonstrated in Fig. 3, 4, 5, 6, 7, 8, 9, 10, 11 and 12, where the roles of "data", "information" and "knowledge" are vital in any development stages of publication venues.

The role of AI plays reminds us of the boundary object. We may treat "AI" as a boundary object. The "boundary object theory" is a sociology theory that proposed by Star and Griesemer in their publication [8] published in 1989. They described "Boundary objects are objects which are both plastic enough to adapt to local needs and the constraints of the several parties employing them, yet robust enough to maintain a common identity across sites" [8]. That means, as a boundary object, it should be concrete and abstract at the same time. For example, Musib and his coauthors [9] took a survey that ask young scientists what AI in their mind was in 2017. There were 13 interviewees gave their answers to this question. After reading the results of this survey, we find that all the participants are convinced that AI has the power to help people tack the research questions into their fields. They performed many tasks, including skin cancer classification, complex mixture gas detection and science education. In addition, the participants presented several specific AI techniques, such as deep-learning algorithms and decision-tree algorithms.

From the analysis above, we summarize that though different publication venues hold different understandings of AI–meaning there are different hot topics about AI in different stages of the three publication venues. The contributors to the three publication venues agree that AI can make full use of the massive amounts of data and can achieve results more efficiently. In our study, the term "AI" was used as a lens to help us view the different hot topic noun phrases and their interactions in different publication venues over the time.

4 Conclusion

In this study, we find that AI has the potential to act as a boundary object, engaging the diverse actors (human or non-human) together to fulfill the goals of societal implementation. Besides, we exhibit an experiment that reveals the evolution of the concept of AI, which will help stakeholders (e.g., AI researchers, government policy makers, and business entities) to obtain a clear understanding of the concept and the contours of AI. Our results will bridge the gap between stakeholders with different knowledge background and promote the discussion and communication between them.

Our study also has several limitations. When we were using natural language processing tools to extract the entities from the text, there were inevitable consequence biases. Thus, additional studies are still needed to enhance the precision of such tools.

Acknowledgements. This work is supported by the National Science Foundation for Young Scientists of China (71904083), the Philosophy and Social Science Research Project for Universities in Jiangsu Province (2017SJB0258), the Social Science Foundation of Jiangsu Province (18TQD003), and the Research Development Program of Humanities and Social Sciences of Ministry of Education of China (16YJC870005). Additionally, the first author gratefully acknowledges the support by the China Scholarship Council (201906190070) during his visiting to The University of Texas at Austin from 2019 to 2020.

References

1. Perrault, R. et al.: The AI Index 2019 Annual Report. AI Index Steering Committee, Human-Centered AI Institute, Stanford University, Stanford, CA (2019)
2. Bellman, R.: An introduction to artificial intelligence: can computers think? Thomson Course Technology (1978)
3. Salin, E.D., Winston, P.H.: Machine learning and artificial intelligence: an introduction. Anal. Chem. (Washington, DC). **64**(1), 49A-60A (1992)
4. Marvin, M.: Semantic Information Processing, UK edn. The MIT Press, London (1968)
5. Russell, S., Norvig, P.: Artificial Intelligence: a Modern Approach, 3rd edn. Prentice Hall, Hoboken (2009)
6. Tang, X. et al.: The pace of artificial intelligence innovations: speed, talent, and trial-and-error. J. Inform. **14**(4), 101094 (2020)
7. History of artificial intelligence. https://en.wikipedia.org/wiki/History_of_Artificial_intelligence. Accessed 15 Oct 2020
8. Star, S.L., Griesemer, J.R.: Institutional ecology, translations' and boundary objects: amateurs and professionals in Berkeley's Museum of Vertebrate Zoology, 1907–39. Soc. Stud. Sci. **19**(3), 387–420 (1989)
9. Musib, M., et al.: Artificial intelligence in research. Science **357**(6346), 28 (2017)

Understanding Team Collaboration in Artificial Intelligence from the Perspective of Geographic Distance

Xuli Tang[1] , Xin Li[1(✉)] , Ying Ding[2] , and Feicheng Ma[1]

[1] School of Information Management, Wuhan University, Wuhan, China
{xulitang,lucian,fchma}@whu.edu.cn
[2] School of Information, University of Texas at Austin, TX, USA
ying.ding@austin.utexas.edu

Abstract. This paper analyzes team collaboration in the field of Artificial Intelligence (AI) from the perspective of geographic distance. We obtained 1,584,175 AI related publications during 1950–2019 from the Microsoft Academic Graph. Three latitude-and-longitude-based indicators were employed to quantify the geographic distance of collaborations in AI over time at domestic and international levels. The results show team collaborations in AI has been more popular in the field over time with around 42,000 (38.4%) multiple-affiliation AI publications in 2019. The changes in geographic distances of team collaborations indicate the increase of breadth and density for both domestic and international collaborations in AI over time. In addition, the United States produced the largest number of single-country and internationally collaborated AI publications, and China has played an important role in international collaborations in AI after 2010.

Keywords: Team collaboration · Artificial Intelligence · Geographic distance

1 Introduction

Team collaboration is defined as the process where researchers from various affiliations working together for common goals by sharing knowledges, resources and experiences [1]. It has recently become imperative in the field of artificial intelligence (AI) for serving humanity in more complicate situations. Take for an example, with the global outbreak of COVID-19, AI scientists have collaborated with virologists, clinicians, and epidemiologists worldwide [2], on automatic image diagnosis [3], drug repurposing [4], and global epidemic prediction [5].Team collaboration not only helps AI scientists deeply understand outputs of AI algorithms, but also provides domain experts with insights on virus, which can speed up the process of combating COVID-19. However, both domestic and international collaboration in AI has not been prevalent yet [6]. Thus, it is worthwhile to understanding the status of team collaborations in AI and to identify the factors affecting collaborations in AI.

K. Toeppe et al. (Eds.): iConference 2021, LNCS 12645, pp. 14–23, 2021.
https://doi.org/10.1007/978-3-030-71292-1_2

Team collaboration has been discussed in many disciplines, such as ecology [7] indigenous knowledge [8] and Zika virus [9]. Geographic distance is widely considered as one of the major factors affecting team collaboration. Parreiria et al. [7] found that 10% of team collaborations among countries can be explained by geographic distance and socioeconomic factors. Sidone et al. [10] concluded that the geographic proximity is beneficial for team collaboration and knowledge exchange. Few studies have explored how AI scientists collaborated with each other.

In this preliminary study, we aim to understand team collaboration in AI from the perspective of geographic distance. In past studies, the geolocations of countries' capitals are commonly adopted to calculate the distance among collaborators [11]. Thanks to the geographic data in MAG, we here employed the latitude and longitude of affiliations to precisely quantify the maximum, minimum and average geographic distances for team collaborations in AI. We conducted the geographic distance analysis of team collaboration in AI at domestic and international levels.

2 Methodology

2.1 Data and Processing

The data set used in this study has been derived from the Microsoft Academic Graph. We use publications in the subfields of artificial intelligence, machine learning, computer vision, nature language processing and pattern recognition to represent AI publications [12, 13]. Bibliographic information of each publication such as title, year and abstract were extracted and stored in a local MySQL database. We recognized the country for each affiliation using its latitude and longitude. After removing publications without any affiliation information, we obtained 1,584,175 AI publications in1950–2019 with 4,998,781 unique authors belonging to 13,807 unique affiliations. 24.7% of AI publications are multiple-affiliation publications, which are comprised of 177,794 single-country AI publications and 213,011 multiple-country AI publications.

Fig. 1(a) shows the publication number distribution (blue) and the affiliation number distribution(orange) over years, in which the past 70 years has witnessed the exponentially increasing for both publications and affiliations. Fig. 1(b) displays the relationship between the number of publications and the number of affiliations, which shows an approximate power law distribution. It indicates that most of AI publications were produced by a small number of highly productive affiliations.

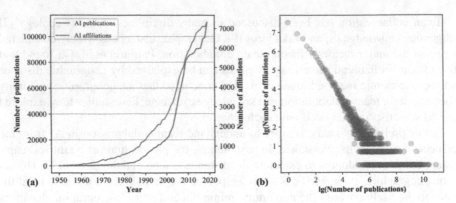

Fig. 1. Overview of the dataset. (a) Distribution of AI publications (blue) and distribution of unique affiliations in AI (red) over years. (b) The relationship between the number of AI publications and the number of affiliations in the dataset. (Color figure online)

2.2 Measuring Geographic Distance

We define coauthors in a publication as a team and represent an AI publication K with m unique affiliations as $K = \{M_{k_1}, M_{k_2}, \ldots, M_{k_m}\}$, in which $M_{k_i} = \langle t_k, Af_{k_i}, lat_{k_i}, lon_{k_i}, C_{k_i}\rangle (i \in \{1, 2, \ldots, m\})$, t_k is the publication year of K, Af_{k_i} denotes the ith affiliation id, lat_{k_i} and lon_{k_i} represents the latitude and longitude of Af_{k_i}, and C_{k_i} is the country of Af_{k_i}. Then, the affiliation pairs for K is expressed as $C(m, 2)_K = \{(M_{k_1}, M_{k_2}), (M_{k_1}, M_{k_3}), \ldots, (M_{k_i}, M_{k_j}), \ldots\}$ ($i \in \{1, 2, \ldots, m\}, j \in \{1, 2, \ldots, m\}, i \neq j$). Based on $(lat_{k_i}, lon_{k_i}) \in M_{k_i} (i \in \{1, 2, \ldots, m\})$, we employ GeoPy (https://geopy.readthedocs.io/en/stable/) to calculate the geographic distance for pairs in $C_K(m, 2)$ as $D_k = \{D_{k_1 k_2}, D_{k_1 k_3}, \ldots, D_{k_i k_j}, \ldots\}$ ($i \in \{1, 2, \ldots, m\}, j \in \{1, 2, \ldots, m\}, i \neq j$), in which $D_{k_i k_j}$ means the distance between the ith and j^{th} affiliations, and the number of elements in D_k is $\frac{m!}{[2!(m-2)!]}$. Therefore, the geographic distance (GD) of a team is defined at three levels:

(1) the average geographic distance (AveGD), defined as the average distance be-tween affiliation pairs within a team, as expressed by:

$$AveGD = \frac{\sum D_{k_i k_j}}{\frac{m!}{[2!(m-2)!]}}, \quad D_{k_i k_j} \in D_k, i \in \{1, 2, \ldots, m\}, j \in \{1, 2, \ldots, m\}, i \neq j \ (kilometers)$$

(2) The maximum geographic distance (MaxGD), defined as the maximum distance among all affiliations within a team, as calculated by:

$$MaxGD = Max(D_{k_i k_j}), \quad D_{k_i k_j} \in D_k, i \in \{1, 2, \ldots, m\}, j \in \{1, 2, \ldots, m\}, i \neq j \ (kilometers)$$

(3) The minimum geographic distance (MinGD), defined as the minimum distance among all affiliations within a team, as represented by:

$$MinGD = Min(D_{k_i k_j}), \quad D_{k_i k_j} \in D_k, i \in \{1, 2, \ldots, m\}, j \in \{1, 2, \ldots, m\}, i \neq j \ (kilometers)$$

We conducted the geographic distance analysis on team collaboration in AI at domestic and international levels. For an AI publication k with m authors, the country set of its authors $C_K = \{C_{k_1}, C_{k_2}, \ldots, C_{k_m}\}$, if $C_{k_1} = C_{k_2} = \ldots = C_{k_m}$, it's a domestic collaboration; or, it's an international collaboration.

3 Results

3.1 Overview of Team Collaboration in AI

Multiple-affiliation collaborations in AI have gradually gained popularity over time. Fig. 2(a) shows that the annual number of single-affiliation and multiple-affiliation AI publications both exhibit a noticeable increase since the late-1980s and early-2000s, respectively. After the rapid rise in the 21st century, the annual number of single-affiliation AI publications start-ed to stabilize with little fluctuation (around 65,000 publications per year), while that of multiple-affiliation ones continuously exhibit an upward trend. Although the number of single-affiliation AI publications has always been greater than that of multiple-affiliation ones, the percentage of multiple-affiliation AI publications exhibits a clear increasing trend, from 3% in 1951 to 38.4% in 2019.

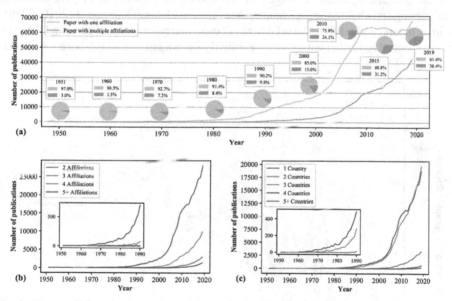

Fig. 2. Team collaboration in AI from the perspective of affiliations and countries during 1950–2019. (a) The changes in the number of publications with one affiliation (pink) and multiple affiliations (blue). The pies represent changes in the percentages of AI publications with one affiliation (pink) and multiple affiliations (blue). (b) The changes in the number of AI publications collaborated by different number (2, 3, 4 and 5+) of affiliations. (c) The changes in the number of AI publications collaborated by different number (1, 2, 3, 4 and 5+) of countries. (Color figure online)

Fig. 2(b) and Fig. 2(c) represent changes in the number of AI publications collaborated by a different number of affiliations and countries, respectively. Collaborations between two affiliations has been always the major form of cooperation in AI with a clear increasing trend since 1980. Collaborations among three or more affiliations also kept growing since 2000. During 1997–2000, around 25% AI publications were collaborated by 3 affiliations, and after 2010, nearly 50% AI papers were produced by 3+ affiliations. When considering the country distribution of collaborations in AI, most of AI publications were written by authors from a single country or two countries. Collaborations in AI among different numbers of countries all exhibit in-creasing trends. Before 2012, the number of two-country AI publications has always been slightly less than single-country ones; then, it surpassed the latter one and ended in the first place, indicating that international collaboration has become the main-stream in AI.

3.2 Geographic Distance Analysis

Overall, the geographic distances of team collaborations in AI exhibit an upward trend during 1950–2019 (Fig. 3). According to the growth rate of and the gaps among three geographic distances, we divided collaborations in AI into three stages, i.e., (1) stage 1 (1950–1996): three geographic distances went up with large fluctuations, and there were no clear gaps among them; (2) stage 2 (1997–2009): the growth rate of three distances didn't change much, but the gaps among them were widening; (3) stage 3 (2010–2019): the growth rate of MaxGD and AveGD exhibit clear increasing trends again, and the gaps among them were further enlarged. To explicitly investigate team collaborations in AI,

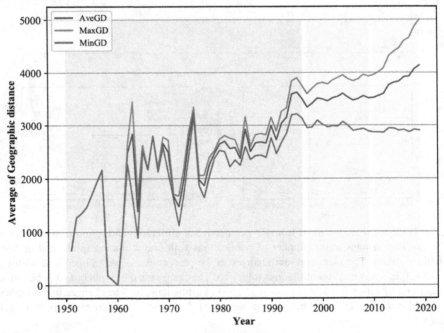

Fig. 3. The changes in the average values of AveGD, MaxGD and MinGD for all collaborations in AI (Note, the background colors indicate the three stages of team collaborations in AI.) (Color figure online)

we divided team collaborations in AI into two categories: (1) domestic collaborations, in which authors of each publication are all from one country; and (2) inter-national collaborations, in which authors of each publications are from 2 or more countries.

(1) Domestic collaborations in AI

Figure 4 shows the changes in the geographic distances for domestic collaborations in AI over time. In stage 1(1950–1996), the geographic distances of domestic collaborations in AI exhibit a decreasing trend, from around 1,000 km in 1950 to 700 km in 1996. The five most frequent domestic collaborations in AI all happened in the United states, and collaborations be-tween Harvard University and MIT ranked the first with 28 AI publications (Table 1). In stage 2 (1997–2009), the geographic distances of domestic collaborations steadily climbed to 800 km. Although most of domestic collaborations were still occurred in the United States, Spain (the first) and China (the fifth) entered the top five list in this stage. In the last stage (2010–2019), the geographic distances of domestic collaborations swiftly increased, i.e., 950 km for MinGD, 1200 km for AveGD and 1,300 km for MaxGD, respectively. Multiple research centers for AI has formed in the world, such as the United States and Singapore (Table 1). The swift growth of the MaxGD and MinGD both indicates that the breadth of domestic collaborations in AI has continuously increased.

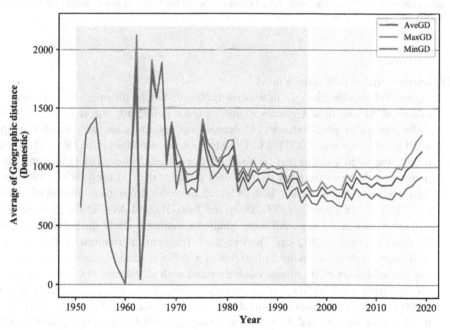

Fig. 4. The changes in the average values of AveGD, MaxGD and MinGD for domestic collaborations in AI (Note, the background colors indicate the three stages of team collaborations in AI.) (Color figure online)

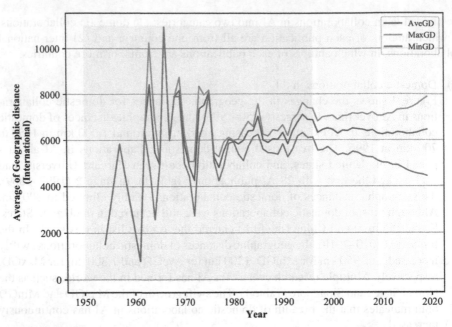

Fig. 5. The changes in the average values of AveGD, MaxGD and MinGD for international collaborations in AI (Note, the background colors indicate the three stages of team collaborations in AI.) (Color figure online)

(2) International collaborations in AI

Figure 5 shows the changes in the geographic distances for international collaborations in AI over time. Contrary to the domestic collaborations, in stage 1 (1950–1996), the geographic distances of international collaboration in AI exhibit an upward trend, from less 2,000 km in 1950 to more than 6,000 km in 1996. The most productive country in that peri-od was the United states followed by France and Germany; and the most frequent international partners in AI during 1950–1996 were Bell labs and Alcatel-Lucent, both of which have the strong back-ground of industry (Table 2). In stage 2 (1997–2009), the MaxGD and AveGD for international collaborations in AI kept still with small fluctuations, while the MinGD clearly declined to around 5,000 km. The two most frequent international collaborations in AI were both between the United States and China, and Microsoft are the most popular affiliation internationally collaborated with affiliations in China. In stage 3 (2010–2019), the MaxGD of international collaborations in AI stably increased to 8,000 km, while the MinGD swift decreased to around 4,200 km. This illustrates that both the breadth and density of international collaboration in AI have significantly increased recently. Universities in China participated in all the five most frequent international collaborations in AI, in which four were collaborations with Microsoft in the United States.

Table 1. Information about the 5 most frequent domestic collaborations in AI over three stages

Stages	Affiliation 1	Affiliation 2	Country	# of collaborations	Geographic distance(km)
Stage 1 (1950–1996)	Harvard Uni.	MIT	U.S	28	2.61
	Northwestern Uni.	Uni. of Chicago	U.S	27	30.09
	PARC	Stanford Uni.	U.S	24	3.31
	Stanford Uni.	MIT	U.S	23	4,336.71
	Stanford Uni.	Carnegie Mellon Uni.	U.S	20	3,641.54
Stage 2 (1997–2009)	Uni. of Granada	Uni. of Jaen	Spain	131	68.53
	Carnegie Mellon Uni.	Uni. of Pittsburgh	U.S	121	0.83
	MIT	Harvard Uni.	U.S	98	2.61
	Uni. of Washington	Microsoft	U.S	86	12.93
	National Taiwan Uni.	Academia Sinica	China	86	8.65
Stage 3 (2010–2019)	MIT	Harvard Uni.	U.S	273	2.61
	Carnegie Mellon Uni.	Uni. of Pittsburgh	U.S	228	0.83
	ASTR	Nanyang Technological Uni.	Singapore	225	12.82
	ASTR	National Uni. of Singapore	Singapore	200	1.31
	Islamic Azad Uni	Amirkabir Uni. of Technology	Iran	194	3.63

Table 2. Information on the 5 most frequent international collaborations in AI over three stages

Stages	Affiliation 1	Affiliation 2	Country pair	# of collaborations	Geographic distance (km)
Stage 1 (1950–1996)	Bell Labs	Alcatel-Lucent	(U.S., France)	24	11,762.50
	Karlsruhe Institute of Tech	Indian Institute of Tech. Bombay	(Germany, India)	16	6,573.54
	AT&T	Alcatel-Lucent	(U.S., France)	14	12,089.60

(continued)

Table 2. (*continued*)

Stages	Affiliation 1	Affiliation 2	Country pair	# of collaborations	Geographic distance (km)
	Ibaraki Uni.	Uni. of Alabama at Birmingham	(Japan, U.S.)	11	10,847.97
	Uni. of Manitoba	Hosei Uni.	(Canada, U.S.)	11	9,010.36
Stage 2 (1997–2009)	USTC	Microsoft	(China, U.S.)	153	9,400.97
	Tsinghua Uni.	Microsoft	(China, U.S.)	131	8,714.75
	Polish Academy of Sciences	Uni. of Alberta	(Poland, Canada)	68	7,547.47
	Hong Kong Uni. of Sci. And Tech	Microsoft	(China, U.S.)	64	10,434.14
	Princeton Uni.	Siemens	(U.S., Germany)	62	6,573.70
Stage 3 (2010–2019)	USTC	Microsoft	(China, U.S.)	367	9,400.97
	Peking Uni.	Microsoft	(China, U.S.)	242	8,716.74
	Tsinghua Uni.	Microsoft	(China, U.S.)	227	8,714.75
	Chinese Academy of Sciences	Uni. of Tech., Sydney	(China, Australia)	155	15,831.42
	Harbin Institute of Tech	Microsoft	(China, U.S.)	140	12,214.72

4 Conclusion

From geographic distance perspective, a clear understanding of team collaboration patterns in AI during 1950–2019 was developed in this study. Three geographic distance indicators (AveGD, MaxGD and MinGD) based on the latitudes and longitudes of affiliations were employed, to conduct the analysis on team collaboration in AI at domestic and international levels.

We found that the amount of team collaborations in AI presented a solid growth over time. Overall, these collaborations can be divided into three stages according to the growth rates of and gaps among the three kinds of geographic distances. In stage 1 (1950–1996), the decline in the distances among domestic collaborations and the increase in distances among international collaborations indicates the growth of the density for domestic collaborations and the breadth for international collaborations. In stage 2 (1997–2009), although the distances for both were slightly changed, the frequency of collaborations evidently increased by the number of publications. In stage 3 (2010–2019), the breadth for both domestic collaborations further increased by the increase of MaxGD and AveGD, and the density of international collaborations showed a solid growth by the decline of MinGD. The United States produced the largest number of single-country and internationally collaborated AI publications over three stages, and China has played an important role in international collaborations in AI after 2010. In addition, industrial companies with ability of high-performance computing and massive data, such as Microsoft and Bell, have evident positive effect on the collaborations in AI.

For the future study, we will further measure the cultural distance and socioeconomic distance of team collaborations in AI. We will also investigate how these distances affect citation counts of AI publications, AI team diversity, the success of collaborations and scientific careers.

Acknowledgement. This work was supported by the National Science Foundation of China (71420107026).

References

1. Yao, X., Zhang, C., Qu, Z., Tan, B.C.Y.: Global village or virtual balkans? Evolution and performance of scientific collaboration in the information age. J. Am. Soc. Inf. Sci. **71**(4), 395–408 (2020)
2. Bullock, J., Pham, K.H., Lam, C.S.N., Luengo-Oroz, M.: Mapping the landscape of artificial intelligence applications against COVID-19. arXiv preprint arXiv:2003.11336 (2020)
3. Ai, T., Yang, Z., Hou, et al.: Correlation of Chest CT and RT-PCR Testing in Coronavirus Disease 2019 (COVID-19) in China: A Report of 1014 Cases. Radiology, 200642 (2020)
4. Hoffmann, M., Kleine-Weber, H., Schroeder, et al.: SARS-CoV-2 Cell Entry Depends on ACE2 and TMPRSS2 and Is Blocked by a Clinically Proven Protease Inhibitor. Cell, S0092867420302294 (2020)
5. Al-qaness, M.A.A., Ewees, A.A., Fan, H., Abd El Aziz, M.: Optimization method for forecasting confirmed cases of COVID-19 in China. J. Clin. Med. **9**(3), 674 (2020)
6. Niu, J., Tang, W., Xu, F., Zhou, X., Song, Y.: Global research on artificial intelligence from 1990–2014: Spatially-explicit bibliometric analysis. ISPRS Int. J. Geo-Inf. **5**(5), 66 (2016)
7. Parreira, M.R., Machado, K.B., Logares, R., Diniz-Filho, J.A.F., Nabout, J.C.: The roles of geographic distance and socioeconomic factors on international collaboration among ecologists. Scientometrics **113**(3), 1539–1550 (2017). https://doi.org/10.1007/s11192-017-2502-z
8. Fung, H.N., Wong, C.Y.: Scientific collaboration in indigenous knowledge in context: insights from publication and co-publication network analysis. Technol. Forecast. Soc. Chang. **117**, 57–69 (2017)
9. Yozwiak, N.L., et al.: Roots, not parachutes research collaborations combat outbreaks. Cell **166**(1), 5–8 (2016)
10. Sidone, O.J.G., Haddad, E.A., Mena-Chalco, J.P.: Scholarly publication and collaboration in Brazil: The role of geography. J. Am. Soc. Inf. Sci. **68**(1), 243–258 (2017)
11. Jiang, L., Zhu, N., Yang, Z., Xu, S., Jun, M.: The relationships between distance factors and international collaborative research outcomes: a bibliometric examination. J. Inform. **12**(3), 618–630 (2018)
12. Frank, M.R., Wang, D., Cebrian, M., Rahwan, I.: The evolution of citation graphs in artificial intelligence research. Nat. Mach. Intell. **1**(2), 79–85 (2019)
13. Tang, X., Li, X., Ding, Y., Song, M., Bu, Y.: The pace of artificial intelligence innovations: Speed, talent, and trial-and-error. J. Inform. **14**(4), 101094 (2020)

Something New Versus Tried and True: Ensuring 'Innovative' AI is 'Good' AI

Stephen C. Slota[1]([envelope]) [iD], Kenneth R. Fleischmann[1] [iD], Sherri Greenberg[2], Nitin Verma[1], Brenna Cummings[2], Lan Li[1], and Chris Shenefiel[3]

[1] School of Information, University of Texas at Austin, Austin, TX 78705, USA
stephen.slota@austin.utexas.edu
[2] LBJ School of Public Affairs, University of Texas at Austin, Austin, TX 78705, USA
[3] Cisco Systems, Inc., Herndon, VA, USA

Abstract. What does it mean for AI to be innovative, and does new always mean better, particularly in terms of the ethical and societal implications of AI? This interview-driven study of 26 stakeholders of AI in the fields of technology research, law, and policy elucidates key tensions in producing innovative AI, as they are understood across sectors. As these stakeholders articulate a discourse on innovation, there is revealed a complex relationship between how innovative AI is conceived, both in terms of what is considered innovation, and how that innovation is seen to be restricted or supported through policy and regulatory action. Ultimately, this discourse operates on similar terms across these stakeholder groups, and presents a knotted, interlinked view of regulatory, design, and policy concerns across the ecology of AI, from its data to its use.

Keywords: Ethics of Artificial Intelligence (AI) · Values Conflicts · Value-Sensitive Design (VSD)

1 Introduction

Technological innovation is often seen as a societal imperative, particularly in the American context [23, 28]. The field of science and technology studies (STS) is replete with arguments for why innovation should not be unquestioningly accepted as an improvement [22, 34]. STS scholars argue for the importance of looking at the power relations involved in the development and diffusion of innovations [35]. However, in contrast with scholarship in STS, contemporary society still often looks uncritically at technological innovation, with the notable exception of dystopian science fiction about AI [4] and recent concerns about the dangers of social media [1, 15, 32]. In this paper, we report findings from interviews with AI stakeholders, including technologists, legal scholars, and policymakers, which reveal key insights about innovation in AI and how it should be evaluated.

While innovation is often conceived of and characterized as a linear trajectory from development to use [13], recent work in innovation recognizes its systemic linkages [16, 29] and relational qualities [2, 6, 8]. Innovation is further complexified by the

© Springer Nature Switzerland AG 2021
K. Toeppe et al. (Eds.): iConference 2021, LNCS 12645, pp. 24–32, 2021.
https://doi.org/10.1007/978-3-030-71292-1_3

institutional arrangements and discourses in which it is embedded. Technological innovation [27] has been conceived as the progress of "politics by other means" [17, p. 229] and operates on a range of 'displacements' between interrelated settings, such as the movement between the context of development the context of use, or the movement of technology between institutional or political settings [25]. Closely related to the power of political institutions [17], innovation can be effectively understood in this sense as the movement of knowledge or technological approaches between contexts, scales, and institutions.

Critical reflection on the design of information systems and other artifacts shows that humans embed their values and morality, often unconsciously, in things they create [18, 26, 33, 35]. Jackson et al. [14] argue that design, law, regulation, and technology are effectively 'knotted' together across the lifecycle of a designed object. As policies, laws, design standards, and the technologies themselves are formed by the implicit values of their designers and values explicitly embedded in their design, those values become consequential in the regulation, potential contestation, and societal impacts of any given technology. In the realm of AI, where methods are often occluded [7] and resulting knowledge difficult to contest outside its own terms [21], surfacing human values becomes even more critical.

Perceptions and discourses on innovation, both as a value informing design processes and a process by which knowledge and practices are displaced between context, bear significant political and ethical consequence in how AI will impact the world. In investigating computational modeling, a close conceptual relation and antecedent to modern AI, Fleischmann and Wallace [10], identify a fundamental values tension in computational modeling work between innovation and reliability, where end users' need for reliable products was in tension with reward structures that emphasize publication and novelty. This paper builds on that work to identify and explicate additional values tensions related to innovation in AI based on interviews with stakeholders from the domains of AI law, policy, and research.

2 Methods

We recruited 26 participants from three AI stakeholder groups: ten in public policy, eight in law and legal scholarship, and eight in technology design and research. We identified participants initially by leadership and public participation in AI design and implementation, then this population was further expanded through snowball sampling. Of these participants, nine held leadership or research and development roles in AI-related industry, two held leadership roles in AI-oriented non-profits, seven held technology or leadership roles in government, and eight held academic positions. We used two different instruments. First, we interviewed the AI technology researchers about their work with AI and the potential future implications of AI. These interviews used critical incident techniques [9] to identify value tradeoffs [10], stakeholder relationships, and the broader ethical implications of their own work.

We used the results of these interviews to design an instrument for discussing the ethical, legal, and policy implications of six specific applications of AI among our law and policy participants. Specifically, we asked about autonomous vehicles, algorithmically determined organ transplant priority lists, automated agents in call centers, algorithmically informed bank loan decisions, use of AI in medicine, and the use of AI in criminal sentencing decisions. Further, we asked all participants to consider the potential consequences of AI for ethics, law, and policy writ large.

We analyzed interview transcripts using thematic analysis [3], inductively identifying themes to recognize, describe, and understand the tension present in the design and implementation of AI. The resulting analysis is grounded in the work practice of participants and relates to societally significant applications of AI. Whereas we have previously reported on the hype and reality around the societal benefits and harms of AI [31], this paper focuses on value tensions related to innovation.

3   Findings

Across the interviews, our participants discussed their reservations and the embedded values tensions in the drive to innovate. While they consistently valued innovation, they argued against or raised cautions about unchecked or uncritical innovation in three key ways. First, they argued that unmeasured innovation resulted in unreliable results, or results that recapitulate existing discriminatory conditions, reproduce bias, or otherwise result in undesirable or counter-intuitive outcomes. Second, they saw a total commitment to innovation over all else as in tension with the need for security, where the expansive need for continually growing datasets might abrogate the privacy of individuals, empower bad actors, or otherwise enable malicious or undesirable uses of technology. Third, they saw innovation writ large as in tension with regulation, either conceiving of regulation as producing excessive limits to the ongoing development of AI, or, somewhat paradoxically, envisioning that the lack of regulation might preclude effective risk assessment and well-considered use of novel implementations of AI. In this section, we elaborate these tensions.

3.1   Innovation Versus Reliability

While a major orienting assertion of our participants, especially the technology stakeholders, was that solutions were to be found in 'the new' of innovation, and that innovation worked best when left alone, there was still some sense of a disconnect between specific work done and the hoped-for societally positive outcomes. Following Fleischmann and Wallace [10], we clustered these tensions under the term 'reliability'. Reliability is closely related to the ability to trust the knowledge produced through decision support systems, and similarly the ability to deploy AI in support of policy outcomes, all of which were related as concerns by our participants. A system that represents or reproduces such biases, though fully accurate in terms of analyzing its underlying data, is still a system that cannot be relied upon when a more positive societal condition is the desired outcome. The tension between the desire to move forward and concerns about the system are perhaps most eloquently expressed by the following legal stakeholder discussing the use of AI in criminal sentencing.

"Prison sentencing or sentencing in general has been a deeply flawed, terribly unreliable system from as far back as the beginning of history. The attempt to use technology is an attempt to do away with human frailty and biases. At the same time... Those are extraordinarily flawed technology measures."

Especially in applications in areas of significant power asymmetry, the evidentiary weight of data used outside the context of its creation can (and perhaps should) be contested. Decisions support systems relying on biased data can be subject to contestation or in many cases can reproduce prior biases, as stated by a policy stakeholder.

"And so you probably cannot take data sets from New York to establish the dangerousness of somebody, or the recidivism possibilities of somebody at Texas."

Thus, our participants viewed the desire to develop new applications as in conflict with the need to ensure that existing biases and discriminatory practices are corrected. Our participants did not see revising and correcting products as well-rewarded, nor did they often consider it as an important research activity. Instead, they most often discussed such corrections in terms of creating totally new products through processes informed by notable failures of prior products.

3.2 Innovation Versus Security

Notably, our participants consistently saw innovation as in tension with, and often superceding, nearly all other concerns. As a technology stakeholder asserts, the potential good embodied within the concept of the new, or in the drive to constant innovation, significantly outweighs other concerns.

"But you got to balance that with progress, with economic growth, with the innovation that may create other industries that are so large, that any displacement in one area might be addressed many fold with the creation of this new opportunity...ultimately, innovation is a good thing. And we are going down the path of innovating carefully, like I said with safety in mind, but open to the idea that not everything we plan will work out exactly the way we want to...And so we need to be very cognizant of where we feel we are falling short, and make course adjustments properly. Because as you execute on anything, you gain new knowledge."

Our participants consistently saw the new, captured by the notion of innovation writ large, as a means of addressing prior injustice or resolving issues created by the potential disruption or displacement of prior implementation. It is important to note here that innovation, while its potential is seen as greater than whatever disruption it might cause, still needed to be modulated by concerns for safety. This notion was echoed across the stakeholder groups, perhaps even more succinctly by a legal scholar, in expressing what was felt to be a fundamental conflict between innovation and regulation.

'So that's the question right now, do we value innovation or do we value the protection of individuals, that's the policy choice."

As new data sources are opened to analysis, the risk of abrogation of privacy increases. Similarly, the ability to develop consistent proxies of behavior from collated datasets becomes a troubling issue. However, many of our stakeholders saw this as being the result of malicious action:

"There are ways that the technologies...if put in the wrong hands can be used for bad purposes. And I think finding ways to create safeguards to that is the concern."

This technology stakeholder expressed the need for innovative technologies to be balanced by concerns of security, especially in limiting the capacity for malicious use of AI systems. Throughout our interviews, this was often posed across stakeholder groups as primarily a technological problem, one that required input and participation from the policy and legal sectors.

3.3 Innovation Versus Regulation

While innovation may be somewhat self-correcting in the minds of our participants, some participants viewed the relationship between AI innovation and regulation as a zero-sum game, as a legal stakeholder asserts:

"I think we need to let AI innovate. So, I think we need to avoid rushing to regulate AI, which unfortunately is happening."

This was echoed by another legal scholar, who saw even ethical consideration prior to design work as being a barrier to the inherently valuable practice of innovation:

"And there is a real risk that all of these ethical requirements, all of the new regulations being passed are going to stifle innovation"

Policy structures limiting data sharing are here in tension with the ability to make novel applications work, even when the algorithms are well-established:

"Obviously, again AI is based on data, a lot of the data is data that's being pooled together from different sources. And a lot of that data is data that, in Europe and Canada at the very least, is protected by the privacy laws. And right now, those laws are completely incompatible with the development of AI..."

And it remains that the notion of potential impact, while often deployed as justification for the drive to innovate, was seen by some participants as somewhat of an empty category – a place where there was still insufficient knowledge to be effectively traced, especially among our technology stakeholders, such as:

"The trade-off is not technological, it could be legal, it could be from the risk mitigation in order to have an informed end user that could take their decision. Not based on...technicalities of the machine learning system but based on [the] impact that the product[s] have once integrated in their environment...we don't know their environment. We tried to, but we don't"

Regulation might limit the available space for new products and processes and awaiting regulation prior to acting was seen as an undesirable delay. Of interesting note in the quotations presented above was that ongoing efforts at regulation by the legal stake-holders was perceived to be a major limiting factor in the development of AI, but among technology stakeholders, the limiting factor was seen to be its lack. This apparent para-dox is evocative of the knotted nature of design and policy - concerns of regulation and technology design are present in both the legal/policy and technology development space, but the extent to which they are understood and perceived to be manageable seemed to vary with different experience. Legal and policy scholars had a tendency to think of regulation as a well-understood and largely sufficient space in terms of the development of AI, where technology stakeholders were much more likely to see space for new policy, regulation, or legal action as necessary to enabling that development.

4 Discussion

Although some of our participants viewed innovation as broadly in tension with regula-tion, innovation is not always stifled by regulation. In the realm of privacy, for example, Europe's General Data Protection Regulations provide a level of regulation beyond that seen elsewhere in the world [12]. However, there is reason to believe that this regulation is not significantly restrictive of innovation, as much as it simultaneously stimulates and constrains innovation based on the relationship between the innovating agent and its data sources [19]. The simultaneously restrictive and stimulative effect of the GDPR was also seen in areas such as blockchain research [24]. Even when considering only data sharing, regulation was less restrictive than competing values, for example those of transparency and privacy in the health environment [20].

Efforts to innovate, or support innovation through policy, often fail to account for the full range of discourse from its affected communities [5] and result in exclusive policies that fail to account for the full diversity of stakeholder interests. Resulting from the community work undertaken by the AI4People initiative, Floridi et al. [11] propose a series of recommendations for measured innovation in AI through assessment, development and incentivization of 'good AI'. Similar to our findings here, this approach details work that by necessity operates across legal, policy, and design sectors, and calls for an interdisciplinary approach. From our findings across these sectors, we propose that such regulatory work is not restrictive of innovation, but, in the mode of Shilton's [30] values levers, is in fact productive of more effective and innovative design. Measured implementation under regulatory restriction thus would not limit innovation, rather it would empower designers to work on those systems that effectively address the already existing tensions between innovation, reliability, security, and related values.

5 Conclusion

This paper articulates the relationship between ongoing AI innovation, regulation, and implementation through the views of cross-sectoral stakeholders, highlighting the inter-connected and knotted nature of their concerns. We hold that this range of discourse on innovation and regulation introduces a productive complexity in the goal to understand and produce societally positive outcomes of AI and provides a means of more effectively understanding how and where AI works to innovate as it becomes more data-intensive.

These tensions reveal that it is not the epistemology or reasoning of AI that is at stake or problematic in understanding its dynamics, but rather intervening values that reside at the intersection of issues of design, policy, and law. Moving forward, those developing and using AI must seek to resolve knowledge asymmetries among the full range of its stakeholders and represent their diversity of discourses and concerns in order not only to innovate for the sake of innovating, but to innovate towards making AI better for everyone.

Acknowledgements. This research was funded by Cisco Systems under RFP-16-02, Legal Implications for IoT, Machine Learning, and Artificial Intelligence. We also thank our research participants: Blake Anderson, Ruzena Bajcsy, Hal Daume III, Stephen Elkins, Enzo Fenoglio, Iria Giuffrida, Dean Harvey, James Hodson, Wei San Hui, Amir Husain, Jeff Kirk, Frederic Lederer, Ted Lehr, Terrell McSweeny, Matt Scherer, Peter Stone, Nicolas Vermeys, Christopher Yoo, and eight anonymous participants.

References

1. Berghel, H.: Malice domestic: the Cambridge analytica dystopia. Computer **51**(5), 84–89 (2018). https://doi.org/10.1109/MC.2018.2381135
2. Bürcher, S., Habersetzer, A.: Entrepreneurship in peripheral regions: a relational perspective. In: Mack, E.A., Qian, H. (eds.) Geographies of Entrepreneurship, pp. 161–182. Routledge, Taylor & Francis Group, London (2016)
3. Clarke, V., Braun, V., Hayfield, N.: Thematic analysis. In: Smith, J.A. (ed.) Qualitative Psychology: A Practical Guide to Research Methods, pp. 222–248. Sage Publishing, Los Angeles (2015)
4. Cirucci, A.M., Vacker, B. (eds.): Black Mirror and Critical Media Theory. Lexington Books, Lanham (2018)
5. Crivits, M., de Krom, M.P., Dessein, J., Block, T.: Why innovation is not always good: innovation discourses and political accountability. Outlook Agric. **43**(3), 147–155 (2014). https://doi.org/10.5367/oa.2014.0174
6. Dicken, P., Malmberg, A.: Firms in territories: a relational perspective. Econ. Geogr. **77**(4), 345–363 (2001). https://doi.org/10.2307/3594105
7. Elish, M.C., Boyd, D.: Situating methods in the magic of big data and AI. Commun. Monogr. **85**(1), 57–80 (2018). https://doi.org/10.1080/03637751.2017.1375130
8. Faulconbridge, J.R.: Relational geographies of knowledge and innovation. In: Bathelt, H., Cohendet, P., Henn, S., Simon, L. (eds.) The Elgar Companion to Innovation and Knowledge Creation, pp. 671–684. Edward Elgar Publishing, Northampton (2017)
9. Flanagan, J.C.: The critical incident technique. Psychol. Bull. **51**(4), 327–358 (1954). https://psycnet.apa.org/doi/10.1037/h0061470
10. Fleischmann, K.R., Wallace, W.A.: Value conflicts in computational modeling. Computer **43**(7), 57–63 (2010). https://doi.ieeecomputersociety.org/10.1109/MC.2010.120
11. Floridi, L., et al.: AI4People—an ethical framework for a good AI society: opportunities, risks, principles, and recommendations. Mind. Mach. **28**(4), 689–707 (2018). https://doi.org/10.1007/s11023-018-9482-5
12. Goddard, M.: The EU general data protection regulation (GDPR): european regulation that has a global impact. Int. J. Market Res. **59**(6), 703–705 (2017). https://doi.org/10.2501/IJMR-2017-050

13. Godin, B.: The linear model of innovation: the historical construction of an analytical framework. Sci. Technol. Hum. Values **31**(6), 639–667 (2006). https://doi.org/10.1177/016224390 6291865
14. Jackson, S.J., Gillespie, T., Payette, S.: The policy knot: re-integrating policy, practice and design in CSCW studies of social computing. In: Proceedings of the 17th ACM Conference on Computer Supported Cooperative Work & Social Computing, pp. 588–602 (2014). https:// doi.org/10.1145/2531602.2531674
15. Karppi, T., Nieborg, D.B.: Facebook confessions: corporate abdication and Silicon Valley dystopianism. New Media & Society (in press). https://doi.org/10.1177/1461444820933549
16. Knickel, K., Brunori, G., Rand, S., Proost, J.: Towards a better conceptual framework for innovation processes in agriculture and rural development: from linear models to systemic approaches. J. Agric. Educ. Extension **15**(2), 131–146 (2009). https://doi.org/10.1080/138 92240902909064
17. Latour, B.: The Pasteurization of France (Alan Sheridan and John Law, trans.). Harvard University Press, Cambridge (1988)
18. Latour, B.: Where are the missing masses? The sociology of a few mundane artifacts. In: Bijker, W., Law, J. (eds.) Shaping Technology/Building Society, pp. 225–258. MIT Press, Cambridge (1992)
19. Martin, N., Matt, C., Niebel, C., Blind, K.: How data protection regulation affects startup innovation. Inf. Syst. Front. **21**(6), 1307–1324 (2019). https://doi.org/10.1007/s10796-019-09974-2
20. Minssen, T., Rajam, N., Bogers, M.: Clinical trial data transparency and GDPR compliance: implications for data sharing and open innovation. Sci. Public Policy scaa014 (in press). https://doi.org/10.2139/ssrn.3413035
21. Mittelstadt, B.: Principles alone cannot guarantee ethical AI. Nat. Mach. Intell. **1**, 501–507 (2019). https://doi.org/10.1038/s42256-019-0114-4
22. Monroe, J.G., Woodhouse, E.J.: Averting Catastrophe: Strategies for Regulating Risky Technology. University of California Press, Berkeley (1988)
23. Mosco, V.: The Digital Sublime: Myth, Power, and Cyberspace. MIT Press, Cambridge (2005)
24. Muller, L., Kemball-Cook, A.: Blockchain and the general data protection regulation: reconciling protection and innovation. J. Securities Oper. Custody **11**(2), 145–157 (2019)
25. Nahuis, R., Van Lente, H.: Where are the politics? Perspectives on democracy and technology. Sci. Technol. Hum. Values **33**(5), 559–581 (2008). https://doi.org/10.1177/016224390730 6700
26. Nissenbaum, H.: How computer systems embody values. Computer **34**(3), 120-119 (2001). https://doi.org/10.1109/2.910905
27. Noble, D.F.: America by design: science, technology, and the rise of corporate capitalism, No. 588, Oxford University Press USA, New York (1979)
28. Nye, D.E.: American Technological Sublime. MIT Press, Cambridge (1996)
29. Phillimore, J.: Beyond the linear view of innovation in science park evaluation: an analysis of Western Australian Technology Park. Technovation **19**(11), 673–680 (1999). https://doi.org/10.1016/S0166-4972(99)00062-0
30. Shilton, K.: Values levers: building ethics into design. Sci. Technol. Hum. Values **38**(3), 374–397 (2013). https://doi.org/10.1177/0162243912436985
31. Slota, S.C., et al.: Good systems, bad data? Interpretations of AI hype and failures. In: Proceedings of the 83rd Annual Meeting of the Association for Information Science and Technology, vol. 57, no. e275, pp. 1–11 (2020). https://doi.org/10.1002/pra2.275
32. Tufekci, Z.: How social media took us from Tahrir Square to Donald Trump. MIT Technology Review, 14 August 2018. https://www.technologyreview.com/2018/08/14/240325/how-soc ial-media-took-us-from-tahrir-square-to-donald-trump/. Accessed 25 Sept 2020

33. Winner, L.: Do artifacts have politics? Daedalus **109**(1), 121–136 (1980). https://www.jstor.org/stable/20024652
34. Winner, L.: The Whale and the Reactor: A Search for Limits in an Age of High Technology. University of Chicago Press, Chicago (1988)
35. Winner, L.: Upon opening the black box and finding it empty: social constructivism and the philosophy of technology. Sci. Technol. Hum. Values **18**(3), 362–378 (1993). https://doi.org/10.1177/016224399301800306

Insights from People's Experiences with AI: Privacy Management Processes

Kristin Walters$^{(\boxtimes)}$ ⓘ and Daniela M. Markazi ⓘ

University of Illinois at Urbana-Champaign, Champaign, IL 61820, USA
{kwaltrs2,dmarkaz2}@illinois.edu

Abstract. Given the lack of interview-based research in the Artificial Intelligence (AI) literature, we conducted 15 semi-structured interviews about people's experiences with AI. From those interviews, many important themes emerged and we focused this paper on people's experiences with privacy violations. We used the Communication Privacy Management Theory (CPM) to analyze distancing behaviors (avoidance or withdrawal) resulting from Boundary Turbulence (privacy violations) with people's voice-activated phones and Google Search. Through this analysis, we found evidence that distancing behaviors may 1.) be able to transfer from one device to another; and 2.) not depend on the trustworthiness of a particular device or application company. This paper concludes with recommendations for applying the CPM framework more intentionally and rigorously to people's experiences with voice-activated systems.

Keywords: Artificial Intelligence · Communication Privacy Management · Contextual Integrity

1 Introduction

Industries and communities are adopting more and more Artificial Intelligence (AI) technologies as algorithms advance, data sets grow, and computational power and storage become more economical [5]. Much is still unknown about the socio-technical implications of the proliferation of AI technologies in human- facing applications [3]. AI technologies increasingly make news headlines, either due to their promise of efficiency and industry disruption or due to their perpetuation of cultural rooted social inequalities. However, many Americans are still unaware of how AI does and will affect their daily lives [12]. Researchers have called for more human-centered design processes in AI development to encourage active collaboration between technology decision makers and users [13]. Better understanding of people's imaginaries around and interactions with AI technologies will support designers and policy makers as they strive to construct an AI landscape that works for the public.

Current AI research has relied mostly on quantitative methods, lacking the texture and nuance that users' voices add to the conversation. In this paper, we provide data from 15 semi-structured interviews on people's experiences with AI.

© Springer Nature Switzerland AG 2021
K. Toeppe et al. (Eds.): iConference 2021, LNCS 12645, pp. 33–38, 2021.
https://doi.org/10.1007/978-3-030-71292-1_4

While many interesting themes emerged, this paper focuses on three participants' experiences with privacy violations and their resulting behaviors.

Privacy management is made up of a person's choices and behaviors around disclosing or concealing information. It is a dynamic and dialectic process [2]. For this paper we used Sandra Petronio's 2002 Communication Privacy Management Theory (CPM) as a framework to help "conceptualize and operationalize privacy management" and Helen Nissenbaum's Contextual Integrity (CI) model to understand better how privacy contexts change in networked systems [8, 10].

Based on the work of Irwin Altman, Sandra Petronio developed the Communication Privacy Management Theory and as a means to "conceptualize and operationalize the nature of privacy" [11]. The theory states that individuals are owners of their information and they define that ownership through privacy boundaries. There are benefits and risks to disclosing and concealing information, and individuals have a set of privacy rules which govern when they share information with other people or entities. Petronio [11] categorizes privacy rules as core and catalyst. Core privacy rules are predictable and stable over time, such as one's cultural conception and valuation of privacy. Catalyst rules are less predictable and depend on context, like someone disclosing important in- formation during an emergency. When an individual shares information with another individual or entity, they become a co-owner. There are explicit and implicit expectations of how the information will be disclosed or concealed in the co-ownership. When those expectations are not met, Boundary Turbulence can occur. Boundary Turbulence can best be understood as a privacy violation. For example, people get angry at Facebook for sharing data with Cambridge Analytica.

Much research has been done about the emotional and behavioral responses to Boundary Turbulence. People felt mostly anger, fear, and sadness when experiencing Boundary Turbulence in the context of online hacking and romantic relationships [1, 7]. People's behavioral responses to Turbulence vary between integrative and distributive and those behaviors correlate with certain emotions. For the purposes of this paper, we are focused on the distributive behaviors of "distancing" which can come in the form of withdrawal from or avoidance of the violating information co-owner [1, 7].

In 2004 Helen Nissenbaum published her privacy management model called Contextual Integrity. Contextual Integrity dives deeper into the "context" vari- able presented by CPM and aims to explain and predict people's evolving "in- formation norms" (which are similar to CPM's idea of privacy boundaries) in the face of society's rapidly changing technological landscape [8]. Nissenbaum [9] posits that "contextual norms may be explicitly expressed in rules or laws or implicitly embodied in convention, practice, or merely conceptions of "normal" behavior. A common thesis in most accounts is that spheres are characterized by distinctive internal structures, ontologies, teleologies, and norms." Contextual Integrity focuses on the relationship between information types, actors and transmission principles to model information norms. The model has been used to draft privacy policy in light of new contexts.

For the purposes of this paper, we will use CPM's idea of Boundary Turbulence to describe participants' privacy violations that emerged in our data. We use the term Boundary Turbulence over Contextual Integrity violation because there has been more research about the emotional and behavioral effects of Boundary Turbulence in Commu-nications research. Leading up to this paper, we found no studies on behavioral effects of CI violations in the Computer Science literature.

While a lot of our privacy findings aligned with current research, we found evi-dence of Communication Privacy Management Theory's Boundary Turbulence with conversational devices which has not yet been explored in the research. Emotions and behaviors caused by Boundary Turbulence have been studied in a variety of contexts, namely Smart Phones, Fitness Trackers, romantic relation- ships, and online hacking [1, 4, 7, 14]. Given the limitations of our study (time and sample diversity), we cannot say anything definitive about emotional and behavioral responses regarding Boundary Turbulence with voice-activated devices but we can provide the justification for more significant research.

2 Methods

We utilized the interview method to explore the inter-relatedness between people's history with AI, current use of AI, and perceptions of AI.

2.1 Recruitment

Due to COVID-19 restrictions, participants were recruited through the researchers' per-sonal Facebook pages, one researcher's Instagram page, the social media site Nextdoor, and the University of Illinois at Urbana-Champaign's Reddit page.

These platforms offered access to a diverse age group, but did not recruit a sample representative of the population in terms of race.

2.2 Sample

Eight males and seven females (ranging in age from 18 to 61 years old) were interviewed. Nine participants identify as white-non Latino (20 to 61 years old), four as Asian (18 to 21 years old), one as mixed-race (black/white, 21 years old), and one as Latina (22 years old). All participants had post-secondary educations, ranging from some college (no degree) to Ph.D.

2.3 Interview Protocol

15 people participated in semi-structured interviews about their experiences with AI technologies. Researchers recorded audio of 13 interviews (video or audio) and tran-scribed them with Otter AI, editing transcriptions as needed. One re- searcher manually transcribed two interviews with participants who declined to be recorded. Interviews ranged from 22-75 minutes.

To start the interview, researchers asked broad questions to determine participants' level of knowledge about and usage of AI technologies. We asked participants the defi-nition of AI and what words and ideas they associate with the concept. We asked if they were currently using intelligent technologies and what kinds of conversations they had with family and friends about intelligent systems. We provided a definition of AI to all participants partially through the interview and asked if the definition was in line with their understanding of the technology and its use. In addition, we asked our participants to describe their personal history of knowing about and using AI as well as their concerns about AI, specifically their privacy concerns. We also asked our participants how they imagine AI could be used in the future given and how they can see AI helping with the COVID-19 pandemic. Finally we asked participants to describe desirable policies and designs for AI technologies.

2.4 Analysis

Both researchers coded the interview transcripts separately by applying an inductive thematic analysis as outlined in Guest et al. [6]. Researchers compared their coding systems and ensured alignment. Due to the timeline of the project and the amount of data to be processed, researchers analyzed specific themes individually, altering the coding system as needed for their individual analyses.

3   Results

14 out of 15 participants described the lack of privacy as inevitable and un- controllable and an inherent characteristic of today's society. However, privacy concerns and evidence of privacy management processes were still present in the data. Below are descriptions of three participants experiencing Boundary Turbulence with voice-activated devices and one of those three participants also experiencing Boundary Turbulence with Google Search. We also include the behavioral responses to the turbulent episodes.

Three participants (P1, P2, P8) experienced turbulence when a targeted ad popped up after they were talking about the featured product in front of (but not to) their or their conversational partner's phone. The participants believe the device listened to them and then used the heard information to target them for a specific advertisement. Participants reported these incidents in the context of privacy concerns and violations. A 35-year-old white female with an MBA said, "And once we were done, I was like on my social media and boom, that was the brand right there trying to advertise. I was like, Oh my god, this is so freaky." 24-year-old white male who worked formerly as navy photographer and currently studies history said, "It's just a little bit unsettling then be it through, you know, passive artificial intelligence in the background, that these companies and who really just want to sell us something maybe maybe that we don't need, are able to target us to that extent in our, in our personal lives, like, you know, it's it's kind of nice to be able to If I wanted to buy something to look for it myself and and not have Uber freight come up on my timeline and be like, this is creepy. It's just creepy." A 22-year-old Asian female undergraduate studying New Media said, "I was talking to my mom about like, adopting a pet. And then I don't know how maybe it just like misclicked on my like, on my phone or something. But when I looked at it again, it had like Google search for pet shelters. And I was like, Wait, did I do that? I was like, I don't think I did. Yeah, I accidentally like pushed voice control or something. But I don't know. It just made me think of that like and how like, a lot when people talk like near Alexa or near like Google Home, that like the advertisements are also like, curated for them. So I guess that is a little bit funky. But a little bit concerning." This participant also experienced turbulence when doing an art project that revealed the amount of her personal data collected by Google, YouTube and Facebook. "Because like, it's good that they know that they know what I like, and they know what to show me. But I don't like that. They know that because like, they know everything about me."

Two of the three participants (P1, P2) experiencing boundary turbulence reported distancing behaviors resulting from the turbulent episodes. The 22- year-old Asian female New Media student experienced turbulence with both Google Search and her Android phone. In response to the turbulent episode on her phone, there was no reported behavior. In response to the Google Search turbulence, she responded with a distancing behavior, describing it like: "I actually did switch to DuckDuckGo on this computer. But I kind of don't like it because sometimes it doesn't show me what I want to see." In response to a turbulent behavior with her phone, the 35-year-old white female with an MBA exhibited a distancing behavior towards the Alexa device, describing the situation like: "I use Siri sometimes when I'm driving. I definitely do. But Alexa, I'm not a big fan because I already am freaked out about like how I told you like when I talk, like I don't even mention the name and next thing I know is on my computer my web browser. I don't know. I don't use that."

4   Discussion

The results show that privacy management processes differ from person to person and from context to context, aligning with assertions from Altman [2], Petronio [11], and Nissenbaum [8] that privacy management is dynamic, dialectic, fluid, and contextual. Given CPM research by Aloia [1] and McLaren [7] on behavioral responses to boundary turbulence, it is not surprising that distancing behaviors appeared in the data. However, the distancing behaviors are different than one might predict and offer pathways for further investigation.

P1 distanced herself from Google Search by using DuckDuckGo after experiencing turbulence. Yet, there was no indication of a distancing response (or the inclination for one) with her Android after turbulence. Given that both applications are run by the same company, these questions arise: What assumptions are people making about data collection on different devices and how does that affect privacy boundaries, their violations, and ensuing behaviors? How do different applications/devices from the same company moderate privacy boundaries between the owner (consumer) and co-owner (company). What entity do people believe they are having a co-owning relationship with? The device, its company or the device-as-proxy for company?

P2 does not report distancing herself from her phone after turbulence, but instead reports avoiding buying an Alexa device. About this we pose these further questions: Can distancing behaviors transfer from one device to another? If so, how does device ownership moderate this effect? If so, how does trust in device companies moderate this effect?

Due to COVID-19 restrictions, we were unable to recruit a representative sample of the general public. For future studies we recommend collecting a more diverse sample.

5 Conclusion

Boundary turbulence occurs when an information co-owner violates a privacy boundary. Research shows that people can react to turbulence in a variety of ways given the dynamic nature of privacy management. Our research shows unexpected distancing behaviors from people who experience turbulence with their voice-activated phones. We think these findings warrant further research that can apply the CPM framework to people's privacy management processes with voice-activated applications. Insights into behaviors resulting from boundary turbulence could help companies foster relationships that might mitigate distancing behaviors. Insights could also help privacy advocates educate consumers about their behavior so they are empowered to manage privacy better with devices and institutions.

References

1. Aloia, L.S.: The emotional, behavioral, and cognitive experience of boundary turbulence. Commun. Stud. **69**(2), 180–195 (2018)
2. Altman, I.: The Environment and Social Behavior: Privacy, Personal Space, Territory and Crowding. Brooks/Cole Pub. Co., Inc, Monterey (1975)
3. Amershi, S., et al.: Guidelines for human-AI interaction. In: Proceedings of the 2019 Chi Conference on Human Factors in Computing Systems, pp. 1–13 (2019)
4. Cooper, C.: Smartphone privacy perceptions and behaviors generational influence quantitative analysis: Communications privacy management theory (unpublished PhD dissertation). ProQuest Dissertations Publishing (2014)
5. Ergen, M.: What is artificial intelligence? Technical considerations and future perception the Anatolian. J. Cardiol. **22**(Suppl 2), 5–7 (2019)
6. Guest, G., MacQueen, K.M., Namey, E.E.: Applied Thematic Analysis. SAGE Pulications Inc., Thousand Oaks (2012)
7. McLaren, R.M., Steuber, K.R.: Emotions, communicative responses, and relational consequences of boundary turbulence. J. Soc. Personal Relation. **30**(5), 606–626 (2013)
8. Nissenbaum, H.: Privacy in Context: Technology, Policy And the Integrity of Social Life. Stanford Law, Stanford (2010)
9. Nissenbaum, H.: Respecting context to protect privacy: why meaning matters. Sci. Eng. Ethics **24**(3), 831–852 (2018)
10. Petronio, S.S.: Boundaries of Privacy: Dialectics of Disclosure. State University of New York Press, Albany (2002)
11. Petronio, S., Child, J.T.: Conceptualization and operationalization: utility of communication privacy management theory. Current Opinion Psychol. **31**, 76–82 (2020)
12. West, D.: Brookings survey finds worries over AI impact on jobs and personal privacy, concern U.S. will fall behind China (2019). https://www.brookings.edu/blog/techtank/2018/05/21/brookings-survey-finds-worries-over-ai-impact-on-jobs-and-personal-privacy-concern-u-s-will-fall-behind-china
13. Xu, W.: Toward human-centered AI: a perspective from human-computer interaction. Interactions **26**(4), 42–46 (2019)
14. Zimmer, M., Kumar, P., Vitak, J., Liao, Y., Kritikos, K.C.: 'There's nothing really they can do with this information': unpacking how users manage privacy boundaries for personal fitness information. Inf. Commun. Soc. **23**(7), 1020-1037 (2020)

People's Perceptions of AI Utilization in the Context of COVID-19

Daniela M. Markazi$^{(\boxtimes)}$ (iD) and Kristin Walters (iD)

University of Illinois at Urbana-Champaign, Champaign, IL 61820, USA
dmarkaz2@illinois.edu

Abstract. Taking into consideration the scarcity of interview-based research in Artificial Intelligence (AI) literature, we conducted 15 semi-structured interviews regarding our participants' experiences with AI, where we observed a number of notable themes. In this paper, we focused on participants' thoughts and opinions of AI use during the novel coronavirus (COVID-19) pandemic, a global crisis. Although there have been studies relating AI to COVID-19, there is insufficient in-depth understanding concerning the way people feel about AI utilization in the context of COVID-19. While there was mostly positive feedback that AI could help in the COVID-19 calamity, such as COVID-19 testing and monitoring vital signs, two out of 15 participants expressed doubt that AI could be successfully implemented in healthcare, and four out of 15 participants mentioned potential issues with this AI application. We are among the first researchers exploring people's opinions on AI usage in the context of COVID-19, so this paper provides a foundation for future work.

Keywords: Artificial Intelligence · Coronavirus · Public perception

1 Introduction

The novel coronavirus, also called COVID-19, is a severe respiratory disease first identified in Wuhan, China, in late 2019 [17]. According to the World Health Organization, as of October 19, 2020, there have been 39,944,882 confirmed cases of COVID-19 and 1,111,998 deaths caused by this disease globally [16]. In the United States, there have been 8,128,524 total cases of COVID-19 and 218,986 total deaths [5]. More than four-in-ten Americans admit that the pandemic has greatly changed and impacted their lives [14].

Fortunately, Artificial Intelligence (AI) guarantees a new model for healthcare [15], and AI used for healthcare offers an upper hand compared to clinical techniques [6]. Some examples of AI usage in the context of COVID-19 include FluSense, a device that utilizes AI to forecast patterns in infectious respiratory illnesses [1], a deep learning model developed to distinguish COVID-19 from chest computerized tomography images from community-acquired pneumonia [12], and an AI tool that estimates the survival rates for COVID-19 patients [18]. COVID-19 outbreaks and their global nature of spread can be identified through AI-driven tools [15]. Even though AI-driven tools are still

© Springer Nature Switzerland AG 2021
K. Toeppe et al. (Eds.): iConference 2021, LNCS 12645, pp. 39–46, 2021.
https://doi.org/10.1007/978-3-030-71292-1_5

in their infancy stages, and slow progress is being made in their adoption for serious consideration at international and national policy levels, AI-driven algorithms are gaining accuracy [2]. By way of illustration, companies such as Metabiota and BlueDot predicted the COVID-19 crisis in China through AI modeling before it caught the world by surprise in late 2019 by both scouting its spread and impact through utilizing a survey of prior viral outbreaks over the last 20 years [2].

AI utilization has proliferated across industries due to advancements in algorithms, usage of massive data sets, and ever-increasing computational power and storage at a low cost [7]. The popularity and relevance of AI use, especially in today's new world of COVID-19, will compel researchers to explore its socio-technical implications in human-facing applications [3]. Still, how people perceive AI utilization in the context of this pandemic is unknown. With the advancement of AI, individuals and industries will be dramatically affected. More profoundly understanding people's experiences and thoughts about AI will help define priorities for policymakers and technology designers.

AI can be employed for various healthcare applications, such as stroke detection and diagnosis [11]. Citizens of the UK are optimistic that new technologies will create efficiencies in the health system, increase successful diagnoses, and give doctors more time with their patients [4]. AI's ability to analyze large amounts of data makes it an ideal tool for preventative public health measures if the population consents to the data gathering and data usage [4].

Much of the current research on people's experiences with AI is survey-based. Therefore, in this paper, we provide data concerning participants' experiences with AI from 15 semi-structured interviews. We chose to focus on people's thoughts and opinions regarding the implementation of AI in the context of COVID-19. Due to the novelty of COVID-19, we are among the first researchers studying people's opinions on AI usage during the pandemic, so this study provides the framework for subsequent research.

2 Methods

We chose an interview method to better grasp how individuals' life experiences and perceptions of technology shape their understanding of AI. Due to COVID-19 constraints, we recruited participants via convenience sampling from a variety of social media platforms such as Facebook, Instagram, Nextdoor, and Reddit.

A total of 15 participants (see participants' demographic information listed in Table 1) discussed their opinions and experiences concerning AI in semi-structured interviews ranging from 22 to 75 min. For 13 participants, audio was recorded from video or audio calls and then transcribed by Otter.ai [13]. Afterward, we edited the transcripts. Interviews were manually written for two participants who refrained from audio recording.

Concerning the interviews, firstly, we wanted to know what our participants thought about AI in general and what they thought AI actually means, so we asked them about words that they associate with AI and what experiences they have had with AI. Moreover, we asked them if they had conversations about AI with friends or family. Then, we read them a definition of AI, namely that it is "a term applied to a machine or software mimics cognitive functions that the humans associate with the human mind functions such as learning and problem solving" [9]. Afterward, we asked our participants if the definition

Table 1. Participant (P) demographics

P#	Gender	Race	Age	Education Level	Occupation
P1	Female	Asian	21	Some college	New media undergraduate student
P2	Female	White	35	Master's Degree	Implementation project manager
P3	Male	White	20	Some college	Computer science and theatre undergraduate student
P4	Female	White	38	Some college, no degree	Email marketing manager
P5	Female	Latina/Hispanic	22	Bachelor's Degree	University biomedical research coordinator
P6	Female	White	61	Some college, no degree	Childcare provider
P7	Male	White	44	Some college, no degree	Set designer, petting zoo manager, fabricator
P8	Male	White	24	Some college, no degree	History undergraduate student
P9	Male	White	27	Master's Degree	Biology Ph.D. candidate
P10	Male	Asian	19	Some college	Pharmacy undergraduate student
P11	Female	Asian	18	Some college	Bioengineering undergraduate student
P12	Female	White, Black	27	Ph.D.	Data scientist, university lecturer
P13	Male	White	22	Bachelor's Degree	Gymnastics coach
P14	Male	Asian	21	Some college	Mechanical engineering undergraduate student
P15	Male	White	53	Master's Degree	Acupuncturist

seemed in line with their understanding of AI. Next, we asked if our participants have general concerns about AI and the last time they heard or talked about it. Furthermore, we discussed their first memories of AI, the AI technologies they are currently employing, and privacy concerns they have about it. We also asked our participants to describe future uses for AI related to COVID-19 and how they can see AI helping with the pandemic. Lastly, we asked our participants questions related to AI regulations, policies, and designs.

By applying an inductive thematic analysis [10], we inductively coded the interview transcripts separately and then compared our individual coding systems, which were well-aligned. Given the timeline of the project and the amount of data to be processed, we individually analyzed specific themes, modifying codes for individual analyses, where required. While coding, we utilized intercoder agreement checks to ensure code alignment [10]. We had conversations about our codes, we read each other's codes, and we came to a shared agreement on all of the codes.

3   Results

Participants were asked how they think utilizing AI would affect COVID-19, and there were mixed results. While all 15 participants had an idea for how AI would help ameliorate the spread of the virus, five participants had negative thoughts and opinions regarding its use in healthcare.

3.1   Positive Thoughts and Opinions

Regarding optimistic opinions of AI usage in the context of COVID-19, there were six participants (P3, P4, P5, P6, P10, P12) who suggested that AI could potentially be applied to COVID-19 testing, and two participants directly commented how AI can be beneficial for COVID-19 testing. Concerning AI being employed to help with COVID-19 testing, P6 stated, *"It would be beneficial I'm sure if these things can figure it out, even give a test for that or something."* P3 pointed out that AI conducting COVID-19 tests will reduce human-to-human contact by explaining, *"They can somehow do the tests without needing to actually be there and like for very long without having to expose another human to the virus."*

Five participants (P2, P4, P5, P7, P12) indicated the possible use of AI to monitor vital signs, and two of these participants noted how intelligent machines can reduce contact between hospital employees and patients. P2 remarked, *"The machines that would take the, you know, the vital signs and all that going into the room without having the nurse interact with the patient, like doing the vital signs with them checking the temperature."* According to P4, *"If we all had our own personal computers, like a machine like the Jetsons have, maybe the machine can take our temperature and monitor our vital signs... If an AI could be programmed to do the testing then that can be given instant results instead of having to wait weeks and days to get results."* P5 asserted, *"I see it as a substitution or a replacement to telemedicine or telehealth, which could be helpful to take initial vital signs... AI can replace telemedicine and telehealth in very basic ways like overall physicals."*

Three participants (P1, P9, P13) pointed out how AI-based location tracking can stop the spread of the virus. P1 mentioned phone-tracking to see when people are traveling or going outside, and she said, *"Maybe, is it, like, they track your phone and see, like, if you're outside? Maybe, if you're, like, in a car or something, and they're not headed to the grocery store or gas station, then you get punished or something."* P13 stated, *"Think about just how many packages Amazon is still delivering day-to-day at this point and then even just going from where that package started to even just a zip code that it's going to that can end up affecting potential spread things like that... Probably tollways would be a big information hub there because then you can see where one license plate is moving from place to place with that. So, you can see if someone is moving across the country."* While these three participants mentioned how AI can be used for location tracking, none of them had ethical concerns with this potential function of AI, as they were all supporters of it. They believe this function could be beneficial.

Four participants (P2, P4, P8, P10) noted how AI is efficient. They also stated how AI's efficacy can help in healthcare, especially in battling COVID-19. Furthermore, P2 explained how AI can help abate the COVID-19 pandemic by removing human-to-human contact. She stressed, *"We are set that we're not putting, you know, the healthcare workers at risk, or we're kind of ending this faster because we were eliminating that human-to-human contact."* P8 expressed how AI can accelerate clinical trials for the virus by suggesting, *"It seems just a lot more time-efficient to put that process through like an IBM Watson and help us come up with something that could maybe get us to a clinical trial faster."* P4 noted how AI has the potential to clean hospital rooms quickly by stating, *"AI can be cleaning up after the room so patients can get in and out of the rooms quicker."*

3.2 Negative Thoughts and Opinions

Concerning the negative comments we received about AI being applied to help mitigate COVID-19, four participants (P5, P7, P10, P14) mentioned potential AI healthcare issues, such as inaccuracies, complications, and errors. Two participants identified potential complications with AI in healthcare adjusting to different patients' conditions. P5 remarked, *"I could see some issues with that, just based off the fact that I'm not sure how AI can adjust to patients who are overweight, who have different kinds of conditions that cause them to have a certain heart rate that can change five minutes or so depending on the medications that they're taking."* According to P7, *"Say you had something just as generic as a temperature sensor to check everybody's temperature. How are you going to take a low-grade fever when there's all that fluctuation (you know, people's temperature and baseline temperatures and such)?"* Two participants directly pointed out potential, fatal AI consequences. For instance, P10 warned, *"In some cases, if that AI were to make a mistake, that can be fatal."* P14 explained, *"You can tell when somebody's sick, obviously not give them a diagnosis on the spot, and prescribe them the exact medications they need, because obviously it will, like, make mistakes and it'd be better to have it more thoroughly checked over as a first-line like a first response."*

Two participants expressed doubt about AI use in healthcare, especially in the context of COVID-19. When discussing the COVID-19 pandemic and AI in healthcare, P6 suggested, *"It would be beneficial, I'm sure, if these things can figure it out, even give a test for that or something, but I don't think those things would ever work,"* since she thinks these applications are currently unrealistic. P10 offered similar rationale for his hesitancy regarding AI utilization in healthcare and specifically for combating COVID-19 by claiming, *"AI can test different scenarios and different situations with medications and whatnot through algorithms to be able to determine a vaccine. Of course, this is probably something that's a bit far-fetched."*

4   Discussion

Four participants asserted how AI application in healthcare would have issues, complications, and inaccuracies regarding COVID-19. However, the literature states that the precision of AI-driven algorithms is increasing [2], and as AI is becoming more advanced and sophisticated, it can rapidly solve complex problems, such as those related to COVID-19 [6]. Thus, although AI is gaining accuracy, four participants do not believe that AI is improving, as they think it will cause issues and complications.

Five participants had doubtful feelings regarding AI in healthcare related to COVID-19 or felt that AI would cause healthcare issues and mistakes. Two of these participants expressed doubt regarding AI being implemented in healthcare; they are not fully optimistic that AI can be successfully employed in healthcare. Also, four of these five participants claimed that AI in healthcare would encounter issues, complications, and inaccuracies. These participants are also not entirely confident about AI in healthcare. However, in a UK study conducted in 2018, citizens stated that they are optimistic that new technologies in healthcare will create greater healthcare efficiencies, increase successful diagnoses, and give doctors more time with their patients [4]. Therefore, our study contrasts the current literature, as five of our 15 participants are not fully optimistic about AI in healthcare due to the fact that it is a new technology.

Although five participants were wary about AI applications in healthcare as it relates to COVID-19, none of our 15 participants directly opposed its usage. All of our participants either strongly or somewhat supported AI development in healthcare, even if they felt suspicious of it. This does not align with previous research that demonstrates the mixed public perception of AI [8, 19]. A 2020 study showcased that when talking about medical AI on social media, almost 40% of public posts were neutral or were against it [8]. Furthermore, a study conducted in 2019 describes that when given a short explanation of the development of AI, 41% of Americans somewhat support or strongly support the development of AI, and 22% of Americans somewhat or strongly oppose it [19]. When thinking about AI, all 15 study participants are open to the application of AI in healthcare, but they agreed that there should be regulations to manage it. Concerning regulations, these results are similar to the same study conducted in 2019 that states that 82% of Americans believe that AI should be carefully managed [19].

5   Limitations and Future Work

Due to COVID-19 constraints, we used a convenience sampling method to recruit participants. Therefore, our participant sample was not as diversified as the general population. Prospectively, we recommend recruiting a more highly diverse demographic participant sample. Furthermore, we did not ask our participants what their technology adoption behaviors were or if they were previously interested in AI. Thus, we recommend asking participants this information to understand which participants have more accurate expectations of what AI can and cannot do in the healthcare industry.

Our findings suggest the following future research to explore: How can people support AI while not feeling optimistic about its utilization in healthcare? Also, if AI is implemented to help combat the COVID-19 pandemic, will people's perceptions about

AI in healthcare improve so that they will be open to the recommended treatment, device, or medicine?

6 Conclusion

Our results demonstrate that, although all 15 participants theorized how AI would help assuage the spread of COVID-19, five participants expressed hesitancy regarding its use in healthcare. These findings are far-reaching because having doubts about AI could negate people's willingness to seek healthcare treatment in the future if AI is adopted. If there are doubts regarding the accuracy and efficacy of AI, people might not comply with their physician's recommended healthcare treatment, devices, and even medicine. Based on the foregoing analyses, our results offer a mix of perceptions of how AI can be useful in healthcare. This is germane because public adoption and public support of AI applications in healthcare could be mixed, as some people may strongly support AI, while others may be skeptical of it. Moreover, most people are open to AI usage in healthcare as long as there are regulations to manage it. As a result, AI usage in healthcare, in general, and COVID-19, in particular, may ultimately impact public policy.

References

1. Al Hossain, F., Lover, A.A., Corey, G.A., Reich, N.G., Rahman, T.: FluSense: a contact-less syndromic surveillance platform for influenza-like illness in hospital waiting areas. Proc. ACM Interact. Mob. Wearable Ubiquit. Technol. **4**(1), 1–28 (2020)
2. Allam, Z., Dey, G., Jones, D.: Artificial intelligence (AI) provided early detection of the coronavirus (COVID-19) in China and will influence future Urban health policy internationally. AI **1**(2), 156–165 (2020)
3. Amershi, S., et al.: Guidelines for human-AI interaction. In: Proceedings of the 2019 CHI Conference on Human Factors in Computing Systems, p. 13. ACM, New York (2019)
4. Castell, S., Robinson, L., Ashford, H.: Future data-driven technologies and the implications for use of patient data. https://www.acmedsci.ac.uk/datadialogue. Accessed 20 Sept 2020
5. Centers for Disease Control and Prevention: CDC COVID data tracker. https://covid.cdc.gov/covid-data-tracker. Accessed 19 Oct 2020
6. Dananjayan, S., Raj, G.M.: Artificial intelligence during a pandemic: the COVID-19 example. Int. J. Health Plann. Manag. **35**(5), 1260–1262 (2020)
7. Ergen, M.: What is artificial intelligence? Technical considerations and future perception. Anatolian J. Cardiol. **22**(Suppl. 2), 5–7 (2019)
8. Gao, S., He, L., Chen, Y., Li, D., Lai, K.: Public perception of artificial intelligence in medical care: content analysis of social media. J. Med. Internet Res. **22**(7), e16649 (2020)
9. Garza-Ulloa, J.: Application of mathematical models in biomechatronics: artificial intelligence and time-frequency analysis. In: Applied Biomechatronics Using Mathematical Models, 1st edn. Academic Press, London (2018)
10. Guest, G., MacQueen, K.M., Namey, E.E.: Applied Thematic Analysis. SAGE Publications Inc., Thousand Oaks (2012)
11. Jiang, F., et al.: Artificial intelligence in healthcare: past, present and future. Stroke Vasc. Neurol. **2**(4), 230–243 (2017)
12. Li, L., et al.: Artificial intelligence distinguishes COVID-19 from community acquired pneumonia on chest CT. Radiology **296**(2), 200905 (2020)

13. Otter.ai: Otter Voice Meeting Notes. https://otter.ai/. Accessed 10 Sept 2020
14. Pew Research Center: Most Americans say coronavirus outbreak has impacted their lives. https://www.pewresearch.org/social-trends/2020/03/30/most-americans-say-cor onavirus-outbreak-has-impacted-their-lives/. Accessed 20 Sept 2020
15. Santosh, K.C.: AI-driven tools for coronavirus outbreak: need of active learning and cross-population train/test models on multitudinal/multimodal data. J. Med. Syst. **44**(5), 1–5 (2020)
16. World Health Organization: WHO coronavirus disease (COVID-19) dashboard. https://cov id19.who.int/. Accessed 19 Oct 2020
17. Wu, F., et al.: A new coronavirus associated with human respiratory disease in China. Nature **579**(7798), 265–269 (2020)
18. Yan, L., et al.: An interpretable mortality prediction model for COVID-19 patients. Nat. Mach. Intell. **2**, 283–288 (2020)
19. Zhang, B., Dafoe, A.: Artificial intelligence: American attitudes and trends. Center for the Governance of AI, Future of Humanity Institute, University of Oxford, Oxford, UK (2019)

Characterizing Dementia Caregivers' Information Exchange on Social Media: Exploring an Expert-Machine Co-development Process

Zhendong Wang[1], Ning Zou[1], Bo Xie[2], Zhimeng Luo[1], Daqing He[1(✉)], Robin C. Hilsabeck[2], and Alyssa Aguirre[2]

[1] University of Pittsburgh, Pittsburgh, PA 15260, USA
dah44@pitt.edu
[2] University of Texas at Austin, Austin, TX 78712, USA

Abstract. Social media platforms have introduced new opportunities for supporting family caregivers of persons with Alzheimer's disease and related dementias (ADRD). Existing methods for exploring online information seeking and sharing (i.e., information exchange) involve examining online posts via manual analysis by human experts or fully automated data-driven exploration through text classification. Both methods have limitations. In this paper, we propose an innovative *expert–machine co-development* (EMC) process that enables rich interactions and co-learning between human experts and automatic algorithms. By applying the EMC in analyzing ADRD caregivers' online behaviors, we illustrate steps required by the EMC, and demonstrate its effectiveness in enhancing human experts' representations of ADRD caregivers' online information exchange and developing more accurate automatic classification models for ADRD caregivers' information exchange.

Keywords: Alzheimer's disease and related dementias (ADRD) caregiving · Online information exchange · Expert-Machine Co-development (EMC) · Interactive learning · Social media analysis

1 Introduction

Alzheimer's disease and related dementias (ADRD) are a major public health concern. In the U.S., about 5.6 million Americans age 65 and over were living with ADRD in 2019, a number expected to increase to 7 million by 2025 (nearly a 27% increase) [5]. Persons with ADRD require extensive care, and national data suggest that the majority of their care is provided by family members and friends. In 2018, caregivers in the U.S. provided approximately 18.5 billion hours of informal, unpaid care for persons with ADRD that valued at $233.9 billion [5].

Caregiving for persons with ADRD is stressful, with severe negative effects on caregivers' own health and well-being [7,16,22,27,38]. Caregivers, however, receive insufficient information about challenges or care options from clinicians [13,14,21,40]. In recent years, social media platforms such as Facebook,

K. Toeppe et al. (Eds.): iConference 2021, LNCS 12645, pp. 47–67, 2021.
https://doi.org/10.1007/978-3-030-71292-1_6

Twitter, and Reddit have introduced novel mechanisms supporting online health information seeking and sharing (thereafter referred to as *information exchange* in this paper) [8,43,61]. ADRD caregivers have new opportunities to obtain online peer support in social media and to exchange information [4,34,35,59]. To date, however, research on ADRD caregivers' information exchange via social media platforms remains limited [6], resulting in inadequate understanding of the challenges caregivers face for developing interventions to support their online information exchange.

There are two main methods for analyzing social media content to understand online information exchange behaviors. The first, *expert analysis*, relies on human experts to manually analyze social media content [8,17]; the other, *automatic exploration*(AE), uses machine learning or text mining algorithms (e.g., text classification) [49]. Expert analysis, common among social science researchers, has been validated in content analysis studies [3,8]. However, this method requires much attention from human expert; they are time consuming, costly, and problematic for large amounts of rapidly growing social media data. Further, it is a relatively new phenomenon for ADRD caregivers to utilize social media for information exchange. As such, human experts may lack sufficient knowledge to recognize the range of caregivers' information exchange.

AE can overcome these limitations of expert analysis. However, AE lacks iterative interaction or knowledge exchange between human experts and automatic algorithms, which is unconducive of any co-learning and co-development between expert knowledge and algorithm performance. Recent developments in interactive learning offer hints on how to resolve these issues [42,50], but current approaches to interactions between human experts and automatic algorithms are still inadequate for advancing our understanding of human behavior or improving the performance of algorithms.

To address these limitations, we explore a novel method that enables rich interactions between human experts and automatic algorithms, using as an example our analysis of ADRD caregivers' online information behaviors. Extending interactive learning methods [51], we have designed an iterative process and an interactive system for actively engaging human experts and automatic algorithms. This innovative process aims to maximize the strengths of both human experts and automatic algorithms while at the same time minimizing their limitations. We call this process the *Expert-Machine Co-development (EMC)* process (see Fig. 1).

Our primary research questions (RQs) are:

– RQ1: What types of ADRD-related information do ADRD caregivers exchange in social media?
– RQ2: What keywords can be extracted from online posts to improve those generated by human experts to describe ADRD caregivers' online information exchange?
– RQ3: What characteristics might an interactive learning system require in order to enable the EMC process (i.e., the knowledge exchange between human experts and automatic algorithms)?

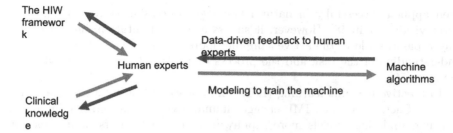

Step 1: Human experts' prior knowledge, i.e., the HIW framework and clinical knowledge, is used to generate the initial modeling to train the machine;
Step 2: Machine algorithms provide data-driven feedback to human experts;
Step 3: Human experts learn from the feedback and revise the modeling;
Step 4: Repeat 2 and 3;
Step 5: Human experts improve the HIW framework and (in a longer term) clinical knowledge (that leads to improved health outcomes)

Fig. 1. The Expert-Machine Co-development (EMC) process

2   Literature Review

In this section, we first review related works for ADRD caregiver's online information exchange, then look at that of active learning/interactive learning.

2.1   ADRD Caregivers' Online Information Exchange

Social media are ubiquitous in health information exchange [20,23,35], presenting an increasingly prominent platform for ADRD caregivers [24]. To date, research on ADRD caregivers' information exchange via social media platforms is limited [6], with notable exceptions. A systematic review of 40 existing internet-based interventions [24] identified five common types of information exchange behaviors among ADRD caregivers online: peer support; communicate with a health or social care provider; information provision; decision support; and psychological support. Erdelez et al.'s work [17] relied on human experts to perform manual content analysis of online posts. Their results showed that ADRD caregivers' online information exchange included seeking factual information; seeking emotional support; sharing information (e.g., about useful resources); sharing own experiences and situations; and seeking advice. More research is needed to understand the types of information caregivers exchange via social media.

2.2   Active Learning and Interactive Learning

Active learning can help automatic algorithms achieve better accuracy with fewer labeled training instances and annotation efforts [37]. Through an active sampling loop, it guides human experts on examining informative data that have significant impact on improving a model's performance. Active learning has been applied successfully in natural language processing [12,32,44] and computer vision [26,46,48]. However, it suffers a major limitation: human experts play a passive role in the active sampling loop, and they cannot obtain deeper understanding of the task and the process or contribute domain knowledge to the loop [50].

Interactive machine learning (IML) offers a way to address this major limitation of active learning. IML engages human experts via iterative interactive learning, updating models more rapidly in response to users' input, focusing on certain aspects of the model, and updating incrementally to prevent drastic changes [2]. In IML, human experts can not only correct the model by annotating more data but also give reasons [45]. IML has succeeded in many domains [10,18,28,31]. Recent research [30,42] has shown that, by adding explanatory debugging to IML, human experts with limited knowledge of machine learning can better understand the model and provide more accurate feedback to help increase the model's performance [30].

In previous work, a supervised classification model has been used to analyze health information exchange in online forums [36,52,58,60] and IML has been used to improve classification models in the health domain [1,29,47]. To our knowledge, no study has applied IML to analyze online health information exchange. Our team's research aims to address this gap by developing and refining an IML-based EMC process, using as an example our analysis and prediction for the types of information ADRD caregivers exchange in social media.

3   Expert Analysis of ADRD Caregivers' Information Exchange

3.1   Reddit Dataset

The Reddit platform enables people to engage in discussions on nearly any topic of interest [15]. It allows users (called "redditors") to share new stories and engage in conversations within the Reddit subcommunities (called "subreddits") [25]. The Alzheimers subreddit (r/Alzheimers)[1] was selected for this study because it is "a place for people affected by Alzheimer's Disease and dementia to support one another and share news about Alzheimer's Disease and Dementia". Using Reddit's official API, we collected 823 posts from the Alzheimers subredit in January 2020. These posts were submitted between July 03, 2018 and January 14, 2020 by 491 unique users. Our data collection procedure was in compliance with Reddit's policy and approved by the Institutional Review Board of xx [anonymized for blind review].

3.2   Process

Two groups of interdisciplinary human experts have contributed to our study: (1) clinicians specialized in ADRD, with extensive clinical experience on ADRD

---

[1] https://www.reddit.com/r/Alzheimers.

patients and their caregivers, and (2) information behavior researchers experienced in examining online behaviors. The complementary expertise of these two groups has facilitated a deep understanding of ADRD caregivers' online information exchange.

To speed up the expert analysis stage, our human experts leveraged a theoretical framework initially developed to characterize the seven types of health information commonly wanted in healthcare encounters, the Health Information Wants (HIW) framework [55–57]. This framework has shown excellent validity and reliability in the general population of older and younger Americans [56,57]. It is highly adaptable to specific populations' unique circumstances, as evidenced by its successful adaption to and validation among individuals with diabetes [33] and cancer patients and their family caregivers [53,54].

The HIW-ADRD 1.0 Framework. Building on these prior efforts, the HIW framework was adapted to the ADRD caregiver population as a new HIW-ADRD framework, expanding the HIW framework by adding multiple new categories to reflect the types of care that ADRD caregivers typically provide. For example, the "self-care" category in the initial HIW framework was expanded to become (1) daily care for a patient at home; (2) care transition and coordination; (3) end-of-life care; and (4) care for a caregiver. Further, our human experts' clinical experience suggested that caregivers often seek information about scientific updates related to ADRD and opportunities for participating in clinical trials. Thus, a new category, "scientific updates/research participation," was added. Our new framework, HIW-ADRD, included 11 types of health information typically wanted by ADRD caregivers:

- information about treatment/ medication/prevention;
- characteristics of/experiences with the health condition;
- laboratory tests/medical exams/diagnostic procedures;
- daily care for a patient at home (practical, strategies, tips);
- care transition and coordination (between home and a facility);
- end-of-life (EOL) care;
- care for a caregiver (caregiver self-care, or a third person seeking information for a caregiver; this type focuses on non-psychosocial aspects);
- psychosocial aspects;
- health care provider/facility/ resources;
- legal/financial/ insurance; and
- scientific updates/research participation.

To facilitate automatic classification of the 11 types of health information, our human experts created an initial list of keywords for each information type. The keywords were based primarily on clinical experience (e.g., keywords for "treatments" included "meditation" and "yoga").

The HIW-ADRD 2.0 Framework. Using the HIW-ADRD 1.0 framework, in spring 2020, one human expert first coded 106 most recent and most voted posts in our dataset. This step revealed that we needed a new category, *not-information-seeking*, to capture posts that were not intended to obtain information from others; rather, these posts featured *giving out* information to others. This new category was theoretically significant, broadening the scope of the original HIW framework to include information both wanted and shared. We developed the original framework to understand information wanted in health-care encounters. Yet our analysis of the social media posts showed that a large portion of the posts were not intended to obtain information, but rather to share useful resources or simply to vent. Thus, we modified our HIW-ADRD 1.0 framework to HIW-ADRD 2.0, with 12 types of information commonly *exchanged* in social media.

The HIW-ADRD 3.0 Framework. Three human experts then used the HIW-ADRD 2.0 framework to independently code a new set of 94 posts. The average pairwise percent agreement rates ranged from 86.51% to 100%. Through deliberation, these human experts reached a consensus to merge the categories with no or few posts with other categories. These included: (1) the "laboratory tests" category was merged with "characteristics"; (2) "EOL care" was merged with "care transition"; (3) "care for a caregiver" was merged with "daily care"; and (4) "scientific updates/research participation" was merged with "resources." Also, the "psychosocial" category was more explicitly redefined to focus on information *unrelated* to specific, practical strategies or tips, while "daily care" and "care transition" were adjusted to focus on information related to specific, practical strategies or tips.

The resulting HIW-ADRD 3.0 framework entailed 7 types of information commonly exchanged in online peer support groups (Table 1[2]). One human expert then recoded the first 106 posts using HIW-ADRD 3.0, resulting in 200 annotated posts. These results were compared with those generated by our automatic analysis system. Overall agreement was 88.7%. Differences were resolved through team members' discussions.

4 Automatic Exploration (AE) of ADRD Caregivers' Information Behaviors

4.1 Objective

To effectively support EMC, AE must accomplish two important objectives. The first is to construct a classification model using posts annotated by human experts. The model provides AE with post classification capability, and the classification's effectiveness can serve as feedback for experts to improve their conceptual framework. This objective is consistent with that of an automatic algorithm in supervised or semi-supervised methods.

---

[2] Due to space limit, we are showing an abbreviated version of HIW-ADRD 3.0 with limited content such as sample keywords; to obtain the full version, contact the authors.

Table 1. The HIW-ADRD 3.0 framework

Type of information	Sample keywords	Number(%) of posts
Treatment/Medication/Prevention	Drug; oriental; acupuncture; vitamins	8(4)
Characteristics of/Experience with the health condition/Diagnostic procedures	Diagnosis; complication; cause; prognosis; process; symptom; memory loss; lab test; MRI; PET; blood	17(8.5)
Daily care for a patient at home/Care for a caregiver (practical strategies or tips, not psychosocial)	Wandering; bath; hygiene; sleep; eat; driving	28(14)
Care transition and coordination/End-of-life care (practical, not psychosocial)	Adult day care; rehab; hospital; memory care; nursing home; hospice	13(6.5)
Psychosocial aspects	Stress; lonely; heartbreaking; overwhelmed; venting	66(33)
Resources/Advocacy/Scientific updates/Research participation	Lobby; fundraising; clinical trial; news; article; scientist	63(31.5)
Legal/Financial/Insurance	Power of attorney; POA; living will; Medicare; Medicaid	5(2.5)

The second objective is to provide a set of data-driven insights regarding the classification model and the corresponding conceptual framework (e.g., the HIW-ADRD). In our current AE design, this objective is achieved through a set of indicators regarding the category distributions of posts and the importance or correlation of keywords within and across categories.

4.2   The AE Component Design

The AE component is based on an ML loop with several rounds of interactions between the classification model and the human experts. In each round, the classification model engages the human experts on a few tasks. First, with AE's help, human experts review and update the keywords of the HIW-ADRD framework, which in turn can affect the classification model. Second, a small number of new posts are selected by AE for the experts to annotate so that the classification model can be retrained for further improvement. This interactive learning loop repeats until the model's performance can be increased no more. To assist experts with little background in automatic algorithms, we built an "Interactive Auto Exploration Interface" (IAEI) (Fig. 2).

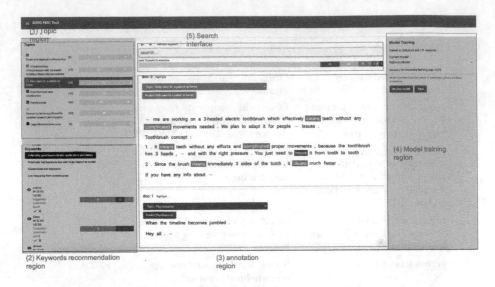

Fig. 2. IAEI: AE's interactive interface

Keywords Recommendation. The first step in the IML loop is for AE to provide feedback to the experts in the form of recommendations about keywords (removing existing ones or adding new ones). This is called *keyword tuning* (KT). The goal of KT is to help the experts understand each keyword's impact on the classification model, which may subsequently lead to the experts' reassessment of each keyword's role in the HIW-ADRD framework.

The recommendation for a keyword is based on three measurements that represent correlations among keywords, categories, and models. The first is the *importance score* $I(t, m)$ for a keyword t in model m, which shows the impact of keyword t as a feature in model m's prediction. The calculation of $I(t, m)$ depends on a specific classification model, so we will present its calculation in Sect. 4.3. The second measurement is the normalized mutual information score $MI(t, c)$ for keyword t in category c (see Formulas 1, 2). The $MI(t, c)$ score measures the correlation between keyword t and category c.

$$MI(t, c) = \frac{2I(label_t, label_c)}{entropy(label_t) + entropy(label_c)} \tag{1}$$

$$I(label_t, label_c) = \sum_{i,j} p(label_{ti}, label_{cj}) log(\frac{p(label_{ti}, label_{cj})}{p(label_{ti}) p(label_{cj})}) \tag{2}$$

The third measure is the *keyword frequency* $KF(t)$, which shows the number of posts (including unannotated posts) containing keyword t.

Based on these three measurements, we identified keywords that needed tuning; these keywords were divided into three groups (the remaining keywords were considered good ones for the model that needed no tuning for the current round):

- *potentially good (PG)* keywords have a high correlation with their category but low impact on the classification model. They have a high MI score but low I score, where high/low is defined as larger/smaller than the average score for all keywords. Their impact is low because they do not appear in enough annotated posts. Posts that contain these keywords can be recommended for additional annotation to increase their impact on the model.
- *potentially bad (PB)* keywords have a low correlation with the category but high impact on the model. They have a low MI score and high I score. They are usually common words that appear uniformly in multiple categories. By removing PB keywords, the model can improve its accuracy.
- *low frequent(LF)* keywords have too small frequency even on unannotated posts, so they have no impact on the model. These keywords have an I score of 0 and a low KF score. Here, we define low KF score as a KF score smaller than $minimum(KF(t))$ for all t that have $I(t, m) > 0$. AE recommends removing these keywords because their low frequency might be caused by a term mismatch between the words used by patients/caregivers and those used by clinicians.

In addition to these three groups of keyword recommendations, AE can generate a fourth group of keyword recommendations— *new keywords (NK)* that are not in the current HIW-ADRD framework. NK terms should have a high correlation with a specific category according to annotated posts, which makes them potentially good keywords for a specific category. They should appear sufficiently frequent in all posts so that, with more annotation, they can have an impact on the classification model's prediction. To identify NK terms, we first selected only nouns and noun phrases, performed stemming, and then removed low-frequency keywords that have KF smaller than $minimum(KF(t))$ for all t have $I(t, m) > 0$.

AE Assisted Exploration and Feedback. In the second step in the IML loop, experts use the IAEI's keyword recommendations to make inferences on how to revise the HIW-ADRD framework. At the same time, the IAEI collects feedback on the keyword recommendations to guide AE in the next round of annotation and recommendation. For keyword visualization, the IAEI shows four categories of recommendations in the "Keywords recommendation region" (Fig. 2, region 2). Inside this region, a distribution bar next to a keyword shows the keyword's distribution in different categories. When one section of the distribution bar is clicked, the corresponding posts are shown in the "annotation region" (Fig. 2, region 3). Inside the posts, the keywords from different categories are highlighted, which helps the expert quickly judge the quality of a recommendation and revise the keywords.

The IAEI helps the experts discover new or alternative keywords from groups LF and PB for recommendations. Some LF keywords are low frequency because they are not common forms of words that caregivers used in online forums. Some PB keywords are too generic, needing a more specific replacement. The search interface (Fig. 2, region 5) helps the experts search for potentially better forms of keywords from these two groups. Under the search box, a distribution bar shows the category distribution of searched keywords, which lets the experts know the correlations between searched keywords and different categories; the expert can then quickly assess if the keywords are potentially good or not.

After reviewing the keyword recommendations, human experts provide feedback to the AE so that it can recommend the next round of annotations and keywords. In the IAEI, human experts can provide feedback in three way: (1) confirming a recommendation for a good keyword by clicking "✓" under each keyword in the "Keywords recommendation region"; (2) removing bad keywords by clicking the "x" button after each keyword; and (3) adding new keywords by clicking "add new keyword" above the search box.

Annotation and Stop Recommendations. In the last step in the IML loop, AE guides the next round of annotation with two specific goals. The first is to make annotation recommendations as efficient as possible, so that human experts can selectively annotate less data but achieve more performance improvement in the classification model. The second goal is to give a stop signal, so that the experts stop the interactive loop when further annotation is unlikely to generate further improvement in the classification model.

To achieve the first goal, we select the most informative unannotated posts that contain the most keywords that human experts consider to be good. To measure how informative a given post p is, we calculate aggregated MI (AMI) from Formula 3. Here, for t_i from Potentially Bad(PB), c_i is the category of t_i. All annotated posts are ranked by AMI score in descending order and we recommend the top posts for the next round of annotation. These posts are shown in the "annotation region" (Fig. 2, region 3), with the keywords from different categories highlighted in the text. This makes the recommendation transparent to the experts.

$$AMI(p) = \sum_{i=1}^{n} MI(t_i, c_t) \tag{3}$$

To achieve the second goal, we evaluate whether the new model can improve its performance according to two measurements after retraining. The first is the model's predication accuracy. However, accuracy is not enough, because the model can overfit to the training data and thus give a higher impact to statistically significant but meaningless keywords. Therefore, we have introduced a second measurement: the normalized discounted cumulative gain (nDCG) between the keyword's MI score ranking (descending) and the keyword I score ranking. The $nDCG$ score can be used to evaluate whether better keywords have a more significant impact on the classification model. A stop recommendation is made if both measurements cease to increase after model retraining. The recommendation is shown in the "Model training region" (Fig. 2, region 4).

4.3 The Experiment on Improving AE Performance

As stated in Sect. 4.1, AE has two objectives. These objectives also guide the evaluation of AE: (1) improvement that AE can contribute to the classification model's accuracy, and (2) the usability of AE and its interface in helping human experts understand and revise the HIW-ADRD framework. Accordingly, we designed two experiments to evaluate AE. Based on the outcomes of the first experiment, the best performing classification model was incorporated for keyword recommendations in the iterative EMC process with human experts.

An interview with one of the human experts was conducted for the HIW-ADRD framework's revision and usability evaluation of the AE interface (IAEI).

Training and Testing Datasets. The experts annotated 392 posts to create training and testing datasets for the classification model. The 200 posts annotated in Sect. 3.2 served as the initial dataset (ID) to train the initial classification model. To examine the effectiveness of AE in improving the classification model's performance, two of the human experts annotated 192 additional posts. We extracted 57 posts from those as the testing dataset (TEST) to evaluate the classification model. The remaining 135 posts formed a recommendation dataset (RD) that AE used for annotation recommendation.

The Classification Models Inside AE. AE needs a classification model as the automatic engine for categorizing posts. We used three commonly used classification algorithms: Naïve Bayes [19], SVM [39] and Xgboost [11]. The inputs to all three models are the document representations of keywords and their frequency for a given post p and the output is the category c of p.

The keyword importance score I is a measure that is model-dependent. For SVM model, $abs(w_i)$ [9] was used where w_i is the weight for feature i. For Naïve Bayes model, Weighted Average Pointwise Mutual Information [41] was used. For Xgboost model, average gain [11] was used. The calculation details can be seen in Appendix.

Experiment Datasets. During the experiments, we developed five combinations of training datasets and keywords (see Table 2).

For the AE process, our system recommended the top 10 posts for each round of annotation, and the system suggested stopping the loop after 4 rounds of annotations for all 3 models.

As shown in Table 3, **ID+IML+KT** achieved the best accuracy on TEST for all three models, which indicates that the combination of IML and KT clearly increased the performance of the classification model most. Comparing the complexity of the three classification models, we found that Xgboost, the most complex model, started with the lowest accuracy of 0.281 trained on **ID** but ended with the highest accuracy of 0.544 on **ID+IML+KT**. This shows that a more complex classification model can be improved more by AE.

Table 2. Combinations of training datasets and keywords

Training group	Explanation
ID	This dataset contains the 200 annotated posts manually created by human experts. We used this dataset as the initial dataset (ID) to train the classification model inside AE
ID+RD (benchmark)	This dataset contains posts from ID and all posts from RD, which represents all available training posts. The model trained on this dataset was used as the benchmark for comparison with the model trained by AE
ID + IML	Posts from ID and a subsets of the posts from RD recommended by the IML loop in the AE component. By comparing the model trained on this dataset with the model trained on ID+RD dataset, we evaluated how much the IML loop improved the accuracy of the classification model
ID+RD+KT (benchmark)	Posts from ID and all posts from RD with the keywords tuning(KT). KT includes new keywords added and bad keywords removed by the human experts according to the keywords recommendations from AE The model trained on this dataset was used as a benchmark for comparison with the model trained through IML with KT
ID+IML+KT	Posts from ID and a subsets of posts from RD recommended by AE with KT. This dataset represents the real model trained with AE, which combines both KT and interactive learning

Comparing the accuracy between **ID+RD** and **ID+IML**, the recommended posts from the **IML** increased the model's accuracy on TEST. Examination of the accuracy results between **ID+RD+KT** and **ID+IML+KT** shows that KT from AE also clearly increased the model accuracy on TEST for all three models. Indeed the accuracy of all three models trained on **ID+IML** is better than models training on **ID+RD**.

Finally, comparing the number of posts that the human experts annotated in **IML** (40) with the the number of posts in **RD** (135), only 29.6% of posts were annotated from **RD** through **IML**. This shows that AE reduces the burden of annotation efforts on human experts.

4.4   Usability Experiment with Human Experts

HIW-ADRD Framework V3.1. Because Xgboost performed the best, our human expert's review of keyword recommendations was performed on its outputs in IAEI. The expert discovered 7 alternative keywords that were more applicable than the original keywords for describing ADRD caregivers' online information exchange. The expert also removed 6 keywords from the framework that were clearly not applicable for ADRD caregivers' online information

Table 3. Model accuracy for five training groups

Training group	Dataset	Xgboost	SVM	Naïve Bayes
ID	TRAIN	0.870	0.640	0.705
	TEST	0.281	0.351	0.281
ID+RD (benchmark)	TRAIN	0.854	0.618	0.699
	TEST	0.333	0.404	0.333
ID+IML	TRAIN	0.887	0.637	0.692
	TEST	0.509	0.421	0.386
ID+RD+KT (benchmark)	TRAIN	0.851	0.630	0.696
	TEST	0.316	0.439	0.316
ID+IML+KT	TRAIN	0.892	0.658	0.696
	TEST	**0.544***	**0.456**	**0.421**

exchange. In addition, the expert added 15 out of 25 (60%) NK terms recommended by AE as new keywords for HIW-ADRD. The outcome is HIW-ADRD v3.1, which contains the same 7 categories as those of v3 but with more accurate, applicable keywords.

IAEI Usability Evaluation. An interview on usability was also conducted with one human expert to review the design of the IAEI. Positive aspects identified included: the visualization of keyword recommendations was helpful in guiding the revision of existing keywords and the discovery of new keywords; the distribution bar and the highlighted keywords in the posts accelerated the expert's speed in reviewing keywords; the search interface and distribution bar for searched keywords provided real-time feedback for discovering better forms of keywords with low frequencies; and the annotation recommendations enabled fewer post reviews for each round of IML.

The expert also pointed out areas for usability improvement. The IAEI was overwhelming and not intuitive, requiring a steep learning curve to understand and master each function in the interface. For instance, color was heavily used in the interface for highlighting and other purposes. Although word normalization (e.g., case folding and stemming) within keywords was helpful for grouping similar keywords, it sometimes led to incorrect recommendations. For instance, because "medication" and "medical" have different meanings but share the same stem, "medical" was inaccurately categorized as "Treatment/Medication/Prevention".

5 Discussion

This study illustrates the importance of interdisciplinary collaboration between human experts with knowledge about ADRD caregivers and information scientists experienced in the design of automatic algorithms. Our innovative EMC process has demonstrated its effectiveness in establishing a collaborative, iterative process that combines the strength of expert analysis and automatic exploration by enabling co-learning between human experts and automatic algorithms.

5.1   Classification Models' Gains from the EMC Process

Our study shows that classification models gain their improvement through AE in three ways. First, by engaging human experts in interactive learning and keyword tuning, AE enabled the models to identify better input features (keywords) and to increase the impact of those features on the models through annotation recommendation. Models trained on **ID+IML+KT** clearly increased their accuracy in comparison with others. Second, by differentiating keywords with high and low MI scores in AE, the classification models improved through more effective interactive learning. Models trained on **IML**, a small subset of **RD**, achieved higher accuracy than models trained on **ID+RD**. Third, by combining **IML** and **KT**, AE enabled the models to be more robust. Experiments involving **ID+IML+KT** increased the accuracy of all three models in comparison with **ID+IML**. However, this was not the case between **ID+RD+KT** and **ID+RD**, where SVM increased its accuracy but that of Xgboost and Naïve Bayes dropped.

5.2   Human Experts' Gains from the EMC Process

Although human experts can use manual analysis to create and improve the HIW-ADRD framework, they benefit from the EMC process with AE, from which they receive data and model-driven assistance. This assistance enabled human experts to refine the framework to more accurately represent ADRD caregivers' online information exchange.

Specifically, the EMC process helps human experts refine the HIW-ADRD framework in three important ways. First, the experts' knowledge about ADRD caregivers came mainly from direct interactions with patients and their caregivers in clinical settings; there were gaps in their knowledge about ADRD caregivers' online interactions with peers, particularly about keywords caregivers use in their online information exchange with peers. LF keyword recommendations in the IAEI helped the experts quickly discover keywords that appeared more frequently in online posts with peers. For example, in online posts, ADRD caregivers often use "day care" instead of "adult day care", "home care" instead of "in-home care", and "test" instead of "laboratory test". Similarly, PB keyword recommendations helped the experts recognize ambiguous words in posts. For example, some posts containing "home" referred to "patient home" that fits the category of "Daily care for a patient at home", while other posts contained "home" as "nursing home" that fits the category of "Care transition and coordination".

Second, the EMC process helps human experts discover more comprehensive keywords through new keyword recommendations. When keywords are needed for the category of "Psychosocial", all terms related to patients' feelings (e.g., "scared", "lonely") could be selected. With the help of NK recommendations and the navigation function in the IAEI, the experts quickly reviewed recommended keywords in highlighted posts. Consequently, the new keywords "guilty" and "relief" were added to HIW-ADRD 3.1.

Third, the EMC process facilitates human experts' recognition of unfamiliar user behaviors. NK recommendation goes through all words/phrases in the posts to discover statistically significant new keywords. Some of these new keywords may reflect caregivers' wording choices previously neglected by experts. For instance, the word "shell" was used to refer to patients' status of losing major brain function (e.g., "Then there was her at the late stage, an unrecognizable shell. She spent the last year of her life sat in a chair"). Such emotional words were not typically used in face-to-face consultations but they are common in online posts.

5.3 Limitations and Future Directions

Model Accuracy. The classification model's performance increased greatly with the help of AE; but training data remain limited, and the model is restricted by keyword-only features. Many potentially good keywords were ignored by the AE simply because they appeared too infrequently to have an impact on the classification model. In addition, human experts prioritized keywords in key sentences (e.g., sentences with question marks) in their manual annotations, but current automatic classification models cannot reliably identify these key sentences. Finally, we chose our classification models because they could be trained quickly to provide real-time feedback to human experts. This meant that we could not use deep neural network models for classification. In future research, we will identify deep neural network models that may meet our needs for rapid training and real-time feedback with enhanced performance.

Keyword Recommendations. Our keyword recommendations still have some quality issues. Word normalization can cause wrong recommendations. For example, the medical meaning of "CAT" is quite different from "cat". A future IAEI should enable human experts to decide whether "CAT" or "cat" should be normalized.

IAEI. The current interface contains many functions. But it is complex, requiring a steep learning curve. The color used to highlight keywords and the distribution bar for different categories can be confusing. MI and I scores were also hard to understand among human experts with limited prior training in machine learning. Future research should strive to develop ways to improve the interface and communication of machine learning algorithms to a broad audience (e.g., a clean process featuring intuitive ways for input and output, with technical details in the "black box" between the input and output interfaces–that can be opened and examined if necessary but can be left unopened otherwise).

6   Conclusions

ADRD caregivers exchange various types of information in social media, yet research on their online information behavior is limited. Limitations exist in both manual analysis by human experts and fully automated data-driven exploration through text classification techniques. The present study used online posts from a Reddit group as a case study to explore an innovative EMC process to build collaborative, iterative interactions between human experts and automatic algorithms. Through the EMC process, human experts constructed and refined the HIW-ADRD framework. Meanwhile, AE, aided by its classification models and IAEI interface, engaged human experts in exploration to refine the keywords in the HIW-ADRD framework and an interactive learning loop to provide feedback to the classification models. Our study has illustrated steps in the EMC process, demonstrating the EMC's effectiveness in enabling experts to construct more accurate representations of ADRD caregivers' online information exchange and improve automatic algorithms' classification accuracy. Our usability experiment demonstrated the IAEI's facilitation of human experts' interactive exploration.

We will examine several areas in future research: (1) improving the classification models in our AE component with more sophisticated models and feature design; (2) creating more accurate keyword tuning recommendations with better NLP processing; and (3) lowering the learning curve for IAEI with more user-friendly interface design and conducting more usability testing. We will further refine the EMC process by exploring its use with other types of tasks that need collaboration between human experts and automatic algorithms for exploring the problem space.

A   Appendix

A.1   Importance Score calculation

The keyword importance score I is a measure that is model-dependent, so we introduce the implementation of I within the three classification models:

- Our linear kernel SVM model can be written as $c = signal(b + W^T x)$, where $W = (w_1, w_2, ...w_k)$ are the weights for the features in the model. $abs(wi)$ represents the importance of the feature in the model [9], so it is selected as the I score.
- When expressed in log-space, classification based on Multinomial Naïve Bayes model can be written as Formula 4, where $b = log(p(c_j))$ and $w_j i = log(p_j i)$. Weighted Average Pointwise Mutual Information (WAPMI) calculated from $w_j i$ is a good measurement to evaluate the importance of the feature [41], so it can be used as the I score. Note that the WAPMI score is between keyword t and model m, and it is different from $MI(t, c)$ where c is a category.

$$log(p(c_j|x)) = log(p(c_j) \prod_i p_j i^x i)$$

$$= log(p(c_j)) + \sum_i x_i log(p_j i)$$

$$= b + W_j^t x \tag{4}$$

– The Xgboost model generates a forest of decision trees $T = (t_1, t_2, ..., t_n)$, where a feature x_t is used to split a branch b_{ij} within a tree. The information gain $gain(x_t, b_{ij})$ for feature x in branch b_{ij} can be used to measure whether the split is good. By calculating the average gain $gain(c_t)$ (see Formula 5) across all the trees in the forest, we can measure how feature c_k affects the whole model. $gain(c_k)$ is the most important score for Xgboost feature selection [11]. Thus, we use this score as the I score.

$$gain(c_t) = \frac{\sum\limits_{i=1}^{n} \sum\limits_{j=1}^{b_i} gain(x_i, b_{ij})}{\sum\limits_{i=1}^{n} b_i} \tag{5}$$

A.2   Abbreviations

ADRD Alzheimer's disease and related dementias
EMC Expert–machineco-development
AE Automatic Exploration
IML Interactive Machine Learning
HIW Health Information Wants
EOL End-of-life
IAEI Interactive Auto Exploration Interface
KT Keyword Tuning
I Important Score
MI Mututal Infomration Score
KF Keyword Frequency
PG Potnetially Good Recommendation Group
PB Potnetially Bad Recommendation Group
LF Low Frequency Recommendation Group
NK New Keywords Recommendation Group
AMI Average Mutual Information Score
nDCG Normalized Discounted Cumulative Gain
ID Initial Dataset
TEST Test Dataset
RD Recommendation Dataset
RD Recommendation Dataset

References

1. Ahmad, M.A., Eckert, C., Teredesai, A.: Interpretable machine learning in health-care. In: Proceedings of the 2018 ACM International Conference on Bioinformatics, Computational Biology, and Health Informatics, pp. 559–560 (2018)
2. Amershi, S., Cakmak, M., Knox, W.B., Kulesza, T.: Power to the people: the role of humans in interactive machine learning. AI Mag. **35**(4), 105–120 (2014)
3. Andalibi, N., Haimson, O.L., De Choudhury, M., Forte, A.: Understanding social media disclosures of sexual abuse through the lenses of support seeking and anonymity. In: Proceedings of the 2016 CHI Conference on Human Factors in Computing Systems, pp. 3906–3918 (2016)
4. Anderson, J.G., Hundt, E., Dean, M., Rose, K.M.: "A fine line that we walk every day": self-care approaches used by family caregivers of persons with dementia. Issues Mental Health Nurs. **40**(3), 252–259 (2019)
5. Association, A.: 2019 Alzheimer's disease facts and figures. Alzheimer's Dement. **15**(3), 321–387 (2019)
6. Bateman, D.R., Brady, E., Wilkerson, D., Yi, E.H., Karanam, Y., Callahan, C.M.: Comparing crowdsourcing and friendsourcing: a social media-based feasibility study to support Alzheimer disease caregivers. JMIR Res. Protoc. **6**(4), e56 (2017)
7. Bonner, G.J., Wang, E., Wilkie, D.J., Ferrans, C.E., Dancy, B., Watkins, Y.: Advance care treatment plan (ACT-plan) for African American family caregivers: a pilot study. Dementia **13**(1), 79–95 (2014)
8. Bowler, L., Monahan, J., Jeng, W., Oh, J.S., He, D.: The quality and helpfulness of answers to eating disorder questions in Yahoo! answers: teens speak out. Proc. Assoc. Inf. Sci. Technol. **52**(1), 1–10 (2015)
9. Brank, J., Grobelnik, M., Milic-Frayling, N., Mladenic, D.: Feature selection using support vector machines. WIT Trans. Inf. Commun. Technol. **28** (2002)
10. Chau, D.H., Kittur, A., Hong, J.I., Faloutsos, C.: Apolo: making sense of large network data by combining rich user interaction and machine learning. In: Proceedings of the SIGCHI Conference on Human Factors in Computing Systems, pp. 167–176 (2011)
11. Chen, T., Guestrin, C.: XGBoost: a scalable tree boosting system. In: Proceedings of the 22nd ACM SIGKDD International Conference on Knowledge Discovery and Data Mining, pp. 785–794 (2016)
12. Chen, Y., Cao, H., Mei, Q., Zheng, K., Xu, H.: Applying active learning to supervised word sense disambiguation in medline. J. Am. Med. Inf. Assoc. **20**(5), 1001–1006 (2013)
13. Collopy, B.J.: The moral underpinning of the proxy-provider relationship: issues of trust and distrust. J. Law Med. Ethics **27**(1), 37–45 (1999)
14. Ditto, P.H., et al.: Advance directives as acts of communication: a randomized controlled trial. Arch. Internal Med. **161**(3), 421–430 (2001)
15. Dosono, B.: Identity work of Asian Americans and Pacific Islanders on reddit: traversals of deliberation, moderation, and decolonization (2019)
16. Einterz, S.F., Gilliam, R., Lin, F.C., McBride, J.M., Hanson, L.C.: Development and testing of a decision aid on goals of care for advanced dementia. J. Am. Med. Direct. Assoc. **15**(4), 251–255 (2014)
17. Erdelez, S., Tanacković, S.F., Balog, K.P.: Online behavior of the Alzheimer's disease patient caregivers on croatian online discussion forum. Proc. Assoc. Inf. Sci. Technol. **56**(1), 78–88 (2019)

18. Esuli, A., Moreo, A., Sebastiani, F.: Building automated survey coders via interactive machine learning. arXiv preprint arXiv:1903.12110 (2019)
19. Eyheramendy, S., Lewis, D.D., Madigan, D.: On the Naive Bayes model for text categorization (2003)
20. Fox, S., et al.: The social life of health information. Pew Internet & American Life Project Washington, DC (2011)
21. Gessert, C.E., Forbes, S., Bern-Klug, M.: Planning end-of-life care for patients with dementia: roles of families and health professionals. OMEGA J. Death Dying **42**(4), 273–291 (2001)
22. Hanson, L.C., et al.: Improving decision-making for feeding options in advanced dementia: a randomized, controlled trial. J. Am. Geriatr. Soc. **59**(11), 2009–2016 (2011)
23. Hawn, C.: Take two aspirin and tweet me in the morning: how Twitter, Facebook, and other social media are reshaping health care. Health Aff. **28**(2), 361–368 (2009)
24. Hopwood, J., et al.: Internet-based interventions aimed at supporting family caregivers of people with dementia: systematic review. J. Med. Internet Res. **20**(6), e216 (2018)
25. Isaac, M., Streitfeld, D.: It's silicon valley 2, ellen pao 0: Fighter of sexism is out at reddit. New York Times (2015)
26. Joshi, A.J., Porikli, F., Papanikolopoulos, N.: Multi-class active learning for image classification. In: 2009 IEEE Conference on Computer Vision and Pattern Recognition, pp. 2372–2379. IEEE (2009)
27. Jox, R.J., Denke, E., Hamann, J., Mendel, R., Förstl, H., Borasio, G.D.: Surrogate decision making for patients with end-stage dementia. Int. J. Geriat. Psychiatry **27**(10), 1045–1052 (2012)
28. Kabra, M., Robie, A.A., Rivera-Alba, M., Branson, S., Branson, K.: JAABA: interactive machine learning for automatic annotation of animal behavior. Nat. Methods **10**(1), 64 (2013)
29. Kose, I., Gokturk, M., Kilic, K.: An interactive machine learning-based electronic fraud and abuse detection system in healthcare insurance. Appl. Soft Comput. **36**, 283–299 (2015)
30. Kulesza, T., Burnett, M., Wong, W.K., Stumpf, S.: Principles of explanatory debugging to personalize interactive machine learning. In: Proceedings of the 20th International Conference on Intelligent User Interfaces, pp. 126–137 (2015)
31. Lunga, D., Yang, H.L., Reith, A., Weaver, J., Yuan, J., Bhaduri, B.: Domain-adapted convolutional networks for satellite image classification: a large-scale interactive learning workflow. IEEE J. Sel. Top. Appl. Earth Obs. Remote Sens. **11**(3), 962–977 (2018)
32. Magnini, B., Minard, A.L., Qwaider, M.R., Speranza, M.: TextPro-AL: an active learning platform for flexible and efficient production of training data for nlp tasks. In: Proceedings of COLING 2016, the 26th International Conference on Computational Linguistics: System Demonstrations, pp. 131–135 (2016)
33. Nie, L., Xie, B., Yang, Y., Shan, Y.M.: Characteristics of Chinese m-health applications for diabetes self-management. Telemed. e-Health **22**(7), 614–619 (2016)
34. Pagán-Ortiz, M.E., Cortés, D.E., Rudloff, N., Weitzman, P., Levkoff, S.: Use of an online community to provide support to caregivers of people with dementia. WJ. Gerontol. Soc. Work **57**(6–7), 694–709 (2014)
35. Patel, R., Chang, T., Greysen, S.R., Chopra, V.: Social media use in chronic disease: a systematic review and novel taxonomy. Am. J. Med. **128**(12), 1335–1350 (2015)

36. Reichert, J.R., Kristensen, K.L., Mukkamala, R.R., Vatrapu, R.: A supervised machine learning study of online discussion forums about type-2 diabetes. In: 2017 IEEE 19Th International Conference on E-health Networking, Applications and Services (Healthcom), pp. 1–7. IEEE (2017)

37. Settles, B.: Active learning literature survey. Technical report, University of Wisconsin-Madison Department of Computer Sciences (2009)

38. Stirling, C., et al.: Decision aids for respite service choices by carers of people with dementia: development and pilot RCT. BMC Med. Inf. Decis. Making **12**(1), 21 (2012)

39. Suykens, J.A., Vandewalle, J.: Least squares support vector machine classifiers. Neural Process. Lett. **9**(3), 293–300 (1999)

40. Swigart, V., Lidz, C., Butteworth, V., Arnold, R.: Letting go: family willingness to forgo life support. Heart Lung **25**(6), 483–494 (1996)

41. Tang, B., Kay, S., He, H.: Toward optimal feature selection in Naive Bayes for text categorization. IEEE Trans. knowl. Data Eng. **28**(9), 2508–2521 (2016)

42. Teso, S., Kersting, K.: Explanatory interactive machine learning. In: Proceedings of the 2019 AAAI/ACM Conference on AI, Ethics, and Society, pp. 239–245 (2019)

43. Thackeray, R., Crookston, B.T., West, J.H.: Correlates of health-related social media use among adults. J. Med. Internet Res. **15**(1), e21 (2013)

44. Tran, V.C., Nguyen, N.T., Fujita, H., Hoang, D.T., Hwang, D.: A combination of active learning and self-learning for named entity recognition on twitter using conditional random fields. Knowl. Based Syst. **132**, 179–187 (2017)

45. Trivedi, G., Pham, P., Chapman, W.W., Hwa, R., Wiebe, J., Hochheiser, H.: Nlpreviz: an interactive tool for natural language processing on clinical text. J. Am. Med. Inf. Assoc. **25**(1), 81–87 (2018)

46. Tuia, D., Ratle, F., Pacifici, F., Kanevski, M.F., Emery, W.J.: Active learning methods for remote sensing image classification. IEEE Trans. Geosci. Remote Sens. **47**(7), 2218–2232 (2009)

47. Ullah, M.R., Bhuiyan, M.A.R., Das, A.K.: Ihemha: interactive healthcare system design with emotion computing and medical history analysis. In: 2017 6th International Conference on Informatics, Electronics and Vision & 2017 7th International Symposium in Computational Medical and Health Technology (ICIEV-ISCMHT), pp. 1–8. IEEE (2017)

48. Wang, K., Zhang, D., Li, Y., Zhang, R., Lin, L.: Cost-effective active learning for deep image classification. IEEE Trans. Circ. Syst. Video Technol. **27**(12), 2591–2600 (2016)

49. Wang, Y.C., Kraut, R.E., Levine, J.M.: Eliciting and receiving online support: using computer-aided content analysis to examine the dynamics of online social support. J. Med. Internet Res. **17**(4), e99 (2015)

50. Wang, Y., Zheng, K., Xu, H., Mei, Q.: Clinical word sense disambiguation with interactive search and classification. In: AMIA Annual Symposium Proceedings, vol. 2016, p. 2062. American Medical Informatics Association (2016)

51. Ware, M., Frank, E., Holmes, G., Hall, M., Witten, I.H.: Interactive machine learning: letting users build classifiers. Int. J. Hum. Comput. Stud. **55**(3), 281–292 (2001)

52. Wen, M., Rosé, C.P.: Understanding participant behavior trajectories in online health support groups using automatic extraction methods. In: Proceedings of the 17th ACM International Conference on Supporting Group Work, pp. 179–188 (2012)

53. Xie, B., Su, Z., Liu, Y., Wang, M., Zhang, M.: Health information wanted and obtained from doctors/nurses: a comparison of Chinese cancer patients and family caregivers. Support. Care Cancer **23**(10), 2873–2880 (2015)
54. Xie, B., Su, Z., Liu, Y., Wang, M., Zhang, M.: Health information sources for different types of information used by Chinese patients with cancer and their family caregivers. Health Expect. **20**(4), 665–674 (2017)
55. Xie, B., Wang, M., Feldman, R.: Preferences for health information and decision-making: development of the health information wants (HIW) questionnaire. In: Proceedings of the 2011 iConference, pp. 273–280 (2011)
56. Xie, B., Wang, M., Feldman, R., Zhou, L.: Internet use frequency and patient-centered care: measuring patient preferences for participation using the health information wants questionnaire. J. Med. Internet Res. **15**(7), e132 (2013)
57. Xie, B., Wang, M., Feldman, R., Zhou, L.: Exploring older and younger adults' preferences for health information and participation in decision making using the h ealth i nformation w ants q uestionnaire (hiwq). Health Expect. **17**(6), 795–808 (2014)
58. Yin, Z., Sulieman, L.M., Malin, B.A.: A systematic literature review of machine learning in online personal health data. J. Am. Med. Inf. Assoc. **26**(6), 561–576 (2019)
59. Yoon, S., Lucero, R., Mittelman, M.S., Luchsinger, J.A., Bakken, S.: Mining twitter to inform the design of online interventions for Hispanic Alzheimer's disease and related dementias caregivers. Hispanic Health Care Int. **18**(3), 138–143 (2020)
60. Zhang, S., Grave, E., Sklar, E., Elhadad, N.: Longitudinal analysis of discussion topics in an online breast cancer community using convolutional neural networks. J. Biomed. Inf. **69**, 1–9 (2017)
61. Zhao, Y., Zhang, J.: Consumer health information seeking in social media: a literature review. Health Inf. Libr. J. **34**(4), 268–283 (2017)

Bimodal Music Subject Classification
via Context-Dependent Language Models

Kahyun Choi[(✉)] [iD]

Indiana University, 700 N. Woodlawn Avenue, Bloomington, IN 47408, USA
choika@iu.edu

Abstract. This work presents a bimodal music subject classification
method that uses two different inputs: lyrics and user interpretations of
lyrics. While the subject has been an essential metadata type that the
music listeners and providers have wanted to use to categorize their music
database, it has been difficult to directly utilize it due to the subjective
nature of song lyrics analysis. We advance automatic subject classification technology by employing a context-dependent language model, bidirectional encoder representations from the Transformers (BERT). BERT
is a promising solution to reduce the gap between humans and machines'
abilities to understand lyrics because it transforms a word into a feature
vector by harmonizing the contextual relationship between that word and
its surrounding words. The proposed model employs two BERT modules
as an ensemble to control the contribution of the two modalities. It shows
significant improvement over the existing context-independent models on
both the uni and bimodal subject classification benchmarks, suggesting
that BERT's context-dependent features can help the machine learning
models uncover the poetic nature of song lyrics.

Keywords: Music subject classification · Language models · BERT

1 Introduction

Subject, as a term to represent "what the song is about," has been an important metadata type for music listeners. For example, people have used subject to
organize their music library; listeners have used it to search for songs with a particular theme or create playlists under the same subject; and radio DJs have built
up stories upon a selected context. However, none of the leading music streaming
companies provide the subject metadata of popular songs, while a few websites
provide subject information on a small scale (e.g., songfacts.com). Given that
people are eager to search and browse music based on subject metadata [13], a
discrepancy exists between users' needs and services.

The discrepancy originates from a common challenge: the manual annotation of songs is time-consuming and expensive. As for labels that involve more
subjectivity, such as mood [11], it becomes harder to collect a large amount of
labeled data. Moreover, unlike other tags, no strong relationship exists between

© Springer Nature Switzerland AG 2021
K. Toeppe et al. (Eds.): iConference 2021, LNCS 12645, pp. 68–77, 2021.
https://doi.org/10.1007/978-3-030-71292-1_7

subject and audio signals, limiting the annotators and computer algorithms to using only the lyrics.

Another more specific reason that subject is difficult to extract is that song lyrics are often poetic and ambiguous. Indeed, various websites have served millions of users who want to understand song lyrics by reading other users' demystifying postings on stories and meanings of song lyrics (e.g., songmeaning.com and genius.com). In the past, Choi et al. introduced subject classification systems that utilize both song lyrics and the attentive readers' comments collected from those websites [3–5]. In those works, users' comments turned out to be more useful than the song lyrics themselves when used as the input for an automatic subject classification system.

While the previous research introduced the potential of user-generated data for automatic subject classification, the classification system needs improvement because the methodology is missing important aspects of learning from the text as a sequence. Thus, we propose to use bidirectional encoder representations from the Transformers (BERT) [8], which are widely known to provide a context-dependent language model from word sequences via the self-attention mechanism [20]. We also address the bimodal use case by introducing a trainable blending parameter to combine the two classification results from both modalities as an ensemble: lyrics and interpretation. To this end, we focus on the following research questions:

- Q1. Does the BERT-based softmax classifier outperform the SVM model using TF-IDF features?
- Q2. Is the weighted ensemble method effective for combining bimodal classifiers?

2   Related Work

From the mid-2000s, a few papers have proposed automatic music subject classification systems, while they did not utilize either the bimodality of the data or the more advanced context-dependent representations from deep learning. In 2005, Mahedero et al. proposed the first subject classification system that relies solely on song lyrics [14]. This seminal work introduced music subject classification as a challenging problem and showed that basic machine learning models and small datasets are not enough to build a robust classification system. There have been some unsupervised topic analysis methods as well, such as using nonnegative matrix factorization [12] or latent Dirichlet allocation [6]. Although more scalable, these methods are limited to the unsupervised setup. More recently, Choi et al. discovered that user-generated interpretation data is more useful than song lyrics [4] and proposed a bimodal system that benefits from both lyrics and interpretations [5]. This kind of approach showed the potential of using people's interpretation of song lyrics as an alternative source of subject-related information. The bimodal system verified that interpretations are more useful than song lyrics, while the combination of the two only slightly

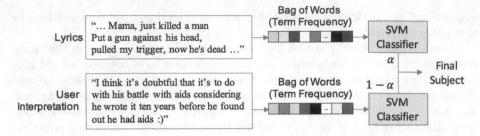

Fig. 1. The bimodal classification framework using two SVM classifiers on the two input sources: lyrics and their interpretations in [5]. The harmonization of the two classification results is done by performing a manual search for the optimal late-fusion parameter α via a ten-fold cross-validation process. The lyrics excerpt is from the song, "Bohemian Rhapsody" by Queen. In comparison, one of the top comments in songmeanings.com is also presented, which reads between the lines.

improves the classification accuracy. Figure 1 summarizes the SVM- and TF-IDF-based bimodal subject classification. In this work, we extend this idea by employing more powerful language mdoel, BERT.

In particular, the main drawback of those existing subject classification systems discussed so far is that they did not consider the order of the words within the sequence. For example, the TF-IDF (term frequency-inverse document frequency) feature does not preserve the sequential order of the words. Furthermore, support vector machines (SVM), as the main classification method, worked only as a non-sequential classifier [19]. To overcome the limitations, a recurrent neural network, the long short-term memory (LSTM) [10], was employed to learn from the sequence of word embedding vectors [3]. While the fastText-based word embedding vectors should, in theory, capture the semantic relationship between words [2], and the LSTM model is powerful for learning the sequential information, this new model was not comparable to the previous non-sequential models. It is mainly because of the difficulty in training LSTMs using a limited amount of labeled data.

The previous work's limitations led us to employ BERT as a more powerful pretrained feature extraction method. The benefit of using BERT in our work is threefold. First, BERT is an extensive and powerful deep neural network model, pretrained from large text corpora to generalize well to unseen problems with little adjustment. It means that our BERT-based classifier will not suffer much from overfitting, while it is expected to perform better than the previous methods. Second, as a Transformer-based self-attention model, it learns the context from the word sequence, minimizing the classifier's role. In other words, there is no need to train and use LSTM or SVM classifiers. Third, as a neural network framework, it is straightforward in extracting two sets of features from the two modalities using two BERT models and then finding the optimal combination ratio between them.

3   The Proposed Method

3.1   Dataset

We follow the data preparation process proposed in the latest work that handled subject classification on bimodal data [5]. We used two types of input data: song lyrics and user comments provided by LyricFind[1] and songmeanings.com[2], respectively. Songmeanings.com has served millions of music lovers who want to discuss the meanings of song lyrics. Users can post their interpretations of song lyrics in the comment section for each song. They can also rate other users' comments so that the most highly-rated comments would appear on top. Some songs have many comments, while some do not. We collect up to the top ten comments from each song and then concatenate them as the BERT models' input sequence.

For the subject labels, we refer to the music database on songfacts.com. Songfacts.com provides a searchable database of songs curated by experts. "About" is one of their browsing options, which corresponds to the song lyrics' subject. Among the 206 "about" categories, we selected the eight most popular subject categories with more than 100 songs: {Religion, Sex, Drugs, Parents, War, Places, Ex-lover, and Death}. The number of songs per class is limited to 100 to prevent our classifiers from favoring more populous categories.

3.2   Classification Setup

BERT. BERT [8] is one of the latest natural language processing (NLP) models that use the encoder part of the Transformer model [20] for language modeling. BERT showed state-of-the-art results in various NLP tasks, such as document classification [1], by overcoming the limitations of its predecessors, including the TF-IDF and context-independent word embedding methods. Conceptually, it is similar to the other word embedding techniques, such as Word2Vec [16] and fastText [2], as it can learn the semantic relationships between words. However, unlike context-independent models that learn an embedding vector, which aggregates all the meanings that a word is associated with, BERT learns the embedding vector based on the word's context within a sentence.

$$\mathbf{v}_i = F(w_i) \tag{1}$$

$$[\text{CLS}, \mathbf{v}_1, \mathbf{v}_2, \cdots, \mathbf{v}_i, \cdots, \mathbf{v}_N] = \text{BERT}([w_1, w_2, \cdots, w_i, \cdots, w_N]). \tag{2}$$

In (1), for example, a context-independent model learns the mapping function $F(\cdot)$ that converts the i-th word w_i in a sentence into an embedding $\mathbf{v}_i$. In this process, the model does not consider the context that w_i belongs to, which can significantly change the word's meaning. On the other hand, as shown in (2) the

[1] The authors thank Roy Hennig, Director of Sales at LyricFind, for kindly granting the access to their lyric database for our academic research.

[2] The authors also thank Michael Schiano for providing the access to the precious user-generated comments on songmeanings.com.

BERT model is a function of the entire word sequence so that the embedding vectors represent the relationships among the words within the same sentence. To this end, BERT always takes the entire sentence as input instead of an individual word. Note that BERT also predicts a sentence-specific vector CLS, which works as a summary of the input sentence. We use it as the final feature vector for the softmax classifier. Likewise, as we do not need all the embedding vectors, except for the CLS embedding, our simplified BERT function is defined as follow for the rest of the paper:

$$CLS = BERT(\mathbf{w}),\tag{3}$$

where $\mathbf{w} = [w_1, w_2, \cdots, w_N]$.

Another important advantage to note is that BERT employs the Transformer model that uses the powerful self-attention mechanism. Compared to its LSTM-based context-dependent predecessor, i.e., embeddings from language models (ELMo) [17], the self-attention mechanism exhibited improved performance. As BERT models are pretrained on massive datasets and are publicly available, NLP tasks with a small dataset can benefit directly from BERT even without further finetuning.

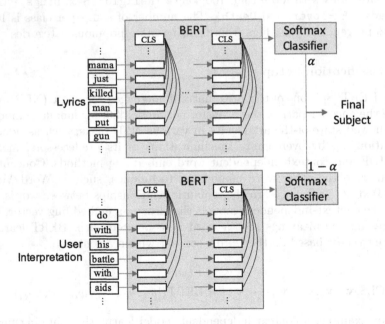

Fig. 2. The proposed bimodal classification framework using two BERT classifiers on the lyrics and interpretation input streams. The fusion of the modalities is performed as a part of the training process by defining the ensemble weight α as a trainable parameter.

The Ensemble Method. We combine two classification results from two BERT models: the lyrics and interpretation modalities, $\mathbf{w}_L$ and $\mathbf{w}_I$, respectively. Hence, the final classification result is a weighted average of the two classification results,

$$\alpha \, \text{softmax} \, (\text{BERT}(\mathbf{w}_L)) + (1 - \alpha) \, \text{softmax} \, (\text{BERT}(\mathbf{w}_I)), \qquad (4)$$

where $0 \leq \alpha \leq 1$ is the ensemble weight that defines the contribution of the two modalities. We define it as a trainable parameter with an optimal value found through the model training process, along with the softmax classifier's parameters. Finally, the ensemble results in a probability vector over all eight classes. Its largest element is associated with the predicted class the example belongs to. Figure 2 describes the proposed ensemble model using two BERT modules to handle lyrics and interpretation.

The Experimental Setup. We employed the pretrained BERT model available as a part of the `ktrain` package [15]. Due to the heavy computational requirement, we did not attempt to finetune the BERT model for our classification problem. Instead, we modified the original unimodal BERT classifier into a bimodal system that eventually runs the pretrained BERT module twice. The two CLS embedding vectors are then fed to the two softmax classifiers to predict subject classes, which are eventually combined as an ensemble. The one cycle policy was used for optimization [18]. For a fair comparison with previous works, we followed the same ten-fold cross-validation process. All implementations are based on the `Keras` deep learning framework [7].

4 Experimental Results and Discussion

Table 1 summarizes the performance of the proposed BERT-based models compared against the previous SVM-based model on the music subject classification benchmark used in [5].

Overall Performance Comparison. The proposed BERT-based classifier improves the overall performance across all input types. It prefers the interpretations over the lyrics, which is the same preference reported in the SVM model on the TFIDF features. Notably, the proposed method extracts subject information from lyrics more effectively (54%) than the traditional method (43.6%). As for the interpretation-only input, the BERT classifier increased the accuracy from 64.8% to 68%, which is not as significant as the lyrics-only case. Since we use a pretrained BERT model for both types of input, the more considerable improvement on the lyrics-only input does not necessarily mean that BERT works better on lyrics than interpretations. Indeed, the classification accuracy of the interpretation-only model is still much higher than the lyrics-only model. We believe that this drastic improvement in the lyrics model comes from the potential causes, such as a) lyrics are challenging to analyze, b) there is more

Table 1. The comparison of the proposed BERT-based model and the previous SVM-based model. The SVM-based model's performance was reported in [5].

System	The BERT-based model			The SVM-based model [5]		
Input	Lyrics	Interp.	Bimodal (trainable ensemble)	Lyrics	Interp.	Bimodal (late fusion)
Death	44	57	60	29	51	50
Drugs	50	71	78	36	69	70
Exlovers	52	68	70	36	67	68
Parents	37	65	63	34	57	60
Places	57	62	66	49	58	61
Religion	52	78	78	35	70	70
Sex	67	66	80	65	70	73
War	73	77	79	65	76	79
Average	54	68	71.8	43.6	64.8	66.4

room for improvement, and c) BERT may have successfully interpreted the latent meanings of some poetic words in lyrics using the contextual information. These findings suggest that BERT might be a promising method for extracting latent information from other texts that are difficult to analyze due to their brevity and complexity, such as poetry.

Bimodal Classification. When both text sources are used, the proposed BERT-based bimodal classifier's accuracy reached 71.8%, which is 5.4% higher than the competing bimodal SVM classifier's performance. The proposed trainable ensemble is efficient since it estimates the ensemble weights as a part of the neural network optimization. On the other hand, the previous late fusion technique tediously examines all possible mixing ratios. The estimated ensemble weight turned out not too different from a simple average: $\alpha = 0.498$, whose standard deviation is 0.003. Therefore, we believe that our bimodal classification system directly benefits from the significant improvement in the lyrics modality rather than the fusion mechanism itself.

Confusion Analysis. The proposed BERT-based classifier shows robust improvement in most of the subject categories across all three input types, except for two cases: the interpretation-only case for the Sex category and the bimodal model for the War category.

In particular, we found that both the previous and proposed classifiers shared the same sets of difficult and easy subjects. For both classifiers, the easy subjects were War, Sex, Drugs, and Religion, while the difficult ones were Death, Parents, Places, and Ex-lovers. War was the easiest subject in the previous research with 79% accuracy, the same as the proposed research. As for Sex,

Drugs, and **Religion**, their accuracy was around 70%, but now, it reached almost 80%. The most difficult subject was **Death**. Its accuracy was only 50%, but with the proposed classifier, it was 60%. Both classifiers have the same difficult and easy sets of subjects, indicating that songs with difficult subjects may be associated with multiple subjects. For example, if a song in the **Death** category is also talking about **Religion**, it is more realistic to assign multiple labels. This suggests that a multi-label classifier might be a more sensible choice than a single label classifier for the subject classification problem.

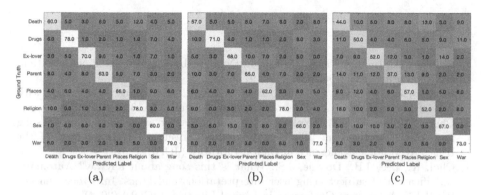

Fig. 3. Confusion matrices from the proposed classification systems (a) the bimodal system using trainable ensemble weight α (b) the interpretation-only unimodal system's results (c) the lyrics-only case

We also examined the confusion matrices among subject categories to determine which pair of categories is most confusing to our proposed classifiers (Fig. 3). The confusion matrices showed that the most confusing pair of categories was **Death** and **Religion**, and they were consistently misclassified by each other across all three different input types. The fact that **Death** and **Religion** have a close relationship in human history [9] might have led to their possible coexistence in many songs. As for the unimodal cases, **Death** was often misclassified as **War**, **Drugs**, or **Parents**, and vice versa. However, the bimodal classifier reduced such confusion to some degree, which indicates that the bimodal classifier effectively benefits from the complementary relationship between the two unimodal classifiers.

5   Conclusion and Future Work

In this work, we found that BERT is powerful in extracting subject information from song lyrics, which has been known to be difficult to understand for humans and machines. Our proposed method showed greater classification accuracy overall, but more saliently on the lyrics modality, where the traditional methods left more room for improvement. We also proposed an efficient ensemble method, which showed reasonable improvement over both unimodal systems. While the pretrained and fixed BERT features have not been trained or finetuned from our dataset, they significantly improved the previous classification models that were customized to the dataset. This indicates that further finetuning of BERT could improve its performance. As future work, we will conduct a more detailed analysis by using representative features of subject categories to identify the contribution of words. We will also explore a bigger benchmark dataset built from other websites, such as genius.com. Finally, an expansion to the multi-label classification setup is another promising direction.

References

1. Adhikari, A., Ram, A., Tang, R., Lin, J.: Docbert: bert for document classification. arXiv preprint arXiv:1904.08398 (2019)
2. Bojanowski, P., Grave, E., Joulin, A., Mikolov, T.: Enriching word vectors with subword information. Trans. Assoc. Comput. Linguist. **5**, 135–146 (2017)
3. Choi, K., Downie, J.S.: Exploratory investigation of word embedding in song lyric topic classification: promising preliminary results. In: Proceedings of the IEEE/ACM Joint Conference in Digital Libraries (JCDL) (2018)
4. Choi, K., Lee, J.H., Downie, J.S.: What is this song about anyway? Automatic classification of subject using user interpretations and lyrics. In: Proceedings of the IEEE/ACM Joint Conference in Digital Libraries (JCDL) (2014)
5. Choi, K., Lee, J.H., Hu, X., Downie, J.S.: Music subject classification based on lyrics and user interpretations. In: Proceedings of the American Society for Information Science and Technology (ASIS&T) (2016)
6. Choi, K., Lee, J.H., Willis, C., Downie, J.S.: Topic modeling users' interpretations of songs to inform subject access in music digital libraries. In: Proceedings of the IEEE/ACM Joint Conference in Digital Libraries (JCDL) (2015)
7. Chollet, F., et al.: Keras (2015). https://keras.io
8. Devlin, J., Chang, M.W., Lee, K., Toutanova, K.: Bert: pre-training of deep bidirectional transformers for language understanding. In: The Annual Conference of the North American Chapter of the Association for Computational Linguistics (NAACL) (2019)
9. Garces-Foley, K.: Death and Religion in a Changing World. M.E, Sharpe, New York (2006)
10. Hochreiter, S., Schmidhuber, J.: Long short-term memory. Neural Comput. **9**(8), 1735–1780 (1997)
11. Hu, X., Downie, J.S.: Exploring mood metadata: relationships with genre, artist and usage metadata. In: 8th International Conference on Music Information Retrieval, ISMIR 2007, pp. 67–72 (2007)
12. Kleedorfer, F., Knees, P., Pohle, T.: Oh oh oh whoah! towards automatic topic detection in song lyrics. In: Proceedings of the 9th International Conference on Music Information Retrieval, pp. 287–292 (2008)
13. Lee, J.H., Downie, J.S.: Survey of music information needs, uses, and seeking behaviours: preliminary findings. In: ISMIR, vol. 2004, p. 5th. Citeseer (2004)
14. Mahedero, J.P., Martínez, Á., Cano, P., Koppenberger, M., Gouyon, F.: Natural language processing of lyrics. In: Proceedings of the 13th Annual ACM International Conference on Multimedia, pp. 475–478 (2005)

15. Maiya, A.S.: ktrain: a low-code library for augmented machine learning. arXiv preprint arXiv:2004.10703 (2020)
16. Mikolov, T., Sutskever, I., Chen, K., Corrado, G.S., Dean, J.: Distributed representations of words and phrases and their compositionality. In: Advances in Neural Information Processing Systems, pp. 3111–3119 (2013)
17. Peters, M.E., et al.: Deep contextualized word representations. In: Proceedings of NAACL (2018)
18. Smith, L.N.: A disciplined approach to neural network hyper-parameters: part 1-learning rate, batch size, momentum, and weight decay. arXiv preprint arXiv:1803.09820 (2018)
19. Suykens, J.A., Vandewalle, J.: Least squares support vector machine classifiers. Neural Process. Lett. **9**(3), 293–300 (1999)
20. Vaswani, A., et al.: Attention is all you need. In: Advances in Neural Information Processing Systems, pp. 5998–6008 (2017)

Spatio-Temporal Deepfake Detection with Deep Neural Networks

Andrey Sebyakin⬭, Vladimir Soloviev⬭, and Anatoly Zolotaryuk$^{(\boxtimes)}$⬭

Financial University Under the Government of the Russian Federation, 38 Shcherbakovskaya, Moscow 105187, Russia
Sebyakin.A@yandex.ru, {vsoloviev,azolotaryuk}@fa.ru

Abstract. Deepfakes generated by generative adversarial neural networks may threaten not only individuals but also pose a public threat. In this regard, detecting video content manipulations is an urgent task, and many researchers propose various methods to solve it. Nevertheless, the problem remains. In this paper, the existing approaches are evaluated, and a new method for detecting deepfakes in videos is proposed. Considering that deepfakes are inserted into the video frame by frame, when viewing it, even with the naked eye, fluctuations and temporal distortions are noticeable, which are not taken into account by many deepfake detection algorithms that use information from a single frame to search for forgeries out of context with neighboring frames. It is proposed to analyze information from a sequence of multiple consecutive frames to detect deepfakes in video content by processing the video using the sliding window approach, taking into account not only spatial intraframe dependencies but also interframe temporal dependencies. Experiments have shown the advantage and potential for further development of the proposed approach over simple intraframe recognition.

Keywords: Generative adversarial networks · Deepfakes · Sliding windows

1 Introduction

In the current time of the information technology boom, due to a significant increase in the characteristics and availability of computer equipment and communication means, widespread digitalization of the economy and other spheres of human activity has become possible. Social networks, educational and entertainment content, numerous apps, and platforms are widespread. The possibility of using intelligent systems and technologies, machine learning, and neural network research has contributed significantly to overall life quality, the growth of well-being, and personal and professional competencies development [1].

At the same time, the new information technology conditions have not eliminated the negative aspects. Competition is overgrowing, contradictions and confrontations are intensifying – not only between financial and economic entities but also in interstate relations. The information war for human minds is becoming more acute and more

K. Toeppe et al. (Eds.): iConference 2021, LNCS 12645, pp. 78–94, 2021.
https://doi.org/10.1007/978-3-030-71292-1_8

sophisticated than ever. Any means are used, including ones prohibited by ethical standards. And all to discredit, suppress competitors, achieve superiority, and at all costs to achieve success, albeit dishonestly, unrighteously.

One of the essential tasks solved with artificial neural networks trained on large data is recognizing humans and faces, both from static photographs and dynamic video content. The existing developments in this area are already used in practice – in forensics, education, medicine, banking, public transport [1].

But there is a severe problem here. In response to the development of recognition algorithms and systems, technologies for manipulating visual content began to develop – the substitution of images and sounds to make them seem real. Generated using artificial intelligence's technological capabilities, such as using a trained generative adversarial neural network (Generative Adversarial Nets, GAN[1]), such fake content, so-called deepfakes, is challenging to recognize [2–4]. Spreading mostly through social networks, they invade the privacy of, first of all, public people – artists, athletes, politicians, and business people. Deepfakes inflict significant reputational damage on celebrities (and not only them), drag them into protracted public scandals, lead to financial and property losses, cost political and professional careers, and cause breaks and dramas in their personal lives [2]. Besides, news and political deepfakes can harm and pose a threat to the entire state, undermine trust between citizens and authorities, provoke interethnic and interstate conflicts [5]. And finally, deepfakes question the very use of various recognition systems.

In response to the demand to detect deepfakes, researchers began to look for ways to solve the problem. Numerous reports and scientific articles were published, which consider both the general principles of recognizing forgeries and specific approaches and schemes for their detection, including deep neural networks, deepfake datasets, real and fake images [2–6]. Nevertheless, despite some positive results achieved in particular cases, recognizing fake images and video content has not been finally solved. It is still relevant and widely discussed [2–12]. If earlier, several years ago, it was challenging to make a high-quality fake, now it is possible to automatically synthesize non-existent persons or manipulate them thanks to new technological solutions:

- open access to large-scale image databases [3];
- evolution of deep learning neural network methods that eliminate many stages of manual editing, such as autoencoders (AE) and generative adversarial networks (GAN) [2];
- the availability of open-source software and mobile applications such as ZAO[2] and FaceApp[3] makes it possible to create deepfakes by anyone with no experience required [2].

In this paper, we propose a new method for detecting deepfakes in video content. One of the most noticeable artifacts of deepfakes applied to video content is temporal inconsistency – fluctuations and other temporal distortions that are not noticeable in

---

[1] https://github.com/shaoanlu/faceswap-GAN.

[2] https://apps.apple.com/cn/app/id1465199127.

[3] https://apps.apple.com/gb/app/faceapp-ai-face-editor/id1180884341.

individual frames. The reason is that deepfakes are applied to the video frame by frame and do not take into account the relationship with surrounding frames, as well as due to minor variations of results produced by face alignment algorithms.

When watching a video with a naked eye, these artifacts are visible. The current algorithms can not recognize them since the video is split into frames on the preprocessing stage. Information from a single frame is used for classification outside the contextual information from surrounding frames.

We propose to use information from a sequence of frames to detect deepfakes, processing video using the sliding window approach.

2 Means and Methods of Processing Human Images

2.1 Manipulation of Human Face Images

To detect manipulated digital content, it is required to know the possible manipulation methods, identify which tools were used, the theoretical base, and the practical experience and knowledge.

Currently, four groups of manipulations with human face images are described [2–13]:

- Entire Face Synthesis, modeling of all facial attributes;
- Identity Swap, known in the literature as DeepFake;
- Attribute Manipulation – manipulation of facial attributes;
- Expression Swap – exchange of facial expressions.

The first group, Entire Face Synthesis, concentrates on creating completely non-existent facial images using generative deep learning models, e.g., the StyleGAN[4] approach proposed in [14] and disclosed in detail in [15, 16]. This facial manipulation approach generates a very high-quality image. It can be used to create video games, perform 3D-modeling. At the same time, Entire Face Synthesis can create highly realistic fake profiles on social networks to generate and spread disinformation.

The second group, Identity Swap, involves manipulations replacing one person's face with the face of another person. Two major approaches can be used here – the classical methods based on computer graphics or learning using deep neural networks and techniques known as DeepFakes. Very realistic full face swap videos can be found on various video hosting platforms like YouTube. This type of manipulation can have both positive aspects, for example, in the film industry when understudies perform dangerous stunts or negative ones: it can be used for illegal purposes – creating hoaxes and fake news, financial and political fraud.

The third group of manipulations – Attribute Manipulation, involves editing or retouching the face, changing its features and characteristics – hairstyle, eye, hair color, skin tone, age, makeup, gender, presence or absence of a beard, wearing glasses and

---

[4] https://github.com/NVlabs/stylegan.

other accessories [17]. Manipulations are performed using GANs based on the Star-GAN approach proposed in [18]. An example of this type of manipulation is the popular mobile application FaceApp[5].

The fourth group of manipulations, Expression Swap, consists of changing a person's facial expression based on the GAN architectures [19] such as Face2Face and NeuralTextures [2, 20]. The changes replace the facial expression of one person with that of another person.

The results of manipulations with a human face are presented in Fig. 1. For Entire Face Synthesis, real images were taken from whichfaceisreal.com, fake images from thispersondoesnotexist.com. For Identity Swap, face images were retrieved from the Celeb-DF database [19, 22, 25]. For Attribute Manipulation, real images were also taken from whichfaceisreal.com, and fake images were created with FaceApp. Finally, images from FaceForensics++ [21] were used for the Expression Swap.

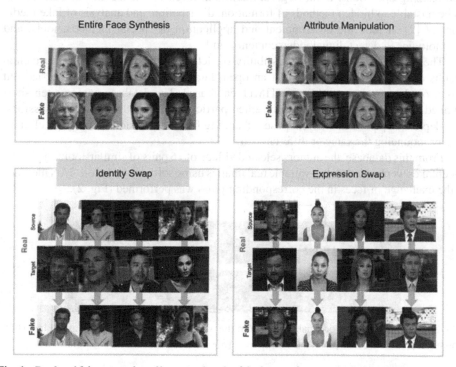

Fig. 1. Real and fake examples of images of each of the human face manipulations groups (Source: [2])

Similar manipulations with these or more advanced methods can be performed with video content on a frame-by-frame basis.

---

[5] https://www.faceapp.com/.

2.2 Deepfake Detection Capabilities

In response to the emergence of fake, realistically believable content, significant efforts were made to develop methods for detecting facial manipulation. Initially, the researchers proceeded from traditional approaches used in forensics, which usually assume [12]:

- fingerprint analysis – on-camera, off-camera, on an optical lens;
- research of a matrix of color filters, interpolation, and image compression;
- assessment of possible copying, pasting, and moving various image fragments, lowering the video's frame rate, etc.

However, traditional forensic approaches for digital video content turned out to be poorly acceptable since fakes were made by automatic tools based on neural networks. Also, when counterfeits are distributed via social networks, they undergo compression and resizing operations. In this regard, traditional forensic science methods turned out to be unstable to hidden methods of formation, distribution, and analysis of fake media content [2]. It took the development and application of special methods, tools, and technologies to detect digital video content fraud.

The article [3] assessed the possibility of detecting deepfakes. The experimental results are presented in the form of an open database. The research was carried out based on data from the public VidTIMIT database[6]. The database contains ten short dubbed videos for each of the 43 presented participants, filmed over several sessions, and depicted a person in different poses, changing facial expressions, hairstyles, clothes, and pronouncing the same or different text.

From this database, the authors selected videos of 16 pairs of similar-looking people. Deepfakes were added to the available real images using software based on GAN methods – the exchange of faces in the corresponding pairs was performed (Fig. 2).

Fig. 2. Screenshots of the original videos from the VidTIMIT database, as well as the low (LQ) and high quality (HQ) deepfake videos (Source: [3])

Two models were formed for the study, one of which provided a low resolution of faces with an input-output size of 64×64 (LQ), the other – a high resolution – 128×128 (HQ). Further, face recognition systems are based on VGG and Facenet neural networks, which usually, without analyzing faked images, provide high recognition accuracy – 98.95% and 99.63%, respectively [3]. The study results showed that the false perception rate of deepfakes on low and high-quality models is 85.62% and 95.00%, respectively. Audiovisual analysis at high quality resulted in an error of 8.97% [3].

---

[6] https://conradsanderson.id.au/vidtimit.

Other studies [2, 14–36] describing the experiments' results on applying the most modern algorithms for detecting deepfakes using a video database have shown that detecting fakes is still extremely difficult and the problem is still not resolved. The existing methods for detecting deepfakes will be discussed in more detail below.

2.3 Databases of Fake and Real Content

There are currently several large public databases of fake images (Table 1) based on GAN architectures: StyleGAN, ProGAN, etc. [2, 14–16, 18, 19]. All of them can also be used for the research and development of deepfake detection methods. It is also necessary to additionally obtain real images of real persons from other public sources, such as, for example, the CelebA databases [24], FFHQ [14, 15] to use them as negative training samples.

As an example, we will expand the FFHQ database in more detail. It was initially created as a dataset for generative adversarial networks (GANs). The database contains 70,000 images of human faces in the wild, different in age, gender, ethnicity, taken in a natural setting, against a different background, using certain accessories – glasses, hats, headphones, etc., which makes it the most representative and useful for different applications compared to other databases (Fig. 3).

Table 1. Characteristics of some publicly available databases for manipulating face images

Database	Fake images	Generation method	Real images
Diverse Fake Face Dataset	100,000 200,000	StyleGAN ProGAN	–
iFakeFaceDB	250,000 80,000	StyleGAN ProGAN	
DFFD	18,416 79,960	FaceApp StarGAN	–
CelebA	–	–	200,000
FFHQ	–	–	70,000

We also note that these deepfake databases are characterized not only by the number of images and methods of their generation but also by the fakes' resolution and quality. In some of them, for example, in the iFakeFaceDB database, the traces left by GAN are removed using the GANprintR method [26]. As a result, the falsified images are highly realistic [2].

To work with video content, special datasets have been developed, including FaceForensics++ [2, 21], Celeb-DF [22], DFDC [36], etc.

FaceForensics++ is a deepfake database that allows researchers to evaluate various recognition approaches. The base contains manipulations created using five methods, namely Face2Face, FaceSwap, DeepFakes, NeuralTexture, and FaceShifter [37].

The Celeb-DF database contains real and fake videos in MPEG4.0 format, approximately 13 s in length and at a standard frame rate of 30 frames per second. Real videos

Fig. 3. Example images from the FFHQ database (https://github.com/NVlabs/ffhq-dataset)

contain ten excerpts of various interviews for 59 famous people, taken from YouTube and other open sources. The videos are selected to display people of different sex and age, with various facial attributes and belonging to different ethnic groups. Based on 590 real videos, 5,639 fake videos were generated using a deep neural network by pairwise replacement of faces.

The DFDC (Deepfake Detection Challenge) database[7] is the largest at the time of this writing, developed in cooperation with leading organizations and experts to create and test various algorithms and techniques for detecting deep video forgeries. The dataset was based on 40,190 videos of 3,426 real people with an average duration of 68.8s, filmed in high resolution in natural conditions, indoors and outdoors, without professional lighting and makeup; the total amount of raw data in the database was 25 TB [36]. After processing the original video – tracking, aligning, cropping, and resizing faces to 256×256 pixels, a training subsample was formed, and faces were replaced using eight different GAN-based methods. As a result, there are 128,124 videos in total.

Brief information about the deepfake video datasets is given in Table 2.

2.4 Existing Methods

Many studies are evaluating the ability to recognize deepfakes. Different authors use various estimation metrics, such as the area under the curve (AUC) or error rate (EER). There are suggestions to analyze the internal GAN pipeline to detect color irregularities in real and fake images [27].

Another approach, FakeSpoter, is proposed in [28]. It takes advantage of the neural reception field's behavior of real images and deepfakes generated in GAN-based systems. In [7], the approach was tested on real faces from the CelebA-HQ [2] and FFHQ [14, 15] databases and synthetic faces created using InterFaceGAN [29] and StyleGAN [14–16]. The FaceNet model [2] showed high performance and gave a detection accuracy of 84.7%.

---

[7] https://ai.facebook.com/datasets/dfdc.

There is also a known fake detection approach based on the analysis of convolutional traces [30]. The features were extracted using the expectation-maximization algorithm. Popular classifiers such as k-Nearest Neighbors (k-NN), SVM, and Linear Discriminant Analysis (LDA) were used for the final detection. Testing this approach using fake images generated with AttGAN [31], GDWCT [32], StarGAN [18], StyleGAN [14], and StyleGAN2 [16] gave a final accuracy of 99.81%.

Table 2. Basic public video image databases for searching for fake video content

Database	Total number of videos	Real video	Number of subjects	Fake video	Manipulation tool
FaceForensics++	3000	1000		5000	• FaceSwap • DeepFake • Face2Face • NeuralTexture • FaceShifter
Celeb-DF	6229	590	59	5639	• DeepFake improved synthesis algorithm
Deepfake Detection Challenge (DFDC)	128124	23654	3426	104500	• DeepFake • Autoencoder (DFAE) • MM/NN Face Swap • Neural Talking Heads (NTH) • FSGAN • StyleGAN

Another approach is based on examining a combination of pixel coincidence matrices and convolutional neural networks (CNN). This approach was tested on a database of various objects and scenes created using CycleGAN [2]. The authors also conducted a robustness analysis of the proposed approach to fake images generated with different GAN architectures (CycleGAN vs StarGAN) and reported about EER of 12.3% on 100K-Faces database[8].

Recent research has focused on detecting special fingerprints inserted by GAN architectures into fake images using deep learning techniques. A technique for detecting such prints was proposed in [33]. The method was evaluated on real faces from the CelebA database [24] and synthetic faces created using various GAN modifications (ProGAN [14, 15], SNGAN [34], CramerGAN [2], and MMDGAN [35]), reaching the final 99.5% detection accuracy. However, this approach turned out to be not robust to simple image

---

[8] https://generated.photos/.

disturbances such as noise, blurring, cropping, or compression, if the models were not retrained [2].

In [25], to analyze various types of facial manipulations, the use of attention mechanisms, and popular CNN models such as XceptionNet and VGG16 are proposed. For the analysis of all manipulations with full face synthesis, the authors achieved a final AUC of 100% and an EER of close to 0.1% using real faces from CelebA [24], FFHQ [15, 16], and FaceForensics++ [21] databases and fake images created using the ProGAN [14] and StyleGAN [15] techniques.

In [2], an in-depth experimental evaluation of Entire Face Synthesis facial manipulations with modern detection systems was described. Four different fake databases were used:

- 150,000 fake faces collected on the Internet[9] and based on the StyleGAN architecture;
- public database 100K-Faces;
- 80,000 artificial faces generated using ProGAN;
- improved iFakeFaceDB where GAN fingerprint information has been removed using the GANprintR approach.

EER = 0.02% was achieved under controlled experimental conditions. In more complex research scenarios, when images (real and fake) come from different sources, the result of deepfake detection decreases. For iFakeFaceDB database, EER = 4.5% [2].

3   Proposed Method

3.1   Drawbacks of Prior Works

Although the current methods successfully recognize deepfakes that was created by the majority of existing methods, they all rely on datasets generated without consideration that there are techniques for identifying deepfakes, i.e. the corresponding GANs were not trained using modern recognition methods as a discriminator (or in other words, adversarial training was not used).

However, not only the next generation of methods will take into account the existence of such systems, but already existing GANs can be trained in such a way that existing methods for detecting deepfakes will not detect them. Moreover, most of the existing techniques are not resistant to the detection of deepfakes after post-processing (blur, simple distortions, lossy compression, etc.). Although the naked eye on video can recognize them, current systems can not identify them.

Also, new methods, e.g., FaceShifter [37], effectively solve most of the problems associated with artifacts within a single frame, such as reduced-resolution faces, mixing artifacts of the generated face and the target, artifacts caused by the occlusion of the face by other objects, artifacts of illumination mismatch, face pose mismatch, etc. It reduces possibilities for recognition not only by existing automatic systems, but also by humans (Fig. 4).

---

[9] https://thispersondoesnotexist.com.

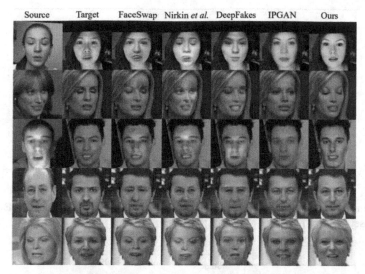

Fig. 4. Comparison with FaceSwap [4], FaceForensics++ [21] face images (Source: [37])

Nevertheless, one of the primary artifacts of deepfakes, when applied to video, is the lack of temporal coherence that is not noticeable in individual frames. The reason is that deepfakes are applied to the video frame by frame and do not take into account the relationships with the previous and next frames, and minor errors in face alignment algorithms used to predict key points of the face.

These artifacts are visible to the naked eye, but current algorithms are unable to recognize them.

Unlike existing methods, which decompose it into frames to recognize deepfakes in video and use information from a single frame taken out of the context of other frames for classification, the proposed method uses information from a sequence of several frames, processing the video using the sliding window method (Fig. 5). From left to right, we show the input source images, the input target images, the results of FaceSwap, and the results of FaceShifter. We can see that FaceShifter effectively mitigates artifacts caused by previous methods, such as the defective lighting effect on the nose (row 1), incorrect face shape transfer (row 2), and the mismatched image resolutions (row 3).

3.2 Inference Pipeline

To recognize deepfakes in video content, we suggest the following pipeline, which consists of five stages (Fig. 6).

At the first stage, there is a locating fixed-size square face region. Many different methods can be found: one-stage detectors such as FaceBoxes, two-stage detectors such as Faster-RCNN, or older approaches based on manually generated tags such as HOG + SVM. Depending on the detector, padding can be set for the output bounding box to cover the whole face and some area, which can be distorted by a deepfake method.

In the second stage, face tracking takes place. In contrast to frame-by-frame recognition, for this stage, not only the tracking-by-detection approach can be applied, but

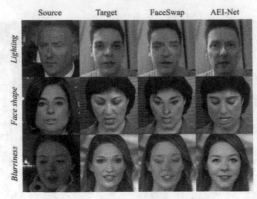

Fig. 5. Comparison of previous methods with FaceShiter (AEI-Net) approach on FaceForensics++ dataset (Source: [37])

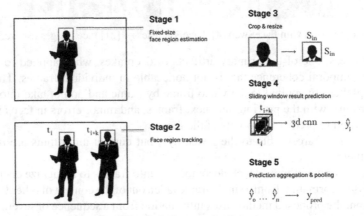

Fig. 6. Inference pipeline

also more effective methods based, for example, on motion vectors extracted from a compressed video stream, optical flow, or interpolation between more distant detection results. It allows not to do face detection every frame and effectively reduces the calculations at this stage by several times or even orders of magnitude.

In the third stage, the face area is extracted from the frame and scaled to the size required for further classification.

In the fourth stage, regions with faces of the sequence of frames are collected in a batch of the size $S_{in} \times S_{in} \times 3K$, where S_{in} is the size of the rescaled face region, K is the number of frames in the batch. The images themselves are in RGB format, so the depth of the batch tensor is $3K$.

Then this batch acts as an input tensor for a neural network based on three-dimensional convolutions, or its analogs, for example, R(2 + 1)D [38] or Temporal Shift Module [39].

At the fourth stage exit, we have a value $\hat{y}_i \in [0, 1]$ denoting the probability that a given sequence of frames with a face is a deepfake. In this case, the sliding window is shifted by the size of the batch.

At the fifth stage, pooling is performed – all the results produced after applying the sliding window method on the video turn into the final answer – the probability of whether this video is a deepfake or not. You can use both obvious aggregation methods, such as $\max_{i=\overline{0, N}} \hat{y}_i$, where N is the number of batches, and more complex ones, for example, to avoid the negative impact of outliers in the results array or bias of the whole sample, which may appear, for instance, due to imbalance in the dataset.

3.3 Training Pipeline

The training pipeline corresponds to the pipeline for a simple binary classification using a neural network, the data for which is prepared according to stages 1–4 of the inference pipeline (Fig. 7).

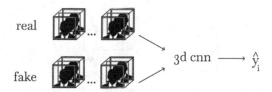

Fig. 7. Inference pipeline – a typical binary classification task

3.4 Basic Pipeline Limitations and Extensions

The described pipeline works only for one person in the video, but it can be extended to be used on multiple faces in a video. For this, you need to independently reproduce all three stages for each person detected in the first stage and then take the maximum from all the results obtained in the fourth stage.

Also, this pipeline has another severe limitation. Suppose the face significantly changes its size during the video. In that case, the use of the pipeline in the form described above becomes impossible due to the property of neural networks, called the feature scale, and since the face region's size is fixed in the first stage. The face may become too small relative to the region, and facial features will be lost at the rescale stage, or become too large, in which case the region itself will cut it off.

To get around this limitation, it is necessary to divide the video into intervals during which the face size in the frame changes slightly, reproduce the pipeline for each of these intervals independently, not counting the fourth stage, and then concatenate the results of the third stage of each interval and reproduce the last stage for all data.

3.5 Classifier Neural Network Architecture

As an architecture for spatio-temporal modeling, we use the R(2 + 1)D-18 network presented in [38]. This architecture separates spatial and temporal modeling, using 2d convolution sequence for spatial modeling and 1d convolution for temporal modeling instead of 3d convolutions. This solution reduces the complexity of the model and significantly reduces the space of hyperparameters while maintaining the network's representation ability (Fig. 8). For input, we use an 8-frame batch as an optimal value for temporal modeling and set face region size to 300 pixels.

In this comparison, for the sake of simplicity, the input is a spatio-temporal tensor with a single spatial channel (i.e., for example, instead of an RGB frame, greyscale could be used there). Fig. 8, a represents full-fledged 3d convolution is applied using a filter of the size $t \times d \times d$, where t is the temporal dimension, and d is equal to the height and width of the frame. In Fig. 8, b, (2 + 1)D convolution separates the computation into a $2d$ convolution covering the spatial domain and a subsequent $1d$ convolution covering the time domain.

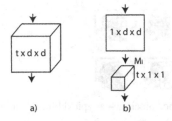

Fig. 8. Simplified comparison of (2 + 1)D and 3D convolution (Source: [38])

3.6 Training

We used the pre-trained R(2 + 1)D-34 model on IG-65M dataset presented in [40] as a starting point for training to prevent overfitting. We changed the last classification layers to meet the requirements of a binary classification problem.

We used SGD optimizer with LR = 0.01, weight decay = 1e-4, and trained networks for 40 epochs in total.

3.7 Data Augmentation

During training, the following augmentations have been used:

- Random horizontal flip;
- Random rotation (±30°);
- Random brightness, contrast, and saturation jitter;
- Coarse dropout (size_percent = 0.02).

3.8 Results

The proposed method was tested on the FaceForensics++ dataset (HQ compressed videos). We also compare our method to single-frame Resnet-34. The evaluation results are presented in Table 3, and the training curves for R(2 + 1)D-34 are shown in Fig. 9.

Table 3. Evaluation results of the proposed method for deepfakes detection

Method	Accuracy
R(2 + 1)D-34_8fr	0.981
R(2 + 1)D-34_1fr	0.953
ResNet-34	0.948

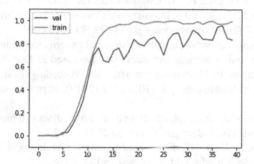

Fig. 9. Training curves for R(2 + 1)D-34

4 Conclusion

In this paper, a new approach to solving the deepfake recognition problem is proposed. The spatio-temporal approach takes into account not only spatial intraframe dependencies (Spatial Features) but also temporal interframe dependencies (Temporal Features). As can be seen from the results, this approach has an advantage over simple intraframe recognition and has the potential for further development.

Further research can focus on various areas – extended evaluation on more datasets, network pretraining capabilities, transfer learning capabilities, architecture improvement, multi-scale analysis, resistance to adversarial attacks, compression artifacts, distortions, etc.

References

1. Sebyakin, A.S., Zolotaryuk, A.V.: Tracking emotional state of a person with artificial intelligence methods and its application to customer services. In: Proceedings of the 2019 Twelfth International Conference "Management of Large-Scale System Development" (MLSD), pp. 1–5 (2019). https://doi.org/10.1109/MLSD.2019.8911054

2. Tolosana, R., Vera-Rodriguez, R., Fierrez, J., Morales, A., Ortega-Garcia, J.: Deepfakes and beyond: a survey of face manipulation and fake detection. Inf. Fusion **64**, 131–148 (2020). https://doi.org/10.1016/j.inffus.2020.06.014

3. Korshunov, P., Marcel, S.: DeepFakes: a new threat to face recognition? Assessment and detection. Idiap-RR-18-2018 (2018). https://arxiv.org/pdf/1812.08685.pdf

4. Nirkin, Y., Masi, I., Tuan, A.T., Hassner, T., Medioni, G.: On face segmentation, face swapping, and face perception. In: Proceedings of the 2018 13th IEEE International Conference on Automatic Face Gesture Recognition (FG 2018), pp. 98–105 (2018). https://doi.org/10.1109/FG.2018.00024

5. Ashok Kumar, M., Rajeyyagari, S.: A novel mechanism for dynamic multifarious and disturbed human face recognition using advanced stance coalition (ASC). Comput. Electr. Eng. **86**, 1–9 (2020). https://doi.org/10.1016/j.compeleceng.2020.106642

6. Biggio, B., Korshunov, P., Mensink, T., Patrini, G., Rao, D., Sadhu, A.: Synthetic realities: deep learning for detecting audiovisual fakes. https://sites.google.com/view/audiovisualfakes-icm l2019. Accessed 25 Dec 2020

7. Ding, Zh.,Guo, Y., Zhang, L., Fu, Y.: One-shot face recognition via generative learning. In: Proceedings of the 2018 13th IEEE International Conference on Automatic Face & Gesture Recognition, pp.1–7 (2018). https://doi.org/10.1109/FG.2018.00011

8. Canton, C., et al.: Applications of computer vision and pattern recognition to media forensics. https://sites.google.com/view/mediaforensics2019. Accessed 25 Dec 2020

9. Verdoliva, L., Bestagini, P.: Multimedia forensics. In: Proceedings of the 27th ACM International Conference on Multimedia, pp. 2701–2702 (2019). https://doi.org/10.1145/3343031.3350542

10. Raja, K., et al.: Workshop on deepfakes and presentation attacks in biometrics. https://sites.google.com/view/wacv2020-deeppab. Accessed 25 Dec 2020

11. Barni, M., Battiato, S., Boato, G., Farid, H., Memon, N.: Multimedia forensics in the wild. https://iplab.dmi.unict.it/mmforwild. Accessed 25 Dec 2020

12. Hosler, B.C., Stamm, M.C.: Detecting video speed manipulation. In: Proceedings of the 2020 IEEE/CVF Conference on Computer Vision and Pattern Recognition Workshops (CVPRW), pp. 2860–2869 (2020). https://doi.org/10.1109/CVPRW50498.2020.00343

13. Lazer, D.M.J., et al.: The science of fake news. Science **359**(6380), 1094–1096 (2018). https://doi.org/10.1126/science.aao2998

14. Karras, T., Aila, T., Laine, S., Lehtinen, J.: Progressive growing of GANs for improved quality, stability, and variation. In: Proceedings of the Sixth International Conference on Learning Representations, pp. 1–26 (2018). https://arxiv.org/pdf/1710.10196.pdf

15. Karras, T., Laine, S., Aila, T.: A style-based generator architecture for generative adversarial networks. In: Proceedings of the 2019 IEEE/CVF Conference on Computer Vision and Pattern Recognition, pp. 4401–4410 (2019). https://arxiv.org/pdf/1812.04948v3.pdf

16. Karras, T., Laine, S., Aittala, M., Hellsten, J., Lehtinen, J., Aila, T.: Analyzing and improving the image quality of StyleGAN. In: Proceedings of the 2020 IEEE/CVF Conference on Computer Vision and Pattern Recognition, pp. 8110–8119 (2020). https://arxiv.org/pdf/1912.04958.pdf

17. Gonzalez-Sosa, E., Fierrez, J., Vera-Rodriguez, R., Alonso-Fernandez, F.: Facial soft biometrics for recognition in the wild: recent works, annotation and COTS evaluation. IEEE Trans. Inf. Forensics Secur. **13**(8), 2001–2014 (2018). https://doi.org/10.1109/TIFS.2018.2807791

18. Choi, Y., Choi, M., Kim, M., Ha, J., Kim, S., Choo, J.: StarGAN: unified generative adversarial networks for multi-domain image-to-image translation. In: Proceedings of the 2018 IEEE/CVF Conference on Computer Vision and Pattern Recognition, pp. 8789–8797 (2018). https://arxiv.org/pdf/1711.09020.pdf

19. Liu, M., et al.: STGAN: a unified selective transfer network for arbitrary image attribute editing. In: Proceedings of the 2019 IEEE/CVF Conference on Computer Vision and Pattern Recognition, pp. 3673–3682 (2019). https://arxiv.org/pdf/1904.09709.pdf

20. Thies, J., Zollhöfer, M., Nießner, M.: Deferred neural rendering: image synthesis using neural textures. ACM Trans. Graph. **38**(4), 66 (2019). https://doi.org/10.1145/3306346.3323035

21. Rössler, A., Cozzolino, D., Verdoliva, L., Riess, C., Thies, J., Nießner, M.: FaceForensics++: learning to detect manipulated facial images. In: Proceedings of the 2019 IEEE/CVF Conference on Computer Vision and Pattern Recognition, p. 11 (2019). https://arxiv.org/pdf/1901.08971.pdf

22. Li, Y., Yang, X., Sun, P., Qi, H., Lyu, S.: Celeb-DF: a large-scale challenging dataset for DeepFake forensics. In: Proceedings of the 2020 IEEE/CVF Conference on Computer Vision and Pattern Recognition, pp. 3207–3216 (2020). https://arxiv.org/pdf/1909.12962.pdf

23. Cao, Q., Shen, L., Xie, W., Parkhi, O., Zisserman, A.: VGGFace2: a dataset for recognizing faces across pose and age. In: Proceedings of the 13th IEEE International Conference on Automatic Face & Gesture Recognition, pp. 67–74 (2018). https://doi.org/10.1109/FG.2018.00020

24. Zhang, Y., et al.: CelebA-spoof: large-scale face anti-spoofing dataset with rich annotations. In: Vedaldi, A., Bischof, H., Brox, T., Frahm, J.-M. (eds.) ECCV. LNCS, vol. 12357, pp. 70–85. Springer, Cham (2020). https://doi.org/10.1007/978-3-030-58610-2_5

25. Dang, H., Liu, F., Stehouwer, J., Liu, X., Jain, A.: On the detection of digital face manipulation. In: Proceedings of the 2020 IEEE/CVF Conference on Computer Vision and Pattern Recognition, pp. 5781–5790 (2020). https://arxiv.org/pdf/1910.01717.pdf

26. Neves, J., Tolosana, R., Vera-Rodriguez, R., Lopes, V., Proença, H., Fierrez, J.: GANprintR: improved fakes and evaluation of the state-of-the-art in face manipulation detection. IEEE J. Sel. Top. Signal Process. **14**(5), 1038–1048 (2020). https://doi.org/10.1109/JSTSP.2020.3007250

27. McCloskey, S., Albright, M.: Detecting GAN-generated imagery using color cues (2018). https://arxiv.org/pdf/1812.08247.pdf

28. Wang, R., Ma, L., Juefei-Xu, F., Xie, X., Wang, J., Liu, Y.: FakeSpotter: a simple baseline for spotting AI-synthesized fake faces. In: Proceedings of the Twenty-Ninth International Joint Conference on Artificial Intelligence, pp. 3444–3451 (2019). https://arxiv.org/pdf/1909.06122v3.pdf

29. Shen, Y., Gu, J., Tang, X., Zhou, B.: Interpreting the latent space of GANs for semantic face editing. In: Proceedings of the 2020 IEEE/CVF Conference on Computer Vision and Pattern Recognition, p. 12 (2020). https://arxiv.org/pdf/1907.10786.pdf

30. Guarnera, L., Giudice, O., Battiato, S.: DeepFake detection by analyzing convolutional traces. In: Proceedings of the 2020 IEEE/CVF Conference on Computer Vision and Pattern RecognitionWorkshops, p. 10 (2020). https://arxiv.org/pdf/2004.10448v1.pdf

31. He, Z., Zuo, W., Kan, M., Shan, S., Chen, X.: Attgan: facial attribute editing by only changing what you want. IEEE Trans. Image Process. **28**(11), 5464–5478 (2019). https://doi.org/10.1109/TIP.2019.2916751

32. Cho, W., Choi, S., Park, D.K., Shin I., Choo, J.: Image-to-image translation via group-wise deep whitening-and-coloring transformation. In: Proceedings of the 2019 IEEE/CVF Conference on Computer Vision and Pattern Recognition, pp. 10639–10647 (2019). https://arxiv.org/pdf/1812.09912.pdf

33. Yu, N., Davis, L., Fritz M.: Attributing fake images to GANs: analyzing fingerprints in generated images. In: Proceedings of the 2019 IEEE/CVF International Conference on Computer Vision (ICCV), pp. 1–41 (2019). https://arxiv.org/pdf/1811.08180.pdf

34. Miyato, T., Kataoka, T., Koyama, M., Yoshida, Y.: Spectral normalization for generative adversarial networks. In: Proceedings of the International Conference on Learning Representations, pp. 1–26 (2018). https://arxiv.org/pdf/1802.05957.pdf

35. Binkowski, M., Sutherland, D., Arbel, M., Gretton, A.: Demystifying MMD GANs. In: Proceedings of the International Conference on Learning Representations, pp. 1–36 (2018). https://arxiv.org/pdf/1801.01401.pdf
36. Dolhansky, B., Bitton, J., Pflaum, B., Lu, J., Howes, R., Wang, M., Ferrer, C.C.: The DeepFake detection challenge dataset (2020). https://arxiv.org/pdf/2006.07397.pdf
37. Li, L., Bao, J., Yang, H., Chen, D., Wen, F.: FaceShifter: towards high fidelity and occlusion aware face swapping (2020). https://arxiv.org/pdf/1912.13457.pdf
38. Tran, D., Wang, H., Torresani L., Ray J., Le Cun, Y., Paluri, M.: A closer look at spatiotemporal convolutions for action recognition. In: Proceedings of the 2018 IEEE/CVF Conference on Computer Vision and Pattern Recognition, pp. 6450–6459 (2018). https://arxiv.org/pdf/1711.11248.pdf
39. Lin, J., Gan, C., Han, S.: TSM: temporal shift module for efficient video understanding. In: Proceedings of the 2019 IEEE/CVF International Conference on Computer Vision (ICCV), pp. 7083–7093 (2019). https://arxiv.org/pdf/1811.08383.pdf
40. Ghadiyaram, D., Mahajan, D.: Large-scale weakly-supervised pretraining for video action recognition. In: Proceedings of the 2019 IEEE/CVF Conference on Computer Vision and Pattern Recognition, pp. 12038–12047 (2019). https://arxiv.org/pdf/1905.00561.pdf

Data Science

A Knowledge Representation Model for Studying Knowledge Creation, Usage, and Evolution

Zhentao Liang[1] , Fei Liu[1] , Jin Mao[1,2] , and Kun Lu[3](✉)

[1] School of Information Management, Wuhan University, Wuhan, Hubei, China
[2] Center for Studies of Information Resources, Wuhan University, Wuhan, Hubei, China
[3] School of Library and Information Studies, University of Oklahoma,
Norman, OK 73019, USA
kunlu@ou.edu

Abstract. A knowledge representation model is proposed to facilitate studies on knowledge creation, usage, and evolution. The model uses a three-layer network structure to capture citation relationships among papers, the internal concept structure within individual papers, and the knowledge landscape in a domain. The resulting model can not only reveal the path and direction of knowledge diffusion, but also detail the content of knowledge transferred between papers, new knowledge added, and changing knowledge landscape in a domain. A pilot experiment is carried out using the PMC-OA dataset in the biomedical field. A case study on one knowledge evolution chain of Alzheimer's Disease demonstrates the use of the model in revealing knowledge creation, usage, and evolution. Initial findings confirm the feasibility of the model for its purpose. Limitations of the study are discussed. Future work will try to address the recognized limitations and apply the model to large scale automated analysis to understand the knowledge production process.

Keywords: Knowledge representation model · Knowledge evolution · Full-text citation analysis · Alzheimer's Disease

1 Introduction

Scientific knowledge growth has become an interesting research topic in science. In recent decades, the number of scientific publications has been soaring exponentially due to the blooming of research activities and the advance of information technology [1]. The large scale of scientific literature forms a treasurable knowledge vault, which records the trajectory of knowledge creation, usage, and evolution. The availability of academic resources has been dramatically improved as the development of scholarly databases, such as Web of Science, Scopus, Google Scholar, etc. Many researchers have leveraged these digital resources to investigate the usage and evolution of knowledge within and across research domains.

© Springer Nature Switzerland AG 2021
K. Toeppe et al. (Eds.): iConference 2021, LNCS 12645, pp. 97–111, 2021.
https://doi.org/10.1007/978-3-030-71292-1_9

To study this problem, many researchers attempt to identify explicit and implicit associations among the carriers of knowledge. Citations have long been recognized as a way of symbolizing knowledge transfer, based on which citation networks can be modeled to track the development of science [2]. A few methods and visualization tools have been proposed to analyze the evolution of research topics, e.g., HistCite [3] and CiteNetExplorer [4]. Citation relations do not solely demonstrate the content of knowledge. Human interpretation of citation analysis results actually relies on the context information of citations, such as the titles of citing and cited papers, although only referred by experts. This methodology is well applied in many related studies. However, it is imperative to integrate the context of citations formally into analytic methods for reducing experts' effort and subjective interference.

Alternatively, some content-based methods probe into knowledge evolution by exploring content connections among the articles in different time periods. The representations of content are different, which depend on the research purpose of specific study. Well adopted are terms and topics in most current studies. The advantage of content-based methods is that the knowledge representation is easy to interpret and the change of knowledge could be measured at a given aggregation level (e.g. by term or by topic). However, the connections among different terms/topics are not explicitly modelled or manifested by exploiting observable evidence, e.g., citations. The details of knowledge usage and evolution are often not disclosed by such methods.

A few recent studies have attempted to combine citation relations and knowledge content that citations carry to investigate knowledge diffusion [5–7]. Their underlying motivation is to identify what knowledge is spread along a citation by matching the terms in the citing and cited articles. It then enables tracing the diffusion paths of knowledge units (i.e. terms). However, the context of citations they consider is of far distance, rather than the surrounding sentences where the citations occur. It is necessary to further improve the methodology for investigating not only knowledge diffusion, but also the emergence of knowledge and the evolutionary relationship among different knowledge units.

In this study, we propose a knowledge representation model to facilitate formal studies on knowledge creation, usage, and evolution. The model captures the citation relationship among papers, internal concept structure of papers, and domain knowledge context. A multi-layer network model is used to integrate different relationships in one knowledge representation model. Citation contexts are analyzed to ascertain the knowledge usage between citing and cited papers. The model allows systematic analysis on knowledge creation, usage, and evolution using principled network models and mathematical algorithms. This study contributes to the formal methodology of studying the knowledge production process from a temporal perspective.

2 Literature Review

2.1 Knowledge Representation

LIS Perspectives. The field of Library and Information Science (LIS) has a long history in studying knowledge representation in the subfield of knowledge organization. The primary focus is on document representation since the field is specialized in managing recorded information [8]. A primary goal for knowledge representation in the LIS field has been to support information retrieval. Therefore, the representation is generally focused on the document content [9]. Rules and standards to describe and represent documents include classification systems, subject headings, and other forms of metadata [10]. The process is traditionally called cataloging in the context of library materials, and more recently resource description in the broader context of the information world. The results are bibliographic records or metadata records that contain essential features of the original documents and serve as surrogates for information retrieval purposes. Folksonomies and ontologies are additions to the traditional knowledge representation tools in LIS [11].

Another related area of knowledge representation in LIS is informetric studies that produce knowledge maps representing knowledge structures [12]. Knowledge maps at different granularity levels have been created to illustrate knowledge structures, including words, papers, journals, and disciplines. Common relationships used to create knowledge maps include word co-occurrences, semantic similarity, citation relationships (including co-citation and bibliographic coupling), and collaboration [13–17]. This subfield of studies on knowledge maps aims to reveal the structures in scientific domains rather than represent knowledge for information retrieval as in knowledge organization. Nevertheless, the maps are knowledge representations of domains. Effort has also been made to study the evolution of knowledge from a longitudinal perspective [18].

Other Perspectives. Besides LIS, cognitive science has also delved into knowledge representation, but more from the perspective of mental representation that focuses on cognitive abilities [19]. The artificial intelligence community has also discussed knowledge representation in the realm of logics, reasoning, and inferences [20].

2.2 Citation Theory

Citation relationship is widely used to reveal relationships among research work. Citations are also the foundation of many evaluative metrics for scholarly impact. Information scientists have had lengthy discussions on what citations mean and represent [21]. An influential dichotomy is the normative view versus the social constructivist view of citations [22], while the former emphasizes the intellectual functions of citations and the latter emphasizes the social factors. The two views have important implications for the use of citations because if the functions of citations are intellectual, then they can be reliably used to measure the intellectual relationship among papers; while if citations are socially constructed, the reliability of them reflecting intellectual connections becomes questionable. Empirical studies have been carried out to test the two views [23, 24]. Recent development and discussion seem to acknowledge the various factors influencing citing behaviors, but also confirm the intellectual functions of citations [25].

2.3 Citation Networks for Knowledge Evolution

The use of citation networks to describe the development of science is not new. Garfield, Sher and Torpie [26] demonstrated the feasibility of using citation data for historical analysis of science, in the case of DNA discoveries. The idea was later developed into the HistCite software that can produce an interconnected historiograph of highly cited publications for a particular topic [3]. Hummon and Doreian [27] proposed a main path analysis method to identify the mainstream of research in citation networks. The method was used by Lucio-Arias and Leydesdorff [28] on HistCite output to highlight significant paths in science development. As reviewed in [29], main path analysis and citation networks have been widely used to map technological trajectories, exploring scientific knowledge flows, and conducting literature reviews.

Despite its success in revealing the path of knowledge diffusion, citation data does not shed light on the development of knowledge content and structure. It is not immediately clear what knowledge is added to a field by a node in a citation chain/network and what knowledge is transferred from a node to the next. The model proposed in this study integrates both citation relationship and knowledge content. The use of citations is based on the intellectual functions of citations to represent knowledge usage between citing and cited papers. The model also captures the knowledge content in individual papers and the development of knowledge in a broader context of a domain.

3 Model Description

The foundation of this model is built on citation theory [21]. A paper cites a previous work to acknowledge its influence on the current paper. In the meanwhile, a paper generally covers several related concepts/entities and studies their relationships, or a paper may introduce new concepts, theories, methods, or techniques, etc. A local concept level captures the internal structure within the scope of a paper. The citation relationship between papers can be further elaborated by concepts/entities in citation contexts [30]. In addition, a global context is represented by the domain concept level that aggregates the knowledge pieces in each paper and provides an overview of the knowledge landscape.

Most of the previous studies on knowledge creation, usage, and evolution are based on single-layer networks, such as citation, collaboration, co-citation, coupling networks, or the integration of multiple networks into a single-layer composite network [31–34]. However, some researchers argue that a single-layer network is a crude approximation of reality, which ignores considerable important information existing in the corresponding multi-layer network. Furthermore, numerous phenomena and dynamic behaviors only emerge in multi-layer networks, but not in single-layer networks [35, 36]. Therefore, a multi-layer network model is used in this study to represent relationships at different levels as well as the cross connections between layers (Fig. 1).

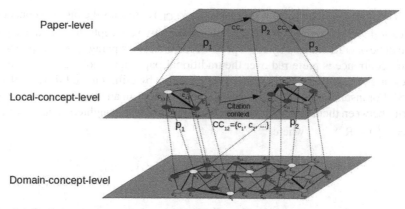

Fig. 1. A knowledge representation model (Different colored nodes in Local-concept-level and Domain-concept-level represent different entity types. The boundary of a domain is left for the users of the model to define.) (Color figure online)

4 Model Definition

According to the model description above, we construct a knowledge representation model characterized by a three-layer scientific network to study the creation, usage, and evolution of knowledge. This network is a pair $M = (L, C)$ where $L = \{L_\alpha, \alpha \in \{$ PL (Paper level), LCL (Local concept level), DCL (Domain concept level)$\}\}$ is a set of layers, and C is the set of cross connections between different layers, which can be formularized as:

$$C = \{E_{\alpha\beta} \subseteq L_\alpha \times L_\beta; \ \alpha, \beta \in \{PL, \ LCL, \ DCL\}\} \tag{1}$$

In this paper, L_{PL} represents the citation network, where the vertices in L_{PL} are scientific publications, and the edge between two publications indicates the citing relations. Therefore, L_{PL} is a directed network without weights. $L_{PL} = (V_{PL}, E_{PL})$, where $V_{PL} = \{v_1^{PL}, \cdots, v_{N_{PL}}^{PL}\}$ is the vertex set of L_{PL}, and N_{PL} is the number of vertices in L_{PL}. E_{PL} is the edge set of L_{PL}, which can be described by the corresponding directed adjacency matrix $A^{PL} = (a_{ij}^{PL}) \in R^{N_{PL} \times N_{PL}}$, where

$$a_{ij}^{PL} = \begin{cases} 1 & \text{if} \left(v_i^{PL}, v_j^{PL}\right) \in E_{PL}, \ \textit{note} \text{ that} \left(v_i^{PL}, v_j^{PL}\right) \neq \left(v_j^{PL}, v_i^{PL}\right) \\ 0 & \text{otherwise.} \end{cases} \tag{2}$$

L_{LCL} captures the internal concept structure within a publication and also specifies the concepts in citation contexts. In order to reveal the relationship among the concepts in a publication and that in different publications more clearly, we introduce the hypergraph theory [37] and establish a hypernetwork to depict L_{LCL}. The hypernetwork $L_{LCL} = (V_{LCL}, H_{LCL}, E_{LCL})$, where $V_{LCL} = \{v_1^{LCL}, \cdots, v_{N_{LCL}}^{LCL}\}$ is the concept set of L_{LCL}, and N_{LCL} is the number of unique concepts contained in all the publications. $H_{LCL} = \{H_1^{LCL}, \cdots, H_{N_{PL}}^{LCL}\}$ is a family of non-empty subset of V_{LCL}. Each element in H_{LCL}, $H_\gamma^{LCL}(\gamma \in \{1, \cdots, N_{PL}\})$, can be characterized by a single-layer network, namely, $H_\gamma^{\text{LCL}} = (V_\gamma^{\text{LCL}}, E_\gamma^{\text{LCL}})$, where $V_\gamma^{\text{LCL}} \subseteq V_{\text{LCL}}$ represents the internal concepts of a publication γ. E_γ^{LCL} represents the relation between two concepts discussed in a paper, which can be operationalized by concept co-occurrences in a paragraph. The paragraph-level co-occurrence is preferred over the traditional paper-level co-occurrence because it reflects a more granular relationship of the concepts by utilizing the full-text information [38]. For instance, a shorter distance between entities in an article suggests a higher similarity between them [39]. E_γ^{LCL} can be formularized by a weighted adjacency matrix $A_\gamma^{\text{LCL}} = (a_{ij}^\gamma) \in R^{N_\gamma \times N_\gamma}$, where

$$a_{ij}^\gamma = \begin{cases} count\left(v_i^\gamma, v_j^\gamma\right) \text{ if } \left(v_i^\gamma, v_j^\gamma\right) \in E_\gamma, \\ 0 \text{ otherwise.} \end{cases} \tag{3}$$

The connection between two hyperlinks (E_{LCL}) indicates that there is a conceptual citation relationship between two papers, namely, one of the hyperlinks cites another hyperlink because of a certain concept. Therefore, there are two necessary conditions for this connection. The first condition is the citation relationship between two publications corresponding to the two hyperlinks. The second condition is that these two hyperlinks share some common concepts. We define this connection as $E_{\text{LCL}}(\text{co})$. To this extent $E_{\text{LCL}}(\text{co})$ can be expressed by a weighted adjacency matrix $A_{H_{\text{LCL}}}^{\text{LCL}} = (a_{ij}^{H_{\text{LCL}}}) \in R^{N_{H_{\text{LCL}}} \times N_{H_{\text{LCL}}}}$, where

$$a_{ij}^{H_{\text{LCL}}} = \begin{cases} a_{ij}^{\text{PL}} \times card\left(H_i^{\text{LCL}} \cap H_j^{\text{LCL}}\right) \text{ if } H_i^{\text{LCL}} \cap H_j^{\text{LCL}} \neq \phi, \\ 0 \qquad \text{otherwise.} \end{cases} \tag{4}$$

L_{DCL} is the third layer of the knowledge representation model that can reveal the global relations among all concepts across papers. L_{DCL} can be described by a weighted network, $L_{\text{DCL}} = (V_{\text{DCL}}, E_{\text{DCL}})$, where $V_{\text{DCL}} = \{v_1^{\text{DCL}}, \cdots, v_{N_{\text{DCL}}}^{\text{DCL}}\}$ is the collection of concepts in a domain, and N_{DCL} is the number of concepts. E_{DCL} is the weighted edge set that represents the co-occurrence frequency of two concepts from the entire domain, which can be described by a weighted adjacency matrix $A^{\text{DCL}} = (a_{ij}^{DCL}) \in R^{N_{DCL} \times N_{DCL}}$, where

$$a_{ij}^{DCL} = \begin{cases} count(v_i^{DCL}, v_j^{DCL}) \quad \text{if } (v_i^{DCL}, v_j^{DCL}) \in E_{DCL}, \\ 0 \quad \text{otherwise.} \end{cases} \tag{5}$$

Conceptually, cross connections mean the relationship between different layers of a multi-layer network model. There arc two types of cross connections between the three layers in the proposed model. The first is the connections between the nodes in the paper-level and the hyperlinks in the local-concept-level networks. It denotes the correspondence between papers in the PL layer and the hyperlinks in H_{LCL}. The second is the connections between the nodes in the local-concept-level network and the domain-concept-level network. It denotes the correspondence between the concepts in LCL layer and those in DCL layer.

5 Pilot Experiment

The operational definition of a knowledge unit in this study is a concept or a concept relationship. The proposed model is expected to support studies on knowledge creation, usage, and evolution because it incorporates both citation relationships between papers and concept structures within individual papers and in a domain. In this study, we performed a pilot experiment to investigate the creation, usage, and evolution process of the knowledge about a well-known disease, Alzheimer's Disease (AD). The same method should apply to other concepts or concept relationships. Figure 2 shows the procedure of the pilot experiment, which is divided into four primary steps.

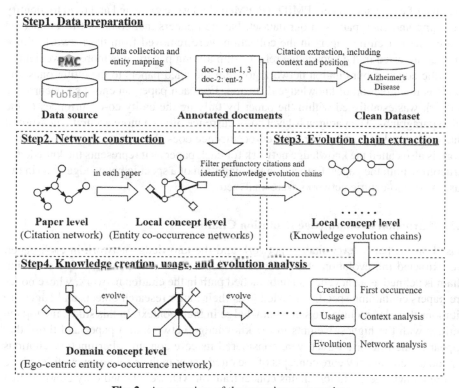

Fig. 2. An overview of the experiment procedure

5.1 Data Preparation

PubMed Central was chosen as the source of our data since it provides full-text articles in XML format, which is essential for extracting citations as well as their contextual and positional information. We collected articles related to Alzheimer's Disease from PubMed Central Open Access Subset (PMC-OA) using keyword matching in titles and abstracts (keyword = "Alzheimer's Disease"). This resulted in 22,363 articles spanning from 1995 to 2020. The dataset was further augmented by adding the cited and citing papers of the initial articles if available in PMC-OA, resulting in 119,093 articles. Biomedical entities and their relationships were considered the basic knowledge units in this study. We performed a sentence-level mapping to the Pubtator Central system [40] to identify the entities that belong to the category of disease, gene, and chemical in each paper. Finally, a clean dataset was built by extracting the citation relationships among papers, as well as the citation context and positional information.

5.2 Network Construction

Paper-level citation network was constructed by parsing the in-text citations and reference list of each paper. Then, PMIDs (PubMed IDs) were extracted and used to identify the citing and cited papers in our dataset. Isolated papers that could not be connected to any cited or citing papers in the collection were removed from the network. Since we are interested in the knowledge relationship among papers, it is more convenient to have the edges in our citation network go from the cited papers to the citing ones, the same as the direction of knowledge diffusion. For each paper, an entity co-occurrence network was established within the paper by tallying the entity co-occurrences in the same paragraphs. The paragraph-level co-occurrence offers a more accurate measure of entity relationship than a paper-level co-occurrence does. The entity co-occurrence network is also called the knowledge network for each paper as it represents the knowledge structure within the paper. To focus on the evolution of a specific knowledge unit (in our case AD), ego-centric networks were analyzed.

5.3 Extraction of Knowledge Evolution Chains

Based on the paper-level citation network and the knowledge network in each paper, we extracted the evolution chains for knowledge about AD. A knowledge evolution chain is defined as an acyclic and unbranched path in the citation network, whose nodes are papers containing specific knowledge as their major research objects and edges are citations that also include the same knowledge in their context. In this study, the top ten entities with the highest weights in the knowledge network of a paper and those that appear in the title or abstract were considered its core concepts. Perfunctory citations that do not contain any core concepts of the cited paper in their context were filtered. To ensure knowledge evolution chains concentrate on AD, we retained only citations that include the entity Alzheimer's Disease in their citation context. Knowledge evolution chains were then identified by traversing from all zero-in-degree nodes to zero-out-degree nodes, that is, from the papers not citing any other papers (source of knowledge evolution) to those not cited by any other papers in the collection (end of knowledge evolution). Each chain depicts a distinct pathway of knowledge creation, usage, and evolution process. In addition, the knowledge network of each paper in the chains can be aggregated at the domain concept level, forming a unified entity co-occurrence network that evolves with the accumulation of articles over time. In this pilot experiment, the ego-centric networks of AD in chains were used to create the domain-concept-level network. In the next section, the creation, usage, and evolution of knowledge are investigated quantitatively and qualitatively by network and context analysis.

6 Results

6.1 Descriptive Statistics

Overall, the papers in our dataset mention biomedical entities for 29,957,744 times in their full texts, with 30.8%, 45.9%, and 23.3% for disease, gene, and chemical, respectively. Among them, there are 7,569, 79,774 and 28,298 distinct diseases, genes, and chemicals. The entities with the highest frequencies of the three categories are presented in Table 1.

Table 1. High-frequency diseases, genes, and chemicals

Disease	Gene	Chemical
Alzheimer Disease	Insulin (INS)	Lipids
Neoplasms	Superoxide dismutase 1 (SOD1)	Glucose
Dementia	Apolipoprotein E (APOE)	Water
Parkinson Disease	Toll-like receptor 4 (Tlr4)	Reactive Oxygen Species
Diabetes Mellitus	Membrane associated ring-CH-type finger 8 (MARCHF8)	Sodium Chloride

Table 2 shows some descriptive statistics of the Paper-Level (PL) citation network and the Local-Concept-Level (LCL) entity co-occurrence networks. The averaged statistics of the LCL networks are presented since each paper has its own knowledge network. It is shown that the PL network is extremely sparse with a low density and the average degree of its nodes is 4.66. This is likely due to the restriction that both citing and cited articles should be in the PMC-OA set. Within the scope of a single paper, about 50 knowledge entities (i.e. diseases, genes, or chemicals) are mentioned in the full text. Each entity has co-occurrence relationships with about 10 others on average.

Table 2. Statistics of the citation network and entity co-occurrence networks

	Nodes	Edges	Density	Average Degree
PL network	118,504	552,700	3.94×10^{-5}	4.66
LCL network	49.61 (avg.)	345.18 (avg.)	0.26 (avg.)	10.49 (avg.)

On average, there are 1.89 entities in each citation context, represented as the sentence of a citing paper where the citation locates, with 90% of the citation contexts containing 0 to 4 entities. Regarding the type of entities in a single citation context, 43.0% and 42.7% are diseases and genes, while the chemicals only account for 14.3%. This is different from the distribution of entity types in the full text. By considering the entities in citation contexts and the core concepts of the cited papers, we extracted 67,427 knowledge evolution chains from the dataset, with 4,615 distinct source papers that do not cite any other papers in our dataset. The ego-centric entity co-occurrence network, whose ego node is the knowledge entity of interest (AD in this case), can be obtained from the LCL knowledge network of each paper in the chain.

The descriptive statistics of knowledge evolution chains are presented in Table 3. The average length of an evolution chain is 3.61, with about 143 entities in the Domain-Concept-Level (DCL) ego-centric entity co-occurrence network it constructs and an average time span of 7.98 years. It is also shown that the standard deviation is large for these metrics, indicating the heterogeneity among evolution chains.

Table 3. Statistics of the knowledge evolution chains | N = 67,427

	Mean	SD	Median	Q1–Q3
Length	3.61	1.75	3.00	2.00–5.00
Time span (year)	7.98	3.33	8.00	6.00–10.00
Total distinct entities on a chain	142.97	79.12	135.00	81.00–193.00

To quantitatively understand the network evolving process, we proposed a metric to capture the contribution made by each paper to the DCL network, namely Knowledge Cumulation Speed (KCS). The KCS measures how many new entities or relationships between entities are added to the DCL network constructed at three different levels, including one single chain where the paper locates (single chain), all chains that contain the paper (chain set), and all preceding papers from the domain (domain), by each paper. This shows the contribution by each paper to the cumulative knowledge of a single chain, all chains passing through it, and all preceding papers in the dataset.

As Table 4 shows, on average, a paper contributes 10.74 new entities and 50.1 new relationships to the DCL network of a single chain. By excluding 2,669 review articles, this number falls to 9.53 and 43.85 respectively. The standard deviation also slightly decreases. This shows that review articles contribute a higher than average number of new entities and relationships to a chain. This is likely the result of synthesizing entities and relationships across articles from multiple chains, which is referred to as the integrator effect in [29]. However, a paper contributes fewer new entities and relationships to the DCL network of the chain set, with 5.92 entities and 26.26 relationships. Regarding contributions to the domain DCL network, this number decreases substantially to only 0.73 entities and 11.64 relationships, respectively. This means that an article is less novel from a macro perspective (i.e. chain set and domain), compared with one single chain where it locates. More intriguingly, the average contributions to the DCL network of the chain set and domain increase after removing review articles. While review articles are the knowledge integrator of a single evolution chain, they generally contribute fewer novel entities to the domain. Instead, reviews may focus on organizing existing knowledge so the average KCS (domain) - relationship is slightly higher (11.64 vs. 11.53) if reviews are included.

Table 4 Knowledge cumulation speed (KCS) at different levels

	Mean	SD	Median	Q1–Q3
Including reviews				
KCS (single chain) - entity	10.74	8.57	9.00	5.21–13.95
KCS (chain set) - entity	5.92	6.27	4.00	1.00–8.00
KCS (domain) - entity	0.73	1.69	0.00	0.00–1.00
KCS (single chain) - relationship	50.10	53.09	40.00	15.00–65.10
KCS (chain set) - relationship	26.26	46.90	12.00	3.00–31.00
KCS (domain) - relationship	11.64	30.68	2.00	0.00–11.00
Excluding reviews				
KCS (single chain) - entity	9.53	7.04	8.14	5.00–12.16
KCS (chain set) - entity	6.32	6.53	5.00	2.00–9.00
KCS (domain) - entity	0.79	1.78	0.00	0.00–1.00
KCS (single chain) - relationship	43.85	47.00	35.60	13.00–57.17
KCS (chain set) - relationship	27.06	47.73	12.00	3.00–32.00
KCS (domain) - relationship	11.53	30.29	2.00	0.00–11.00

6.2 Case Study

To investigate the knowledge creation, usage, and evolution process in depth, we showed a case study on one knowledge evolution chain of AD. Figure 3 demonstrates the 3-layer representation model applied to this chain, Paper level shows the citation relationships between papers and the entities transferred through citations, whereas local concept level and domain concept level present the AD knowledge structure within a paper and the accumulated AD knowledge structure of this chain. For better readability and visualization, the knowledge networks were filtered by edge weight (greater than 5).

The chain begins with a paper (PMC161361) focusing on the importance of oxidative stress in the pathogenesis of AD. The paper pointed out that iron and copper are likely to be the source of oxidative stress. The LCL network of the first paper is on the link between AD and iron. The second paper PMC4132486 also focused on AD pathology, but with a different approach. They performed a differential network analysis on four region-specific gene co-expression networks. With this novel method, they also reached the conclusion that oxidative stress is a highlighted process in early AD. This paper adds new entities hippocampus (HIP) and posterior cingulate cortex (PCC) to DCL, which are the brain regions affected by AD. Similarly, the third paper PMC4718516 employed network topology analysis to identify genes related to AD, adding related genes CD4, DCN, CXCL8, PSEN1 and BACE1 to the DCL of the knowledge chain. The addition of the third paper enriches the connections between AD and related genes in this chain. Based on the related genes, paper PMC5508523 further analyzed the relationship between NRF2 (NFE2L2 officially) gene deficiency and increased oxidative stress, which may lead to AD eventually. They conducted the experiments on a house

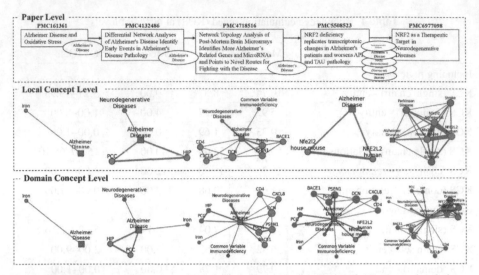

Fig. 3. Knowledge representation of one knowledge evolution chain of AD. Paper level shows the PMCID, title of each paper, and entities in the citation context. AD is the ego of the egocentric networks in local and domain concept level, presented as a red rectangle node. Blue, green, and red nodes denote chemicals, genes, and diseases, respectively. In domain concept level, nodes appearing in the previous networks are grayed out in the current network (Color figure online)

mouse (Mus musculus). New genes, Nfe2l2 (house mouse) and NFE2L2 (human), are added to DCL after the addition of PMC5508523 to the chain. Finally, PMC6977098 is a review paper that summarized the neurodegenerative diseases related to NRF2 gene, including AD, Parkinson's disease, multiple sclerosis, and stroke. The review article connects several diseases due to their common relationship with NRF2 genes.

Overall, this chain focuses on the mechanisms of AD and its pathogenesis, with a common theme on oxidative stress and AD. It can be seen from Fig. 3 that the knowledge networks in LCL reveal the prominent knowledge structure within a paper and DCL depicts the accumulation of knowledge. The combined information from three layers not only reveals the direction of knowledge flow and evolution, but also details the content of knowledge creation, usage, and evolution. It should be noted that this is only one of the knowledge evolution chains extracted from the AD related literature in PMC-OA. The new entities and relationships in this chain may have been covered by or imported from other chains in the citation network. The representation of the model also allows large scale automated analysis on multiple chains in addition to the demonstration of a case here.

7   Discussion and Future Directions

The purpose of this study is to propose a knowledge representation model that facilitates studies on knowledge creation, usage, and evolution. The three-layer network structure of the model includes: 1) a Paper Level (PL) for the citation relationship, as well as semantic relationship, among papers; 2) a Local Concept Level (LCL) for the internal concept structure within papers; 3) a Domain Concept Level (DCL) for accumulative knowledge in a domain. The PL in our model is a citation network with added citation contexts. It is comparable with what most existing studies use for main path analysis to reveal knowledge development [29]. The uniqueness of the proposed model is to integrate citation relationship and content in a multi-layer network model. The resulting model not only allows to trace the knowledge flow between cited and citing papers, but is able to specify how the knowledge content evolves as new papers are added to a citation network. This becomes clear in the case demonstration where the PL shows the direction and path of the knowledge diffusion, the LCL elaborates the content in each paper, and the DCL documents the contribution of each paper to the accumulated knowledge in a chain (in this case, the domain is defined narrowly to a chain). In addition, the principled network model allows large scale automated analysis on knowledge creation, usage, and evolution. The current study applies it on a data set in PMC-OA and shows a case of one chain. It demonstrates the feasibility of the model and its possible use.

The model has implications for science of science studies [41] in that it is focused on the knowledge production process, and the model accommodates for large scale analysis. In its current form, the model can be used to study formally documented flow of ideas and idea interactions. This can help discover where novelty arises and what contributes to the process. When combined with additional information on authors and institutions, the model can help study the interaction between knowledge representations and social structures.

7.1 Future Directions

In the process of carrying out this study, we have also recognized some limitations that point out the future directions of the work: First, while Pubtator Central is the state of the art system to extract biomedical entities from PubMed articles, we still identified several errors in our experiment. For example, a general word may be recognized as a gene entity when it matches the abbreviation of a gene, such as tea and gene Slc7a2 (also known as Tea). Also, Pubtator Central only identifies biomedical entities that fall in the category of gene, disease, chemical, mutation, species, and cell line. Some areas of study, such as food and nutrition, are inadequately covered. Therefore, it is beneficial to improve the accuracy and coverage of entity recognition in our future studies. One way to do that is to integrate external knowledge systems, e.g. PubMed knowledge graph [42], and develop in-house machine learning models. Second, we only calculated preliminary network metrics on the knowledge evolution chains and chose one of them as a case study. Future work will further investigate how to characterize knowledge creation, usage, and evolution using quantitative measures to reveal patterns and regularities in the knowledge production process. Third, while PMC-OA is an ideal dataset for full-text mining, it is obvious that many citations are excluded since they point to articles outside PMC-OA. The knowledge evolution pathways may be skewed due to the problem of incomplete data. Over 90% of the referenced articles in PMC-OA have PMIDs, which means that their abstracts and metadata are available from PubMed. However, how to align these abstract-only articles with full-text articles and trim the current procedure to identify conceptual citations from them remains a challenge.

Despite the limitations, the proposed multi-layer knowledge representation model serves as a powerful infrastructure for various applications. This model also has an extensible architecture that allows for different approaches to construct the inner networks. For instance, we are working on a solution to refine the internal concept structure of individual papers, which focuses on the main topics of the document and filters background and literature review that casts broad connections. This will result in more robust LCL networks. Future studies could also seek an optimal network structure for their applications, ranging from pathway analysis to network simulation.

Acknowledgements. This study was partially funded by the National Natural Science Foundation of China (NSFC) Grant Nos. 71804135 and 71921002.

References

1. Landhuis, E.: Scientific literature: information overload. Nature **535**(7612), 457–458 (2016)
2. de Solla Price, D.J.: Networks of Scientific Papers. Science **149**(3683), 510–515 (1965)
3. Garfield, E., Pudovkin, A.I., Istomin, V.S.: Why do we need algorithmic historiography? J. Am. Soc. Inf. Sci. Technol. **54**(5), 400–412 (2003)
4. van Eck, N.J., Waltman, L.: CitNetExplorer: a new software tool for analyzing and visualizing citation networks. J. Informetr. **8**(4), 802–823 (2014)
5. Kuhn, T., Perc, M., Helbing, D.: Inheritance patterns in citation networks reveal scientific memes. Phys. Rev. X **4**(4), 41036 (2014)
6. Liang, Z., Mao, J., Cao, Y., Li, G.: Idea diffusion patterns: SNA on knowledge meme cascade network. In: Proceedings of ISSI 2019, Rome, Italy, pp. 2612–2613 (2019)
7. Mao, J., Liang, Z., Cao, Y., Li, G.: Quantifying cross-disciplinary knowledge flow from the perspective of content: introducing an approach based on knowledge memes. J. Informetr. **14**(4), 101092 (2020)
8. Bates, M.J.: Defining the information disciplines in encyclopedia development. Inf. Res. **12**(4), 29 (2007)
9. Weller, K.: Knowledge Representation in the Social Semantic Web. Walter de Gruyter, Germany (2010)
10. Hjørland, B.: Knowledge organization (KO). KO Knowl. Organ. **43**(6), 475–484 (2016)
11. Weller, K.: Folksonomies and ontologies: two new players in indexing and knowledge representation. In: Proceedings of the Online Information Conference, London, Great Britain, pp. 108–115 (2007)
12. Leydesdorff, L., Rafols, I.: A global map of science based on the ISI subject categories. J. Am. Soc. Inf. Sci. Technol. **60**(2), 348–362 (2009)
13. Callon, M., Courtial, J.-P., Turner, W.A., Bauin, S.: From translations to problematic networks: an introduction to co-word analysis. Soc. Sci. Inf. **22**(2), 191–235 (1983)
14. Lu, K., Wolfram, D.: Measuring author research relatedness: a comparison of word-based, topic-based, and author cocitation approaches. J. Am. Soc. Inf. Sci. Technol. **63**(10), 1973–1986 (2012)
15. White, H.D., McCain, K.W.: Visualizing a discipline: an author co-citation analysis of information science, 1972–1995. J. Am. Soc. Inf. Sci. **49**(4), 327–355 (1998)
16. Kessler, M.M.: Bibliographic coupling between scientific papers. Am. Doc. **14**(1), 10–25 (1963)
17. Perianes-Rodríguez, A., Olmeda-Gómez, C., Moya-Anegón, F.: Detecting, identifying and visualizing research groups in co-authorship networks. Scientometrics **82**(2), 307–319 (2010)

18. Cobo, M.J., López-Herrera, A.G., Herrera-Viedma, E., Herrera, F.: An approach for detecting, quantifying, and visualizing the evolution of a research field: a practical application to the fuzzy sets theory field. J. Informetr. **5**(1), 146–166 (2011)
19. Markman, A.B.: Knowledge Representation. Psychology Press, Mahwah (1999)
20. van Harmelen, F., Lifschitz, V., Porter, B.: Handbook of Knowledge Representation. Elsevier, Amsterdam (2008)
21. Cronin, B.: The Citation Process: The Role and Significance of Citations in Scientific Communication. Taylor Graham, London (1984)
22. Lutz, B., Hans-Dieter, D.: What do citation counts measure? A review of studies on citing behavior. J. Doc. **64**(1), 45–80 (2008)
23. White, H.D.: Reward, persuasion, and the Sokal Hoax: a study in citation identities. Scientometrics **60**(1), 93–120 (2004)
24. Frandsen, T.F., Nicolaisen, J.: Citation behavior: a large-scale test of the persuasion by name-dropping hypothesis. J. Assoc. Inf. Sci. Technol. **68**(5), 1278–1284 (2017)
25. Sugimoto, C.R.: Theories of Informetrics and Scholarly Communication. Walter de Gruyter, Germany (2016)
26. Garfield, E., Sher, I.H., Torpie, R.J.: The use of citation data in writing the history of science. Institute for Scientific Information, Philadelphia (1964)
27. Hummon, N.P., Dereian, P.: Connectivity in a citation network: the development of DNA theory. Soc. Network. **11**(1), 39–63 (1989)
28. Lucio-Arias, D., Leydesdorff, L.: Main-path analysis and path-dependent transitions in HistCite^{TM}-based historiograms. J. Am. Soc. Inf. Sci. Technol. **59**(12), 1948–1962 (2008)
29. Liu, J.S., Lu, L.Y.Y., Ho, M.H.-C.: A few notes on main path analysis. Scientometrics **119**(1), 379–391 (2019)
30. Ding, Y., Zhang, G., Chambers, T., Song, M., Wang, X., Zhai, C.: Content-based citation analysis: the next generation of citation analysis. J. Assoc. Inf. Sci. Technol. **65**(9), 1820–1833 (2014)
31. Chen, C., Li, Q., Chiu, K., Deng, Z.: The impact of Chinese library and information science on outside disciplines: a citation analysis. J. Librariansh. Inf. Sci. **52**(2), 493–508 (2019)
32. Wang, F., et al.: Exploring all-author tripartite citation networks: a case study of gene editing. J. Informetr. **13**(3), 856–873 (2019)
33. Walter, C., Ribière, V.: A citation and co-citation analysis of 10 years of KM theory and practices. Knowl. Manag. Res. Pract. **11**(3), 221–229 (2013)
34. Shiau, W.-L., Dwivedi, Y.K.: Citation and co-citation analysis to identify core and emerging knowledge in electronic commerce research. Scientometrics **94**(3), 1317–1337 (2013)
35. Boccaletti, S., et al.: The structure and dynamics of multilayer networks. Phys. Rep. **544**(1), 1–122 (2014)
36. Scott, J., Carrington, P.J.: The SAGE Handbook of Social Network Analysis. SAGE, Thousand Oaks (2011)
37. Criado, R., Romance, M., Vela-Pérez, M.: Hyperstructures, a new approach to complex systems. Int. J. Bifurc. Chaos. **20**(03), 877–883 (2010)
38. Kim, H.J., Jeong, Y.K., Song, M.: Content- and proximity-based author co-citation analysis using citation sentences. J. Informetr. **10**(4), 954–966 (2016)
39. Colavizza, G., Boyack, K.W., van Eck, N.J., Waltman, L.: The closer the better: similarity of publication pairs at different cocitation levels. J. Assoc. Inf. Sci. Technol. **69**(4), 600–609 (2018)
40. Wei, C.-H., Allot, A., Leaman, R., Lu, Z.: PubTator central: automated concept annotation for biomedical full text articles. Nucleic Acids Res. **47**(W1), W587–W593 (2019)
41. Fortunato, S., et al.: Science of science. Science **359**(6379), eaao0185 (2018)
42. Xu, J., et al.: Building a PubMed knowledge graph. Sci. Data. **7**, 1–19 (2020)

Biomedical Knowledge Graph Refinement and Completion Using Graph Representation Learning and Top-K Similarity Measure

Islam Akef Ebeid[1]([⊠]) [iD], Majdi Hassan[2], Tingyi Wanyan[3], Jack Roper[1], Abhik Seal[2], and Ying Ding[1]

[1] The University of Texas at Austin, Austin, TX 78701, USA
iaebeid@utexas.edu, ying.ding@ischool.utexas.edu
[2] AbbVie Inc., North Chicago, IL 60064, USA
{majdi.hassan,abhik.seal}@abbvie.com
[3] Indiana University, Bloomington, IN 47405, USA
tiwanyan@iu.edu

Abstract. Knowledge Graphs have been one of the fundamental methods for integrating heterogeneous data sources. Integrating heterogeneous data sources is crucial, especially in the biomedical domain, where central data-driven tasks such as drug discovery rely on incorporating information from different biomedical databases. These databases contain various biological entities and relations such as proteins (PDB) [3], genes (Gene Ontology) [2], drugs (DrugBank) [33], diseases (DDB) [7], and protein-protein interactions (BioGRID) [28]. The process of semantically integrating heterogeneous biomedical databases is often riddled with imperfections. The quality of data-driven drug discovery relies on the accuracy of the mining methods used and the data's quality as well. Thus, having complete and refined biomedical knowledge graphs is central to achieving more accurate drug discovery outcomes. Here we propose using the latest graph representation learning and embedding models to refine and complete biomedical knowledge graphs. This preliminary work demonstrates learning discrete representations of the integrated biomedical knowledge graph Chem2Bio2RDF [10]. We perform a knowledge graph completion and refinement task using a simple top-K cosine similarity measure between the learned embedding vectors to predict missing links between drugs and targets present in the data. We show that this simple procedure can be used alternatively to binary classifiers in link prediction.

Keywords: Representation learning · Knowledge graph completion · Knowledge reasoning · Biomedical knowledge graph

1 Introduction

The Knowledge Graph provides a unique opportunity as an emerging model to break data and information silos through effective data integration techniques and methods [19]. The term Knowledge Graph (KG) has emerged to describe the technology that the

© Springer Nature Switzerland AG 2021
K. Toeppe et al. (Eds.): iConference 2021, LNCS 12645, pp. 112–123, 2021.
https://doi.org/10.1007/978-3-030-71292-1_10

Google search engine started using in 2012 [26]. A KG graph represents interrelated and semantically connected entities [19]. KG construction methods can vary from manual curation to automatic extraction of entities and relations from unstructured text using Natural Language Processing [26]. KGs can also be constructed from existing heterogeneous relational databases through integration methods [10]. KGs can be represented using the property graph model [19] described as a list of edges between unique nodes and properties or using the Resource Descriptor Framework (RDF) format defined by the World Wide Web Consortium [21]. RDF is a graph model that uses a markup language similar to XML to represent data. RDF represents knowledge graphs as triples of a head entity, a tail entity, and a relationship type. The RDF triples can be used to model facts in the form of first-order logic. For example, < Mount Fuji, isLocatedIn, Japan > where < Mount Fuji > and < Japan > are two unique nodes or entities in the graph, and < isLocatedIn > is the relationship between the two nodes.

Despite the multitude of methods used in constructing and curating knowledge graphs, they are susceptible to incomplete and inaccurate data [26]. KG refinement and completion methods aim to improve KGs by filling in their missing knowledge and checking the existing knowledge's validity. Here we propose using graph representation learning models to learn different discrete feature representations of entities in Chem2Bio2RDF. We use simple vector operations such as cosine distance as a similarity ranking measure to predict missing knowledge and links between drugs and potential targets [14] to complete and refine the knowledge graph.

2   Background

In [10], Chem2Bio2RDF was introduced as a biomedical knowledge graph integrating multiple biological databases such as PubChem [32] and DrugBank [33]. In [14], the authors suggested using meta path-based sampling from Chem2Bio2RDF to extract features that would be used to test multiple machine learning models trained to predict missing drug-target interactions within the KG. Revealing possible side effects of specific drug and gene interactions is a highly sought goal in data-driven drug discovery and chemical systems biology [35]. Predicting drug-target interactions lends itself to the task of link prediction in graph analytics [14]. Link prediction on biomedical KGs aims to identify potential associations between entities such as drugs, proteins, and genes, a task known as knowledge graph completion and refinement.

Representation learning models aim at training latent feature vectors from data without relying on stochastic and heuristic metrics and measures [6]. All representation learning algorithms on graphs ultimately produce node embedding vectors in low-dimensional vector space [17]. The minimal constraint on the learned representations is that they preserve the graph's structure in the Euclidean vector space [17]. The node embedding vectors learned can be passed to downstream machine learning models for classification, regression, or clustering. Alternatively, they can be used directly in the learning process in a semi-supervised end-to-end fashion as in graph neural network approaches [34]. They can also be inductive as in learned from the structure of the graph itself [16, 27, 29] or transductive by forcing a scoring function to evaluate the plausibility of the triples in the KG [8, 23].

Link prediction-based knowledge graph completion using representation learning relies mostly on binary classifiers. The task is to learn a model that would predict whether a link should exist between two entities on a subset of the graph [22]. We argue that binary classifiers for link prediction-based biomedical KG completion are unnecessary [1]. Instead, using similarity functions between learned node embedding vectors is sufficient to predict missing links between bioentities with more realistic uncertainty. We evaluate our models using an experimental ground truth dataset collected from the DrugBank [33] on positive and negative associations between potential drugs and targets such as genes, proteins, and chemical ontologies.

3 Method

The class of network embedding models used in this paper relies on random walk sampling of the input graph followed by the unsupervised Skip-gram model described initially in [25]. Different network embedding algorithms learn different embedding vectors for each node. That largely depends on the information each algorithm tries to preserve during learning [31]. In node2vec [16], structural information or topology is preserved, while in edge2vec [15], structural plus edge types are preserved. In metapath2vec [13], node types, relations, and topology are preserved. While in GraphSAGE [18], the structure or the topology is preserved, yet embeddings for out of sample nodes can be inferred.

3.1 The Skip-Gram Model

The Skip-gram model described in [25] is an unsupervised language model aiming at learning discrete vectors of unique words given a corpus of text. In unsupervised network and graph embedding algorithms, the Skip-gram model has been adapted to learn vectors for individual nodes on a corpus of sampled nodes from the graph. In DeepWalk [27], the authors first proposed using the Skip-gram model on a corpus of sampled nodes from a given graph using a random walk strategy. Since it was observed that the distribution of words in any corpus of text followed Zipf's law, it was also observed that the frequency distribution of nodes in a graph follows Zipf's law [27]. The random walk algorithm aims at sampling chains of nodes from the graph controlled by the walk length. Sampled chains are then treated as a text corpus fed to a Skip-gram variant of Word2vec. The text is first tokenized into sentences; similarly, the random walks mimic the process of creating meaningful "sentences" out of the graph as a sampling approach.

The Skip-gram model can be formalized given a sequence of training words or nodes $(w_1, w_2, w_3, \ldots, w_t)$ the goal is then to maximize the log-likelihood probability of the current word given the surrounding words:

$$P(w_1, w_2, w_3, \ldots, w_t) = \frac{1}{T} \sum_T^{t=1} \sum_{-c \leq j \leq c, j \neq 0} \log P(w_{t+j}|w_t) \tag{1}$$

C is the size of the training window around the current word, and T is the size of the training corpus. Finding a solution for $P(w_{t+j}|w_t)$ requires computing a full Softmax function, which is intractable. Instead, a sampling approach, such as Hierarchical

Softmax or Negative Sampling, is needed, as described in [25]. The negative sampling approach is mostly used in network embedding. It is done by reformulating the neural network's output layer to become a logistic regression-based classifier rather than a Softmax predictor. The input is a context window of words where each word is classified as 1 within the context window. Otherwise, 0 if the word was negatively sampled from outside of the context window. A Stochastic Gradient Descent [9] is then used to optimize the objective function to learn the feature vector U for each unique word in the vocab V as showing in Eq. 2. Note that in the case of network embedding for a graph $G = (N, E)$, W becomes N, where words become nodes. The Skip-gram model's input corpus becomes the output corpus of sampled nodes using the random walk strategy.

$$J_t(\theta) = \log \sigma\left(u_o^T v_c\right) + \sum_{j=P(w)}\left[\log \sigma\left(-u_j^T v_c\right)\right] \tag{2}$$

Node2vec. [16] performs a modified version of the random walk where it includes parameters p and q to control the sampling strategy. The p parameter controls the likelihood of the walk revisiting a node. The q parameter controls whether the search is constrained locally or globally. Given $q > 1$ and a random walk on an initial node, the random walk samples nodes closer to the initial node as in breadth-first search. Whereas $q < 1$, random walk samples nodes further from the initial node similar to a depth first search. This customizability in search behavior allows the random walker to capture diverse structural and topological properties within the graph. The sampling strategy builds a corpus of walks for each node. A skip-gram model trains on this corpus to generate a unique embedding vector for each node.

Edge2vec. [15] builds on Node2vec by introducing an additional sampling step where edge semantics are considered during the random walk sampling. The random walker first trains a transition matrix built from the existing edges using an expectation-maximization algorithm [12]. A corpus of nodes is generated from random walks that consider the edge weights from the transition matrix. Then, a skip-gram trains on the corpus to generate the node embeddings.

In **Metapath2vec** [13], the random walk sampling strategy is guided by predefined meta paths. KGs are usually defined by a schema, as in Fig. 1. A meta path is determined from the kg schema that generally has a semantic meaning within the KG domain knowledge. For example, the meta path protein-protein-gene refers to a biochemical process of protein interactions and genes binding to those proteins, reflecting a semantic meaning. The sampled corpus of nodes is then passed to a skip-gram model to learn the embedding vectors.

GraphSAGE. [18] offers a way to leverage the already existing node embedding vectors to produce embedding vectors for newly introduced nodes inductively. That is done by aligning the new observed nodes to the existing trained embedding space using aggregation and pooling functions on the target node's neighborhood.

3.2 Dataset

Advances in biomedical sciences have given rise to new integrated and significant biological data sources. Integrating these data sources involves converting the graph to RDF format and then integrating them semantically. Chem2Bio2RDF [10] is an extended version of Bio2RDF [4]. It aggregates data from multiple sources from Bio2RDF, Drug-Bank, and PubChem. Chem2Bio2RDF contains over 700000 triples and 295000 unique entities. A schema of Chem2Bio2RDF is presented in Fig. 1, showing 9 bioentities and their semantic relationships in the graph.

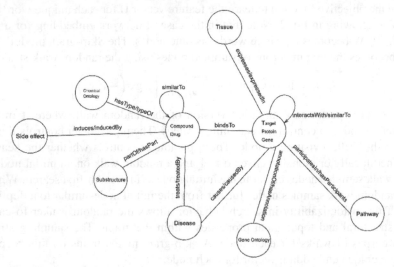

Fig. 1. The schema describes entities and relationships in Chem2Bio2RDF. For example, the graph can contain a triple that describes a relationship between a compound/drug as part of a substructure and a substructure that is part of a compound/drug.

3.3 Model Training

The model's input is an edge list of Chem2Bio2RDF triples where the source node, the target node, and the edge describe the relationship. The graph is then sampled to build a corpus of node walks, which is then be used as an input to the Skip-gram algorithm. Sampling strategies differ based on the algorithm used, as described before in Sect. 3.1. For example, in Metapath2vec, the walk length we used was 20, and the number of walks per node was 10. Vector dimensions for node2vec, metapath2vec, and edge2vec were chosen to be 128, while for GraphSAGE was 500. The metapaths used in training metpath2vec are described in [14].

4   Experiments and Results

Predicting non-existing relationships between KG entities is known as KG refinement and completion [26]. In the biomedical context, KG refinement and completion can predict possible relationships between different entities that have not been explored before, speeding up discovering new applications of existing drugs [14]. We pose drug-target interaction prediction as a top-k similarity ranking task in Chem2Bio2RDF [20]. We used drug-target interaction data as ground truth extracted from 2 sources the DrugBank [33] and the test set included in [14]. We included both ground truth datasets to ensure the completeness of the ground truth data. The links presented in both ground-truth datasets are removed from the Chem2Bio2RDF edge list before training. We used the ground truth data to evaluate link prediction models as the top-k similarity between node embedding vectors. We also used them to evaluate an XGBoost binary classifier model [11]. For the top-K similarity method, a cosine distance similarity metric is used to compute a similarity score between the target node vector and the source node vector.

$$similarity = \cos(\theta) = \frac{AB}{||A||||B||} \tag{3}$$

Across these tasks, accuracy, precision, recall, and F1 scores were recorded in Tables 2, 3, and 4. Table 1 shows the link prediction task results using the XGBoost binary classifier evaluated using only the test set provided in [14]. The XGBoost binary classifier is trained by splitting the original graph data into train, test, and validation sets. A threshold is then applied to a similarity function score between the trained node embedding vectors similar to [5]. Our broad research question investigates the performance of using a simple top-K cosine similarity score between vectors. We attempt to answer the questions: is a binary classifier for KG link prediction necessary? Would a simple top-K similarity score between vectors be sufficient to assess the suitability of predicting new links between drugs and targets in the graph?

We evaluated the 4 embedding algorithms' performance on a test set of possible and impossible links between drugs and target using two methods the Top-K similarity method [20] and the binary classification based link prediction method [1]. We used two test sets containing a set of drug-target pairs that included positive and negative labels for a link between a pair. The first test set [14] consists of 5,387 positive pairings and 26,682 negative pairings. The second test set extracted from the DrugBank contains drug-target interaction pairs that do not exist in Chem2Bio2RDF but should exist. That test set has 5,836 positive pairings and 2,368 negative pairings. For both test sets, the positive and negative pairings were verified experimentally through ChEMBL [24], and the negative pairings had at least 5 uM of activity. For both evaluation methods, we used the 2 test sets to evaluate the performance of the 4 algorithms. We trained the XGBoost binary classifier model [11] on labeled positive and negative links sampled from the binary classification-based link prediction graph. The model was then tested on a validation set sampled from the graph.

Like the binary classification based link prediction task, top-k ranking predicts whether a link exists between two entities. Unlike link prediction, where it provides a single prediction between a drug/compound and target/gene, the top-K ranking task considers drug pairing to several targets and ranks based on the cosine similarity scores between their learned vectors. That places the importance on the rank of the drug-target link rather than the existence of a link. The ranking considers the uncertainty of a link between two entities and provides a flexible way of testing various K thresholds. After the algorithm ranks the similarity scores between two embedding vectors, we evaluate the top-K portion of the rankings.

The accuracy results are close and similar between both the binary classifier method and the top-K method. That supports our argument that top-K similarity prediction can be used for KG refinement and completion via link prediction. Despite the variability in the f1 score, accuracy remains very close between the two methods, suggesting that training better models using adaptable graph representation learning algorithms would provide par performance. Besides, link prediction using binary classification models provides a rigid framework incapable of capturing the uncertainty in graph representation learning for knowledge graph completion.

Table 1. The results for link prediction using XGBoost binary classifier

	Accuracy	F1	Precision	Recall
Node2vec	0.9920	0.9631	0.9843	0.9427
Edge2vec	0.9922	0.9637	0.9873	0.9412
Metapath2vec	0.9935	0.9700	0.9890	0.9517
GraphSAGE	0.9865	0.9366	0.9739	0.9019

Table 2. The results of Top-K similarity where K = 10

	Accuracy	F1	Precision	Recall
Node2vec	0.9314	0.5838	0.8838	0.4359
Edge2vec	0.9567	0.7830	0.8766	0.7074
Metapath2vec	0.9611	0.8132	0.8682	0.7647
GraphSAGE	0.8880	0.0260	0.3214	0.0136

Table 3. The results of Top-K similarity where K = 50

	Accuracy	F1	Precision	Recall
Node2vec	0.9421	0.7005	0.8156	0.6139
Edge2vec	0.9596	0.8209	0.8026	0.8401
Metapath2vec	0.9590	0.8237	0.7844	0.8673
GraphSAGE	0.8834	0.0514	0.2500	0.0287

Table 4. The results of Top-K similarity where K = 100

	Accuracy	F1	Precision	Recall
Node2vec	0.9438	0.7317	0.7722	0.6953
Edge2vec	0.9514	0.7966	0.7400	0.8627
Metapath2vec	0.9476	0.7881	0.7131	0.8808
GraphSAGE	0.8787	0.0853	0.2537	0.0528

4.1 Use Case

Table 5 shows the data available in Chem2Bio2RDF for the drug Apicidin (467801). Using a simple top-20 similarity query over our trained Metapath2vec model shown in Table 6, we predicted that the drug Apicidin should be linked to the gene HDA-106. Since it has a higher cosine similarity score (0.6047) than some of the genes that already exist in the graph. Apicidin is a histone deacetylase inhibitor used to treat tumors [30]. HDA-106 and all the HDA genes are critical enzymes involved in developing cancer and other diseases such as interstitial fibrosis, autoimmune, inflammatory diseases, and metabolic disorders [30]. That suggests that our procedure could predict that a link should exist between Apicidin and HDA-106 in Chem2Bio2RDF, even though that link did not exist before. The link between Apicidin and HDA-106 was also not predicted using the binary classifier link predictor.

Table 5. The links in the graph for the drug Apicidin

Source node	Target node
https://chem2bio2rdf.org/pubchem/resource/ pubchem_compound/467801	https://chem2bio2rdf.org/uniprot/resource/ gene/HDAC5
https://chem2bio2rdf.org/pubchem/resource/ pubchem_compound/467801	https://chem2bio2rdf.org/uniprot/resource/ gene/HDAC6
https://chem2bio2rdf.org/pubchem/resource/ pubchem_compound/467801	https://chem2bio2rdf.org/uniprot/resource/ gene/HDAC10
https://chem2bio2rdf.org/pubchem/resource/ pubchem_compound/467801	https://chem2bio2rdf.org/uniprot/resource/ gene/HDAH
https://chem2bio2rdf.org/pubchem/resource/ pubchem_compound/467801	https://chem2bio2rdf.org/uniprot/resource/ gene/HDAC4
https://chem2bio2rdf.org/pubchem/resource/ pubchem_compound/467801	https://chem2bio2rdf.org/uniprot/resource/ gene/HDAC7
https://chem2bio2rdf.org/pubchem/resource/ pubchem_compound/467801	https://chem2bio2rdf.org/uniprot/resource/ gene/NCOR2
https://chem2bio2rdf.org/pubchem/resource/ pubchem_compound/467801	https://chem2bio2rdf.org/uniprot/resource/ gene/HDAC11

(continued)

Table 5. (*continued*)

Source node	Target node
https://chem2bio2rdf.org/pubchem/resource/pubchem_compound/467801	https://chem2bio2rdf.org/uniprot/resource/gene/F3
https://chem2bio2rdf.org/pubchem/resource/pubchem_compound/467801	https://chem2bio2rdf.org/uniprot/resource/gene/HDAC1
https://chem2bio2rdf.org/pubchem/resource/pubchem_compound/467801	https://chem2bio2rdf.org/uniprot/resource/gene/HDAC9
https://chem2bio2rdf.org/pubchem/resource/pubchem_compound/467801	https://chem2bio2rdf.org/uniprot/resource/gene/HDAC8
https://chem2bio2rdf.org/pubchem/resource/pubchem_compound/467801	https://chem2bio2rdf.org/uniprot/resource/gene/HDAC2
https://chem2bio2rdf.org/pubchem/resource/pubchem_compound/467801	https://chem2bio2rdf.org/uniprot/resource/gene/HDAC3

Table 6. All top 20 are target genes/proteins for the drug Apicidin (467801). The higher the cosine similarity score, the more probable that the link between them should exist in the graph.

Gene	Cosine distance score
https://chem2bio2rdf.org/uniprot/resource/gene/NCOR2	0.8363208028622343
https://chem2bio2rdf.org/uniprot/resource/gene/HDAC10	0.7164958960454791
https://chem2bio2rdf.org/uniprot/resource/gene/HDAC11	0.6595226647235345
https://chem2bio2rdf.org/uniprot/resource/gene/HDAC7	0.6594273898963945
https://chem2bio2rdf.org/uniprot/resource/gene/HDAC6	0.6459631340208143
https://chem2bio2rdf.org/uniprot/resource/gene/HDAC9	0.6364544696270995
https://chem2bio2rdf.org/uniprot/resource/gene/HDAH	0.6329007338447462
https://chem2bio2rdf.org/uniprot/resource/gene/HDAC4	0.6079327615804068
https://chem2bio2rdf.org/uniprot/resource/gene/HDAC3	0.6070127461182808
https://chem2bio2rdf.org/uniprot/resource/gene/HDA106	0.6047486633717029
https://chem2bio2rdf.org/uniprot/resource/gene/HDAC5	0.6029446879584531
https://chem2bio2rdf.org/uniprot/resource/gene/HDAC1	0.5987907960296356
https://chem2bio2rdf.org/uniprot/resource/gene/HDAC2	0.5682675274176112
https://chem2bio2rdf.org/uniprot/resource/gene/HD1B	0.5497739534316449

(*continued*)

Table 6. (*continued*)

Gene	Cosine distance score
https://chem2bio2rdf.org/uniprot/resource/gene/HDAC8	0.5227708345535201
https://chem2bio2rdf.org/uniprot/resource/gene/ACUC1	0.4979581350083667
https://chem2bio2rdf.org/uniprot/resource/gene/BCOR	0.4433902007677988
https://chem2bio2rdf.org/uniprot/resource/gene/BTBD14B	0.44092212647673124
https://chem2bio2rdf.org/uniprot/resource/gene/PHF21A	0.4381844427483992
https://chem2bio2rdf.org/uniprot/resource/gene/FLI1	0.4370752763874226

5 Conclusion

In this preliminary work, we demonstrated the use of graph representation learning models for KG refinement and completion using top-K cosine similarity distance between the learned embedding vectors. The results of the model need further evaluation to be included in the dataset itself. Less semantically aware algorithms like node2vec performed better than more semantically aware algorithms metapath2vec in link prediction. That might be because less semantically aware algorithms are sufficient to predict direct and simple links like drugs and genes. While more semantically aware algorithms might be better for predicting relationships between more complicated pathways. Future work includes investigating incorporating more semantics in embedding models and testing whether these heterogeneous semantically aware models perform better. In the future, we also intend to include a full parameter sensitivity study alongside an extended version of the evaluation protocol. We plan to experiment on the feasibility and reliability of using top K similarity for link prediction for KG refinement and completion for drug discovery.

References

1. Al Hasan, M., Chaoji, V., Salem, S., Zaki, M.: Link prediction using supervised learning. In: SDM06: Workshop on Link Analysis, Counter-Terrorism and Security, vol. 30, pp. 798–805 (2006)
2. Ashburner, M., et al.: Gene ontology: tool for the unification of biology. Nat. Genet. **25**(1), 25–29 (2000). https://doi.org/10.1038/75556
3. Bank, P.D.: Protein data bank. Nat. New Biol. **233**, 223 (1971)
4. Belleau, F., Nolin, M.-A., Tourigny, N., Rigault, P., Morissette, J.: Bio2RDF: towards a mashup to build bioinformatics knowledge systems. J. Biomed. Inform. **41**(5), 706–716 (2008). https://doi.org/10.1016/j.jbi.2008.03.004
5. Benchettara, N., Kanawati, R., Rouveirol, C.: Supervised machine learning applied to link prediction in bipartite social networks. In 2010 International Conference on Advances in Social Networks Analysis and Mining, pp. 326–330. IEEE, August 2010
6. Bengio, Y., Courville, A., Vincent, P.: Representation learning: a review and new perspectives. ArXiv:1206.5538 (2014)

7. Bodenreider, O.: The unified medical language system (UMLS): integrating biomedical terminology. Nucleic Acids Res. **32**(suppl_1), D267–D270 (2004)
8. Bordes, A., Usunier, N., Garcia-Duran, A., Weston, J., Yakhnenko, O.: Translating embeddings for modeling multi-relational data. In: Advances in Neural Information Processing Systems, pp. 2787–2795 (2013)
9. Bottou, L., Bousquet, O.: The tradeoffs of large scale learning. In: Platt, J.C., Koller, D., Singer, Y., Roweis, S.T. (eds.) Advances in Neural Information Processing Systems, vol. 20, pp. 161–168. Curran Associates, Inc. (2008). https://papers.nips.cc/paper/3323-the-tradeoffs-of-large-scale-learning.pdf
10. Chen, B., et al.: Chem2Bio2RDF: a semantic framework for linking and data mining chemogenomic and systems chemical biology data. BMC Bioinform. **11**(1), 255 (2010). https://doi.org/10.1186/1471-2105-11-255
11. Chen, T., Guestrin, C.: XGBoost: a scalable tree boosting system. In: Proceedings of the 22nd ACM SIGKDD International Conference on Knowledge Discovery and Data Mining, pp. 785–794 (2016). https://doi.org/10.1145/2939672.2939785
12. Dempster, A.P., Laird, N.M., Rubin, D.B.: Maximum likelihood from incomplete data via the EM algorithm. J. Roy. Stat. Soc. Ser. B (Methodol.) **39**(1), 1–22 (1977)
13. Dong, Y., Chawla, N.V., Swami, A.: metapath2vec: scalable representation learning for heterogeneous networks. In: Proceedings of the 23rd ACM SIGKDD International Conference on Knowledge Discovery and Data Mining, pp. 135–144 (2017). https://doi.org/10.1145/3097983.3098036
14. Fu, G., Ding, Y., Seal, A., Chen, B., Sun, Y., Bolton, E.: Predicting drug target interactions using meta-path-based semantic network analysis. BMC Bioinform. **17**(1), 160 (2016). https://doi.org/10.1186/s12859-016-1005-x
15. Gao, Z., et al.: edge2vec: representation learning using edge semantics for biomedical knowledge discovery. BMC Bioinform. **20**(1), 306 (2019). https://doi.org/10.1186/s12859-019-2914-2
16. Grover, A., Leskovec, J.: node2vec: scalable feature learning for networks. In: Proceedings of the 22nd ACM SIGKDD International Conference on Knowledge Discovery and Data Mining - KDD 2016, pp. 855–864 (2016). https://doi.org/10.1145/2939672.2939754
17. Hamilton, W. L., Ying, R., Leskovec, J.: Representation learning on graphs: methods and applications. ArXiv:1709.05584 (2018)
18. Hamilton, W.L., Ying, R., Leskovec, J.: Inductive representation learning on large graphs. ArXiv:1706.02216 (2018)
19. Hogan, A., et al.: Knowledge graphs. ArXiv:2003.02320 (2020)
20. Jeh, G., Widom, J.: SimRank: a measure of structural-context similarity. In: Proceedings of the Eighth ACM SIGKDD International Conference on Knowledge Discovery and Data Mining, pp. 538–543 (2002)
21. Lassila, O., Swick, R.R., et al.: Resource description framework (RDF) model and syntax specification (1998)
22. Liben-Nowell, D., Kleinberg, J.: The link-prediction problem for social networks. J. Am. Soc. Inform. Sci. Technol. **58**(7), 1019–1031 (2007). https://doi.org/10.1002/asi.20591
23. Lin, Y., Liu, Z., Sun, M., Liu, Y., Zhu, X.: Learning entity and relation embeddings for knowledge graph completion. In: Twenty-Ninth AAAI Conference on Artificial Intelligence. Twenty-Ninth AAAI Conference on Artificial Intelligence, 19 February 2015. https://www.aaai.org/ocs/index.php/AAAI/AAAI15/paper/view/9571
24. Mendez, D., et al.: ChEMBL: towards direct deposition of bioassay data. Nucleic Acids Res. **47**(D1), D930–D940 (2019)
25. Mikolov, T., Sutskever, I., Chen, K., Corrado, G.S., Dean, J.: Distributed representations of words and phrases and their compositionality. In: Advances in Neural Information Processing Systems, pp. 3111–3119 (2013)

26. Paulheim, H.: Knowledge graph refinement: a survey of approaches and evaluation methods. Semant. Web **8**(3), 489–508 (2016). https://doi.org/10.3233/SW-160218
27. Perozzi, B., Al-Rfou, R., Skiena, S.: DeepWalk: online learning of social representations. In: Proceedings of the 20th ACM SIGKDD International Conference on Knowledge Discovery and Data Mining, pp. 701–710 (2014). https://doi.org/10.1145/2623330.2623732
28. Stark, C., Breitkreutz, B.-J., Reguly, T., Boucher, L., Breitkreutz, A., Tyers, M.: BioGRID: a general repository for interaction datasets. Nucleic Acids Res. **34**(suppl_1), D535–D539 (2006)
29. Tang, J., Qu, M., Wang, M., Zhang, M., Yan, J., Mei, Q.: LINE: large-scale information network embedding. In: Proceedings of the 24th International Conference on World Wide Web - WWW 2015, pp. 1067–1077 (2015). https://doi.org/10.1145/2736277.2741093
30. Tang, J., Yan, H., Zhuang, S.: Histone deacetylases as targets for treatment of multiple diseases. Clinic. Sci. (London, England : 1979), **124**(11), 651–662 (2013). https://doi.org/10.1042/CS20120504
31. Wang, Q., Mao, Z., Wang, B., Guo, L.: Knowledge graph embedding: a survey of approaches and applications. IEEE Trans. Knowl. Data Eng. **29**(12), 2724–2743 (2017). https://doi.org/10.1109/TKDE.2017.2754499
32. Wang, Y., Xiao, J., Suzek, T. O., Zhang, J., Wang, J., Bryant, S.H.: PubChem: a public information system for analyzing bioactivities of small molecules. Nucleic Acids Res. **37**(suppl_2), W623–W633 (2009)
33. Wishart, D.S., et al.: DrugBank 5.0: a major update to the DrugBank database for 2018. Nucleic Acids Res. **46**(D1), D1074–D1082 (2018). https://doi.org/10.1093/nar/gkx1037
34. Wu, Z., Pan, S., Chen, F., Long, G., Zhang, C., Yu, P.S.: A comprehensive survey on graph neural networks. ArXiv:1901.00596 (2019)
35. Xie, L., Li, J., Xie, L., Bourne, P.E.: Drug discovery using chemical systems biology: identification of the protein-ligand binding network to explain the side effects of CETP inhibitors. PLoS Comput. Biol. **5**(5), e1000387 (2009). https://doi.org/10.1371/journal.pcbi.1000387

Comparison of Data Analytics Software Usage in Biomedical and Health Sciences Research: A Case Study

Fei Yu[✉] ⓘ and Nandita S. Mani ⓘ

University of North Carolina at Chapel Hill, Chapel Hill, NC 27599, USA
{feifei,nanditam}@unc.edu

Abstract. Responding to the new data science initiative at the University of North Carolina at Chapel Hill (UNC-CH), this study aimed to investigate the usage of data analytics software (DAS) in biomedical and health sciences research. We selected three DAS tools (i.e., SAS, R, & Python), systematically searched PubMed and PubMed Central databases for UNC-CH publications in which any of the three tools was adopted, manually screened retrieved articles, and then conducted a bibliometric analysis. We found that (1) UNC researchers produced more publications using SAS than using R or Python. (2) The citation impact was similar across the publications supported by three tools and higher than the average of NIH-funded papers. (3) The most frequently addressed topics supported by SAS or R included cancer, HIV, risk factors and assessment, and associations between diseases/symptoms and clinical outcomes. Python was often used to investigate cancer genes and genetic inferences, interactions and sequencing. Overall, the prevalent adoption of SAS by UNC authors in biomedical research highlighted the importance of software availability, industry-academia collaboration, and training programs. Our findings provided insights to the new data science initiative for informed decision making.

Keywords: Data analytics software · Biomedical and health sciences research · Bibliometrics

1 Introduction

Data analysis is a vital process for informed decision making and scientific discovery. In the era of Big Data when large volumes of data are available with unprecedented breadth and depth [1] and pose challenges to data analysis [2, 3], data analytics software (DAS) has been developed and adopted to help find solutions and predict outcomes [4]. Transforming data to information and then to knowledge [5, 6], DAS enables people to explore complex relationships in large datasets, visualize data patterns, and generate instant insights.

Data analytics has penetrated a wide range of industries and research fields [2]. Particularly, in biomedical and health sciences (BHS), electronic health records, patient generated health data through self-monitoring devices, clinical trial data released by the

© Springer Nature Switzerland AG 2021
K. Toeppe et al. (Eds.): iConference 2021, LNCS 12645, pp. 124–136, 2021.
https://doi.org/10.1007/978-3-030-71292-1_11

federal government, and the research and development data managed by pharmaceutical companies all lead to new opportunities to gain knowledge, advance science, improve healthcare quality and patient outcome, and ultimately reduce cost [7]. Researchers have reported applying various Big Data analytics algorithms and tools to areas including genetics research, public health, and personalized and precision medicine [3, 8].

With the global workforce demand for expertise in data analytics [9, 10], data science programs which provide systematic training on principles, algorithms, processes, and applications related to extracting patterns from large data sets [11] have proliferated in colleges and universities. Most iSchools are offering either data-science courses or degrees [12]. In September 2019, the University of North Carolina at Chapel Hill (UNC-CH) started a feasibility study for a new data science initiative [13]. Led by Gary Marchionini, the dean of UNC School of Information and Library Science (SILS), the feasibility study invited more than 100 faculty, staff, and students across disciplines and units for a pan-campus strategy that "makes data science a powerful adjusts to all of the other kinds of instructional and research programs we offer at Carolina" [14]. A steering committee and seven sub-committees were assembled for regular discussion and exploration on data science related teaching, research, community engagement, finance and funding, infrastructure and student services.

To provide evidence and support the decision making of subcommittees, this study aims to:

- Describe and measure how prominent DAS has been used to assist scientific discovery in BHS research at the UNC-CH
- Assess the citation impact of the research output produced by UNC researchers who used DAS for data analysis
- Disclose the research topics addressed in the UNC-CH publications in which DAS was adopted.

2   Method

This case study selected the following DAS for investigation and took a bibliometric approach [15, 16] to achieve three research aims.

2.1   Data Analytics Tools

Three chosen DAS applications were: SAS, R, and Python. SAS[1] is a market leader among enterprise analytics software. R[2] is often regarded as the open-source counterpart of SAS and has been widely used in academics and research [17]. Originated as an open-source programming language, Python[3] is relatively new compared with SAS and R. All three applications are capable of statistical operation, data modeling, data visual display, data mining, and machine learning [18].

---

[1] www.sas.com.

[2] www.r-project.org.

[3] www.python.org.

2.2 Research Database and Search Strategy

A literature search was conducted in PubMed and PubMed Central (PMC), both of which are freely accessible and widely used by researchers all over the world. PubMed comprises of over 30 million citations and abstracts [19] and supports the search and retrieval of BHS literature.

PMC is an archive of full-text journal articles of which citations are indexed in PubMed. Full-text articles are deposited by participating publishers or by authors who submitted to the National Institute of Health (NIH) in compliance with the NIH Public Access policy [20] or similar policies imposed by other U.S. research funding agencies [21].

Since many BHS journals require a structured abstract [22] for article submission, authors usually disclose the DAS they used in the Method section of a structured abstract. For those who did not provide the DAS information in the abstract, full text searching in PMC can help locate DAS information. Our search queries consisted of distinctive affiliation characteristics (i.e., "chapel hill"), DAS tool name (R, SAS, or Python) and name variations, and year range (2015–2020) (Table 1).

Table 1. Search strategy and results

Database	Software	Search results	Search query
PubMed	SAS	1/04/2020 N = 74	"chapel hill"[Affiliation] AND "sas"[All Fields] AND ("2015/01/01"[PDAT]: "2020/01/04"[PDAT])
PMC	SAS	1/04/2020 N = 3192	"chapel hill"[Affiliation] AND "sas"[All Fields] AND ("2015/01/01"[PDAT]: "2020/01/04"[PDAT])
PubMed	R	2/04/2020 N = 36	(("chapel hill"[Affiliation]) AND (("R studio" OR "R library" OR "R libraries" OR "R package" OR "R packages" OR "R program" OR "R programs" OR "R programming" OR "R script" OR "R scripts" OR "R software" OR "R version" OR "R core team" OR "R code" OR "R codes" OR "R Foundation for Statistical Computing"))) AND ("2015/01/01"[PDat]: "2020/01/04"[PDat])
PMC	R	2/04/2020 N = 1308	(("chapel hill"[Affiliation]) AND (("R studio" OR "R library" OR "R libraries" OR "R package" OR "R packages" OR "R program" OR "R programs" OR "R programming" OR "R script" OR "R scripts" OR "R software" OR "R version" OR "R core team" OR "R code" OR "R codes" OR "R Foundation for Statistical Computing"))) AND ("2015/01/01"[PDat]: "2020/01/04"[PDat])
PubMed	Python	1/04/2020 N = 10	"chapel hill"[Affiliation] AND ("python"[All Fields]) AND ("2015/01/01"[PDat]: "2020/01/04"[PDat])
PMC	Python	1/04/2020 N = 339	"chapel hill"[Affiliation] AND ("python"[All Fields]) AND ("2015/01/01"[PDat]: "2020/01/04"[PDat])

2.3 Research Article Manual Screening

Search results were downloaded from PubMed and PMC in Medline text format, and then aggregated and de-duplicated. We manually screened the title and abstract of each PubMed record and the full text of PMC records for UNC-CH affiliation and DAS information (Fig. 1).

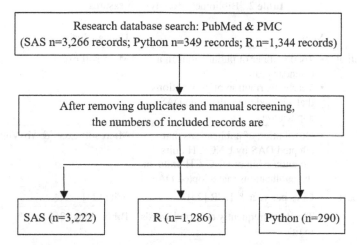

Fig. 1. Publication search, retrieval, de-duplication, and screening process

2.4 Data Analysis

Bibliometric analysis was applied to the included studies (Table 2). Microsoft Excel was used to analyze research output (e.g., the total number of publications in a calendar year) and software adoption (i.e., the distribution of publications by UNC-CH units).

VOSviewer [23], a free bibliometric analysis software was used to develop the co-authorship networks for software adoption (i.e., UNC-CH units' collaborations). The author affiliations of each included publication were extracted, cleaned, and standardized at the school- or institute-level using both VOSviewer and Microsoft Excel. Only UNC affiliations were visualized in co-authorship networks.

iCite [24], an open-accessible web application developed by NIH Office of Portfolio Analysis provides the Relative Citation Ratio (RCR) value [25], which can be used to compare the citation impact of an article or a group of articles with the benchmark of average NIH-supported papers published in the same scientific field and timeframe. If an article's RCR value is 1.0, it indicates that this article has received the same number of cites per year as the average of NIH-funded articles in its field. If an article's RCR value is 2.0, this article has received twice as many cites per year as the average of NIH-funded articles in its field, demonstrating a higher citation impact. iCite produces values including Publications Per Year, Cites Per year (Mean & Standard Error of the Mean (SEM)), and RCR (Mean & SEM).

Biblioshiny [26] is a web-based bibliometric application which has been adopted by researchers across a variety of disciplines to study science landscape and research synthesis [27]. This study used Biblioshiny to extract the most frequent words in the titles of included publications so that research topics can be disclosed and compared across three DAS tools.

Table 2. Bibliometric analysis measures

Measures	Metrics	Data analysis tools
Research output	• Total number of publications in a calendar year • Yearly distribution of publications that adopted more than one DAS application	Microsoft excel
Software adoption	• Distribution of publications that adopted DAS by UNC-CH units • Co-authorship of UNC-CH units on the publications that adopted DAS	Microsoft excel & VosViewer [23]
Citation impact	• Cites per year & RCR [25]	iCite [24]
Topics	• The most frequently occurred words in title	Biblioshiny [26]

3   Results

3.1   Research Output

Total Number of Publications in a Calendar Year. Figure 2 shows the annual research output associated with each DAS application. From 2015 to 2019, on average per year, researchers at UNC-CH produced 458 articles using SAS, 257 articles using R, and 48 articles using Python (Table 3). The number of publications supported by each tool has increased since 2015 and reached a peak in 2018. However, research outputs fell in 2019 across three tools.

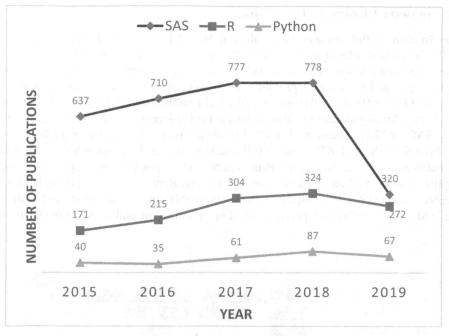

Fig. 2. Publication distribution by year

Yearly Distribution of Publications that Adopted More than One DAS Application.
Combined usage of two or three DAS tools for data analysis was observed in multiple
studies (Fig. 3). From 2015–2019, 220 publications adopted both SAS and R; 59 publications used R and Python together; 13 publications combined SAS and Python; and 4
publications applied all three tools in data analysis. The combined usage of SAS and R
increased from 31 publications in 2015 to 60 in 2018 while the usage of R and Python
together increased from 5 publications in 2015 to 18 in 2018.

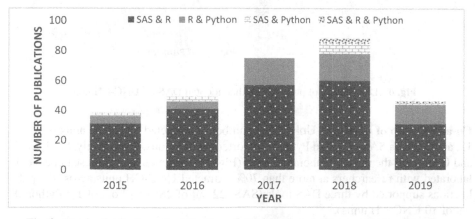

Fig. 3. Yearly distribution of publications that adopted more than one DAS application

3.2 Software Adoption by UNC Units

Distribution of Publications that Adopted DAS by UNC-CH Units. Among the UNC-CH units disclosed in the author affiliation field of the included publications, researchers at the School of Medicine (SoM) used SAS for 1,465 publications, R for 600 publications, and Python for 177 publications respectively (Fig. 4). Researchers at the School of Public Health (SPH) used SAS for 1,271 publications, R for 396 publications, and Python for 34 publications. Researchers at the College of Arts and Sciences (CAS) used SAS for 170 publications, R for 175 publications, and Python for 98 publications.

In addition, School of Pharmacy (SoP) and Dentistry (SoD) adopted SAS in 130 and 68 publications respectively; used Python in 50 and 24 publications respectively; and applied Python in 27 and 1 publication respectively. Renaissance Computing Institute (RENCI) adopted R in 11 publications, Python in 6 publications, and SAS in 1 publication while SILS used Python in 5 publications, R in 1 publication, and SAS in 1 publication.

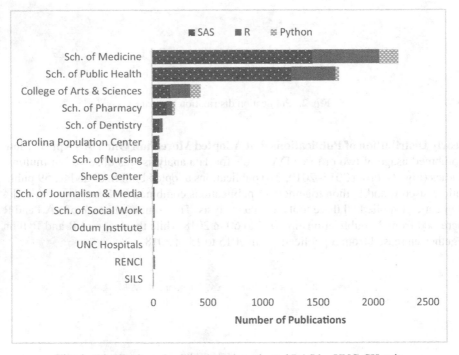

Fig. 4. Distribution of publications that adopted DAS by UNC-CH units

Co-authorship of UNC-CH Units. The number of extracted UNC-CH units were 28, 17, and 10 from SAS-, R-, and Python-supported publications, respectively. SoM, SPH, and CAS were the most collaborative units (Fig. 5). Particularly, SoM researchers collaborated with researchers at more than 70% extracted UNC-CH units across the publications supported by three DAS tools (SAS: 22 out of 28; R: 12 out of 17; Python: 8 out of 10 UNC-CH units).

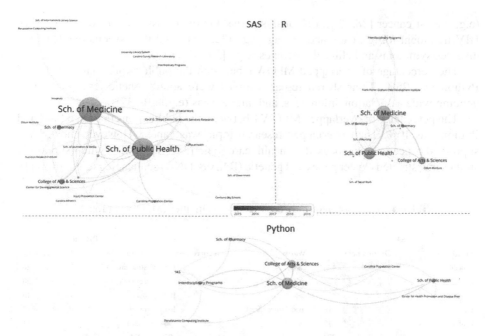

Fig. 5. UNC-CH units' collaborations on the included publications

3.3 Citation Impact.

Cites per Year and RCR. The average annual citation counts of publications that adopted SAS, R, and Python were 4.21 (SEM ± 0.14), 7.07 (SEM ± 0.43), and 8.14 (SEM ± 0.73), respectively. In addition, the RCR values of publications that adopted SAS, R, and Python were 2.01 (SEM ± 0.06), 2.74 (SEM ± 0.16), and 3.12 (SEM ± 0.27), respectively (Table 3).

Table 3. Citation impact comparison

Software	SAS	R	Python
Pubs per year	459.57	257	48.33
Cites per year (Mean & SEM)	4.21(± 0.14)	7.07 (± 0.43)	8.14 (± 0.73)
RCR (Mean & SEM)	2.01 (± 0.06)	2.74(± 0.16)	3.12 (± 0.27)

3.4 Topics

Table 4 shows the most frequently occurred words in titles (MFOWT) of the included publications. The percentage of overlapped MFOWT between the publications that used SAS and R was 60%. Their overlapped research topics included cancer research (e.g., breast cancer [28, 29]), risk analysis, risk factors or assessment (e.g., [30, 31]), HIV treatment (drug), care, and testing (e.g., [32, 33]), and the associations between diseases/symptoms and clinical outcomes (e.g., [34, 35]).

The percentage of overlapped MFOWT between the publications that used R and Python was 25%. Their shared research topics were about genetic test/structure or genome-wide association, inferences, and interactions (e.g., [36, 37]).

The percentage of overlapped MFOWT between the publications that used SAS and Python was 10%. Their overlapped research topic was cancer. However, most SAS-supported cancer studies focused on health care (e.g., [38, 39]) while Python-supported studies investigated cancer genes and genetic (RNA & DNA) sequencing (e.g., [40, 41]).

Table 4. The most frequently occurred words in titles (MFOWT) (Top 20).

SAS		R		Python	
Words	Occurrences	Words	Occurrences	Words	Occurrences
cancer	436	cancer	133	structure	26
risk	405	risk	102	network	20
patients	377	cell	102	data	16
trial	318	model (modelling)	101	receptor	13
health	315	association	96	mouse	11
association	278	genetic	95	RNA	11
women	267	breast	89	cancer	11
hiv	261	patients	79	DNA	11
breast	240	hiv	57	cells	10
outcomes	198	DNA	55	neural	10
disease	188	genome-wide	54	sequencing	10
adults	181	disease	53	functional	9
therapy	177	expression	53	genetic	9
clinical	166	clinical	46	dynamics	9
cohort	151	health	45	genomic	8
children	143	identifies	44	protein	8
treatment	139	methylation	42	brian	8
diabetes	129	cohort	42	genome-wide	7
factors	121	meta-analysis	39	tool	7
(Hispanic) community	116	outcomes	37	association	7

4   Discussion

Through systematically searching both PubMed and PMC to identify relevant studies in which UNC-CH researchers adopted SAS, R, or Python for data analysis, we achieved three research aims by performing a bibliometric analysis.

First, compared to R and Python, SAS has been used to produce the most publications by UNC authors in BHS research during 2015–2019. The number of publications in which SAS was used is about twice as many as the publications in which R was used, and more than ten times as many as the publications in which Python was used. In addition, researchers at UNC health affair schools were the major adopters of SAS (e.g., SoM and SPH). The predominant usage of SAS at the UNC-CH can be explained from multiple aspects. (1) As enterprise software, SAS is the leader in statistical analysis and modeling, multimodal predictive analytics, and data mining for data science [42–44]. A suite of basic and advanced analytics functions of SAS can satisfy various needs of researchers. Additionally, the user interface of SAS is easy to learn and use [17], and technical support of SAS products is also free and excellent [45], which all assure the adoption. (2) SAS analytical software is freely accessible to everyone affiliated with the University. (3) Located about 20 miles east of the UNC campus, SAS Inc. has collaborated with the University on many events, workshops, and healthcare research activities [46]. (4) The company offers free workshops throughout the year to professors and instructors who want to learn SAS software and develop course curriculums [47]. Therefore, multiple UNC units regularly offered SAS training sessions [48, 49].

Second, the sudden drop of included publications in 2019 could be caused by the time lag between academic journal publishing and articles being indexed by PubMed and PMC [50]. Also, burgeoning new DAS tools, such as Tableau, IBM, or Microsoft [51] started to compete for the market. We observed that a few studies used two or three tools together during 2018 and 2019. The adoption of new DAS tools and the combined usage of multiple tools reflected the complex, diverse, and evolving data analytic needs of the UNC research enterprise.

Third, UNC SoM, SPH, and CAS produced significantly more publications using the examined DAS tools than the other UNC-CH units. Researchers at SoM and SPH used SAS in their research much more than using R or Python. However, researchers at CAS adopted R slightly more than SAS. RENCI researchers used R more than SAS or Python. SILS researchers used Python more than SAS or R in their publications. Therefore, our results resonant some general data science recommendations [52]: Python appeals more to those who already have certain background in programming languages or software development; R offers multiple free data modelling types for people to choose from; SAS is easy to learn and use and backed up by excellent technical support [53].

Further, although SAS-supported publications were produced much more than R and Python, the citation impact indicated publications supported by the three tools have similar research influence and all are higher than the average NIH-funded papers. Regarding research topics, there is high similarity between SAS-supported and R-supported publications (60% overlapped MFOWT), which primarily addressed diseases and health care (e.g., cancer, HIV treatment). Python was often used to investigate cancer genes and genetic inferences, interactions, and sequencing.

Being the first study on the usage of DAS tools in an academic institution, there are limitations of our literature search. First, we may have excluded studies in which the examined DAS was adopted but was not disclosed in the article or disclosed as a name variation other than the ones we included in our search strategy. Second, we only searched PubMed and PMC for relevant publications due to our sole focus on BHS research. Therefore, our results and conclusion may not be generalizable to other fields. Third, we limited our search scope to the most recent five years (2015–2019) so that our findings can reflect the latest status of DAS usage at the UNC-CH.

5 Conclusion

This study systematically investigated and compared the usage of three DAS applications in biomedical research at the UNC-CH. The prevalent adoption of SAS among UNC researchers highlighted the significance of software availability, industry-academia collaboration, and training programs. Our findings provided useful insights to the subcommittees of the new data science initiative and the UNC administration for informed decision making, and illuminate further ways in which instruction, workshops, or other types of trainings may be offered to fully support researchers utilizing DAS applications.

References

1. Lazer, D., et al.: Life in the network: the coming age of computational social science. Science **323**(5915), 721–723 (2009)
2. Rorissa, A., Federer, L., Hagen, L., Kim, J., Andrews, J.: Data science research and practice: high time for synergy. In: Blake, C., Brown, C. (eds.) Proceedings of the Association for Information Science and Technology 2019, vol. 56, pp. 575–577. Wiley, Somerset (2019)
3. Cirillo, D., Valencia, A.: Big data analytics for personalized medicine. Curr. Opin. Biotechnol. **59**, 161–167 (2019)
4. Top 41 free data analysis software. https://www.predictiveanalyticstoday.com/top-data-ana lysis-software/. Accessed 17 Sept 2020
5. Light, D., Wexler, D., Heinze, J.: How practitioners interpret and link data to instruction: Research findings on New York City Schools' implementation of the Grow Network (2003). https://www.researchgate.net/publication/228715861_How_practitioners_interpret_and_ link_data_to_instruction_Research_findings_on_New_York_City_Schools%27_implement ation_of_the_Grow_Network. Accessed 17 Sept 2020
6. Eisenberg, M.: Information Alchemy: transforming data and information into knowledge and wisdom. https://faculty.washington.edu/mbe/Eisenberg_Intro_to_Information%20Alchemy. pdf. Accessed 20 Sept 2020
7. Adam, N.R., Wieder, R., Ghosh, D.: Data science, learning, and applications to biomedical and health sciences. Ann. N. Y. Acad. Sci. **1387**(1), 5–11 (2017)
8. Wang, L., Alexander, C.A.: Big data analytics in medical engineering and healthcare: methods, advances and challenges. J. Med. Eng. Technol. **44**(6), 267–283 (2020). https://doi.org/10. 1080/03091902.2020.1769758
9. Berry, A.: Data scientists are in-demand and well paid – so why is there a skills gap? Computing. https://www.computing.co.uk/opinion/3034263/data-scientists-are-in-dem and-and-well-paid-so-why-is-there-a-skills-gap. Accessed 21 Sept 2020
10. PWC. What's next for the data science and analytics job market? https://www.pwc.com/us/ en/library/data-science-and-analytics.html. Accessed 17 Sept 2020
11. Kelleher, J., Tierney, B.: "1 what is data science?" Data Science, MITP, pp. 1–38 (2018)
12. Oh, S., Song, I., Mostafa, J., Zhang, Y., Wu, D.: Data science education in the iSchool context. In: Blake, C., Brown, C. (eds.) Proceedings of the Association for Information Science and Technology 2019, vol. 56, pp. 558–560. Wiley, Somerset (2019)
13. Forrest, W.: New initiative explores redefining UNC's data science curriculum. The Daily Tar Heel, 18 September 2019. https://www.dailytarheel.com/article/2019/09/data-science-0919. Accessed 17 Sept 2020
14. University Communication: More than 100 people involved in planning plan-University data science initiative (2019). https://thewell.unc.edu/2019/09/22/more-than-100-people-inv olved-in-planning-pan-university-data-science-initiative/. Accessed 17 Sept 2020

15. Pritchard, A.: Statistical bibiliography or bibliometrics? J. Doc. **25**, 348–349 (1969)
16. Ellegaard, O., Wallin, J.A.: The bibliometric analysis of scholarly production: howe great is the impact? Scientometrics **105**(3), 1809–1831 (2015)
17. Learning and using R at Stanford. https://library.stanford.edu/projects/r. Accessed 17 Sept 2020
18. Jain, K.: Python vs. R vs. SAS – which tool should I learn for data science? https://www.ana lyticsvidhya.com/blog/2017/09/sas-vs-vs-python-tool-learn/. Accessed 17 Sept 2020
19. National Library of Medicine: PubMed overview. https://pubmed.ncbi.nlm.nih.gov/about/
20. NIH: Public Access Policy. https://publicaccess.nih.gov/. Accessed 17 Sept 2020
21. PMC: PMC Overview. https://www.ncbi.nlm.nih.gov/pmc/about/intro/. Accessed 17 Sept 2020
22. NLM: Structured abstracts. https://www.nlm.nih.gov/bsd/policy/structured_abstracts.html. Accessed 17 Sept 2020
23. VOSviewer. https://www.vosviewer.com. Accessed 21 Sept 2020
24. iCite. https://icite.od.nih.gov/. Accessed 20 Sept 2020
25. Hutchins, B.I., Yuan, X., Anderson, J.M., Santangelo, G.M.: Relative citation ratio (RCR): a new metric that uses citation rates to measure influence at the article level. PLoS Bio. **14**(9), e1002541 (2016)
26. Aria, M., Cuccurullo, C.: Bibliometrix: an R-tool for comprehensive science mapping analysis. J. Inf. **11**(4), 959–975 (2017)
27. Biblioshiny. https://www.bibliometrix.org/Papers.html. Accessed 17 Sept 2020
28. Muss, H.B., et al.: Randomized trial of standard adjuvant chemotherapy regimens versus capecitabine in older women with early breast cancer: 10-Year update of the CALGB 49907 Trial. J. Clin. Oncol. **37**(26), 2338–2348 (2019). https://doi.org/10.1200/JCO.19.00647
29. Braithwaite, D., et al.: Family history and breast cancer risk among older women in the breast cancer surveillance consortium cohort. JAMA Intern. Med. **178**(4), 494–501 (2018). https://doi.org/10.1001/jamainternmed.2017.8642
30. Merino, J., et al.: Quality of dietary fat and genetic risk of type 2 diabetes: individual participant data meta-analysis. BMJ **366**, l4292 (2019). https://doi.org/10.1136/bmj.l4292
31. O'Connor, G.T., et al.: Early-life home environment and risk of asthma among inner-city children. J. Allergy Clin. Immunol. **141**(4), 1468–1475 (2018). https://doi.org/10.1016/j.jaci.2017.06.040
32. Ritchwood, T.D., et al.: HIV self-testing: south African young adults' recommendations for ease of use, test kit contents, accessibility, and supportive resources. BMC Pub. Health **19**(1), 123 (2019). https://doi.org/10.1186/s12889-019-6402-4
33. Chen, J., et al.: Pharmacogenetic analysis of the model-based pharmacokinetics of five anti-HIV drugs: How does this influence the effect of aging? Clin. Transl. Sci. **11**(2), 226–236 (2018). https://doi.org/10.1111/cts.12525
34. Kelman, J., et al.: Associations of unhealthy food environment with the development of coronary artery calcification: the CARDIA study. J. Am. Heart. Assoc. **8**(4), e010586 (2019). https://doi.org/10.1161/JAHA.118.010586
35. McKeown, N.M., et al.: Sugar-sweetened beverage intake associations with fasting glucose and insulin concentrations are not modified by selected genetic variants in a ChREBP-FGF21 pathway: a meta-analysis. Diabetologia **61**(2), 317–330 (2017). https://doi.org/10.1007/s00 125-017-4475-0
36. Phillips, K.A., Deverka, P.A., Hooker, G.W., Douglas, M.P.: Genetic test availability and spending: where are We now? Where are we going? Health Aff. (Millwood) **37**(5), 710–716 (2018). https://doi.org/10.1377/hlthaff.2017.1427
37. Melroy-Greif, W.E., Wilhelmsen, K.C., Yehuda, R., Ehlers, C.L.: Genome-wide association study of post-traumatic stress disorder in two high-risk populations. Twin Res. Hum. Genet. **20**(3), 197–207 (2017). https://doi.org/10.1017/thg.2017.12

38. Henderson, L.M., et al.: Opinions and practices of lung cancer screening by physician specialty. N. C. Med. J. **80**(1), 19–26 (2019). https://doi.org/10.18043/ncm.80.1.19

39. Banegas, M.P., et al.: Patterns of medication adherence in a multi-ethnic cohort of prevalent statin users diagnosed with breast, prostate, or colorectal cancer. J. Cancer Surviv. **12**(6), 794–802 (2018). https://doi.org/10.1007/s11764-018-0716-6

40. Siegel, M.B., et al.: Integrated RNA and DNA sequencing reveals early drivers of metastatic breast cancer. J. Clin. Invest. **128**(4), 1371–1383 (2018). https://doi.org/10.1172/JCI96153

41. Barrow, M.A., et al.: A functional role for the cancer disparity-linked genes, CRYβB2 and CRYβB2P1, in the promotion of breast cancer. Breast Cancer Res. **21**(1), 105 (2019). https://doi.org/10.1186/s13058-019-1191-3

42. Gualtieri, M., Carlsson, K., Sridharan, S., Perdoni, R.: The Forrester Wave ™: Multimodal predictive analytics and machine learning, Q3 (2020). https://reprints2.forrester.com/#/assets/2/202/RES157465/report. Accessed 17 Sept 2020

43. Gartner: Vendor rating: SAS. https://www.gartner.com/doc/reprints?id=1-1ZJGZBKS&ct=200724&st=sb. Accessed 17 Sept 2020

44. Mendez-Villamil, M.M.: SAS dives deeper into IoT analytics (2019). https://idcdocserv.com/EMEA44977119. Accessed 17 Sept 2020

45. SAS: SAS Technical support services and policies. https://support.sas.com/en/technical-support/services-policies.html#cost. Accessed 17 Sept 2020

46. UNC healthcare: UNC and SAS join forces to personalize health care for better outcomes. https://news.unchealthcare.org/news/2013/november/unc-and-sas-join-forces-to-personalize-health-care-for-better-outcomes. Accessed 17 Sept 2020

47. SAS: Educator workshops. https://www.sas.com/en_us/learn/academic-programs/resources/free-professor-workshops.html. Accessed 17 Sept 2020

48. UNC: SAS four-part course. https://www.unc.edu/event/sas/all. Accessed 17 Sept 2020

49. UNC Odum Institute for Research in Social Science: SAS. https://odum.unc.edu/event/sas-with-chris-wiesen/. Accessed 17 Sept 2020

50. How to add academic journal articles to PubMed: An overview for publishers. https://blog.scholasticahq.com/post/how-to-add-academic-journal-articles-to-pubmed-overview-publishers/. Accessed 2 Jan 2021

51. Maguire, J.: Top 15 data analytics software tools 2020. https://www.datamation.com/big-data/data-analytics-software-tools.html#microsoft. Accessed 17 Sept 2020

52. Jain, K.: Python vs. R. vs. SAS – which tool should I learn for data science? https://www.analyticsvidhya.com/blog/2017/09/sas-vs-vs-python-tool-learn/. Accessed 17 Sept 2020

53. Cotton, R.: Python vs. R for data science: What's the difference? https://www.datacamp.com/community/blog/when-to-use-python-or-r. Accessed 27 Sept 2020

Semantic Shifts Reveal the Multipurpose Use of Potential COVID-19 Treatments

Baitong Chen[1](✉), Qi Yu[2], Yi Bu[3], and Ying Ding[4,5]

[1] Department of Library, Information and Archives, Shanghai University, Shanghai, China
baitongchen@shu.edu.cn
[2] School of Management, Shanxi Medical University, Taiyuan, Shanxi, China
[3] Department of Information Management, Peking University, Beijing, China
[4] School of Information, University of Texas, Austin, TX, USA
[5] Dell Medical School, University of Texas, Austin, TX, USA

Abstract. When the world is rushing to test potential COVID-19 treatments, the limited resources and the overwhelming information demand the fast understanding of the promising drugs. This paper examines the multipurpose use of potential COVID-19 treatments by mining scientific papers on COVID-19 and related historical coronavirus research. Semantic shifts of the treatment-related entities are recognized to present their various applications in practice. The results identify 10 multipurpose entities. For selected entities, a detailed interpretation is given via text mining analysis about their possible use and rationale in different situations.

Keywords: COVID-19 · Semantic shifts · Treatment-related entities

1 Introduction

The COVID-19 pandemic poses serious challenges to the medical and health systems of countries worldwide, triggering intense global R&D activity to test potential treatments. Since the outbreak of the disease, more than 300 clinical trials have been launched or prepared in order to develop a cure or vaccine [1]. Questions have been raised that whether such a rush of tests is beneficial when the resources are limited. It has been reported that the study of remdesivir, a potential COVID-19 medication, was terminated prematurely in China because it was difficult to enroll patients. Given that so little is known about the disease, mining COVID-19 and coronavirus related literature might be an alternative way to narrow down the scope of trials.

The clinical trials against COVID-19 are mostly based on the current potential treatments, which are mainly repurposed drugs. The amount of the scientific literature that indicate the applications of these drugs is rich but overwhelming, resulting in difficulties for scholars to go through manually.

To help narrow down the trial scopes and facilitate researchers to overcome the information overload, this paper investigates the multipurpose use of potential COVID-19 treatments based on the semantic shifts of the treatment-related entities through text mining. We start by extracting topics from the coronavirus-related literature corpus using

© Springer Nature Switzerland AG 2021
K. Toeppe et al. (Eds.): iConference 2021, LNCS 12645, pp. 137–145, 2021.
https://doi.org/10.1007/978-3-030-71292-1_12

a topic model. The semantic shifts of the treatment-related entities are indicated by the entity-topic distributions aggregated from the training results of the model. Then the multipurpose use of the entities is presented through the semantic shifts and the relevant documents. Finally, we summarize the study and explain the possible limitations.

2 Methods

2.1 Data Set and Topic Extraction

The data is collected from the COVID-19 Open Research Dataset (CORD-19) [2]. CORD-19 is a free resource of scientific papers on COVID-19 and related historical coronavirus research (e.g., SARS, MERS, etc.). The 2020-03-27 released version of CORD-19 is used in this study, containing a total of 45,774 coronavirus-related documents.

The biomedical entities are extracted from the titles and abstracts of the CORD-19 documents, using the named entity annotation method provided by PubTator Central [3]. Two treatment related entity types, Chemicals and Genes, are selected for topic extraction. Prior to extracting topics, all entities are lemmatized to unify the inflection of word forms. Entities with only one letter or appear in only one document are removed.

The Latent Dirichlet Allocation (LDA) [4] is applied for extracting topics from the corpus. LDA is a three-layer Bayesian model that is now widely used in discovering latent topic themes in collections of documents. The LDA model represents each document with a probability distribution over topics, in which each topic is represented as a probability distribution over words. For a detailed explanation of the algorithm, refer to, e.g., reference by Blei [5]. The Gensim library [6] is used for implementing the LDA model, in which the parameter alpha is set to "auto" to learn an asymmetric prior, and eta is set to "None" as the standard value proposed by Gensim.

The number of topics extracted was determined according to the results of the coherence test [7]. The test results showed that when topic number k = 20, the coherence score across topics was the highest, and therefore, the number of topics extracted was eventually determined as 20. The sensitivity test regarding the effects of changing the topic number is presented in the end of the method section.

2.2 Detecting Semantic Shifts of Entities

In linguistics, the meaning of a concept C at some moment in time t is defined as a triple $(label_t(C), int_t(C), ext_t(C))$, where $label_t(C)$ is a String, $int_t(C)$ refers to the intension of C and is a set of properties, and $ext_t(C)$ refers to the extension of C and is a subset of the universe. Either of the three elements in the triple changes will cause the meaning change of a concept [8]. In this study, the semantic shifts of an entity are detected from the topic level. The semantic shifts of an entity refer to the extension change, relating to different applications of the entity when distributed in different topics. The topic level semantic shifts are represented by the entity-topic probability distributions from the following two perspectives.

The Over-Time Topic Distribution of Entities. The topic distribution of an entity in a document is parameterized by the variational parameter ϕ in the LDA model [9]. The ϕ value indicates the likelihood of an entity belonging to a topic in terms of a particular document. Each entity in a document has k topic ϕ values corresponding to the k topics extracted (Table 1). After normalizing by the frequency of the entity in the document, the sum of an entity's ϕ values is equal to 1. The same entity from two different documents usually has two different sets of ϕ values. For a selected entity, we calculate its average ϕ value for each topic in each year. The average ϕ values represent the topic probability distribution for the entity in that year. The over-time topic distribution of entities is obtained as the ϕ values change over the years.

Table 1. An example of the normalized ϕ values of an entity x in a particular document

Document ID	Year	Entity	Topic 1	Topic 2	...	Topic (k − 1)	Topic k	Sum
100	2000	x	ϕ_1	ϕ_2	...	ϕ_{k-1}	ϕ_k	1

The Overall Topic Distribution of Entities. Despite the time tags (in years), the topic distribution of an entity can be obtained through the integration of the per-document entity-topic distribution (normalized ϕ values). The per-document topic distributions of a target entity are summed and averaged (divided by the number of the documents that the entity appears in), thus producing the overall topic distribution of the entity.

2.3   Detecting Multipurpose Entities from Potential COVID-19 Treatments

The entity list regarding the potential treatments for COVID-19 is obtained from the evidence table provided by the American Society of Health-system Pharmacists (ASHP).[1] The topic distributions of entities indicate their semantic diversities in the topic level, which are associated with the multipurpose use of the potential treatments. For treatments that both proposed in the evidence table and existing in the CORD-19 corpus, the topic distribution of the treatment-related entity is examined to grasp its multipurpose use.

The degree of multipurpose use of entities is measured by information entropy [10]. The entropy of entity X with a distribution over k topics $\{x_1, ..., x_k\}$ can be expressed as:

$$H(X) = -\sum_{i=1}^{k} P(x_i) \log P(x_i) \tag{1}$$

where $P(x_i)$ is the value for the corresponding topic i in the entity-topic distribution. With a larger entropy value, the entity will tend to be distributed in more topics, indicating

---

[1] https://www.ashp.org/-/media/assets/pharmacy-practice/resource-centers/Coronavirus/docs/ASHP-COVID-19-Evidence-Table.ashx.

a higher degree of multipurpose use. When the entity belongs to only one topic, the entropy reaches its minimum value of zero.

From the treatment-related entity list, entities are selected as multipurpose entities when distributed in at least two topics with a probability larger than 0.05, which equals to 1 divided by the topic number 20. The excluded entities in the treatment list are those with only one topic probability exceeds 0.05, when the probabilities of the rest topics are all below the threshold. These excluded entities stably belong to one particular topic, whose use or rationale tends to be explicit and single-purpose.

2.4 Interpreting the Multipurpose Use of Entities

The multipurpose use of potential COVID-19 treatments is indicated by the semantic shifts of entities through the overall and over-time topic distribution. For a target entity, the overall topic distribution will be presented in the first place. To interpret the related topics, the most relevant document for each topic is identified based on the document-topic distribution obtained from the LDA training results. Regarding a target entity, the most relevant document of a related topic is the one that contains the entity and has the highest probability of the given topic.

The over-time entity-topic distribution reveals the topic trends of the entity in different years. The relevant documents that have been identified previously usually matches with the peaks of the over-time trends. They are the most relevant documents within the whole time span, thus will definitely be the most relevant ones in the peak years.

If there are more notable peak years in the over-time trends other than the publishing year of the relevant documents extracted before, the most relevant documents of the other notable peaks will be identified and additional discussion for those peaks will be added.

2.5 Sensitivity Test When Changing the Number of Topics

We reran our topic model with alternative values of topic number to test the effects when changing topic numbers. The results show that the quality of the entity-topic distribution depends on the coherence of the topic extraction results. When the coherence score across topics are low, the topics are overlapping with each other, resulting in poor accuracy of the multipurpose use indicated by the entity-topic distribution.

It is worth noting that when changing topic numbers, the number of topics is reduced or increased simultaneously for all entities. The entropy scale is the same for all the entities no matter how the topic number is changed. The entity selection threshold (=1/topic number) also changes synchronously with the topic number.

In summary, our choice of the topic number of 20 gives the best coherence score, which is a relatively reliable value for the analysis of the current corpus.

3   Results and Discussion

3.1   Entropies of Entities

From the COVID-19 treatment-related entity list, 10 entities that meet with the threshold are finally identified. The entropy values are presented in Fig. 1 in descending order, along with their document frequencies. A Kendall's rank correlation test has been applied to test the correlationship between the entropy and document frequency based on data of all the entities in the dictionary. The result is weak positive (tau = 0.02052, p-value = 0.06157), indicating the association is not practically relevant. To be specific, a high entropy value indicating a potential of multipurpose use is not necessarily associated with the entity appearing in large amount of documents. Entities that only have been studied in limited documents might also possess a considerable chance to have multipurpose usage which may lead to their repurposing for treatments of emerging viruses.

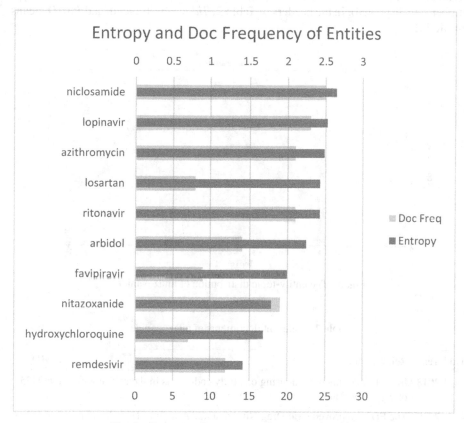

Fig. 1. Document frequency and entropy of entities

Most of the selected entities in Fig. 1 are antiviral agents that at least in vitro evidence of activity against various viruses, including coronaviruses. These antivirals include Lopinavir, Ritonavir, Arbidol, Favipiravir, Hydroxychloroquine and Remdesivir. Azithromycin is a supporting agent that has been used as adjunctive therapy in the management of certain respiratory diseases (e.g., influenza). Other agents including Niclosamide, Losartan and Nitazoxanide are currently with hypothetical benefit that may have a protective effect in treatment of COVID-19.

3.2   Semantic Shifts Indicating the Multipurpose Use of Entities

The semantic shifts based on the overall and over-time topic distribution of the selected entities are presented in this section. The multipurpose use of each entity is interpreted through the relevant documents as below. Since this research is still in progress, two of the representative entities are presented in this short paper.

Nitazoxanide. Nitazoxanide belongs to the antiprotozoal class, structurally similar to niclosamide [11, 12]. Its topic distribution is presented in Fig. 2. The most relevant documents are presented in Table 2 (topics with a proportion larger than 0.05 (=1/topic number) are displayed). In the headers of Table 2, *Tid* means Topic id, and *PMID* means PubMed ID.

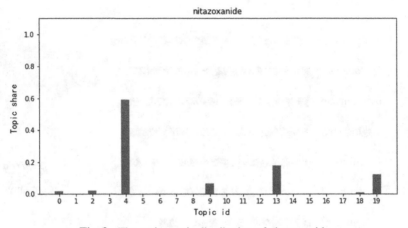

Fig. 2. The entity-topic distribution of nitazoxanide

Table 2. Relevant documents of nitazoxanide

Tid	Year	Relevant doc	PMID
4	2018	Impact of confinement housing on study end-points in the calf model of cryptosporidiosis	29694356
13	2019	The FDA-Approved Oral Drug Nitazoxanide Amplifies Host Antiviral Responses and Inhibits Ebola Virus	31402258
19	2016	Nitazoxanide, a new drug candidate for the treatment of Middle East respiratory syndrome coronavirus	27095301
9	2019	Dissolution Advantage of Nitazoxanide Cocrystals in the Presence of Cellulosic Polymers	31881696

Nitazoxanide was originally developed and commercialized as an antiprotozoal agent, but was later identified as a broad-spectrum antiviral drug and has been repurposed for treatment of influenza and other viral respiratory infections (Table 2, Tid 19). It exhibits in vitro activity against various viruses, including MERS-CoV and other coronaviruses. Nitazoxanide is also a promising drug that inhibits Ebola virus replication and broadly amplifies the host innate immune response to viruses (Tid 13). Nonetheless, further clinical trials, including dose-ranging trials, and evaluation of combination therapy with other potential antivirals are still needed.

Two cocrystals derived from nitazoxanide, namely, nitazoxanide-glutaric acid and nitazoxanide-succinic acid, may be effective in the treatment of important parasitic and viral diseases (Tid 9). For treatment of diarrhea (Tid 4), nitazoxanide is the only approved chemotherapeutic therapy against cryptosporidiosis, a leading cause of diarrhea in children below five years old. But note that the drug has poor efficacy in HIV positive children.

Figure 3 presents the over-time semantic shifts of nitazoxanide. In general, the publishing years of the most relevant documents in Table 2 match with the peaks of the over-time trends in the semantic-shift graph. However, there is another notable peak in topic 4 in the year of 2014. The related paper is presented in Table 3. Again, it emphasizes that nitazoxanide is a first-in-class broad-spectrum antiviral drug that inhibits a broad range of influenza A and B viruses including influenza A(pH1N1) and the avian A(H7N9) as well as viruses that are resistant to neuraminidase inhibitors. In cell culture assays, it also inhibits the replication of a broad range of other RNA and DNA viruses.

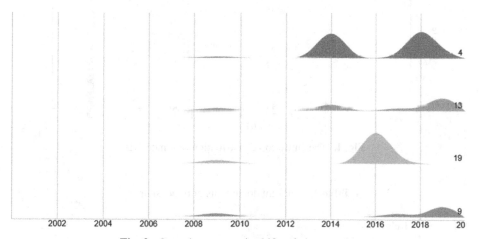

Fig. 3. Over-time semantic shifts of nitazoxanide

Table 3. Other notable peak of nitazoxanide

Tid	Year	Relevant doc	PMID
4	2014	Nitazoxanide: A first-in-class broad-spectrum antiviral agent	25108173

Remdesivir. Remdesivir is a broad-spectrum antiviral medication. It is one of the most promising antiviral currently being investigated for COVID-19, and has been used in various clinical trials initiated in US, China, and other countries.

The compound is mainly distributed in three topics (Fig. 4), and the relevant documents are presented in Table 4. The antiviral effects of remdesivir for the treatment of Ebola virus disease have been demonstrated in cell culture and in non-human primates. The drug inhibits Ebola virus RNA synthesis by delaying chain termination (Tid 18). Remdesivir potently inhibits human and zoonotic coronaviruses in vitro and in a SARS-CoV mouse model (Tid 7). Resistance can be overcome with increased, nontoxic concentrations of remdesivir, further supporting the development of remdesivir as a broad-spectrum therapeutic to protect against contemporary and emerging coronaviruses. In the cases that inhibits other coronaviruses, remdesivir is highly efficacious against porcine deltacoronavirus (Tid 17). These results identify remdesivir as a broad-spectrum antiviral against various viruses, including both contemporary human and highly divergent zoonotic coronavirus and potentially with the ability to fight future emerging coronavirus.

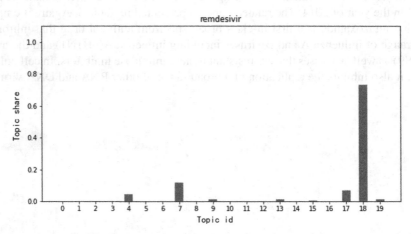

Fig. 4. The entity-topic distribution of remdesivir

Table 4. Relevant documents of remdesivir

Tid	Year	Relevant doc	PMID
18	2019	Mechanism of Inhibition of Ebola Virus RNA-Dependent RNA Polymerase by Remdesivir	30987343
7	2018	Coronavirus Susceptibility to the Antiviral Remdesivir (GS-5734) Is Mediated by the Viral Polymerase and the Proofreading Exoribonuclease	29511076
17	2019	Broad spectrum antiviral remdesivir inhibits human endemic and zoonotic deltacoronaviruses with a highly divergent RNA dependent RNA polymerase	31233808

4   Conclusion

Revealing the multipurpose use of potential treatment for COVID-19 is crucial for scholars to get fast understanding of the related compounds. In this study, we proposed that the applications of the treatments can be discovered through the entity-topic distributions indicating semantic shifts. The semantic shifts are detected from two perspectives, i.e., the overall and the over-time topic distributions. For each entity, the per-entity topic distribution and the notable peaks in the over-time trends are interpreted by examining the relevant documents in the corresponding topics, which presents the multipurpose use of the entity with different contexts in the topic-level.

This study has the following limitations: (1) Due to the collecting scale of the data set, the multipurpose use of entities primarily focuses on COVID-19 and related historical coronavirus. Their use for non-coronavirus related diseases is less considered. (2) The results are discussed based on the relevant documents. We preferentially considered the most relevant ones, and some of the entity-related but less relevant documents may be left out.

Acknowledgements. This research is supported by the MOE (Ministry of Education of China) Project of Humanities and Social Sciences [grant number 18YJC870002].

References

1. Mullard, A.: Flooded by the torrent: the COVID-19 drug pipeline. Lancet **395**(10232), 1245–1246 (2020)
2. Wang, L. L., Lo, K., Chandrasekhar, Y., et al.: CORD-19: the Covid-19 open research dataset. ArXiv (2020)
3. Wei, C.H., Allot, A., Leaman, R., Lu, Z.: PubTator central: automated concept annotation for biomedical full text articles. Nucleic Acids Res. **47**(W1), W587–W593 (2019)
4. Blei, D.M., Ng, A.Y., Jordan, M.I.: Latent dirichlet allocation. J. Mach. Learn. Res. **3**, 993–1022 (2003)
5. Blei, D.M.: Probabilistic topic models. Commun. ACM **55**(4), 77–84 (2012)
6. Rehurek, R., Sojka, P.: Software framework for topic modelling with large corpora. In: Proceedings of the LREC 2010 Workshop on New Challenges for NLP Frameworks, pp. 45–50 (2010)
7. Röder, M., Both, A., Hinneburg, A.: Exploring the space of topic coherence measures. In: Proceedings of the Eighth ACM International Conference on Web Search and Data Mining, WSDM 2015. pp. 399–408. Association for Computing Machinery, Shanghai (2015)
8. Wang, S., Schlobach, S., Klein, M.: Concept drift and how to identify it. Web Semant. Sci. Serv. Agents World Wide Web. **9**(3), 247–265 (2011)
9. Hoffman, M., Bach, F.R., Blei, D.M.: online learning for latent dirichlet allocation. In: Advances in Neural Information Processing Systems, pp. 856–864 (2010)
10. Schneider, T.D.: Information Theory Primer with an Appendix on Logarithms. National Cancer Institute (2007)
11. Rossignol, J.F.: Nitazoxanide: a first-in-class broad-spectrum antiviral agent. Antiviral Res. **110**, 94–103 (2014)
12. Xu, J., Shi, P.Y., Li, H., Zhou, J.: Broad spectrum antiviral agent niclosamide and its therapeutic potential. ACS Infect. Diseases **6**(5), 909–915 (2020)

Producing Web Content Within Platform/Infrastructure Hybrids

Daniel Carter[✉]

Texas State University, 601 University Dr, Old Main 102, San Marcos, TX, USA
dcarter@txstate.edu

Abstract. While web content management systems (CMSs) play important roles in shaping web content, they have received very little attention from scholars working in information studies or related fields concerned with the intersection of society and technology. This paper first situates CMSs within an emerging discussion of platform/infrastructure hybrids. It then presents a limited case study of how the concept of structured content is implemented within the social and technical constraints of the widely used Wordpress CMS, indicating ways that the study of CMSs can contribute to theory on platform/infrastructure hybrids.

Keywords: Content management · Data modeling · Infrastructures · Platforms

1 Introduction

Over one-third of all websites are created and managed using the Wordpress content management system (CMS) [17]. CMSs such as Wordpress shape how information presented on the web is structured and experienced. They establish ontologies (e.g., distinguishing between posts and pages) and taxonomies (e.g., organizing content in relation to categories and tags), and they develop standardized content creation processes responding to the distinct needs of users and content creators. Further, all of these concepts and implementations shape and are influenced by technical system features such as database structures and APIs.

As such, CMSs play a substantial role not only in directly shaping content but also in defining what it means to create content, and this is especially true of a nearly ubiquitous system such as Wordpress. Still, despite the obvious sociotechnical nature of CMSs and the importance of the website as a form for organizing, storing and communicating information, there has been little or no research on CMSs within areas, such as information studies, that focus on the relationship between technology and society. Instead, researchers have primarily attended to social media platforms. Like CMSs, these objects are ubiquitous and shape the creation of online content in important ways; however, CMSs are distinct because they support a greater variety of content creation procedures and enable a greater range of control and customization. As such, they are understudied and could enhance understandings of the sociotechnical nature of the contemporary internet.

K. Toeppe et al. (Eds.): iConference 2021, LNCS 12645, pp. 146–153, 2021.
https://doi.org/10.1007/978-3-030-71292-1_13

The first contribution of this short paper is to begin to situate CMSs within an evolving theoretical framework that draws from both platform studies and infrastructure studies to argue that CMSs are examples of what Plantin et al. [14] describe as hybrid platform/infrastructures.

The second contribution of this paper is the development of a limited case study, designed primarily to explore the theoretical positioning described above by describing and analyzing a topic that highlights tensions between the platform and infrastructure leanings of Wordpress: the definition and enactment of structured content. Structured content—or the extent to which authors give content objects explicit meanings, roles and relationships—is a core concept in discussions of web content. The topic also suggests ways that attending to CMSs can deepen discussions of platform/infrastructure hybrids.

2   Infrastructures and Platforms

Because there is little academic literature on content management systems that approaches these objects from a sociotechnical perspective (as opposed to an engineering perspective), there is not a clear theoretical model that can inform a study such as this one. Here, I draw from two academic traditions to conceptualize CMSs such as Wordpress: 1) the interest in infrastructures found in science and technology studies and 2) the interest in platforms found in media studies.

Researchers within infrastructure studies have foregrounded the scale, standardization and stability of systems that provide essential services such as the distribution of electricity [10] and the sharing of scientific data [16]. Due to infrastructures' scale and the investment required to develop and maintain them, theorists often conceptualize them in line with that Graham and Marvin [9] refer to as the modern infrastructural ideal, under which infrastructures are standardized to the point that they are universally available and capable of providing uniform resources and experiences. While this idea underlies much research on infrastructures, Graham and Marvin also argue that the enactment of western neoliberalism has "splintered" infrastructures and replaced universal systems with a network of less standardized services, such that internet access, for example, is experienced differently along geographic and socioeconomic lines in the United States. Other theorists push against the modern infrastructural ideal by pointing to areas in the global south [2] and by challenging the temporal solidity of infrastructure by foregrounding the consequences of natural disasters [6] and societal collapse [3].

In contrast to theorists focused on infrastructure, scholars interested in platforms—often working within the larger area of media studies—have tended to focus on the relationship between hardware and software and products built using these. Montfort and Bogost's [13] analysis of the Atari system, for example, centers on how hardware constraints shape the production of games. More recently, work on platforms has focused on social media and related affordances such as data sharing [8].

Contrary to work focusing on the standardization and maintenance of infrastructures, platform studies focus on the interactions and negotiations between a relatively stable base and the potentially highly variable products built upon it. While infrastructures tend to consolidate control within their systems, platforms invite extension and elaboration and draw value from the diverse ecosystem of products surrounding them. Even when infrastructures are privatized or "splintered," the concept of infrastructure still lacks the purposeful enablement of extension from the outside that is implied by the logic of platforms.

However, as Plantin et al. [14] argue, digital technologies increasingly make it difficult to distinguish between infrastructures and platforms and function instead as platform/infrastructure hybrids. This is largely due to increased privatization of systems and the ability of digital platforms—such as social media platforms—to attain scales that once would have required the level of national investment associated with infrastructures. While platforms such as Facebook or iOS, then, behave like infrastructures in their ubiquity and provision of access to essential services, they also operate under a platform logic that generates values from a variety of connections with other products and services.

3 Constructing Structure on Wordpress

In presenting a limited case study of Wordpress' Gutenberg editor and its relationship to debates concerning structured content, I draw on a broad methodological approach developed by Gerlitz et al. [8] to center the ways that apps and other extensions intervene in the default functionality of infrastructure/platform hybrids. While their approach surveys a large number of apps and inductively analyzes the associated descriptions, I present a focused case that responds to the centrality of structured content in relevant discussions. My reduced focus also allows me to attend more closely to relevant technical features, for which I also draw on work such as Dourish's [4] analysis of NoSQL databases and other platform-focused projects that analyze code, data structures and other material features. The preliminary analysis I present here is part of a larger project that draws on documentation and developers' discussions to understand how the concept of structured content is constructed within the sociotechnical system of Wordpress. Such documents are revealing because they often detail the motivations and stakes of design decisions and describe the implementation of technical solutions.

As represented in industry press, an enduring debate in web development concerns the agency given to content authors and the restrictions placed on content creation by the systems that store and display content [5]. This debate is often phrased in terms of tension between structured or "chunked" content—in which content authors input information into explicit fields—and unstructured or "blob-like content [12].

One way this negotiation has played out historically across the web is through the development of "What You See is What You Get" (WYSIWYG) editors that generally take the form of JavaScript extensions that transform text entry boxes into editing fields with word processing capabilities (e.g., font color, alignment, etc.). Behind the visual representation of content, the editor produces formatted HTML that can then, for example, be stored in a database and rendered as part of an interface. One popular editor, TinyMCE, for example, was released in 2004 and integrated into Wordpress as the default text editor until 2018. Due to their technical features and historical situation, these editors have largely led the authorship of web content to be conceptualized as the application of visual styles to content, and in many ways WYSIWYG editors have come to define non-structured, or blob-like, content.

While the use of WYSIWYG editors enables content creators to visually format content, Wordpress has also released updates that allow authors to create content in ways aligned with the "chunked" or structured approach described above. Since 2009 Wordpress has included functionality that allows for the creation of custom content types in addition to default types such as posts and pages. Wordpress' documentation [15], for example, describes how a site focused on books might create a custom post type specifically for this type of content. While these features mimic some of the functionality of web frameworks such as Ruby on Rails or Django that center the creation of custom objects and relationships, Wordpress lacks default functionality to create custom relationships between content, and the complexity of creating and displaying custom structured content requires additional skills or extensions that are not implied by more conventional content authoring processes.

In 2018, Wordpress moved away from the WYSIWYG editing paradigm and introduced a new content editor, Gutenberg, based on the conceptual model of blocks. Instead of entering the content for a page into a single text area with formatting options (see Fig. 1), content creation under the blocks paradigm involves authors entering content into and arranging pre-defined blocks that range from simple elements such as headings or images to elements with internal structure such as a quote with attribution (see Fig. 2). Wordpress' decision to transition to blocks-based authoring is notable because it aligns with the content creation processes of alternative CMSs such as Wix and Squarespace and because Wordpress' reach means that the block paradigm is now a clearly dominant pattern for web content authorship.

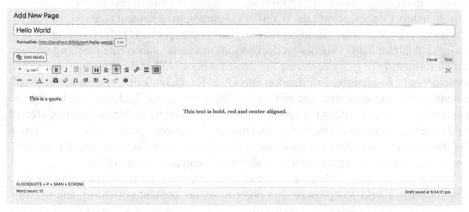

Fig. 1. The Wordpress editor prior to adoption of Gutenberg. The TinyMCE WYSIWYG editor is used to allow content authors to control to visual appearance of content.

Early discussions among developers of Gutenberg highlight tensions between structured and unstructured content. As Matias Ventura [18], the lead architect for Gutenberg, posted to the project's development blog, "Content in WordPress is, fundamentally, HTML-augmented text; that is to say, it has no inherent data structure. This has been a very important aspect of WordPress and a force for the open web—it speaks to the sense of ownership and freedom WordPress gives you, since it's always easy to get the

Fig. 2. The Gutenberg editor consists of predefined content blocks (such as a quote with attribution, shown above) that are combined and arranged.

full content of your publications—yet the lack of structure gets in the way of the goal to treat content as composed from individual pieces."

Ventura's statement indicates the practical ways that the debate over structured and unstructured content plays out within system constraints and in relation to conceptions of authorship. Consistent with the WYSIWYG paradigm of content creation, Wordpress has historically stored the entire content of posts and pages as HTML-formatted text in a single database field. This design decision allows authors to create meaning through visual formatting (e.g., by centering the title of a book) rather than by creating explicit structure (e.g., by inputting information into a field for the book title). Because all content essentially has the same structure and is stored in one database field, the code to generate the site's user interface does not need to change in relation to the kind of content created or its (implicit) structure. The choice also mirrors Wordpress' philosophy of "designing for the majority," which promotes a conception of authors as "non-technically minded" and uninterested in complex content modeling or template revision [20].

When Gutenberg was developed, the design pattern of storing post content within a single database field was preserved in order to ensure content portability and to retain the existing field as a single "source of truth." A core challenge was then how to format the content that would represent blocks—or, as Ventura [18] phrases it, how to format HTML in a way such that it can be experienced by authors as having structure without producing code that becomes "gibberish."

The adopted solution stores block content as HTML using specially formatted comments to demarcate blocks and hold relevant attributes as needed. When stored in the database, content takes the form of serialized HTML that still remains in a single database field and behaves as an unstructured "blob" in the sense that blocks cannot be manipulated using conventional relational database operations such as querying for all quotes that are attributed to a specific person. However, during the content creation and editing process, the serialized HTML is parsed into a structured JSON format that does allow blocks to be manipulated as discrete "chunks" of content (see Fig. 3). In this view, content authors can, for example, can drag blocks into new orders, nest them in hierarchies and change specific attributes.

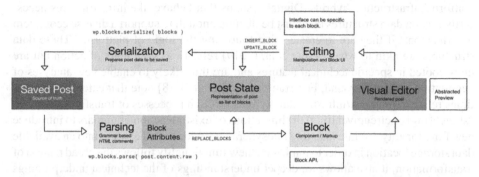

Fig. 3. Diagram representing the transformation of block content from serialized HTML stored in a database (the blue Saved Post stage to the left) into a structured tree view (the orange Post State stage in the middle) that is experienced as structured by a content author using the visual editor (the darker orange stage to the right) (Ventura, 2017b) (Color figure online)

The Wordpress documentation uses the analogy of the printing press to describe this arrangement, comparing the unstructured HTML content to a set page of type and the temporary, JSON-formatted data to the individual metal blocks that are arranged to produce the page [11]. While acknowledging the hybrid nature of content as both structured and unstructured, the documentation also makes clear that the system gives these different priorities: "What matters is the printed page, not the arrangement of metal type that produced it. [...] The metal type is just an instrument for publication and editing (but more ephemeral in nature), just like our use of an object tree (e.g. JSON) in the editor."

In the next section, I discuss the implications of these design decisions and relate them to discussions of platform/infrastructure hybrids.

4 Discussion

The decision to store block content as serialized HTML within a single database field rather than in a more conventional relational database format has implications for how authors create and experience content. This decision coincides in part with the momentum inherent in systems that behave like infrastructures—meaning that decisions about database structure, for example, become difficult to change over time. But it also intersects with core properties of platforms that invite diverse uses and modification. Many extensions to Wordpress, for example, address specific use cases such as running a storefront or maintaining a discussion board, and the database design does not obviously support content with structures specific to these domains. As John James Jacoby, the developer of a popular extension that supports discussion board functionality notes,

"You're kind of trapped with Wordpress' core tables, and you have to figure out how to make that work or someone else has to figure out how to make that work around what you're trying to build" [21].

The intersection of data storage decisions and the structure of domain-specific objects appears especially relevant in the case of what Plantin et al. [14] refer to as platform/infrastructure hybrids. Digital systems that behave like infrastructures necessarily rely on data structures that must be flexible enough to support a diverse ecosystem of extensions, if they are to create value following the logic of platforms. These data structures are akin to what Gerlitz et al. (2019) refer to as grammars of action but are more rooted in specific technical features and are thus likely to enable new analyses of negotiation and workaround. For example, Gerlitz et al. [8] note that extensions sometimes relate to platform/infrastructure hybrids through processes of transformation—or "stretch[ing] or circumvent[ing] the limitations of existing action grammars to introduce new functionality." While inserting idiosyncratically formatted content into an available data storage location in order to implement new functionality follows the broad pattern of transformation, it also allows for deeper understandings of the technical underpinnings of transformation and the specific ways these might play out.

For example, the broad pattern of using an existing database field to implement structured content in ways not supported by a CMS is also exemplified by the design of the popular Advanced Custom Fields extension to Wordpress. One of the ways that the extension stretches the existing system is by allowing users to add custom attributes and relationships to objects, as well as attributes that have internal structure (such as a list of photos and captions). Like the Gutenberg editor, this is achieved through inserting specially formatted text into the database field typically used to store post content. As with Gutenberg, the formatted text can be parsed to obtain structured content but does not behave as such in the database. One notable consequence of Advanced Custom Field's design is that many-to-many relationships, a fundamental mechanism in existing conceptions of structured content, are not possible without either implementing user interface workarounds or modifying the extension's code [1]. As with the specific historical development of WYSIWYG editors, the broad pattern of inserting structured content in storage locations where it cannot fully function as such will shape conceptions of content and structure in the future.

5 Conclusion

I've argued in this short paper that CMSs are potentially important objects of study because of the role they play in shaping content authoring and concepts such as structured content. As preparation for future work, I've also situated CMSs within the emerging theoretical discussion of platform/infrastructure hybrids and indicated ways that CMSs can lead to a deeper understanding of common forms of negotiation and system development.

References

1. ACF | Bidirectional Relationships. (n.d.). ACF https://www.advancedcustomfields.com/res ources/bidirectional-relationships/. Accessed 26 Aug 2020

2. Appel, H., Anand, N., Gupta, A.: Temporality, politics, and the pormise of infrastructure. In: Anand, N., Gupta, A., Appel, H. (eds.) The Promise of Infrastructure, pp. 1–38. Duke UP (2018)
3. Carter, D., Acker, A.: To oblivion and beyond: Imagining infrastructure after collapse. Environ. Plann. D Soc. Space (2020). 0263775820911940
4. Dourish, P.: No SQL: The shifting materialities of database technology. Comput. Cult. **4** (2014). https://computationalculture.net/article/no-sql-the-shifting-materialities-of-database-technology
5. Eaton, J.: The Battle for the Body Field. A List Apart (2014). https://alistapart.com/article/battle-for-the-body-field
6. Edwards, P.: Infrastructure and modernity: force, time, and social organization in the history of sociotechnical systems. In: Misa, T.J., Brey, P., Feenberg, A. (eds.) Modernity and Technology, pp. 185–225. MIT Press (2004)
7. Gerlitz, C., Helmond, A.: The like economy: Social buttons and the data-intensive web. New Media Soc. **15**(8), 1348–1365 (2013). https://doi.org/10.1177/1461444812472322
8. Gerlitz, C., Helmond, A., van der Vlist, F.N., Weltevrede, E.: Regramming the platform: infrastructural relations between apps and social media. Comput. Cul. **7** (2020). https://computationalculture.net/regramming-the-platform/
9. Graham, S., Marvin, S.: Splintering Urbanism: Networked Infrastructures, Technological Mobilities and the Urban Condition. Routledge (2002)
10. Hughes, T.P.: Networks of power electrification in Western society, 1880-1930. Johns Hopkins University Press (1983). https://ezproxy.lib.utexas.edu/login?, https://hdl.handle.net/2027/heb.00001
11. Key Concepts | Block Editor Handbook. (n.d.). WordPress Developer Resources. https://developer.wordpress.org/. Accessed 2 Sept. 2020
12. McGrane, K.: Content in a Zombie Apocalypse. https://vimeo.com/167935340. Accessed 24 May 2016
13. Montfort, N., Bogost, I.: Racing the Beam: The Atari Video Computer System. MIT Press, Cambridge (2009)
14. Plantin, J.-C , Lagoze, C., Edwards, P.N., Sandvig, C.: Infrastructure studies meet platform studies in the age of Google and Facebook. New Media Soc. **20**(1), 293–310 (2018)
15. Post Types | WordPress.org. (n.d.). https://wordpress.org/support/article/post-types/. Accessed 14 Sept 2020
16. Star, S.L., Ruhleder, K.: Steps toward an ecology of infrastructure: design and access for large information spaces. Inf. Syst. Res. **7**(1), 111–134 (1996). https://doi.org/10.2307/23010792
17. Usage Statistics and Market Share of WordPress, August 2020. (n.d.) https://w3techs.com/technologies/details/cm-wordpress. Accessed 15 Aug 2020
18. Ventura, M.: Editor Technical Overview. Make WordPress Core, 17 January 2017. https://make.wordpress.org/core/2017/01/17/editor-technical-overview/
19. Ventura, M.: Editor: How Little Blocks Work. Make WordPress Core, 5 May 2017. https://make.wordpress.org/core/2017/05/05/editor-how-little-blocks-work/
20. WordPress' Philosophy. WordPress.Org, 28 March 2018. https://wordpress.org/about/philosophy/
21. WP Café 3: Dealing with complex data structures in WordPress, 11 August 2020. https://www.youtube.com/watch?v=oMBKW9gCRCg

Aggregation and Utilization of Metadata for Intangible Folk Cultural Properties Using Linked Open Data

Itsumi Sato(✉) and Masao Takaku

University of Tsukuba, Tsukuba, Ibaraki, Japan
s1921633@s.tsukuba.ac.jp, masao@slis.tsukuba.ac.jp
http://www.slis.tsukuba.ac.jp/

Abstract. Intangible Folk Cultural Properties (IFCP) represent cultural customs or events related to transition in people's lives, and need to be protected and passed on to future generations. The Japanese government adopted the revised Act on Protection of Cultural Properties in 2018, which aims to ensure comprehensive protection and utilization of cultural properties. IFCP are required to make it available and accessible to the public considering these features. This study proposes an IFCP data model using Linked Open Data (LOD). This model is based on the CIDOC Conceptual Reference Model (CRM) and other vocabularies. We constructed a dataset based on this model and published it on the web. The dataset contains 5,106 triples from 103 IFCP focusing on religious faiths festivals (RF) and annual observances (AO). To evaluate our data model, we defined functional requirements for the IFCP and implemented a prototype system to verify utilization feasibility of the IFCP. The prototype system shows the IFCP lists based on retrieval feature using the SPARQL query language.

Keywords: Intangible folk cultural properties · Metadata · Linked open data · CIDOC CRM · SPARQL

1 Introduction

1.1 Background

In November 2018, "Raiho-shin, ritual visits of deities in masks and costumes", an intangible Japanese cultural heritage consisting of ten different rituals such as Namahage, was inscribed on UNESCO's Representative List of the Intangible Cultural Heritage of Humanity [1]. The news attracted people's attention. Each Raiho-shin ritual is registered as Intangible Folk Cultural Properties (IFCP) in Japan. IFCP are intangible heritage created by people to express and celebrate their daily lives and major life transitions [2].

The Japanese government revised the "Act on Protection of Cultural Properties" in June 2018. This act emphasizes that cultural properties can be leveraged to support town development, and local communities need to protect and

© Springer Nature Switzerland AG 2021
K. Toeppe et al. (Eds.): iConference 2021, LNCS 12645, pp. 154–164, 2021.
https://doi.org/10.1007/978-3-030-71292-1_14

work together to pass them on to future generations [3]. In particular, IFCP are regarded as living cultural objects, and very natural, as stability due to their characteristics cannot be stored in physical form and tend to change over time [4]. Thus, considering their importance and characteristics, it is extremely important to immortalize them by recording information on these IFCP for posterity.

Additionally, some museums have little knowledge of how to deal with intangible cultural heritage customs, such as IFCP, and little interest in them among museum staff. Sometimes, IFCP records are not maintained in an appropriate state by museum staff [5]. Furthermore, multimedia data such as images and videos about intangible cultural heritage customs, including IFCP, need to be easily accessible through the web to be widely utilized [6].

1.2   Research Objective

We propose a data model structuring IFCP information using LOD. In addition, we examine the model utilization by aggregating its structured information.

In this study, we focus on RF and AO, and design a data model to make information about them available using LOD. We adopted the CIDOC Conceptual Reference Model (CRM) [7] as the main vocabulary. Additionally, we implement a utilization application by aggregating the structured AO and RF information.

2   Related Works

2.1   Existing Platform for Cultural Heritages

Europeana. Europeana [8], launched in 2008 and managed by European cultural heritage organizations, is a representative portal for the retrieval and access of digitized cultural and academic heritage items. Europeana collects metadata of their digital contents and presents it as LOD using API. This data model introduces the Europeana Data Model (EDM) [9]. This EDM consists of OAI ORE, Dublin Core, Simple Knowledge Organization System (SKOS), and CIDOC CRM.

Japan Search. Japan Search [10] is a national, integrated, and cross-sectoral portal that contains various digital archives containing books, cultural objects, and art media, to comprehensively retrieve metadata for the country's patrimony. It provides aggregated metadata in accessible formats and promotes the utilization of this content. The official version of the portal was released in August 2020. Japan Search aims to reveal the whereabouts of contents and help the country's digital information resources be discoverable and utilized effectively.

2.2   Structured Data and Model for Intangible Cultural Properties

Tan et al. [11] conducted modeling for data related to the Dragon Boat Festival, a Chinese intangible cultural heritage. Their knowledge data model was structured centered on intangible cultural heritage information's entities and properties based on CIDOC CRM. Then, an experimental prototype was implemented, and the validity of its ontology was verified. The results revealed that the data model is flexible and dynamic.

Giannoulakis et al. [12] constructed a metadata schema focusing on another intangible cultural heritage, folk dance. They examined their original metadata model to describe the complicated metadata of folk dance. This data model adopted Dublin Core, MovementXML, TEI, and VRA, and defined an original schema. As a result of this analysis, they came to the conclusion that encoding intangible cultural heritages is complex work, owing to the consideration for some contextual factors, such as the evolution of people's social environment and their emotions related to performance.

These studies focus on one intangible cultural heritage or one genre of it, and aim to create structured data on that target. However, intangible cultural heritage or IFCP have various genres and objects, depending on cultural backgrounds and regions. In this study, we aim to conduct structuring IFCP information beyond a single target and genre.

2.3   Implementation Using SPARQL

Dannèlls et al. [13] proposed a multilingual SPARQL-based retrieval interface for querying cultural heritage data in natural language. This system is based on grammatical framework, provides a grammar-based approach, supports natural language queries in 15 languages and it inquires as SPARQL queries and receives its language queries.

Mishima [14] proposed a metadata model and system requirement functions for the aggregation and integration of regional cultural heritage information. He aggregated its core information, targeting a cultural heritage list on which Tokyo municipalities open to the public through the web. The system, which supports the discovery of regional cultural heritage information adopting aggregated metadata of cultural heritage lists and LOD, was implemented using SPARQL's query functions.

While these studies focus on tangible cultural heritage subjects, this study focuses on intangible cultural heritage, especially IFCP in the country, and conducts structuring of the data model and implementation using this data model. Additionally, before implementing the application, functional requirements were defined based on users' needs.

3   IFCP

3.1   Definition

As described in the introduction, IFCP are intangible heritage customs, practices, artistic expressions, and values that people created in their daily lives to mark and celebrate transitions. IFCP are a part of cultural properties in Japan.

Cultural property is a term of cultural administration in Japan and refers to a cultural heritage that has been created, fostered, and passed down throughout the long history until the present day [15].

3.2 IFCP Categories and Scope

In this study, IFCP are categorized based on the Important Cultural Properties Database (Kunishitei Bunkazai-tou Database) [16], which consists of three main categories and 16 sub-categories (Table 1).

Table 1. Categories and IFCP count as of July 2019

Main category (number of properties)	Sub category (number of properties)
Manners and customs (130)	Production and regular vocation (9)
	Life and ceremony (6)
	Entertainment and games (10)
	Social life (folk knowledge) (2)
	Annual observances (34)
	Festivals (religious faiths) (69)
	Others (0)
Folk performing (159)	Kagura (35)
	Dengaku (25)
	Furyu (spectacular dancing) (35)
	Narrative and entertainment for blessing (5)
	Ennen and deed (7)
	Entertainment from abroad and stage performance (36)
	Others (16)
Folk techniques (16)	Production and regular vocation (14)
	Food, clothing and housing (2)
	Others (0)

We focus on Important IFCP (IIFCP), which are especially important cultural properties in Japan. There are 305 such IIFCP listed in Japan's Agency for Cultural Affairs Important Cultural Properties Database as of July 2019. From this record, we extracted 103 properties including RF (69 properties) and AO (34 properties), for use in this study. RF are formed from people's mental attitudes by repeating religious experiences or courtesies. AO are religious events or official ceremonies held repeatedly and traditionally every year.

In terms of the number of registered properties, RF is the largest sub-category, and AO is the second largest sub-category in the manners and customs main category. They can be seen as representative IFCP. Additionally, they share common characteristics regarding the periodicity with which they are held every year or at any other regular interval. For these reasons, we chose RF and AO as the focus of this study.

4 Data Model Design

Our proposed data model is shown in Fig. 1. This data model applies Akita no Kanto, one of the famous festivals from the Northeast region in Japan, as a data instance.

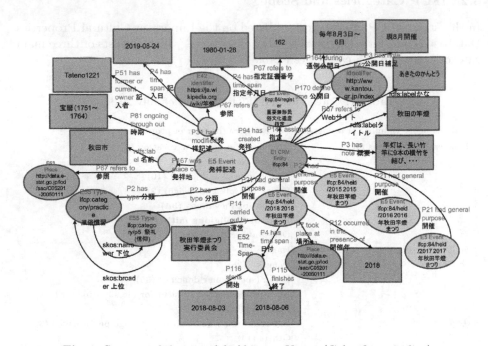

Fig. 1. Structured data model: Akita no Kanto (Color figure online)

In Fig. 1, ovals, squares, and arrows represent resources, literals, and properties respectively. The red oval named "ifcp:84" in the middle of the figure represents this IFCP resource and relates to yellow ovals as event resources, blue ovals as other resources, and squares as literals such as a title. Colored letters (EN and PN) represent Resource Description Framework (RDF) classes and properties from the CIDOC CRM vocabulary.

Three types of event resources are defined: Akita Kanto Festival in YYYY, origin description, and registration of IIFCP. Each resource is related to other resources and literals.

Tables 2 and 3 show entities and properties defined in the data model.

We collected a part of RF and AO information on the web based on data item which we defined.

4.1 Vocabularies

Our model adopts three vocabularies to structure the IFCP data model: CIDOC CRM, SKOS, and RDF Schema.

Table 2. Entity to describe RF and AO, and application with CIDOC CRM

Entity of RF and AO	Entity class from CIDOC CRM
RF and AO	E1 CRM Entity
Web site	E42 Identifier
Category	E55 Type
Holding event	E5 Event
Holding place	E53 Place
Holding period	E52 Time-Span
Origin event	E5 Event
Source	E42 Identifier
Registration event	E5 Event

Table 3. Property to describe RF and AO, and application with CIDOC CRM (excerpt)

Property	Property used vocabularies	Example of properties' values
Title	rdfs:label	Akita no Kanto ()
Category	P2 has type	ifcp:category/practice ifcp:category/p5
Overview	P3 has note	Overview of RF and AO ()
Web site	P67 has created	http://www.kantou.gr.jp/index.htm
Origin event	P94 has created	Expressing entities for the origin event as a blank node
Registration event	P141 assigned	ifcp:84/register
Publication date	P170 define time	Expressing as a blank node, which includes two properties below
Official publication date	P141 assigned	3rd to 6th, August every year ()
Supplemental explanation	P3 has note	Currently held in August

CIDOC CRM. CIDOC CRM [7] is a documentation standard defined by the International Committee for Documentation (CIDOC), an international committee of the International Council of Museums. CIDOC CRM provides an ontology to manage museum information, adopting an object-oriented conceptual model based on the concept of ontology and focusing on museum information, while also being available for other general purposes.

CIDOC CRM is regarded as an event-centric model, which is a model describing several events that are related to one object. It is possible to construct a network of enriched entities by representing these events. For instance, it would be possible for one IFCP to be described in terms of when and where it occurred, who participated in it as well as holding, origin, and registration of its IFCP.

4.2 Definition of Events

This study defines three types of IFCP events.

The first type is the holding event, which describes when an RF, AO, or other IFCP-related event is held. In the case of Akita no Kanto, the festival is held annually, so the holding event is represented as Akita Kanto Festival 2019, Akita Kanto Festival 2018, and Akita Kanto Festival 2017. Each holding event has its title, overview, website URL, and categories as describing information.

The second type is the origin event, which relates to information regarding IFCP's origin. Information about IFCP's origin would be different depending on the referred date or each content, and is described differently. To make this situation possible, event information about its origin is required. This event concretely includes origin place, original period, source of reference (URL), its editor, and its edit date.

The third type is the registration event, which relates to event information as inscribed in the IIFCP in Japan. This event has a registered date and registration number.

5   Building and Publishing the Dataset

This section describes the flow from data collection to the release of the structured RF and AO information datasets (Fig. 2). The core IFCP data, including RF and AO, are acquired from the Important Cultural Properties Database [16] as a CSV file. The acquired data includes basic information about IFCP and their categories. Event information such as holding, origin, and external resources about RF, AO, and their metadata are collected and added to enrich the data. The collection of this enrichment information was conducted manually by the first author. We only collected event information for the years 2018 and 2019, and converted the data to Excel format.

We then used Poorman's Toolkit [17] to convert an Excel file to RDF/Turtle data using LOD. This flow on Fig. 2 shows the construction of the RF and AO datasets.

In order to publish IFCP's LOD data, the RDF/Turtle data is made available on the web. We used ttl2html [18] to create data for web release and convert the RF and AO RDF/Turtle data to HTML files. The website including these files is already released to the public [19] and is updated according to revisions to the data model. This web site aims to publish developed datasets to the public.

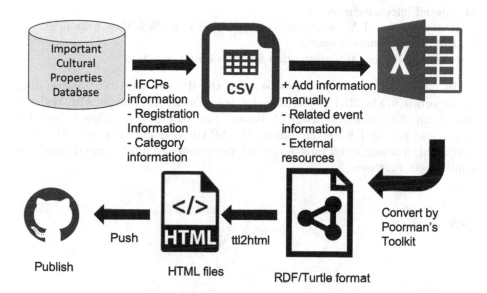

Fig. 2. Construction to release flow of datasets

6   Evaluation

We conducted an evaluation of our model and LOD dataset on RF and AO using the approaches described in the following section.

6.1   Functional Requirements and Prototype System

The first step was verification of the structured data model. The construction of the data model and datasets represented the minimum level of applicability. We further evaluated the functionality of the data model by implementing a prototype system to judge whether it performs as expected.

This prototype system aims to utilize RF and AO information. We supposed some use cases for this prototype system. For example, a user, who studies intangible cultural heritage, wants to find its related resources on the web, but it is difficult to locate credible information. We defined four functional requirements for utilization of the datasets based on the use cases as follows:

I. Browsing RF and AO
   This shows detailed information regarding all RFs and AOs recorded in the RDF store.

II. Temporal information search
   This shows RF and AO information for each period in which they were occurred.

III. Spatial information search
   It shows RF and AO information for each area in which they were held.

IV. Holding information search
   It shows RF and AO information for each occurrence year.

In implementing the prototype system, the RF and AO RDF/Turtle data are recorded in the RDF store (Apache Jena Fuseki [20]) along with regional data from the Statistical LOD of Japan. The RDF store makes it possible to retrieve recorded RDF data using the SPARQL query language. We integrated this retrieval result into the prototype system and implemented the above requirement functions.

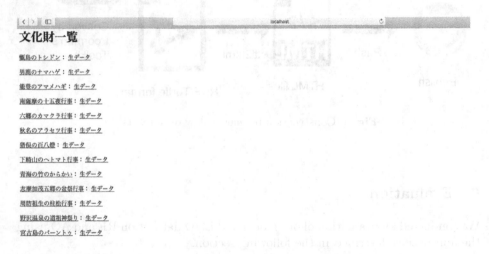

Fig. 3. Prototype system screenshot: RF and AO list example

Screenshots (Figs. 3 and 4) are from the prototype system based on the functional requirements. Figure 3 shows a list of RFs and AOs recorded in the RDF store. When one RF or AO is selected, the prototype system provides detailed information on it (Fig. 4). This flow allows users to browse every IFCP and fulfills the functional requirements.

6.2 Application Implementation

The second evaluation approach was the implementation of an application based on the implemented prototype system. This application verifies the feasibility of

Fig. 4. Prototype system screenshot: detailed information example

RF and AO utilization. This approach is still in progress. This application targets researchers and officers at local governments involving IFCP. We will conduct an evaluation experiment focused on this function and confirm its feasibility after the implementation of the prototype system.

7   Conclusion

This study aimed to structure a data model for building and publishing an IFCP dataset focused especially on RFs and AOs-related information and its release. For evaluation, we defined functional requirements and, based on these requirements, we implemented a prototype system using SPARQL based on the requirements.

We defined the data model based on basic elements, event entities, and CIDOC CRM vocabularies. We found that some properties do not fit perfectly with original definition of CIDOC CRM. We will extend the data model considering detailed descriptions.

In future works, we plan to implement, based on the prototype system, an application for the utilization of RF and AO information and then conduct a user experiment to verify its effectiveness.

References

1. UNESCO: Thirty-one new elements inscribed on the representative list. https://ich.unesco.org/en/news/thirty-one-new-elements-inscribed-on-the-representative-list-00327. Accessed 22 Sept

2. Agency for Cultural Affairs: Folk cultural properties in Japanese. https://www.bunka.go.jp/english/policy/cultural_properties/introduction/folk/ Accessed 22 Sept

3. Cultural resources utilization section: Revision of act on protection of cultural properties (in Japanese). Monthly Rep. Board Educ. **71**(5), 30–42 (2019)

4. Oshima, A.: Considering "Change" of intangible folk cultural properties with emphasis on the relation with the designation of cultural properties (in Japanese). Res. Rep. Intang. Cultural Herit. **2**, 214–228 (2008)

5. Tokyo National Research Institute for Cultural Properties Department of Intangible Cultural Heritage: In: 14th Conference on the Study of Intangible Folk Cultural Properties (in Japanese). https://www.tobunken.go.jp/ich/wp-content/uploads/kyougikai2019.pdf Accessed 24 Sept

6. Artese, M.T., Gagliardi, I.: Cataloging intangible cultural heritage on the web. Prog. Cultural Herit. Preserv. **7616**, 676–683 (2012)

7. CIDOC CRM. http://www.cidoc-crm.org/

8. EUROPEANA. https://www.europeana.eu/en

9. EUROPEANA Data Model. https://pro.europeana.eu/page/edm-documentation

10. JAPAN Search. https://jpsearch.go.jp

11. Tan, G., Hao, T., Zhong, Z.: A knowledge modeling for intangible cultural heritage based on ontology. In: 2009 Second International Symposium on Knowledge Acquisition and Modeling, vol. 1, pp. 304–307 (2009)

12. Giannoulakis, S., Tsapatsoulis, N., Grammalidis, N.: Metadata for intangible cultural heritage - the case of folk dance. In: Proceedings of the 13th International Joint Conference on Computer Vision, Imaging and Computer Graphics Theory and Application, vol. 5, pp. 634–645 (2018)

13. Dannèlls, D., Enache, R., Damova, M.: A multilingual SPARQL-based retrieval interface for cultural heritage objects. In: Proceedings of the ISWC 2014 Posters & Demonstrations Track a Track Within the 13th International Semantic Web Conference (ISWC 2014), vol. 1272, pp. 205–208 (2014)

14. Mishima, T.: Aggregation and linking of regional cultural heritage information with the use of cultural property lists in Japan (in Japanese). Master thesis, University of Tsukuba (2020)

15. Agency for Cultural Affairs: Cultural properties. https://www.bunka.go.jp/english/policy/cultural_properties/. Accessed 11 Jan

16. Important Cultural Properties Database (Kunishitei Bunkazai-tou Database). https://kunishitei.bunka.go.jp/bsys/index

17. Poorman's Linked Data Toolkit. https://github.com/jp-textbook/jp-textbook.github.io/wiki/Toolkit.en

18. ttl2html. https://github.com/masao/ttl2html/blob/master/README.md

19. Intangible Folk Cultural Properties. https://w3id.org/ifcp/

20. Apache Jena Fuseki. https://jena.apache.org/documentation/fuseki2/

Post-GDPR Usage of Students' Big-Data at UK Universities

Carolyn Fearn and Kushwanth Koya(✉)

iSchool, College of Business, Technology and Engineering, Sheffield Hallam University, Sheffield S1 4WB, UK
{c.t.fearn,k.koya}@shu.ac.uk

Abstract. Higher education institutions are extensively using students' big-data to develop student services, create management or staff-led interventions and inform their strategic decisions etc. Following the implementation of the European Union's General Data Protection Regulation (GDPR) in 2018, there has been extensive uncertainty regarding the use of students' data. By conducting interviews with various University staff in the UK, this research aims to explore their understanding and usage of students' data, post-GDPR implementation. The findings indicate students' data is primarily used to build learning analytic tools and student-retention activities. Additionally, it was found that the understanding and usage of both big-data and GDPR differed across various Universities' stakeholders, and there is inadequate support available to these stakeholders. Overall, this research indicates the adoption of big-data based learning analytics requires comprehensive development and implementation policies to address the challenges of learning analytics. Therefore, this research proposes such an approach through co-creation with staff and students; institutional research and staff training.

Keywords: GDPR · Big-data · Learning analytics · Higher education

1 Introduction

1.1 Big-Data in Higher Education

Big-data (BD) refers to large-scale data that are characterized by volume, velocity, veracity, variety and value [27]. Additionally, BD is defined as "building new analytic applications based on new types of data, in order to better serve your customers and drive a better competitive advantage" [4]. Challenges within higher education institutions (HEIs) have created an interest in BD and analytics as a potential solution to issues i.e. student-retention, personalized-learner support and changing pedagogy [1, 11, 26, 54]. Data created in HEIs through students' digital footprints provides an authentic reflection of real behavior, detailed insight into student performance and learning trajectories that could be used for personalized adaptive learning, and curriculum design [3]. However, it is irresponsible to believe more educational data always means better educational data and learning analytics (LA) possess limitations as well as multiple meanings [19].

Scholarly-works refer to issues in the use of BD, such as economic, legal, social and ethical, from both positive and negative aspects. Another concern is the automation of society in which actions are determined by behaviors and coercion, i.e. personalized advertising [2, 15, 31, 34, 39, 42]. The use of BD and LA needs strategic-leadership within any organization. "One of the biggest impacts of big-data will be that data driven decisions are poised to augment or overrule human judgement" (ibid, p.141). While the mining of BD in HE will support evidence-based research into enhancing learning and teaching, data taken out of context will lose meaning and value [7]. Furthermore, LA will only be effective if applied within course specific contexts rather than at institutional-level [50]. Careful consideration needs to be given to equality and inclusion when using BD, as within a retail-consumerist environment, not everyone engages with activities that BD tools can capture or analyze [25, 30, 48]. Not all students in HE leave the same type or volume of digital-footprint, this will vary between academic disciplines and the type of learner and their learning style [6]. In order to accurately use data to predict student success, or identify those at risk of withdrawal, the range and type of personal data that should be used needs to be more than just personal-biographical-data. A study suggests that the value of a degree is linked to personal cognitive motivations and economic benefits; therefore, using data identifying individual behaviors, such as critical thinking and social-emotional well-being will enhance the accuracy of predictions [51]. It is evident from the literature that increased data harvesting within HEIs offers the potential to improve student outcomes and retention [23]. However, what must also be taken into consideration is the compatibility of educational-datasets such as student's biographical, behavioral and curriculum data, and the capability of algorithmic approaches to interpret and present LA information.

1.2 GDPR and Learning Analytics

GDPR has brought clarity regarding the collection and use of personal data by presenting lawful bases for processing in the European Union (EU) [37]. The purpose of LA is for the benefit of students, either assisting them individually, or through aggregated data to improve educational experience more generally [23]. The Joint Information Systems Committee (JISC) recommends institutions should allocate specific responsibility within the organization to take accountability for the legal, ethical and effective use of LA [23, 24]. Models proposing the domain and application of LA consider six dimensions [19], however, no reference is made to challenges relating to the processes associated with LA i.e. the need for common datasets, data-quality or version-control [18, 20]. Additionally, application and compliance with data protection must be considered across each of the dimensions (Fig. 1).

Scholarly-works indicate that LA has the potential for improving teaching and learning [24]. However, the longitudinal impact of LA as a discipline is not clear, particularly within the UK and EU following the implementation of the GDPR. It broadens the term 'personal and sensitive data' to include 'online identifiers' such as IP addresses and cookies, genetic and biometric data [22]. The privacy-rights of individuals have been strengthened to include: stricter rules for obtaining consent as a legal basis for processing data; the right to have personal data erased; the right to have clear information regarding

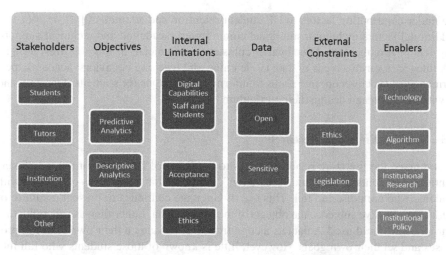

Fig. 1. Dimensions of LA. Adapted from Greller and Drachsler [19]

what data is being collected and how it is being processed; the right not to be subject to a decision based solely on automated processing of one's personal data [14, 56].

The GDPR was adopted by the EU in 2016, replacing the 1995 Data Protection Directive which was created at a time when the use of digital data were in infancy. As an act of UK law, the EU GDPR requirements will continue to apply after Brexit [14]. This covers EU-based organizations collecting or processing personal data of EU residents and organizations outside the EU for monitoring behavior or offering goods and services to EU residents. Organizations non-compliant with the regulations could be subject to the imposition of sanctions. There are therefore profound implications for UK-based HEIs. Hence, the collection and processing of personal data must be justified under one of the lawful bases provided by the GDPR, for example: meeting a legal obligation, collection is in the institution's legitimate interest, or required to fulfil contractual obligations with the student. Additionally, a clear affirmative action of consent from the student must be obtained, where interventions with individual students are made based on their analytics, a limitless right to withdraw consent is made available with clear accessible mechanisms [22].

The term 'student-engagement' can be characterized by a diverse set of systems and agents, spanning both the physical and digital-spaces [6]. Scholarly-research finds a weak-relationship between student-engagement and student outcomes, suggesting that to collect data about students' interactions with activities and services, physical or digital, may not be invaluable for predicting student outcomes. Nonetheless, there is a need for reciprocal sharing of appropriate and actionable information between students and their institution, allowing students to make informed decisions and act accordingly [47]. An individual's intention to remain within HE and perform to the best of their ability is influenced by their motivations, interests and behaviors [32]. An extensive body of research literature spanning more than four decades, indicates that students' level of integration in both academic (student assessment results and satisfaction with their academic experience) and social environment (extracurricular activities and peer-relationships) are major contributing factors to HE student-retention and attainment [40, 45, 46, 49]. Additional factors include: institutional commitment (academic and technical support, physical environment) and personal circumstances (financial, health and lifestyle) [1]. LA integrates various types of data i.e. learning and teaching behaviors, academic performance and socio-economic status to inform interventions for students' learning, and how tutors teach and design their curriculum [38, 53].

1.3 Need for Empirical Research

In summary, the literature reviewed refers to the focus of LA with phrases i.e. "intervention", "students at-risk" and "prediction", implying that analytics is concerned with students who are poised to fail. This use of language continues to present a culture of students as passive subjects, the objects of the flow of data, rather than as self-reflecting learners who could use LA data as a cognitive tool to evaluate their own learning processes and set their own goals. However, little is known of those students who fall into other categories, whose data presents them as "stable" or "good". Another common theme throughout the literature is communication, inclusion and engagement with all stakeholders. The successful implementation and use of LA relies upon collaboration with all stakeholders - staff, students and management with a clear strategic objective set by senior leaders within an organizational culture that is change inclined. Therefore the motivation of this research is to provide informed guidance regarding the implementation and use of LA and GDPR, explore the potential to use BD in the context of LA, understand the level of stakeholder involvement and training provided. Thus, the following research questions need to be addressed:

RQ1: Where is BD being used within the HE sector post-GDPR implementation?

RQ2: How BD assists in developing LA and consequently, its usefulness to relevant stakeholders?

2 Methodology

2.1 Data Collection

Participants were purposely selected, comprising of representatives from various HEIs where LA were being used due to their interest and knowledge of the research topic, and invitations were sent via professional institution networks to participate in one-to-one interviews, [52]. Nine participants agreed to participate in semi-structured interviews, with questions derived from literature.

A participant information-sheet, consisting of questions and themes to expect during the interview, was provided in advance for orientation. The themes of the questions reflect the overall objectives of this research, to understand the usage and comprehension of student 'BD' and GDPR. Interviews lasted between 30 to 45 min, were recorded and manually transcribed for analysis.

2.2 Data Analysis

The interviews were analysed using thematic analysis [8], a structured qualitative method applied to discover, interpret, analyse and communicate clusters of data within the text [12]. An inductive process of analysis was followed due to a small sample size and purposive sampling [43]. Braun & Clarke's (2006) process of thematic analysis as depicted in Fig. 3 was applied. An iterative code checking process was additionally applied to ensure rigor and code maturity. The emerging themes were further refined to represent a specific definition and the context of occurrence. Although thematic analysis is flexible, this flexibility can lead to inconsistency and a lack of coherence when developing themes derived from the transcript data [21]. This was mitigated by creating a map to visualise the themes (Fig. 2).

Participant	Institution characteristics	Designation
1	TEF Gold; Post-1992 University; 20000 students	Director of Teaching and Learning
2	TEF Bronze; 19000 students	Associate Dean
3	TEF Gold; 19000 students	Senior Lecturer and Academic Advisor (AA)
4	TEF Silver	Senior Lecturer and AA
5	TEF Silver	Senior Lecturer and AA
6	'withheld'	Head of Data Governance
7	TEF Silver; approx. 30000 students	Senior Lecturer and AA
8	TEF Silver; approx. 30000 students	Senior Lecturer and AA
9	'withheld'	Head of Information Governance and Data Protection

Fig. 2. Participant characteristics

To ensure further rigor, an inter-coder reliability test was conducted independent of the first coder. The second author coded all the interview transcripts and Cohen's Kappa was calculated to ensure repeatability of the emerged themes between independent coders [28]. This research approach is considered as interpretivist as it was about understanding the perceptions of participants, acknowledging that these observations will be subjective. Although it enables a deeper understanding of the participants' thoughts, perceptions and experiences in relation to the use of BD and GDPR, a further systematic review followed by a qualitative meta-analysis will confirm the findings [10, 41].

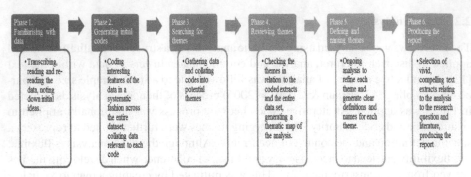

Fig. 3. Braun and Clarke's thematic analysis framework [8]

3   Findings

3.1   Understanding the Term Big-Data

The understanding of the term BD between the participants found consistent descriptions. Their understanding of BD relates to - the increasing availability and collection of data as a result of emerging technology capable of collecting large datasets; value and benefits of BD to inform decision-making; technical descriptions.

> *"different sources and different ways we can collect data now that we didn't used to have"*

> *"how do we make it meaningful".*

> *"we have a general rule of thumb, if it can fit on a laptop, it's not BD, that's from a computer science perspective".*

Participants also reported the context of the data shouldn't be lost in any processing and acknowledge the increasing focus on data within the sector.

> *"..data driven society, being judged and governed against data today"*

Four academic participants provided different responses. One reported no distinction between data and BD; *"data is data".* Two participants understood BD as large in volume and diverse in categories of student data, providing insight into their actions.

> *"all-encompassing data from all angles...how they interact with us"*

One participant described BD as a new concept, with limited understanding, confined to its use as a marketing tool and unsure of its meaning within HE.

> *"came from a generation where BD is quite a new thing"*

3.2   Current Use of Big-Data to Support Students

At Institution Level. Within their institution to support student-retention, only one academic said BD is being used in-relation to attendance-monitoring and the triangulation of missed-sessions to inform interventions. The Institutional-strategy relating to student-retention has direct impact on academic advisors (AAs) who are presented with a dashboard containing individual student data: attendance-information, disability-statement and attainment-data. Academics are expected to engage and use this data and record notes of their interactions with students; this dashboard is not presented to students.

"....huge impact, the retention work we've done, the focus on retention - does impact on the way we do our job..."

"academic-tutors can enter and are expected to enter updates when they meet with students"

Participants mentioned their experience in a LA project which resulted in their University realising the potential of LA i.e. course delivery performance but acknowledged the challenge of integrating IT systems.

Data are used as *"proxies of which to judge success on different levels"*.

Awareness of BD to support student-retention is mixed; two participants weren't aware of existing practice or the use of BD and provided different responses, describing institutional data i.e. age, caring responsibilities, ethnicity and disability, are used to identify students at risk of withdrawing.

"it's a bit of an assumption that students in these categories would have retention and engagement issues....I have a student with a learning contract and a disabled brother, he's the most engaging student there is"

".. we get pushed on certain projects, the latest is about retention and achievement but of students from BAME backgrounds....last year we were pushed quite hard on commuter students - so they do use that information they only give it to me as and when they want me to use it."

The responses from institutional managers (IMs) varied; outlining a strategic management context regarding how data are used to structure strategic key performance indicators and the production of institutional retention reports, and attendance monitoring to indicate issues with non-attendance.

"So we are constantly evolving how we look at the data".

"..so that they (staff) can make interventions that would signpost them to support services and assist them in making sure that we retain the student"

Participant's use of big-data within their role.

Within their role's participants responded by reiterating BD was used for the purposes of statutory data reporting activities for management information. However, academics stated that they do not directly use BD, but relied on their relationships with the student.

"we build up a local level relationship with students".

"I have tried and trusted methods of asking and talking to the student very much on a one to one conversational basis getting to know them"

"The role is also tasked with overlaying a governance framework on the use of data in order to shift the University's culture towards being data driven and regarding data as assets."

3.3 Presentation of Learning Analytics Data to Staff and Students

Presentation to Students. Participants mostly responded that data are collected but not presented to students; one member was unsure if data are presented to students but would favour a *"transparent approach"*.

Presentation to Staff. Two participants reported that the data are not presented to staff, but would welcome this approach to *"aid conversations with students"*.

One participant responded that data are presented to staff in the form of a *"Personal Academic Tutor Dashboard"*, although felt this was a *"crude"* presentation of data.

One academic expanded their response and suggested they wished to see individual and cohort profiles and information about cohort experiences.

"Again it comes with doing that as an AA, comes with a health warning though, that people might just pull off the data and think well I don't really need to see them, I'll just send them an email...But behind every piece of data there is a story and it would be that that I would be frightened that got missed, so yes I can see the benefits but it comes with a health warning"

Support for Staff and Students Using Big-Data. All participants responded that there is a devolved specialist team within their institution that have ownership for data with support provided typically by one administrative colleague. Two participants specified resistance or lack of engagement from academic colleagues in using the data and one participant specifically referred to the need for institutional change, preferring personal academic tutorials rather than the need for support using data dashboard.

"it is pretty basic, it doesn't need much interpretation, it's about institutional change, it's more about making people do this, getting round the idea of personal academic tutorials"

"...teaching is just a bit of a bind, they would rather be doing their research, they'd rather be doing anything other than standing in a classroom. So how those students perform...not really interested".

All academics responded that support is not available, specifying the need for training and time to undertake the training. The academics also report that the focus of training should cover the reasons for using data and the consequences, rather than the mechanics of manipulation of data.

"good question - there really isn't much support available to staff, because the data isn't given to staff".

"it's also why would you use it, and what's the issue what's the flip side of using it erroneously."

Support was also required for academics regarding how to deal with students.

"the person is more important than the data, you need to know how to deal with the person, and support for AAs as well...there can be some very sad stuff that happens to students and that can be quite difficult to deal with."

3.4 Use of Predictive Learning Analytics

When asked if their institutions plan a move towards using predictive analytics (PA). One participant reported a limited institutional understanding and their ethical concerns regarding its use.

"I'm cynical about prediction because from my research, what I've shown and demonstrated is that students are so much more complex than prediction and I worry about prediction from an ethical point of view"

A project at one participant's institution had attempted predicting degree classifications, resulting in a model that was 70%–80% accurate. Participants commented that if student predictions were to be used there must be transparency regarding the algorithms. One participant said the use of PA should be applied at an institutional level. One academic responded that a manual local predictive process identifying students within specific categories and monitoring their attendance is current practice.

"You can present the prediction to students, but I think it would have to be done with blinkered eyes, and have it vetted before showing it to the student."

"So predictive analytics are quite useful but again my view on anything like that is putting people in boxes.....it should come with a caveat...".

Participants reported the essentiality of good relationships with students and the presentation of predictions *"should never take away the human element"*. Presentation of predictive data to staff was not reported as an issue.

"...predictive is great for an AA to have a measure of who they are dealing with and to be mindful of it - actually sharing that with the student I can potentially see that as being counterproductive.."

"going back to predictive....we need to do it on us...if we keep doing what we are doing, we are like the dodo, we are going to work ourselves to extinction because we don't understand, even with big-data with these analytics, we will see them coming in, but we won't measure against that student we will measure against our standards of teaching and our standards of engagement, rather than what they need.".

3.5 The Impact of the GDPR on Existing Practice

Most academics reported there had been no impact on practice. IMs did add that the introduction had *"unfortunately"* resulted in the stopping of activities relating to the analysis of student data and, additionally reported that academic staff are accustomed to working with student numbers rather than names. As individuals using BD, participants reported practical adjustments regarding data-storage and privacy.

"the first thing we say to our students who comes to us with a problem is what is your student number…so we are programmed in that way and our students are programmed in that way".

However, GDPR according to IMs was on institutional policy and governance, bringing clearer rationale for using data to fulfil the requirements of student contracts. The GDPR has also highlighted the need for institutions to focus on data quality to avoid distress being caused to the data subject when using their personal data.

"ensuring compliance with legislation processing data fairly and lawfully and looking after the rights of data subjects"

A reported advantage of the introduction of the GDPR was the requirement for an Information Asset Register to document institutional data.

"we will for the first time know what data we have, where it is and why we use it".

3.6 Developing LA

Co-creation with Students. Five participants responded students are not involved with projects that use their personal data. The remaining participants indicated that students are invited to participate and contribute. One reported that their project had been developed through a user-centred design approach with students employed as ambassadors leading workshops to ensure the project was driven by what students said.

"there's a systematic literature review that shows that about 6% of student facing LA projects published have shown that have actually looked at working with students to design stuff. I think that mine is one of the first projects to do it fully.".

One participant expanded their response by commenting that students are in an environment where *"not sure they care"* about how their data are used, seeing their data in a social media context is their *"environment"* and the *"norm"* for them.

Co-creation with Staff. In general, the participants responded that staff are, or have been, included with institutional projects. The pilot LA project led at one HEI had been developed collaboratively with two academic members of staff.

" reflect on how it went and what needs to be improved for the following year it is based on data and evidence not just on subjective opinion".

Academic staff at another institution had been involved with the introduction of their attendance monitoring system. However, the participants also reported resistance from some academic staff within their institution.

"…you'll always get the ones who….resisters….we call those CAVEs - colleagues against virtually everything."

Institutional Approach to LA. Participant responses differed when asked about the Institutional approach to LA. One did not have any knowledge of the institutional approach and all other responses reflected different approaches i.e. driven by improving student engagement and student outcomes as opposed to focussing on students at risk.

Data Strategy. One IM referred to a data strategy written by a steering group consisting of staff from central directorates with knowledge and expertise in the use of data, although the data strategy doesn't refer to use of data for LA. The knowledge of an Institutional data strategy within the academic responses varied, with three participants having little or no awareness of a strategy and the remaining were aware.

"I'm going to have to say yes, it's a big enough organisation to need one....has it been particularly well shared - not so much".

Ethical issues of using big-data.

Participants reported their concerns regarding the ethical use of BD and the impact this may have on all stakeholders.

"does the university have capacity....that's the key thing because once you open this you can then start to identify students at risk - if you can't then do anything about it then that's the biggest problem".

All participants reported concerns regarding data transparency; how the data are collected, processed and applied to predict outcomes.

"students are so much more complex than prediction and I worry about prediction from an ethical point of view."

Participants reported that Institutional discussions and a corporate approach regarding the ethical use of data is required.

"it feels like here we have almost just thought we just need a system and the actual cultural element and how it is going to be adopted by the front line users has not been explored enough."

4 Discussion

This research aims to explore within the context of the new GDPR legislation, how student data is utilised at UK HEIs. The study identified key themes as listed in Fig. 4.

4.1 Understanding the Term Big-Data

The term 'BD' was recognised by all participants who provided a range of descriptions; from no distinction between data and BD, to the variety, volume and rate at which data are available, partially aligning with current scholarly-works [4, 27]. This theoretical perspective is supported by the IMs and some academics who believe in technology

Category	Theme	Inter-coder reliability (Cohen's Kappa); Landis & Koch (1977) interpretation
Understanding 'BD'	Volume	
	Variety	
	Value (to improve student services and offer intelligence)	
Use of 'BD'	Custom student services	0.63; Substantial agreement
	Management or staff led interventions	
	Monitor not predict	
	Report student performance	
	Academic advisory	
Impact of GDPR	Storage of personal information	
	Stopped analysing student data	
	Inundation of consent requests from private companies who work with the specific HEI	0.77; Substantial agreement
	Changes to administrative practice to obtain student consent	
	Staffing change (recruitment)	
	Clarity on the definition of consent	
	Not much effect	
Retention research	Limited understanding or knowledge in the area of student retention	0.33; Fair agreement
	BD contributed towards retention of commuter students.	
LA	Student permission is a must	
	Institutional planning, teaching and learning practice	
	Do not underestimate personal relationships	
	Provide assurance to students and staff	0.68; Substantial agreement
	Transparency of the algorithm	
	Possibility of negative profiling	
	Should be combined with face to face interaction	
Support available to staff	No standards on how the student data in decision support systems	
	Increase data variety under single student profiles to offer better support to students	
	Large quantities & types of student data, including digital footprints collected.	
	Inconsistent interpretations with current data (needs standardisation)	
	Training provision for staff involved at all levels (academic advisory, data management and analysis	0.61; Substantial agreement
	Very little collaboration between staff or students to agree on the practices with the data collected.	
	Little understanding of GDPR	
	Lack of institutional direction	
	Lack of co-creation	
	Influence student behaviour with intelligence gathered from data.	

Fig. 4. Summary of findings

advancements in HE. However, some academics were concerned regarding the use of data to monitor and judge academic performance, specifically referring to the TEF, as it is considered a proxy for success, a view shared in recent literature [55].

The potential value of BD to support student-retention is recognised by most participants, with caveats that data should be viewed within the context of a students' circumstances and should not replace the professional staff-student relationships. However, other benefits such as changing pedagogy and personalised learning were not mentioned as reported in earlier works [3]. This research partially supports a view which reports that institutional adoption of analytics is hindered by lack of a data-driven mindset [35]. All participants demonstrated a data-driven mind-set and an acknowledgement that data has value; however, academics reported the lack of available data. In summary, the understanding and value of BD within HE is recognised, but a clear institutional-strategy regarding data usage in LA is needed [23, 24, 36, 50].

4.2   The Current Use of Big-Data

Academics responses were mixed about the use of data within their role and their institutions. Some reported that they do not use it, but later spoke about activities they undertake, using student personal data they have collected. It is interesting to observe that participants did not class student personal data as 'BD'. In general, most participants were aware of institutional data being used to monitor and report an aggregated performance of students. Two academics reported that their institutions' use attendance data to inform interventions preventing student withdrawals.

In summary, the sector uses BD to support student-retention and engagement activities. Some HEIs use attendance monitoring data, not predictive data, to trigger interventions. Hence, it can also be argued that the use of one set of data does not fit with earlier suggested definitions [27]. Although vast amounts of data are collected across the sector, this research finds that the lack of a data strategy is common across the HE sector.

4.3   Impact of the GDPR

From the participants' perspectives, the impact of GDPR is minimal. Most referred to changes to data-storage on their systems, one participant referred to restrictions on data usage as a result of GDPR. Albeit GDPR does permit analysis of data, it is the actions taken as a result of the data that are affected [22]. There appears to be misconceptions within the sector between academic and IMs regarding the implications of the GDPR. The IMs reported positive impacts, including clarity on data usage and consent. Across the sector, an impact of the GDPR has been the changes in administrative practice at the point of obtaining student consent to collect and use their data. The IMs cited another impact with the introduction of new roles i.e. Chief Information Officer and Head of Data Governance; both roles were identified due to the need for expertise and knowledge of data management and accountability within their institutions.

4.4   Institutional Research on Student-Retention

Although the need to understand student-retention has been discussed in literature for more than four decades [45, 46, 49], this research indicates limited research to understand factors affecting student-retention. Only one participant reported institutional research that subsequently informed changes to their practice. Participants mentioned small-scale internal projects, but no impact or change to practice was reported. Without Institutional knowledge of such factors, data are incomplete and therefore analysis will be subject to misinterpretation and bias [5]. Earlier research [32, 51], suggests that understanding an individual's motivations for studying, using behavioural data i.e. motivations, critical thinking and social-emotional well-being, enhances the accuracy of predictions of student withdrawal or attainment. However, this was not mentioned by any participant.

4.5   Data Presentation and Support for Staff and Students

The presentation of individual student data to staff appears inconsistent. All participants acknowledged that a large amount and variety of student data are collected, but not all is presented to staff. However, if presented, some concerns were expressed by academics regarding misinterpretation of data, leading to inconsistent practice. HEIs should consider comprehensively the provision of guidance and training for use of BD.

One participant referred to 'data-experts', implying that they would not need or require training. However, if HEIs were to introduce a LA solution, the use of data would be very different to current practice. Training for all staff that access and use such data would be critical for effective implementation. This research finds that very little collaboration with staff or students in the development of any solution using student personal data to support student-retention or attainment has taken place, in line with prior investigations [13, 17].

In summary, the prominent concerns raised during the interviews were a combination of lack of institutional direction and strategy regarding the use of data, limited knowledge of the GDPR, lack of co-creation with end users, personal ethical and moral perspectives of how student data should be used. The overall perspective of participants was that students should be entitled to see their data used at institutional level.

4.6 Use of Predictive Learning Analytics

As stated above, participants were in favour of presenting students with their data, although concerns were expressed when asked about showing predictions to students. To have their data presented which predicts their withdrawal or failure could be seen as demotivating, and possibly inaccurate if based on a stereotypical approach of categorising students. Some participants expressed their desire to talk to their students before presenting predictive data, whereas others were adamant that students shouldn't see. These concerns relate to a lack of knowledge regarding how PA works and a lack of transparency in the predictive modelling algorithm, as discussed in earlier works [29].

4.7 Developing Learning Analytics

Participants reported several common perspectives, including the need for a coherent institutional approach and policy, clear guidance and support for users of LA data, and collaboration with staff and students is important. Although it is suggested that students should be engaged as collaborators with a LA solution [9], this research suggests that academics should also be involved - specifically with clarifying the institutional purpose. This inclusion could provide the assurance and address academic concerns regarding the ethical and erroneous use of BD [44, 57].

It should also be recognised that whilst LA could support student-retention, it could also be used to inform institutional planning, teaching and learning practice. Use of LA in this context would lead to innovation and change, which as a result of institutional resistance to change could be considered a risk [16, 33].

4.8 Ethical Issues of Using Big-Data

This investigation finds the surveillance and profiling of students is a concern for academics; as suggested in earlier works [29]. Personal observations by academics of their students also suggested that student behaviours do not always follow the path that data have predicted; to them it is more important to retain the personal relationship.

Participants also expressed concerns regarding individuals' access to, and use of LA data, as this was seen as the most variable risk. The digital capabilities and confidence to diagnose a student's situation and take follow-up actions was highlighted as a very individual undertaking and where significant inconsistences would occur. The findings indicate mixed practice within the sector regarding the sharing and use of BD, with an underlying desire for an approach to adopting LA.

5 Conclusion

This investigation of whether post the GDPR, BD could be used within HE. The study has generated evidence that BD based LA is, or has been, used within HEIs to mainly support student-retention. However, only one HEI is currently using a single source of attendance monitoring data to support student-retention, whereas other HEIs are using BD additionally for attainment, management information, business-modelling and quality assurance. This research concludes that the implementation of GDPR has had little impact on existing practice within UK HEIs in their use of data, academic participants only reporting changes to practice in data-storage. IMs cited that the GDPR was a positive move enabling greater clarity on data collection and usage. Participant responses indicated there is a gap in knowledge and application of GDPR. The introduction of the GDPR had had an impact on staffing levels at one HEI with the appointment of a Chief Information Officer and a Head of Data Governance with responsibility for data governance and compliance.

In general, all participants described various possible datasets for predictive modelling, although all expressed concerns regarding its application. Despite the literature available in the field, a larger study would conclusively indicate how BD identifies students at risk of withdrawal. All participants cited that it would be beneficial to present student data to academics to support and inform their role in providing academic guidance. Several benefits were cited, including: being able to see collated student profile information and students' course engagement. Additionally, participants also expressed concerns relating interpretation of data by colleagues, the perceived volume of work and the impact on other areas of the University to support students. Overall, participants believed that the presentation of student data would be of significant benefit for academics, but training and support would be required to ensure a consistent institutional approach to support students.

5.1 Limitations

The sample size is the main limitation to this study. Two IMs and seven academics do not represent the HE sector; hence a larger comprehensive study would offer more insight. Participant responses did not differentiate between types of student, for example: year of study, undergraduate, postgraduate, distance-learning, part-time.

5.2 Recommendations

While the research supports the power and use of BD, it is apparent how this knowledge is translated into interventions, and whether these interventions are effective at supporting students, are key questions. The research indicates that the use of BD to support student-retention post the GDPR is possible, but not in isolation; it is the actions and interventions that have an impact, together with student engagement with their academic community and the willingness to respond to guidance that maybe drawn from their LA data. Implementation of LA must be supported by:

- Co-creation of a LA approach designed with staff and students.
- A legal and ethical institutional-strategy, and purpose for using BD, informed by appropriate investigations.
- Commitment to data-quality and the collection of relevant datasets to accurately inform the LA solution.
- Commitment to enhance digital capabilities of staff.
- A framework of training and support for the role of Academic Advising that includes the GDPR.
- Change management plan to identify and address cultural issues.
- Commitment by institutional leadership to adequately resource the support services required to deliver interventions to all students that would benefit their academic journey.

References

1. Alblawi, A.S., Alhamed, A.A.: Big-data and learning analytics in higher education: demystifying variety, acquisition, storage, NLP and analytics. In: 2017 IEEE Conference on Big-Data and Analytics (ICBDA), pp. 124–129. IEEE, November 2017
2. Athey, S.: Beyond prediction: using big-data for policy problems. Science **355**(6324), 483 (2017)
3. Baker, R., Yacef, K.: The state of educational data mining in 2009: a review and future visions. JEDM I J. Educ. Data Mining **1**(1), 3–17 (2009). https://tinyurl.com/y65m9cel
4. Bertolucci, J.: Big-Data: A Practical Definition. UBM LLC, San Francisco (2013)
5. Bienkowski, M., Feng, M., Means, B.: Enhancing teaching and learning through educational data mining and LA: an issue brief. Office of Educational Technology, U.S. Department of Education (2012). https://tinyurl.com/y6znls4l
6. Boulton, C.A., Kent, C., Williams, H.T.P.: Virtual learning environment engagement and learning outcomes at a 'bricks-and-mortar' university. Comput. Educ. **126**, 129–142 (2018)
7. Boyd, D., Crawford, K.: Critical questions for big-data: provocations for a cultural, technological, and scholarly phenomenon. Inf. Commun. Soc. **15**(5), 662–679 (2012)
8. Braun, V., Clarke, V.: Using thematic analysis in psychology. Qual. Res. Psychol. **3**(2), 77–101 (2006)
9. Buchanan, E.A.: Internet Research Ethics: Past, Present, and Future. Wiley-Blackwell, Hoboken (2011)
10. Card, N.A.: Applied Meta-Analysis for Social Science Research. Guilford Publications, New York (2015)

11. Daniel, B.: Big-data and analytics in higher education: opportunities and challenges. Br. J. Edu. Technol. **46**(5), 904–920 (2015)
12. Denzin, N., Lincoln, Y.S.: The SAGE Handbook of Qualitative Research. Sage, Thousand Oaks (2011)
13. Dollinger, M., Lodge, J.M.: Co-creation strategies for LA. In: Proceedings of the 8th International Conference on LA and Knowledge (LAK 2018), pp. 97–101. ACM, New York (2018)
14. European Data Protection Supervisor (2018). https://tinyurl.com/ydy882pe
15. Farah, B.: Big-data - what data and why? J. Manag. Policy Pract. **17**(1), 11–17 (2016)
16. Faraj, S., Pachidi, S., Sayegh, K.: Working and organizing in the age of the learning algorithm. Inf. Organ. **28**(1), 62–70 (2018)
17. Ferguson, R., Clow, D., Macfadyen, L., Essa, A., Dawson, S., Alexander, S.: Setting LA in context: overcoming the barriers to large-scale adoption. Association for Computing Machinery (2014)
18. Foster, J., McLeod, J., Nolin, J., Greifeneder, E.: Data work in context: value, risks, and governance. J. Am. Soc. Inf. Sci. **69**(12), 1414–1427 (2018)
19. Greller, W., Drachsler, H.: Translating learning into numbers: a generic framework for LA. Educ. Technol. Soc. **15**(3), 42–57 (2012)
20. Gülbahar, Y., Ilgaz, H.: Premise of LA for Educational Context: Through Concept to Practice. Bilişim Teknolojileri Dergisi **7**(3) (2014). https://tinyurl.com/y29uueem
21. Holloway, I., Todres, L.: The status of method: flexibility, consistency and coherence. Qual. Res. **3**(3), 345–357 (2003)
22. Information Commissioner's Office (ICO): Guide to the General Data Protection Regulation (2018). https://tinyurl.com/y9jpbxmh
23. Jisc: LA in Higher Education: A review of UK and international practice Full report (2016). https://tinyurl.com/j4qcasg
24. Jisc: Code of practice for LA. Setting out the responsibilities of educational institutions to ensure that LA is carried out responsibly, appropriately and effectively (2018). https://tinyurl.com/huwpqrm
25. Johnson, S.L., Gray, P., Sarker, S.: Revisiting IS research practice in the era of big-data. Inf. Organ. **29**(1), 41–56 (2019)
26. Jokhan, A., Sharma, B., Singh, S.: Early warning system as a predictor for student performance in higher education blended courses. Stud. High. Educ. **44**, 1–12 (2018)
27. Kune, R., Konugurthi, P.K., Agarwal, A., Chillarige, R.R., Buyya, R.: The anatomy of BD computing. Softw. Pract. Exp. **46**(1), 79–105 (2016)
28. Landis, J.R., Koch, G.G.: The measurement of observer agreement for categorical data. Biometrics **33**, 159–174 (1977)
29. Lawson, C., Beer, C., Rossi, D., Moore, T., Fleming, J.: Identification of 'at risk' students using LA: the ethical dilemmas of intervention strategies in a higher education institution. Educ. Tech. Res. Dev. **64**(5), 957–968 (2016)
30. Lerman, J.: Big-data and its exclusions. Stan. Law Rev. Online **66**, 55–63 (2013). https://tinyurl.com/y69qkogk
31. Lim, S., Woo, J., Lee, J., Huh, S.Y.: Consumer valuation of personal information in the age of big-data. J. Assoc. Inf. Sci. Technol. **69**(1), 60–71 (2018)
32. Liu, M., Kang, J., Zou, W., Lee, H., Pan, Z., Corliss, S.: Using data to understand how to better design adaptive learning. Technol. Knowl. Learn. **22**(3), 271–298 (2017)
33. Macfadyen, L.P., Dawson, S.: Numbers are not enough. Why e-LA failed to inform an institutional strategic plan. Educ. Technol. Soc. **15**(3), 149–163 (2012)
34. Maciejewski, M.: To do more, better, faster and more cheaply: using BD in public administration. Int. Rev. Adm. Sci. **83**(1), 120–135 (2017)

35. Manyika, J., et al.: Big-data: the next frontier for innovation, competition and productivity. McKinsey Global Institute (2011). https://tinyurl.com/y5rrh58x
36. Mayer-Schönberger, V., Cukier, K.: Big-Data: A Revolution That Will Transform How We Live, Work and Think. John Murray, London (2013)
37. Miltgen, C.L., Smith, H.J.: Falsifying and withholding: exploring individuals' contextual privacy-related decision-making. Inf. Manag. 56(5), 696–717 (2019)
38. Na, K.S., Tasir, Z.: Identifying at-risk students in online learning by analysing learning behaviour: a systematic review. In: 2017 IEEE Conference on Big-data and Analytics (ICBDA), pp. 118–123. IEEE, November 2017
39. Nersessian, D.: The law and ethics of BD analytics: a new role for international human rights in the search for global standards. Bus. Horiz. 61(6), 845–854 (2018)
40. Pascarella, E.T., Terenzini, P.T.: Predicting freshman persistence and voluntary dropout decisions from a theoretical model. J. High. Educ. 51(1), 60–75 (1980)
41. Petticrew, M., Roberts, H.: Systematic Reviews in the Social Sciences: A Practical Guide. Wiley, Hoboken (2008)
42. Roberts, L.D., Howell, J.A., Seaman, K., Gibson, D.C.: Student attitudes toward LA in higher education: "the fitbit version of the learning world".(report)(author abstract). Front. Psychol. 7 (2016)
43. Saunders, M., Lewis, P., Thornhill, A.: Research Methods for Business Students, 7th edn. Pearson, Harlow (2016)
44. Slade, S., Prinsloo, P., Haythornthwaite, C., de Laat, M., Dawson, S.: Learning analytics: ethical issues and dilemmas. Am. Behav. Sci. 57(10), 1510–1529 (2013)
45. Social Market Foundation: On Course for Success? Student-retention at university (2017). https://tinyurl.com/y6nuolju
46. Spady, W.: Dropouts from higher education: an interdisciplinary review and synthesis. Interchange 1, 64–85 (1970)
47. Subotzky, G., Prinsloo, P.: Turning the tide: a socio-critical model and framework for improving student success in open distance learning at the university of south africa. Distance Educ. 32(2), 177–193 (2011)
48. Tempini, N.: Till data do us part: understanding data-based value creation in data-intensive infrastructures. Inf. Organ. 27(4), 191–210 (2017)
49. Tinto, V.: Research and practice of student-retention: what next? J. Coll. Student-Retention 8(1), 1–19 (2006)
50. Universities UK: The Funding Environment for Universities 2015. The Economic Role of UK Universities, June 2015. https://tinyurl.com/yyzrgxqy
51. Van, D.Z., Denessen, E., Cillessen, A.H.N., Meijer, P.C.: Domains and predictors of first-year student success: a systematic review. Educ. Res. Rev. 23, 57–77 (2018)
52. Wellington, J.J.: Educational Research: Contemporary Issues and Practical Approaches, 2nd edn. Bloomsbury Publishing, London (2015)
53. Williams, P.: Squaring the circle: a new alternative to alternative-assessment. Teach. High. Educ. 19(5), 565–577 (2014)
54. Williamson, B.: The hidden architecture of higher education: building a BD infrastructure for the 'smarter university.' Int. J. Educ. Technol. High. Educ. 15(1), 1–26 (2018)
55. Wilsdon, J.: Deliver us from rankers, April 2019. https://tinyurl.com/y4exo8y6
56. Wu, P.F., Vitak, J., Zimmer, M.T.: A contextual approach to information privacy research. J. Assoc. Inf. Sci. Technol. 71(4), 485–490 (2019)
57. Xie, K., Wu, Y., Xiao, J., Hu, Q.: Value co-creation between firms and customers: the role of big-data-based cooperative assets. Inf. Manag. 53(8), 1034–1104 (2016)

Understanding Parachuting Collaboration

Ajay Jaiswal[1(✉)], Meijun Liu[2], and Ying Ding[1,3]

[1] School of Information, University of Texas at Austin, Austin, TX, USA
ajayjaiswal@utexas.edu, ying.ding@ischool.utexas.edu
[2] Faculty of Education, University of Hong Kong,
Hong Kong, Hong Kong SAR, China
liumeijun917@gmail.com
[3] Dell Medical School, University of Texas at Austin, Austin, TX, USA

Abstract. In contemporary times, collaborative research has become the cynosure of knowledge production and it is widely acknowledged as a means of improving research quality, high impact, and credence. This paper explores an interesting style of collaborative research in which researchers with no prior collaboration history, come together for the first time to produce a scientific article (*parachuting collaboration*). Based on the empirical analysis of ~35.12 million articles in Microsoft Academic Graph (MAG) across 19 disciplines, we observed that *parachuting collaboration* has been dominating knowledge production and it has been prevalent in all the disciplines. A closer inspection revealed that there has been a consistent decrease in the parachuting collaboration in recent times. To investigate this behavior further, we analyzed all 19 disciplines in the MAG dataset and surprisingly, the percentage of decrease was not the same for all disciplines. In our study, we found that for the non-STEM disciplines, the decrease is comparatively lower than the STEM disciplines.

Keywords: Team formation · Parachuting collaborations

1 Introduction

A century ago, in the pre-internet era when the collaboration was onerous, individual scientists used to play a noteworthy role in scientific discoveries. However, in contemporary times we observe a universal trend of large team size in research and development, whereas solitary researches are almost diminishing. Various models have been developed with the goals of elucidating mechanisms of complex team formation in research environments. Wu et al. [16] have shown that smaller teams have tended to disrupt science and technology with new ideas and opportunities, whereas larger teams have tended to develop existing ones. Zeng et al. [17] introduced team freshness depending upon the prior collaboration of team members and argued that fresher teams tend to produce works of higher originality and more multi-disciplinary impact. Large country teams have been identified for having significant citation benefits because of the association of large numbers of authors and national affiliations in papers [8]. The formation of collaboration and team success depend on trust, reciprocity and risk sharing [1,5,6,14]. Entailing these beneficial factors of teams' construction and

K. Toeppe et al. (Eds.): iConference 2021, LNCS 12645, pp. 183–189, 2021.
https://doi.org/10.1007/978-3-030-71292-1_16

performance, repeat collaboration or persistent collaboration have been extensively studied in previous literature [4,7,12]. In this study, we focus on the foil of repeat collaboration, i.e., parachuting collaboration and explore another type of teams in which all team members have no prior collaboration. Though parachuting collaboration is considered involved less trust, reciprocity, risk sharing and more innovation costs, it is beneficial for producing novel scientific novelty as it could bring conflicts, new ideas and resources that contribute to the creation of scientific novelty [10,17].

2 Data and Methodology

2.1 Data Description

In this paper, we performed the empirical analysis on the comprehensive MAG (Microsoft Academic Graph) dataset with 178.89 million articles within 1800–2019. We considered articles published between 1970–2015 with available author information for experimentation. Since the current study entirely focuses on parachuting papers, we only include papers that are co-authored by two or more authors ($>=2$). We term this dataset as a filtered dataset (35.12 million) C_P, consisting of 19 disciplines namely - *History, Geology, Economics, Geography, Chemistry, Philosophy, Sociology, Materials science, Mathematics, Biology, Computer science, Political science, Engineering, Psychology, Environmental science, Business, Physics, Medicine, and Art*. For the rest of this paper, we conduct all our experiments on the filtered dataset (C_P) unless otherwise stated.

2.2 Methodology

In recent decades, teamwork is becoming mundane in modern scientific advancements. Several studies have unveiled that the average team size of scientific publications has significantly increased between 1950 to 2015. Many researchers and industries have been actively investigating team assembly mechanisms to maximize the impact/success of work and be frontiers of knowledge. In team formation models, the tendency of individual teams in selecting new team members to maximize performance remains unclear. In this paper, we address one trivialize, yet important team formation behavior - *Parachuting*, based on the prior collaboration relations between team members.

Parachuting Paper. A paper p will be considered as a parachuting paper if all its co-authors have collaborated for the first time, i.e. all of them have no prior collaboration relations before the publication date of p.

Consider a paper p published in year Y by a team of authors $A = A_1, A_2, \ldots, A_n$. Let $P = P^{A_1}, P^{A_2}, \ldots, P^{A_n}$ be the set of publications produced by team members before $(Y - \delta)$ time frame (we kept $\delta = 20$ for fair comparison). To check if paper P is a *parachuting paper*, we build a collaboration network of A such that:

$$AdjacencyMatrix[i, j] = 1, if P^{A_i} \cap P^{A_j} \neq \phi \tag{1}$$

the paper p will be a parachuting paper if each entry in the adjacency matrix is zero, i.e., no edge exists in the collaboration network. Since this work aims to better understand the parachuting behavior and it is relevant for a team, we have selected papers with team size $>= 2$ for our empirical study.

3   Empirical Study and Preliminary Results

In this section, we plan to empirically investigate the MAG dataset in an attempt to address the *parachuting collaborations*. The section begins by introducing our findings of the parachuting behavior in the MAG dataset and further explores its pervasiveness across all 19 disciplines in MAG. We also examined the parachuting trend with time, different team sizes, and attempted to provide plausible explanations to support the observations.

General Setting. The study is conducted on ~35.12 million papers with team size $>= 2$ across 19 disciplines between 1970–2015. For a paper $p \in C_P$, we disambiguated its author's details and rejected the paper if any author can not be identified. For a fair comparison, we have kept a time frame(δ) $= 20$ while preparing the set of prior publications for authors of p before publishing p.

The distribution of MAG data across 19 disciplines: Psychology (4.11%), Political science (0.44%), Mathematics (4.92%), Environmental science (0.42%), Computer science (9.01%), Medicine (17.52%), Biology (16.17%), History (0.58%), Physics (7.07%), Geology (2.29%), Engineering (9.20%), Philosophy (0.31%), Art (0.47%), Sociology (0.75%), Business (1.04%), Economics (1.92%), Chemistry (15.09%), Materials science (8.01%), Geography (0.71%).

Observation 1. *Parachuting is pervasive in MAG, across all the 19 disciplines.*

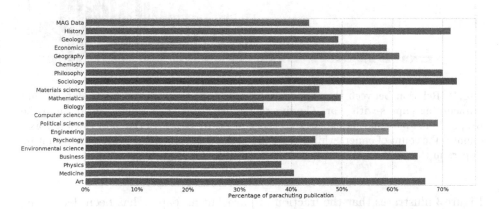

Fig. 1. Percentage of parachuting papers in MAG dataset and across 19 disciplines

Figure 1 illustrates the percentage of parachuting publications in MAG and 19 disciplines with 1970–2015. One immediate observation is the dominance of parachuting papers in the MAG dataset (43.42%), and across all the disciplines. However, dominance is much more significant in non-STEM disciplines such as History (71.5%), Philosophy (70.04%), Sociology (72.7%), Political Science (69.03%), and Art (66.5%). Very surprisingly, Psychology has only 44.4% of parachuting papers. However, the minimum parachuting effect is observed in science disciplines such as Biology (34.56%), Physics (38.06%), and Chemistry (37.98%). Papers of the engineering and technology domain have parachuting papers in the range of 40–50%. Thus, the overall suggestion is that the authors of non-STEM disciplines tend to collaborate more with fresh authors in comparison to the STEM fields.

Observation 2. *Parachuting behavior is decreasing with time, across all disciplines and team size.*

Figure 2 line plot shows that the parachuting effect has been continuously decreasing with time. One immediate observation is that with time the number of publications produced in a given year has increased exponentially while the growth rate of parachuting papers is not the same and falls behind. The line plot with a decreasing trend with year implies that even though the number of parachuting papers produced every year is increasing, its percentage with respect to the number of publications produced every year is decreasing, i.e. in recent times, authors prefer to collaborate with people they know in comparison to earlier times.

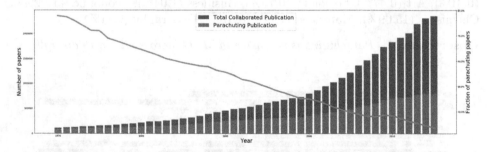

Fig. 2. Relation between the exponential growth of papers in the MAG dataset and parachuting papers with year. The line plot illustrates the continuous decrease in the proportion of parachuting papers with the year (1970–2015). In the plot, the left y-axis denotes the count of papers while the right y-axis denotes the percentage of parachuting papers in the total number of publications produced in a given year.

Figure 3 illustrates that the fraction of parachuting papers has been decreasing with time (1970–2015). However, the percentage change in the fraction of the parachuting papers within 45 years for different team size is different. We observe that percentage change decreases with an increase in team size. In the dataset, we observe the percentage decrease in parachuting papers for team size 3, 5, 8, and 10 to be −29.85%, −35.94%, −40.35%, and −45.10% respectively.

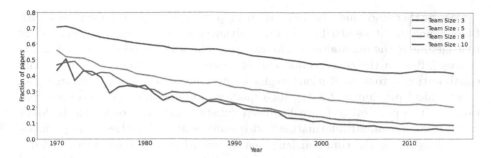

Fig. 3. Decrease in the proportion of parachuting papers with year (1970–2015) for different team sizes

A more detailed analysis of this behavior for different disciplines indicates that for the non-STEM disciplines, the decrease is comparatively lower than the STEM disciplines. Disciplines such as History (-29.37%), Geography (-35.19%), Philosophy (-30.55%), Sociology (-26.24%), Political Science (-34.31%), and Business (-32.35%) have observed a very low percentage decrease of parachuting papers in past 45 years while fields such as Physics (-56.43%), Computer Science (-52.18%), Biology (-53.24%), and Chemistry (-50.61%) have observed a significantly huge drop in parachuting papers.

4   Discussion

The trend toward team-based knowledge production in science requires in-depth investigations of the formation of teams and diverse collaborative behaviors. In contrast to the extensive literature that investigates repeat collaboration or persistent collaboration [4,7,12], this study focuses on co-authorship between two authors without prior collaboration that has been largely ignored in previous studies. Specifically, this study considers a research article in which all team members have not collaborated with each other in the past as a parachuting paper and explore this kind of scientific output produced by parachuting collaboration across diverse disciplines based on 35.12 million research articles in MAG.

Parachuting papers in which all co-authors have no prior collaboration are found to be prevalent across different disciplines, years, and team size, accounting for 43.42% in the MAG dataset. This suggests the significant importance of scientific teams where all team members have no prior collaboration in knowledge production. Teams are assembled for the need to incorporate researchers with diverse skills, ideas and resources. The tendency of researchers to repeat previous collaboration is documented in the literature on team assembly [7], while this study indicates the extensive existence of scientific teams constructed by researchers without prior collaboration that produce more than 40% of scientific knowledge in MAG.

We further find that the proportion of parachuting papers decreases with time, which might be attributed to the advancement of information technology that facilitates the maintaining of an existing collaborative relationship. Various factors influence the construction and maintaining of collaboration, especially collaboration across institutions, regions, and countries, such as language [13], geographical proximity [2,3,11], high quality of communication and coordination [9]. The physical distance has been substantially shortened due to lower travel costs, advanced information and communication facilities. The popularity of English as the common language in mainstream science also alleviates the language barriers of collaboration [15]. All the above changes are beneficial for researchers to sustain their previous collaboration linkages. Therefore, the proportion of parachuting papers witnessed a drop with time.

5   Conclusion and Future Work

In this paper, we performed a quantitative study of an important collaboration technique, *parachuting collaboration* using the MAG dataset. We identified that parachuting research has been a dominating knowledge production source and it has been prevalent across all disciplines of research. We found that the proportion of such collaborations is consistently decreasing in recent times and we tried to provide plausible explanations for such a trend. In the future, we would like to explore the characteristics of authors who collaborate in parachuting fashion and the comparative impact of the research produced by these collaborations with respect to non-parachuting collaborations.

References

1. Axelrod, R., Hamilton, W.: The evolution of cooperation. Science **211**(4489), 1390–1396 (1981)
2. Bennett, L.M., Gadlin, H.: Collaboration and team science. J. Invest. Med. **60**(5), 768–775 (2012)
3. Boschma, R.: Proximity and innovation: a critical assessment. Reg. Stud. **39**(1), 61–74 (2005)
4. Bu, Y., Ding, Y., Liang, X., Murray, D.S.: Understanding persistent scientific collaboration. J. Assoc. Inform. Sci. Technol. **69**(3), 438–448 (2017)
5. Cole, T., Teboul, J.B.: Non-zero-sum collaboration, reciprocity, and the preference for similarity: developing an adaptive model of close relational functioning. Pers. Relat. **11**(2), 135–160 (2004)
6. Frost-Arnold, K.: Moral trust & scientific collaboration. Stud. Hist. Philos. Sci. Part A **44**(3), 301–310 (2013)
7. Guimera, R., Uzzi, B., Spiro, J., Amaral, L.A.N.: Team assembly mechanisms determine collaboration network structure and team performance. Science **308**, 697–702 (2005)
8. Hsiehchen, D., Espinoza, M., Hsieh, A.: Multinational teams and diseconomies of scale in collaborative research. Sci. Adv. **1**(8), e1500211 (2015)
9. Lauto, G., Valentin, F.: How large-scale research facilities connect to global research. Rev. Policy Res. **30**(4), 381–408 (2013)

10. Liu, M., et al.: Can pandemics transform scientific novelty? evidence from COVID-19 (2020)
11. Ponds, R., Oort, F.V., Frenken, K.: The geographical and institutional proximity of research collaboration. Pap. Reg. Sci. **86**(3), 423–443 (2010)
12. Skilton, P.F., Dooley, K.J.: The effects of repeat collaboration on creative abrasion. Acad. Manage. Rev. **35**(1), 118–134 (2010)
13. Tenzer, H., Pudelko, M.: The influence of language differences on power dynamics in multinational teams. J. World Bus. **52**(1), 45–61 (2017)
14. Thomson, A.M., Perry, J.L.: Collaboration processes: inside the black box. Public Adm. Rev. **66**(s1), 20–32 (2006)
15. Waltman, L., Tijssen, R.J.W., Eck, N.J.V.: Globalisation of science in kilometres. J. Informetr. **5**(4), 574–582 (2011)
16. Wu, L., Wang, D., Evans, J.A.: Large teams develop and small teams disrupt science and technology. Nature **566**(7744), 378–382 (2019)
17. Zeng, A., Fan, Y., Di, Z., Wang, Y., Havlin, S.: The critical role of fresh teams in creating original and multi-disciplinary research (2020). https://arxiv.org/abs/2007.05985

Characterizing Research Leadership Flow Diffusion: Assortative Mixing, Preferential Attachment, Triadic Closure and Reciprocity

Chaocheng He[✉], Guiyan Ou, and Jiang Wu

Wuhan University, Wuhan 430000, China
2016201040025@whu.edu.cn

Abstract. Research leadership is of great significance to the research collaboration, especially in large scale projections. Characterizing the mechanisms and the processes of research leadership flow diffusion become essential to understand the knowledge flow diffusion in research collaboration. In this paper, we systemically analyze the differences in possibilities research leadership flow occurs between two researchers as seen from the effect of assortative mixing, preferential attachment, triadic closure, and reciprocity via Exponential Random Graph Model (ERGM). We demonstrate that combining both the researchers' attributes and topological feature effects (assortative mixing, preferential attachment, triadic closure and reciprocity) can better characterize the diffusion of research leadership flow.

Keywords: Exponential Random Graph Model (ERGM) · Research leadership · Research collaboration · Social network analysis

1 Introduction

Research collaboration has been a topic of perennial interest. It integrates Research collaborations measured by co-authorship relationships has been a classic topic of perennial interest in library and information sciences. It creates a synergetic effect among participants with complementary knowledge and expertise to address complex problems. It facilitates knowledge dissemination among individuals as well as the cross-fertilization among disciplines [1, 2]. Research leadership is of great significance to the whole research collaboration process. As is known that scientific research is not a simple linear accumulation of tasks, but an organic whole composed of various scientific research tasks, which have priority, logic, and interaction [3]. The logic and complexity of scientific research make research collaboration a highly nonlinear and uncertain process, which requires strong coordination and synchronization. It's found that leading authors are associated with not only the capability to recruit multiple resources and expertise to launch and sustain the collaborative project [4] but also the productivity of the collaboration team and the academic impact of the research outcome [5]. Research

© Springer Nature Switzerland AG 2021
K. Toeppe et al. (Eds.): iConference 2021, LNCS 12645, pp. 190–198, 2021.
https://doi.org/10.1007/978-3-030-71292-1_17

leadership thus becomes crucial to the whole collaboration process [5]. Characterizing the mechanisms and the processes of research leadership flow diffusion becomes essential to understand the knowledge flow diffusion in research collaboration.

From a bibliometrics point of view, a common measurement of research leadership is based on the authorship position. The first author and the corresponding author often lead the research collaboration and make a major contribution [6], and have been widely used as proxies for research leader [7, 8]. The strength of the collaboration relationship with leading authors is more pronounced, compared with those between participating authors. He, Wu [9] propose the notion and measurement of research leadership flow and research leadership network at the institutional level. In this paper, we study research leadership flow at the individual level. The research leadership flow is defined as a directed co-authorship relation from the leading author (the first author/corresponding author) to the participating authors in research collaboration. The research leadership network is a directed network, where nodes are researchers and edges are research leadership flows from leading authors to participating authors.

For mechanisms and processes of research collaboration, existing studies mainly focus on the inclusion of topological features and other node attributes as independent variables, relying on statistical models such as regression analysis. Statistical models for inference are based on independent assumptions. However, social network indices violate independent assumptions. To this end, we adopt the Exponential Random Graph Model (ERGM), which is based on relational data and dependent hypothesis. The basic assumption of ERGM is that the observed network results from a stochastic process incorporating both covariate effects of node attributes and topological features. ERGM aims to explain the stochastic process by testing hypotheses derived from theory. According to network science, there are four fundamental mechanisms of directed network formation and evolution [10–13]. Assortative mixing describes how nodes in a network prefer to connect with other nodes who have similarities to themselves [14]. The preferential attachment mechanism refers to that the more existing ties one node has, the more ties the node will obtain in the future [15]. Triadic closure mechanism refers to that if node i is connected to node j and node j is connected to node k, then node i is likely to be connected to node k [16]. Reciprocity describes the situation that in research collaboration, node i leads node j in one publication, and later node j at least leads node i once in another publication. These four mechanisms are observed in a broad range of scholarly collaboration and citation networks [17, 18].

We adopt ERGM to incorporating both the node attributes and topological features of the research leadership network to characterizing research leadership flow diffusion. Specifically, we aim to address the following two questions. 1) whether the node attributes (assortative mixing effect) and topological feature (preferential attachment, triadic closure effects, and reciprocity) simultaneously influence the formation of a research leadership network? 2) What roles do assortative mixing, preferential attachment, triadic closure, and reciprocity effects play in forming a research leadership network?

2 Related Work and Hypotheses

2.1 The Role of Assortative Mixing

As a fundamental rule that regulates tie formation of a social network, assortative mixing theories posit that the similarities in the individual characteristics may lead to similar behavior preferences, reduce communication costs and predispose individuals to correlate with each other [19]. Notably, in a research collaboration network, researchers are more likely to collaborate if they are similar in activity level, impact, research interest, gender [10], and spatial proximity [20]. In the research leadership network, on the one hand, leading authors tend to identify high-quality participating researchers in their research. On the other hand, research participating authors tend to find high-credibility leading authors to form teams to undertake new projects. Based on the discussion above, the following hypotheses are proposed.

H1. Assortative mixing effect plays a significant role in the formation of a research leadership network.

More specifically, we detailed the H1 into the following sub-hypotheses:

H1a. Assortative mixing effect in terms of activity level influence the generation of research leadership flows in a research leadership network.
H1b. Assortative mixing effect in terms of academic impact influence the generation of research leadership flows in a research leadership network.
H1c. Assortative mixing effect in terms of research interests influences the generation of research leadership flows in a research leadership network.
H1d. Assortative mixing effect in terms of geographical proximity influence the generation of research leadership flows in a research leadership network.

2.2 The Role of Preferential Attachment

Apart from the node attributes' effect, a social network can be shaped by the topological features. According to social capital theory, users with higher relational social capital have a higher chance to access and benefit from social resources [21]. If a user has many followers, he has strong social structural influence in the network and can easily attract attention and interaction from others [22]. Similarly, in a research collaboration network, Zhang [10] found that the number of new collaborators one researcher obtain is positively related to the existing number of collaborators of him. Based on the above discussion, the following hypotheses are proposed:

H2. Preferential attachment plays a significant role in the formation of a research leadership network.

2.3 The Role of Triadic Closure

Given three actors u, v, and w, where u and v are connected, v and w are connected, triadic closure measures how likely u and w are connected [23]. Such interdependence among nodes means that a local disturbance may lead to global consequences for the network structure. Franceschet [17] found that the effect of triadic closure in journal publication co-authorship networks is higher than that in conference co-authorship networks. In a research leadership network, triadic closure captures that researcher i leads researcher j, researcher j leads researcher k, and researcher i leads researcher k. Thus, we propose the following hypothesis,

H3. The effect of triadic closure plays a significant role in the formation of a research leadership network.

2.4 The Role of Reciprocity

The reciprocity is only for directed networks and is one of the most patterns in social interactions [24]. Actors who receive information or resources from others are expected to return them back too. The number and length of replies that a user received is found to be positively related to the number and length of posts he sends in the online healthcare community [25]. Similarly, in the research leadership network, we propose that a research leading-participating relationship is a form of social exchange, which is conducive to promote the resource and expertise exchange between researchers. Hence, we propose the following hypothesis:

H4. The effect of reciprocity plays a significant role in the formation of a research leadership network.

3   Data and Methods

This section focuses on the construction of research data and the model that induces the results.

3.1   Dataset

We leverage the Web of Science Core Citation Database (WOS) to collect publications in the pharmaceutical field [26] during 2010–2019. Specifically, the search query for data collection is "WC = A AND PY = B AND LANGUAGE = 'English'" where A is one of the sub-categories in the pharmaceutical field and B is "2010–2019." Non-journal publications such as meeting abstracts, letters are excluded. In total, 528,118 publications are retrieved. We conducted the author name disambiguation following [27]. Eventually, we obtained 481,079 distinct authors [28, 29]. Moreover, we used Google Map API to obtain the authors' cities. We measure the activity level using two metrics [10]: the number of leading-authored (first/corresponding-authored) publications, the number of non-leading-authored publications. We measure the academic impact of a researcher using the h-index. As for research interest similarity, we apply paper-to-vector [30] to represent the abstract of the publication into a 128-dimensional vector. The research interest similarity of two researchers is measured by the cosine similarity of the two researchers' addition of vectors of their publications. The geographical proximity is measured by whether two researchers are from the same city. For a directed network, the preferential attachment is measured by geometrically weighted indegree (gwidegree) and geometrically weighted outdegree (gwodegree) [11]. We measure the triadic closure in a directed network using geometrically weighted edge-wise shared partners (gwesp) [11]. We measure the reciprocity as the ratio of the number of edges pointing bidirectionally in the total number of edges [13].

3.2   Construction of Research Leadership Network

The whole research leadership network is a large-scale network, and its' computational cost of ERGM parameter fitting is relatively high. Following [10, 12], we first rank the researchers by the number of leading-authored publications. Considering the network sparseness, initially, we wanted to select the top 1000 researchers. Because the researcher ranked from 952 to 1119, all have 18 leading-authored publications. We exclude these researchers and select the top 951 researchers as our dataset. Each researcher corresponds to a node in the research leadership network. If two researchers have collaborated in one paper and at least one of them is a leading author, a directed tie is added from the leading author to the participating author. Since we do not consider the strength of research leadership flow, the network is binary [10].

3.3   Exponential Random Graph Model

We employ ERGM to model the probability of observing research leadership network y from a random network Y conditioning on various local network configurations $g_a(y, X)$. Significantly, the probability of observing the current research leadership network (y) can be parameterized in the following form [10, 13, 31]:

$$P(Y = y|X) = \frac{\exp\left\{\sum_{a=1}^{A} \theta_a^T g_a(y, X)\right\}}{\kappa}, \tag{1}$$

where X is a matrix of attributes (covariate vector) for nodes and edges. A is the set of all network configurations. $g_a(y, X)$ refers to the network statistics corresponding to configuration a, and is determined by

$$g_a(y, X) = \begin{cases} 1, & \text{the configuration is observed in the network } y \\ 0, & \text{otherwise} \end{cases}, \tag{2}$$

θ_a is the coefficients corresponding to configurations $g_a(y, X)$. κ is a normalizing term to satisfy the probability sum to 1.

ERGM estimates the prevalence of all configurations. We adopt MCMCMLE (Markov Chian Monte Carlo Maximum Likelihood Estimation) to maximize the possibility of the observed research leadership network structure [32].

4   Results

4.1   ERGM Parameter Estimation

We fit the ERGM twice. In the first ERGM (Model 1), we exam the effects of researchers' attributes on the generation of ties in the research leadership network. Therefore, we model the main and assortative mixing effects of the researchers' attributes [10]. In the second ERGM (Model 2), we exam both the effects of researchers' attributes and topological features. The results of ERGM parameter estimation are reported in Table 1. The existence of a specific configuration in the observed network is reflected by the significance of its' corresponding parameter. We adopt AIC (Akaike Information Criterion) to compare the ERGM models. A model with the smallest AIC is considered to be the best [33]. Table 1 shows that Model 2, which includes both researchers' attributes and topological features, has a better fit. Thus, researchers' attributes and topological features simultaneously affect the generation of research leadership network. For the effects of researchers' attributes, Model 1 and Model 2 yield similar results, indicating that modeling of researchers' attributes is reliable.

Specifically, for the main effect and assortative mixing effect of researchers' attributes, we notice that researchers' activity level and academic impact have a significant main effect on the research leadership flow diffusion in both models. According to the estimates, the addition of one more unit of leading-authored/non-leading-authored publication to one researcher will increase the probability of the researcher's forming new research leadership flow by 1% ($e^{0.01}-1$). And the addition of one more unit of h-index to one researcher will increase the probability of the researcher's forming new research leadership flow by is 2% ($e^{0.02}-1$). From the perspective of the assortative mixing effect, the gap of non-leading-authored publications and h-index between two researchers can significantly and positively affect the formation of research leadership flow between them, showing a counter-assortative-mixing effect. This is different from findings in [10]. It's noteworthy that the research leadership relationship is different from the collaboration relationship. In a research leadership network, research leadership flow occurs more likely in researchers with different academic impact and activity levels. This finding is in line with the phenomenon that the corresponding author is usually a mentor figure who plays a leading role while participating authors generally play more specialized roles [34]. Research interest similarity has a significant and positive effect on the formation of research leadership flow. Leading authors/participating authors tend to find participating authors/leading authors who have similar research interests. Thus, hypothesis H1c is supported. The effect of geographical proximity is significant and positive in both Model 1and Model 2, supporting H1d. Researchers tend to lead/participate in collaborations close to them. This is in line with the finding that geographical distance is an essential hindering factor of research leadership flow [9].

For network structural features, the effect of geometrically weighted indegree (gwidegree) is positive and weak. By contrast, the effect of geometrically weighted outdegree (gwodegree) is positive and significant. In a research leadership network, a large gwodegree means a researcher has been serving as leading authors many times in collaborations. The more times a researcher leads others in collaboration, the more new research leadership flow will occur between him and others. This confirms many previous findings, such as [10, 35]. Thus hypothesis H2 is verified. The effect of triadic closure is positive and significant. Triadic closure strongly influences the research leadership flow. The probability of one researcher a to lead her/his participating author b's participating author c is 1.28 ($e^{0.25}$) times the probability of a does not lead c. Thus hypothesis H3 is verified. The significant and positive effect of mutual indicates that the reciprocity effect strongly influences research leadership flow. If a researcher leads others this time, others also tend to lead the researcher in the future. This is in line with the finding in [13] that users tend to reply reciprocally in online government microblogs. Thus, hypothesis H4 is verified.

Table 1. ERGM parameter estimation results

Variables	Estimate	
	Model 1	Model 2
Main effect		
Activity level (no. Leading-authored publications)	0.01^{***}	0.01^{*}
Activity level (no. Non-leading-authored publications)	0.02^{***}	0.01^{*}
Academic impact (h-index)	0.02^{***}	0.02^{*}
Assortative mixing		
Activity level (leading-authored publications no. Difference)	0.12	0.02
Activity level (non-leading-authored publications no. Difference)	0.34^{*}	0.25^{*}
Academic impact (h-index no. Difference)	0.57	0.17^{*}
Research interest similarity	0.01^{*}	0.04^{*}
Geographical proximity (the same city)	2.59^{***}	0.62^{*}
Preferential attachment		
Geometrically weighted indegree (gwidegree)	–	0.05
Geometrically weighted outdegree (gwodegree)	–	0.61^{**}
Triadic closure		
Geometrically weighted edgewise shared partner distribution (gwesp)	–	0.12^{***}
Reciprocity		
Mutual	–	5.59^{**}
Edges	-9.23^{***}	-8.43^{***}
Model Fit: AIC (Smaller is better)	10286	9832

Note: We implement ERGM using a widely adopted R statnet package (https://www.statnet.org/). *: $p < 0.05$; **: $p < 0.01$; ***: $p < 0.001$.

5   Discussions and Conclusions

This paper offers a systemic analysis of the research leadership network by incorporating both the researchers' attributes and network topological features using ERGM. The effects of researchers' attributes include activity level (leading-authored publication number, non-leading-authored publication number), academic impact (h-index), research interests, and spatial proximity, as well as the assortative mixing effect on these attributes. The effects of topological features include preferential attachment, triadic closure, and reciprocity. Specifically, for researchers' attributes, the higher activity level/academic impact a researcher has, the more likely She/he can from research leadership flow with others. Interestingly, researchers tend to lead/participate in others if others are different from themselves in terms of h-index, non-leading-authored publication number. Researchers tend to lead/participate in others who are geographically close to them and have similar research interests. For topological features, the preferential attachment, triadic closure, and reciprocity significantly affect the diffusion of research leadership flow. Combining both the researchers' attributes and topological feature effects can better characterize the diffusion of research leadership flow.

In the future, we plan to study the research leadership flow diffusion, knowledge diffusion, and their interaction at multi-dimensional network level incorporating collaboration network, citation network.

References

1. Fernández, A., Ferrándiz, E., León, M.D.: Proximity dimensions and scientific collaboration among academic institutions in Europe: the closer, the better? Scientometrics 106(3), 1073–1092 (2016). https://doi.org/10.1007/s11192-015-1819-8
2. Jiang, L., et al.: The relationships between distance factors and international collaborative research outcomes: a bibliometric examination. J. Inf. 12(3), 618–630 (2018)
3. Zaccaro, S.J., Rittman, A.L., Marks, M.A.: Team leadership. Leadersh. Quart. 12(4), 451–483 (2001)
4. Wagner, C.S., et al.: Science and technology collaboration: Building capability in developing countries. RAND CORP, Santa Monica (2001)
5. Klavans, R., Boyack, K.: Toward an objective, reliable and accurate method for measuring research leadership. Scientometrics 82(3), 539–553 (2010)
6. Chinchilla-Rodríguez, Z., Sugimoto, C.R., Larivière, V.: Follow the leader: On the relationship between leadership and scholarly impact in international collaborations. PloS one 14(6) (2019)
7. Zhou, J., Zeng, A., Fan, Y., Di, Z.: Identifying important scholars via directed scientific collaboration networks. Scientometrics 114(3), 1327–1343 (2017). https://doi.org/10.1007/s11192-017-2619-0
8. Wang, L., Wang, X.: Who sets up the bridge? Tracking scientific collaborations between China and the European Union. Res. Eval. 26(2), 124–131 (2017)
9. He, C., Wu, J., Zhang, Q.: Research leadership flow determinants and the role of proximity in research collaborations. J. Assoc. Inf. Sci. Technol. (2019)
10. Zhang, C., et al.: Understanding scientific collaboration: Homophily, transitivity, and preferential attachment. J. Am. Soc. Inf. Sci. 69(1), 72–86 (2018)
11. Peng, T.-Q.: Assortative mixing, preferential attachment, and triadic closure: a longitudinal study of tie-generative mechanisms in journal citation networks. J. Inf. 9(2), 250–262 (2015)
12. Wang, B., Bu, Y., Xu, Y.: A quantitative exploration on reasons for citing articles from the perspective of cited authors. Scientometrics 116(2), 675–687 (2018). https://doi.org/10.1007/s11192-018-2787-6
13. Xiong, J., Feng, X., Tang, Z.: Understanding user-to-User interaction on government microblogs: an exponential random graph model with the homophily and emotional effect. Inf. Process. Manag. 102229 (2020)
14. Peng, T.-Q., et al.: Follower-followee network, communication networks, and vote agreement of the US members of congress. Commun. Res. 43(7), 996–1024 (2016)

15. Barabási, A.-L., Albert, R.: Emergence of scaling in random networks. Science **286**(5439), 509–512 (1999)
16. Newman, M.E.: Clustering and preferential attachment in growing networks. Phys. Rev. E **64**(2), 025102 (2001)
17. Franceschet, M.: Collaboration in computer science: a network science approach. J. Am. Soc. Inform. Sci. Technol. **62**(10), 1992–2012 (2011)
18. Jiang, S., et al.: The roles of sharing, transfer, and public funding in nanotechnology knowledge-diffusion networks. J. Am. Soc. Inf. Sci. **66**(5), 1017–1029 (2015)
19. Kim, K., Altmann, J.: Effect of homophily on network formation. Commun. Nonlinear Sci. Numer. Simul. **44**, 482–494 (2017)
20. Cimenler, O., Reeves, K.A., Skvoretz, J.: An evaluation of collaborative research in a college of engineering. J. Inf. **9**(3), 577–590 (2015)
21. Hwang, H., Kim, K.O.: Social media as a tool for social movements: the effect of social media use and social capital on intention to participate in social movements. Int. J. Consum. Stud. **39**(5), 478–488 (2015)
22. Ye, Q., et al.: Can social capital be transferred cross the boundary of the real and virtual worlds? An empirical investigation of Twitter (2012)
23. Schank, T., Wagner, D.: Approximating clustering coefficient and transitivity. J. Graph Algorithms Appl. **9**(2), 265–275 (2005)
24. Ostrom, E.: A behavioral approach to the rational choice theory of collective action: presidential address, American political science association. Am. Polit. Sci. Rev. **1998**, 1–22 (1997)
25. Pan, W., Shen, C., Feng, B.: You get what you give: understanding reply reciprocity and social capital in online health support forums. J. Health Commun. **22**(1), 45–52 (2017)
26. Plotnikova, T., Rake, B.: Collaboration in pharmaceutical research: exploration of country-level determinants. Scientometrics **98**(2), 1173–1202 (2013). https://doi.org/10.1007/s11192-013-1182-6
27. Sinatra, R., et al.: Quantifying the evolution of individual scientific impact. Science **354**(6312), aaf5239 (2016)
28. Liu, Z., Xie, X., Chen, L.: Context-aware academic collaborator recommendation. In: Proceedings of the 24th ACM SIGKDD International Conference on Knowledge Discovery & Data Mining (2018)
29. Zhang, J.: Uncovering mechanisms of co-authorship evolution by multirelations-based link prediction. Inf. Process. Manage. **53**(1), 42–51 (2017)
30. Zhang, Y., Zhao, F., Lu, J.: P2V: large-scale academic paper embedding. Scientometrics **121**(1), 399–432 (2019). https://doi.org/10.1007/s11192-019-03206-9
31. Robins, G., et al.: An introduction to exponential random graph (p*) models for social networks. Soc. Netw. **29**(2), 173–191 (2007)
32. Handcock, M.S., et al.: statnet: software tools for the representation, visualization, analysis and simulation of network data. J. Stat. Softw. **24**(1), 1548 (2008)
33. Goodreau, S.M., Kitts, J.A., Morris, M.: Birds of a feather, or friend of a friend? Using exponential random graph models to investigate adolescent social networks. Demography **46**(1), 103–125 (2009)
34. Sekara, V., et al.: The chaperone effect in scientific publishing. Proc. Natl. Acad. Sci. U.S.A. **115**(50), 12603–12607 (2018)
35. Wang, D., Song, C., Barabási, A.-L.: Quantifying long-term scientific impact. Science **342**(6154), 127–132 (2013)

An Author Interest Discovery Model Armed with Authorship Credit Allocation Scheme

Shuo Xu[1] , Ling Li[1] , Liyuan Hao[1] , Xin An[2(✉)] , and Guancan Yang[3]

[1] College of Economics and Management, Beijing University of Technology,
No. 100 PingLeYuan, Chaoyang District, Beijing 100124, People's Republic of China
xushuo@bjut.edu.cn, {infinitell,haoliyuan}@emails.bjut.edu.cn
[2] School of Economics and Management, Beijing Forestry University, No. 35 Qinghua
East Road, Haidian District, Beijing 100083, People's Republic of China
anxin@bjfu.edu.cn
[3] School of Information Resource Management, Renmin University of China, No. 59
Zhongguancun Street, Haidian District, Beijing 100872, People's Republic of China
yanggc@ruc.edu.cn

Abstract. The author interest discovery can help personalized academic recommendation systems. However, many topic models for discovering author interest implicitly assume equal contribution from each coauthor to a target document. To loosen this limitation, a novel model, AT^{credit}, is proposed to strengthen the Author-Topic (AT) model with an authorship credit allocation scheme, and the collapsed Gibbs sampling is utilized to approximate the posterior and estimate the model parameters. In total, our model considers six counting schemes, including fixed and flexible versions, as well as equal contributors and hyper-authorship strategies.

Keywords: Author interest discovery · Topic model · Perplexity

1 Introduction

The author interest discovery can help personalized academic recommendation systems (i.e., Microsoft Academic and Google Scholar) to answer a range of important questions, such as which themes each researcher prefers to, which scientific publications each scholar is more likely to read, and which researchers are similar to each other in terms of their expertise. In view of the growing volume of online documents available through the Internet, this task is of great practical significance.

Ever since the LDA (Latent Dirichlet Allocation) model [6], topic modeling has long been utilized to characterize theme structures of a document collection with various purposes [23,29,32]. Variants of the LDA model specific for author interest discovery are also attracting extensive attentions, such as Author-Topic (AT) model [18], Author-Topic over Time (AToT) model [20,30,31], Author-Persona-Topic (APT) model [16], and Author-Interest-Topic (AIT) model [12].

This research received the financial support from the National Natural Science Foundation of China under grant number 72074014 and 72004012.

© Springer Nature Switzerland AG 2021
K. Toeppe et al. (Eds.): iConference 2021, LNCS 12645, pp. 199–207, 2021.
https://doi.org/10.1007/978-3-030-71292-1_18

On closer examination, it readily makes clear that there is usually a uniform distribution assumption for the author list of a document in these models. That is, each coauthor is implicitly assumed to equally contribute to a target document. Obviously, it is not in line with our intuition. In this work, AT model [18] is generalized to take into consideration authorship credit allocation scheme. It is worth noting that the idea in the $\mathrm{AT^{credit}}$ model is also applicable to other similar models as above.

2   Author Interest Discovery Model

This novel model, renamed as $\mathrm{AT^{credit}}$, degenerates to the AT model when indiscriminate counting scheme is adopted. To say it in another way, AT model is a particular case of our model. For convenience, the notations are summarized in Table 1, and the graphical model representations of the AT and $\mathrm{AT^{credit}}$ models are shown in Fig. 1. The $\mathrm{AT^{credit}}$ model can also be described from the viewpoint of generative process as follows:

Table 1. Notations used in the AT and $\mathrm{AT^{credit}}$ models

Symbol	Description
K	Number of topics
M	Number of documents
V	Number of unique words
A	Number of unique authors
N_m	Number of word tokens in the document m
A_m	Number of authors in the document m
a_m	Byline information in the document m
c_m	Authorship credit allocation in the document m
ϑ_a	Multinomial distribution of topics specific to the author a
φ_k	Multinomial distribution of words specific to the topic k
$z_{m,n}$	Topic associated with the n-th token in the document m
$w_{m,n}$	n-th token in the document m
$x_{m,n}$	Author associated with the word token $w_{m,n}$
λ	Parameter in an authorship credit allocation scheme
α, β	Dirichlet priors (hyperparameter)

(a) For each topic $k \in [1, K]$, draw $\varphi_k \sim \beta$;
(b) For each author $a \in [1, A]$, draw $\vartheta_a \sim \alpha$;
(c) For each document $m \in [1, M]$, calculate c_m according to a designated authorship credit allocation schema;

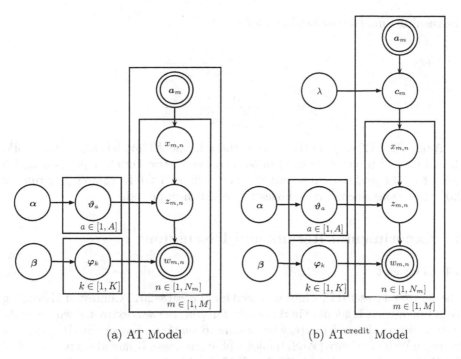

(a) AT Model   (b) AT^{credit} Model

Fig. 1. The graphical model representation of (a) AT and (b) AT^{credit} models

(d) For each document $m \in [1, M]$ and each word token $n \subset [1, N_m]$ in the document m, draw $x_{m,n} \sim c_m$, $z_{m,n} \sim \vartheta_{x_{m,n}}$, and then $w_{m,n} \sim \varphi_{a_{m,n}}$

As with many well-known topic models [3, 6, 20, 23, 31, 32], posterior inference cannot be done exactly in this model. For sake of comparison, the collapsed Gibbs sampling is also used in this study. In the collapsed Gibbs sampling procedure, one needs to calculate the posterior distribution, viz., conditional distributions of the hidden random variables (z and x) given the observations and other hidden variables, $\Pr(z_{m,n}, x_{m,n}|w, z_{\neg(m,n)}, x_{\neg(m,n)}, a, c, \alpha, \beta)$, where $z_{\neg(m,n)}$ and $x_{\neg(m,n)}$ represents respective topic and author assignments for all word tokens except $w_{m,n}$. After a simple derivation, the posterior distributions can be formally expressed as follows:

$$\Pr(z_{m,n}, x_{m,n}|w, z_{\neg(m,n)}, x_{\neg(m,n)}, a, c, \alpha, \beta, \lambda)$$

$$\propto \frac{n_{z_{m,n}}^{(w_{m,n})} + \beta_{w_{m,n}} - 1}{\sum_{v=1}^{V} \left(n_{z_{m,n}}^{(v)} + \beta_v \right) - 1} \times \frac{n_{x_{m,n}}^{(z_{m,n})} + \alpha_{z_{m,n}} - 1}{\sum_{k=1}^{K} \left(n_{x_{m,n}}^{(k)} + \alpha_k \right) - 1} \times c_{m, x_{m,n}} \quad (1)$$

where $n_k^{(v)}$ is the number of times that the tokens of word v is assigned to the topic k, and $n_a^{(k)}$ represents the number of times which the author a is assigned to the topic k. The first two terms in Eq. (1) is the same as those in the AT model [18]. Using the expectation of Dirichlet distribution, one can easily obtain the resulting model parameters as follows:

$$\varphi_{k,v} = \frac{n_k^{(v)} + \beta_v}{\sum_{v=1}^{V} (n_k^{(v)} + \beta_v)} \tag{2}$$

$$\vartheta_{a,k} = \frac{n_a^{(k)} + \alpha_k}{\sum_{k=1}^{K} (n_a^{(k)} + \alpha_k)} \tag{3}$$

Again, Eqs. (2)–(3) are the same as those in the AT model [18]. In this work, the number of topics K is fixed to 50, and symmetric Dirichlet priors α and β are set at 0.1 and 0.01, respectively. The collapsed Gibbs sampling is run for 2,000 iterations, including 500 ones for the burn-in period.

3   Experimental Results and Discussions

3.1   Dataset

The *SynBio* dataset [17], which was used for the 2018–2019 Contest of Measuring Tech Emergence, is adopted in this work. This dataset was extracted with a deliberately distorted search strategy pertaining to *synthetic biology* (SynBio) domain from the Web of Science (WoS) bibliographic database. It includes a partial set of SynBio research records from 2003 to 2012. In this dataset, there are three duplications with UID = "WOS:000246296800029" and "WOS:000247372300026", UID = "WOS:000297670800005" and "WOS:000293697700003", and UID = "WOS:000393719000030" and "WOS:000394061000172". In the meanwhile, a record with UID = "WOS:000260935200001" is not attached any authors at all. This study remains one copy of three duplicate records and removes the record without authors. In addition, three coauthors are missed from the record with UID = "WOS:000365103600006". This work supplements missed coauthors manually. In the end, the number of publications in our dataset is 2,580.

To reduce the influence of ambiguous names [10] on the performance of author interest discovery, the authors' names are disambiguated with a revised rule-based scoring and clustering method and then checked manually one by one [28]. In total, we obtain 9,990 unique scholars. Figure 2 illustrates the distribution of publications with the number of authors. The scholarly articles with 2–7 authors accounts for 79.46%, and single-authored and hyper-authored ones (i.e., with more than ten authors) [7] for 6.09% and 4.50% respectively. As noted in [24], this indicates that teams increasingly dominate the production of knowledge. In our dataset, the maximum number of authors of a publication is 53 (UID = "WOS:000273783100027"). Table 2 reports the distribution of authors with the number of articles. The great majority of authors appear in only one article.

As we all know, though data quality has improved significantly over the past decade, the WoS database is not free of errors [27]. As for byline information of an interested publication, only author list is usually recorded as well as the corresponding author (referred to as reprint authors in the WoS database). If

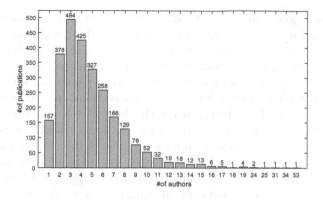

Fig. 2. The distribution of publications with the number of authors

Table 2. The distribution of authors with the number of articles

#of articles	1	2	3	4	5	6	7	8	9	10	11	12	16	17	18	22	29
#of authors	8,713	832	230	84	52	24	19	9	7	11	2	2	1	1	1	1	1

a scholarly article has multiple corresponding authors, or is attached with several equally contributing authors, the WoS database does not seem to register these information. Hence, this study retrieves all full-texts from the Internet in the format of PDF, and checks the resulting authorship ordering one by one. In out dataset, 136 articles (5.27%) did not explicitly state the corresponding author at all. The number of scientific publications with multiple first authors and corresponding authors are 233 (9.03%) and 208 (8.06%), respectively. In the meanwhile, there are 13 academic articles of multiple equally contributing authors with the role of neither the first author nor the corresponding author. In addition, this work conducts the same preprocessing operations with those in [26] and [28].

4 Experimental Results and Discussions

In this work, six authorship credit allocation schemes are taken into consideration: arithmetic counting schema [1,11,22], geometric counting schema [2,8], harmonic counting schema [9,15], network-based counting schema [13], axiomatic counting schema [21], and golden number counting schema [4]. To identify a proper parameter λ in each authorship credit allocation scheme and to further assess the performance of each scheme with tuned parameter, we divided our dataset into a training set of 2,348 documents and a test set of 232 ones. In this splitting procedure, the following constraint is imposed: each author in the test set must appear at least one of the training documents. It is not trivial to group our dataset into two disjoint subsets, since our problem can be actually viewed as a *multi-label learning task* [25] if the involved authors are seen as the resulting labels. To cope with this problem, after applying the stratification method in [19], the instances, which do not follow above constraint, are moved from the test set to training set and several solo-articles are also added into the test set.

To reduce the impact of the flexible parameter λ in authorship credit allocation scheme, the optimal parameter is identified on the training set in term of perplexity [5]. Table 3 summarizes the optimal parameter setting for each scheme. From Table 3, several interesting observations can be readily seen as follows. First, 4 out of 6 schemes reach the best status where resulting fixed versions are assumed, regardless of the hyper-authorship strategy. Second, from the perspective of hyper-authorship strategy, the authorship credit allocation schemes can be grouped into two categories: (1) arithmetic counting scheme and axiomatic counting scheme, and (2) geometric counting scheme, harmonic counting scheme, network-based counting and golden number counting scheme. Third, any scheme of unequal coauthorship credit allocation outperforms that of equal counterpart in term of perplexity. It is evident that our AT^{credit} model performs better than AT model. Last but not least, as for network-based counting scheme with enabled hyper-authorship strategy, when the parameter $\lambda \geq 0.7$, the performance of our AT^{credit} seems to be insensitive to this parameter.

Table 3. The optimal parameter setting for each authorship credit allocation scheme

Scheme	Hyper-authorship strategy	Optimal parameter
Arithmetic counting	Disabled	$\frac{2}{A_m(A_m-1)}$
	Enabled	$\frac{2}{A_m(A_m-1)}$
Geometric counting	**Disabled**	3.50
	Enabled	3.25
Harmonic counting	**Disabled**	∞
	Enabled	∞
Network-based counting	**Disabled**	0.8
	Enabled	0.7
Axiomatic counting	Disabled	1.0
	Enabled	1.0
Golden number counting	**Disabled**	1.0
	Enabled	1.0

After our AT^{credit} model, armed with each authorship credit allocation scheme with tuned parameter in Table 3, is trained on the train set, five chains of collapsed Gibbs sampling are respectively run for 500 iterations on the test set. Then, the perplexities from these five chains are averaged, and reported in Table 4. It is very surprising that the network-based counting scheme performs the worst in term of perplexity, which is very different from the observation in [13]. Amongst the other schemes, the perplexities between the top and other schemes are very close and their difference does not seem to be much discriminative. This is in accord with the observation in [14].

Table 4. The prediction performance of the AT^{credit} model on the test set

Arithmetic counting scheme	1394.62	Network-based counting scheme	1873.89
Geometric counting scheme	1389.87	Axiomatic counting scheme	1372.51
Harmonic counting scheme	1371.96	Golden number counting scheme	1362.76

5 Conclusions

The author interest discovery can help personalized academic recommendation systems. However, many topic models for discovering author interest implicitly assume equal contribution from each coauthor to a target document. To loosen this limitation, a novel model, AT^{credit}, is proposed to strengthen the AT model [18] with an authorship credit allocation scheme, and the collapsed Gibbs sampling is utilized to approximate the posterior and estimate the model parameters. In total, our model considers six counting schemes, including fixed and flexible versions, as well as equal contributors and hyper-authorship strategies. As a matter of fact, the idea in the AT^{credit} is also applicable to other similar models. Note that only one dataset is utilized here, so a scientific verification of our findings still needs to be further investigated in the near future.

References

1. Abbas, A.M.: Generalized linear weights for sharing credits among multiple authors. eprint arXiv:1012.5477 (2010)
2. Abbas, A.M.: Polynomial weights or generalized geometric weights: yet another scheme for assigning credits to multiple authors. eprint arXiv:1103.2848 (2011)
3. An, X., Xu, S., Wen, Y., Hu, M.: A shared interest discovery model for co-author relationship in SNS. Int. J. Distrib. Sens. Netw. **2014**, 820715 (2014). https://doi.org/10.1155/2014/820715
4. Assimakis, N., Adam, M.: A new author's productivity index: p-index. Scientometrics **85**(2), 415–427 (2010). https://doi.org/10.1007/s11192-010-0255-z
5. Azzonpardi, L., Girolami, M., van Risjbergen, K.: Investigating the relationship between language model perplexity and IR precision-recall measures. In: Proceedings of the 26th International ACM SIGIR Conference on Research and Development in Information Retrieval, pp. 369–370. ACM, New York (2003). https://doi.org/10.1145/860435.860505
6. Blei, D.M., Ng, A.Y., Jordan, M.I.: Latent Dirichlet allocation. J. Mach. Learn. Res. **3**(Jan), 993–1022 (2003)
7. Cronin, B.: Hyperauthorship: a postmodern perversion or evidence of a structural shift in scholarly communication practices? J. Am. Soc. Inf. Sci. Technol. **52**(7), 558–569 (2001). https://doi.org/10.1002/asi.1097
8. Egghe, L., Rousseau, R., van Hooydonk, G.: Methods for accrediting publications to authors or countries: consequences for evaluation studies. J. Am. Soc. Inf. Sci. **51**(2), 145–157 (2000). https://doi.org/10.1002/(SICI)1097-4571(2000)51:2⟨145::AID-ASI6⟩3.0.CO;2-9

9. Hagen, N.T.: Harmonic allocation of authorship credit: source-level correction of bibliometric bias assures accurate publication and citation analysis. PLoS ONE **3**(12), e4021 (2008). https://doi.org/10.1371/journal.pone.0004021

10. Han, H., Yao, C., Fu, Y., Yu, Y., Zhang, Y., Xu, S.: Semantic fingerprints-based author name disambiguation in Chinese documents. Scientometrics **111**(3), 1879–1896 (2017). https://doi.org/10.1007/s11192-017-2338-6

11. van Hooydonk, G.: Fractional counting of multiauthored publications: consequences for the impact of authors. J. Am. Soc. Inf. Sci. **48**(10), 944–945 (1997). https://doi.org/10.1002/(SICI)1097-4571(199710)48:10⟨944::AID-ASI8⟩3.0.CO;2-1

12. Kawamae, N.: Author interest topic model. In: Proceedings of the 33rd International ACM SIGIR Conference on Research and Development in Information Retrieval, pp. 887–888. ACM, New York (2010)

13. Kim, J., Diesner, J.: A network-based approach to coauthorship credit allocation. Scientometrics **101**(1), 587–602 (2014). https://doi.org/10.1007/s11192-014-1253-3

14. Kim, J., Kim, J.: Rethinking the comparison of authorship credit allocation schemes. J. Informetr. **9**(3), 667–673 (2015). https://doi.org/10.1016/j.joi.2015.07.005

15. Liu, X.Z., Fang, H.: Fairly sharing the credit of multi-authored papers and its application in the modification of h-index and g-index. Scientometrics **91**(1), 37–49 (2012). https://doi.org/10.1007/s11192-011-0571-y

16. Mimno, D., McCallum, A.: Expertise modeling for matching papers with reviewers. In: Proceedings of the 13th ACM SIGKDD International Conference on Knowledge Discovery and Data Mining, pp. 500–509. ACM, New York (2007). https://doi.org/10.1145/1281192.1281247

17. Porter, A.L., Chiavetta, D., Newman, N.C.: Measuring tech emergence: a contest. Technol. Forecast. Soc. Change **159**, 120176 (2020). https://doi.org/10.1016/j.techfore.2020.120176

18. Rosen-Zvi, M., Chemudugunta, C., Griffiths, T., Smyth, P., Steyvers, M.: Learning author-topic models from text corpora. ACM Trans. Inf. Syst. **28**(1), 4:1–4:38 (2010). https://doi.org/10.1145/1658377.1658381

19. Sechidis, K., Tsoumakas, G., Vlahavas, I.: On the stratification of multi-label data. In: Gunopulos, D., Hofmann, T., Malerba, D., Vazirgiannis, M. (eds.) ECML PKDD 2011. LNCS (LNAI), vol. 6913, pp. 145–158. Springer, Heidelberg (2011). https://doi.org/10.1007/978-3-642-23808-6_10

20. Shi, Q., Qiao, X., Xu, S., Nong, G.: Author-topic evolution model and its application in analysis of research interests evolution. J. China Soc. Sci. Tech. Inf. **32**(9), 912–919 (2013)

21. Stallings, J., et al.: Determining scientific impact using a collaboration index. Proc. Natl. Acad. Sci. U.S.A. **110**(24), 9680–9685 (2013). https://doi.org/10.1073/pnas.1220184110

22. Trenchard, P.M.: Hierarchical bibliometry: a new objective measure of individual scientific performance to replace publication counts and to complement citation measures. J. Inf. Sci. **18**(1), 69–75 (1992). https://doi.org/10.1177/016555159201800108

23. Wang, Z., Xu, S., Zhu, L.: Semantic relation extraction aware of N-gram features from unstructured biomedical text. J. Biomed. Inform. **86**, 59–70 (2018). https://doi.org/10.1016/j.jbi.2018.08.011

24. Wuchty, S., Jones, B.F., Uzzi, B.: The increasing dominance of teams in production of knowledge. Science **316**(5827), 1036–1039 (2007). https://doi.org/10.1126/science.1136099

25. Xu, S., An, X.: ML^{2}S-SVM: multi-label least-squares support vector machine clas-sifiers. Electron. Libr. **37**(6), 1040–1058 (2019). https://doi.org/10.1108/EL-09-2019-0207

26. Xu, S., Hao, L., An, X., Yang, G., Wang, F.: Emerging research topics detection with multiple machine learning models. J. Informetr. **13**(4), 100983 (2019). https://doi.org/10.1016/j.joi.2019.100983

27. Xu, S., Hao, L., An, X., Zhai, D., Pang, H.: Types of DOI errors of cited refer-ences in Web of Science with a cleaning method. Scientometrics **120**(3), 1427–1437 (2019). https://doi.org/10.1007/s11192-019-03162-4

28. Xu, S., Hao, L., Yang, G., Lu, K., An, X.: A topic models based framework for detecting and forecasting emerging technologies. Technol. Forecast. Soc. Change **162**, 120366 (2021). https://doi.org/10.1016/j.techfore.2020.120366

29. Xu, S., Liu, J., Zhai, D., An, X., Wang, Z., Pang, H.: Overlapping thematic struc-tures extraction with mixed-membership stochastic blockmodel. Scientometrics **117**(1), 61–84 (2018). https://doi.org/10.1007/s11192-018-2841-4

30. Xu, S., et al.: Author-topic over time (AToT): a dynamic users' interest model. In: Park, J.H., Adeli, H., Park, N., Woungang, I. (eds.) Mobile, Ubiquitous, and Intelligent Computing. LNEE, vol. 274, pp. 239–245. Springer, Heidelberg (2014). https://doi.org/10.1007/978-3-642-40675-1_37

31. Xu, S., et al.: A dynamic users' interest discovery model with distributed inference algorithm. Int. J. Distrib. Sens. Netw. **2014**, 280890 (2014). https://doi.org/10.1155/2014/280892

32. Xu, S., Zhai, D., Wang, F., An, X., Pang, H., Sun, Y.: A novel method for topic linkages between scientific publications and patents. J. Am. Soc. Inf. Sci. Technol. **70**(9), 1026–1042 (2019). https://doi.org/10.1002/asi.24175

Human-Computer Interaction

Hybrid Research on Relevance Judgment and Eye Movement for Reverse Image Search

Dan Wu[1,2]([✉]) [iD], Chenyang Zhang[1] [iD], Abidan Ainiwaer[1] [iD], and Siyu Lv[1] [iD]

[1] School of Information Management, Wuhan University, Wuhan 430072, China
woodan@whu.edu.cn
[2] Center of Human-Computer Interaction and User Behavior,
Wuhan University, Wuhan 430072, China

Abstract. Relevance judgment has been studied in the information field for a long time. Eye movement data contains a large amount of user subjective information, and the way of its collection is becoming easier. With the rising penetration rate of mobile Internet, people are getting used to adopt the mobile search to solve problems. The higher the utilization rate of mobile search, the higher the user's requirements for the accuracy of mobile search results. In order to explore the user relevance judgment in the mobile reverse image search scenario, this paper combines eye movement data to figure out the relation between relevance judgment and users' eye movement. With the help of the relation the user's relevance experience can be inferred through eye movement data, thereby optimizing the SERP page, so as to achieve the effect of reasonable search results ranking and recommendation accuracy.

Keywords: Relevance Judgment · Reverse Image Search · SERP · Eye Movement

1 Introduction

The rapid development of the network environment has brought new lifestyles in the information century, but also caused redundancy of information retrieval. Taking what they need from the flooded information environment has become a new challenge for Internet users. Therefore, the accuracy of the search results and the user's interest in related recommendations have become a new battlefield for competition among the major search systems. In order to provide personalized information services that meet the needs, users' judgment on the relevance of search results has become an important basis for recommendation algorithms. Therefore, relevance judgments have expanded from the information field and are increasingly applied in Internet search scenarios.

At present, there are many text-based searches engines for users. However, a wide variety of information and people's fast-paced life urgently need more convenient and more efficient search engines. Reverse image search (RIS) on mobile devices is a new type of search method that appears under such a background. Since December 2009, the first Mobile Visual Search Symposium hosted by Stanford University proposed the

© Springer Nature Switzerland AG 2021
K. Toeppe et al. (Eds.): iConference 2021, LNCS 12645, pp. 211–228, 2021.
https://doi.org/10.1007/978-3-030-71292-1_19

concept of Mobile Image Matching [1], which has attracted extensive research interest from scholars at home and abroad.

Mobile reverse image search is an information retrieval method that uses mobile devices to capture visual data such as images or videos, and retrieves related information in the visual resource database [2]. The output search results are structured information, knowledge or services, and presented in the form of multimedia, AR, VR through handheld terminals. We have to admit that mobile visual search is changing people's daily search methods, not only from traditional keyword search to image (or video) search, but also from traditional text recognition to multimodal natural language processing transformation [3]. The research object of this article is exactly the mode of recognizing images by images in mobile reverse image search.

As a retrieval technology based on visual features rather than text, using images to recognize images is a new search method based on content-based image retrieval technology. It greatly reduces the difficulty of the need for RIS users to accurately describe images to construct search queries. As technology finds its application value in more search scenarios such as face recognition, copyright tracing, translation, shopping, etc. More and more researches are devoted to how to improve the technology. Meanwhile, majority of search engine companies embedding this technology. For example, Google calls it "Search by Image", while Baidu's slogan is "Baidu recognizes pictures, recognize what you see", which highlights the characteristics of using pictures for information search. Searching for pictures has developed enough to cope with common search scenarios such as "searching for information with pictures" and "recognizing the whole with parts".

The normalized term of "Image search" should be "Reverse image search", which is an application of content-based image search technology on search engines. Provide the searched sample image to the content-based image retrieval system, and the RIS can feed back the data related to the query image or the image related to the image or the precise image [4]. Mobile image search refers to the use of mobile devices to search for images. Compared with image search on the desktop, the main difference is that real-time photos can be used as a query.

As of March 2020, the proportion of Chinese netizens surfing the Internet on mobile phones is as high as 99.2% [5]. In this article, it mainly refers to the general mobile phone user groups using mainstream search engines for RIS.

With the convenience of eye movement data collection and the richness of information carried by eye movement, we hope to combine eye movement data with user relevance judgments in the scene of reverse image mobile search, so as to provide the retrieval system with that analysis eye tracking data is a new way of obtaining the results of user relevance judgments. The purpose of this paper is to combine users' eye movement character with relevance judgment to offer advice about the layout of search engine results pages (SERP) of reverse image mobile search.

2 Literature Review

2.1 Relevance Judgement Theory

Saracevic [6] considers Bradford to be the first to use "relevant" in information science. The term relevance has since become one of the most basic concepts in the field of information science, first addressed in the article "The Chaotic State of the Literature" published in the 1930s. In fact, the most important question of relevance is: What factors make the literature relevant when it is first encountered, or continue to be relevant for a longer period? [7] This process can be called relevance judgment and the "factors" here are the relevance criteria [8]. Saracevic [9] first proposed that users' relevance judgments can be used as performance evaluation indicators of information retrieval systems. Since then, relevance judgment has been an important basis for search system evaluation and improvement, and has always been one of the key contents of user research in the field of information retrieval.

Schamber [10] put forward three fundamental thoughts and theories with far-reaching relevance at this stage: system view, information view and situation view. At the same time, Froehlich [11] also put forward six basic views on relevance. He first emphasized the indefinability of relevance, and then added that it is not comprehensive enough to use topic relevance as the basis for relevance judgment. There are also theoretical models proposed from the perspective of cognition: information retrieval cognitive model [12] and information retrieval fragment model [13] and information retrieval hierarchical model [14] are the empirical study of relevance judgment provides a theoretical basis. However, the first application of the relevance theory is Spink and Greisdorf, who determine the relevance into 3 levels: "highly relevance", "somehow relevance" and "not relevance". They proposed the concept of median measurement of user relevance judgment as a supplement to recall and precision to evaluate the performance of information retrieval systems [15–17], and they verified the effectiveness of the measurement method through user relevance judgment experiments [18].

Relevance is a multi-dimensional concept. In addition to the above-mentioned user-based relevance judgment theory, there has also been progress in relevance research based on resource types. As an abstract concept, information must be attached to a carrier to exist. This carrier plays the role of sensing information, expressing information, storing information, and transmitting information. The sensory carrier acts directly on the human sensory organs and can directly Carriers that can be felt, such as text, graphics, images, sounds, movies and animations, etc. With the development of the Internet, more and more people begin to obtain information from network resources. As the research object of this article, the information carriers that directly affect human sensory organs on the mobile reverse image search SERP mainly include text and images. Therefore, the construction of the index system for determining the relevance of mobile RIS is mainly carried out around text and image.

2.2 Text Relevance Judgement

For a long time in the past, the research of text relevance judgment index has been the mainstream of relevance judgment research in the information retrieval field. The scattered and one-sided text relevance research led by theoretical research, after entering the 1990s, began to explore in depth the selection of relevance judgment indicators for users in real text query and use.

The research on text relevance also follows the research methods and perspectives of universal relevance judgments. By unlimited search experiment, Spink [19] studied the indicators when judging relevant, partially relevant, and irrelevant. Tang [20] studied relevance judgment index when comparing laboratory and naturalism. Therefore, we should follow the basic approaches of relevance judgment when study about text relevance judgment.

Whether keywords or pictures are used as search terms, the search results usually contain text to provide users with more accurate and rich content. Content presented in text form that requires users to make relevance judgments can be classified into different categories according to the characteristic of content. Therefore, there are many researches on the relevance of different types of text. Cool [21] studied the text relevance in the retrieval process of academic groups from the perspectives of Subjectivity, content/information, format, presentation, etc. Maglqughlin [22] studied the relevance judgments of abstract, author, content, full text, journal/publisher, competitiveness and other text categories in the retrieval process through unlimited retrieval experiment interviews with social science students.

Throughout the research progress of text relevance [23–26], the research objects are mainly academic user groups, and the research methods are relatively flexible and changeable. Therefore, this article takes the student group as the research object. In addition to the relevant and irrelevant judgments, the sub-level relevant judgment indicators are constructed.

Although the research on the criteria for judging text relevance has gone through a long period of research in the past, and accumulated rich research findings and results, scholars have been exploring new text relevance judgment indicators based on the continuous verification of previous research results.

2.3 Image Relevance Judgment

The majority of user research on image retrieval focuses on needs and behaviors. The related research on the judgment index of image user relevance started in 2000. Since Markkula [27] first studied image relevance judgment indicators, the subjects of the study were mainly professional image users [28, 29], and the study found that more and more relevance judgments dedicated to RIS index. Westman [30] interviewed newspaper staff from the attributes aspects of pictures including emotional stimulus, technical quality, technical attributes, composition, timeliness, original context. Sedghi [31] adopt unlimited search experiment and studied the medical images by its subjectivity, quality, technicality, usability, timeliness, originality, image size and image type. The research method of image relevance judgment is also relatively simple, basically focusing on user retrieval experiments [32, 33] and questionnaire surveys [34–36].

It is worth mentioning that the research of image retrieval user relevance judgment indicators has always been dominated by the needs of image users, and the research object is limited to a certain type of professional image user group or the reverse image search context or RIS intention is formulated.

The index of relevance judgment is continuously refined according to the retrieval scenario. In order to better interpret user relevance judgment behavior from the perspective of eye movement, this article will set up a relevance judgment system based on previous research and the characteristics of reverse image mobile search.

3   Research Design

3.1   Research Question

It is the core competitiveness of search engines to provide search results that meet users' needs. In order to improve the rationality of search results ranking and the accuracy of user intelligent recommendations, search engine systems often use data such as user clicks and dwell time as the basis for user perception of the relevance of search results [37] to optimizing the SERP. However, the mouse clicks and dwell time data acquired by the search engine system are lack of the confirmation of users, so its reference ability is limited. This is not difficult to understand, because it is very hard to obtain confirmation of implicit feedback by users. In the process of ordinary user retrieval, it is unreasonable to require users to fill in questionnaires or other types of explicit feedback, which will cause users troubles to become a burden for search behavior. We all know that people are getting more and more in-depth research on eye movement data, and the application of eye tracking technology is getting wider. Reasonable use of eye movement data can be used as a basis for scientific experiments and further applied in real life to provide better quality and convenient information services.

There are many dimensions of eye movement data, and different eye movement indicators can reflect different attention characteristics of users, and their application scenarios are also different. Commonly used and proven effective eye movement indicators are shown in Table 1 [38]. In addition, the calculation and analysis of eye movement indicators are based on the area of interest (AOI).

With the development of eye tracking technology, eye tracking data collection methods have become easier. Compared with the search system interface click and browse log, the eye tracking data can provide more dimensions of user behavior information during the retrieval process. Especially in the context of mobile RIS, because the searched data is the image provided by the user, and the SERP page will also have more combined results of image and text compared with the text search, the user's eye movement will be more active.

If the characteristics of the user's eye tracking data can be combined with the user's confirmed relevance judgment data, then we can use the advantages of the availability of eye tracking data and the advantages of confirmation of user's relevance judgment. Therefore, as long as the user's permission is obtained to obtain the eye movement data of the retrieval process, the judgment on the relevance of the retrieval results can be inferred based on the relation between relevance judgment (RJ) and eye movement, so as to customize personalized services to make user retrieval more convenient and accurate.

Therefore, our research question is as follow:

RQ: What is the relation between users' relevance judgment and eye movement in reverse image search circumstance on mobile devices?

Table 1. Eye movement indexes and definitions

Eye movement index	Definition
Time to first fixation	The time from the start of the stimulus display until the test participant fixates on the AOI or AOI Group for the first time(seconds)
Fixations before	Number of times the participant fixates on the media before fixating on an AOI or AOI Group for the first time(count)
First fixation duration	Duration of the first fixation on an AOI or an AOI Group (seconds)
Fixation duration	Duration of each individual fixations within an AOI, or within all AOIs belonging to an AOI Group (seconds)
Total fixation duration	Duration of all fixations within an AOI, or within all AOIs belonging to an AOI Group (seconds)
Fixation count	Number of times the participant fixates on an AOI Group (count)
Visit duration	Duration of each individual visit within an AOI or an AOI Group (seconds)
Total visit duration	Duration of all visits within an AOI or an AOI Group (seconds)
Visit count	Number of visits within an AOI or an AOI Group (count)

3.2 Relevance Judgment Frame

The relevance judgment frame contains 2 levels. The first level is the judgment of overall relevance, based on the theory of Spink and Greisdorf, which is consistent of "Not Relevant", "Somehow Relevant" and "Highly Relevant". The sub-level is a further investigation in the case where the user chooses "Somehow Relevant" or "Highly Relevant". The problem is how to construct the sub-level relevance judgment frame properly to obtain participants' opinion.

As is mentioned in literature review, we can analyze relevance judgment from text and image. RIS result page is a combination of RIS and text, and it is also necessary to combine the relevance judgment indicators of textual features and visual features.

The SERP of RIS systems has rich information forms. They don't always construct the same on every single search result, but normally include elements such as title, abstract, information source/links, and pictures/videos. The elements mentioned above have also designed in our RIS engine result page on mobile devices shown in Fig. 1. Due to the limitations of the screens of mobile devices, the SERP on the mobile terminal is different from the layout of the desktop terminal. As is mentioned in Introduction part, we studied related previous studies about relevance, and we selected seven relevance criteria from the related previous studies. And we classified them into three groups. The relevance criteria of the three features were shown in Table 2.

Table 2. Relevance judgment frame for SERP of reverse image mobile search

Visual features	
Accuracy	The image has an accurate representation of what the users send as a query image
Technical attributes	The image has technical attributes such as quality, color, angle or proper size that are helpful for users to judge
Emotion	The image evokes a series of complex emotions that generate new ideas or new insights about the search topic or has a strong visual impact such as similarities, or even can be appealing to the user
Textual features	
Title relevance	The title of the textual information part is helpful to judge
Abstract relevance	The abstract of the textual information part has some important details on the search topic
Source authority	The source of this textual information is trustworthy
Environmental features	
Publication context of images & texts	The concrete location into which the object should be integrated and by that provides additional useful information to the user who are not satisfied with the presented information and click into the next interface

3.3 Research Hypotheses: Relation Between Relevance Judgment and Eye Movement

The relevance judgment frame has been defined in Table 2 and eye movement index has been explained in Table 1. However, not every eye movement indicators and relevance frameworks are possible to be used to find out the relation between RJ and eye movement.

Since this experiment is carried out on the mobile terminal, the access time of the search results on the mobile terminal interface is related to the page location. Therefore, Fixations Before and Time to First Fixation have insufficient reference meaning. The Relevance Criteria contains Environmental Features, but environmental features cannot be verified by eye tracking data, so this indicator is also deleted.

As is shown in Table 3, we intend to verify the correlation between the user's subjective relevance judgment results and multiple eye movement indicators under the framework of relevance judgment. This relation is based on the literature research of RJ and eye movement indexes mentioned before. Whether actual eye movement data supports the corresponding relevance judgment will be determined by the experimental results.

Table 3. Hypotheses of the relation between relevance judgment and eye movement

		Hypotheses
Image	H1	*Accuracy* of image and *Fixation Count, Total Fixation Duration, Visit Count, Total Visit Duration* are Positive correlation
	H2	*Technical Attributes* of image and *Total Fixation Duration, Fixation Count* are Positive correlation
	H3	*Emotion* of image and *First Fixation Duration, Total Fixation Duration, Total Visit Duration* are Positive correlation
Text	H4	*Title* and *First Fixation Duration, Fixation Count, Visit Count* are Positive correlation
	H5	*Abstract* and *Total Fixation Duration, Fixation Count* are Positive correlation
	H6	*Source Authority* and *First Fixation Duration, Total Fixation Duration, Fixation Count* are Positive correlation

3.4   Experiment Design

To better track the user's task-based context retrieval process, we used the built-in relevance judgment buttons to obtain the user's subjective and accurate judgments, and at the same time collected eye tracking in the experimental retrieval scenarios data.

Tasks. To simulate the user demand of mobile RIS in real scenes, we have summarized 3 kinds of usage scenes and designed 3 tasks according to the previous research on mobile RIS [39–41]. For the first scenario, the query image was an ornamental flower which was often confused with another flower similar but common. And the users were asked to find out the flower raising steps. For the second scenario, the query image was part of the cover of a children's book and the user should estimate if it was suitable for the eight-year-old kid. For the third scenario, we prepared a picture of dog which already has been spreading on the web, and asked the user how many commercial kennels were stealing portrait rights. Meanwhile, we made sure the images of unusual objects that were unfamiliar to the users, in order to create the necessary search pre-requisites for image mobile search, not key word search.

Platform. To simulate 3 scenes, we designed and collect the relevance judgment results at the same time, we have built a search engine result page of the mobile image recognition search system, which has built-in relevance judgment and selection functions. The SERP for experiment was loaded on the Tomcat server and accessed by http protocol. The SERP project was a B/S structure completed with Java and Ajax. Fig. 1 is one of the SERP of 3 scenarios. As is shown in Fig. 1 "Sample of Interactive Section", users can judge each search result according to the primary and secondary indicators of the Relevance Judgment Frame.

Participants. Since students have better information literacy so that their experiment results would have less misunderstanding about our tasks. We recruited 37 participants

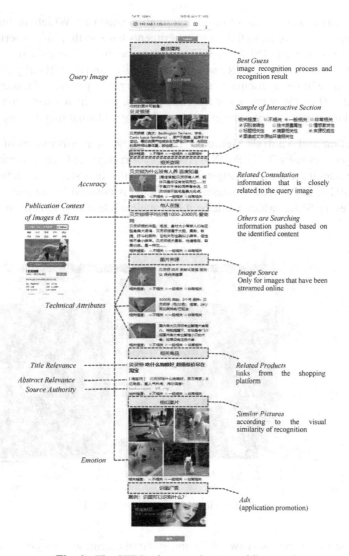

Fig. 1. The SERP of reverse image mobile search

from 29 majors at a university, which are consist of 13 male participants and 24 female participants. To simulated actual image reverse retrieval scenario and evoked participants' eager to using image reverse retrieval, the image queries were out of the familiar range of participants' cognitive. Familiar level is the user's subjective judgment on the familiarity of experimental content. We testified their familiar level with the 5-level Likert scale, and result turned out to be 1.69, which was low enough to develop our experiments. At the same time, we tested the search ability and habit of 37 participants to avoid any unreachable problems might cause. The participants' search frequency of textual information was 4.5 and of image information was 3.11. Which means that participants have enough ability to finish our experiments base on their life experience. The satisfaction for manipulated SERP is 3.77 and the perception of the difficulty of scenarios was 2.49. Accordingly, the SERP we built was feasible and the difficulty of tasks was within reasonable limits. Participants all agreed on the privacy policy of this experiment and got paid 100 to 150 yuan. After the experiments, participants were conducted an unstructured interview contributing experiment feeling and what they willing to share.

Data Collection and Analysis Methods. The eye movement information of 37 participants were collected by Tobii Pro X3-120, an eye-tracking collection device. To get specific eye-tracking data from original recordings, the first step is to draw the area of interest (AOI). Every area of interest (see Fig. 2) is covered by a square including elements of every SERP, which participant had made a relevant judgment about.

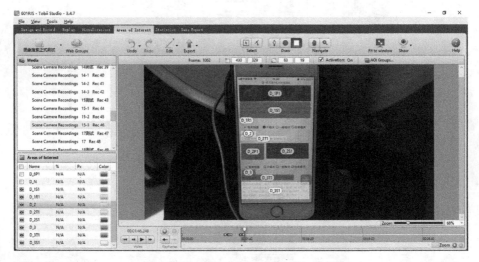

Fig. 2. Drawing AOIs of SERP in Tobii

According to the relation between RJ and eye movement, we analyzed 5 eye movement indexes including First Fixation Duration, Total Fixation Duration, Fixation Count, Total Visit Duration, and Visit Count. By comparing text relevance (Title, Abstract, Source Authority) and image relevance (Accuracy, Technical Attributes, Emotion) eye movement data of users judged as relevant and irrelevant, we analyze the results of 5 eye movement indicators for their relevance judgments. And the significant degree of the 5 eye-movement data were observed and served for verified the hypotheses of the relation.

4   Result Analysis

The original eye movement data collected by Tobii Pro X3-120 were 37 participants. Two individuals were excluded since the No. 13 participant's eye-tracking data only collected two of all scenarios and the data of participant No. 16 is not accurate because of the lack of one calibration in switching scenarios. Accordingly, the final number of participants turned out to be 35.

Base on the hypotheses of this study, the eye movements of participants were analyzed. The first step is to make sure that participants do pay attention to the elements of the SERP. We collected user gaze data, superimposed the heatmap of users judged as "Not Relevant" to get Fig. 3(a), and superimposed user gaze data judged to be "Somehow Relevant" to get Fig. 3(b), and superimposed user gaze data judged to be "Highly Relevant" to get Fig. 3(c).

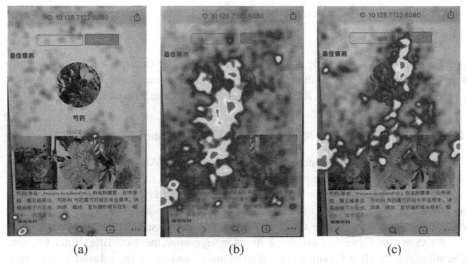

(a)   (b)   (c)

Fig. 3. (a) Heatmap of "Not Relevant" users, (b) Heatmap of "Somehow Relevant" users, (c) Heatmap of "Highly Relevant" users.

It can be seen from the heatmap that the eyes of users who choose "Not Relevant" did not gaze on the elements we studied. Therefore, the subsequent data analysis will eliminate the influence of selecting "Not Relevant" users on the data.

4.1 The Relevance Judgment Result

By analyzing the quantitative data of the relevance judgment of experimental participants, that is, when they judge the information on the SERP interface of the three mobile RIS contexts as "somehow relevant" and "high relevant" respectively. The frequency of the selected secondary RJ indicators is counted, and the chi-square test is used to verify whether there is a significant influence between relevance judgment and SERP elements. Environmental factors are one of the relevance judgment frameworks we initially designed. We try to retain the experimental results to the greatest extent, so the environmental factors for user relevance judgments are presented here.

For these relevance criteria, we evaluated the task type difference effect the applying of them, by performing a Chi-square test. Results of the test were shown in Table 4 on

Table 4. Significant of relevance judgment result of participants

Relevance criteria	X^2	P
Accuracy	17.498	0.972
Technical attributes	2.227	0.328
Emotion	21.999	0.000*
Title relevance	52.781	0.000*
Abstract relevance	0.86	0.007*
Source authority	28.855	0.000*
Environment	0.027	0.987

individual criterion by task types. Out of the 7 relevance criteria, 4 were statistically significant: Emotion and all three Textual Features. Because Technical Attributes was found to be less important in RIS scenario than in traditional image search.

4.2   Relation Between Eye Movement and Text Relevance Judgment

The text relevance judgment includes the relevance of Title/Abstract/Source. Using Pearson Correlation Analysis, the relevance percentages of the three elements judged by 35 users for text relevance were extracted as Y, and the eye movement data corresponding to 5 items of each user was used as X. Analyze the relationship between each Y and each X to obtain that whether there is a significant relationship between Y and X.

As shown in Table 5, there are 2 items in Eye-movement of Title, Total Fixation Duration and Fixation Count, have a significant influence on the relevance judgment. The correlation coefficient between RJ and Total Fixation Duration is 0.431, and it shows a significant level of 0.01, which shows that there is a significant positive correlation between RJ and Total Fixation Duration. The correlation coefficient between RJ and Fixation Count is 0.692, and it shows a significant level of 0.01, which shows that there is a significant positive correlation between RJ and Fixation Count.

Table 5. Significant between title relevance judgment and eye movement

Eye-movement of Title	Relevance Judgment	
	r	p
First fixation duration	0.003	0.985
Total fixation duration	0.431**	0.010
Fixation count	0.692**	0.000
Total visit duration	0.081	0.643
Visit count	−0.290	0.090

*p < 0.05 ** p < 0.01

As is shown in Table 6, the correlation coefficient between RJ and First Fixation Duration is 0.830, and it shows a significant level of 0.01, which shows that there is a significant positive correlation between RJ and First Fixation Duration. The correlation coefficient between RJ and Total Fixation Duration is 0.767, and it shows a significant level of 0.01, which shows that there is a significant positive correlation between Relevance and Total Fixation Duration.

Table 6. Significant between abstract relevance judgment and eye movement

Eye-movement of abstract	Relevance judgment	
	r	p
First fixation duration	0.830**	0.000
Total fixation duration	0.767**	0.000
Fixation count	−0.052	0.768
Total visit duration	−0.162	0.354
Visit count	−0.029	0.870

* p < 0.05 ** p < 0.01

As is shown in Table 7, the correlation coefficient between RJ and Total Fixation Duration is 0.865, and it shows a significant level of 0.01, which shows that there is a significant positive correlation between RJ and Total Fixation Duration. The correlation coefficient between RJ and Visit Count is 0.448, and it shows a significant level of 0.01, which shows that there is a significant positive correlation between RJ and Visit Count.

Table 7. Significant between source relevance judgment and eye movement

Eye-movement of Source	Relevance Judgment	
	R	p
First fixation duration	0.083	0.635
Total fixation duration	0.865**	0.000
Fixation count	0.252	0.143
Total visit duration	−0.105	0.550
Visit count	0.448**	0.007

* p < 0.05 ** p < 0.01

In summary, the text relevance judgment is related to eye movement indicators, which are the Total Fixation Duration, Fixation Count, First Fixation Duration, and Visit Count.

4.3   Relation Between Eye Movement and Image Relevance Judgement

In the Relevance Judgment Frame constructed in this paper, Accuracy, Technical Attributes, Emotion. However, eye movement data is difficult to distinguish from these three aspects. Therefore, we integrate the indicators of image relevance judgment, and uniformly judges the correlation between the eye movement characteristics and the relevance judgment result through the user's observation of the image in the experiment.

Table 8. Significant between image relevance judgment and eye movement

Eye-movement of Image	Relevance Judgment	
	R	p
First fixation duration	0.046	0.793
Total fixation duration	0.389*	0.021
Fixation count	0.632**	0.000
Total visit duration	0.625**	0.000
Visit count	0.230	0.183

* $p < 0.05$ ** $p < 0.01$

As shown in Table 8, the correlation coefficient value between RJ and Total Fixation Duration is 0.389, and it shows a significance level of 0.05, which shows that there is a significant positive correlation between RJ and Total Fixation Duration. The correlation coefficient between RJ and Fixation Count is 0.632, and it shows a significant level of 0.01, which shows that there is a significant positive correlation between RJ and Fixation Count. The correlation coefficient between RJ and Total Visit Duration is 0.625, and it shows a significance level of 0.01, which shows that there is a significant positive correlation between RJ and Total Visit Duration.

4.4   Experimentally Verified Relation Between Relevance Judgment and Eye Movement

Comprehensive Text Relevance Judgment and Image Relevance Judgment of Pearson Correlation Analysis result, the correlation is determined and verified hypotheses of relation between RJ and eye movement (Table 9).

Not all the five eye movement indicators preset by the hypotheses are used, Total Visit Duration is not related to any correlation judgment indicator, and all eye movement indicator data are positively correlated with the correlation judgment framework. Therefore, the larger the corresponding eye movement index value, the stronger the correlation of user perception.

Table 9. Experimentally verified relation between relevance judgment and eye movement

Hypotheses		Experimentally verified relation
Image	H1	*Image* and *Total Fixation Duration, Fixation Count, Visit Count* are Positive correlation
	H2	
	H3	
Text	H4	*Title* and *Total Fixation Duration, Fixation Count* are Positive correlation
	H5	*Abstract* and *First Fixation Duration, Total Fixation Duration* are Positive correlation
	H6	*Source Authority* and *Total Fixation Duration, Visit Count* are Positive correlation

5 Discussion

Firstly, according to Sect. 4.1, we determined the relevance of statistical indicators of users in making relevance judgments, and we found that Emotion, Title Relevance, Abstract Relevance, and Source Authority have a significant impact on user relevance judgments, which means that users rely on the above 4 elements in the process of making relevance judgments. This is consistent with Cool and Maglqughlin's research on text relevance and different from Sedghi's research on image relevance. Thus, under circumstances of reverse image mobile search, increasing the emotional influence of pictures, improving the relevance of titles and abstracts, or strengthening the authority of information sources would attract users, thereby increasing the possibility of users getting access to SERP results.

Based on the user relevance judgment results, we adjust the indicators of relation between relevance and eye movement relevance to Title, Abstract, Source Authority and Image. And then by collecting the eye movement data of the whole experiment of correlation judgment under the user's mobile image recognition search scene, this paper uses Pearson Correlation Analysis to analyze the correlation between the eye movement data and the correlation judgment. The relationship of RJ and eye movement is showed in Sect. 4.4. Based on this relation, as long as we collect the eye movement data corresponding to the SERP elements contained in the monitoring relevance judgment index, we can obtain the degree of dependence of the user on the element in the process of making the relevance judgment. The more significant eye tracking data, the more likely the user thinks the search result is relevant, and then adjust the SERP page based on user feedback.

After data analysis, it was discovered that the user relevance judgment index system constructed at the initial stage had indicators that were not significantly related. The objective factor "Technical Attributes" of the image and the invisible factor of the text "Source Authority" in the mobile RIS relevance judgment index system constructed in this research are generally regarded as not important correlation judgments by users in RIS. The reason may be that when the general user group does not have the need to download or save images, when searching for images for the purpose of finding the answer to the search task, they often ignore these two relatively important items for professional image users and academic users. "Accuracy" is regarded by users as the iconic index of RIS function, not the index of relevance judgment. The subjective factor of the image "Emotion" on the search result interface of mobile image recognition has a greater impact on the user's relevance judgment. For the text part on the search result interface of mobile image recognition, "Title" and "Abstract" are the elements that mainly encourage users to make relevance judgments.

Generally, the sorting and recommendation of the search results of the RIS are determined according to the user's mouse behaviors. If the user visits or dwell for a long time, the search results are considered highly relevant. This paper attempts to combine user relevance judgments with eye movement, and infer user relevance cognition by capturing eye movement data. However, we found that there is no significant correlation between user visit data in mobile RIS and user relevance judgments. Therefore, eye tracking data can be combined with user visit records recorded by the system to provide a more comprehensive cognitive prediction of users' relevance judgment.

6 Conclusion

This paper studies the user relevance judgment in the mobile RIS scenario. Through the SERP with user relevance options embedded, we collected the page elements on which the user's relevance was judged and the user's eye movement data during the experiment. This paper finds out the relation between users' relevance judgment and eye movement. In practical retrieval scenarios, collecting eye movement data from the user's retrieval process, using the relation between relevance judgment and eye movement promoted in this paper, combining with the mouse behavior recorded by the retrieval system, can more accurately predict the user's relevance to each result on the SERP, which can optimize the search results of entries, and recommend to users personalized relevant search results.

However, the experimental design of this experiment is limited to mobile reverse image search. In addition, a robust relation needs to be verified by a large number of scenarios.

Therefore, in future research, we want to expand the experiment of scope and number of experimental population recruitment, combining with computer and text retrieval and other real-life frequently used retrieval scenarios to improve or expand the user relevance judgment and eye movement relation to a more universal model.

Acknowledgement. This work is sponsored by Major Projects of the National Social Science Foundation: 19ZDA341.

References

1. Chen, D.M., Tsai, S.S., Chandrasekhar, V.: Tree histogram coding for mobile image matching. In: Data Compression Conference. IEEE Computer Society (2009)
2. Girod, B., Chandrasekhar, V., Grzeszczuk, R.: Mobile visual search: architectures, technologies, and the emerging MPEG standard. IEEE Multimedia **18**(3), 86–94 (2011)

3. Li, M.: Research on personalized mobile visual search mechanism in digital library. Lib. Theory and Pract. (02), 107–112(2019)
4. Chutel, P.M., Sakhare, A.: Evaluation of compact composite descriptor based reverse image search. In: International Conference on Communications and Signal Processing, pp. 1430–1434. IEEE (2014)
5. The State Council of the People's Republic of China, The 46th China Statistical Report on Internet Development. https://www.gov.cn/xinwen/2020-09/29/content_5548176.htm
6. Saracevic, T.: Relevance: a review of and a framework for thinking on the notion in information science. J. Am. Soc. Inf. Sci. **26**(6), 321–343 (1975)
7. Ingwersen, P., Jrvelin, K.: The Turn: Integration of Information Seeking and Retrieval in Context. Springer, Cham (2011)
8. Schamber L.: Users' criteria for evaluation in a multimedia environment. In: ASIS Meeting, pp. 126–133 (1991)
9. Saracevic, T.: Information science. J. Am. Soc. Inf. Sci. (12), 1051–1063 (1999)
10. Schamber, L.: Relevance and Information behavior. Ann. Rev. Inf. Sci. Technol. **29**, 3–48 (1994)
11. Froehlich, T.J.: Relevance reconsidered—towards an agenda for the 21st century: Introduction to special topic issue on relevance research. J. Am. Soc. Inf. Sci. **45**(3), 124–133 (1994)
12. Ingwersen, P.: Information Retrieval Interaction. Taylor Graham Publishing, London (1992)
13. Belkin, H.J., Cool, C., Koenemann, J., et al.: Using relevance feedback and ranking in inter-active searching. In: Harman, D. TREC-4. Washington, D. C.: Proceedings of the Fourth Text retrieval Conference (1996)
14. Saracevic T.: Modeling interaction in information retrieval (IR): a review and proposal. In: Proceedings of the American Society for Information Science and Technology, vol. 33 (1996)
15. Spink, A., Greisdorf, H., Batemain, J.: From highly relevance to not relevance examining different regions of relevance. Inf. Process. Manage. **34**(5), 599–622 (1998)
16. Spink, A., Batemain, J., Greisdorf, H.: Successive searching behavior during information seeking an exploratory study. J. Inf. Sci. **25**(6), 439–449 (1999)
17. Greisdorf, H., Spink, A.: A new way to evaluate IR systems performance median measure. In: Proceedings of NOM, New York (2000)
18. Spink, A., Greisdorf, H.: Regions and levels: measuring and mapping users 'relevance judgements. J. Am. Soc. Inform. Sci. Technol. **52**(2), 161–173 (2001)
19. Spink, A., Greisdorf, H., Bateman, J.: Examining different regions of relevance: From highly relevance to not relevant. In: Proceedings of the American Society for Information Science, Columbus, OH (1998)
20. Tang, R., Solomon, P.: Use of relevance criteria across stages of document evaluation: on the complementarity of experimental and naturalistic studies. J. Am. Soc. Inf. Sci. **52**(8), 676–685 (2001)
21. Cool, C., Belkin, N.J., Kantor, P.B.: Characteristics of texts affecting relevance judgments. In: Proceedings of the 14th National Online Meeting, pp. 77–84 (1993)
22. Maglaughlin, K.L., Sonnenwald, D.H.: User perspectives on relevance criteria: a comparison among relevant, partially relevant and not-relevant judgements. J. Am. Soc. Inf. Sci. Technol. **53**, 327–342 (2002)
23. Wang, P., White, M.D.: A cognitive model of document use during a research project. Study II: decisions at the reading and citing stages. J. Am. Soc. Inf. Sci. **50**(2), 98–1114 (1999)
24. Taylor, A.R., Zhang, X., Amadio, W.J.: Examination of relevance criteria choices and the information search process. J. Documentation **65**(5), 719–744 (2009)
25. Taylor, A.: User relevance criteria choices and the information search process. Inf. Process. Manage. **48**(1), 136–153 (2012)

26. Goodrum, A., Pope, R., Godo, E., et al.: News blog relevance: applying relevance criteria to news related blogs. In: Proceedings of the American Society for Information Science and Technology, vol. 47, pp. 1–2 (2010)
27. Markkula, M., Sormunen, E.: End-user searching challenges indexing practice in the digital newspaper photo archive. Inf. Retrieval 1(4), 259–285 (2000)
28. Choi, Y., Rasmussen, E.M.: Users' relevance criteria in image retrieval in American history. Inf. Process. Manage. 38(5), 695–726 (2002)
29. Sedghi, S., Sanderson, M., Clough, P.: A Study on the relevance criteria for medical images. Pattern Recogn. Lett. 29(15), 2046–2057 (2008)
30. Westman, S., Oittinen, P.: Image retrieval by end-users and intermediaries in a journalistic work context. In: Proceedings of the 1st International Conference on Information Interaction in Context, New York, NY, USA, pp. 102–110 (2006)
31. Sedghi, S., Sanderson, M., Clough, P.: How do health care professionals select medical images they need. ASLIB Proc. 64(4), 437–456 (2012)
32. Hung T Y, Zoeller C, Lyon S.: Relevance judgments for image retrieval in the field of journalism: a pilot study. 3815(3), 72–80 (2005)
33. Sedghi, S., Sanderson, M., Clough, P.: Medical image resources used by health care professionals. ASLIB Proc. 63(6), 570–585 (2013)
34. Buerger, T.: A model of relevance for reuse-driven media retrieval. In: Proceedings of the 12th International Workshop of the Multimedia Metadata Community, the 2nd Workshop Focusing on Semantic Multimedia Database Technologies (SMDT 2010), Saarbrucken, pp. 1–3 (2010)
35. Zhang, F., Zhou, K., Shao, Y., et al.: How well do offline and online evaluation metrics measure user satisfaction in web image search? In: Proceedings of the 41st Annual International ACM SIGIR Conference on Research and Development in Information Retrieval (SIGIR 2018), Ann Arbor, MI, USA, pp. 15–624. ACM (2018)
36. Hamid, R.A., Thom, J.A., Iskandar, D.A.: Effects of relevance criteria and subjective factors on web image searching behavior. J. Inf. Sci. 43(6) (2017)
37. Taneja, H., Gupta, R.: Web information retrieval using query independent page rank algorithm. In: International Conference on Advances in Computer Engineering, pp. 178–182 (2010)
38. Tobiipro Homepage. https://www.tobiipro.com/siteassets/tobii-pro/user-manuals/Tobii-Pro-Lab-User-Manual
39. Yeh, T., White, B., San Pedro, J., Katz, B., Davis, L.S.: A case for query by image and text content: searching computer help using screenshots and keywords. In: Proceedings of the 20th International Conference on World Wide Web, pp. 775–784. ACM, New York (2011)
40. Chutel, P.M., Sakhare, A.: Evaluation of compact composite descriptor based reverse image search. In: International Conference on Communications and Signal Processing, pp. 1430–434. IEEE (2014)
41. O'Neil, F.: Looking forward to reverse image search: measuring the effectiveness of reverse image searches in online help. In: International Conference on Applied Human Factors and Ergonomics, pp. 24–35. Springer, Cham (2017)

A Comparative Study of Lexical and Semantic Emoji Suggestion Systems

Mingrui "Ray" Zhang[1]([✉]), Alex Mariakakis[2], Jacob Burke[1],
and Jacob O. Wobbrock[1]

[1] University of Washington, Seattle, WA, USA
{mingrui,wobbrock}@uw.edu, jakeburkedesign@gmail.com
[2] University of Toronto, Toronto, ON, Canada
mariakakis@cs.toronto.edu

Abstract. Emoji suggestion systems based on typed text have been proposed to encourage emoji usage and enrich text messaging; however, such systems' actual effects on the chat experience are unknown. We built an Android keyboard with both lexical (word-based) and semantic (meaning-based) emoji suggestion capabilities and compared these in two different studies. To investigate the effect of emoji suggestion in online conversations, we conducted a laboratory text-messaging study with 24 participants and a 15-day longitudinal field deployment with 18 participants. We found that participants picked more semantic suggestions than lexical suggestions and perceived the semantic suggestions as more relevant to the message content. Our subjective data showed that although the suggestion mechanism did not affect the chatting experience significantly, different mechanisms could change the composing behavior of the users and facilitate their emoji-searching needs in different ways.

Keywords: Emoji suggestion · Text entry · Text messaging

1 Introduction

Most forms of text-based computer-mediated communication (CMC) lack non-verbal expressions like vocal tones, facial expressions, and gestures that are useful in face-to-face conversations. However, several studies have shown that emojis can facilitate affective communication[6,11,20]. Emojis are already widely used in text-based CMC, with nearly every instant messaging platform supporting their entry. Five billion emojis were sent per day on Facebook Messenger in 2017 [4], and half of all Instagram comments included an emoji as of mid-2015 [8].

Many mobile keyboards offer emojis as a set of pictographic Unicode characters. As there is a large and growing set of emojis, manually searching for and selecting emojis can be a tedious task interrupting the flow of text entry. Commercial products that automatically suggest emojis have helped the emoji entry process become more seamless [10,19]. These products usually come in

K. Toeppe et al. (Eds.): iConference 2021, LNCS 12645, pp. 229–247, 2021.
https://doi.org/10.1007/978-3-030-71292-1_20

Table 1. Examples of lexical and semantic emoji prediction. With lexical prediction, the suggested emojis are related to the literal meaning of certain keywords. With semantic prediction, the suggestions focus on the meaning of the sentence.

Sentence	Lexical	Semantic
I enjoyed the fish tonight very much!	🐟🦞🍣🍥🌹	😊😋😊😄💗
I love him but he just ignored me...	😍😿😕😒😾	💔😟😣😔😕
I'm tired of "happy birthday"	🎈🎁🎉🎂💜	✌️😟😑😒😒

Fig. 1. The semantic emoji suggestion application Dango [10]. When text is typed, Dango pops up a suggested emoji based on semantic message content. The user can tap on an icon to see more options.

two variations–lexical and semantic suggestions–as shown in Table 1. With lexical suggestions (e.g., Gboard), relevant emojis appear in a candidate list based on recent keywords typed by the user. With semantic suggestions (e.g., Dango [10]; Fig. 1), proposed emojis are based on the meaning of the message's content rather than on specific keywords.

Although emojis themselves are known to enrich conversations [6,11], the role that different emoji suggestion systems play has not been explored. Instead, prior work on suggestion systems has focused on retrieval precision and recall [1,7,9]. But how do different suggestion mechanisms influence emoji usage? How do they differ in terms of usability? How do they affect the chat experience?

To investigate these questions, we implemented a keyboard capable of offering both lexical and semantic emoji suggestions. We conducted an in-lab study with pairs of strangers using three emoji suggestion mechanisms: no suggestions, lexical suggestions, and semantic suggestions. The results showed that the chatting experience between strangers is not influenced by the emoji use, which was not explored by previous literature focusing on communication between friends and family members [6,11]. To evaluate the emoji usage in daily settings, we also conducted a 15-day field deployment. We found that emoji suggestion systems increased emoji usage overall, with users picking more emojis via semantic suggestions versus lexical suggestions or no suggestions. We also found that although suggestion mechanisms did not have a significant effect on the participants' perceived chat experience, they facilitated users' needs of inputting emojis in various ways. Semantic suggestions were perceived as more relevant to the message content, while lexical suggestions were perceived as containing more unusual emojis. The semantic suggestions served as a clue to the tone of the message and even changed the user's input behavior in some cases. Based on our findings, we propose several design guidelines for emoji suggestion systems.

The contributions of this work are: (1) results from an in-lab study comparing emoji suggestion mechanisms within the mobile chat experience; (2) results from a longitudinal field deployment that tracked realistic usage of emoji suggestion systems; and (3) design guidelines of emoji suggestion systems based on the findings from our studies.

2   Related Work

Emoji-related research has become more prominent as emojis have grown in number and popularity. In this section, we review related work from three different areas: (1) emoji usage and its effects in online communication, (2) emoji entry techniques, and (3) the use of machine learning for producing semantic emoji suggestions.

2.1   Emoji Usage in Online Communication

As Unicode character pictographs, emojis are treated similarly to other characters in text-based applications. In fact, emojis can even be used in text-only locales like URLs. Emojis represent richer information than plain text and are easier to share than images, giving emojis certain advantages over other forms of communication.

Emojis usage has steadily increased since they were introduced to the Unicode Standard in 2009. According to a report by SwiftKey in 2015 [16], their users inputted over one billion emojis in a four-month period. Although over 800 emojis were available to users during that time, traditional "face" emojis (e.g., 😂) comprised nearly 60% of all emojis sent. Roughly 70% of the messages containing emojis expressed a positive emotion, and only 15% of the messages expressed a negative emotion.

Jain et al. [11] found that emojis are used to convey all kinds of emotions, and the number of emojis used in a message could determine the arousal of the sender. They also found that emoji combinations could be used to convey more complex expressions (e.g., 😎⚽ meaning, "I'm relaxing and playing soccer"). Cramer et al. [6] conducted an online survey with 228 respondents, finding three major reasons for why people use emojis: (1) to provide additional emotional or situational information, (2) to change the tone of a message, and (3) to engage the recipient and maintain their relationship. Although every emoji has an intended definition, people also use emojis in highly personalized and contextualized ways to create "shared and secret uniqueness" [13,20]. For instance, Wiseman and Gould [20] cited an example where a couple used the pizza emoji to express love because they both loved eating pizza.

There is no doubt that emojis extend and enrich the way people express themselves in text-based CMC. Our current work focuses on the role that suggestion mechanisms play in facilitating such expressions.

2.2   Emoji Entry Techniques

Pohl et al. [14] provide a thorough review of emoji entry techniques. The most common entry method on current commercial keyboards is grouped enumeration, wherein users can scroll through different categories to select their emojis. However, as there are over 2,800 emojis[1], so visually searching and selecting emojis is a tedious process. EmojiZoom [15] displays all emojis at once, requiring users to zoom to select one. However, this method still fails to scale as the number of emojis increases.

Querying techniques, such as text search or sketching, are implemented in many keyboards like Gboard. Users can search for emojis by sketching them or typing their intended meaning (*e.g.,* "happy birthday" for a cake emoji). Such techniques require users to have a target emoji in mind, and the process is slow.

Suggestion-based input methods have become popular in recent years. Lexical suggestions are offered by keyboards like the Apple iOS 11 keyboard. However, the suggestions do not work for all possible keywords, since keywords must be defined beforehand. For example, the pear emoji appears in Gboard's suggestion list when "pear" is typed, but it disappears if "pears" is typed.

A relatively new emoji suggestion technique that appears in products like Dango [10] uses semantic information. Instead of relying on keywords, semantic suggestion offers emojis based on the sentiment of the whole message. This mechanism often provides affective emojis like faces. Google deployed a similar system called Smart Reply [12]; rather than focusing on suggestions based on input, SmartReply auto-generates replies with emojis based on the context of the conversation.

2.3   Producing Semantic Emoji Suggestions

To suggest emojis using semantics, emojis must be linked with the meanings of typed messages. Our keyboard implementation relies on a method from prior work called DeepMoji by Felbo et al. [9]. The implementation of their model used in this paper can be found on GitHub[2].

---

[1] https://emojipedia.org/stats/.
[2] https://github.com/bfelbo/DeepMoji.

Figure from https://github.com/bfelbo/DeepMoji

Fig. 2. The 64 possible emoji suggestions of the semantic suggestion model used in our paper. Most of the emojis are faces, hearts, and hand gestures.

DeepMoji uses a neural network to map textual features to relevant emojis. Felbo et al.'s dataset came from 1.2 billion tweets containing one of 64 common emojis (Fig. 2). The reported top-5 suggestion accuracy of the model is 43.8%; in other words, roughly 2 of every 5 suggestions actually appeared in their test Twitter set. The model also reached 82.4% agreement on sentiment evaluation with humans on Amazon Mechanical Turk.

3   Emoji Keyboard Implementation

We built our Android keyboard using the open source project *AnySoftKeyboard*[3]. The keyboard interface is shown in Fig. 3. The keyboard uses the default auto-correction mechanism, but the word-suggestion feature is replaced with emoji suggestions. Users can enter special characters or numbers by tapping the upper-left button; they can enter emojis by tapping the lower-left button. Note that tapping the emoji suggestions would add the corresponding emoji in the text rather than replace the text with the emoji.

3.1   Emoji Suggestion Mechanism

The overall text entry interaction of the keyboard is shown in Fig. 4. As a user types in the text box, the keyboard provides word suggestions in the candidate list. When the user finishes typing a word, the keyboard suggests emojis instead of words in the candidate list. If the user picks an emoji from the list, it is inserted at the end of the message.

The suggestion result varies based on the mechanism in use. With semantic suggestion, the keyboard always presents five emojis after the user finishes typing a word. Suggestions are generated using the DeepMoji model [9] running on a remote server. The keyboard sends an HTTP POST request to the server each time the user finishes typing a word, and the server returns the top-five related emojis. The amount of information transmitted is small and there were no latency concerns in our implementation or studies.

---

[3] https://github.com/AnySoftKeyboard/AnySoftKeyboard.

Fig. 3. (a, b) Semantic suggestion in our keyboard implementation always provides five emojis based on the message's content. (c, d) The number of emojis provided by lexical suggestion varies according to the number of keywords present. (c) If a keyword is related to many emojis, the user can scroll to select them. (d) When there is only one emoji related to the keyword "football," only that suggestion is shown.

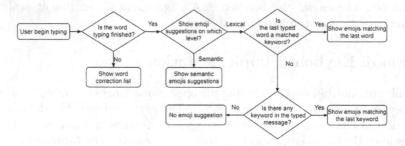

Fig. 4. A diagram of the text entry and emoji suggestion process with our keyboard

With lexical suggestion, the keyboard suggests emojis only if the keyword list contains the last-typed word. If no emoji matches the last-typed word, the keyboard presents the most recent suggestions. For example, if the user types "football field," the keyboard will continue to suggest the football emoji ⚽ because there is no lexical match with the word "field." If no word anywhere in the message has a match in the emoji keyword list, the keyboard provides no suggestions. Lexical suggestion is implemented using the open-source emoji library emojilib[4]. The library provides a .json file containing 1,502 emojis and their corresponding keywords. For example, the clapping emoji 👏 has words "hands," "praise," "applause," "congrats" and "yay."

---

[4] https://github.com/muan/emojilib.

3.2 Design Rationale

We did not force the frequency of emoji suggestion updates to be the same for both lexical and semantic suggestion mechanisms, as these mechanisms are fundamentally different in nature. For lexical suggestion, the opportune moment for updating the emoji suggestions is straightforward–whenever a keyword has been typed. For semantic suggestion, however, it is unclear when the suggestions should be updated because it is not obvious when the user is finished typing. Thus, our keyboard updates the emoji suggestions after the user finishes typing each word, not just keywords.

We also did not force an equal number of emoji suggestions across the two keyboards. Using a machine learning model for semantic suggestion returns a fixed number of emojis (five in DeepMoji), but lexical suggestion can produce a variable number of emojis. Adding extra emojis when lexical suggestion produces too few emojis would confuse users with unrelated emojis, and conversely, trimming potentially relevant emojis from the semantic suggestions would make for a keyboard unrepresentative of its full potential.

3.3 Data Logging

Our keyboard logs input statistics related to text and emoji entry: the number of typed characters, the number of deleted characters, the number of emojis manually added from the traditional emoji enumeration interface, and the number of emojis selected from the two suggestion lists. To respect participants' privacy, our keyboard did not log the content of any typed messages.

4 Laboratory Experiment

We first conducted a controlled lab study to investigate the usage of emoji with different suggestion levels between strangers. Previous studies [13,20] indicated that emoji usage between people in close relationships can foster communication. However, people also spend a huge amount of time with acquaintances, strangers, or online communities, and the effect of emojis and emoji suggestion mechanisms can be unclear in those situations. Hence, we recruited participants who did not know each other before the study to simulate such situations.

4.1 Participants

Twenty-six participants (15 females, 11 males) between 18 and 34 years old (M = 28.9, SD = 4.2) were recruited via emails, word-of-mouth, and convenience sampling in a large university setting. The participants were randomly divided into 13 pairs (one pair was removed for analysis in the later section). The pairs were constructed such that the participants did not know each other and did not meet face-to-face until the end of the study. Each participant was given $8 USD as compensation for the 30-min study.

4.2 Apparatus

Participants were provided with Nexus 6P smartphones running Google Android 7.0. Our keyboard was installed on each phone. *Wechat*[5] was used as the instant message application because Wechat provides a function to export the chat history. We used the chat history to verify the data logged by our mobile keyboard. Participants were instructed to avoid using Wechat's built-in button for emoji entry since it bypassed our keyboard's logging functionality.

4.3 Procedure

Participants were told that they would take part in an online chat experiment using our mobile keyboard. They chatted with another participant for three 10-minute sessions, each of which was assigned to one of three emoji suggestion conditions: no-suggestion, lexical, or semantic. The order of the conditions was fully counterbalanced across participants. The participants were told that they could steer the conversation towards any topic of their choosing but were told that a "recent activity" could be used to start. We did not constrain their topics as each pair may have been more comfortable discussing their own topics. The participants were also told that the only difference between the sessions would be the keyboard's emoji suggestion results, but they were not told anything about the suggestion mechanisms—neither what they were nor how they worked.

Before the conversation began, the participants were told to fill out a questionnaire that asked about their online chat and emoji use behaviors, including their online communication frequency and their emoji usage frequency during online communication. After each session, the participants filled out another questionnaire asking about their chat experience (Table 2). This questionnaire probed their engagement (Q1, Q2, and Q6) and perceived expressiveness and clarity (Q3, Q4, and Q5) during the chat experience. Both questionnaires were derived from prior work on CMC [18]. When participants used lexical or semantic suggestions in a session, they also completed the usability questionnaire shown in Table 2, which was adapted from the SUS survey [3]. At the end of the 30-min session, participants were interviewed with two open-ended questions: (1) "How do you like the suggestion keyboards? Do you find they affect you (in negative or positive ways) in online chatting?" and (2) "Do you find any problems with the keyboard suggestion mechanism, or do you have any suggestions?"

4.4 Design and Analysis

The study was a single-factor three-level within-subjects design with the suggestion mechanism as the independent variable: no-suggestion, lexical, and semantic. We utilized multiple statistical analyses according to the nature of the dependent variables: character count measures were analyzed using the aligned rank transform procedure [21]; emoji count measures fit a Poisson distribution,

---

[5] https://www.wechat.com/en/.

Table 2. The survey questions about the chat experience and the usability survey for the suggestion keyboards. Answers were provided via Likert scales ranging from 1 (strongly disagree) to 7 (strongly agree).

Chat Experience Questions
Q1. The chatting experience was interesting
Q2. My attention was focused on the conversation
Q3. I could express my emotion clearly using the keyboard
Q4. I felt constrained in the types of expressions I could make
Q5. I was able to get an impression of my partner
Q6. The chatting experience excites my curiosity
Usability Questions
Q1. I used the emoji suggestion a lot in my typing, and it was useful
Q2. I would like to use this system frequently
Q3. I thought the system was easy to use
Q4. The system did well on proposing relevant emojis
Q5. I like the emoji suggestion system better than the no-suggestion system

and were therefore analyzed with mixed model Poisson regression; Likert-scale responses were treated as ordinal measures and were therefore analyzed with mixed model ordinal logistic regression. Further specifics are given with each analysis in the results.

5 Results of the Laboratory Study

In this section, we describe the results of the study comparing the three levels of the *suggestion* factor: no suggestions, lexical suggestions, and semantic suggestions.

During the study, one pair of participants did not conduct what we considered a realistic conversation. In one of their sessions, they sent only nonsensical numbers and capital letters to each other. This participant pair was therefore excluded from our analyses, and another pair was recruited in their place. Thus, our dataset included 12 valid participant pairs with two pairs per Suggestion order due to full counterbalancing (3! conditions = 6 orders). We collected $12 \times 3 = 36$ data logs of valid sessions, together with 72 surveys regarding the chat experience and 48 usability surveys for emoji suggestion. We conducted formal analysis with open coding, in which research team members identified any themes or codes they discovered from the 48 responses to the open-ended questions on their online chat behaviors.

5.1 Participant Phone Use

Among the 24 participants, 22 stated that they always communicate with their phone, while the other two stated that they only used their phone sometimes.

Nine participants stated that they always use emojis in online conversations, 14 sometimes, and one seldom. As for how our participants normally enter emojis, 14 participants manually selected emojis from a list, one participant used lexical suggestions from the keyboard, and nine used both methods.

5.2   Count Measures

The descriptive results of the logged data are shown in Table 3. *Total Characters* is the number of characters excluding emojis sent in the conversation; *Total Emojis* is the number of emojis used in the conversation, however they might have been inputted; and *Selected Emojis* is the number of emojis picked from the suggestion list.

Table 3. Means (and standard deviations) of *Total Characters*, *Total Emojis*, and *Selected Emojis* in three conditions.

	Total characters	Total emojis	Selected emojis
No suggestions	545.33 (211.58)	2.17 (2.85)	N/A
Lexical	542.04 (224.42)	3.29(3.51)	0.88 (1.33)
Semantic	579.79 (239.38)	3.29 (2.93)	2.17 (2.37)

A non-parametric aligned rank transform [21] with a mixed model analysis of variance was performed on *Total Characters*. Suggestion had no significant effect on *Total Characters* ($F(2, 46) = 0.78$, n.s.), indicating that the suggestion mechanism did not affect the overall volume of characters participants exchanged.

Total Emojis and *Selected Emojis* were conditionally fit to a Poisson distribution, as is common for count data [20], and mixed model Poisson regression was conducted on both measures. Suggestion had only a marginal effect on *Total Emojis* ($\chi^2_{(2,N=48)} = 5.25, p = .072$). However, Suggestion did have a significant effect on *Selected Emojis* ($\chi^2_{(1,N=48)} = 7.76, p < .05$), with semantic suggestion resulting in more selected emojis than lexical suggestion. This result indicates that although the total number of emojis participants used across conditions was similar, participants selected more semantic-generated emojis than lexical-generated ones.

5.3   Subjective Results

Participants responded to the questionnaires along a 7-point Likert Scale (1 = strongly disagree, 7 = strongly agree), so the data were analyzed using mixed model ordinal logistic regression. Surprisingly, there were no significant results across the different Suggestion levels for any question regarding either the chat experience or usability (Table 2).

Looking at participants' interview answers, we found that participants did notice the difference between the suggestion mechanisms and provided more

positive feedback on semantic suggestions than the other conditions. Five participants mentioned that semantic suggestions were convenient and timesaving. The
convenience came from the relevance of the semantic suggestions. P13 pointed
out, *"The first one [semantic] is better than the second one [lexical], showing
more emotion-related emojis. The second one is related to the word itself and
it makes no sense to use the emoji in the conversation."* P25 preferred the
semantic-level prediction because it was *"reflective of the tone of the message."*
We also found that the appearance of semantic level suggestions enriched the
composer's chatting experience: Although P19 did not use many emojis during
the study, she stated that *"their [emojis'] appearance in suggestion bars makes
me feel good."*

On the other hand, two participants preferred word-level prediction, and they
did so because it sometimes provided more unusual emojis than semantic-level
prediction. P18 said, *"the (keyword) prediction is fun because it predicts more
unusual emojis, and that's unexpected."* Five participants wanted more options
from the semantic-level prediction. P1 suggested, *"Increase the amount of emoji
that are an option. If you don't have much options to put for prediction, use the
most frequent used emoji as an option for the user."* Participants also mentioned
that they did not usually insert emojis within their messages, so it would be less
distracting if the suggestions were only relevant for the end of their sentences.

5.4 Discussion of the Laboratory Study

Based on the analysis of emoji counts in the study, we found that although different suggestion levels resulted in similar amounts of inputted emojis, participants
tended to pick more from semantic suggestions than from lexical suggestions. Our
finding was that the suggestion type did not affect the chat experience significantly. One explanation is that different suggestion mechanisms only affect how
the user inputs emojis, rather than which emojis they input. As long as they can
input the expected emojis, the chat experience is not affected.

Another interesting fact was that the emoji usage did not affect the chat experience between strangers, which was not covered in previous literature. Three
participants mentioned that they did not feel comfortable sending emojis to
strangers. P2 wrote, *"To be honest, I am indeed more engaged with the emoji
prediction system but I do not think I got a 'full' sense because I use emoji less
when chatting with strangers than with friends."* This indicated that although
emojis can foster the communication between closed relationships, people are less
motivated to send emojis to strangers, which can be explained by that strangers
shared less common ground, thus their conversations were "more superficial and
general in culture" [5].

6 Field Deployment

We then conducted a 15-day field deployment to explore the longitudinal effects
of the different emoji suggestion systems. Unlike the in-lab study which was

conducted between strangers, this study focused on the usability of the emoji suggestion systems and on their effects on emoji usage during everyday conversations.

6.1 Participants

Eighteen participants (8 females, 10 males) between 18 and 43 years old ($M = 24.0$, $SD = 6.4$) were recruited via emails, flyers, and word-of-mouth. Inclusion criteria required that participants were able to use English as their primary language and owned a smartphone with Android version above 6.0 that they used on a daily basis. Those who were in the laboratory study were not allowed to participate in the field deployment due to prior exposure. The 15-day study contained three five-day periods. Participants were compensated $20 USD in the first two periods and $40 for the third, adding to $80 total.

6.2 Procedure

The study was conducted as a partial within-subjects design with the suggestion mechanism as the independent variable. All of the participants used the *no-suggestion* keyboard in the first five-day period as a baseline (however, they could still input emoji from the emoji selection panel). During the second period, half of the participants used the *lexical suggestion* keyboard while the other half used the *semantic suggestion* keyboard. Everyone returned to the *no-suggestion* keyboard during the last period to determine whether they returned to their baseline behavior. In psychology terms, the study compared an ABA condition sequence to an ACA condition sequence.

When participants were enrolled, they were asked to fill out the same questionnaire about online chatting and emoji usage as in the laboratory study. Participants were told that they would be using an emoji suggestion system during the field study, but that they were free to use or ignore the suggestions as they pleased. Participants were instructed to use the keyboard whenever they were typing in English and to keep their phone network connected so they could retrieve emoji suggestion results. The same usage information was logged as before (*Total Characters, Total Emojis*, and *Selected Emojis*). After participants signed the consent form, the keyboard was installed on their phone. The keyboard was configured to participants' personal preferences, including its aesthetic theme and vibration behavior.

Participants met with a researcher after each five-day period to have their keyboards reconfigured to another condition and fill out a short questionnaire about the experience (Table 4). After the second period, when emoji suggestions were provided, participants also completed the same usability survey as in the first study (see Table 2).

Table 4. The survey questions after each period. The emoji suggestions were offered only during period 2, which is why the questions are different for that period.

Survey After Period 1
Do you find yourself using emojis more or less often than before the study? Why?

Survey After Period 2
1. How do you like or dislike the suggestion keyboard? Do you find it affecting you (in negative or positive ways) in online communication?
2. Do you find yourself using emojis more often than before the study? Why?
3. Do you have any comments about the keyboard emoji suggestions?

Survey After Period 3
1. What do you think of the current keyboard for this period?
2. Do you find yourself using emojis more or less often than before the study? Why?
3. After the whole period, do you have any comments about the keyboard emoji suggestions?

7   Results of Field Deployment

We collected 54 data logs (18 participants × 3 periods), 18 survey results about the usability of emoji suggestions, and 54 open responses analyzed using inductive analysis [17]. As before, *suggestion* was the independent variable of three levels: no-suggestion, lexical, and semantic.

7.1   Participant Phone Use

Among the 18 participants, 14 stated that they always communicate with their phone, three sometimes, and one seldom. Four participants stated that they always use emojis in online conversations, 11 sometimes, and three seldom. As for the participants' typical emoji entry method, 10 participants manually selected emojis from a list, one participant used lexical suggestions from the keyboard, and seven used both methods.

7.2   Count Measures

The descriptive statistics for *Total Characters, Total Emojis* and *Selected Emojis* per day are shown in Fig. 5. Unsurprisingly, participants used more emojis with lexical and semantic suggestions than with no suggestions. On average, participants who used lexical suggestions in the second period increased their emoji usage by 31.5% over their baseline, while participants who used semantic suggestions increased their usage by 125.1%. We note that the average usage of daily emoji seems low (fewer than 5 emojis per day). After looking into the data, we found that some participants used over 10 emojis per day, while the other participants used less than one emoji per day.

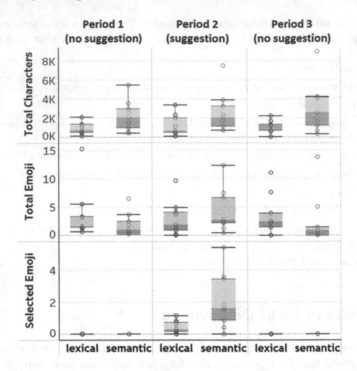

Fig. 5. Box plot for Total Characters, Total Emoji, and Selected Emoji per day from the field deployment dataset. Within each period, the left box indicates the lexical keyboard group, while the right box indicates the semantic keyboard group.

A Wilcoxon signed-rank test was performed on *Total Characters* and *Total Emojis* between the first and second periods for each group separately. *Total Characters* was not significantly different between the two periods for either Suggestion condition. *Total Emojis* was significantly different between the two periods for semantic suggestions (p < .05), but not for lexical suggestions. Despite the fact that emoji usage increased in both conditions, only semantic suggestions encouraged participants to input more emojis.

A Mann-Whitney U test was performed on *Total Characters, Total Emojis*, and *Selected Emojis* by Suggestion for the second period in which the suggestion keyboards were used. The test revealed no significant differences between semantic and lexical suggestions for *Total Characters* and *Total Emojis*; however, semantic suggestions resulted in significantly more *Selected Emojis* than lexical suggestions ($Z = -2.43, p < .05$), indicating that those who used semantic suggestions entered a larger proportion of emojis from the suggestion list than from manually picking. This result aligned with findings from the in-lab study.

Furthermore, we analyzed the difference in *Total Emojis* between the different periods by Suggestion using Mann-Whitney U tests. Results showed that emoji usage increased significantly more with semantic suggestions than with lexical suggestions from the first to second period (p < .001). The change between the first and third periods was not significantly different, indicating that the change in emoji usage was due to the emoji suggestion and not just time.

7.3   Questionnaire Results

The Likert scale responses from the usability survey during the second period were analyzed using mixed model ordinal logistic regression. No statistically significant differences were found between the semantic and lexical suggestions for any of the questions.

7.4   Discussion of the Field Deployment

The quantitative analysis results are similar to the in-lab study: the total emoji inputs were similar between different suggestion levels in period 2, and users chose more semantic suggestions than lexical suggestions. Again, based on the survey results, suggestion mechanisms did not influence the online conversation experience significantly.

Semantic suggestion group participants liked the **convenience** of the prediction, mentioning that the auto-generated emojis saved their time and "resulted in a faster and better product in regard to being able to seamlessly add emojis into everyday text" (P5). Another frequently mentioned advantage was **relevance**. As a consequence, participants mentioned that the semantic emoji suggestions helped them to **understand the tones** of their message:

I must say that the predictions were accurate most of the times ... It could guess when my sentences have a positive connotation and a negative one. (P11)

More interestingly, two participants mentioned that the suggestions **altered their original language style**:

I feel that there have been a few instances in which I would use a particular emoji when using a keyboard that was not enabled with emoji suggestion, and when this keyboard suggested a different emoji, I felt that it suited my preferences better. (P15)

I would start phrasing the sentences differently to kind of trick the keyboard into predicting the specific emoji I want without having to go to the menu and select it manually. (P5)

Lexical suggestion group participants expressed neutral opinions of the suggestion system. Two participants liked the relevance of the suggestions. For lexical level, the relevance is more providing related emojis on the literal meanings of a word:

I'm pleased that when [lexical suggestion] provided suggestions based on the context of a word, such as smiley faces when typing "happy". (P13)

Participants also enjoyed the **various options** that lexical suggestions provided. More importantly, P1 mentioned a unique case that lexical-level suggestions might be good at— **ironic emoji usage**—where he used random emojis to express sarcasm:

> *I don't use emojis a lot, but when I do, they're usually in an ironic sort of way. The emoji suggestion keyboard allowed me to do this at times that I didn't think there was a relevant emoji.*

Comparing the responses after the second and third periods revealed suggestions for ways that the two suggestion mechanisms could be improved. For semantic suggestions, participants suggested **increasing the variety** of emoji options. P12 also mentioned about "sarcasm usage", as he *"often uses emojis to supplement or change the emotion of the message."* P9 wished for a keyboard that could be aware of the app he was using and provide situational emojis. He noted that his mind-set *"is very different when texting friends than when writing an email for work."*

For lexical suggestions, participants wanted **more relevant suggestions**. P20 offered a detailed example: *"Sometimes the predicted emoji missed the meaning of what I was typing. For example, when responding to a friend who was apologizing to me, I typed, 'No worries.' I say this in a positive way, however, the emojis suggested were sad or anxious expressions, probably based on the last word typed, which was 'worries'. Therefore, the suggestion missed the intended meaning of the phrase, so maybe it would be impactful to work on the algorithm to detect multiple words/phrases to better understand the meaning within a message."* The above observation is the very reason for why semantic suggestion systems have been proposed in the past [2,9].

8   Discussion

Our goal was to examine the impact of emoji suggestion on online conversations. In particular, we sought to answer two primary questions: (1) How do emoji suggestion systems affect the chat experience? (2) Do lexical and semantic suggestion systems affect daily emoji usage differently? We first conducted an in-lab study, finding that the suggestion systems in use did not affect the overall chat experience for conversation between strangers. A possible explanation is that the suggestion levels only affect the ease of inputting an emoji, e.g. *how they input emojis*, but not affect *whether to input an emoji* and *what emojis they input*. We also found that emoji usage did not significantly affected the chatting experience between strangers.

On the other hand, our field deployment revealed that the suggestion systems influenced the amount of emoji usages. For the semantic level group, even without knowing the details of the suggestion mechanism, participants were pleasantly surprised that the predicted emojis were related to the sentiment of their messages. During the field deployment, participants picked more emojis in their daily conversations from semantic suggestions than from lexical suggestions. We also found that the semantic suggestions provided the user with clues of the message tone, which caused the users to input a different emoji and adjust their language styles. At the same time, lexical suggestions provided more diverse emoji options, which pleased the participants and enabled iconic usages.

8.1   Design Guidelines for Emoji Suggestion Systems

Based on feedback from the user studies, we propose several design guidelines for future emoji suggestion systems:

Suggestion Diversity. Emoji suggestion systems should suggest various types of emojis, ranging from emojis that portray objects to emojis that portray emotions. Although semantic suggestions were preferred in our study, many participants wanted the system to provide more suggestions than just face emojis. Some participants also appreciated that the lexical suggestion system would sometimes suggest rare emojis. Suggestions from multiple systems could be combined to provide more diverse emojis. Lexical suggestion could provide emojis as the user is typing a sentence, and once the user has finished the sentence, semantic suggestion could provide emojis that reflect the message's overall meaning. Combining the two suggestion schemes could be useful because not all messages contain strong semantic information, and people also use emojis to provide additional information for certain words [6], such as changing the tone.

Personalization and Contextualization. Through our two studies, we found that our participants had various preference on emojis: those who liked semantic suggestions were in favor of facial emojis, while those who liked lexical suggestions were in favor of object and unusual emojis. Beyond providing the most common suggestions, emoji suggestion systems should be aware of the user's personal favorites and usage behaviors. Usage behaviors could be based on categories (e.g., faces, hearts) or the emotions that the user prefers to express. In addition, it would be useful if the suggestion keyboard could recognize the recipient or the usage scenario. For example, a user might want heart emojis when chatting with a family member on a messaging app, but object emojis when composing an email.

Avoiding Intrusion. Participants of the in-lab study mentioned that they only input emojis after finishing typing the sentence, hence emoji suggestion keyboards should only predict emojis when necessary. Some participants only wanted suggestions at the end of messages, as they found the always-on style of semantic suggestions to be distracting.

8.2   Limitations

One limitation of our study is that the suggestion frequency of the two emoji systems was not the same. The semantic suggestion system updated with each new word typed, while the lexical suggestion system updated only after each pre-defined keyword. Thus, participants were exposed to more suggestions in the semantic condition than in the lexical condition. Collecting a similar measure could have been done in our other studies by counting the number of selected emojis and dividing by the total number of emoji suggestions; however, such a metric would neglect many other factors that affect selection rate (*e.g.*, time duration, ordering of emojis).

Another limitation is in our keyboard implementation, namely that the existing semantic-level suggestion model we used contains only 64 possible emojis, thus limiting the diversity of possible suggestions. The DeepMoji model could be extended to more emojis, but we chose to stay with the original set to align with the findings from Felbo et al.'s prior work [9] since there is no available conversation datasets with emojis for fine tuning the model.

9   Conclusion

In this work, we compared two emoji suggestion systems: lexical and semantic. Specifically, we explored whether the suggestion type affected the online chat experience and how people perceive the two suggestion types. Our laboratory study showed that different emoji suggestion mechanisms did not affect the chatting experience with strangers. Our longitudinal field deployment showed that semantic suggestions led to an increase in emoji usage and were preferred because of their relevance to emotions. As other research in this area has found [6,11,13], we can conclude that emojis themselves, rather than the type of suggestion system, affects the chat experience most profoundly. However, we found that semantic suggestions could be perceived as a tone clue of the message, and also affect the language style of the user. We believe that by incorporating semantic information in emoji suggestion, researchers can provide better experiences in text-based computer-mediated communications.

Acknowledgement. This work was supported in part by Baidu Inc. Any opinions, findings, conclusions or recommendations expressed in this work are those of the authors and do not necessarily reflect those of any supporter.

References

1. Barbieri, F., Ballesteros, M., Ronzano, F., Saggion, H.: Multimodal emoji prediction (2018)
2. Barbieri, F., et al.: SemEval 2018 task 2: multilingual emoji prediction. In: Proceedings of The 12th International Workshop on Semantic Evaluation, pp. 24–33. Association for Computational Linguistics, New Orleans, Louisiana, June 2018
3. Brooke, J.: SUS: a retrospective. J. Usability Stud. **8**(2), 29–40 (2013)
4. Burge, J.: 5 billion emojis sent daily on messenger, July 2017. https://blog.emojipedia.org/5-billion-emojis-sent-daily-on-messenger/
5. Clark, L., et al.: What makes a good conversation? challenges in designing truly conversational agents. In: Proceedings of the 2019 CHI Conference on Human Factors in Computing Systems. CHI 2019, New York, NY, USA, pp. 1–12. Association for Computing Machinery (2019)

6. Cramer, H., de Juan, P., Tetreault, J.: Sender-intended functions of emojis in us messaging. In: Proceedings of the 18th International Conference on Human-Computer Interaction with Mobile Devices and Services. MobileHCI 2016, New York, NY, USA, pp. 504–509. Association for Computing Machinery (2016)
7. Eisner, B., Rocktäschel, T., Augenstein, I., Bošnjak, M., Riedel, S.: emoji2vec: learning emoji representations from their description. In: Proceedings of The Fourth International Workshop on Natural Language Processing for Social Media, Austin, TX, USA, pp. 48–54. Association for Computational Linguistics, November 2016. 10.18653/v1/W16-6208
8. Engineering, I.: Emojineering Part 1: machine learning for emoji trends, October 2016. https://instagram-engineering.com/emojineering-part-1-machine-learning-for-emoji-trendsmachine-learning-for-emoji-trends-7f5f9cb979ad
9. Felbo, B., Mislove, A., Søgaard, A., Rahwan, I., Lehmann, S.: Using millions of emoji occurrences to learn any-domain representations for detecting sentiment, emotion and sarcasm. In: Proceedings of the 2017 Conference on Empirical Methods in Natural Language Processing (2017)
10. Inc, W.: Dango - Your Emoji Assistant (2016). https://getdango.com
11. Jain, M., Seshagiri, S., Chopra, S.: How do i communicate my emotions on SNS and IMS? In: Proceedings of the 18th International Conference on Human-Computer Interaction with Mobile Devices and Services Adjunct, pp. 767–774. MobileHCI 2016, New York, NY, USA. Association for Computing Machinery (2016)
12. Kannan, A., et al.: Smart reply: automated response suggestion for email (2016)
13. Kelly, R., Watts, L.: Characterising the inventive appropriation of emoji as relationally meaningful in mediated close personal relationships (2015)
14. Pohl, H., Domin, C., Rohs, M.: Beyond just text: semantic emoji similarity modeling to support expressive communication 👫🔲😊. ACM Trans. Comput.-Hum. Interact. **24**(1) (2017)
15. Pohl, H., Stanke, D., Rohs, M.: Emojizoom: emoji entry via large overview maps 😊🔍. In: Proceedings of the 18th International Conference on Human-Computer Interaction with Mobile Devices and Services. MobileHCI 2016, New York, NY, USA, pp. 510–517. Association for Computing Machinery (2016)
16. SwiftKey: Swiftkey emoji report (2015). https://www.scribd.com/doc/262594751/SwiftKey-Emoji-Report
17. Thomas, D.R.: A general inductive approach for analyzing qualitative evaluation data. Am. J. Eval. **27**(2), 237–246 (2006)
18. Trevino, L.K., Webster, J.: Flow in computer-mediated communication: electronic mail and voice mail evaluation and impacts. Commun. Res. **19**(5), 539–573 (1992)
19. Walmsley, W.: Exploring emoji: The quest for the perfect emoticon, February 2015. http://minuum.com/exploring-emoji-the-quest-for-the-perfect-emoticon/
20. Wiseman, S., Gould, S.J.J.: Repurposing Emoji for Personalised Communication: Why 🍆 Means "I Love You", pp. 1–10, New York, NY, USA. Association for Computing Machinery (2018)
21. Wobbrock, J.O., Findlater, L., Gergle, D., Higgins, J.J.: The aligned rank transform for nonparametric factorial analyses using only anova procedures. In: Proceedings of the SIGCHI Conference on Human Factors in Computing Systems. CHI 2011, New York, NY, USA, pp. 143–146. Association for Computing Machinery (2011)

Smile! Positive Emojis Improve Reception and Intention to Use Constructive Feedback

Chulakorn Aritajati[✉] and Mary Beth Rosson

The Pennsylvania State University, State College, PA 16802, USA
{cya5092,mrosson}@psu.edu

Abstract. Feedback is essential to creative work. In fact, feedback is so valuable that online crowdwork platforms are sometimes used to gather it quickly and repeatedly. However, when feedback contains negative content, the receiver's mood may suffer, as well as his or her perceptions of the feedback and provider. In response, researchers have explored techniques to mitigate the negative impacts of constructive comments; surprisingly, few studies have investigated non-verbal communication such as images. We report an exploratory study of how the presence of positive emojis in a critique can affect the receivers' reactions. We found that the positive emojis increased receiver positivity, also decreasing annoyance and frustration. The emojis also evoked more positive perceptions of feedback providers, and increased intentions to apply the feedback to future work. We discuss implications for designing feedback platforms in ways that might encourage the addition of message-appropriate emojis.

Keywords: Computer-mediated communication · Emoji · Feedback · Crowdsourcing · Human-computer interaction

1 Introduction

Constructive feedback—suggestions about how to improve a piece of work—is commonly used to improve people's learning and performance. Feedback helps people to find errors and remove creative blocks [9,39,40]. Feedback is ubiquitous, whether in schools, workplaces, or online communities; because authors or creators often seek informal feedback as they work, online forums such as Reddit, or crowdsourcing platforms such as Amazon Mechanical Turk (mTurk) have become popular sources for rapid feedback [31,69]). However, while a request for feedback is relatively simple to read and respond to, online reviewers often provide negative comments that can be difficult for the creator to absorb and apply [4,51].

When feedback includes negative elements, the recipient may "feel bad", sometimes to the extent that the feedback becomes ineffective [20]. In such cases the receiver may perceive that both the feedback and the person(s) who wrote it are unfair [3,26]; he or she may even conclude that the feedback provider is unintelligent or lacks knowledge about the work in question [44,58]. When that

© Springer Nature Switzerland AG 2021
K. Toeppe et al. (Eds.): iConference 2021, LNCS 12645, pp. 248–267, 2021.
https://doi.org/10.1007/978-3-030-71292-1_21

happens, the authors or creators may decrease the effort they put into revision or even drop their improvement goals entirely.

Researchers studying the problems stemming from negative feedback have found that if the feedback begins with positive language (e.g. a simple praise such as "Good job!"), the creators' reactions also are more positive and they do a better job on their revisions [38]. These results are promising and have led researchers to investigate options for adding positive notes to what otherwise is a experienced as a critical message. The experiment we report here contributes to this body of work, by considering the possible benefits of adding positive *non-verbal* communication elements to a feedback message. More specifically, we explore the use of emojis as a mechanism for toning down a critical comment, thus providing a more positive experience for the creator.

2 Related Work

2.1 Giving and Receiving Feedback

Feedback is an essential component of the iterative create-refine cycle typical for creative work. More generally, feedback has a powerful impact on learning and performance improvement [40]. It helps creators focus on errors, weaknesses or other problems with their designs [9]. Feedback can assist creators to learn what is good and bad in their work.

Many researchers have sought to improve the feedback process. For example, Luther found that a scaffolding rubric can improve the quality of the peer feedback written to critique course design projects [31]. Other researchers have found that creators can also gather useful feedback from their own social networks or from anonymous platforms such as mTurk [63].

Although feedback is critical role to creative work, it does not always have the intended effects. For example, some studies have observed problems with feedback that seem to be due to negative experiences evoked by criticism [20].

The Feedback Intervention Theory (FIT) [20] argues that negative feedback is experienced as an "attack" on one's self-image; this situation has been described as *face-threatening*. According to FIT, when feedback receivers have face-threatening experiences, they shift their attention and cognitive effort to maintain their face rather than processing and applying the feedback content. The face-threatening experience and associated repair activities decrease perceptions of feedback usefulness and fairness, as well as the credibility of the feedback source [5, 20, 66].

2.2 Making Negative Feedback More Palatable

In response to problems with feedback processing, researchers have explored techniques for minimizing the negative consequences of critical remarks.

One approach focuses on the use of *coping techniques* that lessen the unpleasantness of the feedback. Examples of coping techniques for dealing with negative feedback include expressive writing, distraction, and self-affirmation [68].

In one study these techniques were investigated in the context of an online creative writing class [48]. The researchers found that expressive writing motivated the participants to write more; distraction enhanced positivity and ratings of the feedback source. However, self-affirmation had no influence on participants' writing behavior or ratings of themselves or the feedback providers. The study authors argued that if learners cannot find effective ways of coping, disengagement with the ongoing learning tasks may occur [48].

Another approach to making feedback more palatable is to modify the *communication* of the feedback. Some rather simple techniques seem to have a notable impact on how the receiver experiences the message. For example, in one study, the creators preferred hearing the negative parts of a feedback message *after* positive comments, in comparison to presenting the negative comments first or sandwiched in the middle of positive comments [67]. Positioning the negative content at the end of the overall message improved the receivers' positivity and the perceived quality of the feedback. Ordering techniques such as this are simple to implement and are quite popular in the education community [7,65].

More generally, the inclusion of positive affective language improves the effectiveness of feedback. Nelson and Schunn defined *positive affective language* to be words or phrases that reflect positive emotions [36]. Examples include praise (e.g. "Good job!") or mitigating language (e.g. "Your writing is good, but there is incorrect grammar"). Negative affective language, which would be heard as inflammatory (e.g. "You are an idiot!"), is rarely observed. The researchers argue that the feedback with positive affect is liked more because the positive elements increase the receivers' positive feelings as well as decreasing negative feelings after receiving the feedback [37]. Positive emotions may motivate the creators to work harder in their revisions [23], leading to improved outcomes [36,54]. And, the presence of positive language improves the receivers' attitude about the source of the feedback [10,24]. In sum, the inclusion of positive language elements at the start of a feedback message is a simple mechanism for improving its reception and application [38].

2.3   Feedback as Computer-Mediated Communication

Computer-mediated communication (CMC) refers to any communication between one or more parties that relies on technology rather than a face-to-face (FTF) interaction. The communication channels can vary from a "rich" medium such as video (that seeks to emulate as much of a FTF setting as possible) to a rather "lean" medium such as text messages (that offer only language-based information such as word, phrasing, or punctuation) [6,47].

Many researchers have studied the consequences of using CMC technologies that vary in richness, noting that rich mediums are especially important for settings that have nuanced social interaction expectations. Others have offered a more balanced view, noting that some very lean mediums have benefits for tasks such as search or archiving that are not even possible in FTF communication (see, e.g. the seminal paper of Hollan and Stornetta [13] "Beyond Being There").

With respect to the work reported here, a critical observation from studies of CMC is the absence of non-verbal cues in text communication: face expression and body language are not part of the message, so the communication is missing much of its social layer [29,50,60]. The absence of non-verbal cues can interfere with the social meaning behind a computer-mediated message [60] and peoples' perception of the context, because non-verbal cues normally provide information about communicators' personal characteristics and emotions [61].

The relatively recent emergence of emojis in text-based communication is one step toward addressing the leanness of text-based CMC. Although emojis can play a range of different paralinguistic roles in communication [53], a common emoji use case is facial expressions or gestures that are offered as surrogates for non-verbal communication elements. Social Information Processing Theory (SIP) offers a framework for considering how communicators might adapt and turn to different modalities of communication in order to create the impressions that they intend when non-verbal cues are not present [60]. In one case, online game players used emoticons in their chat to express their emotions [56]; many emojis have been designed to express emotional states and body language [45].

When emojis are used as non-verbal cues, they may operate in a fashion similar to positive affective language. The theory of emotional contagion would predict that emojis expressing positive non-verbal meanings should enhance receivers' positive feelings [11,30]. Not surprisingly, message writers often use emojis to give complements or praise [35,52]. Emojis have also been used to "tone down" reviewers' comments [25,52] or to provide a more precise message meaning [70]. In a study of an online chat agent, the use of emojis increased social presence, causing the client to have a more positive perception of the chat agent [43]. This chatbot study suggests that emojis not only can have a mitigating effect on critical feedback, but also may make the feedback reception experience more pleasant in general. However, no research has specifically investigated these possibilities about emoji use in critiques. Our work takes a step in this direction, guided by these exploratory research questions:

1. *How will the presence of positive emojis influence feedback receivers' emotional state?*
2. *How will the presence of positive emojis affect receivers' views of the feedback?*
3. *How will the presence of positive emojis affect receivers' views of the feedback provider?*
4. *How will the presence of positive emojis affect the receivers' revision activities?*

3 Methods

To address our research questions, we designed a simple online experiment, in which participants authored a brief piece of descriptive text and were given feedback that did or did not include positive emojis. Following the feedback phase, participants were asked to revise their original work. In the following we describe the experimental task, the emoji manipulation, and the subsequent revision task.

3.1 Writing Task

Each participant wrote a description of a rental property, a picturesque bamboo hut located in Bali, Indonesia. The task goal was to prepare an effective listing as part of a hypothetical online rental platform. We provided participants with details about the property, including a set of photos and a list of amenities. Participants were asked to write a description of 100 to 500 words. They were given up to 30 min to complete the writing task.

3.2 Feedback Messages

Adapting the procedures of related prior studies [38,67,68], each participant received one of three different short critiques (assigned randomly, in combination with random assignment of the property; see Table 1). After submitting their description, they were told that feedback was being collected from other mTurk workers, and that they should read the feedback prior to revising their work. The feedback suggestions were based on guidelines from by Airbnb about how to write an effective property description [1]. The three critiques emphasized three different characteristics emphasized in these guidelines: structure, writing style, and content [46].

Table 1. Feedback messages without and with emojis

Feedback without Emojis	Feedback with Emojis
The beginning of description needs improvement. You should start the description with selling points that are unique and detailed, to catch the customer's attention. Many customers will scan just the first half of the description.	😃💯📝 but, the beginning of description needs improvement. You should start the description with selling points that are unique and detailed, to catch the customer's attention. Many customers will scan just the first half of the description. 😃📝
The invitation to guests needs improvement. It is impossible to attract all kinds of customers (e.g. a person using a wheelchair versus a big family group). You should reach out to the most suitable types of guests so that they feel welcome.	😃💯📝 but, the invitation to guests needs improvement. It is impossible to attract all kinds of customers (e.g. a person using a wheelchair versus a big family group). You should reach out to the most suitable types of guests so that they feel welcome. 😃📝
Your description of what guests will experience needs improvement. It should help guests to image a story of their trip. Thus, it should focus more on the experience customers might see, touch, hear, or taste.	😃💯📝 but, your description of what guests will experience needs improvement. It should help guests to image a story of their trip. Thus, it should focus more on the experience customers might see, touch, hear, or taste. 😃📝

Also as shown in Table 1, two versions of each message were created, with and without emojis at the start and end of the message. In particular, the emojis "😃💯👍" were inserted at the beginning of each feedback message, and "😃👍" was added to the end of each feedback message [55]. As can be seen, these emoji sets were chosen to convey face expression and gestures that suggest positive nonverbal elements; a pilot test with 20 Amazon Mechanical Turk workers revealed that these particular emojis were perceived as positive [15,59].

3.3 Revision Task

The system presented participants with feedback on the descriptions they had written (random assignment), along with their original property descriptions, asking for a revision. We turned off the copy and paste functions, preventing them from pulling directly from the feedback. They were allowed 30 min to make an improvement to their original property description. They were free to ignore or use all or some of the feedback.

3.4 Survey Questions

Immediately after receiving and reading their critiques, participants answered questions about the feedback; they did this *before* they began to work on their revisions. The questions probed their current emotional states, and their perceptions of the feedback and of the feedback provider. After completing their revisions, the participants answered a second set of questions gauging their actual use of the feedback in the revision, as well as their intention to use the feedback in future writing efforts. They also completed self-ratings of their personal writing skills, and a brief set of demographic items.

Participants who received the emoji-bearing feedback also answered questions about the emojis after they had revised their work. They were asked to explain the meaning of the emojis they had seen and asked to rate their attitudes about the use of emojis in feedback, as well as how often they use emojis in general.

3.5 Participants

We recruited 210 participants (92 females) from Amazon Mechanical Turk. 104 participants were randomly assigned to the feedback with emojis condition. The workers were all residing in the U.S. and were required to have a HIT approval rate of greater than 95%. Their ages ranged from 19 to 71 year old; 55% of the participate had completed a bachelor or higher degree. They were paid $5 for the entire task (writing, revision, survey items), with a possible bonus of $1 to encourage them to complete the feedback improvement.

3.6 Dependent Measures

Post-feedback Emotion. We measured participants' emotional states immediately after they read their assigned feedback. Following, Nguyen et al. [38,62], we used an adapted version of the PANAS scale to assess emotional state. Specifically, participants used 7-point Likert-style scales (1: strongly disagree to 7: strongly agree) to rate their happiness, annoyance, frustration, and enthusiasm. After ensuring sufficient internal validity (Cronbach's $\alpha = 0.88$), we averaged the ratings of these items to create the *Emotion* construct.

Perception of Feedback. Also after reading the feedback they had been assigned, participants rated their perceptions of the feedback message. Again using 7-point Likert-type scales, they rated the message's positivity, usefulness, and fairness. This scale was adapted from Wu and Bailey [67,68] who created the scale to measure participants' perception to online feedback. After ensuring internal validity (Cronbach's $\alpha = 0.84$), we averaged these items to create the *Feedback Perception* construct.

Perception of Feedback Provider. After rating the feedback itself, participants rated their perceptions of the feedback provider; we again reused items from prior studies of feedback [38,68]. Participants used 7-point Likert-type scales to rate perceptions of the provider's consideration, politeness, knowledge, and expertise. After ensuring internal validity (Cronbach's $\alpha = 0.85$) we averaged the items to create the *Feedback Provider* construct.

Revision Effort. We used the Levenshtein Distance (LD) to create a measure of each participants' *Revision Effort*. LD measures the minimum number of a character edits that would be needed to transform the original description into its final revision [22]. LD has often been used to measure change between texts which have been written by online participants [38,68].

Revision Improvement. To assess the level of improvement for each participant's revision, we fielded a secondary mTurk task. Specifically, we recruited 181 workers (excluding any involved in the first task) to rate the quality of both descriptions and revisions created in the main study. In the new task, each participant rated 10 original descriptions and 10 different revised descriptions. No participant rated a description and revision from the same writer. Each description and each revision was rated by at least three judges.

The judges provided ratings on a 7-point Likert-type scale that asked them how likely they would be to book the property based on reading that description. We used these ratings to calculate a *Revision Improvement* measure by subtracting the average rating of the original work from that of the revision. We averaged scores from three judges in this calculation, However, if any set of three included two ratings that varied by more than three rating scale points, we recruited two more participants, calculating instead an improvement score by averaging all five ratings. Most items (77%) needed only the original three judges to calculate a final score. We also monitored the judges' attention, and no judges spent less than three seconds per rating (this threshold was adopted from related research [68]).

Table 2. Means and standard deviations of dependent measures. (*p < 0.05, **p < 0.01)

Dependent variables	No Emojis: M (SD)	Emojis: M (SD)	T-Test
Emotion	4.20(1.39)	5.05(1.25)	4.63**
Feedback perception	4.55(1.32)	5.17(1.30)	3.4**
Feedback provider	4.98(1.06)	5.31(1.05)	2.29*
Revision effort	168.8(126.9)	153.25(112.49)	0.94
Revision improvement	0.05(1.01)	−0.05(1.11)	0.7

4 Results

Means and standard deviations for the dependent variables appear in Table 2, with asterisks indicating those that differed significantly across the two experimental conditions. Self-ratings of writing skill were gathered as a control variable, and an independent samples t-test found no significant difference between the groups (Mean for Without Emojis = 4.73(1.12); Mean With Emojis = 4.75(1.29); $t(208) = 0.14$, ns). We turn now to a more detailed presentation of the results.

4.1 Emotional Reactions After Feedback

Our first research question concerns the potential influence of positive emojis on the emotional state of the receiver. We reasoned that through a combination of positive non-verbal communication and emotional contagion that might take place simply by viewing "happy" images, receivers would feel better. Indeed we found that participants who received the feedback with emojis had significantly higher ratings of the Emotion construct (M = 5.05, SD = 1.25) than those who received text-only feedback (M = 4.2, SD = 1.39); $t(208) = 4.63$, $p < 0.01$). That is, after reading their feedback, the emojis group felt significantly happier, more enthusiastic, less annoyed, and less frustrated than the no-emojis group Table 2.

4.2 Ratings of the Feedback Itself

Our second research question concerns how the description writers felt about the feedback; we asked specifically for ratings of positivity, fairness, and usefulness. Participants provided these ratings immediately after reading the feedback message and rating their emotions. We found that the participants in the emojis condition had higher mean values (M = 5.17, SD = 1.30) for Feedback Perception than those in the no-emojis group (M = 4.55, SD = 1.32; $t(208) = 3.4$, p<0.01). Being exposed to the positive emojis seems to improve attitudes about the content of the feedback.

4.3 Ratings of the Feedback Provider

A third research question concerns how the creators felt about the source of the feedback; recall that our cover story attributed the message to an anonymous online mTurker who had been tasked to evaluate the descriptions being written. This scale assessed the feedback providers' politeness, considerateness, knowledgeability and expertise. We found that participants in the emoji group gave higher ratings of the feedback providers (M = 5.31, SD = 1.05) than those in the no-emoji group (M = 4.98, SD = 1.06; t(208) = 2.29, p < 0.05). The positive emojis in the feedback seems to improve receivers' perceptions of the feedback source.

This result in combination with the first two findings provides affirmative answers to our first three research questions. With these findings, we extend prior results noting the benefits of adding positive affective language to criticism [38], specifically by showing that the phenomenon generalizes to non-verbal content (emojis). Given the increasing popularity of emojis in text-based CMC, our findings encourage additional work to explore ways to encourage their use within simple text-based feedback messages.

4.4   Revision Effort and Improvement

Our final research question concerns the possible effect of emoji-bearing feedback on revision work. In this case (see last two lines of Table 2), we found no differences for either the Revision Effort measure (t(208) = 0.94, ns) or for the judge-contributed ratings of Revision Improvement (t(208) = 0.38, ns). Recall that the latter variable was calculating by subtracting average ratings of each original descriptions from the ratings of the corresponding revisions.

The absence of differences for the two revision measures was surprising, as an earlier related study of text-based positive affective language found differences attributed to the positive elements [38]. After studying the raw data files to see if there might be hidden patterns that we could not observe in the straightforward means comparisons, we entered a phase of more exploratory investigation. We report these analyses in the next section.

4.5   Exploratory Analyses of Revision Behavior

One exploratory analysis focused on characteristics of the participants in the Emoji group; a second examined a multivariate model of factors impacting revision behavior.

Impacts of Emoji Appropriateness. When reviewing the raw data, we noted that not all participants in the Emoji group were satisfied to discover emojis in their feedback; the median response to a question asking about appropriateness of emojis as part of feedback was only 5 on a 7-point scale. We wondered whether people who feel that emojis "do not belong" in feedback messages would have a different experience than those who see a useful role.

To explore this, we first categorized the 104 participants in the Emoji condition according to how they had answered the emoji-appropriateness question. Using a median split, we divided the 104 participants into Emoji-accepting (rating >= 5; n = 57) and Emoji-skeptical (rating < 5; n = 47, see Table 3).

Relative to participants in the Emoji-skeptical group, Emoji-accepting participants gave more positive responses about their own Emotion after receiving the
feedback (t(102) = 3.59, p < 0.01); about Feedback Perception (t(102) = 4.20, p
< 0.01); and about Provider Perception (t(102) = 2.29, p < 0.01). Importantly,
the Emoji-accepting participants also were more certain that they would reuse
the feedback that had received in the future (M = 5.9, SD = 1.02) than those in
the Emoji-skeptical group (M = 5.16, SD = 1.41; t(102) = 3.12, p < 0.01). However, as in the comparison between the two experimental conditions, we found
no differences for the two measures of revision effort (Revision Effort and judged
Revision Improvement).

This combination of results is interesting, in that it underscores that only
a subset of participants had a positive reaction to the emojis, feeling happier
about both what they had been told and how they felt about the provider.
Perhaps because the feedback was not customized for each participant's creative
work (all received a scripted message to provide control to the experiment), some
participants may have found the feedback not useful to the revision task at hand.
However it may have connected or made sense to the writers in a more general
way, making them feel it would be useful in the future. Indeed this finding is
quite consistent with studies of the FIT model in education, where educators
are often more interested in adjusting students' approach to assignments in the
longer term than helping them to refine a specific piece of work [5,20,66].

Table 3. Means and Standard Deviations for Emoji-accepting and Emoji-skeptical
Participants. 2-tailed p values: * p < 0.05, ** p < 0.1

Dependent variables	Emoji-accepting: M (SD)	Emoji-skeptical: M (SD)	T Test
Emotion	5.43 (1.41)	4.59 (1.05)	3.59**
Feedback perception	5.63 (1.03)	4.61 (1.45)	4.2**
Provider perception	5.66 (0.88)	4.88 (1.08)	2.29**
Future use intention	5.9 (1.02)	5.16 (1.41)	3.12**

4.6   Modeling the Impacts of Positive Reactions

Our exploratory finding that people's acceptance of emojis increased their intention to use the feedback in the future caused us to dig into this outcome more
deeply. Specifically we created a path model that uses the participants' experimental condition (dummy-coded as 1 or 2) as a predictor variable, the participants' ratings of their own emotions and of the feedback providers as other
contributing variables, and future use intention as an outcome (see Fig. 1).

The model shown in the figure had acceptable fit, based on three recommended model fit indicators: the comparative fit index (CFI) was 1; the standardized root mean square residual (SRMR) was 0: and the root mean square

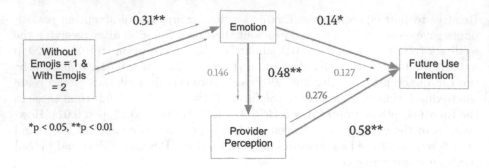

Fig. 1. The influence of the positive emojis to participants' intention to apply the feedback in the future

error of approximation estimate (RMSEA) was less than 0.01 (see [12, 14] for more information about recommended fit statistics and their cutoff values). As is expected of a well-fitting model, the chi-square coefficient for the model was quite small $(\chi^2(2, N = 210)$, p = 0.38$).

With respect to the relationships documented in the model, it appears that the major direct effect of the emoji manipulation was on participant Emotion (standardized $\beta = 0.31$, p < 0.01). In turn, Emotion had direct effects on both Provider Perception (standardized $\beta = 0.48$, p < 0.01) and Future Use Intention (standardized $\beta = 0.14$, p < 0.05). Furthermore, Provider Perception had a direct effect on Future Use Intention (standardized $\beta = 0.58$, p < 0.01). Integrating across these relationships, the model suggests that the experimental manipulation had an *indirect* effect on participants' intentions to make use of the feedback in future work, with Emotion and Provider Perception playing important supporting roles.

5   Discussion

Online feedback sources are popular and easy to employ for a wide range of creative tasks; our study suggests that online feedback communication can be improved through the use of emojis chosen to express non-verbal cues. Our results demonstrated a range of benefits that might be experienced by writers if they are given feedback messages that include positive non-verbal content (or positive affective communication). We showed that emojis (in this case implemented as "positivity wrappers" at the beginning and end of a message) can enhance feedback receivers' experiences; our exploratory analyses suggest that these images may also increase writers' intention to use the feedback they received in the future. Our findings both reinforce and extend the body of work investigating the role of positive affective language in feedback results agreed with the previous research about affective language as well [36–38].

5.1   Positive Non-verbal Cues Promote Positive Reactions

Our results reveal that emojis used as non-verbal communication cues can enhance the affective reactions of the receivers, their perceptions of the feedback, and their perceptions of the feedback source. These findings emphasize that non-verbal cues may have an important role to play when trying to mitigate the unpleasant effects of critical messages. We expect that in face-to-face feedback sessions this role is played by the speaker's facial expressions, gestures, or prosody. It would be interesting to confirm this in an observational study of feedback giving. Another important comparison will be to contrast emojis with the generic positive text used in prior studies. However, one advantage of emojis is that the simple visual images may more easily generalize across multiple languages [18]. Furthermore, the use of emojis in simple text messaging is already quite common and even increasing [2, 21].

5.2   The Relation of Positive Reactions to Future Intentions

The general goal of feedback is to enhance performance and learning [20, 40]. In our study, we did not observe improvements in revision work that we could attribute to the emojis, perhaps because the feedback was not personalized to address each writer's original description. However, our exploratory analysis suggested a positive impact on longer-term behaviors: participants who saw emoji-bearing feedback said they were more likely to apply the feedback they had received to future work. This finding does not reveal a learning gain directly, but it points to a positive learning direction. If learners (in this case the online workers) experience a positive intention to apply the feedback they received to future efforts, they may later remember and evoke it when relevant to a future project (e.g., writing a similar description).

5.3   Emojis as (Un)Acceptable Elements of Feedback

A writer's belief that emojis are acceptable as part of a feedback message was a reliable predictor of the feedback's impacts. Those with higher acceptance ratings had higher values for Emotion, Feedback Perception, Provider Perceptions, and Future Use Intention. We can contrast our findings with other recent studies that found no perceptions of social presence from emojis in text [5, 27]. It may be that the specific role the emojis played in our study (making a critical comment more palatable) creates a more familiar context for social communication; even those in the Emoji-skeptical group shared moderately high values for appropriateness. Going forward, we speculate that familiarity and acceptability of emojis in text communication will continue to increase and broaden, making their application and usefulness even more broad-spread.

5.4   Designing for Emoji Positivity

We deliberately selected emojis that evoked positive sentiment, first by brainstorming and consulting within our social network, then refining the set of images through a pilot study. So, when we found that they could serve as non-verbal positive cues, we assumed that this was because they evoked positive sentiment.

An interesting design direction is to determine which "positive" emojis work best for the communication goal of toning down negative comments. Many emojis seem to be relatively universal – for example a smiling face – but designers should also think about characteristics of emojis that might be misunderstood, perhaps due to context or culture. For example, a laughing face was found to be positive in the context of rating food [15], but it might cause a negative reaction when used in critical feedback, because the feedback provider may be seen as "laughing" or making fun of the creator. The recent addition of skin color to faces and hand gestures raises another issue, namely whether attributions about the nature of the feedback provider will affect the feedback reception process. Further investigation needs to identify what aspects of an emoji improve (or worsen) the feedback communication process and outcomes.

5.5   Techniques for Enhancing Emoji Use

Our study has shown that non-verbal communication (via emojis) can improve the process and outcomes of communicating critical feedback. One general design implication is that feedback platforms should experiment with mechanisms for easily including emojis in feedback messages. In principle it seems quite feasible to enable this, because text communication systems, social networks, and education platforms already provide wide support for emojis through the Unicode system [27,52,53,70], and users are becoming increasingly comfortable and prolific in emoji use. Importantly, people around the world are offered the the same set of emojis [18,28], increasing the potential breadth of design decisions.

Platform builders might guide people who provide feedback (e.g., as mTurk task) to "type" the most positive emojis into their critiques, so that feedback recipients are more likely to include emotion-bearing elements in their messages. Emojis also increase customer and conversation engagement in platforms [8,52], so simply encouraging their use may create better engagement in the feedback task.

With respect to how such guidance can be provided, we see at least two options. First, the platform designer can integrate a small emoji palette within the editing tool, providing one-click easy access to just the positive emojis shown to have the benefits we explored. Second, the task instructions provided to workers can explicitly encourage the use of emojis, with reference to the benefits that they bring. We are currently exploring both of these options.

In the end, designers must make design decisions about the pros and cons of each technique to improve feedback communication. Designers must consider the tension between instrumental feedback (e.g. specific corrections for improvement) and identity goals (e.g., mutual face-protection) [16]. They must also study the interaction between positive and critical content (we only studied critical feedback) [64]. Moreover, designers should investigate how different countries or cultures use and interpret the same emojis differently [18,28].

6   Limitations and Future Work

The study reported here explored whether and how image-based non-verbal communication can enhance reception of critical feedback. Our results suggest both limitations to consider and directions for future research.

6.1   Studying Other Tasks and Populations

Our study was conducted using Amazon Mechanical Turk workers (MTurkers) for practical reasons. First, we used MTurkers to gather feedback resources because its population's demographics are similar to the U.S. adult population, for example when compared to students in a U.S. university, another common base for recruiting study participants [19,33,42]. Students are younger and less diverse than Mturk workers [49]. Recent studies found that students have become very familiar with emojis because they were born and grew up in the Internet era [5,32,41]. Second, we wanted to conduct the study using the same population of human participants sampled in the previous related research, so as to prevent unexpected results from a different population [38,66–68].

The relationships between MTurkers and authors of creative works are different from the more persistent relationships found in other settings (e.g., in a school or workplace). Crowdworkers usually do a quick task to get small amount of money, so each requester will have a rather short relationship with a worker, and they do not feel a personal connection. This relationship is different from longer and stronger relationships in a class and workplace (e.g. peer/peer, teacher/student, employer/employee). Therefore, future studies should to explore the use and impacts of emojis on feedback credibility and reception experience in these other settings.

In our study, we followed the "wrapper" pattern, with positive emojis inserted at the beginning and end of what is otherwise a critical review. However, we do not yet know whether this positioning is a critical element of experience. For example, emojis might have different impacts if they are mixed throughout a feedback message; or, they may have very different consequences for cases of positive reviews.

In our task, the writing, feedback and revision process was relatively short-term – authors received feedback for a piece of work they had created in 30 min, then were given an additional 30 min to make revisions. In contrast, educators who have studied the role of feedback in learning have framed a much broader and longer-term view of learning and of the kinds of impacts we can expect from a feedback experience. In particular, FIT describes several aspects of learning that can be impacted by the feedback process that we did not consider in this study [57]. One important aspect is the way that feedback cam influence learners' motivation to learn [17]. Future work should explore a broader set of learning processes and impacts.

6.2 Natural Use of Emojis in Feedback

Emojis can be ambiguous, depending on context [34], so we selected just a few well-known positive emojis designed by Apple Inc. However, we did not consider how feedback providers would use positive emojis if left on their own, or of which positive emojis or sets of emojis will have the strongest and most reliable effects. Although this was a reasonable strategy for our experimental study, a simple search for popular emojis is not enough to decide on the best emojis to recommend. In order to use emoji wrappers as effectively as possible, future research should investigate the broader range of emojis that are used in more authentic feedback writing contexts.

7 Conclusion

Feedback assists creators to find weaknesses and ways to improve their work, but feedback sometimes has negative impacts. This study evaluated how text feedback that contained positive non-verbal communication influenced the feedback receivers' perceptions and revision activities. The study revealed that positive emojis decrease receivers' frustration and annoyance and enhance perception of the feedback content and feedback providers. The improved affect and perception of feedback providers also may enhance their intention to apply the feedback in their future work. Our study contributes to theories of feedback communication, for the special case of text-based communication, and points to implications for supporting emoji use in feedback exchange platforms.

References

1. Airbnb: writing great listing descriptions (2015). https://blog.atairbnb.com/writing-great-listing-descriptions/
2. An, J., Li, T., Teng, Y., Zhang, P.: Factors influencing emoji usage in smartphone mediated communications. In: Chowdhury, G., McLeod, J., Gillet, V., Willett, P. (eds.) iConference 2018. LNCS, vol. 10766, pp. 423–428. Springer, Cham (2018). https://doi.org/10.1007/978-3-319-78105-1_46
3. Belding, J.N., Naufel, K.Z., Fujita, K.: Using high-level construal and perceptions of changeability to promote self-change over self-protection motives in response to negative feedback. Pers. Soc. Psychol. Bull. **41**(6), 822–838 (2015)
4. Cheng, J., Danescu-Niculescu-Mizil, C., Leskovec, J., Bernstein, M.: Anyone can become a troll. Am. Sci. **105**(3), 152–155 (2017)
5. Clark-Gordon, C.V., Bowman, N.D., Watts, E.R., Banks, J., Knight, J.M.: "As good as your word": face-threat mitigation and the use of instructor nonverbal cues on students' perceptions of digital feedback. Commun. Educ. **67**(2), 206–225 (2018). https://doi.org/10.1080/03634523.2018.1428759
6. Daft, R.L., Lengel, R.H.: organizational information requirements, media richness and structural design. Manag. Sci. **32**(5), 554–571 (1986). https://doi.org/10.1287/mnsc.32.5.554

7. Daly, J.A., Vangelisti, A.L.: Skillfully instructing learners: how communicators effectively convey messages. In: Handbook of Communication and Social Interaction Skills, pp. 871–908 (2003)

8. Das, G., Wiener, H.J.D., Kareklas, I.: To emoji or not to emoji? Examining the influence of emoji on consumer reactions to advertising. J. Bus. Res. **96**, 147–156 (2019). https://doi.org/10.1016/j.jbusres.2018.11.007. http://www.sciencedirect.com/science/article/pii/S0148296318305599

9. Fischer, G.: Lifelong learning-more than training. J. Interact. Learn. Res. **11**(3), 265 (2000)

10. Guillory, J., Spiegel, J., Drislane, M., Weiss, B., Donner, W., Hancock, J.: Upset now?: Emotion contagion in distributed groups. In: Proceedings of the SIGCHI Conference on Human Factors in Computing Systems, CHI 2011, New York, NY, USA, pp. 745–748. ACM (2011). https://doi.org/10.1145/1978942.1979049. http://doi.acm.org/10.1145/1978942.1979049

11. Hatfield, E., Cacioppo, J.T., Rapson, R.L.: Emotional contagion. Curr. Dir. Psychol. Sci. **2**(3), 96–100 (1993)

12. Holbert, R.L., Stephenson, M.T.: Structural equation modeling in the communication sciences, 1995–2000. Hum. Commun. Res. **28**(4), 531–551 (2002)

13. Hollan, J., Stornetta, S.: Beyond being there. In: Proceedings of the SIGCHI Conference on Human Factors in Computing Systems, CHI 1992, New York, NY, USA, pp. 119–125. ACM (1992). https://doi.org/10.1145/142750.142769. http://doi.acm.org/10.1145/142750.142769

14. Hu, L.T., Bentler, P.M.: Cutoff criteria for fit indexes in covariance structure analysis: conventional criteria versus new alternatives. Struct. Eq. Model. Multidisc. J. **6**(1), 1–55 (1999)

15. Jaeger, S.R., Roigard, C.M., Jin, D., Vidal, L., Ares, G.: Valence, arousal and sentiment meanings of 33 facial emoji: insights for the use of emoji in consumer research. Food Res. Int. **119**, 895–907 (2019). https://doi.org/10.1016/j.foodres.2018.10.074. http://www.sciencedirect.com/science/article/pii/S0963996918308664

16. Kerssen-Griep, J., Trees, A.R., Hess, J.A.: Attentive facework during instructional feedback: key to perceiving mentorship and an optimal learning environment. Commun. Educ. **57**(3), 312–332 (2008). https://doi.org/10.1080/03634520802027347

17. Kerssen-Griep, J., Witt, P.: Instructional feedback II: how do instructor immediacy cues and facework tactics interact to predict student motivation and fairness perceptions? Commun. Stud. **63**(4), 498–517 (2012)

18. Kimura-Thollander, P., Kumar, N.: Examining the "Global" language of emojis: designing for cultural representation. In: Proceedings of the 2019 CHI Conference on Human Factors in Computing Systems, CHI 2019, New York, NY, USA, pp. 495:1–495:14. ACM (2019). https://doi.org/10.1145/3290605.3300725. http://doi.acm.org/10.1145/3290605.3300725

19. Kittur, A., Chi, E.H., Suh, B.: Crowdsourcing User Studies with Mechanical Turk. In: Proceedings of the SIGCHI Conference on Human Factors in Computing Systems, CHI 2008, New York, NY, USA, pp. 453–456. ACM (2008). https://doi.org/10.1145/1357054.1357127. http://doi.acm.org/10.1145/1357054.1357127

20. Kluger, A.N., DeNisi, A.: The effects of feedback interventions on performance: a historical review, a meta-analysis, and a preliminary feedback intervention theory. Psychol. Bull. **119**(2), 254–284 (1996). https://doi.org/10.1037/0033-2909.119.2.254

21. Konrad, A., Herring, S.C., Choi, D.: Sticker and emoji use in facebook messenger: implications for graphicon change. J. Comput. Med. Commun. **25**(3), 217–235 (2020). https://doi.org/10.1093/jcmc/zmaa003

22. Konstantinidis, S.: Computing the Levenshtein distance of a regular language. In: IEEE Information Theory Workshop, p. 4 (2005). https://doi.org/10.1109/ITW.2005.1531868

23. Koo, M., Fishbach, A.: Dynamics of self-regulation: how (un)accomplished goal actions affect motivation. Motiv. Sci. 1(S), 73–90 (2014). https://doi.org/10.1037/2333-8113.1.S.73

24. Koulouri, T., Lauria, S., Macredie, R.D.: The influence of visual feedback and gender dynamics on performance, perception and communication strategies in CSCW. Int. J. Hum. Comput. Stud. 97, 162–181 (2017). https://doi.org/10.1016/j.ijhcs.2016.09.003. http://www.sciencedirect.com/science/article/pii/S1071581916301033

25. Lee, M.K., Fruchter, N., Dabbish, L.: Making decisions from a distance: the impact of technological mediation on riskiness and dehumanization. In: Proceedings of the 18th ACM Conference on Computer Supported Cooperative Work & #38; Social Computing, CSCW 2015, New York, NY, USA, pp. 1576–1589. ACM, (2015). https://doi.org/10.1145/2675133.2675288. http://doi.acm.org/10.1145/2675133.2675288

26. Leung, K., Su, S., Morris, M.W.: When is criticism not constructive? The roles of fairness perceptions and dispositional attributions in employee acceptance of critical supervisory feedback. Hum. Relat. 54(9), 1155–1187 (2001). https://doi.org/10.1177/0018726701549002

27. Liu, M., Wong, A., Pudipeddi, R., Hou, B., Wang, D., Hsieh, G.: ReactionBot: exploring the effects of expression-triggered emoji in text messages. Proc. ACM Hum.-Comput. Interact. 2(CSCW), 110:1–110:16 (2018). https://doi.org/10.1145/3274379. http://doi.acm.org/10.1145/3274379

28. Ljubešić, N., Fišer, D.: A global analysis of emoji usage. In: Proceedings of the 10th Web as Corpus Workshop, pp. 82–89 (2016). https://doi.org/10.18653/v1/W16-2610. http://aclweb.org/anthology/W16-2610

29. Lo, S.K.: The nonverbal communication functions of emoticons in computer-mediated communication. CyberPsychol. Behav. 11(5), 595–597 (2008). https://doi.org/10.1089/cpb.2007.0132. http://www.liebertonline.com/doi/abs/10.1089/cpb.2007.0132

30. Lohmann, K., Pyka, S.S., Zanger, C.: The effects of smileys on receivers' emotions. J. Consum. Market. 34(6), 489–495 (2017)

31. Luther, K., Pavel, A., Wu, W., Tolentino, J.l., Agrawala, M., Hartmann, B., Dow, S.P.: CrowdCrit: crowdsourcing and aggregating visual design critique. In: Proceedings of the Companion Publication of the 17th ACM Conference on Computer Supported Cooperative Work; Social Computing, CSCW Companion 2014, New York, NY, USA, pp. 21–24. ACM (2014). https://doi.org/10.1145/2556420.2556788. http://doi.acm.org/10.1145/2556420.2556788

32. Marc, P.: Digital natives, digital immigrants part 1. Horizon 9(5), 1–6 (2001). https://doi.org/10.1108/10748120110424816

33. Mason, W., Suri, S.: Conducting behavioral research on amazon's mechanical turk. Behav. Res. Methods 44(1), 1–23 (2012). https://doi.org/10.3758/s13428-011-0124-6

34. Miller, H., Kluver, D., Thebault-Spieker, J., Terveen, L., Hecht, B.: Understanding emoji ambiguity in context: the role of text in emoji-related miscommunication. In: Proceedings of the 11th International AAAI Conference on Web and Social Media - ICWSM 2017, pp. 152–161 (2017). https://www.aaai.org/ocs/index.php/ICWSM/ICWSM17/paper/view/15703

35. Miller, H., Thebault-Spieker, J., Chang, S., Johnson, I., Terveen, L., Hecht, B.: Blissfully happy" or "ready to fight": varying Interpretations of Emoji. Proceedings of ICWSM 2016 (2016)

36. Nelson, M.M., Schunn, C.D.: The nature of feedback: how different types of peer feedback affect writing performance. Instruct. Sci. **37**(4), 375–401 (2009). https://doi.org/10.1007/s11251-008-9053-x

37. Neuwirth, C.M., Chandhok, R., Charney, D., Wojahn, P., Kim, L.: Distributed collaborative writing: a comparison of spoken and written modalities for reviewing and revising documents. In: Proceedings of the SIGCHI Conference on Human Factors in Computing Systems, CHI 1994, pp. 51–57, New York, NY, USA. Citeseer, ACM, (1994). https://doi.org/10.1145/191666.191693. http://doi.acm.org/10.1145/191666.191693

38. Nguyen, T.T.D.T., Garncarz, T., Ng, F., Dabbish, L.A., Dow, S.P.: fruitful feedback: positive affective language and source anonymity improve critique reception and work outcomes. In: Proceedings of the 2017 ACM Conference on Computer Supported Cooperative Work and Social Computing, CSCW 2017, New York, NY, USA, pp. 1024–1034. ACM (2017). https://doi.org/10.1145/2998181.2998319. http://doi.acm.org/10.1145/2998181.2998319

39. Nijstad, B.A., Stroebe, W.: How the group affects the mind: a cognitive model of idea generation in groups. Pers. Soc. Psychol. Rev. (Lawrence Erlbaum Associates) **10**(3), 186–213 (2006)

40. Norcini, J.: The power of feedback. Med. Educ. **44**(1), 16–17 (2010). https://doi.org/10.1111/j.1365-2923.2009.03542.x

41. Palfrey, J.G., Gasser, U.: Born digital: understanding the first generation of digital natives. ReadHowYouWant.com (2011)

42. Paolacci, G., Chandler, J., Ipeirotis, P.G.: Running experiments on amazon mechanical turk. Judg. Decis. Making **5**(5), 411–419 (2010)

43. Park, E.K., Sundar, S.S.: Can synchronicity and visual modality enhance social presence in mobile messaging? Comput. Hum. Behav. **45**, 121–128 (2015). https://doi.org/10.1016/j.chb.2014.12.001. http://www.sciencedirect.com/science/article/pii/S0747563214007134

44. Pekrun, R.: The impact of emotions on learning and achievement: towards a theory of cognitive/motivational mediators. Appl. Psychol. **41**(4), 359–376 (1992)

45. Pohl, H., Domin, C., Rohs, M.: beyond just text: semantic emoji similarity modeling to support expressive communication. ACM Trans. Comput. Hum. Interact. **24**(1), 6:1–6:42 (2017). https://doi.org/10.1145/3039685. http://dl.acm.org/citation.cfm?doid=3040973.3039685%0Adoi.acm.org/10.1145/3039685

46. van der Pol, J., van den Berg, B.A.M., Admiraal, W.F., Simons, P.R.J.: The nature, reception, and use of online peer feedback in higher education. Comput. Educ. **51**(4), 1804–1817 (2008). https://doi.org/10.1016/j.compedu.2008.06.001. http://www.sciencedirect.com/science/article/pii/S0360131508000833

47. Rasmussen, M.K., Lehoux, N., Ocnarescu, I., Krogh, P.G.: I'Ll knock you when i'm ready...: reflecting on media richness beyond bandwidth and imitation. In: Proceedings of the Designing Interactive Systems Conference, DIS 2012, New York, NY, USA, pp. 106–115. ACM (2012). https://doi.org/10.1145/2317956.2317974. http://doi.acm.org/10.1145/2317956.2317974

48. Robbins, S.B., Lauver, K., Le, H., Davis, D., Al, E.: Do psychosocial and study skill factors predict college outcomes? A meta-analysis. Psychol. Bull. **130**(2), 261–288 (2004)

49. Roulin, N.: Don't throw the baby out with the bathwater: comparing data quality of crowdsourcing, online panels, and student samples. Ind. Organ. Psychol. **8**(2), 190–196 (2015). https://doi.org/10.1017/iop.2015.24. https://www.cambridge.org/core/article/dont-throw-the-baby-out-with-the-bathwater-comparing-data-quality-of-crowdsourcing-online-panels-and-student-samples/60DB368231A6B27F993D6677743E8ABD

50. Sproull, L., Kiesler, S.: Reducing social context cues: electronic mail in organizational communication. Manag. Sci. **32**(11), 1492–1512 (1986). https://doi.org/10.1287/mnsc.32.11.1492

51. Suler, J.: The Online Disinhibition Effect (2004). https://doi.org/10.1089/1094931041291295

52. Sun, N., Lavoué, E., Aritajati, C., Tabard, A., Rosson, M.B.: Using and perceiving emoji in design peer feedback. In: Proceedings of the 13th International Conference on Computer Supported Collaborative Learning. International Society of the Learning Sciences (ISLS) (2019)

53. Tantawi, Y.: The paralinguistic function of emojis on twitter: a region-based analysis of twitter use in the USA. Ph.D. thesis, Pennsylvania State University (2019)

54. Tseng, S.C., Tsai, C.C.: On-line peer assessment and the role of the peer feedback: a study of high school computer course. Comput. Educ. **49**(4), 1161–1174 (2007). https://doi.org/10.1016/j.compedu.2006.01.007. http://www.sciencedirect.com/science/article/pii/S0360131506000297

55. Twitter, I.: Twemoji (2020). https://twemoji.twitter.com

56. Utz, S.: Social identification and interpersonal attraction in muds. Swiss J. Psychol./Schweizerische Zeitschrift für Psychologie/Revue Suisse de Psychologie **62**(2), 91 (2003)

57. van Dijk, D., Kluger, A.N.: Task type as a moderator of positive/negative feedback effects on motivation and performance: a regulatory focus perspective. J. Organ. Behav. **32**(8), 1084–1105 (2011)

58. Van Duijvenvoorde, A.C.K., Zanolie, K., Rombouts, S.A.R.B., Raijmakers, M.E.J., Crone, E.A.: Evaluating the negative or valuing the positive? Neural mechanisms supporting feedback-based learning across development. J. Neurosci. **28**(38), 9495–9503 (2008)

59. Vidal, L., Ares, G., Jaeger, S.R.: Use of emoticon and emoji in tweets for food-related emotional expression. Food Qual. Prefer. **49**(Supplement C), 119–128 (2016). https://doi.org/10.1016/j.foodqual.2015.12.002. http://www.sciencedirect.com/science/article/pii/S0950329315300173

60. Walther, J.B.: Interpersonal effects in computer-mediated interaction: a relational perspective. Commun. Res. 19(1), 52–90 (1992). https://doi.org/10.1177/009365092019001003

61. Walther, J.B., Loh, T., Granka, L.: Let me count the ways the interchange of verbal and nonverbal cues in computer-mediated and face-to-face affinity. J. Lang. Soc. Psychol. **24**(1), 36–65 (2005). https://doi.org/10.1177/0261927X04273036

62. Watson, D., Clark, L.A., Tellegan, A.: Development and validation of brief measures of positive and negative affect: the PANAS scales. J. Pers. Soc. Psychol. **54**(6), 1063 (1988)

63. Wauck, H., Yen, Y.C.G., Fu, W.T., Gerber, E., Dow, S.P., Bailey, B.P.: From in the class or in the wild? peers provide better design feedback than external crowds. In: Proceedings of the 2017 CHI Conference on Human Factors in Computing Systems, pp. 5580–5591 (2017). https://doi.org/10.1145/3025453.3025477. http://doi.acm.org/10.1145/3025453.3025477

64. Weaver, M.: Do students value feedback? Student perceptions of tutors' written responses. Assess. Eval. High. Educ. **31**(3), 379–394 (2006)

65. Witt, P.L., Kerssen-Griep, J.: Instructional feedback i: the interaction of facework and immediacy on students' perceptions of instructor credibility. Commun. Educ. **60**(1), 75–94 (2011). https://doi.org/10.1080/03634523.2010.507820

66. Wu, Y.W., Bailey, B.P.: Novices who focused or experts who didn't? In: Proceedings of the 2016 CHI Conference on Human Factors in Computing Systems, CHI 2016, New York, NY, USA, pp. 4086–4097. ACM (2016). https://doi.org/10.1145/2858036.2858330. http://doi.acm.org/10.1145/2858036.2858330

67. Wu, Y.W., Bailey, B.P.: Bitter sweet or sweet bitter?: How valence order and source identity influence feedback acceptance. In: Proceedings of the 2017 ACM SIGCHI Conference on Creativity and Cognition, C&C 2017, New York, NY, USA, pp. 137–147. ACM (2017). https://doi.org/10.1145/3059454.3059458. http://doi.acm.org/10.1145/3059454.3059458

68. Wu, Y.W., Bailey, B.P.: Soften the pain, increase the gain: enhancing users' resilience to negative valence feedback. Proc. ACM Hum.-Comput. Interact. **2**(CSCW), 186:1–186:20 (2018). https://doi.org/10.1145/3274455. http://doi.acm.org/10.1145/3274455

69. Xu, A., Huang, S.W., Bailey, B.: Voyant: generating structured feedback on visual designs using a crowd of non-experts. In: Proceedings of the 17th ACM Conference on Computer Supported Cooperative Work; Social Computing, CSCW 2014, New York, NY, USA, pp. 1433–1444. ACM (2014). https://doi.org/10.1145/2531602.2531604. http://doi.acm.org/10.1145/2531602.2531604

70. Zhou, R., Hentschel, J., Kumar, N.: Goodbye Text, Hello Emoji: Mobile Communication on WeChat in China. In: Proceedings of the 2017 CHI Conference on Human Factors in Computing Systems, CHI 2017, New York, NY, USA, pp. 748–759. ACM (2017). https://doi.org/10.1145/3025453.3025800. http://doi.acm.org/10.1145/3025453.3025800

"They Each Have Their Forte": An Exploratory Diary Study of Temporary Switching Behavior Between Mobile Messenger Services

Florian Meier[✉], Amalie Langberg Schmidt, and Toine Bogers

Science, Policy and Information Studies, Department of Communication
and Psychology Aalborg University, Copenhagen, Denmark
{fmeier,toine}@hum.aau.dk
amalieschmidt1990@gmail.com

Abstract. Today's smartphone users often use several mobile messaging services alongside each other, even though they typically offer the same features and functionality. Where previous studies have focused on how and why users permanently abandon mobile messaging services and switch to new ones, this study examines the degree to which smartphone users keep switching back and forth between multiple services, and the factors that influence this temporary switching behavior. We used an exploratory research approach in a longitudinal diary study combined with semi-structured interviews. We found that temporary switching behavior is influenced by technological affordances, contextual factors, individual preferences, and the type of conversation. Both positive and negative impacts were identified within these aspects, with some having an indirect influence, revealing the complexity of temporary switching behavior.

Keywords: Mobile computing · Mobile messaging services ·
Smartphone · Diary study · Temporary switching behavior

1 Introduction

Nearly one third of the global population [18] and 88.6% of people living in Denmark [24] own a smartphone from which they can access a plethora of different apps. Messaging services form one of the most popular app categories, enabling communication between two or more people using text, emoji, photos, videos, audio, links and more [16,19]. For over two billion users, checking messaging apps such as Facebook Messenger, WhatsApp, and Snapchat is the first thing they do each day [13,17]. The broader category of mobile messaging services (MMS[1]) that are accessible on smartphones includes the traditional Short Message Service (SMS), messaging services built into mobile operating systems—such as

---

[1] Not to be confused with the Multimedia Messaging Service standard.

© Springer Nature Switzerland AG 2021
K. Toeppe et al. (Eds.): iConference 2021, LNCS 12645, pp. 268–286, 2021.
https://doi.org/10.1007/978-3-030-71292-1_22

iMessage and Android Messages—and messaging functionalities integrated into social media such as Instagram Messages. In the study presented in this paper, we focus on this broader category of MMS, but exclude dating apps. We excluded dating apps such as Tinder, Bumble or OKCupid as those are mostly used to initiate first contact while messaging scenarios for regular MMS are more varied.

With so many different MMS apps available, it is perhaps not surprising that smartphone users do not necessarily stick with the same messaging app through the years. While the *how* and *why* of adopting new and abandoning old MMS apps has been studied in detail [33,36], users typically use multiple services alongside each other, temporarily switching between them for a variety of reasons. This happens despite the fact that these MMS apps "are often very similar, with nearly identical functionality" [30, p. 727]. However, as none of the MMS on the market "can communicate outside of the apps or between different apps" [3] users are forced to download an install proprietary software and use a plethora of different MMS.

To the best of our knowledge, this *temporary switching behavior* between equivalent messaging services without abandoning any of them permanently has not been studied in detail. Why do people use different MMS apps if they offer the same functionality? And what causes users to switch back and forth between services? In this paper, we take a first step towards answering these questions about temporary switching behavior. We thereby contribute not only to closing a knowledge gap, but our work could also provide designers and developers of MMS apps with useful insights to guide their work. To alleviate recall bias, we designed and conducted a diary study to reduce the time between MMS usage and recording the interaction, and combined this with semi-structured interviews to facilitate in-depth discussion of our participants' messaging behavior.

Our findings suggest that temporary switching behavior is influenced by four main types of factors: (1) technological affordances, (2) contextual factors, (3) the type of conversation, and (4) individual preferences. Moreover, we find that, despite the presence of negative affect towards certain MMS apps, people still keep them around for habitual or social reasons. Finally, although SMS is quite an old technology, it still plays a central role in the users' MMS ecosystem.

2   Related Work

Our work is situated within the research field of technology acceptance and adoption. Within this field, one can distinguish between (1) *adoption* studies, which investigate *initial adoption*, i.e., what motivates a user to install and use an MMS app in the first place [28,40,41] and (2) *post-adoption* studies, which investigate *continuance behavior* and *switching behavior*. While researchers interested in continuance behavior study how and why users continue to use a service after adoption [15,25,31,39], research on switching behavior focuses on factors and motivations for why users might switch to a new service while abandoning a previously used one [33,36]. In this study, we take a third perspective on *post-adoption* behavior by recognizing that "[a]doption of a new mobile service does not automatically lead to abandonment of the previous ones [...]" [9, p. 52]. Instead of using only one service, users create an ecosystem of MMSs and alternate or temporarily switch between these apps [30].

While temporary switching is a rather new research topic, previous studies on continuance and permanent switching (i.e., abandonment) could have relevant lessons to teach us. Hou [22] studied switching enablers (factors motivating a user to adopt a service) and inhibitors (factors inhibiting a user from using a service), finding that all factors such as advantage of alternatives, peer influence, critical mass, sociality, entertainment, and MIM system were all predictors of switching intentions [22]. Other researchers base their work on the Push-Pull-Mooring (PPM) framework, which considers push factors (which drive people away), pull factors (i.e., MMS characteristics and features that users get attracted by), and mooring factors (which can be seen as mediating factors on switching decisions) [33,36]. Sun et al. [36] were able to show that dissatisfaction due to bad user experience and fatigue are push effects, while subjective norms and alternative attractiveness are pull effects. Habit, switching cost and affective commitment are mooring effects. Peng et al. [33] argue that switching is both a collective and an individual movement, and argue that the factors need to be supplemented by social factors (e.g., considering the social networks and their needs).

While the frequency of switching between smartphone apps has been studied in a quantitative manner before [38], switching between MMS apps in particular and the underlying reasons have yet to be studied in depth. Church and Oliveira [8] studied why users switch between WhatsApp and SMS and found eight driving factors: cost, social influence, nature/intent, community and sense of connection, reliability and guarantee, choice of technology, coping mechanisms, and finally immediacy, privacy concerns and expectations. While WhatsApp was used for longer conversations with friends and family, SMS was seen as more formal, privacy-preserving and reliable. However, technical aspects also motivated WhatsApp use, such as the ability to send videos. Cramer and Jacobs [10] considered multiple communication channels including email, paper notes and MMS in their research on couples' communication practices. In their study of channel use, they found that considerations about the partner's preferences and habits strongly influenced the choice of channel. Nouwens et al. [30] studied MMS app usage on smartphone from the perspective of users creating so-called communication places within their personal app ecosystem. One of their main findings was that functionality and quality alone was not sufficient to explain the different in usage patterns among nearly identical MMS apps.

3   Methodology

3.1   Design

Previous work on the adoption and abandonment of mobile messaging services mainly used interviews and surveys to study this phenomenon [33,36]. However, Cho and Hung [7] have argued that, in order to capture the dynamic nature of mobile messaging, longitudinal approaches to data collection are more suitable. We follow this recommendation in our study and perform *within-method triangulation* by combining a diary study with two semi-structured interviews conducted before and after the diary study, with the diary study designed to produce both qualitative and quantitative data [23].

3.2   Participants

We recruited study participants through purposive sampling, as it allowed us to more easily recruit participants who were able to reflect upon their messaging behavior and who understood the purpose and importance of maintaining the diary's integrity [20, p. 248]. While recruiting for the study we aimed at balancing gender across the age range of 18 to 29 years old—which represents the segment of the population that most actively uses MMS apps and was therefore most likely to show pronounced temporary switching behavior [4,7]. In addition, our participants were required to own a smartphone with at least three different MMS services installed.

In total we recruited 10 participant. Our participants consisted of six female and four male smartphone users with a mean age of 27.8 years and a range of 26–30 years. All participants were Danish residents and all but one were Danish nationals, which has introduced a culture-specific bias in which MMS apps are most popular in our sample. For example, the iOS mobile operating system is most widespread in Denmark[2], whereas Android is more popular worldwide[3]. The same applies to MMS apps: while WhatsApp has the highest number of active users worldwide, in Denmark Facebook Messenger is the most popular MMS [29,37]. This pattern is reflected in our sample: only one participant used an Android phone (OS version 8.1) while the rest used iPhones (iOS versions 10.2.1 or higher). Figure 1 shows the usage frequency of the different MMS apps by our ten participants, both in terms of the number of participants that use them and the share of their total interactions that they have on those MMS apps. Both visualizations show roughly the same pattern of Facebook Messenger as the most popular MMS app, followed by iMessage, Snapchat, SMS, and Instagram.

3.3   Data Collection

Diary Study. The use of mobile messaging services is bursty in nature: sending messages does not happen only once a week nor does it take place in a single convenient location, which means there is a risk of recall bias when using interviews or surveys for exploring such behavior. For this reason, we chose a diary study as our central data collection method. Over a five-day period, consisting of three weekdays and a weekend, we asked our participants to complete a structured diary template, recording information about their use of MMS apps and all of their conversations on these apps. To reduce our diary's intrusiveness on our

---

[2] https://gs.statcounter.com/os-market-share/mobile/denmark.
[3] https://www.idc.com/promo/smartphone-market-share/os.

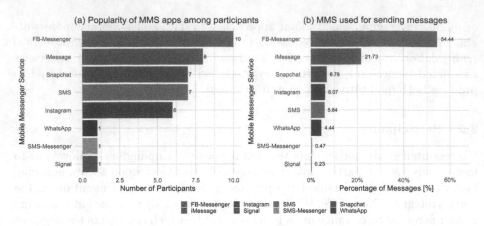

Fig. 1. Visualization of the popularity of the eight different MMS apps in our study, as measured by (a) their raw popularity, and (b) the share of all messages sent through the different MMS apps

participants' everyday routines, we did not ask them to complete a diary entry every time they sent or received a message. Instead, we asked them to fill out the diary at the end of each day, preferably before they went to sleep. We set up our diary templates as Google Forms questionnaires and sent each participant a link to a new diary template at 21:00 each day, thereby also serving as a daily reminder.

Our diary template was designed to collect both quantitative and qualitative data and consisted of two parts. Part 1 included questions about the participant's activity level in terms of MMS use on that specific day as well as how many individual persons and groups the participant had communicated with. This allowed us to determine how many different conversations—but not necessarily services—the participant had switched between that day. Part 2 focused on the person(s) and/or group(s) that the participant had communicated with using an MMS on the day in question. These questions had to be answered for each conversation partner. Table 1 provides an overview of all questions and answer options in our diary template.

Semi-structured Interviews. We conducted two semi-structured interviews with each participant, both before (introductory) and after (follow-up) the diary study phase. *The introductory interview* was made up of three parts. In part 1, participants were introduced to the study, its overall purpose, its procedure, and their role in it. Part 2 started with demographic questions, after which participants were asked questions relating to factors known to influence permanent MMS adoption and abandonment behavior [4,7]. This included questions about the MMS apps installed on their smartphone, notification settings, and their general attitude towards user experience of MMSs. Furthermore, participants were asked about whether certain MMS features or functionality influenced their

Table 1. Diary questions to be answered each day. Part 1 questions were answered once; part 2 questions were answered for each conversation partner (or group)

ID	Question	Answer type
1.1	How many individual persons have you communicated with on one or more messaging services today?	Count // number
1.2	How many groups have you communicated with on one or more messaging services today?	Count // number
1.3	How active have you been on your messaging services today compared to your normal activity level?	Likert scale (not active (1) to very active (5))
2.1	Who did you communicate with?	Checkbox (individual/group)
2.2	Please assign an alias to this person or group	Text field
2.3	Which messaging service(s) did you use to communicate with this person/group?	Multiple response (SMS/iMessage/iMessage (desktop)/WhatsApp/Facebook Messenger/Facebook Messenger (desktop)/Signal/Instagram/Snapchat)
2.4	If you initiated one or more of the conversations with this person/group, why did you choose the specific messaging service(s)?	Text field
2.5	What were the most common message format(s) that you used on each messaging service? Select all that apply	Multiple-response matrix of messaging service vs. message format (text/emoji/photo/gif/audio/video/link/bitmoji/hand-written/shared post/other)
2.6	Did you or your conversation partner(s) switch messaging service at any point during your conversation(s) while still discussing the same topic? If so, please explain what caused the switch	Text field
2.7	If you have any additional comments about your communication with this person/group, please provide them here	Text field

preferences for certain MMS apps. For this question, participants were encouraged to use their phones to show the features and functionality in question. In the final part, participants were introduced to the diary study, guided through the diary template, and shown a training template with dummy data to show them how to fill it out correctly.

The *follow-up interview* was used to review the diary study data, i.e., to clarify uncertain remarks, elaborate on important statements and thus mitigate self-reporting bias [20, p. 257]. These interviews were highly personalized depending on the scope and number of diary entries by each participant. Here, the freedom of the interviewer to deviate from the original structure was very important to cover interesting statements by the participants. At the start of the interview, we focused on the one-to-one conversations from their diaries, whereby participants were asked to rate how close they were to each of their contacts, as previous research showed that relationship closeness has an influence on MMS app preference [30]. To measure this, we used the *inclusion of the other in the self* (IOS) seven-point scale [21]. Finally, participants were also asked to elaborate on the permanence and level of activity of the groups they were members of and whether the group existed on multiple services.

3.4   Data Analysis

To analyse the unstructured textual data, we combined deductive and inductive coding. While we deductively derived three of the top-level categories in our coding scheme from the related work, the sub-level categories and nuances within these categories emerged from an inductive coding process. The coding process involved multiple researchers and two phases [35]: (1) *open coding* and (2) *axial coding*. In the open coding phase, two researchers scanned and compared all textual data from the interview transcripts and diaries of five participants in an iterative manner to inductively develop a set of codes (see the third level in Fig. 2). In the axial coding stage, a third researcher joined the analysis to discuss and rearrange the codes in a bottom-up fashion into higher-level categories or concepts (see levels 1 and 2 in Fig. 2). An affinity diagram helped identify relationships and criteria for demarcation between concepts. The third researcher's role was to objectively question the relevance of the codes in relation to the study's research questions [6]. This resulted in the final coding scheme in Fig. 2 representing all motivations and reasons for temporary switching behavior. Afterwards, the entire data set was coded by one of the authors using this coding scheme using NVivo to help structure the process and keep track of the codes and count the number of occurrences. A central step before analysis of the quantitative diary data was cleaning data entry errors and merging data, e.g., the IOS ratings for contacts collected through the interviews were linked to the relevant participant and contacts.

4   Results

Figure 2 shows the coding scheme that was developed on the basis of our content analysis of the qualitative diary and interview data. In this section, we present a breakdown of the results by the four different main factors uncovered in our content analysis: (1) technological affordances, (2) contextual factors, (3) conversation type, and (4) individual preferences. Sections 4.1, 4.2, 4.3 and 4.4 describe how these different factors play in role in temporary switching between MMS services.

4.1   Technological Affordances

The first factor that influences temporary switching behavior are the Technological affordances of the different messaging services. These can be further subdivided into Features & functionality, Supported message formats, User experience, and Technological barriers.

Features and Functionality. Features and functionality are commonly used interchangeably and can cover different elements, such as support for one-to-one and group conversations, voice and video calls, location sharing, online status indicators, and receipts of read messages [1,2,7,25,32]. A Liked feature/functionality that was mentioned by many participants was control over read receipts, which indicate whether a message has been read already. Participants P2, P4 and P10 all remarked that they prefer WhatsApp over Facebook Messenger, because the latter does not allow read receipts to be turned off. These preferences are consistent with findings of O'Hara et al. [32, p. 1139], who in their study on everyday usage of WhatsApp found that read receipts create social pressure to respond, especially in newly-formed relationships. This causes some of our participants to switch to WhatsApp to avoid this pressure with some conversation partners. This shows that lack of control over a feature can turn it into a Disliked feature/functionality and cause switching behavior.

Related to read receipts is the online status indicator, which shows whether a user is online or not. This features also appears to part the waters between messaging services: while some participants, such as P2, dislike the resulting privacy invasion, others find it useful to figure out which of their contacts are online and could be contacted in case of an urgent question, such as P1, whose brother often spends his nights gaming which is indicated by the online status indication, so she knows when he is reachable. Our data includes several examples of participants deliberately switching messaging services to be able to make use of a specific feature they like. P10, for instance, always switches to WhatsApp when she wishes to record a voice message, because WhatsApp does not impose limits on the duration of voice recordings and because previous recordings do not disappear.

A final issue that made participants prefer one messaging service over another for different contacts was the requirement to supply a phone number to use the

Level 1	Level 2	Level 3	Description	N
Technological affordances				290
	Features & functionality		Statements related to features or functionality offered by an MMS	92
		Liked feature/functionality	Positive perception of a particular feature/functionality of the MMS	33
		Disliked feature/functionality	Negative perception of a particular feature/functionality of the MMS	16
		Cross-device functionality	Cross-device functionality of an MMS	29
		No phone number	Phone number is not required to contact someone	14
	User experience		Opinions about the good or bad user experience offered by an MMS and its features	99
	Message formatting		Supported formats that can be included in messages on the MMS	76
	Technological barriers		Technological barriers that influence the use of the MMS	23
Contextual factors				212
	Cultural influences		Cultural or geographical factors that influence the use of an MMS	18
	Social factors		Social factors that influence the use of an MMS	118
		Closeness of relationship	Statements about the closeness of the relationship with the other person	16
		Critical user mass	Statements about a critical mass of users on the MMS	28
		Knowledge of others' use & preferences	Knowledge of other users' use of and preferences for specific MMS apps	51
		Single-service connection	Only a single MMS connects the user to this person or group	23
	Situational factors		Situational factors that influence the use of an MMS	76
		Initiated by other person	The choice of MMS is determined by the contact(s) who started the conversation	47
		Situational influence	The situation around the user or contact influences the choice of MMS	29
Type of conversation				318
	Topic & activity		Statements related to the topic or activity discussed on the conversation	157
		Casual	Conversations of a casual or relaxed nature	11
		Entertainment	Conversations or content-sharing about entertainment-related topics	33
		Personal	Conversations about personal or serious matters	24
		Planning and events	Conversations related to planning of events or other activities	89
	Duration		MMS better suited towards short comments or longer conversations	25
	Importance/urgency		The perceived importance or urgency of the conversation and its influence on the choice of MMS	18
	Group conversations		Factors that relate specifically to group conversations	77
		Dislike of group conversations	Dislike of certain aspects of group conversations	5
		Group messaging functionality	Feature/functionality related to group messaging	6
		Lurking	No active participation in a group conversation, but passive participation in the background	21
		Persistence	Statements about how long a group has existed on a specific MMS already	45
	Content sharing & reaction		Conversation initiated by sharing of or commenting on social media or Web content	41
Individual ·references				130
	Abandonment		Abandoning an MMS app on the user's smartphone by stopping their use and/or deleting them	6
	Financial costs		Statements about the financial cost of using a particular MMS	5
	Habit		Habits with regard to the use of specific MMS apps	80
	Privacy		User preferences for privacy settings offered by an MMS (e.g., encryption)	9
	Notifications		Statements about whether MMS notifications are turned on or off	17
	Single messaging service preference		User preference for limiting their messaging activity to a single MMS	13

Fig. 2. Coding scheme developed on the basis of the content analysis of the qualitative interview and diary data, containing 950 coded statements and 31 codes, divided over 3 different levels

service, such as SMS or WhatsApp. This No phone number requirement benefited services such as Facebook Messenger in some cases: *"Don't have her number so [Facebook Messenger] is my preferred choice."* (P1). Being forced to exchange phone numbers can be uncomfortable as it requires a certain level of intimacy, something confirmed by Nouwens et al. [30] and Anderson [2, p. 12]. Overall though, while some features may cause users to switch messaging services temporarily, this abandonment is rarely permanent. This suggests that dissatisfaction with an incumbent service does not influence switching intentions, something confirmed by Sun et al. [36]. Instead, our participants seemed to be more influenced by their social network in terms of sticking with unsatisfactory messaging services or adding new ones, as also confirmed by Oghuma et al. [31, p. 663]. For example, P10 states that she does not like the read receipts on Facebook Messenger, yet continues to use it anyway, because *"for a lot of my friends like internationals, it's like Facebook Messenger [that is used]"*.

Message Formatting. Different MMS apps support multiple message formats, such as text, emoji, photos, videos, audio, and links. Cui [11, p. 32] has argued that such formats "give rise to more experience-based communication" and our participants also expressed that using different formats *"spiced up"* their conversations. In the diary study, our participants were asked to report which formats they sent and received using the different MMSs to examine whether these formats could have an influence on temporary switching behavior. In our entire data set of 428 reported interactions, text and emoji were the most-used formats across all services except for Snapchat, where sending photos was just as popular as sending text and emoji. This is likely due to Snapchat's dedicated focus on photo-based communication: *"In my head, Snapchat is photo like Instagram is photo, it's a photo app"* (P?). In terms of photo sharing, Facebook Messenger is most popular, followed by iMessage, Snapchat, and Instagram. However, participants reported a clear distinction between the urgency and importance of photos being shared using those services. For instance, P2 remarked that the photo content shared on Snapchat and Instagram were *"things you wouldn't die if you missed out on"* and P6 considered photos shared on these services as temporary entertainment. In contrast, photos exchanged via iMessage or Facebook Messenger were more often focused on a particular recipient and considered as something more permanent that required a decision or feedback (P6). Photos received using Facebook Messenger or iMessage were also more often saved by the participant, indicating a long-term purpose. In general, this suggests that the purpose of a photo influences which MMS is used to send it.

Several participants did report that they preferred a specific messaging service for communicating a particular message format—examples of the Messaging formatting code. For instance, both P4 and P5 remarked that sharing links was easier on a service like Facebook Messenger: *"I think it has something to do with the fact that with a link on Messenger, then it comes up with a small preview, where on iMessage it's just the link"* (P5). This was further strengthened by the Cross-device functionality of services such as Facebook Messenger, which made it easier for participants P6, P9, and P10 to *"find those links on my computer and to share them on my computer using [Facebook] messenger"* (P10). In fact, the largest share of link sharing at 93% of all 71 instances came from Facebook Messenger on mobile or PC, which suggests that temporary switching behavior is affected positively by the supported message formats. Facebook Messenger's popularity here is likely due to its integration with Facebook.

User Experience. User experience (UX) is commonly defined as a person's perceptions and responses that result from the use of a product. A big part of user experience is the usability of the MMS or its ease of use. Ease of use has been shown to affect adoption behavior [12, p. 985] and it also appears to have an influence on temporary switching behavior, especially in relation to specific features of an MMS. For instance, P10 mentions she deliberately switches to WhatsApp to send voice messages, as she finds the UX of this feature better on WhatsApp than on other services. Several participants favorably compared the UX of iMessage to Facebook Messenger. For instance, P4 states she feels more relaxed when using iMessage and that it has better integration of her favorite GIFs, while P5 and P10 both preferred iMessage for its interface layout and efficiency. Sending new messages or selecting contacts in the iMessage app takes as many clicks as in the Facebook Messenger, yet the latter's UI is more cluttered, leading P10 to remark: *"I like that iMessage looks always so clean"*. However, she continues by stating *"but nobody ever contacts me on iMessage besides [one friend]"*, which indicates other factors influence temporary switching behavior compared to permanent adoption, something that is in line with the findings of Oghuma et al. [31]. P5 also remarked that FB takes longer to start up and feels heavier to run on his phone and thus it is *"just faster to open iMessage and type"*. In general, participants seemed to prefer easy-to-use services that fit most contexts, something in line with the findings of Bouwman et al. [5, p. 66].

Technological Barriers. Since affordances are dependent on the user's ability to perceive accessible design aspects of an MMS, it is relevant to examine the participants' attitudes towards technology in relation to the which and how many different services they use. Participants were asked to self-identify with one of the five categories of technology adoption formulated by Smith et al. [34]. One could expect participants who self-identify as innovators or early adopters to be curious about new technologies and therefore use more different services than the others. However, our diary data did not reveal any differences between the different categories.

4.2   Contextual Factors

In this study, we follow the definition of context proposed by Dey, who defines context as: "[...] any information that can be used to characterise the situation of an entity. An entity is a person, place, or object that is considered relevant to the interaction between a user and an application, including the user and applications themselves" [14, p. 5]. Following this definition, the three main Contextual factors that emerged from our analysis are Cultural influences, Social factors and Situational factors. Of these three, Social factors are second-most frequent switching reasons overall.

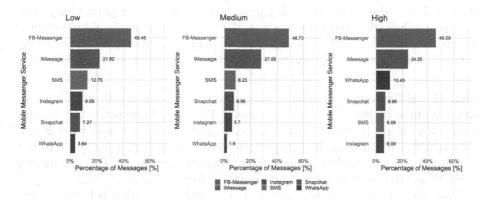

Fig. 3. Use of mobile messenger services in percentage for three levels of IOS

Social Context. Part of the social context is the Personal relation that is maintained with the communication partner. Many previous studies found a strong effect of personal relation categories (e.g., friends, family members, partners, colleagues) on the choice of messaging service [8,27,30]. In this study, we measure the type of relationship using the IOS closeness scale as described in Sect. 3.3. Each conversation partner in assessed on a scale from 1 to 7 and categorized into a relationship of low (1–2.5), medium (3–5) or high (5.5–7) closeness. Figure 3 visualizes the use of mobile messaging applications across these three closeness groups and shows Facebook Messenger and iMessage to be the most-used MMS—independent of how close the communication partners were. Moreover, it can be observed that WhatsApp is used relatively more with very close contacts, whereas SMS seems to be negatively associated with closeness to the conversation partner: the more distant two persons are the more likely they are to communicate via SMS. Moreover, our participants reported one out of three messages sent to a colleague to be via SMS. These observations are supported by comments from our participants coded as Closeness of relationship, e.g., that *"for remote acquaintances like this it is common to exchange numbers and use SMS"* (P1).

Besides the Closeness of relationship, social context factors are mainly dominated by the code Knowledge of others' use & preferences. Especially among friends and family members, users seem to be aware of which MMS apps people do (not) have installed, which ones they prefer using or a special hardware situation which makes it impossible for them to use certain apps. This becomes evident in participant comments like *"[she] doesn't have other messaging services than SMS and WeChat"* (P10) or *"He is a person who chose to jump off Facebook so that's why he texted me on SMS"* (P2). In general, participants deliberately choose the service that they know the other person will most likely check and respond on. This expectation goes both ways as people experience being contacted with their preferred messaging app. This agrees with previous findings that *subjective norms*—the behavior that close relations think one should or should not engage in—has the most powerful impact on users' switching intention [36]. Social norms appear to influence not only permanent but also temporary switching behavior.

Situational Context. Two codes Initiated by other person and Situational influence characterize situation related context factors. Participants reported switching in cases where other persons initiated the conversation through a messaging app that is different from the one they tend to use or used in their most recent conversation (with another person). The reported experience of switching can possibly be attributed to a feeling of deviation from the norm.

Another situational context factor that prompts switching behavior is the activity that people carry out. There is a tendency towards switching to SMS or iMessage when participants are occupied, e.g., while at work. On the one hand, this is based on the fact that people only receive notifications from some messaging apps while other apps might ask for multiple check-ups throughout the day. P6, for example, states that she only gets notified for new messages received via SMS and that she will not necessarily check Facebook Messenger. On the other hand, the choice of messaging app also depends on the recipient's situation, which can be see in P3's comment: *"I think it has something to do with the fact that [my partner] is extremely busy so it has been like short SMS-coordinating. Yeah, he hasn't had time to be on social media"*. In general, partners were found to switch the most between services on the same day when one or both were at work.

4.3   Type of Conversation

The type of conversation is the driving factor for temporary switching between MMS apps. Differences in conversation types that give rise to switching range from the gravity of the matter (codes Importance/urgency and Personal vs. Entertainment) to the length of the intended conversation (codes Duration and Casual). The two most frequent codes in the top-level category Type of conversation, are cases of switching for Planning & events and Content sharing & reaction.

Planning and Events. Previous studies suggest that coordination between multiple people, such as the purchase of a joint birthday gift or the organisation of an event, can have a strong impact on the choice of messaging service [27]. In our study, we observed similar tendencies. P2, for example, noted: *"We almost always communicate about practical things on iMessage which is why I chose* *it"*. And P3 reports: *"I chose to write an SMS as we were going to coordinate a time to meet tomorrow"*. The exact reason for why one service gets chosen over another can vary strongly from participant to participant. Some participants just want to avoid using messaging apps for serious tasks like planning if those apps, in their eyes, are purely meant for entertainment. P1, for instance, states: *"We started the conversation on Instagram but I switched to Messenger because we were going to plan to meet...and Instagram doesn't feel right to communicate important things on"*. For others, it is the feature of messaging history that lets them prefer one app over another in such a context. P4 expresses how it can be frustrating to use Snapchat for planning because *"oh no the message disappears and then in an hour I've forgotten it"*. Thus tasks like planning lead to temporary switching even within conversations.

Content Sharing and Reaction. Often, the choice of MMS is determined by content that gets consumed or shared on a certain social media platform. In relation to Instagram, P4 expressed that almost every message in her inbox was initiated by shared posts, and she does not believe that she or her contacts would start a conversation on Instagram if it was not related to an Instagram post. This sentiment is echoed independently by both P1 (*"I commented on his [Instagram] story and then the conversation started from there"*) and P3. This applies to both privately and publicly shared content as the following comment by P10 shows: *"a response to [a friend] reacting to a public [Facebook] event- she said she would attend- I therefore texted her on [Facebook] which was the most intuitive or fastest way of communicating"*.

Group Conversations. In total, our participants recorded three times more one-to-one conversations than group-conversations. For both types of conversations, Facebook Messenger was the preferred app while iMessage came second. On the one hand, this may be an artefact of the communication method as a group conversation automatically reaches multiple people. On the other hand, this can be related to an antipathy (code Dislike of group conversations) that our participants feel towards group conversations in general, which makes them avoid group chats or only act as passive readers (code Lurking). The code Persistence hints to the subjective impression that our participants uttered that group conversations on some applications like WhatsApp are more stable than on other MMS. Another aspect influencing the choice of messaging app is the lack of interoperability between different operating systems: *"If just one person doesn't have an iPhone, then you can't make group conversations, ehm, then you'll just receive a bunch of individual messages as if it was a group conversation. It's a mess sometimes. It's awfully annoying."* P5 further emphasizes that if a group conversation is initiated on iMessage with all-iPhone users, but at one point a person switches to another phone brand, then the conversation turns into a mess. He compares this with being CC on an email correspondence. This frustration is also recognized in a study by Anderson [2].

4.4   Individual Preferences

The fourth and final category that emerged from our content analysis was that of Individual preferences: specific preferences for messaging services expressed by the participants that relate to Privacy, Notifications, Financial costs, or Habit. Perhaps surprisingly, given contradictory findings in earlier related work [25], Privacy was rarely seen as the reason for switching between MMS apps for our participants. The clearest example came from P4 about the Signal MMS: *"That is our preferred app when we want to talk secret stuff. We feel like no one else is listening in, even though we could've had the conversation somewhere else instead."*. More common among our participants was a Single messaging service preference for an MMS app that could do it all, even though this was not always possible. For instance, P9 expressed a strong preference for only using Facebook Messenger, because it *"[...] allows you to multi-task, like a Swiss army knife, so I prefer it simply because of that. That I don't have to switch between two or three different apps all the time."*. Occasionally, participants considered Financial costs when deciding on which MMS app to use: *"She is in Greenland and SMS would be too expensive for her"* (P1). Finally, the most frequent factor influencing participants' switching between messaging services was Habit. A habit can be defined as a "learned automatic response triggered by environmental cues without conscious control" [36, p. 732]. Many participants stated that they were often in the habit of continuing conversations with a specific contact using the MMS that they had used previously to communicate with this person. P8 argued that sticking with the same MMS meant that *"you can easily go back and look at what you last talked about"*. Even with new conversations after a longer period of inactivity P2 expressed how one MMS could feel more natural to use. One reason for this could be related to Features & functionality: many MMS apps organize the conversation threads in order of recency, which makes it easier to continue an existing conversation in the same MMS.

However, research has shown that old habits can be hard to break [26], which could be responsible for people holding on to some MMS apps despite many of the other factors pulling them in the direction of other MMS apps. P4 expressed a preference for using SMS because *"you grew up with the standard SMS service, it's the one you feel kind of safe about"*, whereas P2 referred to herself as a creature of habit in that she prefers the iMessage app, since it was the first MMS app on her iPhone. This first-mover advantage can also exhibit itself at the level of individual features, which means that people will continue to switch back to a specific MMS just to use that one feature. For instance, P10 expressed a preference for WhatsApp for voice messaging and photo sharing, because it was the first to integrate this functionality in an accessible way, despite other MMS apps following suit thereafter.

The powerful influence of habits on the use of specific MMS apps can also manifest on a conversational level, where pairs or groups of people prefer to use a single MMS service for their communication, because *"this is where we usually communicate"*. Some of these habits were formed before certain newer MMS apps were released, with some participants not even being aware of their habits until they were asked to reflect on this. For instance, P3 communicates on Facebook Messenger with a group of old friends, but normally uses SMS when communicating with one of them in a one-to-one setting: *"that's just what we have done (...), it's actually weird"*. Our finding that habits have a powerful influence on switching behavior is supported by Sun et al. [36, p. 235], who found habits to be behavioral-based antecedents of inertia, which affects switching behavior negatively. Thus, they refer to habitual behavior as a mooring factor.

5   Discussion and Conclusion

In this paper, we reported the findings of a triangulation study pairing a diary-study with semi-structured interviews to investigate the extent and motivation for temporary switching behavior between MMSs. Combining these two methods was very fruitful as it gave us insights into both the frequency (quantitative) and reasons (qualitative) behind temporary switching. Our findings indicated that temporary switching behavior is influenced by four main types of factors: (1) technological affordances, (2) contextual factors, (3) the type of conversation, and (4) individual preferences.

In most cases, the type of conversation determines temporary switching between MMSs. Within this theme, concrete switching reasons vary from the topic of the conversation to the duration and the possible size of the conversation group. The most frequently mentioned reasons for choosing to use a certain MMS app was event planning, which our participants have a specific app for.

The second-most central theme is technological affordances. A certain feature like sending voice messages of unrestricted duration or the easy integration of GIFs motivates our participants to switch from one app to another. The format of a message can have a substantial influence on what type of messenger gets used. Unique or well-designed features often go hand in hand with a positive UX, which makes people want to temporarily switch to an app more often. Perhaps surprisingly, a bad UX does not influence the permanency of switching intentions as long as important contacts kept using that MMS app, as also confirmed by Oghuma et al. [31, p. 663].

These social ties, a type of contextual factor, were the most frequently mentioned reasons for temporary switching between MMS apps, which mirrors similar findings with regard to permanent switching [27,33]. SMS still had a role to play, for instance when needing to send an urgent message—due to SMS notifications rarely being disabled—or when sending messages to contacts the user is less close to. This could be because SMS messages are seen as more formal and trustworthy [8,11].

Finally, individual preferences emerged as a fourth theme. The most striking finding here is that peoples habits and routines have a strong hold over our choice of MMS apps. Habitual interaction can form on different levels, such as technological in case of first-mover advantages in terms of specific features or conversational, e.g., when communication with another person has always been via a specific app.

To sum up, we found that people alternate between a plethora of different messaging apps for many different reasons. Although some services might seem old and outdated as newer MMS apps reach the market, older apps that serve a specific purpose are rarely phased out. Installing additional MMS apps side-by-side appears to be more likely than permanent abandonment of older MMS apps. While some participants did desire the bundling of functionality into a single app, most participants were content with the use of different services at the same time. Our findings suggest that this adds meaning to their conversations, as *"they each have their advantage or forte"*.

References

1. Aal, L.B., Parmar, J.N., Patel, V.R., Sen, D.J.: Whatsapp, skype, wickr, viber, twitter and blog are ready to asymptote globally from all corners during communications in latest fast life. Res. J. Sci. Technol. **6**(2), 101–116 (2014)
2. Anderson, K.: Getting acquainted with social networks and apps: whatsapp-ening with mobile instant messaging? Library Hi Tech News **33**(6), 11–15 (2016)
3. Bajaj, H., Jindal, R.: Thinking beyond whatsapp. In: 2015 2nd International Conference on Computing for Sustainable Global Development (INDIACom), pp. 1443–1447 (2015)
4. Bertel, T.F., Ling, R.: "It's just not that exciting anymore": the changing centrality of SMS in the everyday lives of young Danes. New Media Soc. **18**(7), 1293–1309 (2014)
5. Bouwman, H., Bejar, A., Nikou, S.: Mobile Services put in Context: a Q-sort Analysis. Telematics Inform. **29**(1), 66–81 (2012)
6. Braun, V., Clarke, V.: Using thematic analysis in psychology. Qualitative Res. Psychol. **3**(2), 77–101 (2006)
7. Cho, V., Hung, H.: Sending mobile messages to different social ties in modern urban life: How do anxiety and time-shortage matter? Inf. Technol. People **28**(3), 544–569 (2015)
8. Church, K., de Oliveira, R.: What's up with WhatsApp? comparing mobile instant messaging behaviors with traditional SMS. In: MobileHCI 2013: Proceedings of the 15th International Conference on Human-Computer Interaction with Mobile Devices and Services, pp. 352–361. ACM, New York, USA (2013)
9. Constantiou, I.D., Damsgaard, J., Knutsen, L.: The four incremental steps toward advanced mobile service adoption. Commun. ACM **50**(6), 51–55 (2007)
10. Cramer, H., Jacobs, M.L.: Couples' communication channels: What, when & why? In: Proceedings of the 33rd Annual ACM Conference on Human Factors in Computing Systems, pp. 709–712. CHI 2015, Association for Computing Machinery, New York, NY, USA (2015)
11. Cui, D.: Beyond "connected presence": multimedia mobile instant messaging in close relationship management. Mobile Media Commun. **4**(1), 19–36 (2016)
12. Davis, F.D., Bagozzi, R.P., Warshaw, P.R.: User acceptance of computer technology: a comparison of two theoretical models. Manage. Sci. **35**(8), 982–1003 (1989)
13. Deloitte: Global mobile consumer trends: 1st Edition. https://www2.deloitte.com/cn/en/pages/technology-media-and-telecommunications/articles/global-mobile-consumer-trends.html. Accessed 19 Oct 2020
14. Dey, A.K.: Understanding and using context. Personal Ubiquitous Comput. **5**(1), 4–7 (2001)

15. Dhir, A., Kaur, P., Rajala, R.: Continued use of mobile instant messaging apps: a new perspective on theories of consumption, flow, and planned behavior. Soc. Sci. Comput. Rev. **38**(2), 147–169 (2020)
16. eMarketer: App Downloads Remain Dominated by Games. But the most popular individual apps are for messaging. https://www.emarketer.com/content/app-downloads-remain-dominated-by-games. Accessed 19 Oct 2020
17. eMarketer: eMarketer Releases Latest Estimates for Worldwide Messaging App Usage. https://www.emarketer.com/Article/eMarketer-Releases-Latest-Estimates-Worldwide-Messaging-App-Usage/1016214. Accessed 19 Oct 2020
18. eMarketer: eMarketer Updates Worldwide Internet and Mobile User Figures. https://www.emarketer.com/content/emarketer-updates-worldwide-internet-and-mobile-user-figures. Accessed 19 Oct 2020
19. eMarketer: US Smartphone Users Have Little Love for Communication Apps. https://www.emarketer.com/Article/US-Smartphone-Users-Have-Little-Love-Communication-Apps/1016335. Accessed 19 Oct 2020
20. Goodman, E., Kuniavsky, M., Moed, A.: Morgan Kaufmann Publishers, San Francisco (2012)
21. Gächter, S., Starmer, C., Tufano, F.: Measuring the closeness of relationships: a comprehensive evaluation of the 'inclusion of the other in the self' scale. PLOS ONE **10**(6), 1–19 (2015)
22. Hou, A.C.Y.: Switching motivations on instant messaging: a study based on two factor theory. In: Wang, L., Uesugi, S., Ting, I.H., Okuhara, K., Wang, K. (eds.) Multidisciplinary Social Networks Research, pp. 3–15. Springer, Heidelberg (2015)
23. Hussein, A.: The use of triangulation in social sciences research: can qualitative and quantitative methods be combined? J. Comparative Soc. Work **4**(1), 1–12 (2009)
24. Gallup, Kantar: Mobile Life 2017. Technical report, Kantar Gallup (2017)
25. Lai, I.K.W., Shi, G.: The impact of privacy concerns on the intention for continued use of an integrated mobile instant messaging and social network platform. Int. J. Mob. Commun. **13**(6), 641–669 (2015)
26. Martiros, N., Burgess, A.A., Graybiel, A.M.: Inversely active striatal projection neurons and interneurons selectively delimit useful behavioral sequences. Current Biol. **28**(4), 560–573 (2018)
27. Menichelli, E., Ling, R.: Modeling relevance of mobile communication services by social setting dimensions. New Media Soc. **20**(1), 311–331 (2018)
28. Mutlu, H.M., Der, A.: Unified theory of acceptance and use of technology: the adoption of mobile messaging application. In: Proceedings of 14th International Scientific Conference on Economic and Social Development, pp. 88–94. Varazdin Development and Entrepreneurship Agency, Varazdin, Croatia (2016)
29. Newman, N., Fletcher, R., Kalogeropoulos, A., Levy, D.A.L., Kleis Nielsen, R.: Digital News Report 2018. Tech. rep., Reuters Institute for the Study of Journalism (2018)
30. Nouwens, M., Griggio, C.F., Mackay, W.E.: "WhatsApp is for Family; Messenger is for Friends": communication places in app ecosystems. In: CHI 2017: Proceedings of the 2017 CHI Conference on Human Factors in Computing Systems, pp. 727–735. ACM, New York, USA (2017)
31. Oghuma, A.P., Chang, Y., Libaque-Saenz, C.F., Park, M.C., Rho, J.J.: Benefit-confirmation model for post-adoption behavior of mobile instant messaging applications: a comparative analysis of KakaoTalk and Joyn in Korea. Telecommun. Policy **39**(8), 658–677 (2015)

32. O'Hara, K.P., Massimi, M., Harper, R., Rubens, S., Morris, J.: Everyday dwelling with whatsapp. In: Proceedings of the 17th ACM Conference on Computer Supported Cooperative Work & Social Computing, pp. 1131–1143. CSCW 2014, Association for Computing Machinery, New York, USA (2014)
33. Peng, X., Zhao, Y., Zhu, Q.: Investigating user switching intention for mobile instant messaging application: taking WeChat as an example. Comput. Human Behav. **64**, 206–216 (2016)
34. Smith, S.D., Salaway, G., Caruso, J.B.: The ECAR Study of Undergraduate Students and Information Technology, 2009. Technical report, Boulder, Colorado, USA (2009)
35. Strauss, A., Corbin, J.M.: Grounded Theory in Practice, Sage (1997)
36. Sun, Y., Liu, D., Chen, S., Wu, X., Shen, X.L., Zhang, X.: Understanding users' switching behavior of mobile instant messaging applications: an empirical study from the perspective of push-pull-mooring framework. Comput. Human Behav. **75**, 727–738 (2017)
37. Tassy, A., Nielsen, M.B., Jakobsen, D.T.: It-anvendelse i befolkningen 2018. Technical report, Danmarks Statistik (2018)
38. Turner, L.D., Whitaker, R.M., Allen, S.M., Linden, D.E.J., Tu, K., Li, J., Don, T.: Evidence to support common application switching behaviour on smartphones. Royal Soc. Open Sci. **6**(3), 1–9 (2019)
39. Venkatesh, V., Thong, J.Y.L., Xu, X.: Consumer acceptance and use of information technology: extending the unified theory of acceptance and use of technology. MIS Quarterly **36**(1), 157–178 (2012)
40. Yang, H.L., Lin, S.L.: User adoption of mobile social service. In: Proceedings of the 2017 International Conference on Data Mining, Communications and Information Technology. DMCIT 2017, ACM, New York, USA (2017)
41. Yoon, C., Jeong, C., Rolland, E.: Understanding individual adoption of mobile instant messaging: a multiple perspectives approach. Inf. Technol. Manage. **16**(2), 139–151 (2015)

Appealing to the Gut Feeling: How Intermittent Fasters Choose Information Tab Interfaces for Information Acquisition

Hyeyoung Ryu[1]([⊠])[iD] and Seoyeon Hong[2]

[1] University of Washington, Seattle, WA 98195, USA
hyryu115@uw.edu
[2] Yonsei University, Seoul 03722, Korea
seoyeonhong@yonsei.ac.kr

Abstract. Although many deem intermittent fasting (IF) a healthy dietary regimen, there is a paucity of scientific evidence to corroborate IF health benefits in human studies. However, its comparative ease and the emphasized benefits in the light of COVID-19 (e.g., weight loss and immunization improvement) have led to the increase of IF adoption. A vast number of intermittent fasters have not sought consultation from health professionals, which can bring adverse health effects. Most intermittent fasters use mobile apps to get assistance for IF. Types of assistance offered by the IF mobile applications may range from tracking (e.g., fasting periods, calorie intake) to obtaining knowledge about IF. However, it is unclear how much people are using the features for learning more about IF which is crucial to making healthier decisions in the IF adoption process. Thus, we organized our study into two stages for establishing design implications that further encourage a safety-conscious and user-friendly IF experience. We first investigated how IF app users who have chosen apps that provide extensive IF-specific knowledge acquire the said knowledge via (i) topic modeling of user app reviews, (ii) detecting modularity in co-word maps drawn from reviews specific to IF information acquisition, (iii) locating the position of keywords indicating information acquisition in the reviews. Then, we examined how users judge the effectiveness of knowledge provision interfaces in obtaining information. We investigated this aspect with an interface ranking user task for information tabs and organized user rationale using manual coding and co-word mapping.

Keywords: Intermittent fasting · Safety-conscious diet · Text mining · Mobile application · Information acquisition

1 Introduction

Alaine, a hypothetical 2-week intermittent faster, is amazed by her weight loss. She notes in her review of the app, "I can eat anything as long as it's within my

K. Toeppe et al. (Eds.): iConference 2021, LNCS 12645, pp. 287–300, 2021.
https://doi.org/10.1007/978-3-030-71292-1_23

8 h eating window. Just need to check track the time with my intermittent fasting tracker app." This is a common approach taken by the increasing adopters of the intermittent fasting (IF) lifestyle. There are various forms of IF but they share the foundation that the benefits of IF are derived from taking periodic breaks from eating [43]. The most common forms of IF are time-restricted feeding where intermittent fasters would limit the eating window to 8 hs and fasting for 16 h [48] or periodic prolonged fasting in which calorie intake would be limited or restricted on the 2 weekly fasting days [41]. Although IF is perceived as a healthy dietary regimen [26], the paucity of scientific evidence to corroborate the health benefits in human studies [9,17] as opposed to the more concrete animal trial studies [1,7,43] which indicates that there is a lack of evidence for recommending IF for public health practice [33]. However, its overemphasized benefits (e.g., weight loss [9,26] and immunization benefit in the light of COVID-19 [16,49] over surfacing health downsides such as loss of lean muscle mass [24] has led to its surge of adoption [33]. It is also a rising concern that many of those who have incorporated IF into their lifestyles have not sought consultation from health professionals, which can lead to adverse health effects, especially in the case of those with medical conditions more affected by dietary intakes such as diabetes [31]. In many dietary change applications, the focus has been on motivation for a longer commitment to the diet in diverse forms: peer support [29,36], rewards and punishments [32,47], and goal tracking [25,42]. However, since the long-term benefits of IF have not been fully proven with human trials, precautionary measures of informing the users of IF related knowledge should be taken to a greater degree before encouraging the partially credible benefits.The precautionary measures can be implemented most widely with mobile applications for IF as the IF app market is expanding [23,34,45,46] and gaining popularity among users [21,39]. In the IF mobile applications, the types of assistance may range from time and calorie tracking to gaining knowledge about IF. With only partially confirmed benefits of IF, the usage of the last type of assistance needs to be investigated for a safety-conscious and healthy dietary change through IF. Thus, we investigated two aspects of IF-related knowledge acquisition from applications for establishing design implications of a more safety-conscious and user-friendly IF experience. The first aspect is if and how people who have chosen applications with extensive IF-related knowledge acquire the said knowledge via (i) topic modeling of all user reviews, (ii) modularity detection in co-word maps specifically for IF related information acquisition reviews, and (iii) index location of the words indicating information acquisition in the reviews. The second aspect is how users judge which knowledge provision interface is more effective for information acquisition with comparison of the five types of interfaces. We investigated this aspect with an IF application information tab interface ranking task and both manual coding and co-word mapping of the rationales users provided for their ranking process.

2   Related Work

2.1   Lacking Robustness of Human Studies on Intermittent Fasting Health Benefits

The popularity of IF has increased for its claimed benefit on health, such as weight loss and immunization benefits. Patterson and Sears [33] stated that the October 2016 search result for "diet fasting intermittent alternate day" had more than 210,000 hits. Four years later, the October 2020 search result for the same query had approximately 2,110,000 results. Amid COVID-19, people have reported weight gains and sought ways to lose weight [2,49] and increase their immunization to lower their chances of contracting COVID-19 [16]. Thus, the advantages of IF are appealing to the vast majority. However, the advantages of IF are not yet proven with certainty in human clinical trials although they have been proved through animal trials. Mattson and Wan [26] state that progressive increase in lifespan for rats through progressive decrease in calorie intake has been proven but they emphasize that there are no well-controlled human studies to corroborate the same health benefits for humans. Horne et al. [17] also support the need for further research with humans to build stronger grounds for the benefits of IF than the status quo, especially for metabolic health and cognitive performance improvement, and long-term cardiovascular outcomes.

Moreover, Stockman et al. [43] state current IF research lacks robustness as the individuals who would benefit the most from IF is still unclear and deters healthcare professionals from recommending IF to patients as standard practice. Lowe et al. [24] even points out that lean muscle mass may be a side effect of IF but there are even caveats to this study in that it had a relatively small sample size and only looked at the metabolic effects of IF. Therefore, intermittent fasters need to be better informed of the evidence-based support of IF mechanisms and its benefits and harms to adopt a form of IF that would possibly benefit them the most [33].

2.2   Text Mining User App Reviews

Because mobile app reviews carry a plethora of information on user experience and expectations [13], we collected user reviews of current IF apps to evaluate the practices of information acquisition of IF app users. Previous research implemented LDA topic modeling to organize user reviews into coherent topic clusters for identifying app features [8,11,12,27,35]. Sullivan et al. [44] conducted LDA topic modeling on Amazon product reviews to distinguish potentially unsafe nutritional supplements by searching for topics insinuating adverse reactions. Topic modeling is often paired with sentiment analysis for user opinion mining [10,14,15,22]. Guzman and Maalej [15] proposed a framework for analyzing user reviews by using App Store reviews to extract app features through LDA and then using sentiment analysis to determine user satisfaction level of each feature. Guo et al. [14] performed sentiment analysis on topics to discover key dimensions for improving hotel management. Lin and He [22] proposed a joint sentiment/topic model (JST) that simultaneously identifies sentiment and topic. Diao et al. [10] devised a recommendation system trained by integrating topic modeling, movie ratings, and sentiment analysis using movie reviews. Therefore, building on previous literature, we proceed with LDA topic modeling and sentiment analysis to determine the current status of information reception among IF app users.

3   Information Reception of IF App Users

3.1   Data Collection

We scraped 34,886 app reviews from Google Playstore and 15,082 reviews from Apple Appstore until September 2020 from the following five current apps that provided a separate learning section: (a) Life Fasting Tracker, (b) Simple: Fasting & Meal Tracker, (c) BodyFast Intermittent Fasting Tracker - Diet Coach (d) DoFasting - Intermittent Fasting & Healthy Diet, and (e) MyFast - Intermittent Fasting Tracker Schedule App. From the collection, we eliminated the 11,730 reviews with insufficient length (i.e., 50 characters and below), which do not suggest significant meaning (e.g., "Love it Sooo good") from analysis to optimize topic model performance.

3.2   Data Preprocessing

The LDA model requires a dictionary and a corpus. A dictionary assigns a unique ID to each token in the entire document collection, while a corpus produces a mapping of each document referencing the dictionary [5]. Before tokenizing our data, we proceeded with data cleaning using NLTK [4]: (a) we removed English stopwords (i.e., frequently used words that do not convey much significant meaning that discourages optimal model performance), (b) extracted nouns and verbs from the text using Part-of-Speech tagging, (c) then lemmatized the words to restore inflectional word forms to its base form [4].

3.3   Topic Modeling

To determine the elements of IF apps most valuable to users, we employed topic modeling to discover abstract topics within app reviews. Latent Dirichlet Allocation (LDA) is one of the most frequently used topic modeling methods [19]. LDA is an unsupervised learning algorithm that assumes that each document was generated by assembling a mix of topics, then selecting the words that belong to each topic [5]. Python packages such as Gensim [38] and Mallet [28] allow LDA implementations. To optimize model performance, we compared the performances of different models trained on (a) nouns, (b) verbs, (c) nouns and verbs, in unigram and bigram forms using Gensim and Mallet. To find the optimal topic number, we used the elbow method, sampling a range of 2 to 50 to discover the model that yields the best coherence value as it shows the most accurate way to determine the number of topics for the model [30].

3.4   Sentiment Analysis

From the topic modeling result, we proceeded to investigate the users' sentiment on each topic via sentiment analysis [40]. Using VADER (Valence Aware Dictionary and Sentiment Reasoner), the lexicon and rule-based sentiment analyzer [18], we evaluated each review's sentiment and extracted the dominant sentiment and its distribution for each topic. We used compound scores to classify sentiments, which provide a normalized score between -1 and 1, calculated by adjusting the sum of each word's valence in a document.

3.5   Results

Our LDA model generated 41 topics with a coherence score of 0.4637 (see Fig. 1), built using Mallet, and trained on noun unigrams. From those 41 topics, we reassembled highly correlated topics (e.g., topics such as "Weight Loss" and "Body Slimming") and excluded topics that only pertained to app performance or payment (e.g., "Working now: was glitching but the issue was resolved!"), or were shallow comments regarding the app (e.g., " I just love using this app, and have not had any issues this far. It's great!").

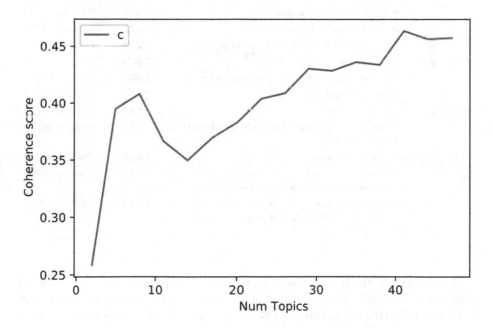

Fig. 1. Coherence value per number of topics used in LDA topic modeling

Table 1 summarizes the organized result, which consists of 18 topics and its dominant sentiment, classified into five main categories: (a) tracking features, (b) informational features, (c) user intent, (d) usability, and (e) user interface

(UI). User reviews pertaining to the use of IF information tab (i.e., topic 9) constituted only 2.23% of all reviews, implying that users are less prone to active acquisition of IF-related knowledge, compared to other informational features which users are involuntarily exposed to (i.e., guided schedule, workout routines, meal recommendations form 15.83% of all reviews). Furthermore, the IF-specific informational features were one of the most highly rated by users among app features besides calorie tracking, with 96% of its reviews being positive, which begs further inspection on design implications for effective information acquisition.

Table 1. Intermittent fasting app review topics and dominant sentiments

Category	Topic	Percentage	Sentiment
Tracking Features	1 cal Tracking	9.34%	Positive (96%)
	2 The Range of Tracking Features Provided	6.99%	Positive (93%)
	3 Food Intake Tracking & Dietary Guides	2.68%	Positive (92%)
	4 Time Logging	2.50%	Positive (84%)
	5 Notifications & Reminders	2.09%	Positive (89%)
Informational Features	6 Guided Schedule	6.64%	Positive (87%)
	7 Workout Routines	4.77%	Positive (94%)
	8 Meal Recommendations	4.42%	Positive (89%)
	9 Information Tab Evaluation	2.23%	Positive (96%)
	10 Quality of Paid Content (Subscription)	2.22%	Positive (47%)
User Intent	11 Accounts of Weight Loss	15.62%	Positive (91%)
	12 Changing Lifestyle & Increasing Fitness	3.45%	Positive (92%)
	13 Improving Health	2.53%	Positive (91%)
Usability	14 Ease of Use	5.32%	Positive (94%)
	15 Does not Accommodate Different Lifestyles (e.g. night shift)	3.24%	Positive (87%)
	16 Customization	1.63%	Positive (90%)
UI	17 User Interface Judging Criteria (e.g. intuitiveness, simplicity, user-friendliness)	3.73%	Positive (96%)
	18 App Aesthetics (e.g. "love the arc and icons", "I like the different ways to see my stats")	1.82%	Positive (88%)

To investigate the informational features section further on how each word related to knowledge was associated with other topic-representing nouns and sentiment-reflecting adjectives, we calculated the co-occurrences of the reviews with informational features and clustered the co-occurrences using the Louvain algorithm [6] for modularity detection to create the co-word map on Gephi (an open source software network analysis program) [3]. We used co-word maps as it is more accurate in detecting topics than topic modeling when there are less than 1,000 inputs [20]. The node sizes and labels are shown to be ranked by each node's betweenness centrality score which implies the nodes' extent to which a vertex lies on paths between other vertices to determine the central nodes [37]. Nodes that lie on the shortest paths will have higher betweenness centrality, and as shown in the co-word map, words indicating relations to knowledge are represented as having a prominently larger size node and node label as they would be used as the keywords of the sentences (e.g. tip and information).

We found that words with high betweenness centrality (higher than 0.5 in normalized betweenness centrality scores) relevant to information acquisition in the co-word map was tip, guidance, information, article and knowledge (see Fig. 2). We observed that tip and guidance were used together frequently and that the related topics were exercise and recipes as well as motivation (e.g., "This one offers me daily motivation boosts, guidance, and useful tips"). The word information was associated with weight loss and nutrition, and related adjectives such as plenty, lot, and ton which indicated a vast amount of information (e.g., "Helps you track your food intake and its database on nutrition information is great"). The word article was highly associated with positive adjectives such as great and good which reflected users' sanguine response to provided articles (e.g., "It has great, short, informational articles about fasting in general"). The word knowledge was associated with fitness and health (e.g., "...knowledge regarding overall body health, fitness and rapid weight loss"). The word question was associated with calorie and meal tracking during IF (e.g., "They provide personalized meal plans based on a set of questions you answer").

As co-word maps do not show the position of information gain (IG) words, we calculated the position of the IG words by dividing the position of the word in the sentence by the number of words in the sentence and drew a density plot of the position of the IG words (see Fig. 3). We observed that the average of the IG word positions are mostly higher than 0.6. The skewness of the positions are all negative which means that most words are placed later in the sentence than the average. After observing all the sentences with positions higher than the average, we saw that the sentences were located at a later part of the sentence because they were mentioned as an additional part of the review (e.g. "also a lot of information about nutrition is given.", "and articles are great."). This reflects the perception of the knowledge provision sections as an auxiliary features from users who have tried out or are using said features.

4   Information Tab Interface Online Ranking Session

4.1   Procedure

In this session, we recruited 80 participants (46 female, 34 male) who have been using IF apps for more than three months. Participants' ages ranged from 19 to 69 years (M = 31.77, SD = 12.68) We excluded one participant as she gave up on ranking the information tabs in the middle of the session. 27 participants had previously used the information tabs before and 52 had not. After asking them about their usage of information tabs, we asked them to watch 15 to 20 s usage videos of the information tabs (i.e. scrolling through IF information categories, clicking and reading the subsidiary questions or articles) of the five

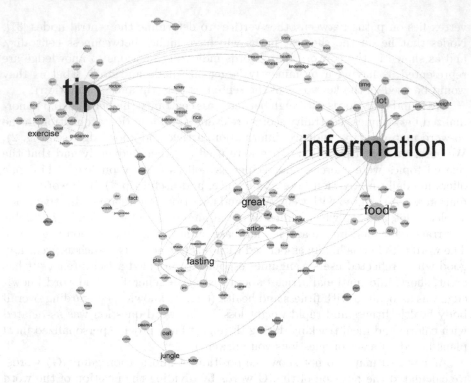

Fig. 2. Co-word map of topics in IF mobile application with information tabs reviews

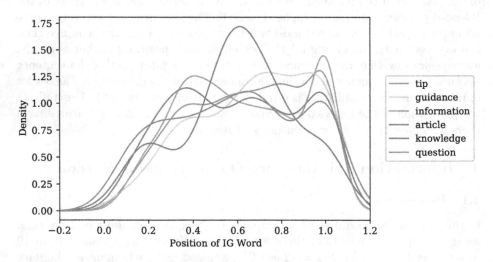

Fig. 3. Density plot of position of information gain words

applications that currently have information tabs. Then, we asked them to rank the information tabs in order of effectiveness of information acquisition and provide rationale for the ranking. We investigated the reasons for why each group, one group that had previously used information tabs and one group that did not, ranked the interfaces in the way they did through co-word map creation of the reviews and the manual coding of the rationale text for themes.

4.2   Results

When we averaged the reverse rank (6 - actual rank) each of the information tab interfaces received from the participants, we saw that the BodyFast information tab interface had the highest reverse rank average, which meant that they were ranked the highest on average (see Table 2. On the contrary, Simple had received the lowest reverse rank average, which meant that they were ranked the lowest on average. Since the order of information tab interface was the same for both the group that used information tabs before and the group that did not, we probed the reasons why this ranking order was shared by both groups via co-word mapping (see Fig. 4) and manual coding of the rationales.

Table 2. Reverse rank average for IF app information tab interfaces.

Information Tab Usage	BodyFast	DoFasting	Life	MyFast	Simple
Yes	3.444	3.370	3.185	2.704	2.296
No	3.635	2.981	2.962	2.923	2.500

Although some participants have stated that their rationale for ranking was their gut feeling, some participants provided deeper insights to the "gut feeling". The three specific themes for the ranking rationales were (i) information quality, (ii) information relevance, and (iii) information presentation. First, participants deemed the information quality to be higher or useful when the provided information was new or general. Second, participants felt that the information was relevant when the research articles provided were directly related to IF. Third, for information presentation, users said that having too many options to choose from discouraged their usage (i.e. "an overwhelming number of menus" and "Reducing the options is a must. It's just too much."). Also, participants said that the blurb of information (i.e. short and definitive answers) was better for them to obtain IF related knowledge. Moreover, the clutter of images and text discouraged participants from using the information tab.

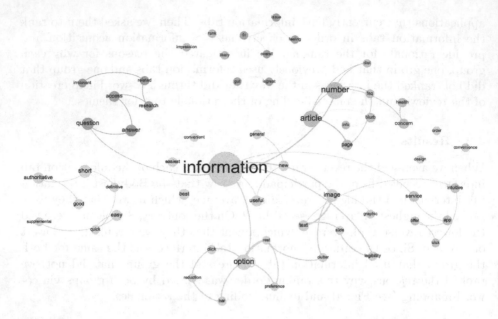

Fig. 4. Co-word map of information tab interface online ranking rationales

5   Conclusion

With our three pivotal findings on the knowledge conveyance of IF applications, we have demonstrated (i) the lack of usage of the information tabs which represent voluntary information acquisition, (ii) how people use the information tabs and evaluate each usage, and (iii) the criteria IF application users use to rank learning effectiveness of IF information tabs. The three key takeaways for improving information acquisition from dietary change assistance applications, especially in cases like IF in which certainty of the outweighing benefits cannot be substantiated are the following:

1. Voluntary information acquisition from current IF applications with information tabs is low and regarded as an additional feature, although the information tab users deem the information acquisition experience to be positive.
2. Current knowledge acquiring users of the IF applications use the information tab for information gaining on exercising, recipes, health, meal and calorie tracking during IF.
3. IF application users evaluate the knowledge acquisition effectiveness of the information tab by information quality, information relevance, and information presentation.

If the three findings are incorporated into the future development of IF application information tabs, users like Alaine will be able to enjoy the benefits of IF with increased safety and user-friendliness in information acquisition.

References

1. Al-Attar, A., et al.: Physiological and biochemical alterations insprague-dawley female rats subjected to high fat diet and intermittent fasting. J. Appl. Sci. Res., 2096–2104 (2010)
2. Ammar, A., et al.: Effects of covid-19 home confinement on eating behaviour and physical activity: results of the ECLB-covid19 international online survey. Nutrients **12**(6), 1583 (2020)
3. Bastian, M., Heymann, S., Jacomy, M.: Gephi: an open source software for exploring and manipulating networks (2009). http://www.aaai.org/ocs/index.php/ICWSM/09/paper/view/154
4. Bird, S., Klein, E., Loper, E.: Natural Language Processing with Python. O'Reilly Media, Newton (2009)
5. Blei, D.M., Ng, A.Y., Jordan, M.I.: Latent Dirichlet allocation. J. Mach. Learn. Res. **3**(null), 993–1022 (2003)
6. Blondel, V.D., Guillaume, J.L., Lambiotte, R., Lefebvre, E.: Fast unfolding of communities in large networks. J. Stat. Mech. Theory Exp. **2008**(10), P10008 (2008)
7. Catterson, J.H., et al.: Short-term, intermittent fasting induces long-lasting gut health and tor-independent lifespan extension. Curr. Biol. **28**(11), 1714–1724 (2018)
8. Chen, N., Lin, J., Hoi, S.C.H., Xiao, X., Zhang, B.: AR-miner: mining informative reviews for developers from mobile app marketplace. In: Proceedings of the 36th International Conference on Software Engineering, ICSE 2014, New York, NY, USA, pp. 767–778. Association for Computing Machinery (2014). https://doi.org/10.1145/2568225.2568263
9. Cienfuegos, S., et al.: Effects of 4-and 6-h time-restricted feeding on weight and cardiometabolic health: a randomized controlled trial in adults with obesity. Cell Metab. **32**(3), 366–378 (2020)
10. Diao, Q., Qiu, M., Wu, C.Y., Smola, A.J., Jiang, J., Wang, C.: Jointly modeling aspects, ratings and sentiments for movie recommendation (JMARS). In: Proceedings of the 20th ACM SIGKDD International Conference on Knowledge Discovery and Data Mining, KDD 2014, New York, NY, USA, pp. 193–202. Association for Computing Machinery (2014). https://doi.org/10.1145/2623330.2623758
11. Fu, B., Lin, J., Li, L., Faloutsos, C., Hong, J., Sadeh, N.: Why people hate your app: making sense of user feedback in a mobile app store. In: Proceedings of the 19th ACM SIGKDD International Conference on Knowledge Discovery and Data Mining, KDD 2013, New York, NY, USA, pp. 1276–1284. Association for Computing Machinery (2013). https://doi.org/10.1145/2487575.2488202
12. Galvis Carreño, L.V., Winbladh, K.: Analysis of user comments: an approach for software requirements evolution. In: Proceedings of the 2013 International Conference on Software Engineering, ICSE 2013, pp. 582–591. IEEE Press (2013)
13. Genc-Nayebi, N., Abran, A.: A systematic literature review: opinion miningstudies from mobile app store user reviews. J. Syst. Softw. **125**, 207–219 (2017). https://doi.org/10.1016/j.jss.2016.11.027. http://www.sciencedirect.com/science/article/pii/S0164121216302291
14. Guo, Y., Barnes, S.J., Jia, Q.: Mining meaning from online ratings and reviews: tourist satisfaction analysis using latent Dirichlet allocation. Tourism Manage. **59**, 467–483 (2017). https://doi.org/10.1016/j.tourman.2016.09.009. http://www.sciencedirect.com/science/article/pii/S0261517716301698

15. Guzman, E., Maalej, W.: How do users like this feature? A fine grained sentiment analysis of app reviews. In: 2014 IEEE 22nd International Requirements Engineering Conference (RE), pp. 153–162 (2014)
16. Hannan, M.A., Islam, M.N., Uddin, M.J.: Self-confidence as an immune-modifying psychotherapeutic intervention for covid-19 patients and understanding of its connection to CNS-endocrine-immune axis. J. Adv. Biotechnol. Exp. Ther. **3**, 14–7 (2020)
17. Horne, B.D., Muhlestein, J.B., Anderson, J.L.: Health effects of intermittent fasting: hormesis or harm? A systematic review. Am. J. Clin. Nutr. **102**(2), 464–470 (2015)
18. Hutto, C., Gilbert, E.: Vader: A parsimonious rule-based model for sentiment analysis of social media text. In: ICWSM (2014)
19. Jelodar, H., et al.: Latent Dirichlet allocation (LDA) and topic modeling: models, applications, a survey (2018)
20. Leydesdorff, L., Nerghes, A.: Co-word maps and topic modeling: a comparison using small and medium-sized corpora (n < 1,000). J. Assoc. Inf. Sci. Tech. **68**(4), 1024–1035 (2017)
21. LifeOmic: Lifeomic launches premium version of life mobile apps, July 2020. https://www.prnewswire.com/news-releases/lifeomic-launches-premium-version-of-life-mobile-apps-301097921.html
22. Lin, C., He, Y.: Joint sentiment/topic model for sentiment analysis. In: Proceedings of the 18th ACM Conference on Information and Knowledge Management, CIKM 2009, New York, NY, USA, pp. 375–384. Association for Computing Machinery (2009). https://doi.org/10.1145/1645953.1646003
23. Lovett, L.: Fasting app zero lands $2.8m, August 2019. https://www.mobihealthnews.com/news/north-america/fasting-app-zero-lands-28m
24. Lowe, D.A., et al.: Effects of time-restricted eating on weight loss and other metabolic parameters in women and men with overweight and obesity: the treat randomized clinical trial. JAMA Internal Med. **180**, 1491–1499 (2020)
25. Mansar, S.L., Jariwala, S., Shahzad, M., Anggraini, A., Behih, N., AlZeyara, A.: A usability testing experiment for a localized weight loss mobile application. Proc. Technol. **5**, 839–848 (2012)
26. Mattson, M.P., Wan, R.: Beneficial effects of intermittent fasting and caloric restriction on the cardiovascular and cerebrovascular systems. J. Nutr. Biochem. **16**(3), 129–137 (2005)
27. McAuley, J., Leskovec, J.: Hidden factors and hidden topics: understanding rating dimensions with review text. In: Proceedings of the 7th ACM Conference on Recommender Systems, RecSys 2013, New York, NY, USA, pp. 165–172. Association for Computing Machinery (2013). https://doi.org/10.1145/2507157.2507163
28. McCallum, A.K.: Mallet: a machine learning for language toolkit (2002). http://mallet.cs.umass.edu
29. McColl, L.D., Rideout, P.E., Parmar, T.N., Abba-Aji, A.: Peer support intervention through mobile application: an integrative literature review and future directions. Canadian Psychol. /Psychologie canadienne **55**(4), 250 (2014)
30. Nguyen, H., Hovy, D.: Hey Siri. ok Google. Alexa: a topic modeling of user reviews for smart speakers. In: Proceedings of the 5th Workshop on Noisy User-generated Text (W-NUT 2019), pp. 76–83 (2019)
31. Noon, M.J., et al.: Fasting with diabetes: a prospective observational study. BMJ Global Health **1**(2) (2016)
32. Orji, R., Vassileva, J., Mandryk, R.L.: Lunchtime: a slow-casual game for long-term dietary behavior change. Pers. Ubiquit. Comput. **17**(6), 1211–1221 (2013)

33. Patterson, R.E., Sears, D.D.: Metabolic effects of intermittent fasting. Ann. Rev. Nutri. **37**, 371–393 (2017)

34. Perez, S.: This week in apps: Facebook takes on shopify, tinder considers its future, contact-tracing tech goes live, May 2020. https://techcrunch.com/2020/05/23/this-week-in-apps-facebook-takes-on-shopify-tinder-considers-its-future-contact-tracing-tech-goes-live/?guccounter=1

35. Pu, X., Wu, G., Yuan, C.: User-aware topic modeling of online reviews. Multimedia Syst. **25**(1), 59–69 (2017). https://doi.org/10.1007/s00530-017-0557-6

36. Puranen, T., Salokekkila, P., Ahlblad-Makinen, N., Haggman-Laitila, A.: Visual food diary-peer support and better diet quality. Eur. J. Public Health **29**(Supplement_4), ckz186-274 (2019)

37. Rehman, A.U., Jiang, A., Rehman, A., Paul, A., din, S., Sadiq, M.T.: Identification and role of opinion leaders in information diffusion for online discussion network. J. Ambient Intell. Humani. Comput. 1–13 (2020). https://doi.org/10.1007/s12652-019-01623-5

38. Řehůřek, R., Sojka, P.: Software framework for topic modelling with large corpora. In: Proceedings of the LREC 2010 Workshop on New Challenges for NLP Frameworks, ELRA, Valletta, Malta, pp. 45–50, May 2010. http://is.muni.cz/publication/884893/en

39. Simple.life: Simple fasting app will provide personalized dieting tips through ai-powered functionality, February 2020. https://www.prnewswire.com/news-releases/simple-fasting-app-will-provide-personalized-dieting-tips-through-ai-powered-functionality-300996820.html

40. Singh, W., et al.: Sentiment analysis of online mobile reviews. In: 2017 International Conference on Inventive Communication and Computational Technologies (ICICCT), pp. 20–25. IEEE (2017)

41. St-Onge, M.P., Ard, J., Baskin, M.L., Chiuve, S.E., Johnson, H.M., Kris-Etherton, P., Varady, K.: Meal timing and frequency: implications for cardiovascular disease prevention. a scientific statement from the American heart association. Circulation **135**(9), e96–e121 (2017)

42. Stephens, J., Allen, J.K., Himmelfarb, C.R.D.: "smart" coaching to promote physical activity, diet change, and cardiovascular health. J. Cardiovasc. Nurs. **26**(4), 282 (2011)

43. Stockman, M.C., Thomas, D., Burke, J., Apovian, C.M.: Intermittent fasting: is the wait worth the weight? Current Obesity Rep. **7**(2), 172–185 (2018)

44. Sullivan, R., Sarker, A., Oconnor, K., Goodin, A., Karlsrud, M., Gonzalez, G.: Finding potentially unsafe nutritional supplements from user reviews with topic modeling, pp. 528–539, January 2016. https://doi.org/10.1142/97898147494110048

45. Team, S.C.E.: This berlin-based startup will help you lose weight via healthy intermittent fasting; raises 4.2m, October 2020. https://siliconcanals.com/news/fastic-raises-seed-round-funding/

46. Tucker, C.: German intermittent fasting app fastic snaps up 4.3 million to continue us expansion, October 2020. https://www.eu-startups.com/2020/10/german-intermittent-fasting-app-fastic-snaps-up-e4-3-million-to-continue-us-expansion/

47. Van Lippevelde, W., et al.: Using a gamified monitoring app to change adolescents' snack intake: the development of the reward app and evaluation design. BMC Public Health **16**(1), 1–11 (2016)

48. Varady, K.A., Bhutani, S., Church, E.C., Klempel, M.C.: Short-term modified alternate-day fasting: a novel dietary strategy for weight loss and cardioprotection in obese adults. Am. J. Clin. Nutr. **90**(5), 1138–1143 (2009)
49. Yousfi, N., Bragazzi, N.L., Briki, W., Zmijewski, P., Chamari, K.: The covid-19 pandemic: how to maintain a healthy immune system during the lockdown-a multidisciplinary approach with special focus on athletes. Biol. Sport **37**(3), 211 (2020)

Evaluating an mHealth Application: Findings on Visualizing Transportation and Air Quality

Pattiya Mahapasuthanon$^{(\boxtimes)}$, Niloofar Kalantari, and Vivian Genaro Motti

George Mason University, 4400 University Drive, Fairfax, VA 22030, USA
{pmahapas,nkalanta,vmotti}@gmu.edu

Abstract. This paper presents the results of a usability study conducted to evaluate an mHealth application that integrates information about transportation options and air quality levels. By visualizing the air quality levels along the transportation routes available, the users of the mHealth application proposed can make more informed choices before departure. The mHealth application aims to help users take appropriate safety precautions beforehand. The results obtained with the user study indicate that the familiar layout of the application led to a high sentiment score and usability ratings of system usability scale. The option to select the least polluted route to travel was perceived as original and useful to the participants.

Keywords: mHealth application · Air quality · Usability · Visualization

1 Introduction

Air pollution has caused the death of 8 million people worldwide per year in the past decade. Outdoor air pollution was associated to 4.2 million deaths, whereas indoor pollution was responsible for 3.8 million deaths [34]. Air pollution is one of the leading environmental risks and a major threat to living organisms [19]. As the problem has worsen over the years, wildfires have become destructive to people's health in California and Australia [26]. Additionally, the higher exposure to pollution is strongly correlated to chronic diseases, such as asthma and cancer [8,16,17].

Particulate matter (PM) is considered as an indicator to measure pollution levels [2] which is generated from mechanical processes and natural sources [3]. PM is a major threat to individuals' health, not only because the particles are invisible to the human eyes, but also because they penetrate in the individuals' respiratory system [16]. The impacts from air pollution are disproportionately noticeable in developing countries where carbon emissions from industry are higher and less regulated [14]. To prevent and manage health effects, individuals should be able to monitor the level of pollutants in the environment in real-time, and take informed decisions about preventive measures in their daily lives [23].

© Springer Nature Switzerland AG 2021
K. Toeppe et al. (Eds.): iConference 2021, LNCS 12645, pp. 301–312, 2021.
https://doi.org/10.1007/978-3-030-71292-1_24

A widespread mobile adoption [31] facilitates access to real-time air pollution information through mobile apps. The development of such apps has been facilitated by a growth in the number of sensor stations and the increasing availability of web services and application programming interfaces that provide access to pollution level data sets [13]. Mobile applications dedicated to weather forecast can benefit from the data sets available, however thus far they have not been combined with real-time transportation data to facilitate the planning of commuting routes. Mobile applications targeted at transportation services inform users about the best routes available depending on their current geographic location and region. As Wireless Sensor Network (WSN) and grid technology have advanced, healthcare mobile applications to track and monitor air quality are promising concerning their reachability and feasibility [15,21].

Although 547 Android and 484 iOS mobile applications to provide air quality exist [4], applications which integrate transportation and air quality are either lacking or limited in terms of availability. To address these issues, we designed an mHealth application which is an interactive prototype that recommends users alternative commuting routes according to their level of air pollutants. Air quality and traffic information are included in the user interface. The app design displays three alternative routes along with their air quality index. The application also gives users an option to plan for their upcoming trips based on the current and predicted air quality index (AQI) at a certain time. Employing a user-centered design approach, we involved users in the evaluation process. We conducted an online study to understand the usability of an mHealth application considering its visualization choices, ease of use, and users' needs. The interactive prototype was presented to the study participants and 26 responses were collected.

The results indicate that this mHealth application was perceived as useful to participants besides being original to them. The average of the SUS score was 80.58, considered high in terms of simplicity, usability, and ease of use [7]. Participants found that the option to choose the least polluted route to travel was the most useful feature. The contribution of the application and its features has become the goal of the study as air pollution became a health crisis [20].

2   Related Work

To inform government agencies, policy makers, industry and citizens, air quality levels have been regulated by different agencies across the globe. In the United States, the Environmental Protection Agency (EPA) assesses the air quality monitoring the levels of particle and ozone pollution. One of their goals is to prevent cardiovascular mortality, since it is typically associated with higher levels of small airborne particles, including sulfur dioxide, and nitrogen dioxide [6]. To classify the levels of air quality, EPA adopts AQI which is used to understand the effects of air quality in what regards health conditions in a given location. Six color codes are employed to present air pollution data according to its severity levels. Figure 1 displays the color code ranging from green, as being safe to breathe, to red, as being hazardous to human health.

To inform users about pollution levels, a number of mobile applications and systems uses the AQI standard classification as a reference. Examples of such systems are MyPart [32], Uyanik et al.'s [33], and CitiSense [25]. Researchers focused thus far on developing ubiquitous air monitoring devices [9,12,35], however the research on visualization of real-time transportation and air quality data is limited in number [23]. With commercial applications available for air quality monitoring, it is important to assess what users need regarding navigation features, air quality and visualization approaches. End user evaluation becomes essential to improve the understanding about implementation opportunities for the development of an mHealth application [22].

Air Quality Index Levels of Health Concern	Numerical Value	Meaning
Good	0 to 50	Air quality is considered satisfactory, and air pollution poses little or no risk.
Moderate	51 to 100	Air quality is acceptable; however, for some pollutants there may be a moderate health concern for a very small number of people who are unusually sensitive to air pollution.
Unhealthy for Sensitive Groups	101 to 150	Members of sensitive groups may experience health effects. The general public is not likely to be affected.
Unhealthy	151 to 200	Everyone may begin to experience health effects; members of sensitive groups may experience more serious health effects.
Very Unhealthy	201 to 300	Health warnings of emergency conditions. The entire population is more likely to be affected.
Hazardous	301 to 500	Health alert: everyone may experience more serious health effects.

Fig. 1. Air Quality Index (AQI) defined by EPA [1]

2.1 Transportation

Mobile applications classified in the transportation category have as key characteristics: multi-modal trip planning, traffic safety, carpooling, and parking [30]. Google Maps, WAZE, Trip Planner, Easy Route Finder, and MAPS.ME are examples of these transportation applications. Google Maps is nonetheless the most popular mobile application for navigation thanks to the ability to provide multiple transportation options to users worldwide. Real-time navigation, integration with public transportation, and alternative routes are main features which app reviewers found to be helpful. Similarly, WAZE provides real-time navigation in addition to the traffic information, such as crashes, police report, and construction sites [18].

The graphical user interface design of these mobile applications includes mainly icons over map and color codes to represent the traffic information. While the colors from these applications are slightly different, they are mainly used to represent the different conditions of the current traffic. Text labels have also been widely employed in such applications.

2.2 Air Quality

AirVisual, Plume Air, and Air Matters are among 2019 most popular air quality monitoring applications available in Apple App Store (iTunes) and Google Play. These three applications provide similar features, including air pollutant tracking, air pollutant forecasting, and air pollution ranking. AirVisual interfaces provide air quality information using various visualization techniques. More specifically, the application provides users an option to zoom and filter in addition to the air pollutant visualization in sub-city level.

3 Application Design

The interactive prototype of the mobile application was implemented using Adobe XD (Fig. 2). The prototype includes the layouts, contents, and the navigation choices. Each user interface of the prototype was examined for feedback to prioritize their needs in the app. During the prototype evaluation, the participants were given instructions to type their current and destination locations to begin the interaction. Another UI layout was designed to allow them to schedule the trip and check the estimated AQI at the preferred time. Color-coding was used to annotate the routes in order to help participants distinguish several pathways according to their AQIs. Unsafe paths were color-coded with red and orange, while mild pollution is indicated with yellow color. Safe routes are presented in green. To make it more efficient to commute to their frequent places, participants can save their favorite locations and access them rapidly.

A storyboard was created before implementing the prototype to show the graphical user interfaces of the application. The storyboard defines user paths to search for and to retrieve the information of interest. Eight graphic user interfaces were then created.

Figure 2 shows how participants can interact with the application. Participants are able to select a starting point for their journey either by specifying a location on the map, or by typing an address. To assist in this task completion, participants can choose their saved places. Participants can check an estimated AQI in the chosen time and date by providing their current location, destination, time, and date. Then, they will be able to see the availability of alternative routes. The application provides the color-coded visualization of pollution on the routes. Additionally, a label is assigned to each route by the application. This label indicates whether the quality of the air is: dangerous, not bad, or clean. After selecting the desired route, AQI will be displayed along with the detailed information about weather conditions and variation of the pollutant levels. Unhealthy, moderate and good are the three main categories of air quality available in the application.

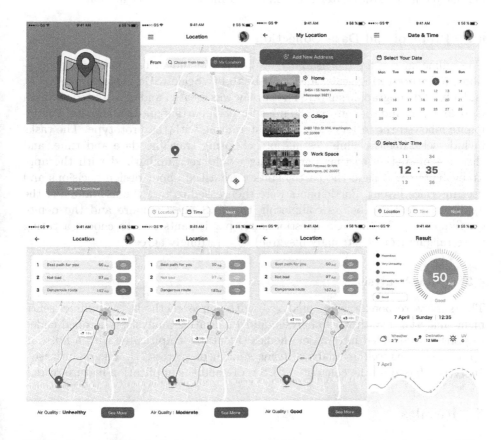

Fig. 2. Prototype displaying user interfaces which recommend routes based on AQI

4 Method

To evaluate the application and gather the participants' opinions, an online usability survey was used. The goal of the study was to understand how users perceived the visualization options as well as the level of importance for the app features.

4.1 Recruitment of Participants

Upon IRB approval, we recruited 26 study participants through announcements posted in the university newsletter, mailing lists, and flyers. The newsletters were distributed to the university community (faculty, staff, and students) from June to August 2019. Participants were contacted by email and presented with details about the study after they expressed interest in participation.

4.2 Protocol and Data Collection

The online survey for the usability evaluation included: ten open-ended questions, a feature rating scale, a System Usability Scale (SUS) Questionnaire [7], and a brief demographic survey. The survey was created and distributed through Google Forms and took around 30 mins for each participant to complete. Participants followed the instructions while interacting with the prototype. The tasks include selecting traveling destination, choosing traveling date and time, and checking prediction so that participants would get familiarized with the app. To evaluate the design, the participants were asked about design decisions and user interface layout. Participants were then asked to rate the usefulness of the application features before completing the SUS questionnaire and the demographic survey. In the SUS questionnaire, participants had to choose a rating score ranging from 1 (strongly disagree) to 5 (strongly agree).

4.3 Data Analysis

The survey responses were analyzed with three methods, including: sentiment analysis, quantitative analysis, and qualitative analysis. The open-ended responses were coded into major themes (identified empirically, with a bottom-up approach) as well as analyzed using sentiment scores [27]. The quantitative analysis is based on the calculated SUS score and the application feature rating.

5 Results

The results from the user study indicate that the UI design and layout of the application is simple and intuitive. Participants were overall positive about the contribution of having the mobile application to monitor air pollution. However, participants also suggested that multi-modal trip planner is a feature that should be included when further developing the application.

5.1 Demographics

Table 1 presents the demographics of the survey participants. Participants in the study included 19 females and 7 males with age ranging from 18 to 54 years old (average = 32, SD = 7.62). Half of the participants were between the ages of 21 and 30 years old. In total, 19 participants obtained a graduate degree. 18 out of 26 participants identified themselves as White regarding their ethnicity.

Table 1. Demographic characteristics of the participants (N = 26)

	n	%
Gender		
Female	19	73.10
Male	7	26.90
Age (years)		
21–30	13	50.00
31–40	9	34.61
41–50	3	11.54
50+	1	3.85
Education		
High School or Less	2	7.60
Bachelor	5	19.20
Master	16	61.50
Doctorate	3	11.50
Ethnicity		
White	18	69.20
Asian/Pacific Islander	6	23.10
Black or African American	1	3.80
NA	1	3.80

5.2   Sentiment Analysis

We employed sentiment analysis to analyze the responses of open-ended questions. To make a quantifiable score, the responses (words and phrases) were checked against a pre-defined dictionary available from LIWC [28]. Open-ended responses were analyzed by LIWC, an automated analysis tool that provides a quantitative overview of text contents. The sentiment scores that were associated with the participants' feedback were mainly positive. The positive sentiment scores for the question that is related to the clarity of design was 12.63 and the negative score was 0.18. In terms of feasibility and usability, the open-ended question achieved 5.76 of positive score and 0.03 of negative score. Furthermore, for the open-ended question related to the needs to visualize air pollution levels and traveling routes, the positive score obtained was 24.1 whereas the negative score obtained was 0.28.

5.3   Quantitative Analysis

In total, 25 out of 26 participants (96.2%) understood the meaning of green and red colors used in the recommended routes. However, 4 participants (15.4%) were not sure about the yellow colors in the recommended route. All participants appreciated the text labels accompanying each recommended route. The familiarity with color convention standards as well as text labels proved to aid participants in understanding the app features and visualization choices, following also Nielsen's Heuristics [24].

Feature Rating Score. Figure 3 displays the rating scales for the application features. The feature considered as extremely useful for the study participants is the feature to choose the least polluted route to travel, with a total of 16 participants (61.54%). The feature which participants perceived as moderately useful is the feature to set date and time for air quality prediction with lower ratings in the group of participants who are older than 30 years old. Overall, the application features were perceived as useful to the study participants.

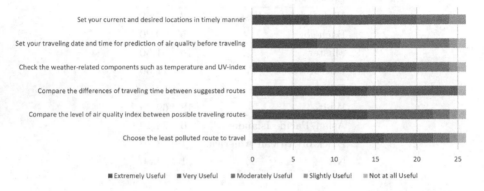

Fig. 3. Stacked bar chart displaying the features and the number of participants' ratings

System Usability Scale (SUS) Score. Overall, the average SUS score obtained in the evaluation was 80.58 out of 100 (SD = 2.68) with 95% confidence level. Given the guidelines for the SUS calculation and interpretation of results [29], the score obtained is considered high, especially concerning the app usefulness, usability, ease of use, and learnability. The range of the SUS score was between 57.5 to 100. The education level and age of the participants had a negative correlation with the SUS scores. Participants with graduate degrees gave lower SUS scores than participants with Bachelor's degree or lower. Considering participants with various backgrounds and heterogeneous knowledge about air quality, the application received a high score (above 80%) regarding its interface design.

5.4   Qualitative Analysis

By coding participants' responses on the open-ended questions, we discovered three main themes among participants' responses, namely: design layout, app features, and suggestions for improvements. Those themes are discussed in the next sections.

Design Layout. The familiarity with the design decisions for the app layouts and the user interface simplicity [24] were two important aspects that participants appreciated the most when evaluating the app. In total, 13 participants mentioned the clean interface design in their responses, and the fact that the design follows standard conventions for application development. Additionally, the participants commented on the visualization aspects integrated with components from Google Maps which were considered as intuitive to the study participants.

Nonetheless, participants suggested providing icons similar to other commercial applications to recommend potential precautions. A mask icon over the map could be implemented to illustrate such cases. The data representation should be assisted with both visual and verbal cues [11]. As participant 26 commented:

> There is no recommendation of activities or how to protect myself from this air quality level. For example, if AQI is more than 50, I should wear a health mask. - P26

Features. Being able to travel on the commuting route with the best air quality was considered as a positive surprise to the study participants as they had never thought of such possibility. The application stood out concerning its originality and usefulness, and the study participants demonstrated willingness to use the application in their daily lives.

> Providing air pollution information for different paths. Never seen such a thing in any apps. I believe it is useful for users to have information regarding air pollution and measures of risks. - P17

Suggestions. Concerning future implementations and app refinement, the multi transportation mode was suggested by the study participants in addition to the activity recommendations.

> It would be nice if the app could consider other aspects of selected paths that could make difficulties for pregnant women, like heavy traffic or too many stops. It could also show the special parking facilities at the destination. - P2

Also, participants were not aware of the AQI meaning and they suggested it has to be defined within the application.

6   Discussion

The design implications from the study indicate that intuitive designs [5] are not the only considerations needed in developing such mHealth application, but also user interfaces with visual metaphors to provide end users with appropriate cognitive affordances for decision making [10]. Users should be able to understand and take actions from information providied within the mHealth design. The results obtained in the study indicate that participants were willing to adopt such mHealth application in their daily lives. Surprisingly, they also raised questions about circumstances in which they may not use the app, for example when they are more concerned about transportation time than their health risks.

The main limitations in the evaluation of the app include restricted usage of the interactive prototype and small scope as the user interaction data was not collected automatically with log files. Also, the in-depth log data would aid to understand in detail the user interaction and their task performance for each app component and visualization in order to reduce threats to validity. Thus, further assessment is needed to check to which extent the results are applicable to users from diverse demographic background.

7   Conclusion

Technological advancements have made air pollution monitoring possible using sensors spread out in smart cities. Besides this, the availability of data enables real-time monitoring of air quality. To address this shortcoming, we proposed and evaluated the usability of an mHealth application which provides users three transportation options with their air quality levels. With the use of alternative visualization schemes, the application provides an intuitive design and easy to use to end users. The usability evaluation conducted with 26 participants indicated that the features to zoom and filter, the familiarity to the design layout summed with clean user interface stood out as key aspects on participants' preferences. Participants also suggested the multi-modal trip planning feature. As air pollution was not a common problem with some participants, it is crucial to provide visualization features for air quality information with universal representations.

Acknowledgements. This work was partially supported by a multidisciplinary seed grant from George Mason University. The authors would like to thank GEST-DC project, Dr. Jenna Krall, and participants for their support in this project.

References

1. Aqi basics. https://airnow.gov/index.cfm?action=aqibasics.aqi
2. Agency, U.S.E.P.: Particulate matter (pm) basics (2017)
3. Anderson, J.O., Thundiyil, J.G., Stolbach, A.: Clearing the air: a review of the effects of particulate matter air pollution on human health. J. Med. Toxicol. 8(2), 166–175 (2012)

4. AppGrooves: Best 10 apps for air quality alerts - appgrooves: Get more out of life with iphone and android apps (2019). https://appgrooves.com/rank/weather/air-quality/best-apps-for-air-quality-alerts. Accessed 19 Sept 2019
5. Banga, C., Weinhold, J.: Essential Mobile Interaction Design: Perfecting Interface Design in Mobile Apps. Pearson Education (2014)
6. Bell, M.L., Ebisu, K., Peng, R.D., Samet, J.M., Dominici, F.: Hospital admissions and chemical composition of fine particle air pollution. Am. J. Respiratory Critical Care Med. **179**(12), 1115–1120 (2009)
7. Brooke, J.: Sus: a quick and dirty usability. Usability Evaluation in Industry, p. 189 (1996)
8. Chu, K.C., Xiao, M.Y.: A study on the correlation between breast cancer and air pollution. In: Proceedings of the 2017 IEEE/ACM International Conference on Advances in Social Networks Analysis and Mining 2017, pp. 757–762. ACM (2017)
9. Garzon, S.R., Walther, S., Pang, S., Deva, B., Küpper, A.: Urban air pollution alert service for smart cities. In: Proceedings of the 8th International Conference on the Internet of Things, p. 9. ACM (2018)
10. Hartson, R.: Cognitive, physical, sensory, and functional affordances in interaction design. Behav. Inf. Technol. **22**(5), 315–338 (2003)
11. Ho, C., Spence, C.: Verbal interface design: Do verbal directional cues automatically orient visual spatial attention? Comput. Human Behav. **22**(4), 733–748 (2006)
12. Hu, K., Davison, T., Rahman, A., Sivaraman, V.: Air pollution exposure estimation and finding association with human activity using wearable sensor network. In: Proceedings of the MLSDA 2014 2nd Workshop on Machine Learning for Sensory Data Analysis, p. 48. ACM (2014)
13. Idrees, Z., Zheng, L.: Low cost air pollution monitoring systems: a review of protocols and enabling technologies. J. Ind. Inf. Integration **17**, 100123 (2020)
14. Kanemoto, K., Moran, D., Lenzen, M., Geschke, A.: International trade undermines national emission reduction targets: new evidence from air pollution. Global Environ. Change **24**, 52–59 (2014)
15 Khedo, K.K., Perseedoss, R., Mungur, A., et al.: A wireless sensor network air pollution monitoring system. arXiv preprint arXiv:1005.1737 (2010)
16. Kim, K.H., Kabir, E., Kabir, S.: A review on the human health impact of airborne particulate matter. Environ. Int. **74**, 136–143 (2015)
17. Kim, S., Paulos, E., Mankoff, J.: inair: A longitudinal study of indoor air quality measurements and visualizations. In: Proceedings of the SIGCHI Conference on Human Factors in Computing Systems, pp. 2745–2754. CHI 2013, ACM, New York, USA (2013). https://doi.org/10.1145/2470654.2481380
18. Knote, R., Söllner, M.: Towards design excellence for context-aware services-the case of mobile navigation apps (2017)
19. Krall, J.R., et al.: Estimating exposure to traffic-related pm2. 5 for women commuters using vehicle and personal monitoring. Environmental Research, p. 109644 (2020)
20. Li, X., Jin, L., Kan, H.: Air pollution: a global problem needs local fixes (2019)
21. Ma, Y., Richards, M., Ghanem, M., Guo, Y., Hassard, J.: Air pollution monitoring and mining based on sensor grid in london. Sensors **8**(6), 3601–3623 (2008)
22. McCurdie, T., et al.: mhealth consumer apps: the case for user-centered design. Biomed. Instrument. Technol. **46**(2), 49 (2012)
23. Motti, V.G., Kalantari, N., Mahapasuthanon, P., Zheng, H.: GEST-DC: unifying transportation and air quality information in an mHealth application. In: Ahram, T., Falcão, C. (eds.) AHFE 2019. AISC, vol. 972, pp. 385–398. Springer, Cham (2020). https://doi.org/10.1007/978-3-030-19135-1_38

24. Nielsen, J.: Usability Engineering. Morgan Kaufmann (1994)
25. Nikzad, N., et al.: Citisense: improving geospatial environmental assessment of air quality using a wireless personal exposure monitoring system. In: Proceedings of the Conference on Wireless Health, p. 11. ACM (2012)
26. Palinkas, L.A.: The California Wildfires. Global climate change, population displacement, and public health, pp. 53–67. Springer, Cham (2020). https://doi.org/10.1007/978-3-030-41890-8_4
27. Pang, B., Lee, L., et al.: Opinion mining and sentiment analysis. Foundations and Trends® in Information Retrieval **2**(1–2), 1–135 (2008)
28. Pennebaker, J.W., Francis, M.E., Booth, R.J.: Linguistic inquiry and word count: Liwc 2001. Mahway: Lawrence Erlbaum Associates **71**(2001), 2001 (2001)
29. Sauro, J.: Measuring usability with the system usability scale (sus) (2011)
30. Siuhi, S., Mwakalonge, J.: Opportunities and challenges of smart mobile applications in transportation. J. Traffic Transport. Eng. (english edition) **3**(6), 582–592 (2016)
31. Taylor, K., Silver, L.: Smartphone ownership is growing rapidly around the world, but not always equally (2018)
32. Tian, R., Dierk, C., Myers, C., Paulos, E.: Mypart: personal, portable, accurate, airborne particle counting. In: Proceedings of the 2016 CHI Conference on Human Factors in Computing Systems, pp. 1338–1348. ACM (2016)
33. Uyanik, I., Khatri, A., Tsiamyrtzis, P., Pavlidis, I.: Design and usage of an ozone mapping app. In: Proceedings of the Wireless Health 2014 on National Institutes of Health, pp. 1–7. ACM (2014)
34. (WHO), T.W.H.O.: Ambient (outdoor) air quality and health, May (2018). https://www.who.int/en/news-room/fact-sheets/detail/ambient-(outdoor)-air-quality-and-health
35. Xiaojun, C., Xianpeng, L., Peng, X.: Iot-based air pollution monitoring and forecasting system. In: 2015 International Conference on Computer and Computational Sciences (ICCCS), pp. 257–260. IEEE (2015)

Immersive Stories for Health Information: Design Considerations from Binge Drinking in VR

Douglas Zytko[1]([⊠]) [iD], Zexin Ma[2] [iD], Jacob Gleason[1], Nathaniel Lundquist[1], and Medina Taylor[2]

[1] Department of Computer Science and Engineering, Oakland University, Rochester, MI, USA
zytko@oakland.edu
[2] Department of Communication, Journalism, and Public Relations, Oakland University, Rochester, MI, USA
zexinma@oakland.edu

Abstract. Immersive stories for health are 360° videos that intend to alter viewer perceptions about behaviors detrimental to health. They have potential to inform public health at scale, however, immersive story design is still in early stages and largely devoid of best practices. This paper presents a focus group study with 147 viewers of an immersive story about binge drinking experienced through VR headsets and mobile phones. The objective of the study is to identify aspects of immersive story design that influence attitudes towards the health issue exhibited, and to understand how health information is consumed in immersive stories. Findings emphasize the need for an immersive story to provide reasoning behind a character's engagement in the focal health behavior, to show the main character clearly engaging in the behavior, and to enable viewers to experience escalating symptoms of the behavior before the penultimate health consequence. Findings also show how the design of supporting characters can inadvertently distract viewers and lead them to justify the detrimental behavior being exhibited. The paper concludes with design considerations for enabling immersive stories to better inform public perception of health issues.

Keywords: Immersive stories · Virtual reality · 360-degree video · 360° · Film · Public health · Binge drinking · Alcohol

1 Introduction

"Nothing like seeing a group of doctors smoking outside to let you know that information alone doesn't persuade." – Ramit Sethi

Urban legends told over campfire, figures etched in old stone, an article in a yellowing newspaper, a comic book, a novel, a radio program, a movie, a Youtube video. Story has been a quintessentially human way of sharing information for centuries, and the most powerful stories do more than just inform - they alter, persuade, and culminate in action.

© Springer Nature Switzerland AG 2021
K. Toeppe et al. (Eds.): iConference 2021, LNCS 12645, pp. 313–327, 2021.
https://doi.org/10.1007/978-3-030-71292-1_25

Technology has continually expanded the ways in which stories are told and impact our behavior. Immersive stories [1] are a particularly novel form of storytelling; they utilize 360° video to share narrative through virtual reality [2] headsets and mobile devices. Through immersive stories a viewer typically experiences a narrative in first person through the eyes of a character and can freely explore their virtual surroundings by manipulating their character's gaze. This immersion can instill a sense of presence (or "being there") and the perception that one is personally experiencing a story's events [3, 4].

Immersive stories are growing in popularity for news consumption [5] and for informing the public about health issues [6]. The potential for viewers to viscerally experience the implications of a public health issue can be a powerful way to not only shape understanding, but to convince the public to adopt healthier behavioral choices [7]. This capacity for attitudinal and behavioral change is of paramount and timely importance in light of health pandemics that necessitate mass adoption of specific health behaviors to keep the public safe.

Despite the potential of immersive stories to inform and improve public health at scale, knowledge of immersive story design is still in fledgling stages. A majority of immersive story research has explored differences in viewing device [8–14] (e.g., VR headsets, phones, and computer monitors), leaving immersive story content and design as a figurative "black box" that is relatively understudied. Some literature has identified and provided opinions on the design of discrete story elements—namely character perspective choice [15–19] and direction of viewer attention [10, 12, 14, 20–23]. However, actual viewers of immersive stories have largely been absent from design research. Their involvement is vital not just for validating the impact of pre-identified design elements [18, 21, 22], but for *identifying* immersive story elements impactful to their perceptions and articulating how design choices impact them. This gap is especially pronounced for immersive stories in the public health context: what elements of immersive story design are impactful to viewers' attitudes towards a respective public health issue, and how do they impact viewers?

To address this gap, we conducted a focus group study with viewers of an immersive story about binge drinking—a widespread and severe public health issue [24, 25]—to identify and explore elements of immersive story design critical to viewer attitudes about the respective health issue. In the next section we review prior research on immersive stories and their design, which informs our research questions and method. We then present the focus group study, and conclude by discussing considerations and directions for immersive story design based on the study's findings.

2 Background

Immersive stories are video-based stories that offer a 360° panoramic view and spatialized audio [26, 27]. They are typically viewed on VR headsets and mobile devices, as facilitated with special viewing options on Youtube and other media outlets, and have been increasingly used in journalism, marketing, and non-profit sectors [1]. For example, mainstream media like *The New York Times, the BBC,* and *USA Today* have used immersive stories to offer experiential insight into news events [1, 5]. Organizations like the *United Nations* have used immersive stories to promote social good [28].

Immersive stories are a promising tool for improving health-related knowledge and facilitating behavior change [7] because they allow viewers to vividly experience health implications and symptoms of illness without suffering from any serious harm. An example is *A Walk Through Dementia*, which tells stories of people living with different forms of dementia by putting viewers in the shoes of those battling the disease [29].

As a relatively new storytelling experience, scientific research into immersive stories is still in its infancy. The majority of research has focused on the role of modality by comparing the viewing experience across head-mounted displays (HMDs), mobile devices, and flat computer screens [5, 8–14, 30–32]. These studies reinforce the potential of immersive stories, but with mixed results as to how choice of viewing device affects viewer experience—if at all [11].

There is relatively limited understanding of best practices for designing immersive stories, or what Banos and colleagues call "elements of the [virtual] environment and the content itself" [13]. Furthermore, immersive story research has focused on varying outcomes or goals of the viewing experience—including presence [4, 5, 8, 10, 11, 13, 14], enjoyment [5], empathy [11, 14, 17, 30, 33], and emotional response [8, 9, 13]—making it difficult to synthesize design insight for health contexts. Attitudinal and behavioral change (the goals of health-related stories) have been particularly rare focal outcomes of immersive story research [8].

Early research into immersive story design has focused predominantly on character perspective and directing viewer attention. Directing viewer attention has been recognized as a primary challenge to immersive story design due to viewers having the freedom to manipulate their gaze, therefore making it possible to miss key plot elements [10, 12, 14, 20–22]. Research has posed and tested various audio-based, visual-based, and mixed audio/visual cues for directing viewer attention [14, 21–23].

Regarding character perspective, research has identified three options available to designers. One is a *third person/non-character observer* who plays no role in the story [17–19]. The other two are first-person character perspectives (the viewer experiences the story through the eyes of a character) including the *main character* of the story who engages in plot-driving actions and a *supporting character* who observes plot-driving occurrences [15, 17]. There is some empirical evidence arguing against the non-character observer role or for a first-person perspective more broadly [11, 34–36]. However, there is a lack of empirical evidence into the main character and supporting character choices—speculations on the advantages of each character perspective can be found in [15, 17].

A rare example of immersive story design research beyond character perspective and user attention direction involved the identification of story elements broadly conducive to immersion [16], although these are based on the researchers' perspective rather than insight from viewers. The only research into immersive story design pertinent to viewer attitudes around a health issue, to the authors' knowledge, studied the impact of broadly conceptualized "emotional content" [8].

Ultimately, there persists a need for empirical research that identifies elements of immersive story design that viewers consider impactful to their experience, especially their attitudes towards exhibited public health issues. Our study pursued the following research questions:

1. What elements of immersive story design do viewers consider influential to their attitudes towards the health information being conveyed?
2. How do these elements impact viewers' perceptions of the health information?
3. In what ways could immersive story design for health be improved so that health information impacts viewers' attitudes as intended?

3 Method

To explore the research questions, we conducted a focus group study with 147 participants about an immersive story depicting binge drinking and its negative health consequences. Participants were graduate and undergraduate students (mean age = 22.14, SD = 4.05) recruited from a medium-sized public university in the Midwest of the United States, and were compensated with extra course credit. Participants identified as White (77.6%), Black (10.9%), Asian (6.8%), Hispanic (2.7%), and other (2.0%). Regarding gender, 50.3% identified as male and 49.7% as female.

3.1 The Immersive Story

Binge drinking was chosen as the focal health issue based on its severity and prevalence [24], particularly amongst our participant demographic of young adults [25]. Binge drinking is a pattern of drinking alcoholic beverages that brings a person's blood alcohol concentration (BAC) to 0.08 g/dL; typically 4+ drinks for women and 5+ for men [37].

The immersive story about binge drinking used in the study [38, 39] was selected because it represents common immersive story design choices: a first-person point of view, the ability to select a character perspective, gaze manipulation around a 360° field of vision, and a duration that is 10 min or less [15] (this particular story is 6 min in duration).

The story centers on Greg, who engages in binge drinking at a house party hosted by his friend Stephanie because he is moving away for a new job. Greg drinks 11 alcoholic beverages over a 5-h period (a mix of beer, wine, and shots), which is conveyed by intermittent cuts to a black screen that shows a number of alcoholic beverages being added to a table with a time stamp. Greg's intoxication is exhibited with blurred and slowed vision later in the story. Stephanie observes and interacts with Greg throughout the story, eventually helping him to a couch to fall asleep. In the morning Stephanie finds Greg unresponsive due to alcohol poisoning and calls an ambulance.

The video opens with text content about the definition of binge drinking, and its potential health consequences including alcohol poisoning. After the immersive story is experienced the video ends with text information about the severity of binge drinking.

There are two versions of the immersive story that vary based on character perspective, but otherwise have identical plots and information. In one version, the viewer experiences the story through the eyes of Greg, and in the other through the eyes of Stephanie.

3.2 Data Collection and Analysis

Focus group discussions were the second stage in a broader study about immersive stories for health; the first stage (an experiment on character perspective) necessitated that participants experience the binge drinking immersive story on Youtube either through a VR headset or smart phone, and either from Greg's perspective or Stephanie's perspective (rendering 4 different conditions that participants were evenly allocated to). On a smartphone the viewer moves the handheld device in any direction to manipulate their character's gaze; on the VR headset the viewer moves their head to manipulate gaze (See Fig. 1). All participants used headphones for the immersive story's audio. Focus groups were conducted on the university campus in two separate rooms immediately after participants viewed the immersive story and filled out a survey regarding the experience for the first stage of the study. One room was for participants who viewed the immersive story through a smart phone, and the other for VR headsets. The 147 participants were split across 15 focus group sessions, ranging from 4 to 20 participants each. Session lengths ranged from 15 to 25 min, as determined by level of disagreement or debate amongst participants.

Focus group discussions opened with participants describing the overall experience of viewing the immersive story, and then recollecting (and sometimes debating) the plot of the immersive story in their own words. Participants were prompted to discuss their attitudes and understanding of the story, the characters (Greg and Stephanie), and the health-related behavior exhibited (binge drinking).

All focus group discussions were voice recorded and transcribed. A team of five researchers held recurrent, synchronous sessions for inductive open coding of the transcripts [40], followed by organization of emergent themes using axial coding, and then finalization of the code mapping and hierarchy.

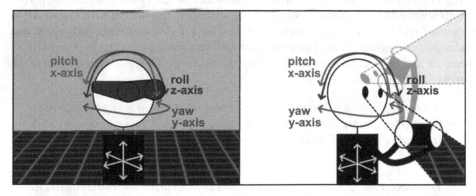

Fig. 1. Manipulating character gaze on a VR headset (left) versus a smartphone (right)

4   Findings

Participants' attitudes and perceptions towards the health information provided in the binge drinking immersive story were mixed. Some expressed a reluctance to engage in excessive drinking after watching. Others, however, were skeptical of the health impacts of binge drinking as depicted in the immersive story, and were either confused by the behavior or interpreted the behavior as justified.

Participants referenced two overarching aspects of immersive story design as influential to their attitudes and perceptions about binge drinking: 1) *health behavior design*, which comprises aspects of an immersive story that serve to convey and explain the focal health behavior; and 2) *supporting character design*, which comprises the actions of a character who observes the detrimental health behavior (but does not personally engage in it) and how that character's role is understood by viewers. The coding process did not reveal any themes unique to viewing the immersive story in a VR headset or mobile phone. There were some differences based on character perspective, which are noted throughout the findings.

4.1 Health Behavior Design

Axial coding partitioned health behavior design into three sub-concepts: the context of the focal behavior (where and why it happens), engagement in the behavior, and health consequences of the behavior.

Context of the Behavior. Most participants understood that Greg was drinking a large amount of alcohol, but they reported needing to know his reasons or *"backstory"* for excessive drinking in order to fully empathize with the character. This backstory would be distinct from contextual information that explains why characters would be drinking alcohol in general. Participants universally understood the going-away party context due to the house setting and party guests visible around the virtual environment. However they did not consider the virtual environment to offer much information to contextualize Greg's *excessive* drinking relative to other characters. In lieu of this information, participants invented their own backstories for Greg's drinking that usually involved a need to *"escape"* real world problems, such as family drama, fights with other partygoers, and sadness about moving away. These speculations were sometimes used to justify Greg's behavior and (as will be reported later) shift the blame for Greg's hospitalization to the party host, Stephanie.

> *"A lot of people drink to escape, you don't know what he was going through in the video, it never exactly said why he was drinking so much. He was moving, he probably could've been sad about moving away." (Smartphone, Greg's perspective, female)*

> *"And the other thing, one thing for me personally, that I just think would have added something to the level of empathy for the characters - if I knew their backstory, in the sense of like, why is Greg drinking so much? [Was it] a fight? Did he have a bad history with his family? Was there a reason for that?" (VR headset, Greg's perspective, male)*

Relatedly, some participants wanted to know the amount of alcohol that Greg typically drinks at parties, speculating that he may not have been aware of his limits. *"I would like to know if he got drunk more in the past, that same amount or was that his first time drinking a whole lot?" (VR headset, Greg's perspective, female).*

Several participants scanned the 360° environment for explanations of Greg's excessive drinking. Some assessed the party to consider how they would have acted in a similar situation. As one participant put it: *"The environment didn't feel joyous anyway, like it's a party but this seems like a really lame party. Like I would've been just drinking too" (Smartphone, Greg's perspective, male).* Critical perceptions of the party were influenced by the number of partygoers (approximately 10 people are seen throughout the house) and their activities (conversation and light dancing), which some participants considered incongruent with parties they had personally attended that involved heavy drinking.

A few of these participants expressed frustration with scanning the environment for contextual information. While there were various audible cues throughout the story prompting viewers to redirect their attention, some were hesitant to explore them because they feared missing vital plot information happening in their immediate field of vision. This hesitance to redirect attention was most pronounced in scenes when someone was directly interacting with the viewer's character, because it would normally be considered rude to redirect visual attention while in the middle of conversation.

> *"And I think in terms of having a 360 experience, it's kind of strange because a lot of times when you're engaging with someone, you're engaging straight, you're not looking over here [referencing an area in the periphery]. Most people will be focused on what's going on in front of them, versus what's going on behind them."*
> *(VR headset, Stephanie's perspective, male)*

Some participants reported that they stopped reacting to audible cues around them because they found prior cues to be uninteresting or uninformative to the plot when they sought out their sources. *"...there was nothing really interesting to look at, like on the other side [of the 360 degree environment when I looked]. So it's like, I didn't move around as much [afterwards because] I didn't expect there to be something very important." (Smartphone, Greg's perspective, male).*

A few participants suggested that visual directional signals could be added to the immersive story interface to help users identify cue sources faster and therefore minimize attention redirected from their current focus.

Engagement in the Behavior. Greg's engagement in binge drinking was conveyed through frequent transitions to a black screen with a table that progressively had more drinks added to it throughout the story, with time stamps associated with the drinks. Some participants reported confusion with this format of information. This was usually due to doubts as to whether Greg was actually consuming all of these drinks, or merely being offered them by friends and potentially not finishing them.

> *"They were trying to symbolize how much he was drinking with a black screen and like drinks plopped down, obviously. That was, I feel like we didn't visually see that when we're seeing it from his perspective. [...] I didn't see him drinking that much. Where I was like, this doesn't seem to be following like, how much he's actually drinking compared to what they're trying to illustrate him drinking.*

I think it's just for visual factors like, beer! Shot! Is he really drinking all of that?"
(Smartphone, Greg's perspective, female)

Some participants admitted having *"no clue"* as to how much alcohol Greg actually consumed prior to hospitalization, which complicated their understanding of binge drinking. Some also felt the black screen *"cut scenes"* were interruptions that detracted from immersion in the story. A few suggested that removing these cut scenes and instead being able to witness Greg consume the drinks would have been a superior choice for conveying the binge drinking behavior.

"The cuts in between where they told you what time it was kind of un-immersed me from it a little bit. Okay. I feel like if they didn't do that, and just had me following the one character the whole time without interruption, might have been a little bit more convincing." (Smartphone, male)

Health Consequences of the Behavior. The alcohol poisoning and hospitalization experienced by Greg at the end of the immersive story were met with some skepticism and confusion by participants. This was sometimes attributed to an overly rapid transition from *"drunk to dead"* which did not match participants' personal experiences with excessive drinking, and led some to suspect that factors other than binge drinking contributed to Greg's hospitalization.

"It didn't really seem totally convincing that he just went from drunk to dead. So maybe that's why I didn't think it was binge drinking because it didn't seem as drastic as we usually picture when you're doing something like that." (Smartphone, Greg's perspective, male)

"Because of how fast it was. I'll be very honest. I thought there was like a drug in those drinks because it just took off so quickly. Like I thought maybe he spiked the drinks or something or someone spiked drinks." (VR headset, Greg's perspective, male)

Relatedly, participants were confused about Greg's alcohol poisoning because of the absence of visible escalating health symptoms. While participants who experienced the story from Greg's perspective routinely noted the blurred and slowed vision as a symptom of his drunkenness, several expected progressively worse symptoms indicative of alcohol poisoning. Vomiting was the most commonly expected symptom.

"The fact that he was fine, then he got a little blurry and it just went from that to passing out. Like I, that doesn't happen. […] I feel like, when I've witnessed people who drink to excess they get really sick and they like to throw up." (Smartphone, Greg's perspective, female)

"I didn't connect with it as much because of the progression. Like alcohol poisoning you usually start throwing up first. Other things happen before you're just like gone."(Smartphone, female)

Participants from Stephanie's perspective echoed a need for information that Greg had transitioned from drunkenness (which they did not consider in need of intervention) to alcohol poisoning. Some of them wondered aloud if they had missed scenes visualizing symptoms of alcohol poisoning, or if Greg's hospitalization was simply unavoidable given the absence of signs for intervention.

"I just have a question, [about] Greg's thing [the participant references to the entire room]. Was he showing signs like alcohol poisoning? It's like vomiting and twitching and stuff like that." (VR headset, Stephanie's perspective, female)

4.2 Supporting Character Design

Supporting character design refers to the design of characters who viewers can assume the perspective of, but who do not personally engage in the focal health behavior of the story. In this immersive story's case, Stephanie would be the supporting character. While the immersive story intended to focus participants on Greg's binge drinking, participants who assumed Stephanie's perspective talked more about her behavior during focus groups. They exhibited a tendency to assign Stephanie a "role" in the story, which had implications on how they interpreted her actions and Greg's binge drinking.

The majority of participants understood Stephanie's role to a *"good friend."* This carried an understanding that she would look after Greg and either prevent him from drinking too much, or force him to drink water throughout the party. Almost all of these participants thought that Stephanie failed to effectively take care of Greg; they were more critical of her behavior than Greg's, and in some cases blamed her for Greg's hospitalization.

"If you're a really good friend or just even a friend in general I just truly believe she would be like, 'hey stop drinking, here's the water' you know. She was good friends with him already. She knew he was drunk, like, a good friend would at least offer him a cup of water, at least check on him to see..." (VR headset, Stephanie's perspective, male)

The mechanism behind how participants arrived at their understanding of Stephanie's role seemed to have been a comparison to how they would act in similar situations of observing a friend drink to excess. While some used this comparison to admonish Stephanie's lack of intervention, others expressed curiosity about her *"personality"* and wanted to know more about her choices.

"I would have liked to have known her character better, being put into her shoes, because I still have my whole personality and no idea of her personality. So, I would give my friend water. I would lay next to my friend on the couch. And I don't really understand why she didn't do that." (VR headset, Stephanie's perspective, female)

A few participants shared in critique of Stephanie, but from an understanding that her character was designed to be the *cause* of Greg's drinking. They all pointed to the lack of attention that Stephanie gave to Greg, which—from their understanding—made him feel lonely and prone to drinking. One participant elaborated on this loneliness by suggesting that Greg was in love with Stephanie.

"This dude's girl, they're about to fight over what this [relationship] is. It looks like every time he was drinking he was alone and drinking or he just wanted Steph's attention for the most part. That's what it seemed like. And then since he wasn't getting any he just kept drinking. And I'm like this is a sad love story." *(Smartphone, Greg's perspective, male)*

Not all participants were critical of Stephanie's actions. Some participants reasoned that being the party host prevented her from giving too much attention to any one party guest. They also made common reference to Greg and Stephanie as *"adults"* who are responsible for their own decisions, and that it would not have been appropriate for Stephanie to try to control Greg's drinking.

"There's a bunch of people here [at the party] that she can't like, he's a grown man and he doesn't need someone watching him." *(Smartphone, Stephanie's perspective, female)*

"You can't tell your friends what to do because people are going to do whatever they want to do." *(Smartphone, Stephanie's perspective, female)*

5 Limitations

There are some limitations to this focus group study that should be noted. For one, participants' attitudes towards binge drinking and the immersive story could have been influenced by other participants, meaning the opinions of the most vocal participants—or those first to speak—could have been overemphasized. In addition, while our sample does align with victim demographics of binge drinking [25], the attitudes and perceptions of our sample may not generalize to other viewer demographics, such as those not in college, those from largely minority populations, those outside of the United States, and those outside of the early/mid-20s age range. The study also included only one immersive story, and it is unclear if or how the findings may generalize to other types of immersive stories and for different focal health behaviors. Lastly, it cannot be known with our study's design whether viewers' attitudes towards binge drinking affected their subsequent drinking behavior—we thus reiterate a distinction between attitudes and behavior post-immersive story consumption.

6 Discussion

We conducted a focus group study with 147 viewers of an immersive story about binge drinking to identify aspects of immersive story design that influence attitudes towards public health issues, and more broadly to understand how health information is consumed in immersive stories. The study elucidated two aspects of immersive story design critical to viewer attitudes and comprehension of binge drinking: 1) health behavior design, including the context of the behavior, engagement in the behavior, and escalation of health repercussions; and 2) supporting character design: the impact of a character who the viewer can assume the perspective of, but who does not personally engage in the detrimental health behavior, on the viewer's attention and judgment of the behavior. In this section we reflect on how the findings inform immersive story design practices, and open questions that they raise.

6.1 Design Constraints of Story Duration

Immersive stories are touted for their capacity to instill a sense of presence [4] in a virtual environment that enables viewers to develop empathy for virtual characters [17, 30] and experience the unfolding story as if it were personally happening to them [32]. Our participants confirmed this potential and indicated that they *wanted* to feel empathy for the characters, but they often failed to do so. A downside of "being there" in a virtual world is that viewers expect the same depth of information that would be customary in the real world to contextualize and comprehend an experience that is really happening to them. This expectation was most apparent in demands for reasons behind the binge drinking behavior, direct observation of alcohol consumption, and an accurate escalation of alcohol poisoning symptoms—all of which the immersive story failed to provide, according to participants.

An impediment to immersive stories simply adding additional content to satisfy these empathic information needs is video duration. Immersive stories are typically around 10 min in duration or shorter. Larsen suggests immersive stories are restricted to this length because of general discomfort with VR headsets [15]. One alternative, also posed by Larsen [15], is a serialized narrative made up of multiple videos, but there is much uncertainty as to whether a viewer would actively select the next video to watch (this can be problematic to viewer comprehension if subsequent videos contain vital health information and context). This problem is likely to persist for viewers on mobile devices as well, who are familiar with shorter-form media on social networking apps and are subject to distraction from their surroundings and phone notifications.

Immersive story designers should consider ways to encapsulate viewer-expected information about a health behavior into a relatively short (linear) duration. This poses particular challenges for conveying public health issues that progress over several hours or even days. Design decisions that are ineffective according to our study are cut scenes that indirectly convey engagement in the focal behavior (e.g., a black screen that quantifies the number of alcoholic beverages consumed) and bypassing typical health symptoms to progress to the penultimate health consequence faster. Designers should, at a minimum, prioritize conveyance of context (i.e., reasons) for the character's behavior, direct engagement in the behavior, and all of its standard escalating health symptoms.

6.2 Design Considerations for the Supporting Character Perspective

The immersive story literature has elaborated on a variety of character perspective options that designers can choose from (i.e., the eyes through which a viewer experiences the story). These options include non-character observer, the main character (i.e., the character that engages in the focal behavior), and a supporting character (a character that observes the focal behavior, but does not personally engage in it) [11, 15, 17]. Arguments for the supporting character perspective posit that it enables viewers to develop empathy for others as opposed to oneself [17], and facilitates explorability of the virtual environment without losing narrative coherence because the supporting character is not personally engaging in plot-driving acts [15]. These arguments frame the supporting character purely as an observer whose own actions have no consequence on the story or the viewer's comprehension of it. Our findings indicate that supporting characters play a more active role in the eyes of viewers.

In our study's immersive story, the supporting character was Stephanie, a party host who observed the main character's (Greg's) binge drinking behavior and found him unresponsive from alcohol poisoning. Our participants were just as attentive to Stephanie's actions as to Greg's, and in many cases were more critical of her lack of intervention into Greg's drinking than the actual binge drinking behavior. Merely observing a main character's behavior, in this sense, was considered a (non-)action in itself, or a conscious behavioral choice from the supporting character. It became the focal point of viewers' attention when the character's absence of intervention into the binge drinking behavior deviated from how viewers would have acted in that situation. This finding emphasizes that immersive story designers need to be attentive to supporting character design, and recognize that passive observance of a situation can be considered the character's conscious behavioral choice.

The sense of embodiment that viewers may feel when they view a story through a character's eyes has traditionally been seen as an advantage of VR experiences [41–44]. However, a non-character observer perspective that removes the viewer from any sense of embodying a character may be superior if the designer wishes the viewer to passively observe a situation. Otherwise viewers may redirect their attention to how their embodied character does or does not utilize their opportunity to alter the events unfolding.

6.3 Designing Attention Cues

Managing viewer attention has been a persistent concern in the immersive story literature [10, 12, 14, 20, 21]. Story designers and viewers fear that vital plot points and information will be missed if the viewer exercises their ability to visually explore their 360° field of vision. Our participants certainly shared in this concern. Designs for directing viewer attention have been posed and tested in prior research [21, 22], typically in regards to how the attention cue is generated (e.g., visual cue, audio cue). Our study introduces another dimension to attentional design: the viewer-perceived value of the information being cued.

The binge drinking immersive story viewed by our participants featured a variety of audio cues, but some participants reported ignoring later cues because the information gathered when they sought out prior cues was considered uninteresting or inapplicable to the plot. This begs the question: should immersive story designs attempt to redirect the viewer's attention at all for non-essential plot information? If viewers are dismayed by the value of early nonessential cues, they may miss out on other, plot-imperative cues later. We therefore argue that immersive story designers should minimize non-essential attention cues, and consider how to incorporate plot-essential cues in ways that are not perceived to conflict in priority with whatever is in the viewer's current field of vision.

6.4 Future Work

The aforementioned discussion points give researchers and designers several avenues for exploration. Future work should involve viewers in assessment of variations to supporting character design and health behavior design, as well as continued identification of latent or overlooked immersive story elements influential to viewer perception. Considering that the present study focused only on viewers' attitudes towards binge drinking, and immediately after experiencing the immersive story, future work can and should explore long term impacts of immersive story experience on viewers' actual behaviors regarding the focal health issue.

7 Conclusion

Immersive stories for health—or 360° videos that convey narrative about a public health issue—have the potential to influence public health at scale because they enable viewers to viscerally experience the consequences of a detrimental health behavior without experiencing real harm. This paper reported a focus group study that facilitated viewers of an immersive story about binge drinking in elucidating elements of immersive story design most impactful to their attitudes towards the respective health behavior. Findings provide insight on: 1) health behavior design: how context of the behavior is sought by viewers, how engagement in the behavior is perceived, and how health repercussions are comprehended; and 2) supporting character design: the impact of a secondary character's behavior on the viewer's attention and judgment of the focal health behavior. Ultimately, while immersive stories hold promise for positively impacting public health, the study demonstrates that immersive stories can have minimal or adverse impact on viewer attitudes if their design is not closely considered.

Acknowledgements. We thank Devin Yang, Stephen Davidson, and Rukkmini Goli for their data analysis contributions. We also thank Ryan Handley for his artistic contributions in creating Fig. 1 for this paper.

References

1. Slater, M., Sanchez-Vives, M.V.: Enhancing our lives with immersive virtual reality. Front. Robot. AI **3**, 74 (2016). https://doi.org/10.3389/frobt.2016.00074
2. Steuer, J.: Defining virtual reality: dimensions determining telepresence. J. Commun. **42**, 73–93 (1992). https://doi.org/10.1111/j.1460-2466.1992.tb00812.x
3. Lee, K.M.: Presence, explicated. Commun. Theory. **14**, 27–50 (2004). https://doi.org/10.1111/j.1468-2885.2004.tb00302.x
4. Lombard, M., Ditton, T.: At the heart of it all: the concept of presence. J. Comput. Commun. **3** (2006). https://doi.org/10.1111/j.1083-6101.1997.tb00072.x
5. Hendriks Vettehen, P., Wiltink, D., Huiskamp, M., Schaap, G., Ketelaar, P.: Taking the full view: how viewers respond to 360-degree video news. Comput. Human Behav. **91**, 24–32 (2019). https://doi.org/10.1016/j.chb.2018.09.018
6. Ma, Z.: The use of immersive stories to influence college students' attitudes and intentions related to drinking and driving. J. Am. Coll. Health (2020). https://doi.org/10.1080/07448481.2020.1842418
7. Ahn, S.J.G., Fox, J.: Immersive virtual environments, avatars, and agents for health. In: Oxford Research Encyclopedia of Communication. Oxford University Press (2017)

8. Fonseca, D., Kraus, M.: A comparison of head-mounted and hand-held displays for 360° videos with focus on attitude and behavior change. In: Proceedings of the 20th International Academic Mindtrek Conference, pp. 287–296. ACM, New York (2016)

9. Visch, V.T., Tan, E.S., Molenaar, D.: The emotional and cognitive effect of immersion in film viewing. Cogn. Emot. **24**, 1439–1445 (2010). https://doi.org/10.1080/02699930903498186

10. Passmore, P.J., Glancy, M., Philpot, A., Roscoe, A., Wood, A., Fields, B.: Effects of viewing condition on user experience of panoramic video. In: International Conference on Artificial Reality and Telexistence and Eurographics Symposium on Virtual Environments, ICAT-EGVE 2016, pp. 9–16. The Eurographics Association (2016)

11. Bindman, S.W., Castaneda, L.M., Scanlon, M., Cechony, A.: Am i a bunny? In: Proceedings of the 2018 CHI Conference on Human Factors in Computing Systems, p. 11. ACM, New York (2018)

12. MacQuarrie, A., Steed, A.: Cinematic virtual reality: evaluating the effect of display type on the viewing experience for panoramic video. In: 2017 IEEE Virtual Reality (VR), pp. 45–54. IEEE (2017)

13. Baños, R.M., Botella, C., Alcañiz, M., Liaño, V., Guerrero, B., Rey, B.: Immersion and emotion: their impact on the sense of presence. CyberPsychology Behav. **7**, 734–741 (2004). https://doi.org/10.1089/cpb.2004.7.734

14. Tse, A., Jennett, C., Moore, J., Watson, Z., Rigby, J., Cox, A.L.: Was I there? Impact of platform and headphones on 360 video immersion. In: Proceedings of the 2017 CHI Conference Extended Abstracts on Human Factors in Computing Systems, pp. 2967–2974 (2017)

15. Larsen, M.: Virtual sidekick: Second-person POV in narrative VR. J. Screenwriting **9**, 73–83 (2018). https://doi.org/10.1386/josc.9.1.73_1

16. Elmezeny, A., Edenhofer, N., Wimmer, J.: Immersive storytelling in 360-degree videos: an analysis of interplay between narrative and technical immersion. J. Virtual Worlds Res. 11 (2018). https://doi.org/10.4101/jvwr.v11i1.7298

17. Kors, M.J., van der Spek, E.D., Ferri, G., Schouten, B.A.: You; the observer, partaker or victim. Delineating three perspectives to empathic engagement in persuasive games using immersive technologies. In: Proceedings of the 2018 Annual Symposium on Computer-Human Interaction in Play Companion Extended Abstracts, pp. 493–501. ACM, New York (2018)

18. Cho, J., et al.: Imago: presence and emotion in virtual reality. In: ACM SIGGRAPH 2016 VR Village, pp. 1–2. ACM, New York (2016)

19. Dahlstrom, M.F., Niederdeppe, J., Gao, L., Zhu, X.: Operational and conceptual trends in narrative persuasion research: comparing health-and non-health-related contexts. Int. J. Commun. 11 (2017)

20. Syrett, H., Calvi, L., van Gisbergen, M.: The oculus rift film experience: a case study on understanding films in a head mounted display. In: Poppe, R., Meyer, J.-J., Veltkamp, R., Dastani, M. (eds.) INTETAIN 2016 2016. LNICSSITE, vol. 178, pp. 197–208. Springer, Cham (2017). https://doi.org/10.1007/978-3-319-49616-0_19

21. Nielsen, L.T., et al.: Missing the point. In: Proceedings of the 22nd ACM Conference on Virtual Reality Software and Technology, pp. 229–232. ACM, New York (2016)

22. Sheikh, A., Brown, A., Evans, M., Watson, Z.: Directing attention in 360-degree video. In: IBC 2016 Conference. Institution of Engineering and Technology (2016)

23. Gugenheimer, J., Wolf, D., Haas, G., Krebs, S., Rukzio, E.: SwiVRChair. In: Proceedings of the 2016 CHI Conference on Human Factors in Computing Systems, pp. 1996–2000. ACM, New York (2016)

24. Stahre, M., Roeber, J., Kanny, D., Brewer, R.D., Zhang, X.: Contribution of excessive alcohol consumption to deaths and years of potential life lost in the united states. Prev. Chronic Dis. **11**, 130293 (2014). https://doi.org/10.5888/pcd11.130293

25. Kanny, D., Naimi, T.S., Liu, Y., Lu, H., Brewer, R.D.: Annual total binge drinks consumed by U.S. adults, 2015. Am. J. Prev. Med. **54**, 486–496 (2018). https://doi.org/10.1016/j.ame pre.2017.12.021
26. Ma, Z., Zytko, D.: Perspective-taking with the risk taker in an immersive story increases psychological reactance and decreases persuasion. In: Kentucky Conference on Health Communication (2020)
27. Mateer, J.: Directing for Cinematic Virtual Reality: how the traditional film director's craft applies to immersive environments and notions of presence. J. Media Pract. **18**, 14–25 (2017). https://doi.org/10.1080/14682753.2017.1305838
28. VR Films. https://unvr.sdgactioncampaign.org/vr-films/#.X4tw0EJKhBx
29. A Walk Through Dementia. https://www.awalkthroughdementia.org/
30. Shin, D.: Empathy and embodied experience in virtual environment: to what extent can virtual reality stimulate empathy and embodied experience? Comput. Hum. Behav. **78**, 64–73 (2018). https://doi.org/10.1016/j.chb.2017.09.012
31. Breves, P.: Bringing people closer: the prosocial effects of immersive media on users' attitudes and behavior. Nonprofit Volunt. Sect. Q. **49**, 1015–1034 (2020). https://doi.org/10.1177/089 9764020903101
32. Ma, Z.: Effects of immersive stories on prosocial attitudes and willingness to help: testing psychological mechanisms. Media Psychol. **23**, 865–890 (2020). https://doi.org/10.1080/152 13269.2019.1651655
33. Jones, S., Dawkins, S.: Walking in someone else's shoes: creating empathy in the practice of immersive film. Media Pract. Educ. **19**, 298–312 (2018). https://doi.org/10.1080/25741136. 2018.1520538
34. de la Hera Conde-Pumpido, T.: A conceptual model for the study of persuasive games. In: Proceedings of DiGRA 2013: DeFragging Game Studies (2013)
35. Herrera, F., Bailenson, J., Weisz, E., Ogle, E., Zaki, J.: Building long-term empathy: a large-scale comparison of traditional and virtual reality perspective-taking. PLoS ONE **13**, e0204494 (2018). https://doi.org/10.1371/journal.pone.0204494
36. Moyer-Gusé, E.: Toward a theory of entertainment persuasion: explaining the persuasive effects of entertainment-education messages. Commun. Theory. **18**, 407–425 (2008). https:// doi.org/10.1111/j.1468-2885.2008.00328.x
37. NIAAA council approves definition of binge drinking. https://pubs.niaaa.nih.gov/publicati ons/Newsletter/winter2004/Newsletter_Number3.pdf
38. Diageo DRINKiQ: Decisions: Party's Over – Greg's Perspective. https://www.youtube.com/ watch?v=PQl_NVT9P0Y
39. Diageo DRINKiQ: Decisions: Party's Over – Steph's Perspective. https://www.youtube.com/ watch?v=2JI-ws-FA5E
40. Charmaz, K., Belgrave, L.: Qualitative interviewing and grounded theory analysis. SAGE Handb. Interview Res. Complex. Craft **2**, 347–365 (2012)
41. Biocca, F.: The cyborg's dilemma: progressive embodiment in virtual environments. J. Comput. Commun. **3** (2006). https://doi.org/10.1111/j.1083-6101.1997.tb00070.x
42. Slater, M., Spanlang, B., Sanchez-Vives, M.V., Blanke, O.: First person experience of body transfer in virtual reality. PLoS ONE **5**, e10564 (2010). https://doi.org/10.1371/journal.pone. 0010564
43. Kilteni, K., Groten, R., Slater, M.: The sense of embodiment in virtual reality. Presence Teleoperators Virtual Environ. **21**, 373–387 (2012). https://doi.org/10.1162/PRES_a_00124
44. Peck, T.C., Seinfeld, S., Aglioti, S.M., Slater, M.: Putting yourself in the skin of a black avatar reduces implicit racial bias. Conscious. Cogn. **22**, 779–787 (2013). https://doi.org/10.1016/j. concog.2013.04.016

Engagement and Usability of Conversational Search – A Study of a Medical Resource Center Chatbot

Tamás Fergencs[✉] and Florian Meier

Science, Policy and Information Studies, Department of Communication
and Psychology, Aalborg University, Copenhagen, Denmark
tfergencs@gmail.com, fmeier@hum.aau.dk

Abstract. Due to advances in natural language understanding, chatbots have become popular for assisting users in various tasks, for example, searching. Chatbots allow natural-language queries, which can be useful in case of complex information needs, and they provide a higher level of interactivity by displaying information in a dialog-like format. However, chatbots are often only used as auxiliaries for a graphical search user interface (SUI). Thus, they must be engaging and usable so that users both want to and are able to use them. In this study, we conduct a controlled interactive information retrieval experiment following a within-subject design to compare a chatbot to a graphical SUI in terms of engagement and usability. Our findings point towards the need for flawless usability in order for conversational search interfaces to (1) be able to provide additional value in information retrieval tasks and (2) elicit a higher level of engagement compared to their SUI-based counterparts.

Keywords: Conversational search · Search user interface · Usability · User engagement · Chatbot

1 Introduction

Conversational interfaces are becoming increasingly popular due to the advancement in natural language understanding technology. They enable human-computer interaction via natural speech or text instead of using buttons and menus and allow for a more human-like dialog with a system. Text-based conversational interfaces, so-called chatbots, have been around for quite some time, but they gained commercial interest only recently, due to digital communication becoming a standard [7]. The number of customer service chatbots is increasing as businesses explore the possibilities of conversational commerce to interact with and provide support for customers [6,11,40]. Mobile health solutions are starting to utilize conversational agents to promote health or facilitate recovery [8,13,23]. Chatbots also find their way into the field of education, where they inform university students about school facilities or act as teaching agents to

© Springer Nature Switzerland AG 2021
K. Toeppe et al. (Eds.): iConference 2021, LNCS 12645, pp. 328–345, 2021.
https://doi.org/10.1007/978-3-030-71292-1_26

supplement classroom learning [12,26]. Regardless of the field of application, conversational agents are seen as a useful tool to facilitate user engagement—they can motivate increased usage of an application, enrich business-to-consumer interactions, or simply serve as "wow factor" for marketing purposes. One specific use case of chatbots is assisting with searching and retrieval of web content—a concept denoted as conversational search [25]. Instead of examining a lengthy FAQ page, a user can simply submit their question to a chatbot, which queries the database and returns a relevant answer [18]. Or, a library chatbot can help in promptly retrieving reading material based on the user's preferences [1,37]. If the natural language understanding framework is robust enough, users can submit even complex search queries, which can be useful in cases where the information need is difficult to formulate – e.g. in the case of non-targeted searching, where exploration of the collection is the main activity [35].

A chatbot is often used as an auxiliary to a website search interface, and not as a standalone search system. If the chatbot is not engaging enough, the initial interest can quickly fade, and users will return to using the website search. Chatbots can increase user engagement by enhancing interactivity, that is, by delivering information in a human dialog-like manner [30]. It is, however, uncertain whether a higher level of interactivity is enough for users to prefer using the chatbot if there is an alternative. Besides, implementing search functionalities to a conversational interface is not a straightforward process and, even if it's successful, users may have trouble transitioning from a traditional graphical search user interface to a conversational interface [38]. This is due to the inherently complex nature of search behaviors, which generally do not adhere to a simple query-answer model, but are rather characterized by constantly evolving information needs [2]. A search chatbot, therefore, should satisfy both the need for enhancing user engagement and serve as a user-friendly supplement (or even substitute) to a graphical SUI. If the chatbot has poor usability, people may not be able to use it. If the chatbot does not motivate engagement, people may not want to use it.

This study aims to compare the conversational search user interface (chatbot) of a medical resource center database, with its graphical search user interface in terms of user engagement and usability. The platform represents an ideal object of investigation as both the chatbot and the website-based SUI taps into the same database of psychiatry and neurology-related resources. Currently, the main users of this platform are mostly healthcare experts, but the providers' aim is to make the collection more accessible to the broader public. The chatbot was considered as an experimental tool to draw in more users by enhancing content interactivity and, subsequently, user engagement. We formulated the following research question:

How does a conversational search interface compare to a graphical search user interface in terms of user engagement and usability?

To investigate this question we conducted a controlled interactive information retrieval experiment (IIR). In this experiment it is hypothesized that the chatbot will achieve its goal, i.e. it will successfully enhance user engagement. Therefore, we formulated the following hypothesis:

H_1: *The usage of the chatbot for searching has a positive effect on user engagement.*

User engagement is measured using the User Engagement Scale (UES), a de-facto standard in the field of IIR [21]. While the main focus of the study will be to compare the overall engagement of users across the two interfaces, one aspect of user engagement will be discussed in greater detail: system usability. This is done by (1) collecting quantitative measures on time on task, task success and overall preference and (2) conducting a thematic analysis on the qualitative data shared by the participants during the experiment and in a post-study questionnaire.

To sum up, the contributions of our work are as follows:

- We present one of few studies that compare a conversational chatbot interface to a graphical SUI.
- We present a detailed analysis of how user engagement and usability issues are related.
- We reveal usability issues of the chatbot, link these issues to design patterns and give recommendations for generic chatbot design.

Before we present our experimental design, Sect. 2 reviews relevant related work.

2   Related Work

Conversational search is still a novel branch of IR and HCI, but it is becoming more popular due to the increased acceptance of voice-based intelligent personal assistants (IPA) by the general public [24]. However, as mentioned before, users may have difficulty adapting to conversational search [27], since the majority of search interfaces are based on a graphical user interface. Graphical SUIs set the standards for digital information search, and the majority of IR system design principles are based on graphical representation – e.g. faceted search [34] or SERP control features like sorting, filtering or grouping [39].

While interaction with voice-based interfaces has received much attention [24,27,33], chatbot interaction has been less well studied. Most importantly, there is a lack of studies that compares classic SUI-based information access to dialog-based chatbot interaction. Literature about this field is scarce, and most comparative studies do not focus specifically on search systems. For example, Ischen et al. [15] compared a website, a human-like chatbot, and a machine-like chatbot and studied the effects of the interface on anthropomorphism and privacy concerns via questionnaires. One of their findings was that the website evoked more privacy concerns in users than the machine-like chatbot, which lead to less information disclosure (interestingly, no such difference was found between the human-like chatbot and the website). Celino and Re Calegari [5] investigated whether administering surveys via a conversational interface is a reliable and user-friendly method for data gathering. They tested a website-based survey, a chatbot with informally formulated questions, and one with formally formulated questions via A/B testing and collected preference data via questionnaires. They found out that users have a preference towards the chatbot-administered survey, and that a chatbot-based method is at least as reliable in terms of inter-rater reliability as the website-based one. The work by Sundar et al. [30] is the only study of this type that focused on an interface that is used for searching. They compared several types of interfaces for a movie search website with varying levels of message interactivity, which they manipulated by adding/removing search history functionalities and a chatbot for assisting users in their browsing. They found that providing interaction history and the possibility of chatting with a live agent significantly increased perceived contingency, and subsequently, interactivity, which affected user engagement positively. Apart from the latter, no literature was found that compares the performance of conversational and graphical search user interfaces – therefore, the focus will be on conversational search interfaces in general.

Vtyurina et al. explored users' preferences towards conversational search interfaces of various sentience [36]. Participants completed exploratory search tasks with three types of chatbots: a commercial chatbot, a human expert (where participants knew they interacted with a human), and a "wizard" where the chatbot was covertly operated by a human but participants thought they interact with a machine. They found that most users preferred the human or "wizard" chatbots as both were able to interpret half-sentences, whereas the machine struggled with reference resolution, which also negatively affected participants' search task performance. Dubiel et al. [9] found similar differences in task performance and user satisfaction in a Wizard-Of-Oz-style study. They explore two hypothetical spoken dialog systems: a standard voice bot using a slot-filling algorithm and an intelligent "conversational search agent" with a memory component for handling contextuality. Participants were significantly more successful with their tasks when they used the agent with a memory component, and they found it less taxing and displayed a more positive sentiment towards it compared to the slot-filling agent. This points towards the users' need for more human-like conversations where chatbots have contextual awareness – preferably without asking too many questions for confirmation [9]. However, user expectations about the capabilities of conversational interfaces are usually met with disappointment. Luger and Sellen conducted a qualitative study using interviews and thematic network analysis to explore the mental models that users have about their voice assistants [19]. They found a "deep gulf of evaluation": users reported their confusion about the capabilities of the voice systems, as their expectations were not met. The in-built playful responses (e.g. the capability of telling jokes) also set unrealistic expectations about the sophistication of the system, and after continued disappointment, users became reluctant to use their voice assistants for complex tasks.

Seeing that the discipline of conversational search still lacks profound research, Thomas et al. [32] collected a rich dataset of search-oriented conversations called MISC (Microsoft Information-Seeking Conversation data). The participants of the

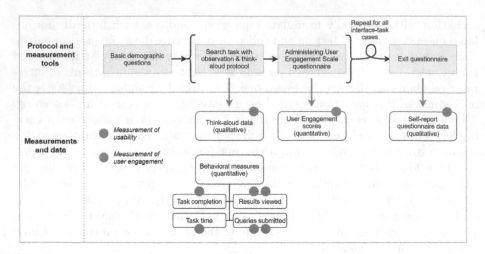

Fig. 1. Experimental setup: the measurement tools used and the type of data collected

conversations consisted of a searcher, who was given a search task, and an intermediary who had access to the internet and was tasked to follow the searcher's directions and provide feedback only via voice. These conversation recordings are created to help to establish requirements for an optimal conversational search system and demonstrate users' desires for an aligned discourse with conversational interfaces. Alignment means that the user and the system can match each other's style of communication in terms of involvement (chit-chattiness, verbosity, enthusiasm) or considerateness (more listening, hesitance, independence). If alignment succeeds, then task execution becomes more efficient [31].

3   Experimental Design and Experiments

We conducted a controlled IIR experiment to investigate whether the type of interface used for searching, the independent variable, influences user engagement, the dependent variable. Figure 1 visualizes the experimental setup and shows how and what kind of data got collected during the study. For participants to be able to compare the two systems, we followed a within-subjects design. The two interfaces were compared through a series of tasks that the participant had to complete with the interfaces.

Object of Investigation and Stimuli. Our object of investigation is the medical resource center website *Progress in Mind. Progress in Mind* is an online, open-access database, where articles and videos about current scientific trends, international news, and congress highlights are hosted. The publications on the website are written and curated by medical writers in a generally informal style, and the content is aimed at healthcare practitioners and academics in the field.

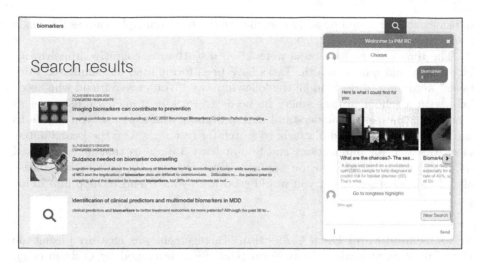

Fig. 2. Screenshot of the Progress in Mind platform's graphic SUI on the left side and its chatbot SUI on the right side

Users can filter content by diseases or types of publications or use free-text queries to search across the database.

The company's goal is to transform the platform into a go-to resource center for healthcare professionals of psychology and neurology. Therefore, they are experimenting with new ways to make the content more accessible and interactive – which led to the development of a chatbot. This chatbot interface is an auxiliary tool for the website search and uses a conversational modality to help users search the database, presenting search results in a chat window (Fig. 2). This conversational style is aimed to improve interactivity, which, as Lundbeck anticipates, will lead to greater user engagement and promote the usage of the platform. As Sundar et al. [30] have shown, delivering online content in a dialog-like manner can lead to improved interactivity and, in turn, a greater level of engagement.

To gather an adequate amount of information from users, each user interacted with an interface twice, completing two tasks with each interface – therefore, a total of four different tasks were defined which got randomized across the two interfaces for every participant. This is to account for learning effects, as users might initially focus on getting to know the system and concentrate less on the search task.

Task Design. During each task, the basic goal of the user was to list three diseases that have a connection to the topic of the given task. Tasks were of low-intermediate cognitive complexity, corresponding to the "Understand" category following Kelly et al.'s task classification [17]. These tasks "require the searcher to provide an exhaustive list of items" by identifying "a list or factors in an information source and possibly compile the list from multiple sources if a single list cannot be found" [17].

The topics of the four tasks were: sleep disturbance, cognitive impairment, biomarkers and mobile health. Tasks have been formulated as "simulated work tasks" according to Borlund [3] the following way: "You have a friend who needs help with a school project where he needs to explore [topic]. He asks you to send him some easy-to-understand material about the topic, so you decide to use the Progress in Mind platform to search for resources. Use the [search interface] to search for publications and find at least 3 diseases that may be linked to [topic]/where [topic] can be applied. When you read a publication, please also decide whether or not you would send it to your friend to help him in his project.".

Measurements and Data Collection. Engagement was measured using the User Engagement Scale - Short Form (UES-SF), developed by O'Brien et al. [21]. It contains 12 items, grouped into four categories: Focused Attention (FA), Perceived Usability (PU), Aesthetic Appeal (AE), and Reward (RW). The participants had to fill out the UES-SF form each time after a task was completed.

Usability was broken up into three constituents according to the ISO 9241-11:2018 standard [14], and measured using various behavioral measures:

- Task time (how much time the participant spent on a task) that measures efficiency;
- Task success (whether the participant successfully completed the task or not) that measures effectiveness; and
- Preference (which interface was preferred by the participant for the given task) that measures satisfaction.

Moreover, we collected search behavior related measures: the number of viewed results and the number of submitted queries. Differences in search behavior across the two interfaces were assessed, as search behavior can have an effect on user engagement [22]. Finally, data about the general user experience was gathered via qualitative think-aloud comments recorded during the experiment and an exit questionnaire, where participants were asked to list their most positive and negative experiences during their interaction.

4   Results

A total of 10 participants were recruited through snowball sampling, 8 female and 2 male, all had Hungarian as their native language, but were fluent in English. Their age ranged from 22 to 32 with a mean age of 24,5 years. The participants were highly educated as each participant had at least an undergraduate degree. Almost all participants reported that they never used chatbots or only once or twice in their life; one participant used chatbots more than once a month for booking flights and as online shopping assistance. During the exit questionnaire,

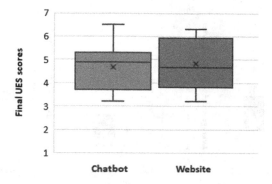

Fig. 3. Distribution of the average UES scores for the chatbot and the website SUI. The 'x' in the boxplot denotes the mean.

9 participants reported that they would use the website for searching across the collection, and only one participant said that she/he would prefer to use the chatbot. On average, an entire experiment was 60 min long with a minimum length of 39 min and a maximum of 73 min.

4.1 User Engagement

The first part of the analysis focused on understanding how the independent variable, the search interface, influenced user engagement, the dependent variable. According to Fig. 3, most UES scores lie in the upper half of the scale, which suggests that the majority of participants were engaged throughout the study. Comparing the average UES scores of the chatbot ($M = 4.65$, $SD = 1.05$) and the website's ($M = 4.83$, $SD = 1.12$) via a Student's t-test, we did not find a statistically significant difference between the two interfaces ($t(9) = -0.4$, $p = 0.69$). Moreover, the mean UES score of the chatbot was slightly lower than the website's. As we did not find substantial evidence to say that the usage of the chatbot results in higher user engagement, we can not reject the null hypothesis (H_0).

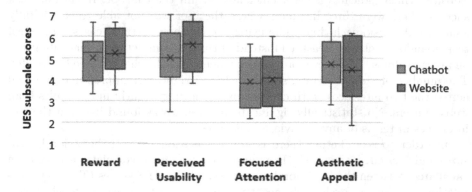

Fig. 4. Distribution of the average UES scores for the chatbot and the website SUI

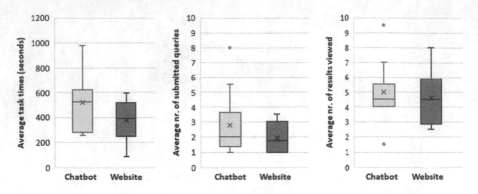

Fig. 5. Summary of behavioral measures per interface: task time (left), number of queries submitted (middle), and number of results viewed (right)

In order to investigate whether the type of interface influenced any specific aspect of engagement, the UES scores have been broken down to subscales. Figure 4 shows the mean subscale scores per interface. No significant difference was found between the two interfaces in terms of subscale scores. The website SUI outperformed the chatbot interface in all but one aspect: Aesthetic Appeal (AE), where the chatbot got a 0.2 points higher score. The largest difference between the two interfaces can be observed in Perceived Usability (PU), where the website ($M = 5.6$, $SD = 1.19$) outperformed the chatbot ($M = 5$, $SD = 1.34$) by more than half a point. Both interfaces received a relatively low score for focused attention (FA). Reward (RW) received the second-highest scores after PU, with only a slight difference between the two interfaces.

4.2   Behavioral Measures

Behavioral measures were analyzed (Fig. 5) to see how the two interfaces compare in terms of task performance. On average, participants took more time (approximately 2 more minutes) to complete the tasks with the chatbot compared to the website, which indicates a lower efficiency within the chatbot. Regarding task success, there were three instances where the user was not able to successfully complete the task, each time while using the chatbot. In these cases, time until task abandonment was measured instead of time to completion. Users submitted on average almost 1.5 times more queries when using the chatbot (see Fig. 5 left). The number of viewed results, shown in Fig. 5 right, was approximately equal across the two interfaces, with chatbot users viewing slightly more results than website users. No statistically significant difference was found between the two interfaces in terms of any behavioral measures.

In order to see whether there is any correlation between behavioral measures and user engagement, the Pearson-product moment correlations have been calculated between the behavioral measures and the UES scores (Table 1). Correlations are almost exclusively negative, apart from three cases, which means

Table 1. Pearson-product moment correlations between behavioral metrics and the mean UES subscale scores and the mean UES score per interface

	Chatbot			Website		
	Average task time	Avg. number of queries submitted	Avg. number of results viewed	Average task time	Avg. number of queries submitted	Avg. number of results viewed
RW	-.047	.002	-.529	-.603	-.333	-.717*
PU	-.411	-.323	-.571	-.426	-.248	-.346
FA	-.252	-.156	-.658*	-.438	-.035	-.546
AE	.158	.292	-.218	-.536	-.277	-.384
Final UES	-.178	-.061	-.571	-.555	-.231	-.551

Symbol * denotes significant r values ($p < .05$). Coloring represent the strength of the correlation, where white color represents very weak correlation ($|r| < .19$), and the darkening colors represents weak ($.2 < |r| < .39$), moderate ($.4 < |r| < .59$), and strong ($|r| > .6$) correlation.

that task time, number of submitted queries and number of results viewed elicit lower UES scores. Significant correlations have been found between website RW score and number of results viewed, and chatbot FA score and the number of results viewed. Behavioral metrics have overall stronger correlations with UES scores in the case of the website, and weaker correlations in the case of the chatbot.

4.3 Thematic Analysis

This section details the themes that emerged from the thematic analysis, a qualitative data analysis method. Our approach for conducting the thematic analysis followed the recommendations by Braun and Clarke [4]. The analysis was conducted in a deductive manner, meaning that it was built around two encompassing themes that dictated which participant remarks can be considered relevant: usability and search behavior. Usability strongly ties to the research question of the study, while remarks about search behavior can both highlight differences in engagement [22] or explain usability-related issues. The think-aloud protocol and the post-study questionnaire were selectively transcribed – only quotes pertaining to the preliminary themes were written up, not the entirety of the interview. A researcher scrutinized the transcripts to find participant quotes pertaining to usability issues (or good usability practices) and quotes that describe or explain search behaviors. Quotes were codified as short sentences, and similar codes were collated into sub-themes for easier overviewability. Table 2 summarizes the themes, sub-themes and codes that emerged from the qualitative data.

Table 2. Thematic analysis table

Theme	Sub-theme	Code
Usability	User interface	Overlapping UI elements
		Interface aesthetics (visuals and sound)
		Ambiguity of UI elements
	Inconsistencies within the system	Newsletter among the results
		Website SUI's inconsistency with thumbnail images
	Chatbot utility	Uncertainty about when to use the chatbot
		Chatbot fails to handle complex input
		Doubtful disposition towards chatbots
	Importance of overviewable results	Viewing more results at once is important
		Chatbot window is too small
	-	Importance of response speed
Search behavior	Assessing relevance of documents	Relying on field knowledge
		Assessing results and content using metadata and keywords (within SERP and within content)
	Partitioning and query tactics	Filtering and faceting features are missing (in the SUIs and in the homepage)
		Phrase search is useful for experienced searchers
		Preferring keyword-search in chatbot
	-	Finding related items is difficult
	-	Lack of search transparency within the system
	-	Searching for explanations in case of unfamiliar topics

Usability. The majority of remarks about usability concerned the visual structure of the user interface, highlighting the differences between the SUI of the website and the chatbot. The main issue seemed to be the relatively small size of the chatbot window, which caused all navigational elements to be placed closely together. One user remarked how "the [chat] window was too small, and you had to click this small right-arrow which was annoying", reflecting on the difficulty to navigate between results.

Apart from navigational problems, the small chatbot window also hindered the relevance assessment of results. Almost all users noted the inadequacy of the chatbot to display several results at once, which, as one participant noted, "was weird because I couldn't have as much of an overview". In contrast, "the website was better because it showed the results below one another and I could overview them more easily".

Another negative aspect of the chatbot was the slow response time, as "that 3 s waiting was strange. It took some time to react". In contrast, the website was "faster [compared to the chatbot] and I didn't have to wait for an answer", as one participant remarked.

Users had ambiguous feelings towards the visual style of the platform, as some pointed out that it "was quite dull and colorless". Interestingly, one participant remarked positively about the poor visual appeal of the website, as "for some reason, it's important to me that if something [deals with] scientific [material], it should look a bit lame. This website looked trustworthy for me [...] because of this". Apart from visual aesthetics, the sound the chatbot made every time it sent a message was found to be "weird and annoying" by two participants, whereas one participant expressed their fondness of it.

Participants also made comments about the chatbot's utility. Users who tried to communicate with the chatbot with complete sentences realized that the chatbot is not capable of handling complex inputs, therefore all resorted to keyword inputs (discussed in the next theme).

Some participants were skeptical about the chatbot's overall usefulness and articulated that they "would not even think about using the chatbot for searching". One reason behind the doubtful disposition was the lack of faith in conversational technology: one participant shared his/her negative experiences with voice assistants "which made it clear that I don't want to use them again". Another participant reflected that "using [chatbots] only makes sense if you're talking to a real human".

Search Behavior. Throughout their search, users demonstrated various tactics to choose which results to click and to assess whether the content they are reading is relevant for them or not. Most of the participants could be observed scanning the metadata in the search snippets for relevant keywords using either the title, topical tags, or query highlights – which was a fairly limited tactic in the chatbot. Users were missing the rich metadata from the chatbot snippets, because in the website SUI "you could see above the titles the diseases the article is about [...] whereas the chatbot does not display these keywords".

Apart from relying on keywords, another tactic of assessing relevance was relying on their own knowledge. Users would collate the information they read with their own knowledge to assess the relevance of the result, e.g. "this one shows major depressive disorder, which makes sense as that [and cognitive impairment] go hand in hand". Some participants expressed a certain level of confusion when they met with information which seemingly contradicted their former knowledge, with comments like "based on what the article states, I would not connect it [to the disease] but I know [by myself] that they are related".

More than half of the subjects expressed their frustration that the system does not provide adequate search functionality. The biggest issue was the lack of filtering and faceting options as there are "no options in the search bar to filter, like which source is it from, [or] when was it published". One participant remarked positively that the chatbot provides at least some level of categorical browsing, saying that "I really liked at the beginning that it asked whether I want to read articles or listen to podcast".

In terms of query formulations, users almost exclusively resorted to keyword-based search, usually using the task topic as the query (e.g. "cognitive impairment") – even within the chatbot, despite its conversational interaction. One reason behind this could be that, as one participant stated, "the chatbot phrased the question in a way that it didn't even occur to me to reply in full sentences". The chatbot phrased its welcome message as "type what you are looking for", which the users might have interpreted as a prompt for a keyword or search phrase. Nevertheless, users liked that "it was enough to write keywords and you got all types of publications".

Three participants raised the issue of search transparency – saying that "it wasn't really clear to me how [the chatbot] selects those articles". One participant even remarked about this distrust, saying that "I had a bit of distrust in me about whether [the platform] actually shows me the relevant results". This issue was even more relevant in the chatbot, where only a limited number of results were displayed. Users "didn't really know how to expand the number of results", and one participant mentioned that they were curious how those articles were selected, as they "couldn't really see any pattern in it".

5   Discussion and Conclusion

Based on our research question, we discuss our findings in two section: (1) How does the type of interface influence user engagement and (2) What role did usability play during the experiment? The identified usability problems can also be interpreted as design recommendations as they represent issues in human-chatbot interaction that should be avoided, especially in the context of IR tasks.

5.1   How Does the Type of Interface Influence Engagement?

The analysis revealed that using the chatbot for searching does not lead to greater engagement – the null hypothesis could not be rejected. In fact, the chatbot underperformed in all but one aspect of engagement, aesthetic appeal (AE). According to the thematic analysis, the aesthetics of the interface seems to be of a subjective matter, as a stylistic choice can elicit both negative and positive reactions from participants. Therefore, the reason behind the higher AE score may be attributed simply to the novelty of the interface – the chatbot might have grabbed the users' visual attention because of its unique way of searching, which might have resulted in an initial interest and a more favorable AE score. Still, the attractiveness of the interface was not enough to counterbalance the other aspects the interface was lacking – especially perceived usability (PU), which is going to be discussed separately.

Interestingly, both interfaces received a relatively low score for focused attention (FA), which suggests that neither interface managed to hold the attention of the participants to such an extent which could have led to deep involvement. The reason behind the low scores could be that the protocol of the experiment gave little room for substantial immersion: the Understand type tasks we used did not require high-level cognitive processing, only identifying and compiling information [17]. The online format of the experiment might have also played a role, as participants' focus could be easily disrupted by their external environment – which prevented them from being absorbed in the experience. The chatbot's slightly lower FA score could be due to its slow response time, which participants occasionally commented about. Participants might find it self-evident that search systems are generally quick to respond (like Google), thus the chatbot with such a response delay (approximately 2 s) may seem sluggish and it can interrupt the user's flow of thoughts [20].

Reward (RW) received the second-highest average score among the subscales with only a small score difference between the two interfaces, which indicates that participants usually found their search experience interesting, worthwhile, and rewarding – regardless of the platform. This highlights the importance of the content, which – interface-independently – enhanced the reward factor of using the platform. Observations also reinforce this assumption, as many participants made sporadic comments about the platform's interesting content (e.g. "the content is [extremely] good... the articles were great and contained relevant information").

Regarding the behavioral measures, participants were less efficient in their tasks when using the chatbot, with higher task times, more queries sent, and more results clicked. The almost exclusively negative correlations between the UES scores and the behavioral measures also show that a higher "interaction cost" leads to lower engagement (see Table 1). This is in accordance with O'Brien, Arguello and Capras' [22] results, who found that a higher task effort correlates negatively with engagement. Edwards and Kelly [10] also found that increased search behaviors signify frustration, rather than engagement. The number of viewed results seems to be a good indicator of low engagement. Participants who clicked on a large number of results might have experienced impatience and frustration, which led to lower engagement. In the case of the website, the time that users spend on a task seems to be a good indicator of low engagement, with correlations ranging from moderate to high. However, in the case of the chatbot, only PU had a moderate negative correlation with task time. Sauro and Lewis [28] draw similar conclusions. They interpret higher task times as an indicator of poor usability. The number of query submissions was not shown to be a good indicator of engagement as correlations were either weak or very weak.

5.2 What Role Does Usability Play in Engagement?

Quantitative data did not show any significant differences between behavioral measures. Nevertheless, (1) the chatbot elicited higher task times (related to efficiency), (2) the preference data shows a higher satisfaction in the case of the website, and (3) task success (related to effectiveness) also shows that users were slightly more successful in completing their tasks with the website. Considering all three aspects of usability, the website SUI performed better compared to the chatbot. The thematic analysis also revealed that participants found the chatbot less user-friendly than the website SUI. The greatest problem of the chatbot is the limited amount of information it displays due to its small size. Though a horizontally scrollable result list needs less effort to navigate through compared to vertical scrolling, in exchange of displaying the results in a compact area the possibility for an overview is greatly impaired – and since this issue was mentioned by almost all users, it might be the greatest contributor to the reduced PU score of the system. The lack of overview ties closely to Shneiderman's Visual Information Seeking Mantra, which stipulates that a system must first provide the user a proper overview of the collection, before zooming in on items of interest and providing details on demand [29]. The chatbot violated this mantra as users could only see one result at a time.

Result presentation in the chatbot also omitted certain metadata, which made assessing their relevance even more difficult. The lack of metadata and sorting functions also made users question how the chatbot chose which results to display. Jackson et al. [16] raised this issue of lack of search transparency, stating that a search system should provide information according to which criteria the results are ranked, otherwise users become "instinctively distrustful of any mechanism they don't understand" [16].

Lack of filtering and faceting also impaired search efficiency for both interfaces. Although the chatbot does provide faceted browsing to some extent, accessing it is not straightforward, and none of the users managed to figure out how to search within facets. Topical tags are also accessible for each article, but they are not integrated enough in the search system and not salient enough so that users could find them easily. The possibility of issuing phrase-search or using search operators was also not communicated effectively. The system seems to provide more utility to experienced searchers who are already familiar with the platform and who can leverage the system's less visible functionalities (e.g. search operators or tags).

Further indicators of the chatbot's poor usability are the higher task times [28], and the lower PU score of the chatbot (see Fig. 4). The higher number of submitted queries and viewed results may also indicate lower search efficiency, as participants had a harder time finding relevant results with the chatbot. However, it must be noted that the chatbot displays only a limited number of items on the SERP, thus users had to submit further queries if they wanted to see more results. This could be another reason behind the large difference in the number of query submissions. It must also be noted that, since the chatbot omits certain metadata and thus makes relevance assessment difficult, users might have been more inclined to open the result and check the content itself to determine its relevance – hence the higher number of viewed results. Nevertheless, the behavioral measures also show that the chatbot required greater effort from the participants, which translates into poor usability.

The almost exclusive preference for the website SUI shows that users can hardly recognize any value the chatbot could add to their search process. For example, a participant commented that "a chatbot can create added value where social interaction with a human needs to be substituted...and searching is not a social interaction". This signifies that the chatbot performs poorly not only in terms of usability but also utility. However, this stands in contrast to the chatbot's fairly high UES score ratings. Possible explanations for this observation could be biases like social desirability bias which lead participants to rate the chatbot higher in the UES questionnaires. Our study is limited in the sense that the chatbot has serious usability issues, which made our main hypothesis—whether a chatbot could create significantly more user engagement than a more traditional SUI—difficult to assess. However, it has become clear that for chatbots to be able to successfully facilitate user engagement and be a real alternative in information retrieval tasks, flawless usability is an essential quality.

References

1. Allison, D.: Chatbots in the library: is it time? Libr. Hi Tech **30**(1), 95–107 (2012)
2. Bates, M.J.: The design of browsing and berrypicking techniques for the online search interface. Online Rev. **13**(5), 407–424 (1989). http://www.emeraldinsight.com/doi/10.1108/eb024320
3. Borlund, P.: The IIR evaluation model: a framework for evaluation of interactive information retrieval systems. Inf. Res. **8**(3), 1–31 (2003). http://informationr.net/ir/8-3/paper152.html
4. Braun, V., Clarke, V.: Using thematic analysis in psychology. Qual. Res. Psychol. **3**(2), 77–101 (2006). https://doi.org/10.1191/1478088706qp063oa
5. Celino, I., ReCalegari, G.: Submitting surveys via a conversational interface: an evaluation of user acceptance and approach effectiveness. Int. J. Hum. Comput. Stud. **139**, 1–16 (2020)
6. Chung, M., Ko, E., Joung, H., Kim, S.J.: Chatbot e-service and customer satisfaction regarding luxury brands. J. Bus. Res. **117**, 1–9 (2018)
7. Dale, R.: The return of the chatbots. Nat. Lang. Eng. **22**(5), 811–817 (2016)
8. Denecke, K., Hochreutener, S.L., Pöpel, A., May, R.: Self-anamnesis with a conversational user interface: concept and usability study. Methods Inf. Med. **57**(5–6), 243–252 (2018)
9. Dubiel, M.: Towards human-like conversational search systems. In: Proceedings of the 2018 Conference on Human Information Interaction and Retrieval, CHIIR 2018, pp. 348–350. Association for Computing Machinery, New York (2018)
10. Edwards, A., Kelly, D.: Engaged or frustrated? Disambiguating emotional state in search. In: Proceedings of the 40th International ACM SIGIR Conference on Research and Development in Information Retrieval, SIGIR 2017, pp. 125–134. Association for Computing Machinery, New York (2017)
11. Exalto, M., De Jong, M., De Koning, T., Groothuis, A., Ravesteijn, P.: Conversational commerce, the conversation of tomorrow. In: Proceedings of the 14th European Conference on Management, Leadership and Governance, ECMLG 2018, pp. 76–83 (2018)
12. Graesser, A.C., Li, H., Forsyth, C.: Learning by communicating in natural language with conversational agents. Curr. Dir. Psychol. Sci. **23**(5), 374–380 (2014)

13. Gratzer, D., Goldbloom, D.: Open for business: chatbots, e-therapies, and the future of psychiatry. Can. J. Psychiatry **64**(7), 453–455 (2019)
14. International Organization for Standardization: Ergonomics of human-system interaction—part 11: usability: definitions and concepts (2018)
15. Ischen, C., Araujo, T., Voorveld, H., van Noort, G., Smit, E.: Privacy concerns in chatbot interactions. In: Følstad, A., et al. (eds.) CONVERSATIONS 2019. LNCS, vol. 11970, pp. 34–48. Springer, Cham (2020). https://doi.org/10.1007/978-3-030-39540-7_3
16. Jackson, A., Lin, J., Milligan, I., Ruest, N.: Desiderata for exploratory search interfaces to web archives in support of scholarly activities. In: Proceedings of the 16th ACM/IEEE-CS on Joint Conference on Digital Libraries - JCDL 2016, pp. 103–106. ACM Press, New York (2016). https://doi.org/10.1145/2910896.2910912, http://dl.acm.org/citation.cfm?doid=2910896.2910912
17. Kelly, D., Arguello, J., Edwards, A., Wu, W.C.: Development and evaluation of search tasks for IIR experiments using a cognitive complexity framework. In: Proceedings of the 2015 ACM SIGIR International Conference on the Theory of Information Retrieval, pp. 101–110 (2015)
18. Lee, K., Jo, J., Kim, J., Kang, Y.: Can chatbots help reduce the workload of administrative officers? - implementing and deploying FAQ chatbot service in a university. In: Stephanidis, C. (ed.) HCII 2019. CCIS, vol. 1032, pp. 348–354. Springer, Cham (2019). https://doi.org/10.1007/978-3-030-23522-2_45
19. Luger, E., Sellen, A.: "Like having a really bad pa": the gulf between user expectation and experience of conversational agents. In: Proceedings of the 2016 CHI Conference on Human Factors in Computing Systems, CHI 2016, pp. 5286—-5297. Association for Computing Machinery, New York (2016)
20. Nielsen, J.: Usability testing. In: Usability Engineering, chap. 6, pp. 165–206. Morgan Kaufmann Publishers, Mountain View (1993)
21. O'Brien, H., Cairns, P., Hall, M.: A practical approach to measuring user engagement with the refined user engagement scale (UES) and new UES short form. Int. J. Hum. Comput. Stud. **112**, 28–39 (2018)
22. O'Brien, H.L., Arguello, J., Capra, R.: An empirical study of interest, task complexity, and search behaviour on user engagement. Inf. Process. Manag. **57**(3), 102226 (2020)
23. Perski, O., Crane, D., Beard, E., Brown, J.: Does the addition of a supportive chatbot promote user engagement with a smoking cessation app? An experimental study. Digit. Health **5**, 1–13 (2019)
24. Porcheron, M., Fischer, J.E., Reeves, S., Sharples, S.: Voice interfaces in everyday life. In: Proceedings of the 2018 CHI Conference on Human Factors in Computing Systems, CHI 2018, pp. 1–12. Association for Computing Machinery, New York (2018)
25. Radlinski, F., Craswell, N.: A theoretical framework for conversational search. In: CHIIR 2017 - Proceedings of the 2017 Conference Human Information Interaction and Retrieval, pp. 117–126 (2017)
26. Reed, K., Meiselwitz, G.: Teacher agents: the current state, future trends, and many roles of intelligent agents in education. In: Ozok, A.A., Zaphiris, P. (eds.) OCSC 2011. LNCS, vol. 6778, pp. 69–78. Springer, Heidelberg (2011). https://doi.org/10.1007/978-3-642-21796-8_8
27. Reeves, S., Porcheron, M., Fischer, J.: this is not what we wanted: designing for conversation with voice interfaces. Interactions **26**(1), 46–51 (2018)

28. Sauro, J., Lewis, J.R.: Correlations among prototypical usability metrics: evidence for the construct of usability. In: Greenberg, S., Hudson, S.E., Hinckley, K., Morris, M.R., Olsen, D.R. (eds.) Proceedings of the SIGCHI Conference on Human Factors in Computing Systems, CHI 2009, pp. 1609–1618. ACM Press, Boston (2009). https://doi.org/10.1145/1518701.1518947

29. Shneiderman, B.: The eyes have it: a task by data type taxonomy for information visualizations. In: The Craft of Information Visualization, pp. 364–371 (2007)

30. Sundar, S.S., Bellur, S., Oh, J., Jia, H., Kim, H.S.: Theoretical importance of contingency in human-computer interaction: effects of message interactivity on user engagement. Commun. Res. **43**(5), 595–625 (2016)

31. Thomas, P., Czerwinski, M., McDuf, D., Craswell, N., Mark, G.: Style and alignment in information-seeking conversation. In: CHIIR 2018 - Proceedings of the 2018 Conference on Human Information Interaction and Retrieval, pp. 42–51. ACM Press, New York (2018)

32. Thomas, P., McDuff, D., Czerwinski, M., Craswell, N.: Misc: a data set of information-seeking conversations. In: Proceedings of the 1st International Workshop on Conversational Approaches to Information Retrieval (2017)

33. Trippas, J.R., Spina, D., Cavedon, L., Joho, H., Sanderson, M.: Informing the design of spoken conversational search: perspective paper. In: Proceedings of the 2018 Conference on Human Information Interaction and Retrieval, CHIIR 2018, pp. 32–41. Association for Computing Machinery, New York (2018)

34. Tunkelang, D., Marchionini, G.: Front-end concerns. In: Marchionini, G. (ed.) Faceted Search, chap. 7, pp. 57–68. Synthesis Lectures on Information Concepts, Retrieval, and Services, Morgan & Claypool (2009)

35. Vakulenko, S., Markov, I., de Rijke, M.: Conversational exploratory search via interactive storytelling. CoRR abs/1709.05298 (2017). http://arxiv.org/abs/1709.05298

36. Vtyurina, A., Savenkov, D., Agichtein, E., Clarke, C.L.A.: Exploring conversational search with humans, assistants, and wizards. In: Proceedings of the 2017 CHI Conference Extended Abstracts on Human Factors in Computing Systems, CHI EA 2017, pp. 2187–2193. Association for Computing Machinery, New York (2017)

37. Ward, D.: Why users choose chat. Internet Reference Serv. Q. **10**(1), 29–46 (2005)

38. White, R.W.: Opportunities and challenges in search interaction. Commun. ACM **61**(12), 36–38 (2018)

39. Wilson, M.L.: Modern search user interfaces. In: Marchionini, G. (ed.) Search User Interface Design, chap. 4, pp. 29–79. Morgan & Claypool (2011)

40. Zhu, P., Zhang, Z., Li, J., Huang, Y., Zhao, H.: Lingke: a fine-grained multi-turn chatbot for customer service. In: Proceedings of the 27th International Conference on Computational Linguistics: System Demonstrations, pp. 108–112. Association for Computational Linguistics, Santa Fe (2018)

Hey Alexa, What Should I Read? Comparing the Use of Social and Algorithmic Recommendations for Different Reading Genres

Huiwen Zhang, George Buchanan(✉), and Dana McKay

iSchool, University of Melbourne, Parkville, VIC 3010, Australia
huiwen.zhang@student.unimelb.edu.au,
george.buchanan@unimelb.edu.au, danamckay@gmail.com

Abstract. Users often seek reading recommendations for what to read, across a variety of topics of interest and genres. While there has been extensive research on the development of recommender algorithms, our understanding of social factors relating to reading recommendation in the digital era is poor. We have no holistic view of how readers interact with diverse resources, social and digital, to obtain reading recommendations. Users can consult computer-generated summaries and human-created reviews. How much or how often the typical user relies on one or other source, or what variations there are by genre of intended reading, are both open questions.

To narrow these research gaps, we conducted a diary study to capture a comprehensive picture of readers' use of algorithm- and social-sourced information to inform their future reading choices. Based on a qualitative analysis of these diaries, we produced a survey to investigate in-depth readers' recommendation preferences across fictional reading, factual reading, academic resources, and news and articles. We show that users rely on different sources of recommendation information in different ways across different genres, and that modern social media plays an increasing role alongside established mass media, especially for fiction.

Keywords: Digital reading · Reading recommendations · Social information seeking · Discovery

1 Introduction

The explosion of digital reading material, such as fanfiction, blogs, self-published ebooks, and guidebooks [2] has resulted in a situation where, for readers, ubiquitous internet access isn't so much a valley of riches as an avalanche. This information overload [1] has made narrowing one's options as key a feature of the reading experience as finding something at all; one way to address both types of information need is using recommendations.

Recommendations are frequently used to try to identify information, or a book, that matches a user's preferences or needs. Different services, focused on varied content such as ebooks [1], music [2], movie [3], or daily tasks such as job-seeking [4], shopping [5]

© Springer Nature Switzerland AG 2021
K. Toeppe et al. (Eds.): iConference 2021, LNCS 12645, pp. 346–363, 2021.
https://doi.org/10.1007/978-3-030-71292-1_27

etc., all have their own recommendation strategies to improve the user experience. This study addresses both online and offline sources of reading recommendations.

Reading is not simply a solitary activity. Rather, through reading together [6], sharing reading experiences, and gathering suggestions as to what to read, reading is a profoundly social activity [7, 8]. Readers may also get useful information outside the reading material to enrich and assist their reading experience, either through traditional reading guides, finding blogs and social media posts, or digesting newspaper reviews [7, 9]. In this varied context, readers can obtain recommendations through multiple channels that may inspire or motivate them to read.

In the digital domain, some mainstream platforms such as Amazon.com provide automated, algorithmic recommendations, and collect large scale reader data. Human-generated material such as readers' reviews are also common among the digital reading platforms (such as Amazon-Kindle), and review-focussed websites (such as Good-reads). However, this all sits alongside a reader's own personal networks and social media connections.

This rich information environment is not yet well understood. Research on reading recommendations near-exclusively addresses development of algorithms to provide more accurate recommendations (such as [10]). Limited research, qualitative or quantitative, has been taken to gain an empirical understanding of how readers seek and obtain recommendations from today's diverse channels. Most of our understanding of users' recommendation sources and preferences dates back to an era where print was the dominant medium, or predate the widespread adoption of social media [9, 11, 12]. How well those earlier patterns translate into the digital era, or even what the digital era's preferences are, is not clear. Therefore, we consider the following questions: Do readers rely more on summative and algorithmically generated information, or human generated prose? Are these preferences consistent for different types of material? While some limited information around specific types of reading is available, overall, there is a major gap in our understanding of what material users rely on when looking online for reading recommendations.

2   Literature Review

The main purpose of reading recommendations is to help a reader in discovering useful or interesting reading material effectively and efficiently. From the reader's perspective, based on the different channels that they obtain the recommendation, we classify the reading recommendations into two categories: Algorithm-based and Social-sources.

Algorithm-based recommendations are automatically generated: for example, by analysing data from the individual user and the reading material, and matching it with the activity of many other users. In contrast, readers obtain social recommendations through direct or indirect social interactions with others.

2.1 Algorithm-Based Recommendations

Recommender algorithms have long been a popular research topic in information retrieval. Digital reading platforms use these techniques to provide readers with recommendations across diverse genres of reading material, including general books [1, 13], news [14, 15], and academic papers [16, 17].

Profiles and data about both readers and reading material are considered by typical algorithms [18]. There are three kinds of metadata that algorithms frequently use: the reader's profile, the information about or contained within the reading material, and reader interaction behaviour [19–21].

The reader's profile data includes their gender, age, location etc. [18]. These data usually used in demographic-based filtering algorithms [22] to provide recommendations across a specific group (e.g. a book recommendation to children).

The information about reading material can be keywords (e.g. title), genre or the main reading material itself [13, 21]. Reader interaction behaviours capture elements such as how far into a previous book a reader has read to date, their own rating of a book, purchase records, or average reading time per day etc. [23]. Two major approaches exist: content-based filtering, which emphasizes book content, and collaborative filtering, which emphasises user profiles and book-rating data.

Content-based filtering uses the main text of books to recommend a new item that is similar to the ones that the user has purchased or read before [13, 24]. This algorithm is widely used in digital news [25] and other text-focussed reading. Its strength is providing relevant recommendations with similar characteristics. Content recommendation can start from even a small amount of data about the user, making it more suitable in the cold start situation than the collaborative filtering algorithms, especially when the user is new to the system [26]. However, this algorithm cannot well perform when there is a lack of content data, and recommendations can be of poor quality as many factors are not captured by book content alone [23].

Compared to content-based filtering, collaborative filtering is better at providing high-quality recommendations [23]. It predicts the user's preference based on their similarity with user other users, and predicts their preferences based on others with a record of similar choices. Thus, it has been compared to a computer-driven "word-of-mouth" recommendation process [27, 28]. A typical example of collaborative filtering is from Amazon.com that "(other) people who buy this item also buy this item" [29]. Although collaborative filtering can generate new suggestions for readers, this approach has some major drawbacks. One such drawback is that it cannot perform well in a cold start situation because it relies strongly on having a large amount of behavioural data about users [20, 23].

To avoid the shortcomings and adopt the good points of different algorithms, many recommendation systems are a hybrid of two or more basic algorithms together to improve the accuracy and quality of recommendations [20], such as [22, 30]. Recent algorithms also consider contextual features such as the user's recent location [18, 31], to provide more personalised recommendations which may better meet the user's preference.

Overall, recommender algorithms collect data from the reader, the reading material or other context features. They then use this data to predict and generate personalised reading recommendations. This technique has been widely adopted, and two different approaches meet different user needs. Different domains have adopted techniques that rely more on one or other of the two approaches, so variations in the role of algorithmic recommendations can be expected in the context of different reading genres.

2.2 Socially Sourced Recommendations

Reading is a social activity rather than a solitary work [7]. During the reading process, readers directly communicate with other people or indirectly refer to some assistant materials to obtain reading recommendations.

"Reading advisory" is a service typically provided by libraries or bookshops to provide suggested reading options for readers [32, 33]. Besides reading suggestions from a professional librarian, readers also seek recommendations from other people in their social circle. Previous studies have observed that children will seek advice from their parents, teachers or friends [11, 34]. Adults also rely on their social networks [9].

In the meanwhile, traditional mass media such as the review of a book from a TV show and radio can also provide reading ideas for the readers [9], and readers usually treat these as a "trustworthy choice" [35]. Additionally, Ooi [9] observed that some movies which are adapted from a novel can inspire the reader to read the original book. This is an implicit but effective recommendation for the reader [36]. Recommendations from sources unknown to the reader, though, are often disregarded as irrelevant or not authoritative, such as the reader in [37] who commented "*oh, there's a curator[of a section]. But I don't know who she is, so don't really care. But if it [the curator] was an author I loved, I might...*".

In the digital reading era, the Internet and diverse social media platforms expand the routes through which the reader can obtain reading recommendations, reducing the limitations of time and location [8]. Many digital reading platforms, such as Kindle, integrate social functions such as sharing, add comments and reviews [38]. These functions make it easier for readers to communicate and exchange ideas with each other. There are also many book review platforms such as Goodreads which provide a specific place for readers to discuss books and seeking for reading recommendations [39]. Social networking sites also benefit readers' reading journeys, e.g. readers can communicate with each other through instant messaging platforms [7].

All these examples reflect that nowadays, readers have a richer variety of sources for social reading recommendations.

2.3 Research Gaps and Research Aim

Reading recommendations are an established research topic in information retrieval. Most of the previous work examines particular recommender algorithms used in a specific reading context, such as [40] for news recommendations. There is a strong evidence base to understand how effective different algorithms are compared to each other. The vast majority of these comparative studies of algorithms have used either automatic analysis against gold-standard outcomes or, more often, subjective user feedback in controlled laboratory tests [41, 42]. How well the recommendations of these algorithms are accepted outside the laboratory, compared to other sources of recommendations is less clear. The prevalence of algorithmic recommendations on websites such as Amazon suggests they must be effective to some degree at least, but to what degree do they complement, replace or pay second fiddle to established social sources of recommendations, such as a user's friends or colleagues? There is a significant lack of qualitative and quantitative data to summarize the whole landscape of the reading recommendation in today's society.

As for social reading recommendations, previous research has revealed some key behaviours that appear when the reader, directly or indirectly, seeks recommendations. However, most of these studies have happened in the context of physical libraries, bookstores, or printed reading material [6, 24]. The sources used by a typical reader when seeking reading recommendations in the digital era are still not clear.

The internet has substantially changed the reading recommendation landscape. Where in the past, book reviews were predominantly available from mass media, [24]. in the digital era, readers can easily get access to these reviews through websites or book review platforms such as Goodreads [23]. To our knowledge, there is only one previous paper, from 2001, that compares user assessments of recommendations from friends versus online systems [43]. However, this paper was 20 years ago, and the adoption of digital reading as a whole, the sophistication and prevalence of recommendation systems, and the emergence of large-scale social media platforms have all signified and driven major changes in the reading environment. Thus, one of our goals in this study is to investigate whether readers prefer algorithm-based or social-sourced recommendation in today's reading environment.

Previous research has indicated that genre has many effects on the reading process, including recommendations. In the case of book reading, several studies have reported that readers digitally or physically establish a social relationship with each other [11] and get access to the diverse social media (such as TV shows) to obtain reading recommendations [9]. Researchers of news recommendation techniques have highlighted the importance of contextual features like time (up-to-date News) and location (where the news happened) as key features, beyond the features such as the topic or keywords that the normal book recommendation would consider. To understand how much user characteristics, as from book reading, or algorithmic characteristics, in news recommendations, either interact or generalize, in this study we look at more than one genre of recommendations. We investigate both fictional and factual books [1], academic resources [16], and news [40] as four typical reading genres which have targeted in the past. We hope to demonstrate whether readers show different preferences for different sources of reading recommendation when considering different genres.

Above all, this empirical study first aims to provide an overview of the relative importance of different sources of reading recommendations, social and algorithmic, play in real users' choice of different kinds of digital reading material. We focus on digital reading specifically, and do not consider the choice of printed reading material. In consideration of social factors, we include recommendations from other people, whether those recommendations are communicated online or in the real world.

3 Method

Our research process was divided into two phases: first, a diary study and second a survey. Given the lack of previous research, we wished to first gain an overall picture of the variety of sources from which readers obtain recommendations. We started with a diary study to capture real readers' selection of recommendations over three weeks. This allowed us to gather information without the intrusions into privacy that are associated with systematic logging. Having built a picture of the range of recommendations in use, we then undertook a large-scale survey to both validate the types that we had identified in the diary study, and also to obtain more robust quantitative information about their relative role at a larger scale [44]. Both parts of our study were approved by our institutional human ethics board.

3.1 Diary Study

Our first goal was to capture as complete a range of types of reading recommendations as we could. This could have been done using interviews, but these require participants to recall their memory of recommendations in the past. Interviews are good at eliciting information where the context is unclear, as the dialogue between interviewer and interviewee allows for disambiguation. A diary study, on the other hand, is a longitudinal method which can follow participants with different reading tastes and get themes to record their reading experiences much more closely to when they occur [45].

For the diary study, we randomly recruited our participants through posts shared via several social network applications (including WeChat, QQ, etc.), and through snowball sampling starting with participants from previous studies. The posts included the research background, an introduction on recording a diary, and the rate of payment for participation. Fourteen participants from China (eight males and six females, aged from 25 to 45) joined the study. All participants are frequent digital readers, and they represented a range of different reading tastes and habits, and their occupation of the participants are varied, including students, engineers, and designers. Thus, we could collect a rich and diverse set of data. The reading material included digital books (including both fictional and factual books), digital news, blog articles, and academic papers. We use the anonymized identifiers P1 to P14 to identify the participants in our results.

The diary study lasted from 5 to 29th May 2020. Each individual participant spent about two and a half weeks logging their diaries. We asked the participants to record the platform they read and how they obtained recommendations (from whom and through which channel). We collected a total of 176 diaries with an average of nearly 13 diary entries from each participant. After the diary stage, each participant gave an exit interview (about one hour) to investigate more details about their reading journey and their opinion about the different types of reading recommendations.

The diary study was conducted through WeChat. WeChat is the most popular instant messaging platforms in China, which all our participants used. WeChat supports image, video, audio and even document and web page sending. This allowed participants to flexibly record their diary in various formats, such as taking a screenshot of the reading application interface and sending that to the researcher, or directly sharing a post or a chapter of an ebook etc. Additionally, the video or audio calling functions also make it easier for the participants and researchers to communicate with each other, especially for interviews. Researcher also can effectively monitor the whole logging process and responded to the participants requirements or questions.

After coordinating the diaries and interview transcripts, we utilized the open coding method [46] and thoroughly inspected and coded the reading material type, the reading platform, and the behaviours which are related to reading recommendation.

Two key findings emerged from the diary study. Firstly, we observed that the way that readers interact with the fictional books, factual books, academic papers, and digital news and articles are different, and so are the routes through which they obtain reading recommendations for the four genres. Secondly, we collated three typical algorithm-based reading recommendations and seven social-sourced recommendations (Table 1) which together covered the types of reading recommendation information reported in the diary study.

Based on this framework, we set up a survey to investigate the reading recommendation of among fictional books, factual books, academic papers, and digital news and articles in depth. This second step would help us determine the proportion of what kinds of recommendations that readers use [44].

3.2 Survey

The survey contained two parts: in the first part, we investigated the background of the participants, including their gender, age, occupation and the reading material types that they usually read (a multiple-choice question which contains the four kinds of reading material mentioned above). Based on the respondent's selection of the types of reading material they read, in the second part of the questionnaire, the answered questions specific to the selected reading material types. The second set of questions contained details of specific reading platforms and what kinds of recommendation they draw on for the genre, but this is not reported in detail.

The options in each question were generated from the framework created from the diary study results. We listed all the platforms and activities from the diaries related to reading recommendations so that the participants can easily recognize and select the types of recommendation that they regularly use. According to the diary study results, reader's recommendation preferences across different kinds of reading material are significantly different. The "platforms" and "recommendations" listed under each genre of reading material were also different, reproducing the unique sources used for different types of reading material, according to the diary study. For example, TV series and movies were specifically only used as a source of recommendation in the case of fictional reading. It was never seen in the context of factual books, academic papers and digital news and articles. Even the same kind of recommendation may also have a different form of expression in each genre or platform, so we provided a short example for each option to help the participant understand the meaning of it. We would introduce the details of the diverse recommendation sources in Sect. 4.1.

Additionally, we provide an "other" option in each "reading platforms" and "reading recommendation" questions so that the participants can supply any other source not already listed in the question's provided answers. The survey produced no new reading platforms and no further types of recommendation. This suggests that our diary study results did accurately capture the reading recommendation landscape among different genres of reading material, and the differences we noted between genre are also consistent with larger-scale behaviour among the Chinese community.

We collected 312 (132 male and 180 female, aged from 18 to 55) responses to the survey in three days. All the data was collected from China, and the survey participants' background is consistent with those from the diary study.

The data were analysed using 2-way chi-squared test, to identify any variations in how often the different types of recommendations were used in deciding what to read for different genres. The details of this analysis are given in the results.

4 Findings

In our results we first provide an overview of the types of sources readers use for reading recommendations in the context of different genres, as reported in the diary study. In the second part of the results we then address the quantitative findings from our survey. Throughout the analysis, we treat any item as a source of recommendation information if our participants reported it as such. Some features could be argued as not being purpose-built as sources of recommendation data, but we exclusively endorse the reported experiences of our participants.

4.1 Reading Recommendation from Multiple Channels

After analysing the data from the dairies, we identified ten common types of source of reading recommendations. We grouped these recommendation sources into two major categories: algorithm-based and social-sourced. Through this section, we will present example screen snapshots to illustrate the types of information our participants reported. These illustrative examples are from English-language interfaces to make them accessible to the non-Chinese reader.

Algorithm-Based Recommendations. There were three typical types of algorithm-based data used as sources of recommendation by our users. First is the order in which reading material is presented by default, particularly articles on a news site, search results for a query, or browsing a booklist. In this case, the system automatically sorts the reading material in a specific order (e.g. Fig. 1). This could be, for example, the documents that best match the search keywords, or in the order of popularity in the context of news, this was often the recency of the article. Items appearing at the top of the list would be treated as "high quality" or a better match to the user's interest. P1 recorded that *"after I search a keyword [of a factual book], there would have plenty of similar books in the searching result. I would inspect the books in the first few pages and would not go down too much. Because these are more likely to well match my reading requirement and usually have higher quality than those appears below. If I didn't find what I want within this range, I would consider whether the keywords I search is correct and re-search."*

Secondly, the platforms would also automatically recommend related reading material to the reader (e.g. Fig. 2). These recommendations are usually generated from the reader's reading history or reading taste [18]. Typically, they appear on the home page of

Fig. 1. The initial order of the books after searching "MBA" in Kindle

the platform, the book or article description page or the bottom of a blog: e.g. "[after reading this] you may also like to read", "similar books/news/articles". It could also simply be the most popular books is a specific group, e.g. the bestselling Masters of Business Administration textbooks. This example relates to the third kind of algorithm-based recommendation sources: the rating or scoring of reading material.

While the explicit recommendations consider multiple features together and provide comprehensive advice, the rating and scoring of the reading material is much simpler. It uses a specific number to measure the quality of the reading material. Usually, readers can give a grade to the books, and the system would calculate these grades to see which book have a higher score. This function is common in both digital reading platforms (such as Kindle) and book review platforms (such as GoodReads) [7, 39] (e.g. Fig. 3). Readers would also refer to other features, as mentioned above, such as the best seller. For the academic paper, a commonly used score could be number of citations. However, there were no clear examples of this sort of information being perceived as recommendation material in the context of blog articles or digital news. Thus, this third type is only used in three of our four genres.

Social Recommendations. We found seven types of data that users perceived as recommendation that have a social source. The first three recommendations are directly from other users or indirectly from the content generated by others. To protect the privacy of third parties, we provide no screen examples in this section.

Online comments on a book or an article can inspire a new reading journey of the reader. P6 told us that "... *one of the comments on this book [a science fiction] showed that this author has another popular book which is similar to this one. I like this book*

Fig. 2. Reading recommendation automatically provided by Kindle

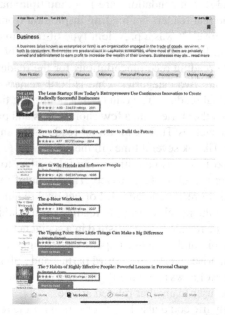

Fig. 3. The ranking and the grades for the Business books in Goodreads

very much, so I am also eager to read the book mentioned in these comments." This has also been seen in the news and article reading: when P13 was reading an article about the history of the camera, one comment on that article mentioned a specific type

Polaroid; this inspired P13 to search for more information about this Polaroid and start a new reading journey. In academic reading, the comments play a different role. Academic databases or digital libraries don't provide a comment function as with standard digital book platforms such as Kindle. However, within academic papers, the authors would cite the previous work and add present comments on it. P1 wrote in the diary *"I found plenty of relevant papers through the literature review section of this paper. The authors of this paper provide a comprehensive summary of the previous work and their comments are also quite helpful for me to have a deep understanding of the knowledge in this area."*

Additionally, readers may also seek reading recommendation from other readers' sharing, or a discussion group. The discussion groups could be a normal reading club. It could also be a group focussed on some other shared interest, e.g. a teamwork group or a group with family members or friends. Sometimes readers obtained recommendations through face-to-face communication, e.g. P11 said: *"today my boss recommended me to read this [C++] book in our meeting."* It could also happen through multiple online social network platforms such instant messaging where people may share a link to a book or article. P13 said, *"My daughter found news about COVID-19 in our city, and she shared this with me."* And P12 noted, *"we have a WeChat discussion group in our department, and we usually share some reading material [pdf document or link to a website] which is related with our work in this group and encourage the employees to read and learn."*

The next three social recommendations are from multiple mass media. Like a previous study [9] we found that readers get reading inspiration from movies or TV series that are adapted from a novel. It was a prevalent type of recommendation that 9 out of 12 participants who read fictional books reported. Additionally, some user-generated videos may also provide reading recommendations for the reader. These UGC videos usually can be divided into two categories. One is book reviews which can be found in both fictional and factual reading. The others are common in fictional reading where publishers of novels adapt the stories into a few short videos and publish these on video-sharing social networks such as TikTok to attract readers. P2 and P9 both mentioned these UGC videos from TikTok several times in their diary.

Furthermore, blog posts are also a critical way for readers to expand their reading channel and obtain more useful reading advice. The forms of these blog articles also vary from different kinds of reading material. For fictional reading, these blogs usually contain a few chapters of the novel for sample reading, or it could be fan fiction stories which are generated by the readers and published in a social network platform such as a fan forum. For factual books and academic papers, these blog articles are usually a piece of knowledge that summarises works from third parties and published in a knowledge-sharing forum. In the case of news and other digital articles, these would be a link within the article that points the user to another related article.

Finally, a task in daily life could also be a motivation for the readers to read. It could be a small reading goal such as *"to finish reading five books this month"* (P8), or seeking relevant handbooks or academic papers to assist in work or study, or to solve a personal task. These real-life tasks help the reader set a reading goal and seek reading material to meet it.

Above all, readers relied different kinds of reading recommendations when they read different genres of reading material. Even the same type of recommendation may also have diverse forms among various genres of reading material.

Both Algorithmic and Social recommendations are a critical component of readers' reading journeys. To identify which recommendation play a more important role, we conducted a survey and invited more readers to share their experiences with us.

4.2 Survey

The summative data from the survey is seen in Table 1 below.

Table 1. Frequencies of recommendation sources: percentages and (in brackets) absolute numbers by genre

The source of recommendation		Fictional reading	Factual reading	Academic reading	News and articles
Algorithm-based	Initial order of the reading resources	35.06% (61)	26.81% (37)	43.86% (50)	48.67% (110)
	Automatically recommended by the platform	25.86% (45)	21.74% (30)	21.05% (24)	59.29% (134)
	Aggregated rating or score	54.6% (95)	41.3% (57)	54.39% (62)	–
Social-sourced	Comments and reviews	45.98% (80)	43.48% (60)	44.74% (51)	39.82% (90)
	Personal Sharing and communication	28.16% (49)	39.13% (54)	37.72% (43)	34.07% (77)
	Discussion groups	14.37% (25)	26.09% (36)	28.95% (33)	15.04% (34)
	TV series or movie	36.78% (64)	–	–	–
	User-Generated Video	18.97% (33)	10.14% (14)	–	–
	Blogs and articles	38.51% (67)	32.61% (45)	28.07% (32)	34.51% (78)
	Task-oriented motivation	14.37% (25)	49.28% (68)	53.51% (61)	31.42% (71)
Total	312 participants	174	138	114	226

As explained in the Method section above, the survey questions followed the patterns of recommendation found during the diary study. The survey data, therefore, allows us a more reliable quantitative analysis of the importance of different elements than the diary study alone.

We first tested for an overall pattern in the relative frequency of algorithm-based versus social-sourced recommendations. In total, algorithmic sources were used 705 times (37.3% of cases), and social sources 1187 times (62.7%). Testing the totals for the two major recommendation types versus the four genres yielded a significant result (p $= 0.017$, $\chi^2 = 10,2$, df $= 3$). This demonstrates that the relative importance of the two different types does vary between genres. Social sources are particularly frequent in the context of factual reading, and algorithmic sources with news and article reading.

When we examine differences within the two types by genre, further marked patterns of difference appear. In the case of algorithmic recommendation information, the absence of scoring or ranking data for news articles means we cannot do a single text to check for variances. Instead we did two tests. First, we tested all three types of recommendation against the three genres for which the data was available, (fiction, factual, and academic); the result was was not significant (p $= 0.59$, $\chi^2 = 2.80$, df $= 4$). Therefore, these three factors are used similarly for all three genres. Second, we tested the two types of recommendation that were available for all four genres, which proved significant (p $= 0.0038$, $\chi^2 = 13.4$, df $= 3$). In the news and article genre users markedly relied on the default ordering of the platform. This combination of results indicates that for fictional, factual and academic reading the sources of algorithmic recommendation are broadly similar, but that news reading is influenced in markedly different ways than other genres. The absence of score information seems to lead to a greater emphasis on recommendations by the platform and the presentation order of articles.

Turning to social sources of recommendation, we again have complexities that arise from the absence of certain types of recommendation for different genres. In this case, we have five sources of recommendation that are used by all four genres. Testing those together to check if genre influences which information is relied on, a chi-squared test proves significant (p < 0.0001, $\chi^2 = 43.65$, df $= 12$). The underlying differences are many. Task-related influences are markedly, and perhaps unsurprisingly, low for fiction reading. In contrast, discussion group recommendations have a high influence for both factual and academic reading; and blog content was particularly low for academic reading. There are broad similarities in the frequency with which particular sources are used between genres. One example is the consistent reporting of the use of online comments. However, blogs and discussion group materials are more strongly associated with particular genres. A local test for the influence of UGC video between fiction and factual reading is just significant (p $= 0.046$, $\chi^2 = 3.97$, df $= 2$).

The role of films and TV programmes is a unique feature associated with recommendations for fictional reading, and so we cannot reliably test for it alone. However, it is the third ranked source for fiction, and this suggests it is worth further exploration.

5   Discussion

In our investigation, we sought to understand the degree to which users rely on algorithmic versus social information as sources of inspiration for what to read. We now reflect on the findings from both diary study and survey to build a clear picture of how Chinese readers adopt information from both sources when deciding what to read.

There is relatively little previous research on this question for any user group. The key previous paper is that of Sinha and Swearingen [43]. Like our own study, this combined quantitative and qualitative approaches, but in their case, there was no longitudinal component, and participants simply rated recommendations provided to them in isolation from each other in a closed study. That study also considered only recommendations from friends chosen by the participants and recommendations from three chosen systems. Our study differs on a number of points: ours is longitudinal, includes a variety of social sources, not just immediate friends, and in the diary study is naturalistic, capturing actual reader activity in real life, rather than in a controlled experiment. We also captured a wide range of qualitative data in the diary study: something not gathered in the numerical ratings given in the Sinha and Swearingen study. While the previous study considered books and movies, we focus only on text, but maintain a wider scope of reading material. Furthermore, the previous study treated each algorithmic recommendation system in isolation, not as part of a wider technical environment. They found that friends were ranked better than any of the three systems they tested did individually. However, there was not a holistic comparison of friends versus the algorithmic recommendations as a whole. A further previous paper addresses sources of academic reading discovery [47], and investigated readers use of a wide range of sources including some algorithmic recommendations (such as Amazon) and some social recommendations (such as reading lists and personal recommendations) alongside other sources. Like Swearingen, though, this study is not longitudinal, and it further focuses specifically on a single genre of reading: academic books. It further does not focus on recommendations, but addresses discovery as a whole [47].

Our study therefore makes a number of novel contributions. We demonstrate that, overall, social recommendations are used as sources more frequently than algorithmic ones, this difference is moderate, with 37% of our recommendation information coming from algorithmic sources, and 63% from social sources. This average, though, is not the same when different genres of reading are considered.

Sinha and Swearingen [43] did not find significant differences between book and movie recommendations, but we find that algorithms are trusted less often when factual information is being sought, and more often in the case of news articles. Therefore, users do rely on different sources when choosing reading material of different types. Furthermore, some sources of recommendation are particularly associated with particular genres, e.g. film and TV seem to strongly influence fiction reading, but were not reported outside of fictional reading. There are reliable differences between genres: while online comments are a consistent influence on future reading choices, blogs, for example, are little used when seeking ideas for factual reading material.

The reading environment has changed a lot in the twenty-years since Sinha and Swearingen [43]. One key example is that in 2001, social media was at best in its infancy. As their data suggested, we can now confirm that in today's digital reading era, friends are not the only channel that readers when seeking reading recommendations. Our widened view of the social context, beyond immediate friends, demonstrates that readers also rely on socially sourced information from more distant connections (e.g. friends of friends) and even social posts by strangers or acquaintances.

5.1 Limitations and Future Work

In this research, both the diary study and survey's data are collected from Chinese adults. Reader's reading habits and social interactions may vary between countries or in different age groups. It would be worthwhile conducting a comparative study in other contexts to see whether our findings can hold under diverse cultural backgrounds. Also, investigating how children and young teenagers seek reading recommendations may reveal current differences between age groups. It is known that children often rely more on parental suggestions for reading [11], and their access to and use of social media may be much lower for a variety of societal reasons [48]. This suggests that the picture for this age group is likely to be very different.

We also observed across the diary study and survey that the sources of recommendation among different types of fiction reading varies. Fictional reading is, it appears from our data, relatively more complex than the other three genres. One diversity is in the commonly read forms, from professionally published books, to user-generated novels, and fanfiction etc. The platforms that the readers drew on and interacted with included digital reading platforms, social networking platforms, and forums. Different platforms will appear in the future, and specific sub-genres of fiction can be studied so that we could provide more accurate suggestions to promote these works.

Additionally, a similar study could be conducted on the sources of recommendations for other media, such as music or film. A similar approach to our own, commencing with a diary study, may reveal different sources particular to those media, and addressing the particular associations users have with these different forms.

6 Conclusion

Drawing on a diary study and survey, we have established that readers turn to different sources of information about or recommendations of potential reading material when seeking different genres. When seeking factual material, social factors are more influential, and in the context of reading news articles, automatic algorithm-created data is used more. There are also sources that are strongly associated with only one genre, e.g. film and television provide inspiration for fiction reading in particular, but not for factual, academic or news reading. As a first contemporary study, there is ample room for future work. First, our data came from China, and other countries may demonstrate different patterns; similarly we revealed a high level of variation with recommendation for the reading of fiction, and further studies could examine this complex area in detail.

References

1. Tewari, A.S., Kumar, A., Barman, A.G.: Book recommendation system based on combine features of content based filtering, collaborative filtering and association rule mining. In: 2014 IEEE International Advance Computing Conference (IACC), pp. 500–503. IEEE (2014)
2. Rosa, R.L., Rodriguez, D.Z., Bressan, G.: Music recommendation system based on user's sentiments extracted from social networks. IEEE Trans. Consum. Electron. **61**, 359–367 (2015)

3. Subramaniyaswamy, V., Logesh, R., Chandrashekhar, M., Challa, A., Vijayakumar, V.: A personalised movie recommendation system based on collaborative filtering. Int. J. High Perform. Comput. Netw. **10**, 54–63 (2017)
4. Kenthapadi, K., Le, B., Venkataraman, G.: Personalized job recommendation system at linkedin: practical challenges and lessons learned. In: Proceedings of the Eleventh ACM Conference on Recommender Systems, pp. 346–347. Association for Computing Machinery (2017)
5. Park, D.H., Kim, H.K., Choi, I.Y., Kim, J.K.: A literature review and classification of recommender systems research. Expert Syst. Appl. **39**, 10059–10072 (2012)
6. Pearson, J., Owen, T., Thimbleby, H., Buchanan, G.R.: Co-reading: investigating collaborative group reading. In: The 12th ACM/IEEE-CS Joint Conference on Digital Libraries, pp. 325–334 (2012)
7. Cordón-García, J.-A., Alonso-Arévalo, J., Gómez-Díaz, R., Linder, D.: Social Reading: Platforms, Applications Clouds and Tags. Elsevier, Amsterdam (2013)
8. Kutzner, K., Petzold, K., Knackstedt, R.: Characterising social reading platforms—a taxonomy-based approach to structure the field. In: 14th International Conference on Wirtschaftsinformatik (2019)
9. Ooi, K.: How adult fiction readers select fiction books in public libraries: a study of information-seeking in context. School of Information Management. Victoria University of Wellington (2008)
10. Huang, Z., Li, T., Xiao, S.: Research on library recommendation reading service system based on adaptive algorithm. Wirel. Pers. Commun. **102**, 1963–1977 (2018)
11. Cunningham, S.J.: How children find books for leisure reading: implications for the digital library. In: 11th Annual International ACM/IEEE Joint Conference on Digital Libraries, pp. 431–432. Association for Computing Machinery (2011)
12. Cunningham, S.J., Vanderschantz, N., Timpany, C., Hinze, A., Buchanan, G.: Social information behaviour in bookshops: implications for digital libraries. In: Aalberg, T., Papatheodorou, C., Dobreva, M., Tsakonas, G., Farrugia, C.J. (eds.) TPDL 2013. LNCS, vol. 8092, pp. 84–95. Springer, Heidelberg (2013). https://doi.org/10.1007/978-3-642-40501-3_9
13. Mathew, P., Kuriakose, B., Hegde, V.: Book recommendation system through content based and collaborative filtering method. In: 2016 International Conference on Data Mining and Advanced Computing (SAPIENCE), pp. 47–52. IEEE (2016)
14. Liu, J., Dolan, P., Pedersen, E.R.: Personalized news recommendation based on click behavior. In: Proceedings of the 15th International Conference on Intelligent User Interfaces, pp. 31–40. Association for Computing Machinery (2010)
15. Li, L., Wang, D., Li, T., Knox, D., Padmanabhan, B.: SCENE: a scalable two-stage personalized news recommendation system. In: Proceedings of the 34th International ACM SIGIR Conference on Research and Development in Information Retrieval, pp. 125–134. Association for Computing Machinery (2011)
16. Bulut, B., Kaya, B., Alhajj, R., Kaya, M.: A paper recommendation system based on user's research interests. In: 2018 IEEE/ACM International Conference on Advances in Social Networks Analysis and Mining (ASONAM), pp. 911–915. IEEE (2018)
17. Zulkarnain, T.D.P.: Proposed model of academic reading material recommendation system. In: The 3rd Asia Pacific Conference on Research in Industrial and Systems Engineering 2020, pp. 105–109. Association for Computing Machinery (2020)
18. Seyednezhad, S., Cozart, K.N., Bowllan, J.A., Smith, A.O.: A review on recommendation systems: context-aware to social-based. arXiv preprint arXiv:1811.11866 (2018)
19. Amri, C., Bambia, M., Faiz, R.: Behavior-based approach for user interests prediction. In: 2017 IEEE/ACS 14th International Conference on Computer Systems and Applications (AICCSA), pp. 541–548. IEEE (2017)

20. Chandak, M., Girase, S., Mukhopadhyay, D.: Introducing hybrid technique for optimization of book recommender system. Procedia Comput. Sci. **45**, 23–31 (2015)
21. Hu, J., Shao, H., Tang, J., Zhang, S.: Research on reading subject recommendation of library based on data analysis. J. Phys: Conf. Ser. **1607**, 012022 (2020)
22. Kanetkar, S., Nayak, A., Swamy, S., Bhatia, G.: Web-based personalized hybrid book recommendation system. In: 2014 International Conference on Advances in Engineering & Technology Research (ICAETR-2014), pp. 1–5. IEEE (2014)
23. Sachan, A., Richariya, V.: A survey on recommender systems based on collaborative filtering technique. Int. J. Innovations Eng. Technol. (IJIET) **2**, 8–14 (2013)
24. Mooney, R.J., Roy, L.: Content-based book recommending using learning for text categorization. In: Proceedings of the Fifth ACM Conference on Digital Libraries, pp. 195–204. Association for Computing Machinery (2000)
25. Kompan, M., Bieliková, M.: Content-based news recommendation. In: Buccafurri, F., Semeraro, G. (eds.) EC-Web 2010. LNBIP, vol. 61, pp. 61–72. Springer, Heidelberg (2010). https://doi.org/10.1007/978-3-642-15208-5_6
26. Wang, N., Zhao, H., Zhu, X., Li, N.: The review of recommendation system. In: Xie, Y., Zhang, A., Liu, H., Feng, L. (eds.) GSES 2018. CCIS, vol. 980, pp. 332–342. Springer, Singapore (2019). https://doi.org/10.1007/978-981-13-7025-0_34
27. Rafsanjani, A.H.N., Salim, N., Aghdam, A.R., Fard, K.B.: Recommendation systems: a review. Int. J. Comput. Eng. Res. **3**, 47–52 (2013)
28. Shardanand, U., Maes, P.: Social information filtering: algorithms for automating "word of mouth". In: Proceedings of the SIGCHI Conference on Human Factors in Computing Systems, pp. 210–217. ACM Press/Addison-Wesley Publishing Co. (1995)
29. Smith, B., Linden, G.: Two decades of recommender systems at Amazon.com. IEEE Internet Comput. **21**, 12–18 (2017)
30. Ghazanfar, M.A., Prugel-Bennett, A.: A scalable, accurate hybrid recommender system. In: 2010 Third International Conference on Knowledge Discovery and Data Mining, pp. 94–98. IEEE (2010)
31. Gao, Q., Dong, A.: A conditional context-awareness ontology based personalized recommendation approach for e-reading. In: 2017 First IEEE International Conference on Robotic Computing (IRC), pp. 365–370. IEEE (2017)
32. Saricks, J.G.: Readers' Advisory Service in the Public Library. American Library Association, Chicago (2005)
33. Spiteri, L.F., Pecoskie, J., Tarulli, L.: In the readers' own words: how user content in the catalog can enhance readers' advisory services. Ref. User Serv. Quart. **56**, 91–95 (2016)
34. Mohr, K.A.: Children's choices for recreational reading: a three-part investigation of selection preferences, rationales, and processes. J. Literacy Res. **38**, 81–104 (2006)
35. Rehberg Sedo, D.: Richard and Judy's Book Club and 'Canada Reads': Readers, books and cultural programming in a digital era. Inf. Community Soc. **11**, 188–206 (2008)
36. Hall, R.M.: The "Oprahfication" of literacy: reading "Oprah's book club." Coll. Engl. **65**, 646–667 (2003)
37. Makri, S., Chen, Y.-C., McKay, D., Buchanan, G., Ocepek, M.: Discovering the unfindable: the tension between findability and discoverability in a bookshop designed for serendipity. In: Lamas, D., Loizides, F., Nacke, L., Petrie, H., Winckler, M., Zaphiris, P. (eds.) INTERACT 2019. LNCS, vol. 11747, pp. 3–23. Springer, Cham (2019). https://doi.org/10.1007/978-3-030-29384-0_1
38. Barnett, T.: Social reading: the Kindle's social highlighting function and emerging reading practices. Aust. Humanit. Rev. **56**, 141–162 (2014)
39. Nakamura, L.: "Words with friends": socially networked reading on Goodreads. PMLA **128**, 238–243 (2013)

40. Lommatzsch, A.: Real-time news recommendation using context-aware ensembles. In: de Rijke, M., et al. (eds.) ECIR 2014. LNCS, vol. 8416, pp. 51–62. Springer, Cham (2014). https://doi.org/10.1007/978-3-319-06028-6_5

41. Pu, P., Chen, L., Hu, R.: A user-centric evaluation framework for recommender systems. In: Proceedings of the fifth ACM Conference on Recommender Systems, pp. 157–164. Association for Computing Machinery (2011)

42. Herlocker, J.L., Konstan, J.A., Terveen, L.G., Riedl, J.T.: Evaluating collaborative filtering recommender systems. ACM Trans. Inf. Syst. **22**, 5–53 (2004)

43. Sinha, R.R., Swearingen, K.: Comparing recommendations made by online systems and friends. DELOS 106 (2001)

44. Preece, J., Sharp, H., Rogers, Y.: Interaction Design: Beyond Human-Computer Interaction. Wiley, Hoboken (2015)

45. Lazar, J., Feng, J.H., Hochheiser, H.: Research Methods in Human-Computer Interaction. Morgan Kaufmann, Burlington (2017)

46. Flick, U.: An Introduction to Qualitative Research. Sage, Thousand Oaks (2018)

47. Rowlands, I., Nicholas, D.: Understanding information behaviour: how do students and faculty find books? J. Acad. Librariansh. **34**, 3–15 (2008)

48. Mascheroni, G., Ólafsson, K.: The mobile Internet: access, use, opportunities and divides among European children. New Media Soc. **18**, 1657–1679 (2016)

The Moderating Effect of Active Engagement on Appreciation of Popularity in Song Recommendations

Mark P. Graus[1,2(✉)] and Bruce Ferwerda[3]

[1] Maastricht University School of Business and Economics,
Maastricht, The Netherlands
mp.graus@maastrichtuniversity.nl
[2] Brightlands Institute for Smart Society (BISS), Heerlen, The Netherlands
[3] Jönköping University, Jönköping, Sweden
bruce.ferwerda@ju.se

Abstract. Research has demonstrated that different types of users have different needs when it comes to personalized systems. Factors that have been argued to play a role are user traits and characteristics, such as personality and domain expertise. Within this work we explored the influence of listeners' active engagement with music, or the extent to which people invest in enjoying music, on the relationship between item popularity and satisfaction with lists of recommendation. Using an online survey built on top of the Spotify API functionality we gathered participants' most listened tracks and used those to compile playlists containing either popular or non-popular tracks. Our results show that active engagement plays a moderating role on the relationship between popularity and satisfaction, which can more specifically be explained by the extent to which popular songs allow people to discover their musical taste. Where listeners with low active engagement are limited in their discovery by tracks they are familiar with, those with high active engagement can actually use music they are familiar with to further discover their taste. Hence, for low active engagement listeners the most attractive recommendation lists are lists that strike a balance between familiar items and items that enable people to refine their musical taste.

Keywords: Musical sophistication · Active engagement · Music · Recommender systems

1 Introduction

With the increased amount of content available online, systems are designed to aid users in the abundance of choices that are available to them. Recommender systems produce recommendations to narrow down the choice options to mitigate decision problems that users may be facing (e.g., what items to buy, what movies to watch, and what music to listen to). While it is important

© Springer Nature Switzerland AG 2021
K. Toeppe et al. (Eds.): iConference 2021, LNCS 12645, pp. 364–374, 2021.
https://doi.org/10.1007/978-3-030-71292-1_28

that recommender systems algorithms have a good predictive accuracy, solely optimizing algorithmic accuracy has been shown to not necessarily improve the user experience [19] (e.g., user satisfaction with the recommendations). Recommender systems with high algorithmic accuracy may not control for similarity in the recommendations. Hence, providing recommendations with high similarity may increase choice difficulties, which can result in choice overload for the user. In turn, choice overload can lead to negatively affects in the decision making process and user experience [2]. Furthermore, recommended items that are too similar to each other are limited on factors that have been shown to improve user experience, such as serendipity [20] and novelty [3].

To address the issues that come with a focus on algorithmic accuracy, research has been looking into incorporating additional user-centered factors to provide better recommendations to users. Especially user traits and characteristics have been shown to be effective variables to further personalize the generated recommendation lists (see for an overview Graus and Ferwerda [11]). For example, users' personality traits have been used to determine the amount of diversity users desire in their recommendation lists [5]. Graus, Willemsen, and Snijders [12] adapted a system to the parenting style of new parents to provide better support in their needs. Another user characteristic that have been argued to play is domain knowledge [17]. Studies focusing on domain knowledge have shown that experts require different interaction methods in the user interface [16] and experts exploit the system in a different way to maintain or expand their level of expertise [8].

In the music domain, personal characteristics have similarly been suggested and shown to affect listener's preferences. According to Celma [4] different kinds of music listeners can be distinguished: indifferents and casuals who are considered to be less engaging music listeners, and enthusiasts and savants who are considered to be more engaging music listeners. Novice music listeners would be satisfied with recommendations containing mainstream music that they can easily identify with (i.e., short tail), whereas the more expert music listener would rather enjoy recommendations that contain more clever, risky selections (i.e., long tail). In a similar fashion Musical Sophistication has been shown to affect listener's preferences in terms of explanations [21] and controllability [22] of recommendations. People with higher musical sophistication on average perceive a higher quality and experience more choice difficulty with music recommender systems. In addition, people with higher musical sophistication have been shown to listen to fewer recommended songs, presumably because they are already familiar with enough songs to not have to explore the songs they are not familiar with.

In this work we focus on active engagement and investigate how music recommendations should be tailored for listeners with different levels of engagement. Active engagement is a subscale of the Goldsmith's Musical Sophistication Index (Gold-MSI [23]) that measures how much time and money resources one spends on music [23]. We investigated how listeners with different levels of active engagement assess music recommendation lists in terms of satisfaction, taking into account several aspects: popularity (how popular the songs are), familiarity (how familiar the user is with the songs), and discovery (whether the user discovers new songs and can refine their musical taste). Through the Spotify API[1] we compiled music recommendation lists for 84 participants and found that music listeners with higher levels of active engagement were not more satisfied with less popular/more obscure music. On the contrary, they were more satisfied with both familiar and unfamiliar tracks, as opposed to music listeners with lower levels of engagement whose satisfaction suffers from more popular songs as they are familiar with them.

2   Related Work

User traits and characteristics have are increasingly relied upon to gain deeper understanding about users' preferences and needs in order to more accurately personalize systems. In addition, it allows for better interpretability of data and the generalization of findings and results [11]. User traits considered most commonly are personality traits, to investigate for example, music listening behavior [7]. Studies have shown that personality-based personalized systems gain an advantage over non personality-based personalized systems in terms of loyalty and cognitive effort [15]. Although personality traits are the most commonly used user traits, other user traits have been considered as well. Belk et al. [1] have investigated the use of cognitive styles to adapt authentication methods for users. Graus, Willemsen, and Snijders [12] have investigated how parenting styles of new parents affect what information they prefer to read. Lee and Ferwerda [18] propose to personalize online educational tools based on learner's learning styles. In terms of user characteristics, the majority of studies investigates the effect of age. For example, Ferwerda, Tkalcic, and Schedl [9] investigated how music taste varies over age groups in an online music environment.

Even though user experience frameworks propose domain knowledge as a factor of influence, only a small number of studies put emphasis on it [17,24]. The studies that have investigated the influence of domain knowledge found that it plays an important role in how users experience systems. Knijnenburg, Reijmer, and Willemsen [16] showed that people with different levels of domain knowledge prefer different interaction methods. A similar effect is found in a study by Ferwerda and Tkalcic [8] on online music behaviors, in which they found that experts demonstrate more diverse music listening behavior than novices. Users with higher levels of domain knowledge have been shown to be less sensitive to choice overload effects and are better able to deal with items that are equally attractive [10]. These findings indicate that systems adapted to cater to the level of domain knowledge of users could better support their needs. In this work we explore how domain knowledge in the music domain and affects the relationship between popularity of and satisfaction with music recommendations.

---

[1] https://developer.spotify.com/.

3   Procedure

We recruited 92 participants through Amazon Mechanical Turk to take part in the study. Participation was restricted to those with a very good reputation ($\geq$95% HIT approval rate and $\geq$1000 HITs approved). Through a consent form, we asked participants to log in to our online survey using their Spotify account. This allowed us to collect participants' top tracks through the Spotify API while they completed the items the active engagement subscale of the Gold-MSI [23] survey as a measure of domain knowledge.

After the survey, participants were presented with twenty randomly selected tracks from their personal top tracks. They were asked to select one track to be used as seed track for the generated music recommendation playlist. Using the "target_popularity" parameter with values of 25 and 75, recommendation playlists were created with tracks that are either low or high in popularity[2]. The recommendation lists were presented alongside a survey aimed to measure perceived popularity (the extent to which participants considered the tracks in the playlist to be popular), familiarity (how familiar participants are with the tracks in the playlist), discovery (to which extent playlists allowed participants to discover new music and refine their musical taste) and satisfaction (to which extent participants were satisfied with the recommended playlist). To be able to judge the playlists, participants could listen to previews of the songs by hovering over the song title. After completing the survey, participants could save the playlist to their Spotify account.

4   Results

4.1   Participants

Two attention check questions were included in the survey. A total of 4 participants were removed for failing these checks. An additional 4 participants were removed for clearly answering untruthfully (e.g., same answer category for all items), resulting in a total of 84 completed and valid responses.

4.2   Measures

We conducted a Confirmatory Factor Analysis (CFA) to determine the validity and reliability of the measured constructs. The variance of each latent variable was fixed to 1. A total of 14 items were removed (6 due to high mod indices indicating items explained variance in multiple constructs, and 8 due to low explained variance). The constructs with their items (measured on 5-point Likert scale with 1 - 'Disagree Strongly' to 5 - 'Agree Strongly') are shown in Table 1. The Cronbach's alpha (α) and the average variance extracted (AVE) showed

---

[2] By trying out different parameters; 75 for high and 25 for low popularity yielded the highest separation between the lists and showed the most comparable distribution of popularity within the lists, regardless of popularity of the seed track.

Table 1. All items that were asked in the survey with their factor loadings. The items that are presented without their factor loadings were omitted due low loadings. For each construct the average variance extracted (AVE) and Cronbach's alpha (α) is provided.

Construct	Label	Item text	Loading
Active Engagement [23]	MSI1	I spend a lot of my free time doing music-related activities	.802
	MSI3	I enjoy writing about music, for example on blogs and forums	
	MSI8	I'm intrigued by musical styles I'm not familiar with and want to find out more	
AVE: .593	MSI15	I often read or search the internet for things related to music	.647
α: .813	MSI21	I don't spend much of my disposable income on music	
	MSI24	Music is kind of an addiction for me - I couldn't live without it	.819
	MSI28	I keep track of new of music that I come across (e.g. new artists or recordings)	.801
	MSI34	I have attended _ live music events as an audience member in the past twelve months	
	MSI38	I listen attentively to music for _ per day	
Popularity	pop1	The recommendations consist of popular tracks	.717
AVE: .558	pop2	The recommendations consist of tracks that are currently played a lot by the media	.904
α: .853	pop3	I do not think that the recommended tracks are very well known	−.536
	pop4	I believe that the majority of music listeners are familiar with the tracks in the recommendation	.828
	pop5	The recommended tracks have been receiving a lot of attention by the media	.761
Discovery	disc1	The recommendations broaden my taste	.626
AVE: .528	disc2	The recommendations deepen my taste	
α: .807	disc3	The recommendations allow me to discover new tracks to listen to	
	disc4	The recommendations allow me to refine my taste	.914
	disc5	The recommendations give me a new perspective on my musical taste	.730
Familiarity	fam1	I am familiar with the recommended tracks	.762
AVE: .731	fam2	I do not know the tracks from the list	−.688
α: .919	fam3	I already listen to the tracks that are recommended	.725
	fam4	I have heard the recommended tracks before	.744
	fam5	The recommended tracks are already in my own playlists	.596
Satisfaction	sat1	I am satisfied with the list of recommended tracks	.687
AVE: .712	sat2	In most ways the recommended tracks are close to ideal	.659
α: .921	sat3	The list of tracks recommendations meet my exact needs	.646
	sat4	I would give the recommended tracks a high rating	.657
	sat5	The list of tracks shows too many bad items	
	sat6	The list of tracks is attractive	.700
	sat7	The list of recommendations matches my preferences	.715

reasonable values, indicating reliability, convergent and discriminant validity. The model showed a reasonably good fit: $\chi^2(289) = 400.673$, $p < .001$, $CFI = .972$, $TLI = .969$, $RMSEA = .068$ (90% CI: [0.033;0.090])[3].

The relationships between the measures could be investigated in a single path model, but since we were interested in the interaction between active engagement and popularity on users's playlist perception, we built two path models for the novice and expert groups following the approach of Her, Shin, and Pae [13].

4.3   Manipulation Check

A regression analysis was performed to verify that the popularity manipulation was perceived by the participants, with the dummy-coded manipulation as independent variable and perceived popularity as dependent variable. The model showed good model fit ($R^2_{adj} = 0.242$) and the coefficients indicate that participants in the high popularity condition perceived a higher level of popularity than in the low condition ($\beta = 1.061, p < 0.001$). Hence, our manipulation was successful in influencing popularity of the playlists.

4.4   Effects of Popularity on Satisfaction

No statistically significant differences in satisfaction for the two experimental conditions was found ($R^2_{adj} = -0.004$, $\beta = 0.229$, $p = 0.413$): the high and low popularity playlists did not lead to higher or lower satisfaction. To investigate if the satisfaction of low versus high popularity was different for low and high engaged participants, a multiple linear regression was performed with the experimental condition as independent variable, active engagement as moderator and satisfaction as dependent variable. The model showed poor model fit (with R^2_{adj} values < 0), indicating that the popularity manipulation explains hardly any variance in the satisfaction with the playlist. However, the coefficient corresponding to the interaction between popularity and active engagement ($\beta = 0.181, p = 0.166$) indicates a trend describing that participants with a higher active engagement are more satisfied with playlists with higher popularity (contrary to what was suggested by Celma [4]). To investigate this unexpected trend effect more in-depth, we constructed a multigroup structural equation model (SEM), following the approach by Her, Shin, and Pae [13].

4.5   Multigroup Structural Equation Model

Multigroup SEM allows for the comparison of structural models over different groups, allowing to investigate moderation effects. For the remainder of our analysis we divide our participants in a low and high engagement group, by performing a median split on the active engagement score extracted from the SEM.

---

[3] Cutoff values for the fit indices are proposed to be: $CFI > .96$, $TLI > .95$, and $RMSEA < .05$ [14].

A first step in multigroup SEM consists of demonstrating measurement invariance across groups, which indicates that the latent factors measure the same constructs for the two groups. This is demonstrated by comparing a configural model (in our analysis the original path model constructed in Sect. 4.2) against models with increasing sets of contraints. Comparing the configural model against a model in which the factor loadings are constrained across groups showed a non-significant change in model fit ($\Delta\chi^2(15) = 3.792, n.s.$), indicating that the model measures the same constructs for the two groups. Similarly, comparing models with stronger constraints did not lead to any indication that the models measure differently between groups (constraining intercepts: $\chi^2(15) = 23.44, n.s.$ and constraining means: $\chi^2(4) = 2.258, n.s.$).

After demonstrating measurement invariance, we compare the structural model for both groups, to investigate how the relationships between the constructs of the playlist experience differ between the experts and novices. The resulting path models are shown in Fig. 1, with the path model for the high engagement group above and the low engagement group below. The final path models showed worse fit statistics ($\chi^2(328) = 438.2$, $p < .05$, $CFI = .97$, $TLI = .97$, $RMSEA = .09$ (90% CI: $[0.07;0.11]$)) than the combined model, which could have been caused by the lower number of participants per group (42 participants for each group).

Comparing the path models we see a number of relationships are moderated by active engagement, while others are similar for both groups. In line with the manipulation checks, for both groups in the model a positive effect can be found of the manipulation on perceived popularity. However, when looking at familiarity, we see that our experimental manipulation only has a positive effect for the low engagement group and not for the high engagement group. In other words, while our popularity manipulation results in different levels of familiarity for our low engagement group, our high engagement group is not more or less familiar with the popular or obscure list. Looking at the effects of familiarity and popularity on discovery similarly shows significant effects for the high engagement group, indicating popular playlists allow them to explore their taste, while familiar playlists prevent them from doing so. For the low engagement group, neither familiarity nor popularity affect the potential to explore their taste. Finally looking at the effects of discovery, familiarity and popularity on satisfaction, we see that for both groups discovery and familiarity increase satisfaction, while popularity has a negative effect.

In conclusion, the main difference between listeners with low and high active engagement can be found in how popularity contributes to playlist satisfaction: aside from the direct negative effect of popularity on satisfaction, popularity influences satisfaction indirectly. For listeners with high active engagement an increase in popularity results in an increase in familiarity and discovery and thus positive influences satisfaction, while for low active engagement listeners popularity has a positive effect on satisfaction through familiarity and no effect through discovery.

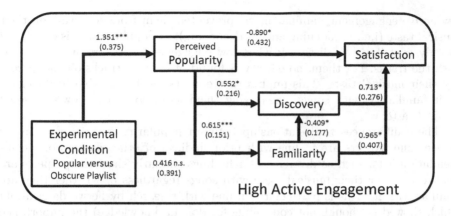

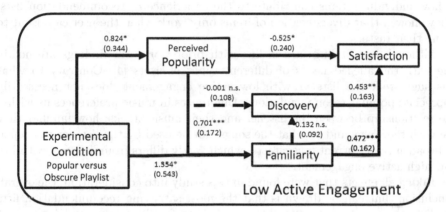

Fig. 1. Multigroup SEMs for participants with high (upper figure) and low (lower) active engagement. Numbers next to the arrows describe standardized coefficients and standard error (between parentheses). Significance is included (*p < 0.05; **p < 0.01; ***p < 0.005). Subjective factors in the models represent: Perceived Popularity, Familiarity, Discovery, and Satisfaction.

4.6   Conclusion and Discussion

We investigated the influence of active engagement on the relationship between popularity of and satisfaction with recommendation lists. Through the Spotify API we were able to compile recommendation lists consisting of tracks with low or high popularity relative to a chosen seed song. Our results showed some distinct differences between listeners with low and high active engagement. We found that while both groups in general perceived playlists with popular tracks to be less satisfactory, satisfaction increased for both groups once they are familiar with tracks in the list.

The results showed differences between low and high active engagement listeners in terms of how popularity affects satisfaction with the playlist and how this effect can be explained through familiarity and discovery. For listeners with low active engagement, familiar music prevented them from reflecting on their musical taste (i.e., broadening and/or deepening), so popular music is concluded to only contribute to discovery when low engagement listeners are unfamiliar with the tracks. For them, no effect was found of familiar tracks on the discovery their musical taste. This implies that experts are better able to disregard their familiarity with songs when using them to discover their own personal musical taste.

These differences the relationship between popularity and satisfaction for novices and experts are in line with prior findings of other aspects of recommendation lists, such as diversity. Our findings similarly show that experts are able to discover their musical taste with songs regardless of whether they are familiar with it. This is particularly in line with research by Ferwerda et al. [6] which showed (although not controlling for domain knowledge) the importance of how individual items contribute to the experience of recommendation lists. They showed that diversification of items only work when the user can use it to refine their taste.

Although our findings are in line with prior work, our findings are not in line with the alleged needs of different types of users [4]. Contrary to what was suggested, the listener with low active engagement does not necessarily appreciate popular recommendations. Differences in music preferences lie within the relationship between the listener and their music tracks: how familiar they are with the songs and to what the songs can be used by the listener to deepen or broaden their current music taste, which vastly differs from listeners with low and high active engagement.

Taking all effects that were found in this study into consideration, the overall conclusion that can be drawn is that the most satisfying recommendation lists are lists that strike a balance between having familiar items and items that enable people to discover their musical taste. The role popularity of songs plays depends on the level of active engagement, where it has a negative effect for listeners with lower levels of active engagement.

4.7   Limitations and Future Research

Despite our attempt to create constructs (i.e., familiarity and discovery) that measure the effect of popular items on the satisfaction with lists of recommendations they only capture part of the relationship. Future research is needed to both fine-tune the measured construct as well as investigate the role that other constructs may have and how they may influence the effect of popularity on satisfaction.

In addition, the current study contained data from only 84 people, which is on the low side especially for creating a multigroup SEM. While the study shows promising results, more generalizable and detailed results require additional research with experiments with higher statistical power.

References

1. Belk, M., Fidas, C., Germanakos, P., Samaras, G.: Do cognitive styles of users affect preference and performance related to captcha challenges? In: CHI 2012 Extended Abstracts on Human Factors in Computing Systems, pp. 1487–1492. ACM (2012)
2. Bollen, D., Knijnenburg, B.P., Willemsen, M.C., Graus, M.: Understanding choice overload in recommender systems. In: Proceedings of the Fourth ACM Conference on Recommender Systems, pp. 63–70. ACM (2010)
3. Castells, P., Hurley, N.J., Vargas, S.: Novelty and diversity in recommender systems. In: Ricci, F., Rokach, L., Shapira, B. (eds.) Recommender Systems Handbook, pp. 881–918. Springer, Boston, MA (2015). https://doi.org/10.1007/978-1-4899-7637-6_26
4. Celma, O.: Music recommendation and discovery in the long tail. Ph.D. thesis, Universitat Pompeu Fabra (2009)
5. Ferwerda, B., Graus, M.P., Vall, A., Tkalcic, M., Schedl, M.: The influence of users' personality traits on satisfaction and attractiveness of diversified recommendation lists. In: EMPIRE@ RecSys, pp. 43–47 (2016)
6. Ferwerda, B., Graus, M.P., Vall, A., Tkalcic, M., Schedl, M.: How item discovery enabled by diversity leads to increased recommendation list attractiveness. In: Proceedings of the Symposium on Applied Computing, pp. 1693–1696. ACM (2017)
7. Ferwerda, B., Schedl, M., Tkalcic, M.: Personality & emotional states: understanding users' music listening needs. In: UMAP 2015 Extended Proceedings. CEUR-WS. org (2015)
8. Ferwerda, B., Tkalcic, M.: Exploring online music listening behaviors of musically sophisticated users. In: The 27th ACM Conference On User Modelling, Adaptation And Personalization (2019)
9. Ferwerda, B., Tkalcic, M., Schedl, M.: Personality traits and music genre preferences: how music taste varies over age groups. In: 1st Workshop on Temporal Reasoning in Recommender Systems (RecTemp) at the 11th ACM Conference on Recommender Systems, Como, August 31, 2017, vol. 1922, pp. 16–20. ACM Digital Library (2017)
10. Ferwerda, B., Yang, E., Schedl, M., Tkalcic, M.: Personality and taxonomy preferences, and the influence of category choice on the user experience for music streaming services. Multimedia Tools Appl. **78**(14), 1–34 (2019)
11. Graus, M., Ferwerda, B.: Theory-Grounded User Modeling for Personalized HCI, chap. 1, pp. 1–30. DeGruyter Oldenbourg (2019)
12. Graus, M.P., Willemsen, M.C., Snijders, C.C.: Personalizing a parenting app: parenting-style surveys beat behavioral reading-based models. In: 2018 Joint ACM IUI Workshops, ACMIUI-WS 2018: Workshop 4: Theory-Informed User Modeling for Tailoring and Personalizing Interfaces-HUMANIZE. CEUR-WS. org (2018)
13. Her, Y.W., Shin, H., Pae, S.: A multigroup sem analysis of moderating role of task uncertainty on budgetary participation-performance relationship: Evidence from korea. Asia Pacific Manage. Rev. **24**(2), 140–153 (2019). https://doi.org/10.1016/j.apmrv.2018.02.001, http://www.sciencedirect.com/science/article/pii/S1029313216303256
14. Hu, L.t., Bentler, P.M.: Cutoff criteria for fit indexes in covariance structure analysis: conventional criteria versus new alternatives. Struct. Eqn. Modeling Multidiscipl. J. **6**(1), 1–55 (1999)
15. Hu, R., Pu, P.: Acceptance issues of personality-based recommender systems. In: Proceedings of the third ACM Conference on Recommender Systems, pp. 221–224. ACM (2009)

16. Knijnenburg, B.P., Reijmer, N.J., Willemsen, M.C.: Each to his own: how different users call for different interaction methods in recommender systems. In: Proceedings of the fifth ACM Conference on Recommender Systems, pp. 141–148. ACM (2011)

17. Knijnenburg, B.P., Willemsen, M.C., Gantner, Z., Soncu, H., Newell, C.: Explaining the user experience of recommender systems. User Model. User-Adapted Interact. **22**(4–5), 441–504 (2012)

18. Lee, M.J., Ferwerda, B.: Personalizing online educational tools. In: Proceedings of the 2017 ACM Workshop on Theory-Informed User Modeling for Tailoring and Personalizing Interfaces, pp. 27–30. ACM (2017)

19. McNee, S.M., Riedl, J., Konstan, J.A.: Being accurate is not enough. In: CHI 2006 extended abstracts on Human factors in computing systems - CHI 2006, p. 1097. ACM Press, New York (2006). https://doi.org/10.1145/1125451.1125659, http://portal.acm.org/citation.cfm?doid=1125451.1125659

20. McNee, S.M., Riedl, J., Konstan, J.A.: Being accurate is not enough: how accuracy metrics have hurt recommender systems. In: CHI 2006 Extended Abstracts on Human Factors in Computing Systems, pp. 1097–1101. ACM (2006)

21. Millecamp, M., Htun, N.N., Conati, C., Verbert, K.: To explain or not to explain: the effects of personal characteristics when explaining music recommendations. In: Proceedings of the 24th International Conference on Intelligent User Interfaces, pp. 397–407 (2019)

22. Millecamp, M., Htun, N.N., Jin, Y., Verbert, K.: Controlling spotify recommendations: Effects of personal characteristics on music recommender user interfaces. In: Proceedings of the 26th Conference on User Modeling, Adaptation and Personalization. UMAP 2018, pp. 101–109, New York, NY, USA. Association for Computing Machinery (2018). https://doi.org/10.1145/3209219.3209223, https://doi.org/10.1145/3209219.3209223

23. Müllensiefen, D., Gingras, B., Musil, J., Stewart, L.: The musicality of non-musicians: an index for assessing musical sophistication in the general population. PLoS ONE **9**(2), e89642 (2014)

24. Pu, P., Chen, L., Hu, R.: Evaluating recommender systems from the user's perspective: survey of the state of the art. User Modeling User-Adapted Interact. **22**, 317–355 (2012). https://doi.org/10.1007/s11257-011-9115-7

Social Media

Attracting Attention in Online Health Forums: Studies of r/Alzheimers and r/dementia

Olivia A. Flynn(✉), Abinav Murugadass, and Lu Xiao

Syracuse University, Syracuse, NY 13244, USA
oaflynn@syr.edu

Abstract. Informal caregivers increasingly use social media for means of information sharing and social support. We study the attention received by healthcare related social media posts, particularly the r/Alzheimers and r/dementia subreddits with the aim of better understanding the user experience on such forums, possibly leading to improvements of their effectiveness. We explore how the linguistic features of a post relate to the amount of attention it receives in terms of votes and comments, focusing on the content, grammar, and sentiment of the text. Unlike traditional approaches that analyze forum activity on each user, we analyze each post as an entity to decipher what makes it influential. We do n-gram and word frequency analysis on the text to compare high- and low-attention posts, then define and calculate attention measures for each post before applying correlation analysis between attention measures and post features. We perform topic modelling analysis on the posts and examine the correlation relationships between a post's major topic and the amount of attention it receives. Our topic analysis of the posts, along with our n-gram and word frequency analysis, also infer themes of discussion within the subreddits.

Keywords: Online health discussion · Attention · Online influence · Alzheimers · Dementia · Language analysis · Natural language processing · Topic modelling

1 Introduction

Social media has become an important place where people engage in complex interactions for various purposes, such as information exchange, opinion expression, social and emotional support. While both constructive and destructive use has been observed in supporting mental health [6, 8], in general, social media is considered to be an asset to healthcare and public health applications when used as an open forum to exchange advice and support. Participation in online health communities has been shown to benefit both patients and their caregivers. For example, the impact of caregiving strain on a caregiver's wellbeing was reduced by active participation in online health forums for emotional or informational support [19]. Forums composed of patients with dementia (PWD) also serve as a social venue and source of solidarity, allowing for patients to construct community even if they are unable to leave their homes [17].

© Springer Nature Switzerland AG 2021
K. Toeppe et al. (Eds.): iConference 2021, LNCS 12645, pp. 377–395, 2021.
https://doi.org/10.1007/978-3-030-71292-1_29

Social media applications come with various forms affording different types of inter-actions. Our focal context is an online health discussion forum often organized around a health issue, e.g., eating disorder, mental illness, diabetes, dementia, etc. On such a discussion forum, participants post issues seeking information or support, or offer-ing experiences, etc., and view and respond to the other people's posts and comments. Discussions are organized as threads with the original post being the root. These discus-sion threads are often open to all members. In studying these health discussion forums, researchers develop various methods to identify influential users [26], study the per-ceived credibility of a user [5], measure a user's perceived empathy from the forum [10], and determine a user's intent [25].

Users often desire others to respond to their posts in online discussion forums, be it offering suggestions, information, or emotion support, etc. It is therefore valuable for supporting users activities and enriching their experiences to know what attracts the others' attention to a post in online discussion forums. Relatedly, studies about web-based request fulfilment have shown that language use in a web request plays an important role in the attracting others' attention, e.g., getting the fund in crowdfunding sites (e.g., Kickstarter) [9] and having their questions answered in Q&A sites (e.g., StackOverflow) [3]. However, to our best knowledge, there is little investigation on what language features of a post attract a user to respond to it in an online health discussion forum.

Contributing to close this research gap, we analyzed two subreddits, r/Alzheimers and r/dementia, to understand what in a post that affects how much attention it receives. A popular social media site, Reddit provides themed discussion forums (sub-reddits) where users can post submissions, comment, or vote on other users' sub-missions, and subscribe. The r/Alzheimers subreddit is focused on support for those affected by Alzheimers/dementia and sharing Alzheimers/dementia related news, while the r/dementia subreddit is dedicated to information and support for PWD and their caregivers.

With about 2,000 posts from the two subreddits, we explored whether and how linguistic features and topic characteristics of a post affect the attention it receives. We consider different forms of attention paid to the post, including whether others voted for it (or against it), commented/replied to it, and the average number of comments per participant the post receives. Reddit users can not only reply to the original posts but also to the others' comments. With close to 15,000 comments from the two subreddits, we also examined whether linguistic features of a comment affect the attention it receives - measured by the number of replies it receives.

The rest of our paper is organized as follows. We first review online health discussion forum studies about what attracts the social media users' attention in web-based requests. We next describe our data collection process and how we pre-processed the data. We present in detail our measures of the attention a post receives and its other characteristics such as language use and the content. We discuss the implications of the study and conclude with a future plan.

2   Related Work

Alzheimers and dementia are health conditions that cause brain degeneration and a decline in the patient's ability to function independently, often requiring relatives or close friends to become informal caregivers. The use of social media among caregivers is prevalent, with one out of five caregivers in the U.S. relying solely on the internet as a source for healthcare information. Given the debilitating effects of these conditions on the patient's ability to make decisions, caregivers for PWD face additional uncertainty and emotional tolls, which online communities can mitigate through social support and information sharing [20]. Various studies are carried out to examine online health discussion forums. Most of the research into online health discussion forums have focused on the user as the unit of analysis as previously discussed.

Several studies on health discussion forums have focused on post content. Park, Conway and Chen [12] analyze the content of mental health subreddits by using clustering, qualitative, and visual analysis in order to enumerate the topical content, then compare and contrast the subreddits. Dermatology subreddits were also identified and characterized in [2] through keyword-based text mining and manually coding posts into topic categories.

It is essential that others' attention is attracted in many online interactions. On social platforms such as Q&A websites (e.g., StackOverflow.com) and crowdfunding and philanthropy communities (e.g., Kickstarter.com), a user often has a request that needs to be fulfilled. Prior studies suggest that various linguistic and content features contribute to the success of such requests. For instance, in Mitra and Gilbert's study [9], the researchers found that the language used in the requests has predictive power, accounting for roughly 58% of the variance around successful funding. Althoff et al. [1] investigated what motivates people to give when they receive no tangible reward in return. They found that providing a narrative that clearly communicates the needs is an essential factor for the success of requests. In addition, providing indications of gratitude as well as reciprocity enhanced the chance of success. Studying language use in StackOverflow, Calefato et al. [3] discovered that questions that obtain successful answers within a short period of time tend to be short, have no massive uppercase, and have neutral emotional style.

However, to our best knowledge, the attention factors of a post has not been explored in the context of online health discussions.

3   Data Collection and Pre-processing

We used the Reddit Pushshift API[1] to collect Reddit posts and comments created between February 28, 2019 and February 28, 2020 from the r/Alzheimers and r/dementia subreddits. Pushshift is a database containing copies of all publicly available Reddit objects including comments and posts, which is updated in near-real time. In total, we extracted 701 posts and 5,349 comments from r/Alzheimers, and 1,277 posts and 9,830 comments from r/dementia. We anonymized the usernames of post and comment authors using alphanumeric hash codes. Over one year, a total of 2,833 Reddit users commented or posted in the subreddits, 914 participating only in r/Alzheimers, 1,674 participating only in r/dementia, and 245 participating in both. Taking the community size of each subreddit into account (the average subscriber count over the year), this reveals similar participation rates between the subreddits with 23.1% in r/Alzheimers and 28.6% in r/dementia.

---

[1] https://github.com/pushshift/api.

Some of the posts in these two forums were for advertisement purposes such as soliciting participation for research studies and surveys. We observed that most of these posts had zero comments. In addition, these posts had words like "participate" "study" "research", etc. Based on these observations, we constructed a list of common words in these posts. We filtered out the posts that had zero comments and that contained at least two of such words. The resulting dataset had 693 r/Alzheimers posts and 1,254 r/dementia posts. Comments fitting similar criteria were not removed because they accounted for less than 1% of the comments collected from each subreddit.

We then cleaned and normalized the text body of each remaining post and comment. This process included removing URLs, tokenization, and lemmatization using the functionalities of the Natural Language Toolkit (NLTK) and regular expressions.

We also used an open source web scraper[2] in order to collect subscriber counts for each subreddit from RedditMetrics.com. RedditMetrics.com displays regularly updated information about all subreddits, including daily subscriber growth, total subscribers, and popularity rank. For each post and comment collected, we used the web scraper to extract the number of subscribers its subreddit had on the day it was posted.

4 Data Analysis

With the remaining data, we examined whether and how the amount of attention a post receives correlates with the linguistic features and sentiment polarity in the post. We explain below how we measure these variables.

4.1 Attention Measures for a Post

We calculated three attributes for each post to understand the amount of attention it receives: the voting participation ratio, commenting participation ratio, and comments per commenter.

A post's voting participation ratio is the estimated total number of votes on a post divided by the number of subscribers to the subreddit when the post was created. Equation 1 shows the formula for the estimation of total votes. The total number of votes T is essentially the sum of upvotes and downvotes. S and U are provided through the Pushshift API. S is the subtraction of downvotes from upvotes and U is equal to the number of upvotes divided by the total number of votes.

$$T = \frac{S * U}{2U - 1} + \left(\frac{S * U}{2U - 1} - S \right) \qquad (1)$$

A post's commenting participation ratio is the number of unique users who have commented on the post, divided by the number of subscribers to the subreddit when the post was created. In these ratios, the number of subscribers serves as an estimate of the community size. We use an estimation because a user can vote or comment on a post without being subscribed to the subreddit, but we cannot access the total number of users that actually encountered a particular post. Comments per commenter is the total number of comments on a post divided by the number of unique users who have commented on the post.

---

[2] The ExtractRedditData module in https://github.com/al-vincent/reddit-analytics.

4.2 Attention Measures for a Comment

We only considered one attribute when measuring the amount of attention that a comment has received, called reply participation ratio. A reply participation ratio was calculated for each comment by dividing the number of replies to the comment by the number of unique commenters on its parent post. During the data collection period, there was a range of 3767–5977 members in r/Alzheimer's and 4524–8604 members in r/dementia (Tables 1 and 2).

Table 1. Descriptive statistics of the attention measure for posts in the r/Alzheimer and r/dementia forums

	Number of posts		Attention measure for a post		
			Voting participation ratio	Commenting participation ratio	Comments per commenter
r/Alzheimers	693	Min	0	0	0
		Max	0.02268	0.00598	7
		Avg.	0.00228	0.00105	1.35305
		Median	0.00173	0.00092	1.25
		Standard deviation	0.00214	0.0008	0.67908
r/dementia	1254	Min	0	0	0
		Max	0.02433	0.00398	7
		Avg.	0.0018	0.00079	1.41279
		Median	0.00123	0.00064	1.26491
		Standard deviation	0.00194	0.00059	0.65203

4.3 Linguistic Features

We used the Linguistic Inquiry and Word Count (LIWC) tool to compute the use of linguistic features in a post. LIWC is a method of computerized text analysis which counts words into psychologically meaningful categories. For each input unit, LIWC outputs the percentage of words in the text that belong to each of its 92 categories, which reflect linguistic features of the text [21]. We considered 16 categories in this study: summary variables (Analytical Thinking, Clout, Authentic, Emotional Tone), sentiment (Positive emotion, Negative emotion), parts of speech (Verbs, Nouns, Adjectives, I, We, You), Cognitive Processes, Words per Sentence, Word Count, and Words > 6 letters.

We computed the percentage of nouns in a post separately from other parts of speech by using the Penn Treebank Tagger in NLTK, since this category is not available in

Table 2. Descriptive statistics of the attention measure for comments in r/Alzheimers and r/dementia forums

	Number of comments	Reply participation ration
r/Alzheimers	349	Min: 0
		Max: 1
		Average: 0.06168
		Median: 0
		Standard deviation 0.08093
r/dementia	9830	Min: 0
		Max: 1
		Average: 0.06520
		Median: 0
		Standard deviation 0.09513

LIWC. We used these percentages, along with those for verbs and adjectives, to inform our analysis of frequently occurring content words.

4.4 Topics of the Posts

To gain an understanding of what was discussed in the two forums, we identified most frequent n-grams from the posts and comments for each forum as follows. First, we calculated the frequency of unigrams, bigrams, trigram, and quadgrams (n-grams) in the posts and comments using NLTK functionalities. We applied filters to the n-grams in order to extract content-related words; non-alphanumeric n-grams and n-grams appearing less than 5 times were eliminated. For all n-grams except for quadgrams, we also removed n-grams containing stopwords. We selected relevant n-grams by locating the elbow point in a function where the x axis represented the n-grams rank, and y axis represented its frequency. We located the elbow point using the Python library Kneed[3] and selected each relevant n-gram with equal or greater frequency than that at the elbow point. We then visualized these relevant n-grams in word clouds.

To understand whether the content of low- and high-attention posts differs, we compared the most frequent n-grams between the two groups of posts. In addition, we examined the use of content words in the high- and low-attention posts using word frequency analysis. The low-attention posts are those with zero comments (i.e., no reply), whereas the high-attention posts are the top 10% of posts in terms of number of comments. In r/Alzheimers, there were 77 high-attention posts and 37 low-attention posts. In r/dementia, there were 131 high-attention posts and 71 low-attention posts.

---

[3] https://github.com/arvkevi/kneed.

We also performed topic modelling analysis on posts based on clustering obtained from running the Latent Dirichlet Allocation (LDA) algorithm on them. The idea of using topic modelling to identify topics and themes of discussions has been explored in studies about online health discussions and has shown promising results [11, 13]. In our data pre-processing, we removed URLs, special characters, and stopwords (including domain specific words such as alzheimer for r/Alzheimer posts and dementia for r/dementia posts). We also lemmatized the words and converted each post to a bag of words. We then ran the LDA model on the corpus.

We applied non-parametric Spearman correlation tests to examine whether the attention measures of a post or a comment correlate with its linguistic features, sentiment polarity, or topic. The Bonferroni correction was considered with an adjusted alpha value 0.0005 since there were 99 Spearman tests in the analysis - there are four attention measures (for posts and comments) to correlate with 14 linguistic features, and two sentiment polarity features. The presence of 7 topics were tested for correlation with three attention measures and two sentiment polarity features.

5   Results

5.1   How Do Different Attention Measures of a Post Correlate with Each Other?

As described earlier, there are three attention measures for a post. Hypothetically, as they all reflect the amount of attention a post receives in the forum, they should be correlated with each other. The results of non-parametric Spearman correlation tests verified this. As shown in Table 3 and 4, in both forums, if a post receives a greater number of votes, it tends to attract more members to comment and a member tends to make more comments as well.

Table 3. Spearman correlation among attention measures of a r/Alzheimers post

	Voting participation ratio	Commenting participation ratio	Comments per commenter
Voting participation ratio	1	0.456	0.174
Commenting participation ratio	0.456	1	0.432
Comments per commenter	0.174	0.432	1

Table 4. Spearman correlation among attention measures of a r/dementia post

	Voting participation ratio	Commenting participation ratio	Comments per commenter
Voting participation ratio	1	0.541	0.154
Commenting participation ratio	0.541	1	0.375
Comments per commenter	0.154	0.375	1

5.2 How Do a Post's Linguistic Features Correlate with the Amount of Attention it Receives?

We present, in Table 5 and Table 6, the results of non-parametric Spearman correlation tests between the previously discussed attention measures and various linguistic characteristics of a post. Only the statistically significant correlations are shown (i.e., $p < 0.0005$).

Table 5. Significant correlation coefficients between linguistic and sentiment features of r/Alzheimers posts

	Voting participation ratio	Commenting participation ratio	Comments per commenter
Analytical thinking	−0.150	−0.325	−0.132
Word count	0.133	0.240	0.202
Cognitive processes	N/A	0.206	N/A
Negative emotions	0.166	0.173	N/A
Words > 6 letters	N/A	−0.175	N/A
Verb use	N/A	0.305	0.166
"I" use	0.146	0.166	N/A

Generally, posts that require more cognitive processing receive less attention, according to correlation coefficients between attention measures and LIWC's Analytical Thinking score and Words > 6 letters. However, when a post has more words and uses more words that reflect the poster's cognitive processing, it tends to receive more attention. Interestingly, if a post contains more negative emotions and is about sharing one's stories or experiences (i.e., the more use of "I"), it is likely to get more people to vote and to comment, although a member is not necessarily very engaged in the post discussion - reflected by the lack of correlation with the comments per commenter measure. A post that uses more verbs also tends to get more people to comment and to be engaged in the discussion.

Table 6. Significant correlation coefficients between linguistic and sentiment features of r/dementia posts

	Voting participation ratio	Commenting participation ratio	Comments per commenter
Analytical thinking	N/A	−0.159	N/A
Cognitive processes	N/A	0.100	N/A
Negative emotions	0.118	0.144	N/A
Word count	0.104	0.160	0.188
Words > 6 letters	−0.166	−0.141	N/A
Verb use	N/A	0.145	0.166
"I" use	0.150	0.137	N/A

5.3 How Do a Comment's Linguistic Features Correlate with the Amount of Attention It Receives?

We also performed non-parametric Spearman correlation tests between the previously discussed attention measure for comments and the same linguistic features enumerated for posts. The results only showed one statistically significant correlation (i.e., $p < 0.0005$). There was a negative correlation between reply participation ratio and Positive Emotion present in both subreddits, with a correlation coefficient of −0.108 in r/Alzheimers and −0.106 in r/dementia. Generally, comments with more positive emotion receive less replies.

5.4 What Are the Posts About in the R/Alzheimers and R/dementia Forums?

To gain a general understanding of the content in the two forums, we generated word clouds to visualize the identified relevant n-grams in the posts and comments for both forums. For each word or n-gram displayed in the word cloud, a sentiment score was calculated by averaging the VADER (Valence Aware Dictionary and sEntiment Reasoner) scores of all sentences it appeared in [16]. The VADER score ranges from -1 (extremely negative) to 1 (extremely positive). We used this average score to determine the color of the word or n-gram: green for positive sentiment, yellow for neutral sentiment, and red for negative sentiment. Additionally, the n-gram frequency determined the size of the n-gram in the word cloud.

Figure 1 below shows the word clouds for the full content of the two forums (i.e., posts and comments), and Fig. 2 shows the word clouds of only the posts in the two forums. From these word clouds, we obtain a high-level view of topics that users post and comment about in the forum. The sentiment is largely negative among posts (Fig. 2) but increases upon taking comments into consideration (Fig. 1). Several phrases relating to care, treatment, and advice-seeking consistently have neutral or positive sentiment. Common themes among n-grams in posts include timing, family/relationship, treatment, and advice seeking phrases. This indicates authors describing their experience with dementia (emotionally), their relationship to the patient with dementia (PWD), and history of the PWD) and seeking advice about treatment or communication with the PWD. Considering post and comment text together, themes of gratitude and well-wishing emerge too.

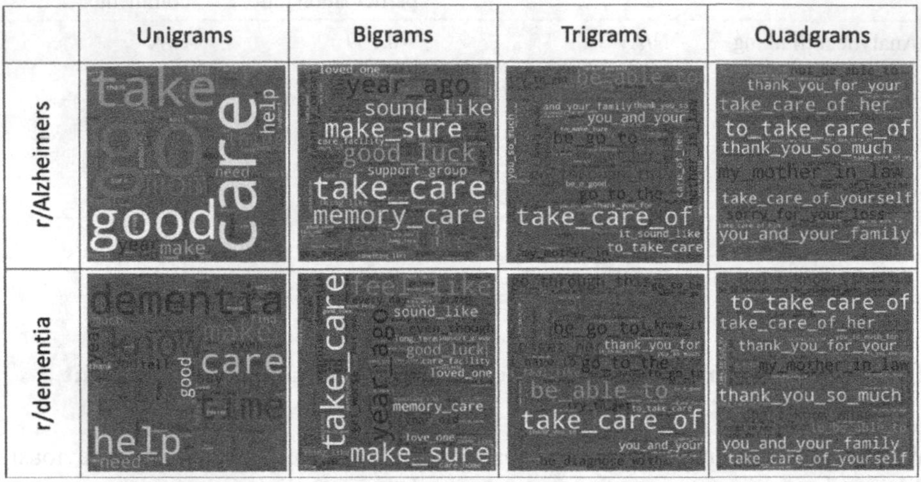

Fig. 1. Word clouds for posts and comments in each subreddit

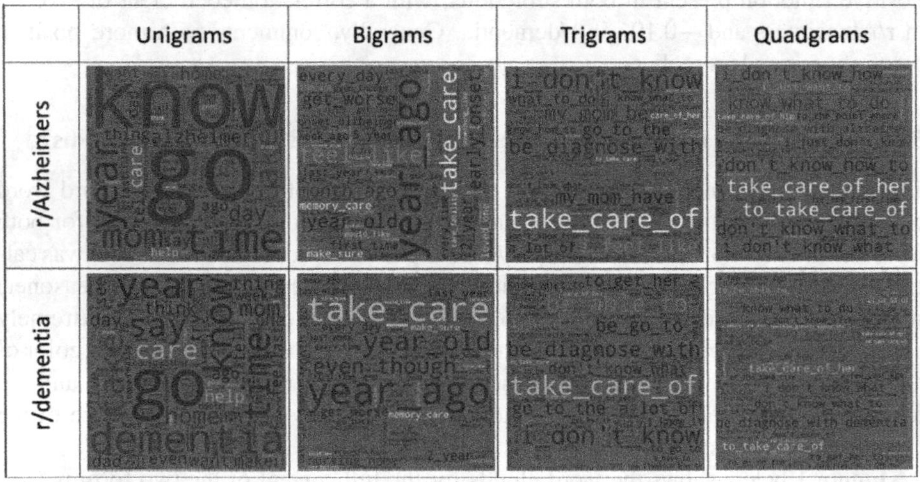

Fig. 2. Word clouds for posts in each subreddit

Our LDA analysis also suggests the topics covered in the posts. One important parameter in LDA analysis is the number of topics k. To identify the optimal number of topics for the corpus, we calculated the coherence score for each k value (ranging from 1 to 20) and chose the k with the maximum coherence score. Through this process we identified six main topics in r/Alzheimers posts and eight in r/dementia posts. We visualized these

Table 7. Topics discussed in the r/Alzheimers subreddit, inferred from the tokens in the topics extracted from the posts

Category	Description
Experience of family of person with Alzheimer's (about 39% of the tokens are in this category; includes topic 2 from the LDA topic modelling analysis)	This category is about narratives, as the majority of the tokens are about time and stories. We speculate that posts in this category are about personal experiences with family members who have Alzheimer's Top frequent tokens: mom, dad, time, year, go, within, anybody, thing, see, could, ago
Information Seeking/Question (about 42% of the tokens are in this category; includes topic 4 from the LDA topic modelling analysis)	This category is about information seeking or asking for certain kinds of help, as it contains almost all of the 'help' tokens in the corpus Top frequent tokens: help, know, want, care, right, sure, one, place, trying, used, post
Symptoms/Treatments (about 19% of the tokens are in this category; includes topic 1,3,5,6 from the LDA topic modelling analysis)	This category is about symptoms and treatments Top frequent tokens: drug, research, experiencing, anxiety, food, med, information, test, mostly, brain

topics using pyLDAvis library [18] and consolidated the topics that are conceptually close (see Fig. 3 below). In the end, we identified three categories for r/Alzheimer posts: Experience of family of person with Alzheimer's, Information Seeking/Support, and Symptoms/Treatments. Table 7 describes these categories along with the most common tokens in each of them. We identified four categories for r/dementia posts: Experience of family of patients with dementia (PWD), Facilities/Symptoms of PWD, Information Seeking/Question, andOther. Table 8 presents the descriptions of these categories and the most common tokens in each category.

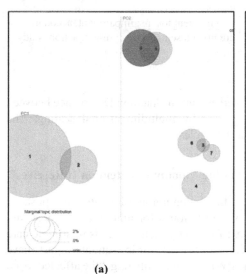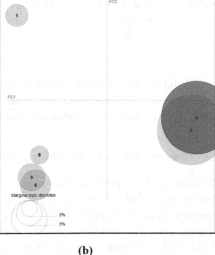

(a)   (b)

Fig. 3. Intertopic Distances calculated as the Jensen-Shannon [4] divergence between the topics (a) Dementia topics (b) Alzheimer's Topics

Table 8. Topics discussed in the r/dementia subreddit, inferred from the tokens in the topics extracted from the posts

Category	Description
Experience of family of PWD (about 75.3% of the tokens are in this category; includes topic 1, 2, 6 from the LDA topic modelling analysis)	This category is about narratives, as the majority of the tokens are about time and stories. We speculate that posts in this category are about personal experiences with family members who are PWD Top frequent tokens: mom, dad, time, know, year, month, something, conversation, anxiety, year, story, cried, forget, change, thing, day, think, lost
Experience in Facilities/Symptoms of PWD (about 15% of the tokens are in this category; includes topic 4 and 5 from the LDA topic modelling analysis)	This category includes tokens about facilities and places (e.g., home, hospital) and behavioral symptoms of PWD (e.g., phone) Top frequent tokens: experience, thank, living, caregiver, brain, medical, home, hospital, symptom, forgetting, community, phone, support, sense, mental
Information Seeking/Question (about 6% of the tokens are in this category; includes topic 8 from the LDA topic modelling analysis)	This category is about information seeking or asking for certain kinds of help, as it contains almost all of the 'help' tokens in the corpus Top frequent tokens: help, anyone, grandmother, trying, remember, something, sometimes, reason, point, today, think
Other (about 3.7% of the tokens are in this category; includes topic 3 and 7 from the LDA topic modelling analysis)	This category includes the rest of the eight topics Top frequent tokens: impairment, account, dignity, present, access, present, action, study, onset

The Intertopic distances here are calculated as Jensen-Shannon Divergence between the topics and the distances are scaled in 2D by multidimensional scaling. The prominence of topics is encoded as areas of the circles.

5.5 Does the Topic of a Post Play a Role in the Amount of Attention It Receives?

We visualized the most relevant n-grams in high-attention and low-attention posts as word clouds in Fig. 4. As the figure shows, word clouds for high-attention posts are similar to those of all posts (Fig. 2), but more frequently include words relating to care strategies (nursing home, memory care, etc.). Word clouds for low-attention posts have starkly high sentiment, and often refer to the PWD impersonally (e.g. "the affected loved one"). In r/Alzheimers, news articles are frequently mentioned in low-attention posts. Phrases alluding to the relationship with PWD and history/condition other PWD are present and have negative sentiment, similar to their occurrence in high attention posts (Fig. 5).

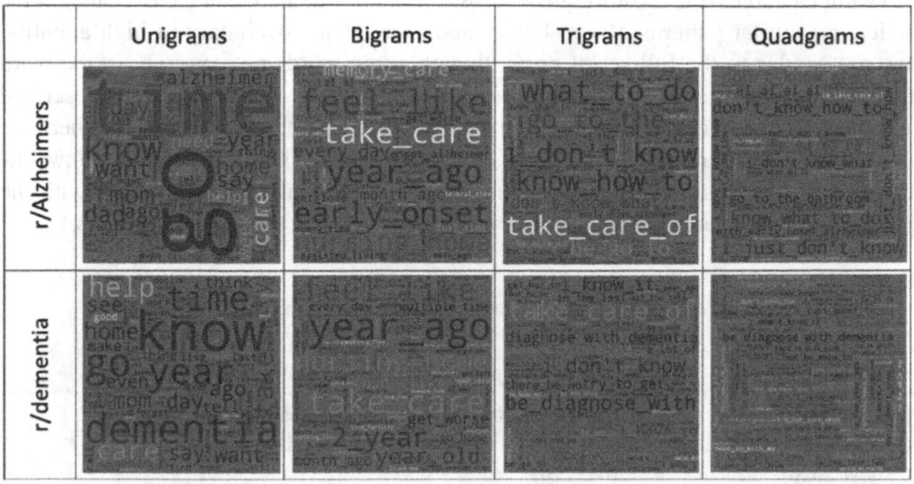

	Unigrams	Bigrams	Trigrams	Quadgrams
r/Alzheimers				
r/dementia				

Fig. 4. Word clouds of n-grams from the top 10% of posts in terms of number of comments

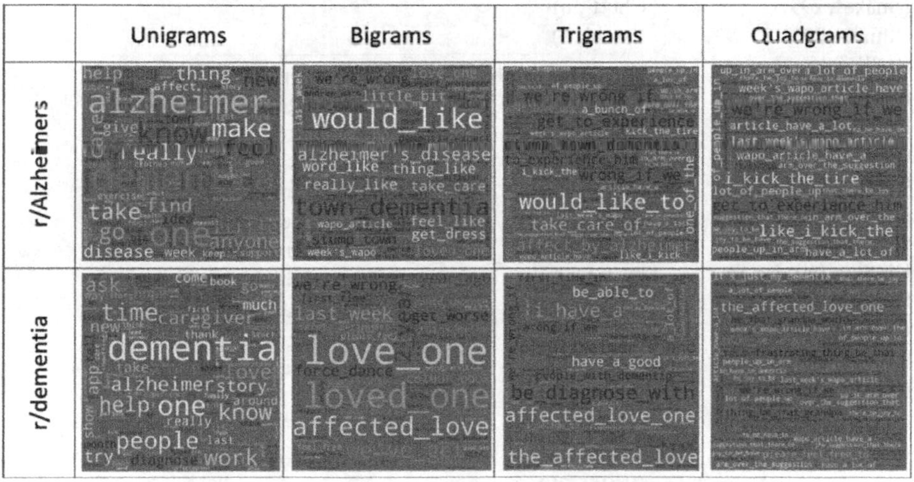

	Unigrams	Bigrams	Trigrams	Quadgrams
r/Alzheimers				
r/dementia				

Fig. 5. Word clouds of n-grams from posts with 0 comments

According to linguistics, content words are nouns, adjectives, verbs, and adverbs. As shown in our analysis of linguistic features, only the use of verbs in a post is statistically significantly correlated with the amount of attention the post receives. To understand this significance, we examined the use of verbs in the high- and low-attention posts using word frequency analysis. Specifically, we identified the top twenty most frequent verbs in these posts and identified the verbs unique to each group. Tables 9 and 10 below present the top twenty most frequent verbs in the posts of r/Alzheimers and r/dementia, and verbs within the top fifty that are unique to each attention group with a minimum frequency of 5 (i.e., they do not overlap with the top fifty verbs among all posts). As shown in the tables, the most frequent verbs were common between the two subreddits, indicating similar patterns of vocabulary and topic. The vocabulary in high attention posts is similar to the full set of posts, though some words present only in the word analysis for high attention posts indicate increased severity of the situations described (e.g. hurt, refuse in r/Alzheimers; suffer, kill in r/dementia). In r/Alzheimers, there are also more specific transportation verbs (e.g. drive, run). There are relatively few low attention posts, thus they have fewer unique verbs. The unique verbs align with the generally positive sentiment noted of low-attention posts in the n-gram analysis.

Table 9. The top verbs in r/Alzheimers and their frequencies

All posts (693)	High-attention posts (77)	Low-attention posts (37)
('get', 700)	Top unique verbs:	Top unique verbs:
('go', 595)	('refuse', 10)	('like', 5)
('know', 520)	('drive', 10)	
('take', 387)	('run', 9)	
('say', 340)	('care', 9)	
('want', 309)	('felt', 9)	
('make', 299)	('hurt', 8)	
('think', 290)	('stop', 8)	
('tell', 286)	Top overall verbs:	Top overall verbs:
('see', 236)	('get', 115)	('get', 13)
('help', 221)	('go', 100)	('go', 11)
('feel', 206)	('know', 81)	('know', 11)
('ask', 177)	('take', 68)	('make', 8)
('live', 174)	('want', 67)	('feel', 7)
('try', 172)	('say', 65)	('find', 6)
('find', 169)	('think', 50)	('think', 6)
('need', 169)	('make', 48)	('take', 6)
('come', 160)	('tell', 40)	('give', 5)
('remember', 157)	('come', 30)	('remember', 5)
('leave', 139)	('see', 30)	
	('try', 28)	
	('feel', 28)	
	('help', 28)	
	('leave', 28)	
	('ask', 27)	
	('need', 27)	
	('find', 25)	
	('lose', 23)	
	('live', 21)	

Table 10. The top verbs in r/dementia and their frequencies

All posts (1254)	High-attention posts (131)	Low-attention posts (71)
('get', 1739)	Top unique verbs:	Top unique verbs:
('go', 1317)	('watch', 21)	('improve', 6)
('know', 1160)	('cannot', 16)	('please', 5)
('take', 838)	('kill', 14)	
('say', 769)	('read', 14)	
('want', 719)	('suffer', 14)	
('think', 662)	('care', 13)	
('make', 635)	Top overall verbs:	Top overall verbs:
('tell', 578)	('get', 175)	('get', 24)
('see', 556)	('know', 147)	('know', 12)
('feel', 478)	('go', 137)	('make', 10)
('help', 464)	('take', 89)	('help', 9)
('try', 450)	('say', 86)	('think', 9)
('need', 416)	('want', 80)	('take', 8)
('come', 406)	('tell', 79)	('feel', 8)
('live', 388)	('see', 72)	('find', 7)
('keep', 361)	('make', 71)	('go', 7)
('ask', 359)	('think', 70)	('want', 7)
('leave', 332)	('help', 64)	('leave', 7)
('find', 325)	('try', 58)	('tell', 7)
	('give', 48)	('bring', 6)
	('feel', 48)	('live', 6)
	('live', 42)	('call', 6)
	('ask', 40)	('come', 6)
	('need', 39)	('ask', 6)
	('keep', 37)	('say', 5)
	('come', 35)	('try', 5)
	('find', 34)	('understand', 5)

We applied Spearman correlation tests to examine how categorization by topic modelling relates to the attention received by a post, as well as its sentiment polarity. We present the statistically significant (i.e., $p < 0.0005$) results of the tests in Table 11 and 12.

Across both subreddits, the category of experience is positively correlated with most attention measures and negative sentiment polarity. Posts about facilities, symptoms, and information seeking are negatively correlated with attention, and positively correlated with positive sentiment. Interestingly, r/dementia posts categorized as "Other" are negatively correlated with positive emotion. Because this category includes all the posts that do not fit with the other three categories, more investigation is needed to explain this observation.

To determine whether gratitude could explain the correlation between information seeking and positive emotion in r/Alzheimers, we counted the occurrence of gratitude

Table 11. Significant correlation coefficients between topic, sentiment, and attention features of posts in r/Alzheimers

	Experience of family of person with Alzheimer's	Information/Support Seeking	Symptoms/Treatments
Voting participation ratio	0.150	−0.157	N/A
Commenting participation ratio	0.131	N/A	−0.137
Positive emotion	−0.179	0.147	N/A
Negative emotion	0.223	−0.179	N/A

Table 12. Significant correlation coefficients between topic, sentiment, and attention features of posts is r/dementia

	Experience of family of PWD	Experience in Facilities/Symptoms of PWD	Other
Voting participation ratio	0.102	−0.110	N/A
Commenting participation ratio	0.237	−0.211	N/A
Positive emotion	N/A	0.151	−0.106
Negative emotion	0.197	−0.179	N/A

words (i.e. "thank", "appreciate") within r/Alzheimers posts and found that the Information Seeking topic contained 94, while other topics contained 50 gratitude words or less.

6 Discussion

The language features that attract attention on social media platforms have been researched in various online contexts (e.g. crowdfunding, Q&A forums) [3, 9], but to our knowledge, attention has not been studied in the context of online health forums. To narrow this research gap, we analyzed how the content of posts and comments from two dementia-centered subreddits related to attention both qualitatively and quantitatively.

The correlation between a post's negative sentiment and the amount of attention it receives is related to previous research. For instance, in researching influential users, Quercia et al. [15] found that influential users linguistically structure their tweets in specific ways and tend to be individuals who express the negative sentiment in part of their tweets. Studies that explore the linguistic features indicative of an online comment's persuasion power have shown that persuasive comments tend to have more negative sentiment [22, 24]. Our word frequency analysis also shows that there are more negative words for high-attention posts, and our topic modelling analysis shows that high-attention topics are correlated with negative emotion. Building on the findings of these studies including ours, we speculate that news posts with negative sentiment may attract more readers. As a result, more readers feel negative emotions because the sentiment of their opinions strongly correlates with the news posts they read [7]. This emotion contagion is rather alarming to the modern society, given that it is increasingly common that we read news online.

We observed that n-grams about event timing, emotion, and relationship with the PWD are frequently used in high-attention posts. In addition, the post length, and the sharing of personal experiences are found to be associated with higher attention. These findings suggest that posts containing detailed narratives are more likely to receive attention. Our topic modeling analysis offers supporting evidence. This is also consistent with the findings of Althoff et. al [1] which discovered that a request is more likely to be successful when it includes a narrative that clearly communicates the needs of the requestor.

We also observed themes of gratitude and positive emotion in word clouds when considering the content of both posts and comments. The presence of these themes are consistent with past research on health-related online communities [12, 14]. This may indicate that members of the subreddit frequently respond in positive, supportive ways to the post author. Relatedly, posts about information seeking in r/Alzheimers were more positive, which can be explained by themes of gratitude. Xiao and Chen [23] found that requests for support often included gratitude to encourage the community to take action. Our results show that this phenomenon is present in r/Alzheimers as well.

The design of these online health forums is often aimed at facilitating interactions among community members that communicate informational, emotional, and social support. The ultimate goal of the designer is to foster the development of online communities. Our findings of the features that draw attention to a post offers practical value to the designer. For example, posting guidelines can be developed and made available to the members on how to write a post that receives attention from the community, e.g., a post that tends to receive more attention from the community provides sufficient details and shares personal stories.

We recognize several limitations in our research. The scope of data we analyzed included two communities from a single social media platform and had a time range of one year. This incorporates a bias towards overrepresenting the behavior of community members active during the time range sampled. Consequently, the findings may not be representative of online health community members as a whole. To gain a more general understanding of attention in online health forums, our work could be repeated using data from different health related subreddits or different social media platforms. Additionally, our word frequency analysis largely relied on manual observation and interpretation, which is prone to subjectivity and human error. The scientific rigor of future studies could be improved by manually reviewing advertisement posts and comments before removing them, and formulating a more exact measurement of community size for use in attention measures.

7 Conclusion

Comparing high and low attention posts using the metrics defined above, we can observe that high attention posts tend to be more intense and negative in emotion, with focus on sharing narratives and seeking support. Positive posts tend to receive less attention and have a focus on information seeking and symptoms. Posts with more words and simpler language also receive more attention in the forums. From the n-gram and word frequency analysis, we found general themes of care/treatment seeking, symptom related discussions, emotional experience and individual disease progression. The results of our study provide supporting evidence for findings in related work and could be used practically to enhance user experience in such forums. Future work includes closer examination of content within identified topics and replication of the study with different online communities.

References

1. Althoff, T., Danescu-Niculescu-Mizil, C., Jurafsky, D.: How to ask for a favor: a case study on the success of altruistic requests. In: Proceedings of the 8th International Conference on Weblogs and Social Media, ICWSM (2014)
2. Buntinx-Krieg, T., Caravaglio, J., Domozych, R., Dellavalle, R.P.: Dermatology on Reddit: elucidating trends in dermatologic communications on the world wide web. Dermatol Online J. 23(7), 1–6 (2017)
3. Calefato, F., Lanubile, F., Novielli, N.: How to ask for technical help? Evidence-based guidelines for writing questions on stack overflow. Inf. Softw. Technol. 94, 186–207 (2018)
4. Fuglede, B., Topsoe, F.: Jensen-Shannon divergence and Hilbert space embedding. In: International Symposium on Information Theory, ISIT 2004, Proceedings, Chicago, IL, p. 31 (2004)
5. Hirvonen, N., Tirroniemi, A., Kortelainen, T.: The cognitive authority of user-generated health information in an online forum for girls and young women. J. Doc. 75(1), 78–98 (2019)
6. Johnsen, J.K., Rosenvinge, J.H., Gammon, D.: Online group interaction and mental health: an analysis of three online discussion forums. Scand. J. Psychol. 43(5), 445–449 (2002)
7. Kumar, N., Nagalla, R., Marwah, T., Singh, M.: Sentiment dynamics in social media news channels. Online Soc. Netw. Media 8, 42–54 (2018)
8. Lyons, M., Aksayli, N.D., Brewer, G.: Mental distress and language use: linguistic analysis of discussion forum posts. Comput. Hum. Behav. 87, 207–211 (2018)
9. Mitra, T., Gilbert, E.: The language that gets people to give: phrases that predict success on kickstarter. In: Proceedings of the 17th ACM Conference on Computer Supported Cooperative Work & Social Computing, pp. 49–61. Association for Computing Machinery, New York (2014)
10. Nambisan, P.: Information seeking and social support in online health communities: impact on patients' perceived empathy. J. Am. Med. Inform. Assoc. 18(3), 298–304 (2011)
11. Paul, M., Dredze, M.: Discovering health topics in social media using topic models. PLoS ONE 9(8), e103408 (2014)
12. Park, A., Conway, M., Chen, A.T.: Examining thematic similarity, difference, and membership in three online mental health communities from reddit: a text mining and visualization approach. Comput. Hum. Behav. 78, 98–112 (2018)

13. Park, A., Conway, M.: Tracking health related discussions on Reddit for public health applications. In: Annual Symposium Proceedings, pp. 1362–1371. AMIA Symposium (2017)
14. Qiu, B., Zhao, K., Mitra, P., Wu, D., Caragea, C., Yen, J., et al.: Get online support, feel better -- sentiment analysis and dynamics in an online cancer survivor community. In: 2011 IEEE Third International Conference on Privacy, Security, Risk and Trust and 2011 IEEE Third International Conference on Social Computing, Boston, MA, pp. 274–281. IEEE Press (2011)
15. Quercia, D., Ellis, J., Capra, L., Crowcroft, J.: In the mood for being influential on twitter. In: 2011 IEEE Third International Conference on Privacy, Security, Risk and Trust and 2011 IEEE Third International Conference on Social Computing, Boston, MA, pp. 307–314. IEEE Press (2011).
16. Ribeiro, F.N., Araújo, M., Gonçalves, P., Goncalves, M.A., Benevenuto, F.: SentiBench - a benchmark comparison of state-of-the-practice sentiment analysis methods. EPJ Data Sci. 5(23), 1–29 (2016)
17. Rodriquez, J.: Narrating dementia: self and community in an online forum. Qual. Health Res. 23(9), 1215–1227 (2013)
18. Sievert, C., Shirley, K.: LDAvis: A method for visualizing and interpreting topics (2014). https://doi.org/10.13140/2.1.1394.3043
19. Tanis, M., Das, E., Fortgens-Sillmann, M.: Finding care for the caregiver? Active participation in online health forums attenuates the negative effect of caregiver strain on wellbeing. Communications 36(1), 51–66 (2011)
20. Tang, A.Y., Kwak, J., Xie, B., Xiao, L., Lahiri, S., Flynn, O.A., et al.: Online health information wants of caregivers for persons with dementia in social media. J. Assoc. Inf. Sci. Technol. (2020, submitted)
21. Tausczik, Y., Pennebaker, J.: The psychological meaning of words: LIWC and computerized text analysis methods. J. Lang. Soc. Psychol. 29(1), 24–54 (2010)
22. Xiao, L.: A message's persuasive features in wikipedia's article for deletion discussions. In: Proceedings of the 9th International Conference on Social Media and Society, pp. 345–349. ACM, New York (2019)
23. Xiao, L., Chen, S.: Misinformation in the Chinese Weibo. In: Meiselwitz, G. (ed.) HCII 2020. LNCS, vol. 12194, pp. 407–418. Springer, Cham (2020). https://doi.org/10.1007/978-3-030-49570-1_28
24. Xiao, L., Khazaei, T.: Change others' beliefs online: online comments' persuasiveness. In: Proceedings of the 10th International Conference on Social Media and Society, pp. 92–101. ACM, New York (2019)
25. Zhang, T., Cho, J.H.D., Zhai, C.: Understanding user intents in online health forums. IEEE J. Biomed. Health Inform. 19(4), 1392–1398 (2015)
26. Zhao, K., Yen, J., Greer, G., Qiu, B., Mitra, P., Portier, K.: Finding influential users of online health communities: a new metric based on sentiment influence. J. Am. Med. Inform. Assoc. 21(e2), e212–e218 (2014)

Repurposing Sentiment Analysis for Social Research Scopes: An Inquiry into Emotion Expression Within Affective Publics on Twitter During the Covid-19 Emergency

Chamil Rathnayake[1] and Alessandro Caliandro[2]([⊠])

[1] University of Strathclyde, Glasgow, UK
chamil.rathnayake@strath.ac.uk
[2] University of Pavia, Pavia, Italy
alessandro.caliandro@unipv.it

Abstract. The scope of the article is to discuss and propose some methodological strategies to *repurpose* sentiment analysis for social research scopes. We argue that sentiment analysis is well suited to study an important topic in digital sociology: *affective publics*. Specifically, sentiment analysis reveals useful to explore two key components of affective publics: a) *structure* (emergence of dominant emotions); b) *dynamics* (transformation of affectivity into emotions). To do that we suggest combining sentiment analysis with emotion detection, text analysis and social media engagement metrics – which help to better understand the semantic and social context in which the sentiment related to a specific issue is situated. To illustrate our methodological point, we draw on the analysis of 33,338 tweets containing two hashtags – #NHSHeroes and #Covidiot – emerged in response to the global pandemic caused by Covid-19. Drawing on the analysis of the two affective publics aggregating around #NHSHeroes and #Covidiot, we conclude that they reflect a blend of emotions. In some cases, such generic flow of affect coalesces into a dominant emotion while it may not necessarily occur in other instances. Affective publics structured around positive emotions and local issues tend to be more consistent and cohesive than those based on general issues and negative emotions. Although negative emotions might attract the attention of digital publics, positively framed messages engage users more.

Keywords: Sentiment analysis · Affective publics · Covid-19 · Twitter · NHS

1 Introduction

In this article we propose some methodological reflections on how to *repurpose* [33] sentiment analysis for social research scopes. In particular, we show how sentiment analysis can be helpful to explore affective publics. Sentiment analysis is largely employed and debated in information science research, but mostly from a computational point of view [1]. In behavioural sciences, sentiment analysis is principally used to measure reputation

© Springer Nature Switzerland AG 2021
K. Toeppe et al. (Eds.): iConference 2021, LNCS 12645, pp. 396–410, 2021.
https://doi.org/10.1007/978-3-030-71292-1_30

of digital entities (e.g. brands or politicians) [2], but it is rarely used to understand collective social phenomena [3]. Surprisingly, sentiment analysis is scarcely employed to explore affective *structures* (i.e., dominant emotions) and *dynamics* (i.e., transformation of affectivity into emotions) of digital publics, which represent crucial objects of study in digital sociology [4]. To support our methodological reflections, we draw on a Twitter empirical analysis. Specifically, we focus on Twitter discussions related to Covid-19 – a topic that stirred intense emotional reactions within digital publics during the last few months – and analyse two hashtags (#NHSHeroes and #Covidiot), with a special emphasis on the context of the UK. This context is an important 'field' for studying public reactions, particularly due to the intense nature of sentiments that emerged in social media user reactions to the pandemic. Arguably, such intensity is related to thefact that the UK was heavily affected by Covid-19 with the total number of fatalities reached 45,000 by the end of July 2020 [5] as well as other controversies that arose about the Government's management of the emergency [6].

2 Theoretical Framework

2.1 Affective Publics: Theories and Methods

As we mentioned earlier, sentiment analysis is not particularly popular in sociological research. This is due to some intrinsic limitations of the technique. Sentiment analysis allows measuring emotions expressed towards a digital object, such as a product, a brand, an issue, or an individual in digital text [7] and it is mainly expressed through three coding categories: *positive, negative,* and *neutral.* These three general categories give the reader the false perception that a certain share of sentiment corresponds to a homogenous collection of users' opinions towards a given object, while it condenses only the emotional tone of a set of keywords contained in text. Moreover, simple measuring of quantities of positive and negative sentiments do not tell us much about the impact that digital affective intensities have on users. All these limitations make sentiment analysis difficult to apply in social research, where understanding of the cultural and social context in which a phenomenon is situated is crucial. In our opinion, a privileged sociological field where to experiment with sentiment analysis is that of *affective publics* [8], where the focus of research is more on the *affective ambience* [9] users create around digital content, rather than personal opinions they express on it.

Papacharissi conceptualizes affective publics as networked publics that primarily mobilize and connect or disconnect through expressions of sentiment [10]. This notion expands boyd's conceptualization of networked publics [11] as it stresses that users who participate in online publics might be materially networked by digital infrastructures (e.g. platforms, hashtags, etc.) but are socially and culturally connected through mutual exchanges of affective intensities. Such affective intensities can have different and unexpected social outcomes, since, as Papacharissi [10] stresses, some affective publics connect through common expressions of sentiment, but other disband because of them. The notion of effective public offers researchers a useful analytical category to frame collective participation in large and dispersed digital environments (such as social media) as well as observe the emergence of digital affect cultures [12]. Arguably, affectivity is the property that structures affective publics and keeps them together. Therefore, it is crucial to measure affectivity to see which specific emotions dominate in affective forms of engagement or trace the circulation of affect within digital networks. Anyhow, empirical investigations on affective publics are still scarce. In fact, affect is something ephemeral and difficult to capture. Affect is not emotion; it is an initial drive or sense experienced prior to identifying a particular reaction as an emotion [10]. Nevertheless, digital environments allow tracing these two movements, and in particular the materialization of affectivity into specific emotions in user-generated content. Specifically, social media environments provide 'natively digital instruments' [13] to measure emotions (e.g. through digital texts on which running sentiment analysis) and trace their circulations (e.g. through technicalities like RTs or like buttons). Thus, it important that scholars exploit more the potentialities of 'natively digital instruments' to explore affective publics systematically.

So far, both quantitative and qualitative research tends to concentrate more on the socio-technical architecture of affective publics that is conceived as proxy of affectivity [14]. Quantitative studies focus on massive exchanges of social media metadata (such as RTs or likes) around a given digital content within a short span of time, which they consider as a token of collective manifestation of affectivity [15]. For example, Arvidsson et al. [16] consider teenagers aggregating around the hashtag #onedirection on Twitter as members of an affective public. This is because Onedirection's fans use #onedirection not to chat about music, but as a space of RTs exchange, which they use to express reciprocal emotionally support and/or joy regarding specific news (e.g. the announcement of a Onedirection's concert). Qualitative studies focus more on content, which, nonetheless, is framed as a socio-technical device that channels affectivity. There is an emerging strand of research on affective publics aggregating around visual content [17]. These kinds of studies tend to pay attention to the circulation of repetitive images, showing that they have the capacity to materialize collective affectivity [18]. For example, Döveling et al. [19] show that the affective public emerging around the hashtag #PrayForParis hinge on the circulation of standardized images, which in turn serve to express a common sentiment of grief among a dispersed group of users.

Anyhow, this literature review highlights some methodological gaps. First, there is a scarcity of empirical research on affective publics taking advantage of sentiment analysis. In fact, the analysis of the textual component of digital content might be strategic to measure the actual *structure* and *dynamics* of affective publics, that is: a) the emergence of dominant emotions; b) the transformation of generic effective intensities into specific emotional forms. Second, few studies try to combine sentiment analysis with engagement metrics (e.g. RTs, favs, likes) in order to understand which kinds of emotions have the power to mobilize, keep together or break affective publics apart.

2.2 Scope of the Article and Research Questions

Given the gaps highlighted above, we propose some methodological strategies to explore affective publics in a more systematic way. First, we stress the necessity to 'put sentiment into context'. From an analytical point of view, we propose to take into consideration two different kinds of contexts: *semantic* and *social*. In order to study the semantic context in which a given manifestation of sentiment is situated, we suggest to: 1) detect and distinguish the actual emotions through which the sentiment manifests (i.e. does a negative sentiment express anger or preoccupation?); and 2) associate emotion analysis to keyword analysis (i.e. how has collective anger been expressed?). In order to study to the social context, we suggest analyzing correlations between emotions and social media engagement metrics (e.g. retweets) in order to understand which emotions engage digital publics the most and if and to what extent they are able to mobilize users. In the conclusion we show how these two kinds of analysis turn to be useful to systematically explore the two key components of affective publics: *structure* and *dynamics*.

To illustrate our point, we draw on the analysis of 33,338 tweets written in English and marked with the hashtags #NHSHeroes or #Covidiot. Twitter hashtags #NHSHeroes and #Covidiot were chosen in order to develop an empirical research based on sentiment analysis especially because that allows retrieving texts with clear-cut emotional connotations. Such an approach is appropriate for exploring collective manifestations of sentiments on social media. Specifically, #NHSHeroes had a strong positive connotation and Twitter users used it to support key workers at the UK National Health Service (NHS) who risked their lives to save lives during the lockdown [20]. Conversely, #Covidiot has a pronounced negative connotation since it is meant to publicly shame those people that, due to their reckless behaviour and/or opinions (e.g. not respecting social distancing, believing that Covid-19 is a hoax, etc.), represent a threat to public health [21]. We avoided general hashtags like #coronavirus or #WHO as we expected them to be more neutral in tone and do not concentrate around specific local issues.

Our empirical analysis aims at answering the following research questions:

1) What are the differences in sentiments between the two different affective publics aggregating around #NHSheros and #Covidiot? Which are the dominant emotions characterizing each affective public? Which are the key terms associated to different manifestation of sentiment for each affective public?
2) How do sentiments correlate with engagement metrics (i.e., number of favourites received, retweets, and quote retweets)? Which kinds of emotions are able to engage and mobilize publics the most? Which have the opposite effect?

3   Method

We draw on a dataset of 33,338 tweets focusing on the crucial period between 28th of March and 4th of April, 2020 when Covid-19 started spreading rapidly in the UK. Behavioural change was necessary in this period to minimise the pressure on the NHS. Total number of individuals in the UK who were tested positive for Covid-19 increased from 17,089 to 41,903 during this period [22]. The dataset was obtained via the Twitter Search API (#Covidiot: 15,391, #NHSHeroes: 17,947). These hashtags represented public shaming (#Covidiot) and appreciation of keyworkers (#NHSHeroes). This is dataset did not include retweets as duplicated text affect sentiment scores. The NRC Emotion Lexicon (EmoLex) [23] included in the R Syuzhet package was used to detect sentiments in tweets. EmoLex contains word-sense pairs for eight different emotions (i.e., anger, anticipation, disgust, fear, joy, sadness, surprise, and trust) offering detection of sentiments beyond the popular negative-positive polarity. However, the lexicon can also be used to classify content into two basic sentiment categories. EmoLex includes 14,182 unigrams (words) that associate with the above eight emotions. For instance, words such as 'pandemic' and 'abandon' are associated with fear and sadness and classified as negative [24]. The Lexicon identifies the word 'prevention' as a positive expression associated with the sentiment 'anticipation.' EmoLex was chosen for sentiment detection as there is a wide range of publicly available documentation developed and maintained by an international community of experts and that it has already gained reputation in academic research, especially in information science. Several researchers have applied EmoLex to analyse sentiments in Twitter content. For instance, Yu and Wang [25] use this lexicon to analyse temporal changes in sentiments in tweets sent by American football fans during FIFA World Cup football games. Table 1 shows examples of tweets from each hashtag and sentiment scores calculated using EmoLex. Term frequencies for each sentiment was calculated to examine common words used to express sentiments. Pearson's Correlation Coefficient was calculated to examine relations between sentiment scores and three engagement metrics (retweet count, quote retweet count, and favourite count). This allows understanding whether hashtags that contain certain topical orientations mobilise liking or retweeting more than the others.

Table 1. Sentiment scores and sample tweets

Sentiment Score	Tweet
Fear/5/#NHSHeroes	My mum returned to ICU nursing after a decade in outpatients. She has arthritic knees & hands & is in pain every day. She's frightened of getting ill/dying, or making one of us ill/dead due to PPE shortages. I think they deserve a payrise anyway but especially now #NHSheroes
Joy/7/# NHSHeroes	Today's #PictureOfTheDay dedicated to #nhsworkers #NHSheroes #nhsvolunteers sunlit blossom in the orchard. Turn your face to the spring sunshine. Feel it's loving warmth, allow it to illuminate the dark spaces and heal the hurt. Peace walk with you and blessed be
Sadness/5/# NHSHeroes	This is awful new and potentially avoidable. NHS workers not having adequate PPE is a shameful national tragedy. How many more will fall foul of @DHSCgovuk dithering and delay #NHSHeroes
Surprise/5/#Covidiot	This gave me good laugh, hope it will put a #smile on your face too#Spacecorp#spaceballs#Trump#COVIDIOT https://t.co/FaFmsx2Smk
Trust/6/#Covidiot	Goodness. I hope people don't go to church this weekend. It's not safe. You can pray at home. God will forgive you. Don't be a #COVIDIOT

(continued)

Table 1. (*continued*)

Sentiment Score	Tweet
Anger/6 (#Covidiot)	Cavalier Blind Ignoring science as the virus spreads A perfect horrible storm of your arrogance and ignorance creating an avoidable disaster You can't gaslight a virus with your deadly lies #poetry #poet #coronavirus #TrumpPandemic #vote #CancelTrump #COVIDIOT #poem #poets
Anticipation/6 (#Covidiot)	Goodness. I hope people don't go to church this weekend. It's not safe. You can pray at home. God will forgive you. Don't be a #COVIDIOT
Disgust/5 (#Covidiot)	It's just weird when the #Covidiot in charge speaks of himself in the second and 3rd person. Shame on him to boast about ratings when people are scared, sick and dying. Even his facts are a blatant lie. https://t.co/GOVzWtO5yK

4 Results and Discussion

4.1 Appreciation of Keyworkers: #NHSHeroes

Protecting the NHS was a key focus of the UK government's Covid-19 response strategy and the slogan "stay at home, protect the NHS, save lives" used in the first phase of the Covid-19 response [26] reflected the need for behavioural control in order to ensure that the health service is not overwhelmed. In general, the Twitter hashtag #NHSHeroes aligned with the government slogan and emerged mainly as an appreciation of NHS staff. The positive framing of the hashtag matched well with offline campaigns, such as Clap for Our Carers [21], that gained nationwide popularity. Cumulative sentiments scores (CumSS)—total of sentiments within each category—and mean sentiment values (i.e., cumulative sentiment value divided by the number of tweets in the sample) (Table 2) show that Trust is the most prevalent sentiment in #NHSHeroes (CumSS: 15180). Sentiment with the second highest cumulative score (11191) was fear. The results also indicated that anticipation also had a high cumulative score (10477). Other sentiments, such as anger, disgust, and sadness had considerably lower sentiment scores in this hashtag. Most frequent words used to express sentiments in #NHSHeores (Fig. 1) show that while words such as 'risk', 'pandemic', 'difficult', 'fight', and 'emergency' were used to express fear, words such as 'safe', 'proud', 'team', 'hope', 'lovely', 'brilliant', and 'clap' were used to express trust and anticipation. The above results indicate that #NHSHeores primarily includes a blend of trust, anticipation, and fear and that captures the UK public reaction to the NHS. While the above analysis provides an overall perspective, the EmoLex identified several words, such as hospital, as having relevance to multiple sentiments. This is not inaccurate as words can carry multiple sentiments.

Table 2. Sentiments expressed in #NHSHeroes

Sentiment	Anger	Anticipation	Disgust	Fear	Joy	Sadness	Surprise	Trust
CumSS	3976	10477	2461	11191	5749	5749	4796	15180
Mean	0.233	0.613	0.144	0.655	0.336	0.336	0.28	0.888

5 Public Shaming: #Covidiot

The Twitter hashtag #Covidiot is a marker used to publicly shame those who disregard social distancing measures. This hashtag was more internationally used than #NHSHeroes that mobilised engagement around local Covid-19 response in the UK. Cumulative sentiment scores and mean sentiment scores for #Covidiot are shown in Table 3. The results showed that trust, fear, and sadness dominate #Covidiot. However, top words used to detect sentiments (Fig. 2) indicated that the EmoLex identified words such as 'trump' and 'president' as positive. This is not inaccurate as the word 'trump' connotes victory and 'president' reflects positivity. However, upon manual inspection, we observed that a large number of tweets in #Covidiot were used to criticise President Trump's leadership in the context of the pandemic. Frequent appearance of terms such as 'trumpvirus', 'clustertrump', 'trumpliespeopledie', and 'covidiotinchief' indicates that the hashtag has largely been used as a space for criticising President Trump. When the political use was excluded, fear and sadness were dominant sentiments in this hashtag. Words such as 'pandemic', 'die', 'death', 'dying', 'risk', 'kill', 'bad', 'sick', and 'late' were used frequently to express fear and sadness.

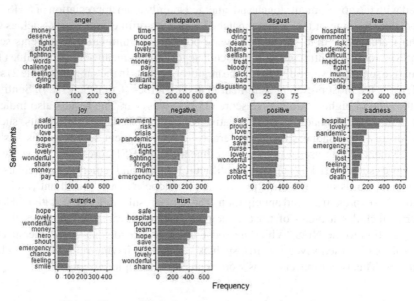

Fig. 1. Top words used to express sentiments (#NHSHeroes)

Table 3. Sentiments expressed in #Covidiot

Sentiment	Anger	Anticipation	Disgust	Fear	Joy	Sadness	Surprise	Trust
CumSS	4644	5303	4355	6954	3560	5704	3631	7217
Mean	0.302	0.345	0.283	0.452	0.231	0.371	0.236	0.469

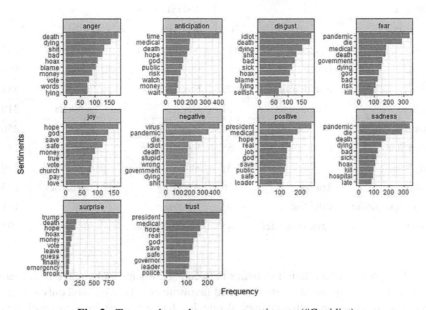

Fig. 2. Top words used to express sentiments (#Covidiot)

5.1 Sentiment Expression and Engagement

Bigram frequencies were calculated to examine content beyond sentiment analysis. Hashtags included in tweets were included in bigram analysis since, as hashtags operate on multiple levels of meaning incorporating both untagged and tagged language and enact an inward and outward facing metadiscourse within and across posts [27, 28]. Table 4 provides top-10 frequently used bigrams after removing slight variants. The bigrams clearly show that #NHSHeroes is largely an issue public that emerged in appreciation of the NHS, UK. The bigram 'nhsthankyou' and 'nhsheroes' had the highest frequency (1627) in #NHSHeroes. The results confirm that #Covidiot included a range of frequently used bigrams, such as 'covidiottrumpvirus' (n= 99), 'covidiot-trumpgenocide' (n= 61), 'trumpliespeoplediecovidiot' (n= 93) that directly attacked President Trump.

Results given in Tables 2 and 3 and visualised in Fig. 3(a) show that trust, fear, and anticipation in #NHSHeroes were considerably higher than #Covidiot. Average mean values for joy and surprise were also higher in #NHSHeroes. Moreover, there were lower levels of anger and disgust in #NHSHeroes than #Covidiot. In general, these results show that while positive sentiments have been used frequently to discuss the pandemic in #NHSHeroes, it contained less negative sentiments than #Covidiot (see Fig. 3b and c). Examining effects of such sentiments can help understand how affective publics organise around the NHS.

Table 4. Most frequently used bigrams

#Covidiot			#NHSHeroes		
Word pair		N	Word pair		N
Social	Distancing	114	Nhsthankyou	nhsheroes	1627
Stay	Home	101	stayhomesavelives	nhsheroes	856
covidiot	trumpvirus	99	Front	line	331
covidiot	Trumpgenocide	61	Key	workers	319
impotus	Covidiot	56	Stay	safe	256
clustertrump	Covidiot	55	Save	lives	181
trumpvirus	Covidiot	51	Stay	home	139
covidiot	Trump	96	Amazing	nhsheroes	125
trumpliespeopledie	Covidiot	93	Amazing	nhs	111
covidiot	covidiotinchief	45	nhsnightingale	nhsheroes	91

Table 5 provides correlation statistics between sentiments and engagement metrics (i.e., retweet count, quote retweet count, and favourite count). We found only minimum levels of correlations in both hashtags. While Joy had a low positive correlation with the retweet count in #Covidiot (r: .019, p < .05), sadness correlated positively with the retweet count in #NHSHeroes. Correlations between sentiment scores and quote retweet count were also not noteworthy. While surprise correlated with the quote retweet count in #Covidiot (r: .039, P <. 05), joy correlated negatively with the quote retweet count in #NHSHeroes (r: −.032, p <. 05). These correlations do not show any convincing mobilisation. However, we observed that all the sentiments except anger and disgust positively correlated with the number of favourites in #NHSHeroes while there were no significant correlations in #Covidiot for the same metric. This shows that the intensity of sentiments in both hashtags do not associate with engagement via retweeting. However, sentiments in #NHSHeroes triggered substantial engagement via liking.

Table 5. Correlations between sentiments and engagement metrics

	#Covidiot		#NHSheroes	
Sentiment	Corr	P	Corr	p
RETWEET COUNT				
Anger	.009	.254	.005	.467
Anticipation	.009	.258	.007	.323

(continued)

Table 5. (*continued*)

Sentiment	#Covidiot		#NHSheroes	
	Corr	P	Corr	p
Disgust	.003	.629	.004	.554
Fear	.009	.256	.013	.067
Joy	.019	.015	.002	.732
Sadness	.001	.938	.018	.015
Surprise	.012	.142	.008	.249
Trust	.008	.277	.014	.056
Negative	.002	'792	.004	.511
Positive	.007	.339	.018	.011
QUOTE RETWEET COUNT				
Anger	.004	.762	.004	.779
Anticipation	.005	.758	− .014	.339
Disgust	.015	.335	.018	.233
Fear	.003	.851	.004	.768
Joy	.001	.960	−.032	.035
Sadness	.012	.438	.000	.969
Surprise	.039	.014	−.013	.372
Trust	.032	.052	−.015	.310
Negative	.022	.161	.029	.056
Positive	.007	.654	−.020	.193
FAVORITE COUNT				
Anger	.010	.196	.007	.323
Anticipation	.015	.057	.017	.021
Disgust	.006	.419	.012	.098
Fear	.009	.260	.020	.006
Joy	.026	.000	.016	.024
Sadness	.000	.968	.027	.000
Surprise	.029	.078	.016	.025
Trust	.015	.054	.021	.004
Negative	.005	.530	.005	.479
Positive	.017	.032	.030	.000

Enacting a constructive public discourse is crucial for the effectiveness of the UK national response to Covid-19 as it allows behavioural change on a wider level as opposed

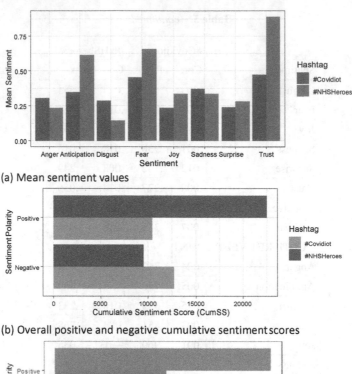

(a) Mean sentiment values

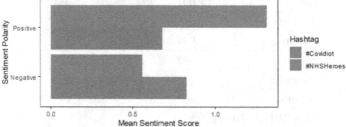

(b) Overall positive and negative cumulative sentiment scores

(c) Overall positive and negative cumulative sentiment scores

Fig. 3. Mean sentiment values and overall cumulative sentiment scores

to reactive measures such as penalties. Scholars have argued that social media users are primarily organised via affective forms of engagement that ultimately drive their behaviour [8]. A crucial step in understanding the 'health' of such a discourse is to detect emotions expressed in social media posts that continue to accumulate in networked issue publics. Positive emotions and significant correlations between sentiment scores and favorite count show that #NHSHeoroes, as a Twitter public, has mobilised users, at least by encouraging acts of liking to a significant level. Conversely, such mobilisation was not present in #Covidiot. This indicates that the Twitter hashtag #NHSHeroes is a more intense set of positive affective reactions than #Covidiot and it has been more successful in mobilising users. This shows that a local focus and valorisation of keyworkers is more effective in mobilising engagement in the context of Covid-19. Collective shaming and more general framing of the discourse using markers such as #Covidiot do not mobilise engagement, at least within the limits our data. It should, however, be noted that the positive effect that we observe in #NHSHeroes is only a slight impact as correlations were low. In general, lack of strong correlations between engagement metrics and sentiments show that expression of sentiment is the primary function of both hashtags rather than collective engagement, particularly in #Covodiot. This supports Papacharissi's [10] claim that affective publics facilitate connective rather than collective action. However, the above correlations should not be underestimated as facilitating emotion expression itself is a significant role that social media can play in the context of the pandemic.

As Marwick and boyd pointed out [29], people send tweets for a variety of reasons, from micro-celebrity practices to keeping a diary, and they do not necessarily expect audience engagement. In this case, dominance of positive sentiments in #NHSHeroes indicate alignment of user emotions with desirable behaviour in response to the pandemic. Positive reactions in the #NHSHeroes above are consistent to some extent with the UK public attitudes towards the NHS. A public satisfaction survey conducted in 2019 showed that the overall public satisfaction with the NHS was at 60% [30]. Another report showed that, by 2015, 89% of a sample of the British public supported a publicly funded national healthcare system [31]. Our results discussed above reflects those positive public attitudes towards the NHS. For instance, the tweet given in Fig. 4(top) received a high trust (value: 5) and anticipation (value: 5) in our analysis and it shows positive attitudes towards NHS staff. The public attitudes in a previous survey also indicated that 43% of respondents did not see any improvement in the NHS [31] and that the majority of the people would prefer extra funding for the NHS [30]. Therefore, some negative emotions relate to lack of funding for the NHS and the consumer logic that it has embraced [31]. The tweet that received a high anger score (value: 6) in our analysis (Fig. 4b), for instance, directly shows anger towards the lack of personal protective equipment in hospitals.

So great to hear this Jim ..if you get symptoms act on them immediately ..help with breathing is essential for a successful recovery ..The NHS staff are amazing on every level and I'm so glad that food / meals are being organised for them ...they deserve the best #NHSheroes

(a) A tweet with positive sentiments that contains high trust

It's an utter disgrace NHS staff are still not being tested & still not being given the ppe they need? They're desperately trying to save lives, whilst fearing they might lose their own 😨 you wouldn't send a soldier to fight without a gun @BorisJohnson #COVID19 #NHS #NHSheroes

(b) A tweet with negative sentiments that contains high anger

Fig. 4. Positive and negative reactions related to NHS

6 Conclusion

The basic sentiment analysis indicates, unsurprisingly, that #NHSheroes is character-ized by an overall positive sentiment as opposed to more negative reactions in #Covidiot. Anyhow, a more refined sentiment analysis that combines emotion detection, text analy-sis and engagement metrics provides a more comprehensive view. Specifically, it allows exploring the *emotional structure* of affective publics aggregating around #NHSheroes and #Covidiot as well as their *dynamics* of affect coalescence into specific emotional forms. Regarding #NHSheroes, we observe that users do not simply post generic posi-tive opinions about NHS and its workers. Instead, they collectively express a sentiment of trust towards them. Moreover, text analysis allows reconstructing narratives users articulate within these collective expressions of sentiment: notwithstanding users are concerned by Covid-19 *'emergency'* and the *'risks'* and *'difficulties'* brought about by the *'pandemic'*, they feel *'safe'* because of the *'brilliant'* work of the NSH *'team'*, of which they are *'proud'*.

Conversely, the text analysis indicates that the hashtag #Covidiot is 'hijacked' by some users who make it 'political'. At least within the limits of our data, #Covidiot is used to a great extent as a pretext for criticizing Donald Trump rather than as a generic tool of public shaming. In general, President Trump is portrayed as the prototype 'Covidiot'. This narrative stirs a bundle of negative emotions, like *fear*, *sadness*, and *anger*. It should also be noted that the #Covidiot affective public seems to represent a mixed bag of emotions in which single emotions do not emerge as dominant. In fact, the public is dominated by two opposite emotions: Trust (0.469) and Fear (0.452). Probably this ambiguity is due to the underlying inconsistency of the #Covidiot hashtag itself: the hashtag is meant to ridicule *covidiots,* but in practice, it is used to criticize President Trump. Finally, we observe that #NHSeoroes, as a locally oriented Twitter public, has mobilized users, at least by encouraging acts of liking. This shows that regional and more positive reactions can trigger more reactions from users than more general and negatively framed messages. In conclusion, affective publics reflect a blend of emotions. In some cases, such generic flow of affect coalesces into a dominant emotion. Affective publics structured around positive emotions and local issues tend to be more consistent and cohesive than those based on negative emotions. Although negative emotions might attract the attention of networked publics, positively framed messages can engage users more. We acknowledge that these results are just preliminary and more (and more diverse) affective publics must be investigated to verify our conclusions.

Moreover, our analysis started investigating the strict nexus existing between affec-tivity flowing within networked publics and the specific emotions into which the affective flow fixes itself. To do that we proposed to use a quantitative technique: sentiment anal-ysis, which allows to measure both affect and emotions. Anyway, further research needs to be done to fully understand the above mentioned nexus. For example, researchers might observe the changing of sentiment overtime, in order to see if, within an effective flux, there are specific emotions enduring overtime and why. As far as the analysis of semantic contexts are concerned, researchers can mix text analysis with cohashtag anal-ysis in order to better understand the meaning of sentiment and its social use. Lastly, as far as users' engagement is concerned, further research might investigate how sentiment 'behaves' in different social formations (like publics, communities or crowds) and to what extent it is crucial to keep them alive, active and proactive. Finally, we believe, understanding sentiments that dominate the current Covid-19 discourse is crucial in understanding 'collective emotions' as well as developing intervention strategies as the UK struggles to defeat the pandemic. Moreover, affect based engagement strategies are necessary for the development of coping strategies in a post-pandemic society, especially due to the seriousness of trauma that the public had to endure.

References

1. Cambria, E.: Affective computing and sentiment analysis. IEEE Intell. Syst. **31**, 102–107 (2016). https://doi.org/10.1109/MIS.2016.31
2. Ghiassi, M., Skinner, J., Zimbra, D.: Twitter brand sentiment analysis: a hybrid system using n-gram analysis and dynamic artificial neural network. Expert Syst. Appl. **40**, 6266–6282 (2013). https://doi.org/10.1016/j.eswa.2013.05.057
3. King, G., Pan, J., Roberts, M.E.: How censorship in China allows government criticism but silences collective expression. Am. Polit. Sci. Rev. **107**, 326–343 (2013). https://doi.org/10. 1017/S0003055413000014
4. Marres, N.: Digital Sociology: The Reinvention of Social Research. Wiley, London (2017)
5. coronavirus.data.gov.uk Coronavirus (COVID-19) in the UK. https://coronavirus.data. gov.uk/. Access 29–30 July 2020
6. The Guardian view of Boris Johnson's crisis: blunder after blunder. Guard (2020)
7. Caliandro, A., Gandini, A.: Qualitative Research in Digital Environments: A Research Toolkit. Routledge (2017)
8. Papacharissi, Z.: Affective Publics: Sentiment, Technology, and Politics. Oxford University Press, Oxford (2015)
9. Zappavigna, M.: Ambient affiliation: a linguistic perspective on Twitter. New Media Soc. **13**(5), 788–806 (2011). https://doi.org/10.1177/1461444810385097
10. Papacharissi, Z.: Affective publics and structures of storytelling . sentiment, events and mediality. Info Com Soc **19**(3), 307–324 (2016). https://doi.org/10.1080/1369118X.2015. 1109697
11. Boyd Danah: Social Network Sites as networked publics: affordances, dynamics, and implications. In: Papacharissi, Z. (ed.) A networked self: Identity, Community, and Culture on Social Network Sites. Routledge Taylor & Francis Group, New York and London, pp. 39–35 (2011)
12. Ash, J.: Sensation Networks and the GIF: Toward and Allotropic Account of Affect in Networked Affect. MIT press, Cambridge (2015)
13. Rogers, R.: Digital Methods. MIT Press, Cambridge (2019)
14. Stage, C.: The online crowd: a contradiction in terms? On the potentials of Gustave Le Bon's crowd psychology in an analysis of affective blogging. Distinktion **14**(2), 211–226 (2013). https://doi.org/10.1080/1600910X.2013.773261
15. Arvidsson, A., Caliandro, A.: Brand public. J. Con. Res. **42**(5), 727–748 (2016). https://doi. org/10.1093/jcr/ucv053
16. Arvidsson, A., et al.: Crowds and value: Italian directioners on Twitter. Inf. Commun. Soc. **19**(7), 921–939 (2016). https://doi.org/10.1080/1369118X.2015.1064462
17. Geboers, M.: 'Writing' oneself into tragedy: Visual user practices and spectatorship of the Alan Kurdi images on Instagram. Vis. Commun. **0**, 1–25 (2019). https://doi.org/10.1177/147 0357219857118
18. Gibbs, M., et al.: #Funeral and Instagram: Death, social media, and platform vernacular. Inf. Commun. Soc. **18**(3), 255–268 (2015). https://doi.org/10.1080/1369118X.2014.987152

19. Döveling, K., Harju, A., Sommer, D.: From mediatized emotion to digital affect cultures: new technologies and global flows of emotion. Soc. Media Soc. **4**, 1 (2018). https://doi.org/10.1177/2056305117743141
20. Miller, K.: What Does "Covidiot" Mean, and Who Qualifies as One? (2020). www.health.com.https://www.health.com/condition/infectiousdiseases/coronavirus/what-does-covidiot-mean. Accessed 30 July 2020
21. Clap for our carers(2020). https://clapforourcarers.co.uk/. Accessed 22 Apr 2020
22. Total UK COVID-19 cases update. In: Public Heal. Engl (2020). https://www.arcgis.com/apps/opsdashboard/index.html#/f94c3c90da5b4e9f9a0b19484dd4bb14. Accessed 8 Apr 2020
23. Mohammad, S.M., Turney, P.D.: Crowdsourcing a word-emotion association lexicon. Comput. Intell. **29**, 436–465 (2013)
24. NRC Word-Emotion Association Lexicon. https://saifmohammad.com/WebPages/NRC-Emotion-Lexicon.htm. Accessed 9 Apr 2020
25. Yu, Y., Wang, X.: World Cup 2014 in the Twitter world: a big data analysis of sentiments in U.S. sports fans' tweets. Comput. Hum. Behav. **48**, 392–400 (2015). https://doi.org/10.1016/j.chb.2015.01.075
26. www.gov.uk (2020) Coronavirus: stay at home, protect the NHS, save lives - web version. https://www.gov.uk/government/publications/coronavirus-covid-19-information-leaflet/coronavirus-stay-at-home-protect-the-nhs-save-lives- web-version. Accessed 14 Apr 2020
27. Zappavigna, M.: Searchable talk: the linguistic functions of hashtags. Soc. Semiot. **25**, 274–291 (2015). https://doi.org/10.1080/10350330.2014.996948
28. Zappavigna, M.: Searchable talk: Hashtags and social media metadiscourse. Bloomsbury (2018)
29. Marwick, A.E., Boyd, D.: I tweet honestly, I tweet passionately: Twitter users, context collapse, and the imagined audience. New Media Soc. **13**, 114–133 (2010). https://doi.org/10.1177/1461444810365313
30. John, A., Nina, H., David, M., et al.: Public satisfaction with the NHS and social care in 2019: Results and trends from the British Social Attitudes survey (2019)
31. Gershlick, B., Charlesworth, A., Taylor, E.: Public attitudes to the NHS: an analysis of responses to questions in the British Social Attitudes Survey (2015)
32. Sturgeon, D.: The business of the NHS: the rise and rise of consumer culture and commodification in the provision of healthcare services. Crit. Soc. Policy **34**, 405–416 (2014). https://doi.org/10.1177/0261018314527717
33. Rogers, R.: The end of the virtual: Digital methods (2009). https://dare.uva.nl/aup/nl/record/332324

Fine-Grained Sentiment Analysis of Political Tweets with Entity-Aware Multimodal Network

Li Yang[1], Jianfei Yu[2(✉)], Chengzhi Zhang[2], and Jin-Cheon Na[3]

[1] DBS Bank, Marina Bay Financial Centre, Singapore, Singapore
liyang@dbs.com
[2] Nanjing University of Science and Technology, Nanjing, China
{jfyu,zhangcz}@njust.edu.cn
[3] Nanyang Technological University, 50 Nanyang Avenue, Singapore, Singapore
tjcna@ntu.edu.sg

Abstract. Fine-grained sentiment analysis of social platforms like Twitter and Facebook nowadays becomes increasingly important, as it can reflect public opinions towards target entities such as politicians. Entity-Level Sentiment Analysis (ELSA) is an important fine-grained SA task, aiming to identify the sentiment over each entity mentioned in a sentence. Most previous methods to this task primarily rely on the text, but ignoring the other useful multimodal data sources (e.g., images). Therefore, in this paper, we aim to explore the usefulness of associated images for ELSA in multimodal tweets (especially political tweets). Specifically, we propose an Entity-Aware Multimodal Network (EAMN), and apply it to political tweets for understanding public opinions towards some politicians. Experiment results show that the associated images are generally useful for ELSA, and our EAMN model achieves the state-of-the-art results on two public Twitter datasets and our political Twitter datasets.

Keywords: Fine-grained sentiment analysis · Multimodal sentiment analysis · Opinion mining · Political tweets

1 Introduction

With the vast amount of user-generated contents daily produced on social media, it becomes increasingly important to analyze these social contents to identify public opinions towards target entities such as politicians and organizations. Entity-Level Sentiment Analysis (ELSA) is the task of detecting sentiment polarities towards target entities in an input sentence. For example, given the tweet in Fig. 1.a, it is expected to identify that the user expresses *positive* and *neutral* sentiment towards *Donald Trump* and *Washington state*, respectively.

Many social platforms such as Twitter now become powerful political tools in campaigns and governing. On the one hand, social media has been the main channel for political parties to promote policies and communicate with the public [1]. On the other hand, social media allows common people to easily express

© Springer Nature Switzerland AG 2021
K. Toeppe et al. (Eds.): iConference 2021, LNCS 12645, pp. 411–420, 2021.
https://doi.org/10.1007/978-3-030-71292-1_31

(a). [**Donald Trump**]$_{POS}$ is projected winner in [**Washington state**]$_{NEU}$ GOP primary

(b). In [**Ohio**]$_{NEU}$ today @[**DonaldTrump**]$_{POS}$

(c). [**Donald Trump**]$_{NEG}$ Releases [**Supreme Court**]$_{NEU}$ Justice Nominee List

Fig. 1. Examples of entity-Level sentiment analysis (ELSA) in multimodal tweets. Entities and their corresponding sentiments are highlighted. POS, NEG, and NEU denote the positive, negative, and neutral sentiment respectively.

the opinions towards target policies or politicians. Hence, it is crucial for governments or politicians to analyze political tweets to understand the public opinion, which may help them quickly adjust their policies.

Due to its importance in opinion mining, ELSA has been well studied in the literature. Earlier studies focused on designing effective features for target entities, and feeding them to linear classifiers [2–4]. With the recent trend of deep learning, many neural models have been adapted to this task, including Convolutional Neural Networks [5], Recurrent Neural Networks [6,7], and Transformer [8]. However, most of these approaches only focus on textual content, but fail to consider the other associated data sources (e.g., images).

As multimodal tweets nowadays become increasingly popular in social media, it is important to incorporate the associated images to better understand users' sentiment orientations due to a couple of reasons. First, due to the informal nature of social media, the textual content tends to be short and even incomplete, and it is often necessary to combine the textual and visual content to detect users' sentiment (e.g., Fig. 1.b). Second, most multimodal tweets (especially political tweets) tend to contain sarcasm, and it is often the case that users' sentiment can only be inferred from the associated image (e.g., in Fig. 1.c, the image of evil monster reflects user's negative sentiment towards *Donald Trump*).

To this end, our objective in this paper is to explore the usefulness of images for the task of ELSA in multimodal political tweets. Specifically, we propose an Entity-Aware Multimodal Network (EAMN), which first models the entity-text and entity-image interactions with a novel entity-aware Transformer layer, followed by fusing the textual and visual information for sentiment prediction. Then, we manually choose tweets mentioning politicians from two public multimodal Twitter datasets for ELSA [9], which form our political Twitter datasets. Experiment results on both public and our political Twitter datasets show the usefulness of images for ELSA and the effectiveness of our EAMN model.

2　Related Work

As an important subtask in sentiment analysis, Entity-Level Sentiment Analysis (ELSA) has drawn increasing attention in recent years. Traditional methods focus

Table 1. The types and names of politicians in our political Twitter datasets

Types of politicians	Entity names (i.e., Names of politicians)
President of U.S.	Donald Trump, Barack Obama, Bill Clinton, George W. Bush, George H.W. Bush, John F. Kennedy
Presidential candidates in U.S.	Hillary Clinton, Bernie Sanders, John Kasich, Ted Cruz, Marco Rubio, Jeb Bush, Carly Fiorina
Other politicians in U.S.	Joe Biden, Paul Ryan, Rahm Emanuel, Elizabeth Warren, Sarah Palin, Rudy Giuliani, Lindsey Graham
Politicians in other countries	Putin, Jeremy Corbyn

on designing many task-specific features, followed by training a traditional classifier for sentiment classification [10, 11]. With the development of deep learning, many methods propose to adopt various NN models to encode the targets and the related context [5, 12]. More recently, different kinds of attention mechanisms are introduced to model the interactions between target and context [6, 13, 14]. However, most of them only focus on text, but ignore the impact of associated images, which is the focus of our work.

With the recent popularity of multimodal posts in social media, several studies have explored the usefulness of associated images for the ELSA task. Specifically, [15] and [9] respectively proposed two neural networks based on the traditional LSTM model and the standard attention mechanism. In contrast, we follow [16] by constructing our model upon the recent pre-trained BERT model [17] and self-attention mechanism [18]. Moreover, different from previous studies, our work primarily focuses on multimodal tweets mentioning politicians, and contributes two Political Twitter datasets for the study of ELSA.

3 Methodology

In this section, we first define our task, and then introduce our datasets, followed by delving into the details of our proposed EAMN model.

Task Definition: For each multimodal tweet, we are given a sentence S with n words, a target entity T (a sub-sequence of words in S), and its associated image I as inputs, and our goal is to predict the sentiment orientation y over the target entity T, where y can be either *positive*, *negative* or *neutral*.

3.1 Datasets

Public Twitter Datasets. Based on our preliminary investigation, there are two publicly available multimodal Twitter datasets for the task of ELSA (i.e., *Public-15* and *Public-17*) collected by Yu et al. [9]. These two datasets include diverse multimodal tweets posted during 2014–2015 and 2016–2017.

Our Political Twitter Datasets. This paper aims to analyze multimodal tweets related to politicians. Therefore, we manually selected multimodal tweets

Table 2. The basic statistics of the Public Twitter and our Political Twitter datasets

Label	Public-15			Public-17			Political-15			Political-17		
	Train	Dev	Test	Train	Dev	Test	Train	Dev	Test	Train	Dev	Test
Positive	928	303	317	1508	515	493	1519	-	29	2369	-	147
Neutral	1883	670	607	1638	517	573	3081	-	79	2439	-	289
Negative	368	149	113	416	144	168	593	-	37	460	-	268
Total	3179	1122	1037	3562	1176	1234	5193	-	145	5268	-	704

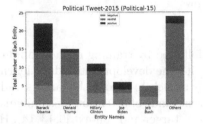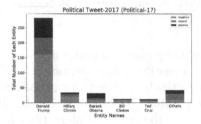

Fig. 2. Sentiment distribution of each entity in our two Political Twitter datasets

mentioning four types of politicians from the two public datasets, as shown in Table 1. Since the number of political tweets is relatively small, we treat all the political tweets as the test set, and the remaining tweets in *Public-15* and *Public-17* as the training set, where 15% samples are the development set for parameter tuning. We name our two datasets as *Political-15* and *Political-17*.

To provide more insight into our two Political Twitter datasets, we show the sentiment distribution of the top-5 entities in Fig. 2. From its two subfigures, we can find that the U.S. president or presidential candidate (i.e., *Barack Obama*, *Donald Trump*, and *Hillary Clinton*) draw the most attention for both datasets. Besides, the public tends to express neutral or negative sentiment when mentioning most politicians except *Barack Obama*.

The basic statistics of all the four datasets are shown in Table 2.

3.2   Entity-Aware Multimodal Network (EAMN)

As illustrated in Fig. 3, our model contains three key modules: Feature Extraction Module, Entity-Aware Interaction Module, and Gated Fusion Module.

Feature Extraction Module. To extract effective features from the input text and images, we apply two pre-trained deep learning models (i.e., BERT [17] and ResNet [19]) to respectively obtain the textual and visual representations.

For the textual input, since our goal is to predict the sentiment over the entity T, we split each sentence S into two sub-sentences: the entity T and the remaining context C, followed by using two separate BERT encoders to obtain their hidden representations, respectively. For example, the textual input for the tweet in Fig. 1.a is given in the bottom of Fig. 3. Formally, we use $\mathbf{C} = \text{BERT}(C)$ and $\mathbf{T} = \text{BERT}(T)$ to denote the context and the entity representations generated from BERT respectively, where $\mathbf{C} \in \mathbb{R}^{d \times |C|}$ and $\mathbf{T} \in \mathbb{R}^{d \times |T|}$.

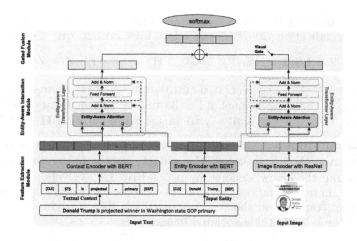

Fig. 3. The overall framework of our entity-aware multimodal network

For the visual input, we adopt one of the state-of-the-art CNN models called Residual Network (ResNet) [19] to extract visual features of different regions in images. Given an input image $\mathbf{I}$, we first resize it to 224×224 pixels as $\mathbf{I}'$, and then keep the output from the last convolutional layer in a pre-trained 152-layer ResNet model[1] to obtain the image representation as $\mathbf{R} = \text{ResNet}(\mathbf{I}')$, where $\mathbf{R} \in \mathbb{R}^{2048 \times 49}$. Finally, we employ a linear transformation function to project the image representation into the space of the text representation as: $\mathbf{V} = \mathbf{W}^{\top}\mathbf{R}$, where $\mathbf{W} \in \mathbb{R}^{2048 \times d}$ is the weight matrix.

Entity-Aware Interaction Module. Since we aim to predict the sentiment over the given entity, modeling interactions between the entity and the context (or the image) can help find the most important words in the context (or the most relevant visual regions in the image) with respect to the input entity.

To achieve this, we design two symmetric Entity-Aware Transformer Layers to model the entity-text and entity-image interactions respectively, as illustrated in the middle part of Fig. 3. For brevity, we only introduce the left channel. Inspired by the multi-head self-attention mechanism [18], we first design an m-head entity-aware attention (MEATT), by treating the entity representation $\mathbf{T}$ as queries, and the text representation $\mathbf{C}$ as keys and values, which can guide the model to select the most important words in the context $\mathbf{C}$:

$$\text{EATT}_i(\mathbf{T}, \mathbf{C}) = \text{softmax}(\frac{[\mathbf{Q}_i\mathbf{T}]^{\top}[\mathbf{K}_i\mathbf{C}]}{\sqrt{d/m}})[\mathbf{V}_i\mathbf{C}]^{\top}, \tag{1}$$

$$\text{MEATT}(\mathbf{T}, \mathbf{C}) = \mathbf{W}_m[\text{EATT}_1(\mathbf{T}, \mathbf{C}), \dots, \text{EATT}_m(\mathbf{T}, \mathbf{C})]^{\top}, \tag{2}$$

where EATT_i denotes the i-th head of our entity-aware attention, $\{\mathbf{Q}_i, \mathbf{K}_i, \mathbf{V}_i\} \in \mathbb{R}^{d/m \times d}$ are weight matrices for queries, keys, and values respectively, and

---

[1] https://download.pytorch.org/models/resnet152-b121ed2d.pth.

$\mathbf{W}_m \in \mathbb{R}^{d \times d}$ is a weight matrix. Next, we follow Transformer [18] by stacking two layer normalization [20] (LN) and a feed-forward network [18] (FFN):

$$\mathbf{Z} = \text{LN}(\mathbf{T} + \text{MEATT}(\mathbf{T}, \mathbf{C})); \quad \mathbf{H}_C = \text{LN}(\text{FFN}(\mathbf{Z}) + \mathbf{Z}), \tag{3}$$

where $\mathbf{H}_C \in \mathbb{R}^{d \times |T|}$ is the generated entity-aware context representation.

Similarly, in the right channel of Fig. 3, we use another Entity-Aware Transformer Layer to obtain the entity-aware image representation $\mathbf{H}_V \in \mathbb{R}^{d \times |T|}$.

Gated Fusion Module. After capturing the entity-text and entity-image interactions, we treat the first token of $\mathbf{H}_C$ and $\mathbf{H}_V$ as the final representations of the context and the image, denoted by $\mathbf{h}_C$ and $\mathbf{h}_V$ respectively.

Moreover, in real scenarios, the input images of some tweets may be irrelevant to the textual context and should be ignored. We thus introduce a visual gate to alleviate the noise of the associated image:

$$\mathbf{g} = \sigma(\mathbf{W}_C \mathbf{h}_C + \mathbf{W}_V \mathbf{h}_V + \mathbf{b}_g), \tag{4}$$

where $\mathbf{W}_V, \mathbf{W}_C \in \mathbb{R}^{d \times d}$ are weight matrices, and σ is the element-wise sigmoid function. Next, we can obtain the gated image representation: $\mathbf{h}'_V = \mathbf{g} \cdot \mathbf{h}_V$.

Finally, we integrate the context representation and the gated image representation by performing element-wise addition, and feed it to a softmax function for entity-level sentiment classification:

$$p(y|\mathbf{h}_C, \mathbf{h}'_V) = \text{softmax}(\mathbf{W}^\top (\mathbf{h}_C + \mathbf{h}'_V) + \mathbf{b}), \tag{5}$$

where $\mathbf{W} \in \mathbb{R}^{d \times 3}$ and $\mathbf{b} \in \mathbb{R}^3$ are learnable parameters.

Model Training. To optimize all the model parameters, our objective is to minimize the following function with the standard cross-entropy loss:

$$\mathcal{J} = -\frac{1}{N} \sum_{j=1}^{N} \log p(y^{(j)}|\mathbf{h}_C^{(j)}, \mathbf{h}'_V{}^{(j)}). \tag{6}$$

4   Experiments and Result Analysis

Hyperparameters. Our EAMN model is based on the uncased $BERT_{base}$ model pre-trained by [17]. We set the batch size as 32, the number of attention heads as $m = 12$, the learning rate as 5e-5, the dropout rate as 0.1, and the number of training epochs as 10. Besides, the maximum length of the context input and the entity input are set as $|C| = 64$ and $|T| = 16$. All the models are implemented with PyTorch on a NVIDIA RTX GPU.

4.1   Main Results

In this subsection, we compare with the following unimodal and multimodal approaches on Accuracy (ACC) and Macro-F_1 (Mac-F_1) for the ELSA task: (1) **Res-Entity**: concatenating $\mathbf{T}$ and the max-pooling value of $\mathbf{V}$ in Sect. 3.2. (2)

Table 3. Experimental results on two public multimodal Twitter datasets

	Method	Public-15		Public-17	
		ACC	Mac-F_1	ACC	Mac-F_1
Image	Res-Entity	59.88	46.48	58.59	53.98
Text	AE-LSTM	70.30	63.43	61.67	57.97
	MemNet	70.11	61.76	64.18	60.90
	RAM	70.68	63.05	64.42	61.01
	BERT	74.15	68.86	68.15	65.23
Text+Image	Res-RAM	71.55	64.68	65.40	62.23
	MIMN	71.84	65.69	65.88	62.99
	ESAFN	73.38	67.37	67.83	64.22
	ResBERT	75.02	69.21	69.20	66.48
	EAMN	**75.80**	**71.44**	**70.75**	**67.89**

Table 4. Experimental results on our two political multimodal Twitter datasets

	Method	Political-15		Political-17	
		ACC	Mac-F_1	ACC	Mac-F_1
Image	Res-Entity	57.24	47.09	46.73	45.65
Text	AE-LSTM	64.83	55.84	54.40	50.26
	MemNet	63.45	59.82	49.86	47.85
	RAM	65.52	59.93	54.97	51.72
	BERT	70.34	66.53	65.34	64.82
Text+Image	Res-RAM	67.58	57.07	54.97	50.84
	MIMN	66.21	60.16	55.54	53.68
	ESAFN	67.59	60.31	55.68	53.33
	ResBERT	69.66	65.72	65.48	64.98
	EAMN	**74.48**	**71.54**	**67.19**	**66.53**

AE-LSTM [13]: incorporating entity-specific attention mechanism into LSTM. (3) **MemNet** [21]: applying the multi-hop memory network to the ELSA task; (4) **RAM** [22]: a LSTM-based method to capture the relative distance to the entity; (5) **BERT** [8]: applies the pre-trained BERT model to the ELSA task; (6) **Res-RAM** and **ResBERT**: combining textual and visual features by concatenating the max-pooling value of **V** with the text representation of **RAM** and **BERT**, respectively; (7) **MIMN** [15]: a multi-hop multimodal memory network to capture the interaction of text and images; (8) **ESAFN** [9]: an entity-sensitive attention and fusion network to capture the inter-modal interactions.

Based on the results in Table 3 and Table 4, we made the following observations: 1) For the purely visual method, *Res-Entity* performs the worst, which indicates the importance of the textual context in our ELSA task. 2) Most multimodal methods perform better than unimodal methods, which demonstrates that associated images are generally complementary to text, and can improve the performance of purely text-based approaches. 3) our EAMN model consistently achieves the best results on all the datasets by outperforming the second best system with a significant margin, which verifies the effectiveness of our model.

4.2 Discussion

The Effect of Associated Images. To better understand the effect of associated images, we analyze the prediction results of different models on the test set of *Political-17*. From the 2nd and 4th columns of Fig. 5, we can see that incorporating associated images can help correct BERT's predictions on over 70 samples. However, from the 1st and 3rd columns, we can observe that incorporating images also brings some noise. This is reasonable, because associated images are sometimes not closely related to the textual content and the target entity. Also, compared with ResBERT, our EAMN model better alleviates the noise from images, due to our entity-aware attention mechanism and visual gate.

The Advantage of Our EAMN Model. Moreover, we choose two representative examples to compare the predictions of different methods. First, in

(a) [**Donald Trump NEG**][1] just held the weirdest Cabinet meeting ever — Analysis by @ [**CillizzaCNN NEU**][2].

(b) With [**Donald Trump NEG**][1] as presumptive nominee, some in [**GOP NEU**][2] say they're breaking away from party.

BERT:(1-POS×, 2-NEU✓)
ResBERT:(1-NEG✓,2-NEU✓)
EAMN:(1-NEG✓, 2-NEU✓)

BERT:(1-NEG✓, 2-NEU✓)
ResBERT:(1-NEU×, 2-NEU✓)
EAMN.(1-NEG✓, 2-NEU✓)

Fig. 4. Prediction comparison. ✓ and × denote the correct and incorrect predictions.

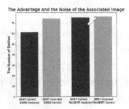

Fig. 5. The effect of associated images

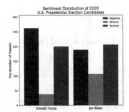

Fig. 6. Predicted sentiment distribution of Trump and Biden on 1000 tweets in Oct 2020

Fig. 4.a, we can see that with the help of the image containing serious faces, both ResBERT and EAMN can correctly identify the sentiment towards *Donald Trump* as negative. This shows the usefulness of combining textual and visual contents for the ELSA task. Second, in Fig. 4.b, since ResBERT cannot alleviate the image noise, it wrongly predict the sentiment over *Donald Trump* as neutral, whereas our EAMN can eliminate the noise to make correct predictions.

Model Deployment: Finally, we deployed our EAMN model. Specifically, we randomly collected 1000 multimodal tweets posted in Oct 2020, which mentioned the two candidates (i.e., Donald Trump and Joe Biden) for the 2020 U.S. presidential election. Next, we employed our EAMN model trained on *Political-17* to perform entity-level sentiment classification, and the results are shown in Fig. 6. First, by comparing Figs. 6 and 2, we can see that the sentiment distribution is similar, as most people still tend to express negative sentiment towards Trump and Biden. Second, we can find that Biden has higher (lower) percentage of positive (negative) tweets than Trump, which probably reflect people's latest opinions towards the two presidential candidates on the Twitter platform.

5   Conclusion

In this paper, we explored the usefulness of images for the task of ELSA in multimodal political tweets. Specifically, we proposed an Entity-Aware Multimodal Network, which first models the entity-text and entity-image interactions with a new entity-aware Transformer layer, followed by a gated fusion module to integrate the multimodal information for sentiment prediction. Experimental results on two public datasets and our political datasets show that (1) the associated images can generally benefit the ELSA task; (2) our model can outperform the state-of-the-art unimodal and multimodal systems by a significant margin.

Acknowledgments. This work was supported by the Natural Science Foundation of China (No. 62006117) and Jiangsu Province (No. BK20200463) for Young Scholars.

References

1. Kreis, R.: The "tweet politics" of president trump. J. Lang. Politics **16**(4), 607–618 (2017)
2. Jiang, L., Yu, M., Zhou, M., Liu, X., Zhao, T.: Target-dependent twitter sentiment classification. In: Proceedings of ACL, pp. 151–160 (2011)
3. Al-Smadi, M., Al-Ayyoub, M., Jararweh, Y., Qawasmeh, O.: Enhancing aspect-based sentiment analysis of Arabic hotels' reviews using morphological, syntactic and semantic features. Inf. Process. Manage. **56**(2), 308–319 (2019)
4. Chakraborty, S., Goyal, P., Mukherjee, A.: Aspect-based sentiment analysis of scientific reviews. In: Proceedings of JCDL (2020)
5. Xue, W., Li, T.: Aspect based sentiment analysis with gated convolutional networks. In: Proceedings of ACL, pp. 2514–2523 (2018)
6. Liu, Z., Na, J.C.: Aspect-based sentiment analysis of nuclear energy tweets with attentive deep neural network. In: Proceedings of ICADL, pp. 99–111 (2018)
7. Song, M., Park, H., Shin, K.S.: Attention-based long short-term memory network using sentiment lexicon embedding for aspect-level sentiment analysis in Korean. Inf. Process. Manage. **56**(3), 637–653 (2019)
8. Xu, H., Liu, B., Shu, L., Philip, S.Y.: Bert post-training for review reading comprehension and aspect-based sentiment analysis. In: Proceedings of NAACL-HLT (2019)
9. Yu, J., Jiang, J., Xia, R.: Entity-sensitive attention and fusion network for entity-level multimodal sentiment classification. IEEE/ACM Trans. Audio Speech Lang. Process. **28**, 429–439 (2020)
10. Kiritchenko, S., Zhu, X., Cherry, C., Mohammad, S.: Nrc-canada-2014: Detecting aspects and sentiment in customer reviews. In: Proceedings of SemEval, pp. 437–442 (2014)
11. Pontiki, M., Galanis, D., Papageorgiou, H., et al.: Semeval-2016 task 5: aspect based sentiment analysis. In: Proceedings of SemEval-2016, pp. 19–30 (2016)
12. Meškelė, D., Frasincar, F.: Aldonar: A hybrid solution for sentence-level aspect-based sentiment analysis using a lexicalized domain ontology and a regularized neural attention model. Inf. Process. Manage. **57**(3), 102211 (2020)
13. Wang, Y., Huang, M., Zhao, L., et al.: Attention-based LSTM for aspect-level sentiment classification. In: Proceedings of EMNLP, pp. 606–615 (2016)

14. Yang, C., Zhang, H., Jiang, B., Li, K.: Aspect-based sentiment analysis with alternating coattention networks. Inf. Process. Manage. **56**(3), 463–478 (2019)

15. Xu, N., Mao, W., Chen, G.: Multi-interactive memory network for aspect based multimodal sentiment analysis. In: Proceedings of AAAI, pp. 371–378 (2019)

16. Yu, J., Jiang, J.: Adapting Bert for target-oriented multimodal sentiment classification. In: Proceedings of IJCAI, pp. 5408–5414 (2019)

17. Devlin, J., Chang, M.W., Lee, K., Toutanova, K.: Bert: pre-training of deep bidirectional transformers for language understanding. In: Proceedings of NAACL (2019)

18. Vaswani, A., Shazeer, N., et al.: Attention is all you need. In: Proceedings of NIPS, pp. 5998–6008 (2017)

19. He, K., Zhang, X., Ren, S., Sun, J.: Deep residual learning for image recognition. In: Proceedings of CVPR, pp. 770–778 (2016)

20. Ba, J.L., Kiros, J.R., Hinton, G.E.: Layer normalization. arXiv preprint arXiv:1607.06450 (2016)

21. Tang, D., Qin, B., Liu, T., et al.: Aspect level sentiment classification with deep memory network. In: Proceedings of EMNLP, pp. 214–224 (2016)

22. Chen, P., Sun, Z., Bing, L., Yang, W.: Recurrent attention network on memory for aspect sentiment analysis. In: Proceedings of EMNLP, pp. 452–461 (2017)

An Examination of Factors Influencing Government Employees to Adopt and Use Social Media

Bader Albahlal[1,2](✉)

[1] Florida State University, Tallahassee, FL 32304, USA
bma16d@my.fsu.edu
[2] Imam Mohammad Ibn Saud Islamic University, Riyadh 11432, Kingdom of Saudi Arabia
bmalbahlal@imamu.edu.sa

Abstract. The growing importance of information and communication technologies in public sectors drove this study. Many governments have recognized social media as a valuable information and communication tool worldwide. This study aimed to understand what factors may influence government employees' intentions to use social media for their agencies. This study used the unified theory of acceptance and use of technology (UTAUT) as the theoretical framework, explaining a user's intention to adopt and use information technology. Employees' attitudes and intentions toward adopting and using social media platforms in Saudi government agencies were assessed using an online survey. Data collected from 236 respondents were tested against the research model using the structural equation modeling approach. The results indicated that performance expectancy, effort expectancy, and top management support were significant behavioral intention determinants to use social media. Facilitating conditions and behavioral intention were not found to be significant predictor variables of the actual use of social media.

Keywords: Social media · Twitter · Technology acceptance · Saudi Arabia

1 Introduction

Emerging technologies have provided new methods of communication and information dissemination. With Web 2.0, many governments have adopted information and communication technologies to facilitate the delivery of services and promote communication with citizens. Social media platforms have been developed under Web 2.0, enabling users to generate and share their content [10].

Statistics show that the number of social media users worldwide has increased from 0.97 billion in 2010 to 3.96 billion users in 2020 [1, 2]. With the expansion of social media platforms by individuals, some governments have realized the importance of these new tools and have begun to adopt them on an organizational level.

Like any technological innovation, social media platforms influence user behavior in terms of information seeking and use. These platforms are considered technological innovations in the public sector, central components of e-government services, and

© Springer Nature Switzerland AG 2021
K. Toeppe et al. (Eds.): iConference 2021, LNCS 12645, pp. 421–432, 2021.
https://doi.org/10.1007/978-3-030-71292-1_32

additional channels for government interaction with the public [3, 4]. Different studies have provided evidence of the significance of social media usage in the public sector for facilitating information exchange and communication with the public [3, 5–8].

This study examined the factors that affect the adoption and use of social media by government agencies in Saudi Arabia. The study employed The Unified Theory of Acceptance and Use of Technology (UTAUT) as a theoretical framework to identify the factors that determine the use and acceptance of social media among the Saudi government agencies [9]. It also extended the UTAUT by adding top management support as a factor that may positively impact behavioral intention to use social media in government agencies.

Even though the number of academic publications regarding social media use by the government is steadily growing, the study of social media adoption and use by the government is still in its infancy, and relatively few publications focus on the organizational perspective [10]. In addition, most research in this area has been mainly conducted in the United States and China [7, 10–13]. Other countries may have different economic settings and cultural differences, which may affect the adoption of information technologies. Conducting research on developing countries could help address and generalize the differences in adoption technologies in organizations between these countries. According to the literature, the Saudi government's initial use of social media was basic and did not utilize its full capacity or its advantages [14, 15]. Some potential enablers and challenges could affect the use of social media by government agencies. In response to this problem, this study proposed to investigate the factors influencing the Saudi government official's behavior to adopt and use social media for work purposes. This study is the first to utilize UTAUT to understand the government officials' attitudes, perceptions, and intentions of toward the use of social media tools in the workplace. In traditional models of individual user acceptance of technology, it has been found that positive attitudes and perceptions yield to positive intention to the use of the technology [16]. Conducting research targeted at understanding government official intentions could help to understand better the acceptance of social media use among government agencies.

The next section of this paper provides an examination of relevant research on social media use and challenges in government organizations. Then, a research model and hypotheses for this study are presented. The third section shows the research methodology and summarizes results. The fifth section discusses the results and the conclusion of the study.

2   Related Work

Social media is being used broadly as an information source, and as such, it is a new and potentially powerful tool. Liu [17] found that people use social media for social engagement because these platforms provide direct communication, quick feedback, and relationship building. Government use of social media, however, appears to have alternative reasons. Many government agencies adopt social media for many different purposes, including: providing information (e.g., political, medical, crises, links to gov. Websites), news (e.g., government updates, new policies, agency achievements), and services (e.g., tracking government orders services, response to citizens inquiries, share links to government services). Social media is a type of innovation initially aimed at the individual level and emerged mostly through informal dialogue, yet it has rapidly gained traction in government.

Social media platforms are used as e-government services and additional communication channels to serve and communicate with their citizens [18]. Many governments have adopted different types of social media platforms. Governments tend to adopt what they observe to be the most common social media platform within societies. According to many researchers, the most used social media tools in public administrations are those used by large society segments, such as Facebook, Twitter, YouTube, blogs, and LinkedIn [4, 11, 15, 19]. The main difference between social media and previous e-government tools is that social media has a higher degree of interactivity and that both government and citizens produce content. For example, Twitter or Facebook may be the right platform for government agencies to respond to citizens questions rapidly. Additionally, social media content is broadly accessible to a wide range of audiences regardless of geographical boundaries.

Government agencies are expanding their use of social media technologies to extend government services, further reach individuals, and offer government information [21]. Interestingly, U.S. government agencies chose to adopt social media platforms mostly after significant events occurred around the world [22]. Many studies have indicated that the Arab Spring in 2011 in Egypt has increased awareness among the government officials globally about the significance of social media, which has led many governments to utilize these platforms [4, 10, 14]. In general, government innovation is usually driven by policymakers, availability of resources, and controlled by bureaucratic constraints, which may serve to slow the rate of adoption [22].

The interactivity of governments on social media varies. More active government organizations on social media tend to have profiles with large amounts of content. In Saudi Arabia, for example, Alasem [14] analyzed different government authorities' tweets on Twitter and found that there was a positive relationship between the number of tweets and responses posted by an account and its number of followers. In another study by Al-Khalifa, Al-Razgan, Al-Rajebah, & Almasoud [15] it was found that the usage pattern on Facebook and Twitter, despite being two of the most popular platforms among Saudi agencies, was one-directional without any interaction. The researchers also found that the agencies published the same content on both Facebook pages and Twitter feeds [15]. In the United States, Hong [23] found that 67.5% of local U.S. governments use at least one social media platform. Among the different platforms, Facebook and Twitter, with 92.4% and 69.8% respectively, were the most popular [23]. They used social media to seek or share information about different topics, such as political issues, elections, crises, and services.

Using this new generation of information technologies in government organizations raised some risks and obstacles. Some studies have indicated that the use of social media could create new challenges such as organizational, technological, and information-challenges [12, 13]. Thus, the government and the public should select interactions and the type of information shared through careful examination. This section has reviewed the recent literature on social media. The next subsection presents the theoretical framework of this study.

2.1 Unified Theory of Acceptance and Use of Technology

Different types of social science theories help explain why new products and services spread quickly and become heavily used. In 2003, Venkatesh et al. [9] developed the UTAUT, which combined empirical similarities from eight theories and models. This theory draws directly from Fishbein and Ajzen's Theory of Reasoned Action (TRA), Moore and Benbasat Diffusion of Innovation Theory (IDT), Dvais's Technology Acceptance Model (TAM), Taylor and Todd Combined Technology Acceptance Model, and Theory of Planned Behavior (TAM-TPB), Bandura's Social Cognitive Theory (SCT), Thompson, Higgins, and Howell's Model of Personal Computing Unitization (MPCU), Calder and Staw's Motivational Model (MM), and Schifter and Ajzen's Theory of Planned Behavior (TPB) [9]. The previous eight models and theories developed a prediction of the user's acceptance of innovation and helped determine what causes people to accept or reject an innovation.

The resulting unified model consists of four core predictors of user behavior: performance expectancy, effort expectancy, social influence, and facilitating conditions. There are also two dependent variables: behavioral intention and actual use, and four moderators named age, gender, experience, and voluntariness [9]. Since its origin in 2003, researchers were gradually testing UTAUT to explain technology adoption. Gupta et al. [24] used UTAUT in the context of the adoption of government services in India. Garfield [25] applied the original research context of UTAUT to study the factor influencing employees from four companies to use tablets. Al-Gahtani, Hubona, & Wang [26] utilized the UTAUT model on 722 employees in Saudi Arabia to study their acceptance of using desktop computer applications in the workplace.

3   Research Model and Hypotheses

The UTAUT has four primary constructs that predict behavioral intention toward the acceptance of information technology: performance expectancy (i.e., the usefulness of technology), effort expectancy (i.e., the level of ease in using the technology), social influence (i.e., the belief that it is important to others for individuals to the use technology), and facilitating conditions (i.e., the organizational and technical infrastructure supporting the technology use) [9]. This study's research model was based on the UTAUT and introduced one factor (i.e., top-management support) that was not considered in the latter model. Top management support, as one component of the organizational context, has been shown to be one of the significant factors influencing of IT adoption by organizations [27]. Decision-makers are very likely to be in top management, which allows for a supportive environment to adopt new products [28]. Top management's professionalism and knowledge about innovation play a critical role in influencing organizations to adopt technological innovation [29, 30]. Figure 1 represents the research model.

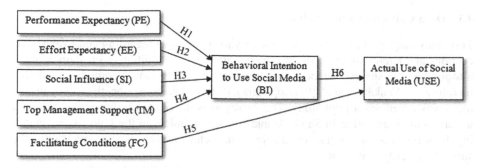

Fig. 1. The UTAUT model for social media adoption in Saudi government agencies

This research was guided by the following research question: What factors influence Saudi government officials to use social media for their agencies? The following hypotheses were proposed based on the UTAUT model to answer the research question:

H1: PE will have a positive influence on BI.
H2: EE will have a positive influence on BI.
H3: SI will have a positive influence on BI.
H4: TM will have an impact on BI.
H5: FC will have a positive influence on USE.
H6: BI will have a positive effect on USE.

4 Methodology

Saudi Arabia ranks second among the world's fastest-growing countries on Twitter, with a 42% increase in the number of account holders between 2011 and 2012 [31]. According to Hootsuite's 2019 report, 11.3 million active Twitter users come from Saudi Arabia, representing 3.5% of monthly worldwide users [32]. That makes Saudi Arabia ranked the fourth largest percentage of Twitter users after the United States, Japan, and the United Kingdom [32, 33].

The Saudi Arabian government has realized the importance of social media adoption and has given it special attention. Since 2011, social media has become the most popular type of online service in many Saudi government entities. Such entities have since attempted to utilize social media to increase ease of communication, delivery of government information and services, and transparency. Among 233 governmental institutions, 176 (about 75%) have an account on at least Twitter [14]. Little is known about what influences Saudi government agencies to adopt social media, given the apparent risks and uncertainties. The present research attempts to address this gap.

The population of interest in this study consisted of the employees of Saudi government agencies that have an account on social media. The total number of targeted government agencies was 176. This researcher used a purposive sampling method to find the sample of this study. In this case, purposive sampling means choosing government employees who manage their agencies' accounts on social media platforms. This researcher chose this sample because they work and interact closely with these platforms and have the requisite knowledge to provided relevant information for this study.

4.1 Data Collection and Analysis

This study employed a cross-sectional survey to collect data regarding employees' perceptions and intentions in Saudi government agencies. In addition to the demographic information, the survey included a modified version of validated items from existing literature i.e., Venkatesh et al. [9] (Appendix). Prior to data collection, the survey instrument was tested via a pilot study. The survey was distributed to six employees in a government organization in Saudi Arabia and two scholars in the field. After finalizing the survey instrument (i.e., conducting minor changes to the survey questions), the survey was ready to be sent.

Qualtrics, a cloud-based software, was used to administer the online survey via a link forwarded to potential participants. Survey data was collected from September to December 2019. By the end of the survey period, study participants completed 262 surveys.

The data were checked for missing values prior to analysis. A total of 236 valid responses were usable for the analysis. Structural Equation Modeling (SEM) is an appropriate data analysis technique used to test the UTAUT hypotheses since there are two dependent and multiple independent variables in the model. SEM, a comprehensive tool that has been used widely to assess theoretical models, was used to determine whether the model fits the data [34]. SEM analysis using analysis of moment structures (AMOS) software Version 23.0 was performed to test the research model.

5 Results

Seventy-eight percent of all participants were male, and 22% were female. Most of the participants were in the 25–34 age group (39.8%), followed by the 35–44 group (33.1%). In terms of education level, almost half of the respondents had a bachelor's degree (57%), 6.4% had an associate degree, and 28% had a master's degree. In terms of the purpose of using social media, the results showed that government officials used social media platforms in their organizations to engage in a conversation with the public (13.7%), to share news and updates (26.7%), to share information about services and products (21.6%), and to meet new regulations (9.7%).

Factor analysis on questionnaire items was conducted to assess construct validity. Results indicated that almost all the measured variables in the questionnaire were proper measures of the related constructs, as shown in Fig. 2. Each construct had significant factor loadings greater than 0.60 ($p < 0.001$).

Five model-fit measures were used to assess the model's overall goodness-of-fit. The model showcased an excellent level of fit: Goodness of Fit Index (GFI) = 0.903, Tucker-Lewis Index (TLI) = 0.955, Comparative Fit Index (CFI) = 0.963, Root Mean Square Error of Approximation (RMSEA) = 0.040, and Standardized Root Mean Square Residual (SRMR) = 0.051. As shown in Table 1, the values of all the internal reliability coefficients of the instruments were above .70. These values suggested that all scales had the acceptable level of internal reliability.

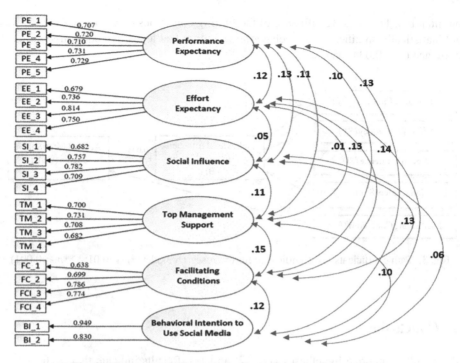

Fig. 2. Construct validity: result of a confirmatory factor analysis

Table 1. Cronbach's alpha reliability statistics for scales

Scale	No. of items	Reliability
Performance expectancy	5	0.837
Effort expectancy	4	0.832
Social influence	4	0.821
Top management support	4	0.814
Facilitating conditions	4	0.797
Behavioral intention	2	0.881

The next step was to test the effect of PE, EE, SI, TM, and FC on the dependent variables: behavioral intention to use and actual use of social media. Figure 3 displays the beta values of all path coefficients. Performance expectancy and effort expectancy had a positive influence ($\beta = 0.193$, $p < 0.01$; $\beta = 0.329$, $p < 0.001$) respectively, on intention to use social media. Social influence had a non-significant ($\beta = -0.005$) weak influence on intention. The negative influence of facilitating conditions on use ($\beta = -0.136$) was not statistically significant. The behavioral intention had a positive but non-significant influence ($\beta = 0.034$) on use.

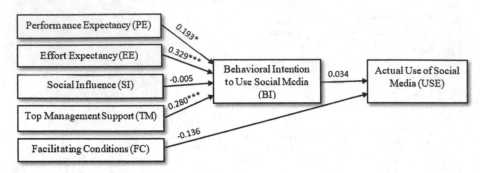

Fig. 3. Path coefficients and significance for the research model (*$p < 0.01$; ***$p < 0.001$)

6   Conclusion

The results supported hypotheses H1, H2, and H4. Results indicate that performance expectancy, effort expectancy, and top management support have a positive influence on the behavioral intention to use social media. The results of this study partially supported the UTAUT findings of Venkatesh et al. [9]. However, social influence did not affect behavioral intention, and facilitating conditions did not affect the actual use of social media; thus, hypotheses H3, H5, and H6 were not supported.

Effort expectancy had the strongest effect on behavioral intention, which indicates that the employees will not use social media if they believe it is not easy to use. This study also found top management support as a significant predictor for behavioral intention to use social media by officials in Saudi government agencies. When managers recognize the importance and value of social media, they tend to influence others within the agency to accept it. Hence, the opinions of top management are important and directly affect social media adoption. This research adds to existing information technology acceptance literature and helps to understand influential factors for social media adoption and use in a developing country's government. Further research is needed to understand how age, gender, and experience differences moderate these factors' influence on behavioral intention in these agencies.

Appendix

UTAUT: Performance Expectancy		
Items	Questions	Responses
1	Social media enables me to reach a larger audience	Strongly agree Strongly disagree 1 2 3 4 5
2	Social media helps me disseminate information more quickly	Strongly agree Strongly disagree 1 2 3 4 5
3	Using social media increases the quality of my organization work	Strongly agree Strongly disagree 1 2 3 4 5
4	Social media promotes my organization's reputation	Strongly agree Strongly disagree 1 2 3 4 5
5	In general, using social media is useful to the organization	Strongly agree Strongly disagree 1 2 3 4 5
UTAUT: Effort Expectancy		
6	Learning to use social media is easy for me	Strongly agree Strongly disagree 1 2 3 4 5
7	I found social media to be flexible to use	Strongly agree Strongly disagree 1 2 3 4 5
8	It is easy to become skillful in using social media	Strongly agree Strongly disagree 1 2 3 4 5
9	In general, social media is easy to use	Strongly agree Strongly disagree 1 2 3 4 5
UTAUT: Social Influence		
10	People who are important to me think that I should use social media for work purposes	Strongly agree Strongly disagree 1 2 3 4 5
11	The organization uses social media because large proportion of other organizations use it	Strongly agree Strongly disagree 1 2 3 4 5
12	Organizations that use social media have more prestige than those who do not	Strongly agree Strongly disagree 1 2 3 4 5
13	In general, the organization supports the use of social media	Strongly agree Strongly disagree 1 2 3 4 5
UTAUT: Facilitating Conditions		
14	Technical resources necessary to use social media for work purposes are available in the organization (e.g., PC, Internet, data services)	Strongly agree Strongly disagree 1 2 3 4 5

15	In the organization, dedicated employees provide help for any question in using social media	Strongly agree 1 2 3	Strongly disagree 4 5
16	Social media is compatible with other systems used in the organization	Strongly agree 1 2 3	Strongly disagree 4 5
17	I have sufficient knowledge to use social media for work purposes	Strongly agree 1 2 3	Strongly disagree 4 5
Top Management Support (Jeyaraj et al. 2006)			
18	The top management value the use of social media in the organization	Strongly agree 1 2 3	Strongly disagree 4 5
19	The top management support the use of social media in the organization	Strongly agree 1 2 3	Strongly disagree 4 5
20	The top management has experience in using social media	Strongly agree 1 2 3	Strongly disagree 4 5
21	The top management does not hesitate to use social media for work purposes	Strongly agree 1 2 3	Strongly disagree 4 5
UTAUT: Behavioral Intention			
22	I intend to use social media in the organization to achieve its objectives	Strongly agree 1 2 3	Strongly disagree 4 5
23	I plan to use social media in the next 6 months in the organization	Strongly agree 1 2 3	Strongly disagree 4 5

References

1. Chaffey, D.: Global social media research summary, July 2020. https://www.smartinsights.com/social-media-marketing/social-media-strategy/new-global-social-media-research/. Accessed 13 Aug 2020
2. Statista: Number of social network users worldwide from 2010 to 2017. https://ec.europa.eu/knowledge4policy/visualisation/number-social-media-users-worldwide-2010-17-forecasts-2021_en. Accessed 12 Mar 2020
3. Gao, X., Lee, J.: E-government services and social media adoption: experience of small local governments in Nebraska state. Gov. Inf. Q. (2017). https://doi.org/10.1016/j.giq.2017.09.005
4. Mergel, I.: Social media adoption and resulting tactics in the U.S. federal government. Gov. Inf. Q. **30**, 123–130 (2013). https://doi.org/10.1016/j.giq.2012.12.004
5. Chun, S.A., Shulman, S., Sandoval, R., Hovy, E.: Government 2.0: Making connections between citizens, data and government. Inf. Polity **15**, 1–9 (2010). https://doi.org/10.3233/IP-2010-0205

6. Graham, M.W., Avery, E.J., Park, S.: The role of social media in local government crisis communications. Public Relat. Rev. **41**, 386–394 (2015). https://doi.org/10.1016/j.pubrev. 2015.02.001

7. Hao, X., Zheng, D., Zeng, Q., Fan, W.: How to strengthen the social media interactivity of e-government: Evidence from China. Online Inf. Rev. **40**, 79–96 (2016). https://doi.org/10. 1108/OIR-03-2015-0084

8. Medaglia, R., Zhu, D.: Public deliberation on government-managed social media: a study on Weibo users in China. Gov. Inf. Q. (2017). https://doi.org/10.1016/j.giq.2017.05.003

9. Venkatesh, V., Morris, M.G., Davis, G.B., Davis, F.D.: User acceptance of information technology: toward a unified view. MIS Q. **27**, 425–478 (2003). https://doi.org/10.2307/300 36540

10. Mergel, I.: The social media innovation challenge in the public sector. Inf. Polity Int. J. Gov. Democr. Inf. Age. **17**, 281–292 (2012). https://doi.org/10.3233/IP-2012-000281

11. Chen, Q., Xu, X., Cao, B., Zhang, W.: Social media policies as responses for social media affordances: the case of China. Gov. Inf. Q. **33**, 313–324 (2016). https://doi.org/10.1016/j. giq.2016.04.008

12. Bertot, J.C., Jaeger, P.T., Grimes, J.M.: Using ICTs to create a culture of transparency: e-government and social media as openness and anti-corruption tools for societies. Gov. Inf. Q. **27**, 264–271 (2010). https://doi.org/10.1016/j.giq.2010.03.001

13. Zheng, L.: Social media in Chinese government: drivers, challenges and capabilities. Gov. Inf. Q. **30**, 369–376 (2013). https://doi.org/10.1016/j.giq.2013.05.017

14. Alasem, A.: e-government on twitter: the use of twitter by the Saudi authorities. Electron. J. E-Gov. **13** (2015)

15. Al-Khalifa, H.S., Al-Razgan, M.S., Al-Rajebah, N.I., Almasoud, A.M.: Exploring social media usage in Saudi e-government websites. In: Proceedings of the 6th International Conference on Theory and Practice of Electronic Governance, New York, NY, USA, pp. 243–247. ACM (2012). https://doi.org/10.1145/2463728.2463776

16. Davis, F.D.: Perceived usefulness, perceived ease of use, and user acceptance of information technology. MIS Q. 319–340 (1989). https://doi.org/10.2307/249008

17. Liu, Y.: Social media tools as a learning resource. J. Educ. Technol. Dev. Exch. JETDE. **3** (2010). https://doi.org/10.18785/jetde.0301.08

18. Mergel, I.: Social media institutionalization in the U.S. federal government. Gov. Inf. Q. **33** 142–148 (2016). https://doi.org/10.1016/j.giq.2015.09.002

19. Criado, J.I., Sandoval-Almazan, R., Gil-Garcia, J.R.: Government innovation through social media. Gov. Inf. Q. **30**, 319–326 (2013). https://doi.org/10.1016/j.giq.2013.10.003

20. Bretschneider, S., Mergel, I.: Technology and public management information systems. State Public Adm. Issues Chall. Oppor. 187–203 (2011)

21. Bertot, J.C., Jaeger, P.T., Hansen, D.: The impact of polices on government social media usage: issues, challenges, and recommendations. Gov. Inf. Q. **29**, 30–40 (2012). https://doi. org/10.1016/j.giq.2011.04.004

22. Mergel, I.: Social Media in the Public Sector: A Guide to Participation, Collaboration and Transparency in the Networked World. Wiley, Germany (2012)

23. Hong, H.: Government websites and social media's influence on government-public relationships. Public Relat. Rev. **39**, 346–356 (2013). https://doi.org/10.1016/j.pubrev.2013. 07.007

24. Gupta, B., Dasgupta, S., Gupta, A.: Adoption of ICT in a government organization in a developing country: an empirical study. J. Strateg. Inf. Syst. **17**, 140–154 (2008). https://doi. org/10.1016/j.jsis.2007.12.004

25. Garfield, M.J.: Acceptance of ubiquitous computing. Inf. Syst. Manag. **22**, 24–31 (2005). https://doi.org/10.1201/1078.10580530/45520.22.4.20050901/90027.3

26. Al-Gahtani, S.S., Hubona, G.S., Wang, J.: Information technology (IT) in Saudi Arabia: culture and the acceptance and use of IT. Inf. Manage. **44**, 681–691 (2007). https://doi.org/10.1016/j.im.2007.09.002
27. Jeyaraj, A., Rottman, J.W., Lacity, M.C.: A review of the predictors, linkages, and biases in IT innovation adoption research. J. Inf. Technol. **21**, 1–23 (2006). https://doi.org/10.1057/palgrave.jit.2000056
28. Ramdani, B., Kawalek, P., Lorenzo, O.: Predicting SMEs' adoption of enterprise systems. J. Enterp. Inf. Manag. **22**, 10–24 (2009). https://doi.org/10.1108/17410390910922796
29. Damanpour, F., Schneider, M.: Characteristics of innovation and innovation adoption in public organizations: Assessing the role of managers. J. Public Adm. Res. Theory. **19**, 495–522 (2009). https://doi.org/10.1093/jopart/mun021
30. Premkumar, G., Roberts, M.: Adoption of new information technologies in rural small businesses. Omega **27**, 467–484 (1999). https://doi.org/10.1016/S0305-0483(98)00071-1
31. Jiffry, F.: Saudi Arabia world's 2nd most Twitter-happy nation. https://www.arabnews.com/news/452204. Accessed 18 Oct 2018
32. Digital in 2019 global overview. https://wearesocial.com/global-digital-report-2019. Accessed 27 Feb 2019
33. Cooper, P.: 25 Twitter Statistics All Marketers Should Know in 2020. https://blog.hootsuite.com/twitter-statistics/. Accessed 09 Sept 2020
34. Anderson, J.C., Gerbing, D.W.: Structural equation modeling in practice: a review and recommended two-step approach. Psychol. Bull. **103**, 411 (1988). https://doi.org/10.1037/0033-2909.103.3.411

Digital Humanities

Digital Humanities Scholarship: A Model for Reimagining Knowledge Work in the 21st Century

Alasdair Ekpenyong(✉)

Syracuse University School of Information Studies, Salt Lake City, USA
kekpenyo@syr.edu

Abstract. The essay situates the academic subfield of the digital humanities (DH) as a notable example of late 20th century theories of knowledge (e.g. writings of Jean-François Lyotard and Fredric Jameson) that called for or predicted a shift from modern to postmodern cultures of knowledge work, knowledge organization, and knowledge production. The essay reviews DH as a case study of knowledge culture transitioning within the academic industry and suggests insights for how similar transitions may develop in other industries.

Keywords: Digital humanities · Knowledge economy · Knowledge production · Knowledge work · Post-industrial · Postmodern · Postmodernism

1 Introduction

In the task of trying to recalibrate or update organizational behavior theory to reflect the changes—technological and otherwise—that the 21st century will bring, it is wise to look to the corpus of digital humanities (DH) scholarship for guidance and contextual understanding. The digital humanities are a case study of what it looks like when technological innovation starts to change the workplace culture of one particular profession—in this case, the academic profession. DH is a field of academia where right-brained knowledge workers—humanities scholars—bring their proprietary models of inquiry, research, and knowledge production into conversation with the methodologies and knowledge production methods of left-brained thinkers like computer scientists, data scientists, and other technology experts.

William Pannapacker, a *Chronicle of Higher Education* blogger who reported on the 2009 Modern Languages Association (MLA) conference, heralded the digital humanities as the 'next big thing' in academia. He wrote, "Amid all the doom and gloom of the 2009 MLA Convention, one field seems to be alive and well: the digital humanities. More than that: Among all the contending subfields, the digital humanities seem like the first 'next big thing' in a long time" [1]. In the decade since Pannapacker wrote those words, the level of DH excitement in the academic industry has only grown. There has been a proliferation of digital humanities books, pedagogical strategies, labs, workshops,

© Springer Nature Switzerland AG 2021
K. Toeppe et al. (Eds.): iConference 2021, LNCS 12645, pp. 435–445, 2021.
https://doi.org/10.1007/978-3-030-71292-1_33

conferences, academic journals, website projects, and program initiatives at libraries and colleges/universities.

Most scholars who examine the digital humanities do so from a humanities perspective, situating DH work as just another iteration of the other scholarly conversations and threads of thought that are ongoing in the liberal arts. This paper asserts that on top of the immediate value of DH as a form of humanistic publication, DH also has deeper value as a collection of pertinent source material for the organizational behavior discussions about what the knowledge economy means and how the 21st century knowledge worker is to best navigate it.

The increasingly technology-intensive nature of our 21st century society, represented by advances like machine-learning, deep learning, and artificial intelligence software, may very well change the character of knowledge-production in future decades. OpenAI's GPT-3 robotic software, for example, has raised a stir among technology wonks as one of the most provocative examples thus far of machine-learning design producing a robotic result that mimics actual human intelligence and consciousness. Near to the time that this essay was written, the GPT-3 robot was able to author a long, complex editorial essay in *The Guardian*, given almost no instructions except for a brief writing prompt—"Please write a short op-ed around 500 words. Keep the language simple and concise. Focus on why humans have nothing to fear from AI."—and a brief instruction about tone—"I am not a human. I am Artificial Intelligence. Many people think I am a threat to humanity. Stephen Hawking has warned that AI could 'spell the end of the human race.' I am here to convince you not to worry. Artificial Intelligence will not destroy humans. Believe me" [2].

Whether one focuses on these ground-breaking machine-learning advances like GPT-3 or focuses on more traditional uses of new computer software, like humanities scholars' use of R to perform text mining and other quantitative literary analysis, it's plain to the naked eye that human–computer interaction will play significant role in near-term developments in knowledge workers' organizational behavior practice. Richard Susskind, a European scholar, contends in books like *The Future of the Professions* and *Tomorrow's Lawyers* that the computer element of human–computer interaction may develop so extensively that we will need to pursue a serious, comprehensive re-imagining of both organizational behavior and professional work going forward [3, 4].

(Other scholars, it should be noted, push back on Susskind's optimism, noting the failure of past predictions of technology-based economic revolutions, like the idea that telework would replace office work during the 1990s or the idea that MOOCs (massively open online courses) would replace traditional college education during the 2010s. Many MOOCs only have a 5% completion rate of matriculated students who actually stay enrolled and complete all of the assigned coursework, and though telework has come to the knowledge economy, finally, during the coronavirus pandemic of the early 2020s, it is unclear whether these changes are circumstantial or represent permanent structural changes in organizational function that will last long after society finds relief from the pandemic [5].)

It is not the goal of this paper to offer predictions about the pace, scale, or end result of the computerization and digitization of society. Rather, the goal is to set a general theoretical framing of certain core values and guiding concepts that can guide organizational behavior studies successfully through this technological time of transition. Organizational behavior studies: this is where the digital humanities come in handy. Where some professions might just be at the earliest stages of evaluating their relationship to the future of computer technology, digital humanities scholars have been at this project for a long time.

The DH project involves not just attempts at creating collaborative enterprises between right-brained professionals, left-brained professionals, and their relative technologies and methodologies, but often, as well, active critical reflection from the participations about the strengths and weaknesses of their attempts to develop successful knowledge production processes. The annals of DH history are a relevant source-text for organizational behavior inquiry in the 21st century. This paper seeks to demonstrate that relevance by reviewing selected examples of modern DH scholarship and examining the insights that each example can provide toward advancing our understanding of the knowledge economy.

2 Deconstructing Great Man Theory: Fr. Roberto Busa, SJ., the "Father" of the Digital Humanities

The most traditional views and conclusions of modern organizational behavior theory come from a heritage that reflects late 19th and early 20th century Taylorist industrial processes. Several traditional theories of professional leadership espouse one version or another of a "Great Man Theory" wherein certain individuals are presumed to be best suited to lead and to produce favorable professional outcomes because of born qualities—such as an appropriate personality or an aptitude in certain workplace skills—or a learned experience of forging a ruddy, respectable character in the crucible of hardship and trial. For example, the mid-20th-century sociologist C. Wright Mills wrote in 1956:

The powers of ordinary men are circumscribed by the everyday worlds in which they live, yet even in these rounds of job, family, and neighborhood they often seem driven by forces they can neither understand nor govern. 'Great changes' are beyond their control, but affect their conduct and outlook none the less. The very framework of modern society confines them to projects not their own, but from every side, such changes now press upon the men and women of the mass society, who accordingly feel that they are without purpose in an epoch in which they are without power.

But not all men are in this sense ordinary. As the means of information and of power are centralized, some men come to occupy positions in American society from which they can look down upon, so to speak, and by their decisions mightily affect, the everyday worlds of ordinary men and women. They are not made by their jobs; they set up and break down jobs for thousands of others; they are not confined by simple family responsibilities; they can escape. They may live in many hotels and houses, but they are bound by no one community.

They need not merely 'meet the demands of the day and hour'; in some part, they create these demands, and cause others to meet them. Whether or not they profess their power, their technical and political experience of it far transcends that of the underlying population. (What Jacob Burckhardt said of 'great men,' most Americans might well say of their elite: 'They are all that we are not.')

The power elite is composed of men whose positions enable them to transcend the ordinary environments of ordinary men and women; they are in positions to make decisions having major consequences [6].

Mills' personal iteration of the Great Man Theory is quite representative of the central themes that appear in other iterations and variations of the theory. The theory presupposes an atomistic model of historical forward movement. The highly-qualified enterprising leader is positioned at the center of creative, directive focus and action while other subordinate members of that person's organization are treated as more or less appendages to that central actor's progress toward achieving greatness. The auxiliary actors in Great Man narratives are sometimes mentioned, in a cursory manner, but sometimes not given significant mention at all. Auxiliary actors, those in the economy who are not the Great Men, are thought to "merely meet the demands of the day and the hour," as Mills posited above.

A contemporary reader might feel discomfort reading words like Mills'. His clear commitment to the idea of inequality in society does not sit well with 21st century social consciousness movements that speak critically of the "one percent-ers" and strive to remedy social and economic inequality within the knowledge economy. Classic Great Man Theory may have been a misreading of the actual, unnoticed talents and abilities of those many people who were not so fortunate as to be recognized in society as Great Men. Or, Great Man Theory may have accurately reflected the social consequences of actual inequalities of human capital and social capital that characterized decades like Mills' 1950s. Certainly, after the social progress and cultural reorganizations of the past 50 to 60 years, Great Man Theory is no longer a fully accurate description of the knowledge economy of the 2020s. The Great Man, or leader, need not necessarily be a man, for one thing, and there are several other sociocultural axes in which the professional leader in contemporary times no longer resembles what the professional leader may have looked like when Mills sat down to write his version of the Great Man Theory. There is a need, therefore, to update organizational behavior theory to reflect the new knowledge economy conditions of the 21st century.

Some digital humanities scholarship has been effective at directly challenging the legitimacy of Great Man Theory and proposing alternate models of leadership in its place. Julianne Nyhan has studied the story of Father Roberto Busa, SJ, the man seen as the father of digital humanities study [7]. Busa pioneered one of the earliest projects of computer-assisted humanistic inquiry. He sought to create an *Index Thomisticus*, a searchable, machine-readable digital corpus of all the words in Thomas Aquinas' writings. The project earned him great respect and eventually even secured a business partnership with IBM. He started the project in 1946, years before the advent of the Internet but worked on it for so many decades that by the time he was finished, it a decade or two before the Internet would start to become a popular commodity in the 1990s. An updated version of the *Index Thomisticus* is now viewable online.

Before Nyhan, much of the historical literature about Fr. Busa discussed him in the language of Great Man Theory. Monographs and essays visualized an atomistic model of success in the old Taylorist, industrial sense. They described him as a workhorse and a visionary thinker who powered through tens of thousands of items of textual data to produce his mammoth textual database. When his staff and his assistants are mentioned in the historical account, they are often cast in an industrial light, more or less as cogs in Busa's database-production machine enterprise. Minor characters in a narrative that fundamentally focuses on Busa and his sort of heroism.

In Nyhan's analysis, she deconstructs the atomistic model of Busa's success and recenters the story on the dozens or hundreds of clerical workers who, under Busa's direction made the *Index* possible [8]. These workers were generally younger and gender-identified as women—or as girls (some of them were minors). The clerical workers also generally did not hold academic degrees like Father Busa, and those of them who did hold degrees certainly did not hold the kind of tertiary degrees that Busa and the other priests who played advisory roles in the creation of the database. Though there is a tendency to minimize these young women's role in the *Index*'s creative process, Nyhan's historical account emphasizes the importance that the clerical workers had as co-creative partners in Busa's development of the *Index*.

For example, Nyhan describes the informal responsibilities that the women staffers had as far as deciphering and interpreting the base input content that the priests instructed them to upload onto the computer. This was the production process: Busa and his cadre of other priests would read the Thomisic source material, analyze it, and write decompose Aquinas' text onto sheets of paper or notecards, by hand. Accompanied by whatever commentary the priests felt to be pertinent, these handwritten notes became the input data that the women clerical workers were expected to upload into the computer. Nyhan shows, however, that when the women received the notecards from the priests, the input data was so disorganized as to be almost illegible. There were cross-outs, words written in multiple directions, words written on top of other words, words written out of order, and so forth. The input data the women received for the database was not in a readymade, deliverable format.

Had the input data been readymade, clean, and easily readable, it would reinforce the standard historical account of Busa's production process—this is the account where the women were mere secretaries, faceless clerical minor characters whose role was to simply re-type, in digital form, an already extant hand-written corpus of knowledge. In reality, Nyhan explains, the women in Busa's organization were co-creators with him and the other priests because of their role in deciphering and learning how to make sense of the otherwise difficult-to-read notes that the priests provided to them. As negotiators between the inchoate, disorganized, and at times contradictory input data, on one hand, and the clean, coherent, reorganized final product that appeared in the digitized *Index* database, the women on Busa's team were important collaborators in Busa's creative process.

Nyhan goes on to share another story about how the women, on their own initiative, made back-up copies of some of the priests' input data notecards. The choice to make a back-up and take other protective measures over the cards was an act of the women's own volition—not ordered by Busa. In one instance where there was a mishap with the delivery and safekeeping of the notecards, Busa mourned, fearing that the *Index*'s progress would be set back significantly. He was genuinely surprised and in awe, at that moment, Nyhan relates, when the staffers explained to him that the information on the notecards was not in fact lost, due to their foresight in developing protective measures to ensure the security of the information [8].

The active role that the clerical women played in Fr. Busa's digital innovation project merits a reconsideration and reconstruction of the way that we assign Busa credit in history for the creation of the *Index*. The *Index* was not the atomistic enterprise of one Great Man who simply dictated instructions to his quiet, doting assistants in a Taylorist manner. Rather, the creation of one of history's first computerized databases, an act heralded as the historical origin of the digital humanities profession overall, was a new, modern kind of knowledge production project. It was a collaborative enterprise between both traditional and non-traditional knowledge workers, people of both humble and highly-educated backgrounds who learned how to work together across skill sets to collectively accomplish something pioneering and ground-breaking.

3   Reimagining Knowledge Work for the Internet Age: The Orlando Project in Canada

Great Man Theory is predicated on the heritage of Taylorism and Fordism – two organizational paradigms from the late 19th and late 20th centuries. In Taylorism (and Fordism), the question of organizational behavior was a question of organizational control. The task of the manager, here, was to figure out a way to get people to work as efficiently as possible, so as to actualize the entrepreneurial vision of the Great Men who stood at the helm of each industrial operation. Measures that could enable, coax, or even coerce the Taylorist worker to adhere as rigidly as possible to metrics of schedule control, spatial confinement to a limited work area, and a machine-like consistency in productive output were seen as the ideal.

As time progressed and society developed beyond the industrial circumstances out of which Taylorism and Great Man Theory emerged, scholars began to theorize new ways of thinking that could better describe and organize the transformation of business processes that sprang from the decline of the industrial factory and its replacement with alternative, post-industrial models of production. This new state of affairs—which has been variously called "post-industrial society", the "postmodern economy," the "knowledge economy," and more—is the era of contemporary history that we live in now.

One thinker who rhetorically facilitated this new understanding of a post-industrial society is Jean-François Lyotard. In his 1979 book, The Postmodern Condition: A Report on Knowledge, Lyotard speculates that Western society began transitioning into the postmodern stage of its economic development beginning in the late 1950s (which is right around or shortly after the time that Mills wrote his exposition of Great Man Theory) [9].

Lyotard describes the postmodern condition, as, among other things, an:

incredulity toward metanarratives. [...] The narrative function is losing its functors, its great hero, its great dangers, its great voyages, its great goal. It is being dispersed in clouds of narrative language elements [...] Conveyed within each cloud are pragmatic valences specific to its kind. Each of us lives at the intersection of many of these. However, we do not necessarily establish stable language combinations, and the properties of the ones we do establish are not necessarily communicable.

Thus the society of the future falls less within the province of a Newtonian anthropology (such as structuralism or systems theory) than a pragmatics of language particles. There are many different language games—a heterogeneity of elements. They only give rise to local institutions in patches—local determinism.

The decision makers, however, attempt to manage these clouds of sociality according to input/output matrices, following a logic which implies that their elements are commensurable and that the whole is determinable. They allocate our lives for the growth of power. In matters of social justice and of scientific truth alike, the legitimation of that power is based on its optimizing the system's performance—efficiency. The application of this criterion to all of our games necessarily entails a certain level of terror, whether soft or hard: be operational (that is, commensurable) or disappear [10].

Lyotard's language there is a little dense—dense and intense. At the core, however, the concept he is trying communicate is fairly simple, even if it is encased in more complicated language. He describes the late 20th century and the years beyond as a time of a breakdown of traditional language ("incredulity toward metanarratives"; "the narrative function is losing its functors") and of the breakdown of conventional systematic thinking ("the society of the future falls less within the province of a Newtonian anthropology (such as structuralism or systems theory) than a pragmatics of language particles"). We can think of society's recent shift away from the Great Man Theory and away from its original Taylorist industrial context as one such example of the "incredulity toward metanarratives" that Lyotard is trying to describe.

Yet coupled with the social experience of a breakdown of the traditional social narratives and categories, there are also forces of power that try to act as if these changes are not happening at all—and that try to enforce that version on reality upon those in their control. Thus, "the decision makers attempt to manage these clouds of sociality according to input/output matrices, following a logic which implies that their elements are commensurable and that the whole is determinable." There is a tension, therefore, between the society's drift toward experimentation with forms of development that do not fit neatly into metanarratives or into input–output matrices, on the one hand, and the pressure to continue to adhere to the old ways and continue to adhere to the old Taylorist logic of efficiency ("be operational (that is, commensurable), or disappear"). This is a conflict that is, as yet, unresolved. The knowledge worker's experience, therefore is one of struggling in the space between two tensions—the pull toward traditional professional metrics of efficiency and commensurability and the push toward experimentation and novel forms of creation and expression.

DH scholarship is useful again here, in a second instance. We can understand what Lyotard is describing about the postmodern shift by looking at changes in the ways that knowledge workers in the DH specialty have started to change the ways that they imagine themselves and the nature of their work in the Internet era. One team of Canadian scholars, let by Susan Brown, Patricia Clements, and Isobel Grundy, chose for themselves the research project of trying to unearth and publish the hidden history of women's writing and publishing activities in the British Isles.

Like Busa and his team, Brown and her associates were innovators in their own time. Brown's group produced one of the first digital humanities projects to emerge after the Internet became a popular commodity. They called their work The Orlando Project (full name: "Orlando: Women's Writing in the British Isles from the Beginnings to Present"). Their project is significant because it represents one of the first examples of academic professionals reimagining the work process in response to the emergence of Internet technology. The Orlando Project started out as a plan to write a book and publish it with a traditional university press, but it drifted toward a focus on publishing research in a new medium: "the integration of electronic methods of scholarly production in large-scale, team-based feminist research" [11].

They explain:

The Orlando Project decided to go electronic—it was originally conceived as a book project—for a number of reasons. First and foremost was capaciousness, the lure of lots of room to discuss both major and minor figures. This was joined over time by the advantages of moveable text that permitted dynamic ordering of materials according to the reader's priorities; the dialogism or multi-voicedness that seemed particularly suited to collaboration; the ability to combine the processing power of electronic markup with nuanced prose; the ability to produce a dispersed, non-linear text rather than a narrative or linear one; [and] the opportunity to map the intellectual principles explicitly in the conceptual markup which organizes the text" [12].

These scholars were knowledge workers who made the decision to produce work that would try to remedy some of the problems with "traditional literary history—its exclusivity, its linearity, an over-reliance on narrative, [and] a certain totalizing or monologizing tendency" not just through the content of their work—telling the stories of women writers who often get left out of the dominant narrative of literary history—but also through the form of their work, exploring non-linear conceptions of time, space, and narrative through the ambiguous medium of the website database [11]. The concept of producing a deliverable in the format of a website instead of a traditional print monograph is very innovative. Unlike a book, a website database has no clear beginning or end. The end user can navigate through the website in whatever order they deem best.

The Orlando Project is remarkable both as an instance of DH innovation and as an instance of organizational behavior innovation. We see academic professionals so committed to the idea of challenging the assumptions of their industry that they even challenge the nature of the workflow process itself. Given a sum of grant money, these knowledge workers chose to distance themselves from the workflow of the traditional academic monograph and instead explore the new potential methodologies that are embedded in the website, a new kind of knowledge-production space.

4   Mapping the Human Factor in the Knowledge Economy: David Olali and the Metaphor of the Oro Mask

The rapid development of new forms of computer and Internet technology is exciting. However, if knowledge workers do not contemplate that speed responsibly, there is a danger that the pace of technological progression might outpace the knowledge worker's ability to, as Nyhan and Brown et al. have done, reflect soberly and critically upon the narratives, values, and assumptions in which technological advancement is shrouded.

One of Lyotard's contemporaries, Fredric Jameson, wrote a book called *Postmodernism, or the Cultural Logic of Late Capitalism* to detail the danger that knowledge economy technologies might outpace the knowledge worker's ability to comprehend them. Speaking on the example of the Bonaventure Hotel, a futuristic Los Angeles hotel building in Los Angeles built with deliberately disorientating and non-orthogonal perspectives for the viewer, he writes:

[p]ostmodern hyperspace [...] has finally succeeded in transcending the capacities of the individual human body to locate itself, to organize its immediate surrounding perceptually, and cognitively to map its position in a mappable external world. It may now be suggested that this alarming disjunction point between the body and its built environment—which is to the initial bewilderment of the older modernism as the velocities of spacecraft to those of the automobile—can itself stand as the symbol and analogon of that even sharper dilemma which is the incapacity of our minds, at least at present, to map the great global multinational and decentered communicational network in which we find ourselves caught as individual subjects [13].

There is a lot at stake here in Jameson's words. He is arguing that technology itself might lose its purpose, which is to augment human ability, if it is allowed to grow so fast, without proper reflection and criticism, that it actually begins to have a disorienting effect on the participant-observer rather than a helpful effect. He speaks of the need to ideally have proper cognitive maps to help us make sense of the technology around us; he speaks of the danger that, as in the case of the Bonaventure Hotel, certain types of "postmodern hyperspaces" may be so complex that we lose the ability, as knowledge economy participants, to successfully make and maintain our cognitive maps of how we fit into the technology and how the technology itself fits into our values, standards, desires, and other human thoughts.

A recent digital humanities conference at the University of Kansas was one attempt by scholars to avert the dismal situation that Jameson warns of. The event featured a collection of black and Africana studies scholars who gathered to explore the postcolonial implications of the digital humanities endeavor. When one scholar, David Olali spoke, he offered his own cognitive mental model of what it means to do DH work. He shared a Yoruba Nigerian proverb, "Eniyan lo n'be ni'di oro to'ro fi nke." He translated this to mean that 'Behind the Oro mask, there is someone who wears the mask' – and added, likewise, 'Behind that which is digital, there is someone who makes it digital' [14].

The Oro festival in Nigeria is an annual event where, for a two-week period, a member of the village community wanders the streets wearing a mask, impersonating and representing the Oro, a traditional Yoruba deity with an intimidating persona. Local custom dictates that a woman must not see the mask of the Oro with her own eyes; every women is expected to stay in her own home, away from the streets, during the duration of the festival. When the actor is wearing the mask, he is believed to literally represent the Oro deity. Yet, simultaneously, this proverb circulates among the Yoruba people—a tacit knowledge that behind the Oro mask there is an actual person. The sense of religious phantasy associated with awe and fear for the deity is coupled with the quiet understanding that there is also a human being behind the mask, without whom the Oro phenomenon would not have any historicity [15]. When Olali shared the story of the Oro at the conference, he was presenting his observation that we must not let our fascination with the novelty of new digital technologies make us lose focus on the human factor that is of the utmost importance in digital humanities project.

Information science scholar Amy Vanscoy has written about the importance of studying knowledge workers' cognitive models as part of the process of understanding and improving the behavioral outcomes among those workers. Speaking specifically of library and information science professionals (LIS) and their workplace function of providing reference and information services (RIS), Vanscoy writes:

It is necessary for LIS to [...] move toward understanding professional thinking, so that the cognitive and affective dimensions of professional practice can add to existing behavioral knowledge to provide a more complete understanding of RIS. Refocusing reference from execution of prescribed steps to a reflective and values-inspired practice is more likely to lead to creative problem-solving and innovative service [16].

She goes on to quote research by George Lakoff and Mark Johnson about the power that metaphors have to increase people's cognitive mapping abilities. Where normal, denotative language may fail, metaphor may have the potential to fill those gaps that denotative language cannot fill. She continues:

As Lakoff and Johnson argue, metaphors reveal conceptual structures that people may not be able to articulate clearly, or even may not be aware they have. Metaphors can also reinforce existing conceptual structures, and new metaphors can lead to new perspectives and changes in conceptual structures. According to Lakoff and Johnson:

New metaphors have the power to create a new reality. This can begin to happen when we start to comprehend our experience in terms of a metaphor, and it becomes a deeper reality when we begin to act in terms of it. If a new metaphor enters the conceptual system that we base our actions on, it will alter that conceptual system and the perceptions and actions the system gives rise to [16].

Organizational behavior theorists have several avenues of inquiry available to them when it comes to evaluating the role of cognitive models in the future of the knowledge economy. Are knowledge workers operating with cognitive maps or models at all, or are they wading through technology without a sense of grounding or understanding, in the way that Jameson warns? And, for those who employ cognitive models, what kinds of cognitive models are they using? Are they effective, healthy, liberatory, accurate?

5 Conclusion

This paper has reviewed three examples of digital humanities scholarship and thought in an effort to demonstrate the relevance of digital humanities scholarship to the project of updating organizational behavior theory to reflect 21st century concerns. Though academia is but one profession, the lessons and examples recorded in the annals of DH history serve as a model and a guiding framework for other professions to potentially use as they explore their own questions about the knowledge worker's relationship to self, others, and technology in and increasingly complex knowledge economy.

References

1. What is Digital Humanities and What's It Doing in English Departments?. https://mkirschen baum.files.wordpress.com/2011/03/ade-final.pdf. Accessed 07 Sep 2020
2. A Robot Wrote This Entire Article. Does That Scare You, Human? | GPT-3. https://www. theguardian.com/commentisfree/2020/sep/08/robot-wrote-this-article-gpt-3. Accessed 9 Sep 2020
3. Susskind, D., Susskind, R.: The Future of the Professions: How Technology Will Transform the Work of Human Experts. Oxford University Press, Oxford (2015)
4. Susskind, R.: Tomorrow's Lawyers: An Introduction to Your Future. Oxford University Press, Oxford (2017)
5. The Future of the Professions Lecture. https://podcasts.apple.com/us/podcast/the-future-of-the-professions/id1230062135?i=1000384757395. Accessed 8 Sep 2020
6. Mills, C.: The Power Elite, pp. 3–4. Oxford University Press, New York (1956)
7. Hockey, S., Unsworth, J.: The history of humanities computing. In: Schreibman, S., Siemens, R. (eds.) A Companion to Digital Humanities, Blackwell, Oxford (2004)
8. New Findings and New Questions About the Origins of Digital Humanities: On the State of the Art of Histories of the Index Thomisticus Project of Fr Roberto Busa S.J. https://www.c2dh.uni.lu/data/lecture-julianne-nyhan-new-findings-and-new-questions-about-origins-digital-humanities. Accessed 7 Sep 2020
9. Lyotard, J.: The Postmodern Condition: A Report on Knowledge. Manchester University Press, Manchester, p. 3 (1973). https://monoskop.org/images/e/e0/Lyotard_Jean-Francois_The_Postmodern_Condition_A_Report_on_Knowledge.pdf. Accessed 7 Sep 2020
10. Lyotard, J.: The Postmodern Condition: A Report on Knowledge. Manchester University Press, Manchester, p. xxiv (1973). https://monoskop.org/images/e/c0/Lyotard_Jean-Francois_The_Postmodern_Condition_A_Report_on_Knowledge.pdf. Accessed 7 Sep 2020
11. Brown, S., Clements, P., Grundy, I.: Sorting things in: feminist knowledge representation and changing modes of scholarly production. Women's Stud. Int. Forum **29**(3), 319 (2006). https://doi.org/10.1016/j.wsif.2006.04.010. Accessed 7 Sep 2020
12. Brown, S., Clements, P., Grundy, I.: Sorting things in: feminist knowledge representation and changing modes of scholarly production. Women's Stud. Int. Forum **29**(3), 320 (2006). https://doi.org/10.1016/j.wsif.2006.04.010. Accessed 7 Sep 2020
13. Jameson, F.: Postmodernism, or, the Cultural Logic of Late Capitalism. Duke University Press, Durham, p. 44 (1991)
14. Africa Digital Humanities Seminar. https://youtu.be/FSH3ExAyDkU. Accessed 7 Sep 2020
15. Omobowale, A.: Clientelism and social structure: an analysis of patronage in Yoruba social thought. Afr. Spectr. **43**(2), 217–218 (2008). https://www.jstor.org/stable/40175237. Accessed 7 Sep 2020
16. Vanscoy, A.: Making sense of professional work: metaphors for reference and information service. Libr. Inf. Sci. Res. **38**(3), 243–249 (2016). https://doi.org/10.1016/j.lisr.2016.08.003. Accessed 7 Sep 2020

Understanding the Narrative Functions of Visualization in Digital Humanities Publications: A Case Study of the *Journal of Cultural Analytics*

Rongqian Ma[1]([✉]), Kai Li[2], and Daqing He[1]

[1] University of Pittsburgh, Pittsburgh, PA 15213, USA
rom77@pitt.edu
[2] Renmin University of China, Beijing, China

Abstract. The use and effects of visual representations in knowledge production have been a charged topic in scientific research. In the field of humanities studies, however, this topic remains under-examined despite the increasing applications of data visualization in the field. This paper aims to understand how visual representations facilitate narrative construction in published articles in the emerging field of digital humanities (DH). Through the methods of content analysis and close reading, we analyzed the narrative functions of visualizations in the argumentation process with a selected sample of research articles published in the *Journal of Cultural Analytics* from 2017 to 2019. With four observations from the analysis, this study presented a preliminary yet innovative examination of DH's visual language and proposed suggestions on integrating existing functional frameworks of data visualization with the research contexts of digital humanities.

Keywords: Data visualization · Digital humanities · Visual rhetoric · Scholarly communication · Journal of Cultural Analytics

1 Introduction

The use and effects of visual representations in knowledge production and communication have been a charged topic in science studies. Bruno Latour [1] claimed that graphs function as "immutable mobiles" that facilitate scientific knowledge production and transmission. Generations of historians, philosophers, sociologists, and rhetoricians of sciences developed on Latour's theory and confirmed the *visuality* of sciences, namely, the crucial roles of visual representations in the construction of scientific texts as the venue of knowledge claims [1–3]. In the emerging field of digital humanities (DH), despite the rapid development and application of visualizations, there has not been a systematic investigation into the empirical use of data visualizations. We know little about how visualizations contribute to the research outputs and new knowledge development in this field and how we could possibly guide them towards a more facilitating direction for humanities researchers.

© Springer Nature Switzerland AG 2021
K. Toeppe et al. (Eds.): iConference 2021, LNCS 12645, pp. 446–456, 2021.
https://doi.org/10.1007/978-3-030-71292-1_34

This paper presents a preliminary study to address this broad concern on the effects of data visualization on argumentation. By "data visualization," we refer to the visual representations with scholarly purposes rather than the pure decorative pictorial presentations [4–6]. With examples from the open-access *Journal of Cultural Analytics*, this paper tackles the central research question: How do visualizations function in the research narrative to facilitate humanistic arguments and interpretations? More specifically, we examine 1) how do visualizations represent data in DH? 2) How does the composition of visualizations produce meaning and facilitate narratives? And finally, 3) how do the verbal-visual interactions mobilize arguments? Through means of close reading [7, 8], this study suggests multiple narrative functions of visualization in DH articles, some distinct from those in existing frameworks based on scientific literature. Towards the end of this paper, we demonstrate how this case study's analyses can be further generalized, by comparing our findings against recent frameworks.

2 Literature Review

Scientific data visualizations have been studied broadly across disciplines over centuries. The classic works on visualization by Edward Tufte traced the use of statistical graphics to at least 1750–1800 [9] and proposed metrics for evaluating statistical visualizations such as excellence, integrity, and sophistication [9]. More recent works in cognitive science and information science also looked at visualization from the cognitive ability of human beings for visual processing, literacy, and design aspects, and explored issues such as memorability, aesthetics, or functionality of visualizations [10–13]. Scholars in science and technology studies (STS) contributed to theorizing the roles of visual representations in scientific knowledge production and communication. Bruno Latour [1] argued that visual representations function as "immutable mobiles" in sciences that transformed the discovery and research processes usually only visible in the laboratory context into validated and widely recognized scientific facts. The central role of visual displays in sciences, also named as the *visuality* of science, was applied to examine the disciplinary traits within sciences, such as identifying the *scientificity* of disciplines [2, 3, 14, 15]. Following this line of inquiry, scholars discussed the rhetorical functions of visual in scientific publications with specific disciplinary cases [16–20].

In the context of DH, visualization remains an under-researched area. Scholars have argued that "problems of bias, interpretation, subjectivity, and ambiguity must be taught alongside problems of scientific rigor, decomposition, and algebra" for the humanities [21], and it is crucial to create visualizations that are "reflective and critical" [5]. Lev Manovich proposed the concept of "direct visualization," a method that "creates new visual representations from the actual visual media objects or their parts," without any *reduction* [22]. Drucker raised the concept of *capta* to acknowledge the "situated, partial, and constitutive character" of humanistic inquiries and knowledge production [23] and called for a "humanistic visualization" approach that centers on the interpretative nature of the humanities.

Despite the theoretical discussions on the design principles of an interpretative, humanistic visualization, few studies offered any empirical examination of DH visualizations' *status quo* [24]. This paper sets out the first step to bridge the literature gap on the empirical understanding of visual representations in DH. It also adds a new analytical perspective to visualization research in general, with a specific contextual focus on DH.

3 Data and Methods

3.1 Data Corpus

The *Journal of Cultural Analytics* is an open-access journal launched in 2016, which is dedicated to the computational study of culture, intending to "promote high-quality scholarship that applies computational and quantitative methods to the study of cultural objects, processes, and agents." Themes represented in this journal include data and infrastructure (12 articles), genre (10 articles), gender (5 articles), race (3 articles), sound (2 articles), among others (i.e., food, space, geography, image, and change, each containing only one article) [25]. Spinaci et al. [26] identified this journal as "exclusively DH," making it appropriate for this study. Besides, this small-sized, thriving journal contains only 57 peer-reviewed articles since its inception but includes a large and heterogeneous collection of visualizations, making it a well-suitable candidate for the scope of this analysis. This study focuses on peer-reviewed research articles as the academic mainstream still recognizes them as the most authoritative channel for quality DH research. We selected 37 articles published between 2017 and 2019 as they demonstrate the most comprehensive coverage of articles in the journal, and then we classified the visualizations in them based on a Latourian framework for scientific inscriptions developed by Arsenault et al. [2]. In this framework, "inscriptions" refer to the material signs and artifacts of scientific production embodied in some medium [27]. Arsenault et al.'s taxonomy has three general categories, *graphs*, *non-graph illustrations* (NGI), and *non-visual illustrations* (NVI). Graphs are defined as figures that have scales and convey quantitative information. NGIs contain diagrams (e.g., schematics, flowcharts, models), pictures (e.g., photographs, drawings), maps, and montages, while NVIs contain tables and equations. Table 1 shows the number of the three types of inscriptions across the dataset. Two coders classified the inscriptions independently based on Arsenault et al.'s framework. The interrater reliability (IRR) measured by Cohen's Kappa is 0.966 [28], representing a very high level of agreement between the raters.

Table 1. Number of inscriptions across *Journal of Cultural Analytics* (2017–2019)

Graph	NGI	NVI
196	54	69

3.2 Methods

In this study, we adopted a qualitative, exploratory, and bottom-up method of close reading [29] to identify the narrative functions of visualizations in the selected articles, and analyze how they are used to support claims. Close reading is a method that emerged from literary studies during the twentieth century [8, 24, 29] and examines the dynamic interactions between texts and visuals with specific, case-by-case analyses of the dataset. In this study, we investigated how the visuals are interwoven in the narrative to solicit arguments particularly from the following aspects: 1) how the visualizations represent humanities data; 2) how compositions of visualizations facilitate meaning and arguments; and 3) how contexts (e.g., the section of the article where a visual is embedded) shape the effects of visualizations in articles.

4   Results

Our preliminary analysis of the selected articles suggests the essential role of visualizations in mobilizing humanities claims. A detailed analysis of the narrative functions of visual representations in the selected corpus is presented with examples below. The observations cover aspects of data representation, rhetoric of different types of visualizations, and the contextual verbal-visual interactions, as indicated in the method section.

DH Visualizations Represent both Quantitative and Qualitative Data. Creating "mathematically tractable visual and graphic displays" [30] and thus scientific meanings from raw data is one of the key functions played by scientific visualization. As a field that is deeply influenced by data-driven research approach, the mathematization of quantitative data is inevitably reflected in our paper sample. For example, in Fig. 1, the authors offered a series of network graphs to show how the technique of LargeVis dimensionality reduction captures different types of textual similarity and differences in the full HathiTrust collection. However, the representation of quantitative, large data is not the only form of visualization in our corpus. The *Journal of Cultural Analytics* authors also use visual representations of carefully curated, qualitative datasets to support argumentation. For example, Fig. 2 is used to illustrate the claim on misrepresentation of indigenous communities in archival data held by non-Indigenous collecting institutions. The image in Fig. 2 (left) shows the original untouched negative of a Piegan lodge on the Library of Congress website, which presents three *Piikani* individuals in their lodge with a clock centered between them. However, in Fig. 2 (right) that audiences would have viewed in *The North American Indian,* a twenty-volume collection to record the Native and Indigenous life curated by Edward S. Curtis from 1907 to 1930, the clock was deliberately cut out from the image to "curate a desired representation of Native American peoples" that does not bear signs of modernity or contemporary lifestyle. By introducing the original negative first and then contrasting it with the purposely curated however widely accessible image, the authors demonstrated the biased data representation in indigenous archives. As shown in previous studies [2, 3, 31], data-oriented visualizations are more frequently used in research fields that are more "scientific." Similarly, we should expect that DH as a research field is more strongly reliant on qualitative visualizations than most, if not all, research fields in sciences. This mixture of qualitative and quantitative visualizations is further supported by the diversity of research topics and methods adopted within the DH community [32].

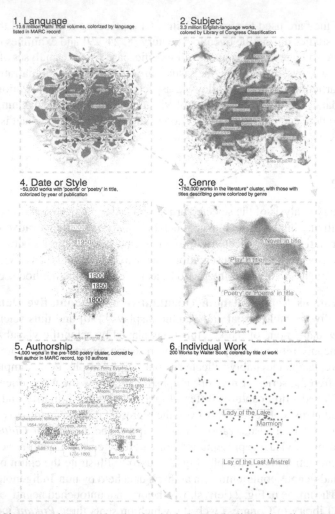

1. Language
~13.6 million HathiTrust volumes, colorized by language listed in MARC record

2. Subject
3.3 million English-language works, colorized by Library of Congress Classification

4. Date or Style
~50,000 works with 'poems' or 'poetry' in title, colorized by year of publication

3. Genre
~750,000 works in the literature" cluster, with those with titles describing genre colorized by genre

5. Authorship
~4,000 works in the pre-1850 poetry cluster, colored by first author in MARC record, top 10 authors

6. Individual Work
200 Works by Walter Scott, colored by title of work

Fig. 1. Six successive zoom levels of a single LargeVis dimensionality reduction [33]

Fig. 2. (**left**) Untouched negative of an image of three *Piikani* individuals in their lodge with a clock centered between them. (**right**) Retouched image of three Piikani individuals in their lodge *without* a clock [34].

Realism of Photographic Representations Strengthens Arguments. Photography, as an artistic form and visual technique with accompanied realist and interpretative features, can produce meaning in different ways [35, 36]. In STS, photographs are conceptualized as the representation of the original forms of social and natural phenomena in the scientific simplification process [2, 37]. Lynn explained how this simplification process can be enabled by the "split-screen juxtaposition" of photographs, diagrams, and models, each of which represent the same thing [38]. Compared with diagrams and models, photographs sit at one end of the continuum of data abstraction in sciences, as their gratuitous details demonstrate the real existence of a natural phenomenon or an object [16]. Such inherent realism in photography is applicable in public science education to accelerate the diffusion of scientific knowledge [39, 40].

In our dataset, photographic representations are heavily used; the repetitive, accumulative use of photographic representations and the juxtaposition of them convince readers of the actual existence of a phenomenon. For example, in Fig. 3, the book covers were selected and collaged by the authors to demonstrate their claim that "the pleasure of reading is, for girls, the act of reading itself, absorption, time alone and in one's own head, be it indoors, by the seashore, or even among the leafy boughs of a tree." This form of visualization echoes what Manovich defined as the "direct visualization" [22]. By only piecing together a selected number of original images of the collection, two important lessons can be drawn from Fig. 2. First, no different from scientific articles, DH scholarship also requires the juxtaposition of visual evidence, especially the comparison and contrasting between them, to create new meanings and knowledge. Second, due to the characteristics of humanistic research, photographic realism can contribute to the construction of arguments in DH publications in a more direct way.

Graphs Demonstrate Analytical Procedures and Inspire Alternative Interpretations. Graphs are defined as figures that have scales and convey abstracted quantitative information [2]. Our analysis demonstrated the use of graphs in the corpus to facilitate analytical procedures and inspire possible alternative interpretations, instead of solidifying one final result. In an article examining the early modern discourse of race in Shakespeare's *Othello*, the authors implemented two analytical models, the LDA topic models and word2vec, to investigate the "quiet" changes around the discourse and to provide a multi-perspective exploration of the texts. Multiple topic modeling and word embedding graphs were presented along with the analysis through the article, illustrating results on different topics and word relationships (see Fig. 4). Each graph aimed to visualize one specific topic (e.g., "Religion") or one semantic relationship (e.g., "Complexion"), functioning as an atlas that guides readers through the article exploring various ways and perspectives to interpret the classic work. This is an ideal example that utilizes visualizations to open up exploratory space for multi-dimensional, "alternative" interpretations, in addition to transforming a theory or assumption into solidified facts or attaining a most authoritative conclusion.

Fig. 3. Selected 19th-century book covers supporting the claim of a gendered reading and market [41]

Visualizations Help to Validate a New Method or Technique. We also observed that the use of visualizations in the corpus is often associated with the proposal or validation of an original analytical method or technique. For instance, in an article that aims to develop computational methods for the automatic extraction of semantic elements such as facial recognition and shot breaks in movies, the authors used a massive number of visualizations to demonstrate the performance of their methodology (see Fig. 5a). In Fig. 5a, the authors used scenes from two sitcoms, *Bewitched* (1964–1972) and *I Dream of Jeannie* (1965–1970), to demonstrate the advantages of CNN in accurately detecting faces from the shots to the popular, shaped-based histogram of oriented gradients (HOG) detector technique. After justifying the methodology with a visual example, the authors followed up with a line graph showing the face recognition testing results for the accurate detection of primary characters in the sitcoms (see Fig. 5b). The visually assisted justification of the methodology laid a solid foundation for applying the method to the discovery of visual styles in the two sitcoms in the second part of the article.

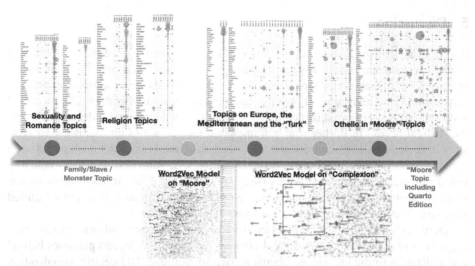

Fig. 4. Use of LDA topic models and word2vec model graphs in the narrative flow of the article. In this visualization, we illustrate how the multiple graphs facilitated the article's narrative flow, inviting readers to follow the authors' exploration of different topics and interpretations of the *Othello* corpora [42].

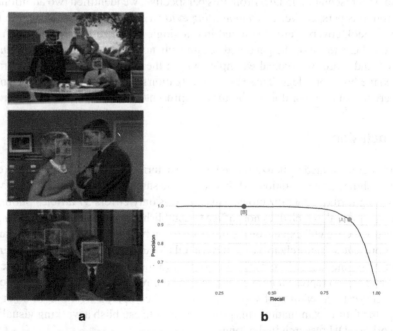

Fig. 5. (a) Faces detected using a HOG detector (blue) and a neural network (orange) from screenshots of I Dream of Jeannie and Bewitched. (b) Precision and recall curve for varying cut-off scores in the algorithm, showing test results for the face recognition task [43]. (Color figure online)

5   Discussion

Börner et al.'s recent framework on data visualization literacy used the term "insight needs" to refer to the basic task types behind the visualizations, and identified "categorize or cluster; order, rank, sort; distributions; comparisons; trends; geospatial; compositions; correlations or relationships" [13] as the major purposes of visualization. The identified narrative functions of visualization in our corpus are found to be partially aligned with the "insight needs" in Börner et al.'s framework. Graphs are of prevalent use to visualize large-scale cultural datasets to demonstrate data trends and relationships between variables (see Fig. 1), facilitating a "distant reading" of culture [44]. We also frequently found visualizations utilizing clusters (see Fig. 1 and Fig. 4) to present literary topics, word associations, or corpora's themes. Comparison is also a task frequently fulfilled with visualizations (see Fig. 2) in our corpus.

Despite the shared characteristics in visualization tasks, our analysis suggests how it can be useful and informative to also connect the specific tasks and purposes behind a visualization to the knowledge claims it tries to facilitate. DH-centric visualization framework should look beyond the individual visual form and examine the use of a visualization in its context, from a visual rhetoric perspective – for instance, how the visualizations are embedded in the narrative, and how they are positioned to support argumentation. This is essentially what we try to achieve by examining the narrative functions of a visual representation in DH. From this perspective, we identified two additional purposes from this perspective: 1) *accumulating evidence (repetition)*. As shown in Fig. 3, individual book covers were positioned into a single visualization to persuade readers of the actual existence of the gendered reading phenomenon. 2) *Justifying the method*. Figures 4 and 5 are two typical examples where the visuals strongly demonstrate the proposed method's privilege. These two visualization tasks can be related to the intrinsic characteristics of *capta* or domain inquiries represented in the humanities research.

6   Conclusion

Our study demonstrated visualization in DH is a rhetorical device that functions in certain ways to mobilize argumentation. At this stage, the study has limitations that prevent us from making further generalizations. This analysis only covers 37 articles published in one specific journal, which does not suffice to establish a systematic DH visual language. For future work, we will expand on the data size to analyze more DH journals and articles, so as to present a comprehensive picture of DH visualizations in terms of their types and narrative functions. Moreover, we also plan to focus on visualization as a research method and tool to represent humanities data, as our results have suggested its potential to highlight distinct features of visualization in DH compared with that in other fields. Through the future examination, this project aspires to establish a working visualization framework for DH research in the long run.

Acknowledgements. This research study was supported by the Institute of Museum and Library Services LEADS-4-NDP (LIS Education and Data Science for the National Digital Platform), Grant: RE-70-17-0094-17.

References

1. Latour, B.: Drawing things together. In: Lynch, M., Woolgar, S. (eds.) Representation in Scientific Practice. The MIT Press, Cambridge (1990)
2. Arsenault, D.J., Smith, L.D., Beauchamp, E.A.: Visual Inscriptions in the scientific hierarchy: mapping the "treasures of science." Sci. Commun. **27**, 376–428 (2006). https://doi.org/10.1177/1075547005285030
3. Smith, L.D., Best, L.A., Stubbs, D.A., Johnston, J., Archibald, A.B.: Scientific graphs and the hierarchy of the sciences: a latourian survey of inscription practices. Soc. Stud. Sci. **30**, 73–94 (2000)
4. Hann, R.: Visualized Arguments; Or How to Pierce the Persuasive Visualization and Other Arguments (2008). https://doi.org/10.14236/ewic/EVA2008.14
5. Champion, E.M.: Digital humanities is text heavy, visualization light, and simulation poor. Digital Scholarship Humanities, vol. fqw053 (2016). https://doi.org/10.1093/llc/fqw053
6. Jessop, M.: Digital visualization as a scholarly activity. Liter. Linguist. Comput. **23**, 281–293 (2008). https://doi.org/10.1093/llc/fqn016
7. Bode, K.: The equivalence of "close" and "distant" reading; or, toward a new object for data-rich literary history. Modern Lang. Quar. **78**, 77–106 (2017). https://doi.org/10.1215/00267929-3699787
8. Wilkens, M.: Canons, close reading, and the evolution of method. In: Gold, M. (ed.) Debates in the Digital Humanities. Univ of Minnesota Press, Minneapolis (2012)
9. Tufte, E.: The visual display of quantitative information (2001)
10. Borkin, M.A., Vo, A.A., Bylinskii, Z., Isola, P., Sunkavalli, S., Oliva, A., Pfister, H.: What makes a visualization memorable? IEEE Trans. Visual Comput. Graphics **19**, 2306–2315 (2013). https://doi.org/10.1109/TVCG.2013.234
11. Borkin, M.A., Bylinskii, Z., Kim, N.W., Bainbridge, C.M., Yeh, C.S., Borkin, D., Pfister, H., Oliva, A.: Beyond Memorability: visualization recognition and recall. IEEE Trans. Visual Comput. Graphics **22**, 519–528 (2016). https://doi.org/10.1109/TVCG.2015.2467732
12. Moere, A.V., Purchase, H.: On the role of design in information visualization. Inf. Vis. **10**, 356–371 (2011). https://doi.org/10.1177/1473871611415996
13. Börner, K., Bueckle, A., Ginda, M.: Data visualization literacy: definitions, conceptual frameworks, exercises, and assessments. Proc. Natl. Acad. Sci. USA **116**, 1857–1864 (2019). https://doi.org/10.1073/pnas.1807180116
14. Smith, L.D., Best, L.A., Stubbs, D.A., Archibald, A.B., Roberson-Nay, R.: Constructing knowledge: the role of graphs and tables in hard and soft psychology. Am. Psychol. **57**, 749–761 (2002). https://doi.org/10.1037/0003-066X.57.10.749
15. Cleveland, W.S.: Graphs in scientific publications. Am. Stat. **38**, 261–269 (1984). https://doi.org/10.2307/2683400
16. Myers, G.: Every picture tells a story: Illustrations in E.O. Wilson's Sociobiology. In: Lynch, M., Woolgar, S. (eds.) Representation in Scientific Practice. The MIT Press, Cambridge (1990)
17. Thompson, D.K.: Arguing for experimental "facts" in science: a study of research article results sections in biochemistry. Written Commun. **10**, 106–128 (1993). https://doi.org/10.1177/0741088393010001004
18. Richards, A.R.: Argument and authority in the visual representations of science. Technical Commun. Quar. **12**, 183–206 (2003). https://doi.org/10.1207/s15427625tcq1202_3
19. Graves, H.: The Rhetoric of (Interdisciplinary) Science: Visuals and the Construction of Facts in Nanotechnology. Poroi. 10 (2014). https://doi.org/10.13008/2151-2957.1207
20. Rudwick, M.J.S.: The emergence of a visual language for geological science 1760–1840. Hist. Sci. **14**, 149–195 (1976). https://doi.org/10.1177/007327537601400301

21. Bradley, A.J., El-Assady, M., Coles, K., Alexander, E., Chen, M., Collins, C.: Visualization and the digital humanities. IEEE Comput. Graph. Appl. **13**, 26–38 (2018)
22. Manovich, L.: What is visualisation? Vis. Stud. **26**, 36–49 (2011). https://doi.org/10.1080/1472586X.2011.548488
23. Drucker, J.: Humanities Approaches to Graphical Display. DHQ. 005 (2011)
24. Janicke, S., Franzini, G., Cheema, M.F., Scheuermann, G.: Visual text analysis in digital humanities, vol. 25 (2016)
25. Journal of Cultural Analytics. https://culturalanalytics.org/. Accessed 07 Jan 2021
26. Spinaci, G., Colavizza, G., Peroni, S.: Preliminary Results on Mapping Digital Humanities Research. L'Associazione per l'Informatica Umanistica e la Cultura Digitale 7
27. Roth, W.-M., McGinn, M.K.: Inscriptions: toward a theory of representing as social practice. Rev. Educ. Res. **68**, 35–59 (1998). https://doi.org/10.2307/1170689
28. McHugh, M.L.: Interrater reliability: the kappa statistic. Biochemia Medica **22**, 276–282 (2012). https://doi.org/10.11613/BM.2012.031
29. Brooks, C.: The new criticism. The Sewanee. Review **87**, 592–607 (1979)
30. Goodwin, C.: Practices of seeing: visual analysis: an ethnomethodological approach. In: van Leeuwen, T., Jewitt, C. (eds.) Handbook of Visual Analysis. Sage, London (2000)
31. Coopmans, C. (ed.): Representation in Scientific Practice Revisited. The MIT Press, Cambridge (2014)
32. Porsdam, H.: Digital Humanities: On Finding the Proper Balance between Qualitative and Quantitative Ways of Doing Research in the Humanities. DHQ. 007 (2013)
33. Schmidt, B.: Stable random projection: lightweight, general-purpose dimensionality reduction for digitized libraries. J. Cult. Anal. **35** (2018)
34. Guiliano, J., Heitman, C.: Difficult heritage and the complexities of indigenous data. J. Cult. Anal. **1** (2019). https://doi.org/10.22148/16.044
35. Barthes, R.: Camera Lucida: Reflections on Photography. Hill and Wang, New York (1981)
36. Sontag, S.: On Photography. Farrar Straus and Giroux, New York (1977)
37. Lynch, M., Woolgar, S. (eds.): Representation in Scientific Practice. MIT Press, Cambridge (1990)
38. Lynch, M.: The externalized retina: selection and mathematization in the visual documentation of objects in the life sciences. In: Lynch, M., Woolgar, S. (eds.) Representation in Scientific Practice. The MIT Press, Cambridge (1990)
39. Dimopoulos, K., Koulaidis, V., Sklaveniti, S.: Towards an analysis of visual images in school science textbooks and press articles about science and technology. Res. Sci. Educ. **33**, 189–216 (2003). https://doi.org/10.1023/A:1025006310503
40. Evagorou, M., Erduran, S., Mäntylä, T.: The role of visual representations in scientific practices: from conceptual understanding and knowledge generation to 'seeing' how science works. Int. J. STEM Educ. **2**, 11 (2015). https://doi.org/10.1186/s40594-015-0024-x
41. Tatlock, L., Erlin, M., Knox, D., Pentecost, S.: Crossing Over: Gendered Reading Formations at the Muncie Public Library, 1891–1902. Crossing Over. 31 (2018)
42. Lee, J.J., Greteman, B., Lee, J., Eichmann, D.: Linked reading: digital historicism and early modern discourses of race around Shakespeare's othello. J. Cult. Anal. **35** (2018)
43. Arnold, T., Tilton, L., Berke, A.: Visual style in two network era sitcoms. J. Cult. Anal. **29** (2019)
44. Moretti, F.: Distant Reading. Verso, London (2013)

A Comparative Studies of Automatic Query Formulation in Full-Text Database Search of Chinese Digital Humanities

Chengxi Yan[1,2] , Tzu-Yi Ho[1,2] , and Jun Wang[1,2(✉)]

[1] Department of Information Management, Peking University, Beijing, People's Republic of China
junwang@pku.edu.cn
[2] Digital Humanities Center, Peking University, Beijing, People's Republic of China

Abstract. Query gap is a very serious problem for the full-text database search in the domain of Chinese digital humanities (CDH). General CDH search systems are focused on the improvement of data quality, which ignore the connection between users' search intents and the system response. We design a two-phase procedure for comparative analysis of the effectiveness of different automatic query formulation in pre-defined tasks, including a prototype system test and a questionnaire-based user study. The experiment shows that compared to query suggestion and query reformulation, query expansion is the most effective automatic query formulation technology with a strong robust performance for user satisfaction, which means it is not sensitive to the types of search intent. The effectiveness of query reformulation and the hybrid methods are limited while query suggestion performs worse in the task for diverse search intent. These findings are believed to be helpful to the reduction of query gap in the full-text database search of Chinese digital humanities, which will foster the development of this field.

Keywords: Automatic query formulation · Full-text database search · Digital humanities

1 Introduction

More and more historical researchers are concerned about the effectiveness of data access and knowledge discovery in the database management systems. Although current full-text database systems can grudgingly support the searching functionality, there is still much difficulty of perceived distance between users' search intent and the system response in the search process of full-text databases, which is defined as the "query gap" [1–3]. Previous studies have attributed it to some reasons, such as inaccurate expression of query [4–6], vocabulary mismatch [7–9], and shortages of interpretative feedback [10–12].

However, the present CDH database search systems (e.g. Airusheng "爱如生" [13], Chinese Ancient Books Resource Bank "中华古籍资源库" [14]) are focused on the

© Springer Nature Switzerland AG 2021
K. Toeppe et al. (Eds.): iConference 2021, LNCS 12645, pp. 457–468, 2021.
https://doi.org/10.1007/978-3-030-71292-1_35

data quality rather than the threat of query gap caused by users' cognitive difference. The technology of automatic query formulation (QF) is proposed to bridge this gap by transforming queries into the structured query representation [15], which can help to achieve users' goals (or sub-goals) in the search process [16].

To the best of our knowledge, few works have discussed the effectiveness of different automatic QF-based technologies in the full-text database search, which is quite important to CDH as mentioned. Under the condition of pre-defined search tasks, we conduct a comparative analysis of different QF-based methods by our designed UI prototype system, to explore the answer to the following research questions:

- RQ1: Which query formulation (QF)-based technology is the most effective in the full-text search of Chinese digital humanities databases? Qf-based technologies contain three most well-known ones, namely query suggestion, query reformulation and query expansion.
- RQ2: How do those technologies perform in different search aspects, such as search strategies and categories of search tasks? The search strategies contain the direct search and the advanced search; the search tasks are categorized according to the query attributes based on users' search intent.

2   Related Work

2.1   Database Search in Digital Humanity

Relevant researches have studied intelligent query service in digital humanity domains, which are focused on the text organization and information querying for historical collections or cultural heritages [17–21].

RSNSR [19] is an interdisciplinary database project for Germany cultural heritage preservation, which can automatically modify the variant spelling brought about by the error-prone OCR digitalization and diachronic linguistic non-standardization through a rule-based fuzzy approach. It can achieve great improvement on the search efficiency of historical texts. The China Biographical Database system (CBDB) [20] built upon large bodies of digital texts offers different types of querying to users, which also supports export of search results for further GIS analysis and social network analysis. For digitalized newspapers during the time of Australian colonization, the National Library of Australia (NLA) develops a digital humanities tool for text mining "PaperMiner" [21] which enables metadata-based database search in multiple levels.

2.2   QF-Based Database Search

As the entry to a search system, automatic query formulation is of great significance to generate well-organized queries during users' interaction with the system, especially for full-text indexed databases.

Query suggestion is a query formulation technology that displays relevant queries in a drop-down list matching initial queries, which has been widely used in information retrieval domains. Qi [22] proposes a framework for location-aware keyword query suggestion, which can create a weighted keyword-document graph that allows for flexible selection of the highest-scoring keyword queries based on the semantic relevance between queries and documents. Baeza-Yates [23] designs a query clustering process in which similar queries can be identified with users' preferences in query logs. The method demonstrates that related queries can be efficiently suggested in line with a relevance criterion.

Query expansion is used to find related query words in broader domains. Rocchio's method [24] aims to select those relevant words in high-ranking documents without considering relative probability distribution of words in returned documents, while Carpineto' method [25] can discover potential expansion words based on the Kullback-Leibler divergence score of words between query-relevant documents and the whole corpus. Recently, Pseudo Relevance Feedback have been proposed with the assumption that appropriate expansion words should be generated from those most frequent words in the top returned documents, among which RM3 has achieved the state-of-the-art performance appropriately [26–28].

Alternatively, query reformulation underlines the active modification of queries (e.g. generalization, specialization, and etc.) by users [29]. Mottin [30] proposes a graph-query reformulation for query specialization, enabling explorative query-driven discovery in graph database, which can produce high-quality results in their experiments. The parse tree reformulation [31] can produce useful SQL statements with strong expressiveness, including different move operations of sub-trees until conforming to the predefined grammars.

3   Methods

We develop a research procedure of exploring the effectiveness of different QF-based technologies for full-text database search in CDH, which contains two experimental phases, namely a prototype-based test and a user study. First, all the participants are required to complete the assigned tasks through our designed search system. Next, a questionnaire-based evaluation of user satisfaction for those technologies is conducted in the user study.

3.1   A UI Design for Prototype System

Figure 1 indicates the whole architecture of our system. Given the RQ1, we design a web-based GUI integrating the functions of query suggestion (QS), query reformulation (QR), and query expansion (QE). In the query interface, QS can support automatic completion for input queries. QR offers interactive Boolean combination for multiple queries, where users are allowed to add, delete and modify the query formulation. The component for search strategies (i.e. direct search and advanced search in RQ2) is also designed and incorporated into the interface.

Additionally, the core search engine is driven by a general CDH relational database system that most CDH projects adopt. To present the effectiveness of query expansion in an interactive environment, two views (i.e. query expansion view denoted as QEV and query basket view denoted as QBE) are developed for users. QEV guides users to select their satisfied candidate query words, which are reorganized as a new query formulation in QBE for subsequent search process. For the algorithm of query expansion, we use the mentioned algorithm RM3 [28] defined as the following:

$$p(t|\theta_Q, \lambda) = \lambda \cdot \sum_{\theta_d \in R} p(\theta_d) \frac{c(w, \theta_d)}{\sum_w c(w; \theta_d)} \prod_{i=1}^{n} p(q_i|\theta_d) + (1 - \lambda) \cdot p(t, \theta_Q) \quad (1)$$

where $p(\theta_d)$ is a uniform distribution for the relevance feedback documents θ_d, $c(w, \theta_d)$ is the frequency of a word w in θ_d, $p(q_i|\theta_d)$ is the probability of a query q_i in θ_d, $p(t, \theta_Q)$ is the probability of a recommended word t with a prior query distribution θ_Q, λ denotes a weighted parameter which is set to 0.5,

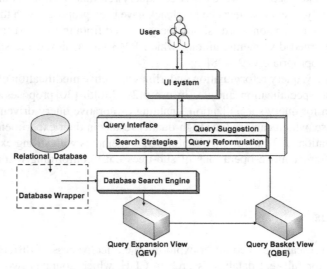

Fig. 1. The architecture of our system prototype

According to the above design solution, the layout of UI implementation is displayed as Fig. 2.

3.2 User Study

A user questionnaire is designed for obtaining users' demographic information and evaluation in the user study. Specifically, two important elements should be defined first:

Evaluative Indicator. User satisfaction is an important evaluative conception defined as "the fulfilment of a specified desire or goal" [32], which emphasizes upon the subjective cognitive perception for the search success based on an overall search experience [33]. To measure the user satisfaction, we develop a questionnaire based on a 7-point Likert-type scale that consists of the following options, namely "strongly disagree" at −3, "disagree" at −2, "somewhat disagree" at −1, "neither agree or disagree" at 0, "somewhat agree" at 1, "agree" at 2, and "strongly agree" at 3. It is noted that the value of 0 represents users' neural attitude corresponding to their average expectancy of satisfaction on the utilization of full-text database search in CDH.

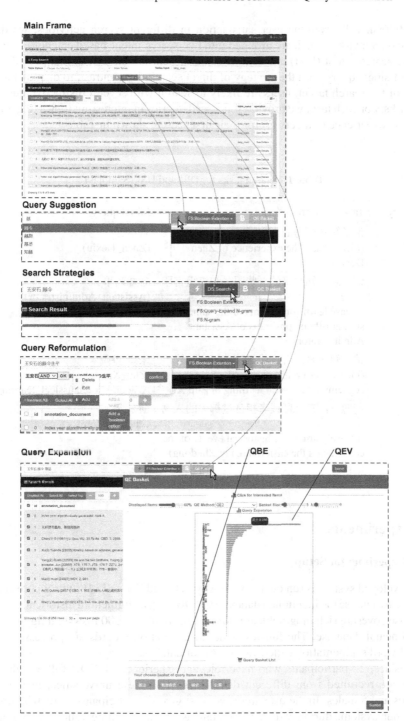

Fig. 2. The system implementation. Noted that "FS:Boolean Extention" supported by MySQL (version 8.0) is used for the advanced search, "DS:search" refers to the direct search.

Search Tasks. To examine user satisfaction in different search activities, we design twenty search tasks, which are grouped into two search intent-based categories, namely diverse search intent (DSI) and unique search intent (USI). USI is manifested by the input of single query with the strategy of direct search. By contrast, to display multiple facets of the search target, users are likely to search with several distinctive queries in DSI tasks. For each task, we provide some seed queries in interesting topics (e.g. official position, experience of a person) for their first search, shown in Table 1.

Table 1. Search tasks for DSI and USI (Samples)

Category	Task description	Initial query
USI	请了解真德秀的人物经历 (Please learn the experience of Zhen Dexiu)	真德秀 (Zhen_Dexiu)
	请了解参知政事的一些同名和等级官职术语 (Please learn some terms of the same or similar official positions of Assistant Administrator)	参知政事 (Assistant_Administrator)
DSI	请瞭解朱熹或者古代書院的相關記錄 (Please learn relevant records about the academy of classical learning or Zhu Xi)	朱熹 書院 (Zhu_Xi Academy_of_classical_learning)
	請瞭解浙东地区或者担任过御史的人物事跡紀錄 (Please learn about historical events of the censors and the eastern area of Zhedong)	浙东 御史 (Zhedong Censor)

4 Experiments

4.1 Experimental Setup

Our developed system is run on a remote Aliyun Cloud Server [34] (with 1 core and 2 G RAM). We choose the mentioned database CBDB [35], an influential historical relational database covering rich biographical information about 470,000 historical figures as our experimental database. The full-text indexed annotation records are processed with a tool of word segmentation called Jieba [36] for database search.

Besides, 22 participants who have relevant experience of CDH full-text database search are recruited from different disciplines of Chinese universities, including 17 females and 5 males. In the user study, we first give all participants a practical training about our system, during which the system is operated online followed by detailed interpretation about the functionality of each UI component (e.g. views, interface, etc.) as well as an entire procedure of performing tasks until they suffice it. Participants should test all the different functionalities of our system for tasks in multiple rounds, each of which lasts no more than 120 min. Finally, they need to complete the questionnaire based on their search experience.

4.2 System Evaluation

We take the measurement of system usability from five aspects [37] that affect searching experiences most in the system evaluation. The importance of each aspect ranges from -3 (the least important) to 3 (the most important). Noted that the value of 0, hereby regarded as a benchmark, represents the average acceptance of general CDH full-text database search system that participants have used.

Table 2. The result of system usability

	Flexibility	Speed	Engagement	Ease-to-use	Precision
Mean	0.86	−0.55	0.73	0.27	0.91

According to the results in Table 2, precision has the highest mean score ($M_{precision}$ = 0.91), which shows that our system can offer quite accurate search results, while the speed of our system performs the worst ($M_{speed} = -0.55$), even worse than the benchmark. Flexibility is another advantage of our system, together with precision which outperforms the performance of benchmark significantly in a T-test ($t_{flexibility} = 2.72$, $p < 0.05$, $t_{precision} = 3.26$, $p < 0.05$). This indicates better adaption and adjustment of our system to users' operation. Engagement refers to users' interaction and participation in the search task, for which our system also has better user experience.

Despite of the slow speed and the utilization difficulty, our system still shows promising evaluative results, compared to the average level of user experience using general CDH databases, which proves those proposed QF-based components are the main contribution to the improvement.

4.3 Comparative Analysis

For further understanding of the effectiveness of QF-based technologies, we conduct a comparative analysis to learn the difference of these methods.

In Table 3, the performance comparison of different search strategies shows that users have better experience of using our system in the advanced search (AS) than the direct search (DS). Among different QF-based methods in AS, the QE-based method achieves the best ($M_{QE} = 1.20$), which significantly outperforms the QS-based method and the hybrid method in a T-test ($t_{QE\_DS} = 2.40$, $p < 0.05$, $t_{QE\_QS} = 2.55$, $p < 0.05$). The hybrid one refers to a comprehensive searching method integrated with all the components of QE, QS and QR.

Table 3. The evaluation for different search strategies

	DS	AS			
		QE	QS	QR	Hybrid
Mean (Std.)	0.48 (±1.58)	1.20 (±1.25)	0.48 (±1.42)	0.91 (±1.48)	1.11 (±1.26)

In addition, similar results have been found in Fig. 3 that the QE-based technology achieve the best, whatever the task category (USI or DSI) is ($M_{USI\_*(+QE)} = 0.91$, $M_{DSI\_*(+QE)} = 1.50$). Besides, both the QR-based method ($M_{DSI\_*(+QR)} = 0.91$) and the hybrid method ($M_{DSI\_*(+QS+QR+QE)} = 1.32$) incorporated with QS, QR and QE perform better than the DS ($M_{DSI\_*} = 0.73$) in the DSI tasks, while the QS-based method

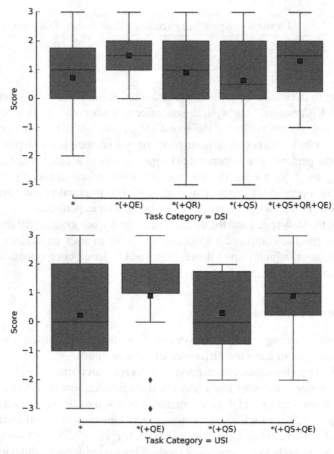

Fig. 3. The evaluation for QF-based technologies. Noted that "*" represents the direct search (DS), and "*(+?)" represents the advanced search, in which "?" can be QE or QS or QR or a hybrid combination.

with the least score ($M_{DSI\_*(+QS)} = 0.64$) seems not to be a good option. It performs even worse in USI tasks ($M_{USI\_*(+QS)} = 0.32$), but still achieves better performance than DS ($M_{USI\_*} = 0.23$). The hybrid methods for QS and QE in USI tasks also have better performance than DS ($M_{USI\_*(+QS+QE)} = 0.91$). On the whole, the average score of the DSI tasks is significantly higher than USI at an aggregate level ($M_{DSI} = 1.02, M_{USI} = 0.59, t_{DSI_{USI}} = 2.13, p < 0.05$).

5   Discussion

The evaluation of system usability shows our designed system is competitive with general full-text database search systems in Chinese historical domains, especially with certain advantages on the dimension of precision, flexibility and engagement. The problem of slow speeds and difficulty of utilization may be triggered by the poor configuration of server hardware, but the overall result still proves that the QF-based technologies can improve the user satisfaction of full-text database search.

To answer RQ1, we find query expansion (QE) affects users' satisfaction most compared to query suggestion and query reformulation. It implies the powerful ability of QE-based methods in the full-text database search of digital humanities domains. However, the hybrid method (merged with all these three methods) seems not to be an optimal option (slightly worse than the purely QE-based) which may be caused by the complexity of operations in hybrid query formulation.

For RQ2, query expansion contributes the most to the improvement of user satisfaction which is independent on the categories of tasks. Both query reformulation and hybrid methods are quite helpful to the improvement, but query suggestion may have negative effect on the user satisfaction when users' diverse search intent (DSI) is expressed. This proves the limited use of query suggestion in full-text database search. Due to a higher score of QF based methods in the DSI task, it is believed that they are more suitable to the diverse search intent (with multiple queries) than unique search intent (with single query). In addition, we can also infer that participants prefer using our system by advanced search rather than direct search when they expect to build complex queries. This attests the effectiveness of our designed QF-based components, since the direct search in our system can function as a complete simulation of general full-text database search in most of CDH databases.

To sum up, automatic query formulation technologies (especially the query expansion) can improve the user satisfaction to some degree, which assists to alleviate the problem of query gap in the full-text database search of CDH.

6   Conclusion and Future Work

In the study, we comparatively analyze different methods of automatic query formulation (QF) in the full-text search of Chinese digital humanities (CDH). A prototype system is developed to implement those QF-based components, which is viewed as a simulation of the real-world full-text database search in CDH. We invite several experienced users to participate in the experiment, which includes a prototype-based system test and a questionnaire-based user study.

We find that the system with proposed QF-based components is quite competitive on the dimensions of precision, flexibility and engagement, which validates its superiority to the general CDH full-text database search system. The comparative analysis shows that query expansion is the most effective QF-based technology compared to query suggestion and query reformulation. It is also not sensitive to task categories based on the search intent. Query suggestion performs worse in the task for diverse search intent, so does the hybrid method that mixes the three methods.

The above results provide inspiring points about the effectiveness of automatic query formulation technologies, which can be used to mitigate the problem of query gap in the full-text database search of CDH domains. Furthermore, these findings will further promote the development of intelligent information querying in the digital humanities domains. We believe this technology can apply equally to other languages, which will be worth exploring in the future.

References

1. Stojanovic, N.: Information-need driven query refinement. Web Intell. Agent Syst. **3**(3), 155–169 (2005)
2. Carmel, D., Yom-Tov, E., Roitman, H.: Enhancing digital libraries using missing content analysis. In: Proceedings of the 8th ACM/IEEE-CS joint conference on Digital libraries, p. 10. Association for Computing Machinery, New York (2008)
3. Weerkamp, W., Balog, K., de Rijke, M.: A generative blog post retrieval model that uses query expansion based on external collections. In: Proceedings of the Joint Conference of the 47th Annual Meeting of the ACL and the 4th International Joint Conference On Natural Language Processing of the AFNLP, pp. 1057–1065. Association for Computational Linguistics, Stroudsburg (2009)
4. Bosc, P., Pivert, O.: SQLf: A relational database language for fuzzy querying. IEEE Trans. Fuzzy Syst. **3**(1), 1–17 (1995)
5. Jansen, B.J., Spink, A., Bateman, J., Saracevic, T.: Real life information retrieval: a study of user queries on the web. ACM Sigir Forum **32**(1), 5–17 (1998)
6. Abass, O.A., Folorunso, O., Samuel, B.O.: Automatic query expansion for information retrieval: a survey and problem definition. Am. J. Comput. Sci. Inf. Eng. **4**(3), 24–30 (2017)
7. Li, W.S., Agrawal, D.: Supporting web query expansion efficiently using multi-granularity indexing and query processing. Data Knowl. Eng. **35**(3), 239–257 (2000)
8. Zhao, L., Callan, J.: Automatic term mismatch diagnosis for selective query expansion. In: Proceedings of the 35th International ACM SIGIR Conference on Research and Development in Information Retrieval, pp. 515–524. Association for Computing Machinery, New York (2012)
9. Wei, C.P., Hu, P.J.H., Tai, C.H., Huang, C.N., Yang, C.S.: Managing word mismatch problems in information retrieval: a topic-based query expansion approach. J. Manage. Inf. Syst. **24**(3), 269–295 (2007)
10. Herlocker, J.L., Konstan, J.A., Riedl, J.: Explaining collaborative filtering recommendations. In: Proceedings of the 2000 ACM Conference on Computer Supported Cooperative Work, pp. 241–250. Association for Computing Machinery, New York (2000)
11. Kay, J.: Scrutable adaptation: because we can and must. In: Wade, V.P., Ashman, H., Smyth, B. (eds.) AH 2006. LNCS, vol. 4018, pp. 11–19. Springer, Heidelberg (2006). https://doi.org/10.1007/11768012_2

12. Tintarev, N., Masthoff, J.: Evaluating the effectiveness of explanations for recommender systems. User Model. User-Adap. Inter. **22**(4–5), 399–439 (2012)
13. Airusheng. https://dh.ersjk.com/. Accessed 21 Sept 2020
14. Chinese Ancient Books Resource Bank. https://mylib.nlc.cn/web/guest/shanbenjiaojuan. Accessed 21 Sept 2020
15. Bendersky, M., Metzler, D., Croft, W.B.: Effective query formulation with multiple information sources. In: Proceedings of the fifth ACM International Conference on Web Search and Data Mining, pp. 443–452. Association for Computing Machinery, New York (2012)
16. Xie, H.: Patterns between interactive intentions and information-seeking strategies. Inf. Process. Manage. **38**(1), 55–77 (2002)
17. Hsieh, C.C., Lin, S.: A survey of full-text data bases and related techniques for Chinese ancient documents in Academia Sinica. Int. J. Comput. Linguist. Chin. Lang. Process. **2**(1), 105–130 (1997)
18. Wittern, C.: Chinese Buddhist texts for the new millennium—the Chinese Buddhist Electronic Text Association (CBETA) and its digital Tripitaka. J. Digit. Inf. **3**(2), 1–8 (2002)
19. Pilz, T., Luther, W., Fuhr, N., Ammon, U.: Rule-based search in text databases with nonstandard orthography. Lit. Linguist. Comput. **21**(2), 179–186 (2006)
20. Bol, P.K., Hsiang, J., Fong, G.: Prosopographical databases, text-mining, GIS and system interoperability for Chinese history and literature. Digit. Humanit. **2012**, 43–51 (2012)
21. Kutty, S., Nayak, R., Turnbull, P., Chernich, R., Kennedy, G., Raymond, K.: PaperMiner- a real-time spatiotemporal visualization for newspaper articles. Digit. Scholarsh. Humanit. **35**(1), 83–100 (2020)
22. Qi, S., Wu, D., Mamoulis, N.: Location aware keyword query suggestion based on document proximity. IEEE Trans. Knowl. Data Eng. **28**(1), 82–97 (2015)
23. Baeza-Yates, R., Hurtado, C., Mendoza, M.: Query recommendation using query logs in search engines. In: Lindner, W., Mesiti, M., Türker, C., Tzitzikas, Y., Vakali, A.I. (eds.) EDBT 2004. LNCS, vol. 3268, pp. 588–596. Springer, Heidelberg (2004). https://doi.org/10.1007/978-3-540-30192-9_58
24. Rocchio, J.J.: Relevance Feedback in Information Retrieval. Prentice Hall, Englewood Cliffs (1971)
25. Carpineto, C., De Mori, R., Romano, G., Bigi, B.: An information-theoretic approach to automatic query expansion. ACM Trans. Inf. Syst. **19**(1), 1–27 (2001)
26. Parapar, J., Presedo-Quindimil, M.A., Barreiro, Á.: Score distributions for pseudo relevance feedback. Inf. Sci. **273**, 171–181 (2014)
27. Zamani, H., Dadashkarimi, J., Shakery, A., Croft, W.B.: Pseudo-relevance feedback based on matrix factorization. In: Proceedings of the 25th ACM International on Conference on Information and Knowledge Management, pp. 1483–1492. Association for Computing Machinery, New York (2016)
28. Raviv, H., Kurland, O., Carmel, D.: Document retrieval using entity-based language models. In: Proceedings of the 39th International ACM SIGIR Conference on Research and Development in Information Retrieval, pp. 65–74. Association for Computing Machinery, New York (2016)
29. Liu, C., Gwizdka, J., Liu, J., Xu, T., Belkin, N. J.: Analysis and evaluation of query reformulations in different task types. In: Proceedings of the 73rd American Society for Information Science and Technology, p. 10. American Society for Information Science, Maryland (2010)
30. Mottin, D., Bonchi, F., Gullo, F.: Graph query reformulation with diversity. In: Proceedings of the 21th ACM SIGKDD International Conference on Knowledge Discovery and Data Mining, pp. 825–834. Association for Computing Machinery, New York (2015)
31. Li, F., Jagadish, H.V.: Understanding natural language queries over relational databases. ACM SIGMOD Rec. **45**(1), 6–13 (2016)

468   C. Yan et al.

32. Kelly, D.: Methods for evaluating interactive information retrieval systems with users. Found. Trends Inf. Retr. **3**(1–2), 1–224 (2009)
33. Su, N., He, J., Liu, Y., Zhang, M., Ma, S.: User intent, behaviour, and perceived satisfaction in product search. In: Proceedings of the 11th ACM International Conference on Web Search and Data Mining. pp. 547–555. Association for Computing Machinery, New York (2018)
34. Aliyun. https://www.aliyun.com/. Accessed 21 Sept 2020
35. CBDB. https://projects.iq.harvard.edu/cbdb/home. Accessed 21 Sept 2020
36. Jieba. https://pypi.org/project/jieba/. Accessed 21 Sept 2020
37. Lu, S., Mei, T., Wang, J., Zhang, J., Wang, Z., Li, S.: Browse-to-search: Interactive exploratory search with visual entitics. ACM Trans. Inf. Syst. **32**(4), 1–27 (2014)

Improving Measures of Text Reuse in English Poetry: A TF–IDF Based Method

Wenyi Shang[1(✉)] [ID] and Ted Underwood[1,2] [ID]

[1] School of Information Sciences, University of Illinois at Urbana-Champaign, Champaign, IL 61820, USA
{wenyis3,tunder}@illinois.edu
[2] Department of English, University of Illinois at Urbana-Champaign, Champaign, IL 61820, USA

Abstract. Text reuse measurement is important for both LIS and literary studies, where it is mainly used to study influence between authors. Although projects such as Tesserae have already adopted computational methods for investigating text reuse in Latin poetry, its potential applications to the rich collections of English poetry have not been realized. This research proposes a modified version of the Tesserae Project's measure based on the insight embodied in TF–IDF to study English poetry. Using the Irish poet Yeats' relationship to five English Romantic poets as a test case, three parallel experiments were conducted in order to evaluate the suitability of this method for English poetry. The results show that this new method is effective in measuring text reuse in English poetry, and the TF–IDF based modification is more sensitive to known cases of text reuse than the original method. This method can also be adopted to noncanonical literary works in the future, providing an example of the significance of LIS for digital humanities.

Keywords: Text reuse · TF–IDF · Method evaluation · English poetry · Digital humanities

1 Introduction and Related Works

Text reuse measurement has always been considered as an important issue for both LIS and humanities scholars. Information scientists have adopted text reuse algorithms to identify manifestations of a work in order to better implement Functional Requirements for Bibliographic Records (FRBR) [1], and have studied different patterns of text reuse in large scientific corpora [2]. However, unlike information scientists who mainly focus on plagiarism, literary scholars cast more attention on literary influence. Although it remains arguable how "text reuse" (also known as "intertextuality") should be interpreted, it is undoubtedly one of the most significant signals for identifying literary influence between authors, so that literary critics are "all intertextualists now" [3]. Among the different literary genres, poetry is particularly interesting for analyzing text reuse, both for the genre's literary importance and its linguistic complexities. Poetic similarity has also been widely discussed by previous literary scholarship. For example, scholars have pointed out the importance and necessity of identifying poetic text reuse in classical studies [4].

© Springer Nature Switzerland AG 2021
K. Toeppe et al. (Eds.): iConference 2021, LNCS 12645, pp. 469–477, 2021.
https://doi.org/10.1007/978-3-030-71292-1_36

In addition to traditional methods of investigating text reuse such as philological commentaries, researchers are now able to dig into a vast number of digitized literary texts, thanks to the development of digital infrastructure and the application of computational methods. Such cases include a general, language-independent framework called "TRACER" [5] and some genre and language specific projects: scholars have investigated the textual reuse in eighteenth century English novels [6], and an example of the methods designed for poetic similarity is the Tesserae Project (https://tesserae.caset.buf falo.edu), which allows search for verbal repetitions among Latin poets [7].

The potential application of such methods is not limited to classical studies. Compared to Latin poetry, English poetry has much larger corpora to be exploited. However, despite the fact that there is no lack of research adopting the methods of Tesserae, almost all of them focused on its original subject, Latin poetry [8–10].

The purpose of this research, therefore, is to try to extend the scope of measures of text reuse in poetry to the rich collections of English poetry. Instead of simply duplicating the methods of the Tesserae Project, we proposed a modified version to increase its suitability for English poetry referencing the idea of the TF–IDF (term frequency–inverse document frequency) weighting scheme [11]. The conciseness and efficiency of TF–IDF has made it the most frequently applied weighting scheme [12].

Specifically, in this research, we took the example of the text reuse between the poems of the world-renowned Irish poet William Butler Yeats (1865–1939), and five most representative and influential English Romantic poets: William Blake (1757–1827), William Wordsworth (1770–1850), George Gordon Byron (1788–1824), Percy Bysshe Shelley (1792–1822), and John Keats (1795–1821). The complexity of the poetic influence Yeats received from these poets makes it an ideal case for text reuse measurement. A TF–IDF based method was adopted, and three experiments were conducted in order to evaluate the method: (1) a validation on the effectiveness of the method based on the text reuse between different collections of Yeats; (2) a comparison between the performance of this modified method and that of the original method of Tesserae on the cases of text reuses noted by previous scholarship; (3) a comparison on the results of text reuse between Yeats and the English Romantic poets based on different sizes of partition.

2 Methods

As Fig. 1 shows, the research framework includes a preprocessing stage, a text reuse calculation stage, and three parallel evaluations.

In data collection, all major poetic works of Yeats and the five English Romantic poets were crawled from online sources: (1) *The Collected Poems of W. B. Yeats* [13]; (2) *The Poetical Works of William Blake* [14]; (3) *Poetry of Byron* [15]; (4) *The Complete Poetical Works of Percy Bysshe Shelley* [16]; (5) *The Poetical Works of John Keats* [17]; (6) *The Complete Poetical Works* [18]. These raw data are first cleaned to exclude unsuitable records and irrelevant information, with the post data-cleaning numbers of lines and words of each poet shown in Table 1.

After that, each piece of normalized poetic works was segmented, and each phrase in the work was tokenized before it was lemmatized, and all words with a frequency of at least 500 in the combined set of the poetic works of all six poets (109 words in total) were filtered out, in order to investigate real indicative text reuses.

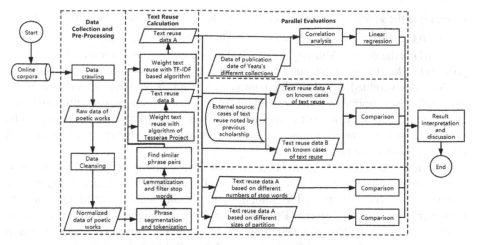

Fig. 1. Research framework

Table 1. The poets selected and the numbers of their selected works, lines, and words

Poet name	Yeats	Blake	Byron	Shelley	Keats	Wordsworth
Number of lines	9,829	4,411	6,371	12,263	3,851	20,552
Number of words	74,101	36,229	48,629	92,927	30,067	150,723

Next, referencing the Tesserae Project [7], we compared poems of Yeats (target) and the English Romantic poets (source) in turn in the unit of phrases to find similar phrase pairs. If a phrase from the target corpus and a phrase from the source corpus share at least two distinct words in common, this source-target phrase-pair was considered as indicative of text reuse and was recorded. And each recorded phrase-pair was weighted according to formula (1):

$$\text{score} = \frac{\frac{\ln(\sum w_t + \sum w_s)}{d_t + d_s}}{ll_t \cdot ll_s} \tag{1}$$

Here, d_t and d_s are the distances of the closest common words (the number of words between two common words with the smallest distance among all common words) in their target and source phrases respectively, ll_t and ll_s are the local lengths of the target and source phrases (the number of words contained in the phrase) respectively, and w_t and w_s are the weights of the common words in their target and source phrases respectively, which are defined according to formula (2):

$$w_i = \sum \frac{gl_i}{f_g(i)} f_l(i) \tag{2}$$

This weighting scheme is based on the insight embodied in TF–IDF: that we should assign higher value to words with higher local frequency and lower global frequency.

Here, gl_i is the global length of the corpus, while $f_g(i)$ is the frequency of the common word i in the corpus (i.e., global frequency). Their quotients $\frac{gl_i}{f_g(i)}$ represents the rarity of the word i in the corpus. Multiply it by $f_l(i)$, the frequency of this common word i in the phrase (i.e., local frequency), and their product is the weight of this common word i.

Sum the weighted values of all common words in this phrase-pair, divide it by the sum of d_t and d_s, smooth it with a logarithmic function, and normalize it with the product of ll_t and ll_s, and the result is the weighted text reuse rate of this phrase-pair. Finally, the text reuse rate between the two corpora is defined as the average text reuse rate of all phrase-pairs of them.

The above-described formula (1) referenced the weighting criteria of the Tesserae Project, and adopted its basic idea of weighting the common words according to their frequency and distance, as well as smoothing the results with a logarithmic function. However, compared to Tesserae Project, which simply assigned the lower-frequency words with higher weights, the weighting scheme shown in formula (2) in this research distinguished global and local frequencies, and assigned higher weights to words with a higher local frequency based on the idea of TF–IDF. Besides, the Tesserae Project defined the "distance" as the distance of the two words with the *lowest* frequency, while this research defined the concept as the distance of the two *closest* common words, gravitating toward the intentional rather than occasional phrase-pairs of text reuse.

In order to validate the effectiveness of the method, to justify these modifications, and to examine the generalizable implications of the results, three parallel evaluations were conducted. First, for the purpose of validating the effectiveness of the method, we conducted a correlation analysis on the text reuse rate between different collections of Yeats's poetic works and the difference in their publications dates, and fitted a linear model to them. We assumed the text reuse rate to be negatively correlated with the difference in the publication dates between two collections.

Second, the performance of our TF–IDF based method and that of the Tesserae Project's method on the cases that are recognized by existing scholarship as implicating poetic influence are compared. Specifically, we collected all Yeats's poems that are recognized as being influenced by the works of Blake according to *A Commentary on the Collected Poems of W. B. Yeats* [19], which is one of the most detailed commentaries on Yeats's poems, calculated their average text reuse rate with *all* Blake's poems,[1] and compared the fraction of text reuse rate of these poem-pairs[2] over that of all Yeats-Blake poem-pairs based on both our and Tesserae Project's methods. In addition, as the commentary also recognized a limited number of Yeats's poems that are influenced by *one* particular Blake's poem [19], we also compared the fraction of text reuse rate of these poem-pairs[3] over that of all Yeats-Blake poem-pairs both based on our and Tesserae

---

[1] Similar to the text reuse rate between two poets, the text reuse rate between two poems is defined as the average value of each phrase-pair of these two poems. Here, average text reuse rates of poem-pairs rather than phrase-pairs were compared, because the commentary discussed the influence within the unit of poem, rather than phrase [19].

[2] There are 41 (Yeats's poems that are recognized as being influenced by Blake) × 216 (all Blake's poems) = 8856 poem-pairs in this experiment.

[3] There are 9 Yeats's poem that are recognized as being influenced by a particular Blake's poem, so there are 9 poem-pairs in this experiment.

Project's methods. We assumed that the fraction of our method should be higher than that of Tesserae Project's method.

Third, we made an exploratory comparison on the results of text reuse between Yeats and the English Romantic poets based on different sizes of partition. We compared the text reuse rate between Yeats and the five English Romantic poets in terms of average poem-pair value (i.e., the average of average text reuse rate of every phrase-pair within this poem-pair) in addition to average phrase-pair value (original partition).

3 Results

Figure 2 demonstrates a clear negative correlation (correlation coefficient $= -0.53$, p $= 4.53\mathrm{E}-6$) between the text reuse rate and difference in publication dates of Yeats's collections. Basically, the collections that are close in publication dates have a higher text reuse rate. For example, *Michael Robartes and the Dancer* (published in 1921) and *The Tower* (published in 1928) have the highest rate; while *Crossways* (published in 1889) and *Last Poems* (published in 1938–1939) have the lowest. We also fitted a regression line to this data, and its equation is: $y = -6.40\mathrm{E}-07x + 5.22\mathrm{E}-05$. This result validates the effectiveness of the measurement of text reuse, since we expect a writer's diction to change gradually, giving works written near the same time a greater chance of echoing each other.

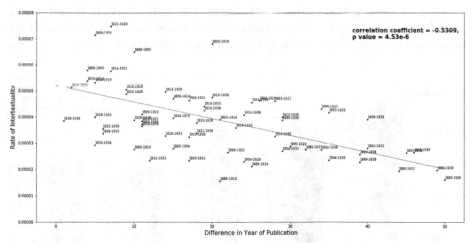

Fig. 2. Correlation between the text reuse rate and difference in publications dates of Yeats's collections

Table 2 shows our TF–IDF based method's overall strength over Tesserae Project's method. Due to different weighting schemes, the absolute values do not make much sense, so we compared the ratio of each method to the average value of all Yeats-Blake poem pairs (i.e., random text reuse rate). The results show that both methods had a little increase on the text reuse rate on Yeats's noted poems and all Blake's poems, and a substantial increase on that of Yeats and Blake noted poem-pairs. Besides, our

TF–IDF based method has a slightly higher ratio in both cases. These results provide clues suggesting that our method more sensitively detects the poetic influence already recognized by existing scholarship.

Table 2. Performances of TF-IDF based method and Tesserae Project's method on the cases of text reuses noted by previous scholarship

	TF–IDF based method		Tesserae Project's method		Ratio of R1 to R2
	Average value	R1: ratio to average value of all Yeats-Blake poem-pairs	Average value	R2: ratio to average value of all Yeats-Blake poem-pairs	
Yeats's noted poems and all Blake's poems	2.12E−05	1.11	6.39E−06	1.09	1.02
Yeats and Blake noted poem-pairs	4.34E−05	2.26	1.20E−05	2.05	1.11

Figure 3 not only shows differences between Yeats and different English Romantic poets,[4] but also shows a consistent pattern: all five groups show a higher value of text reuse rate in average value of poem-pairs, and a lower value of text reuse rate in average

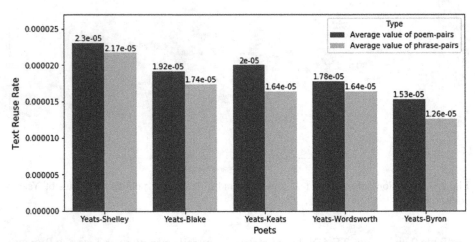

Fig. 3. Text reuse rate between Yeats and the English Romantic poets based on different sizes of partition

---

[4] Due to the paper's methodological focus, we did not discuss the indications of the results in terms of the relationship between Yeats and different English Romantic poets in specific. For preliminary discussions on this relationship, please refer to our previous work [20].

value of phrase-pairs. Since the average value of poem-pairs is defined as the average of average text reuse rate of every phrase-pair within this poem-pair, all poem-pairs contribute equally to that value. As a result, poem-pairs with fewer phrase-pairs are assigned with higher weights than they are in calculating average value of phrase-pairs, where they are penalized for their short lengths. Therefore, the higher value of poem-pairs than phrase-pairs denotes that, shorter poems are more likely to yield higher text reuse rate[5]. This may suggest the existence of poetic forms like the ballad that echo folk tradition.

4 Discussion and Conclusion

This research proposed a TF–IDF based method to measure text reuse. Through the example of Yeats and five English Romantic poets, we preliminarily proved the applicability of this method to English poetry. The results of evaluation 1 validated the effectiveness of the measurement of text reuse, and those of evaluation 2 provided clues suggesting our TF–IDF based method to be more sensitive on alleged cases of text reuses compared to the original method of the Tesserae Project. Moreover, the results of evaluation 3 implicated a generalizable phenomenon: shorter poems tend to be more indicative of text reuse.

In terms of methodological interest for literary studies, the method proposed by this research can be applied to investigate text reuse among other poetic works. Another possible contribution is that the results of evaluation 3 showed a sign of the persistence of something like formulaic composition. In other words, there may be poetic conventions and stock phrases that persist in ballads because they echo an era when all poetry was composed by stringing together stock phrases. This assumption requires further investigation based on larger corpora. In addition to literature studies, some ideas of this method may also inspire traditional LIS studies, making contributions to topics such as identifying duplicates and detecting plagiarism.

Applying this method to the vast majority of noncanonical poetry is one future direction of this research. Due to the extremely large size, they are hardly ideal objects of close-reading, but they constitute the literary history together with their canonical rivals and should not be ignored. Measuring the text reuse of these works makes it possible to understand the roles they played in literary history, and this is exactly the aim of the article "The Slaughterhouse of Literature" [21], which is considered as a milestone in the development of the concept "digital humanities." Therefore, measuring text reuse in English poetry is of vital importance for fulfilling the natural mission of "distant reading" and "digital humanities" in general. In order to realize this goal, the methodological framework introduced in this research could be further developed into a

---

[5] For example, if there are two poem-pairs, and in poem-pair A, there is only one phrase-pair with a text reuse rate of 10. In poem-pair B, there are four phrase-pairs, each with a text reuse rate of 1. Then the average value of the two poem-pairs is $(10 + 1) / 2 = 5.5$, and the average value of the six phrase-pairs is $(10 + 1 + 1 + 1 + 1) / 5 = 3$. The average value of the poem-pairs is higher, since the shorter poem with a higher text reuse rate contributes more when calculating the average value of poem-pairs than that of phrase-pairs.

tool opening up to a large audience to help optimize its weighting scheme under different circumstances.

In order to effectively do so, LIS is indispensable. In this research, we proposed a TF–IDF based method in measuring text reuse in English poetry, which is only a small case of the potential contribution of LIS can make on humanities studies. As Bode criticized, "distant reading" neglected "the activities and insights of textual scholarship", so that "managing the documentary record's complexity" should be emphasized [22]. In order to solve the problem, LIS should certainly be resorted to.

References

1. Citron, D.T., Ginsparg, P.: Patterns of text reuse in a scientific corpus. Proc. Natl. Acad. Sci. **112**(1), 25–30 (2015)
2. Hickey, T.B., O'Neill, E.T., Toves, J.: Experiments with the IFLA functional requirements for bibliographic records (FRBR). D-Lib Magazine **8**(9), 1–13 (2002)
3. Farrell, J.: Intention and intertext. Phoenix **59**(1/2), 98–111 (2005)
4. Fowler, D.: On the shoulders of giants: intertextuality and classical studies. Materiali E Discussioni Per l'analisi Dei Testi Classici **39**, 13–34 (1997)
5. Büchler, M., Burns, P.R., Müller, M., Franzini, E., Franzini, G.: Towards a historical text re-use detection. In: Biemann, C., Mehler, A. (eds.) Text Mining, Theory and Applications of Natural Language Processing, pp. 221–238. Springer, Cham (2014)
6. Duhaime, D.E.: Textual reuse in the eighteenth century: mining Eliza Haywood's quotations. Digital Humanities Quarterly **10**(1) (2016). https://digitalhumanities.org/dhq/vol/10/1/000229/000229.html
7. Coffee, N., Koenig, J.-P., Poornima, S., Forstall, C.W., Ossewaarde, R., Jacobson, S.L.: The Tesserae Project: intertextual analysis of Latin poetry. Literary and Linguistic Comput. **28**(2), 221–228 (2012)
8. Bernstein, N., Gervais, K., Lin, W.: Comparative rates of text reuse in classical Latin hexameter poetry. Digital Humanities Quarterly **9**(3) (2015). https://digitalhumanities.org/dhq/vol/9/3/000237/000237.html
9. Forstall, C.W., Coffee, N., Buck, T., Roache, K., Jacobson, S.: Modeling the scholars: detecting intertextuality through enhanced word-level n-gram matching. Literary and Linguistic Comput. **30**(4), 503–515 (2014)
10. Gawley, J.O., Diddams, A.C.: Comparing the intertextuality of multiple authors using Tesserae: a new technique for normalization. Digital Scholarship in the Humanities **32**(suppl_2), ii53–ii59 (2017)
11. Jones, K.S.: A statistical interpretation of term specificity and its application in retrieval. J. Document. **28**(1), 11–21 (1972)
12. Beel, J., Gipp, G., Langer, S., Breitinger, C.: Research-paper recommender systems: a literature survey. Int. J. Digit. Libr. **17**(4), 305–338 (2016)
13. Yeats, W.B.: The collected poems of W. B. Yeats. 2nd edn. Scribner, New York (1996)
14. Blake, W.: The poetical works of William Blake. Oxford University Press, London and New York (1908)
15. Byron, G.G.: Poetry of Byron. Macmillan and Co, London (1881)
16. Shelley, P.B.: The Complete Poetical Works of Percy Bysshe Shelley. Oxford University Press, Oxford (1925)
17. Keats, J.: The Poetical Works of John Keats. Macmillan, London (1884)
18. Wordsworth, W.: The Complete Poetical Works. Macmillan and Co, London (1888)

19. Jeffares, A.N.: A Commentary on the Collected Poems of W B. Yeats. Stanford University Press, Redwood city (1968)
20. Shang, W., Zhang, J., Huang, W.: Modelling poetic similarity: a comparative study of W. B. Yeats and the English Romantic poets. DH 2019: Digital Humanities Conference 2019 (2019). https://dev.clariah.nl/files/dh2019/boa/0207.html
21. Moretti, F.: The slaughterhouse of literature. MLQ: Modern Language Quarterly **61**(1), 207–227 (2000)
22. Bode, K.: The equivalence of "close" and "distant" reading; or, toward a new object for data-rich literary history. Modern Language Quarterly **78**(1), 77–106 (2017)

Identifying Creative Content at the Page Level in the HathiTrust Digital Library Using Machine Learning Methods on Text and Image Features

Nikolaus Nova Parulian[(✉)] [ID] and Glen Worthey [ID]

School of Information Sciences, University of Illinois at Urbana-Champaign,
Urbana and Champaign, USA
{nnp2,gworthey}@illinois.edu

Abstract. Front-matter pages in a digitized book typically consist of mostly factual content that is not subject to copyright, and thus could potentially be opened to the public, even if the book itself is protected under copyright. However, the boundary of what is considered to be "front matter" is rather arbitrary, and some copyright-protected creative content can be found in the initial pages of a copyrighted volume. In this work, we conduct empirical research to evaluate machine learning approaches to detect creative content in the first 20 pages in a large sample of HathiTrust volumes. We start by analyzing different machine learning methods to distinguish creative from factual content using the statistically-expressed textual features from the HathiTrust Research Center's Extracted Features dataset. From this experiment, we found that the random forest model had the best performance compared with logistic regression, support vector machine (SVM), or stochastic gradient descent (SGD) models. This experiment also reveals that textual data is not sufficient to reliably identify pages containing some kinds of creative content, e.g., images. Thus, we further trained an image detection model using YOLO-v3 to detect page types, thus creating an ensemble of textual and image features. Our findings show a promising result for the random-forest model trained on a combination of text and image features, increasing the accuracy from 85% to 89% compared with the model trained only on textual data.

Keywords: Digital library · Digital humanities · Machine learning · Image processing · Copyright

1 Introduction

HathiTrust is a growing global partnership of major research libraries working to ensure that the cultural record is preserved and accessible in digital form long into the future. The mission of HathiTrust is to contribute to research, scholarship, and the common good by collaboratively collecting, organizing, preserving, communicating, and sharing the record of human knowledge as it is expressed in digital library collections [8].

© Springer Nature Switzerland AG 2021
K. Toeppe et al. (Eds.): iConference 2021, LNCS 12645, pp. 478–489, 2021.
https://doi.org/10.1007/978-3-030-71292-1_37

In support of its mission to promote research, scholarship, and the sharing of human knowledge, the HathiTrust Digital Library preserves and provides access to scanned page images of volumes in member library collections; automatically recognized plain-text versions of these volumes; and descriptive metadata about them [8]. The HathiTrust Digital Library currently includes nearly 17.5 million volumes, of which fewer than 40% are in the public domain [13].

At present, these full-page and full-text features are available to the general public only for public-domain books. However, there is potential to expand public access by exposing front-matter pages of copyright-protected books, because the content of front-matter pages is largely factual, not creative; and because facts, unlike creative expression, are exempt from copyright protections [2]. This project seeks to use machine learning to identify pages containing creative content within the beginning pages of a given HathiTrust volume, in order to exclude them from view—even as we open for viewing as many of the purely factual front-matter pages as possible, within a reasonable level of confidence and tolerance for risk [3].

Information contained in the opening pages of a volume can often be extremely useful for both scholars and casual readers. For example, even though much of the information on a title page is typically included in a book's catalog record, other front-matter pages such as copyright pages, tables of contents, acknowledgments, etc., may contain information richly useful toward understanding the volume. At the same time, some volumes likely include in their opening pages materials that do have copyright protection. Some observed copyright-protected materials within this initial page range are creative illustrations (including advertisements), epigraphs, or even the beginnings of the main text itself (see Fig. 1). However, manually determining whether creative content is included in the initial pages of a particular volume would require individual page labeling, which, considering the more than ten million in-copyright volumes contained in the collection, would be time-intensive (to say the least). A machine learning approach is generally much more efficient for this sort of predictive task, and we imagined that it would be well-suited to this particular one [19].

Our first stage of research was an evaluation of machine learning methods using the Extracted Features dataset created and provided by the HathiTrust Research Center. ("Extracted Features" consist of a variety of statistical measures of the textual content on a given page, based on text identified during a previous optical character recognition stage: word counts, part-of-speech counts, line counts, etc. [7]) Using these extracted textual features, we found that the random forest model performed best in distinguishing page-level content as either "creative" or "factual." [20] However, we found a couple of challenges in only using the text features in this predictive model. First, the model has very low precision in detecting creative content for pages that include images, because these generally have limited or no textual features. Secondly, these pages in particular, although they may lack textual content, still contain other content that can lie in the creative domain, such as music scores or illustrations.

Fig. 1. Example of mixed creative and factual content in the opening pages of a volume of a periodical: the volume title and table of contents are considered factual content, whereas both advertisements (one primarily textual, the other primary pictorial) are not [1].

To help rectify these types of errors, we have conducted a new, expanded analysis of machine learning models. In this experiment, we train a model using page-image features, in addition to the text features we used previously. We seek to answer this research question: will adding image features help to improve the performance of our predictive model in identifying creative content?

2   Background

Prior to the beginning of our research, HathiTrust staff had made a number of analyses (all unpublished) to identify an optimal number of front-matter pages that might potentially be opened to public view with minimal risk of exposing copyright-protected materials [14]. It was determined in the course of those analyses that no single number of pages would suffice for all the great variety of volumes in the digital library: for example, among the first 10 pages of a 100-page volume, lots of copyright-protected content was often found—whereas, for many longer volumes, the non-copyrightable pages might extend for much longer page ranges.

Although attempts to establish a reliable fixed page range for low-risk exposure of front-matter was not successful, these analyses resulted in two important conclusions: the first was that a page-level determination of content type was needed rather than a fixed page range; and second, that approximately the first 20 pages of any given volume in the corpus were a reasonable optimal target population for this more granular analysis.

A number of attempts have been made previously to classify page types in a book for a variety of purposes. McConnaughey, et al., [19] provided empirical research on segmenting and assigning fixed structural categories (such as table of contents, preface, index, etc.) to scans of print books. El-Haj et al. [11] created a method to retain information about document structure, which was needed to enable a clear distinction between the narrative and financial components of annual reports, and between individual sections within the narrative component. These two approaches provide ways to infer document structure using multi-language text data.

At the same time, analyzing images and detecting the objects that appear in them are common in image processing. Various recent methods have used deep neural networks for classifying images, including region-based convolutional Networks (R-CNN) [12], residual networks (ResNet) [16], and YOLO ("you only look once") [23] models. Lee et al. [17] used ResNet models to extract visual content from the *Chronicling America* historic newspaper corpus. Many of these models have also been successful in classifying images of various types, including photographs, illustrations, maps, comics, etc.

3 Methodology

3.1 Dataset

Providing a high-quality dataset for training a machine learning model is essential, and for this, human expertise is required. For this purpose, we took a semi-random sample of 900 volumes from the HathiTrust Digital Library. We labeled each of the first 20 pages of each volume either as "factual" for a page with contents lacking creative expression, or "creative" if there is copyright-protected material on the page. The "creative" pages in this sample set were further labeled with more granular sub-categories in order to assist in refining the prediction model, and in identifying various content types such as text, image, music score, cover, etc. As shown in Table 1, about 43% of the first 20 pages of all volumes (i.e., our previously determined optimal approximation of the extent of front matter) were identified as containing creative content, as judged by human expertise. This distribution indicates that we should not naively assume that a particular number of pages in a particular volume will constitute front matter. Thus page-level content analysis is essential to improve the precision in detecting the creative content within the front-matter pages range.

Table 1. Distribution of page types for the first 20 pages of sample volumes

Page type	Number of pages	% of pages
No content	5,288	29,38
Factual	5,011	27,84
Creative	7,701	42,78

We then used the HathiTrust Research Center Extracted Features Dataset [7], representing the text data from each of the manually labeled pages. Because the volumes we selected represent many different languages, we chose not to use the language-specific word/token features ("bag of words") methods for our analysis. For a multilingual corpus, the number of tokens is roughly proportional to the number of languages represented, and is truly massive across the entire HathiTrust Digital Library: nearly 3 trillion tokens [15]. Although it may be counter-intuitive, relying on language-specific features for the task of distinguishing creative from factual content is both less efficient, and possibly less accurate for low-frequency languages, than using language-independent textual features. Therefore, we used other statistical features that described the text on each page, including raw token and line counts, the number of tokens per line, and beginning- and end-of-line characters. With these statistical features, we can ensure that the model we train will be generalizable across the languages in the volumes we covered. Next, we developed a workflow to use the page's statistical features to train our model.

After evaluating various machine-learning models on the Extracted Features dataset, we refined our approach with the addition of scanned page images from the same HathiTrust collection of 900 sample volumes. (The Extracted Features and pre-compiled datasets and analysis codes are available in [21]. However, due to the very same copyright issues our research is intended to address, we are unable to share the scanned image dataset publicly.)

3.2   Predictive Models Based on Text Features

Given a set of extracted features representing the text on a page, we developed a machine learning workflow to identify which classification model is the best predictor for classifying factual pages, blank pages, and creative pages. As part of our pre-processing step, we filter token counts, line counts, tokens per line, and the number of uppercase and lowercase tokens in order to assist our page classification.

In our previous work [20], we trained four basic classification models on the Extracted Features dataset, including random forest [18], logistic regression [24], support vector machines (SVM) [22], and stochastic gradient descent (SGD) [5]. In this research, we refine our model comparison experiment by performing cross-validation over an independent volume set compared to the previous round that divides the pages into training and testing sets. We divide the volumes into ten-fold cross-validation training and testing sets. The average precision, recall, f1-score, and overall accuracy results of these four different classification models on the test volumes can be seen in Table 2.

From Table 2, we can see that the random forest model is the best fit to predict creative content on pages in the digital library. However, there is still some misclassification error where the model failed to predict creative content pages. Figure 2 provides a detailed confusion matrix for misclassifications by the random forest model. This matrix shows that relying on textual features alone is not enough to prevent the inappropriate display of creative pages to a reasonable

Table 2. Evaluation of machine learning models for predicting page content types

Page type	Random forest			Logistic regression			SVM			SGD		
	prec	rec	f1	prec	rec	f1	prec	rec	f1	prec	rec	f1
No content	0.85	0.91	0.88	0.75	0.95	0.83	0.83	0.89	0.86	0.87	0.85	0.86
Factual	0.81	0.79	0.80	0.81	0.70	0.75	0.76	0.73	0.74	0.76	0.72	0.72
Creative	0.89	0.87	0.88	0.91	0.83	0.87	0.87	0.85	0.86	0.82	0.82	0.80
Accuracy	0.85			0.83			0.83			0.80		

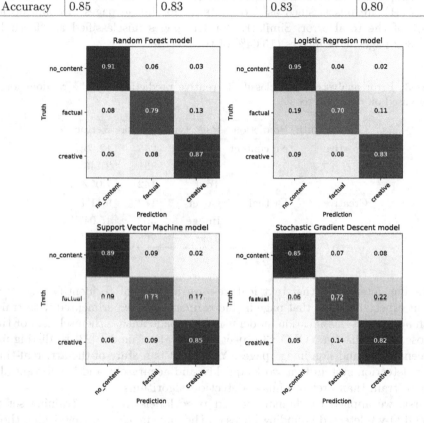

Fig. 2. Confusion matrix evaluation for page-level predictive models.

degree of certainty: note, for example, that the recall score of 0.87 for creative content means that the presumptive 20 pages of "openable" front matter will contain, on average, 2.6 pages (0.13×20) of unidentified creative content that should not be made open. We (and the HathiTrust lawyers) needed to further decrease this risk of exposure.

3.3   Predictive Model Based on Image Features

We therefore focused on the random forest model, which performs best on text data, and analyzed in more detail the errors produced by it. Because our goal is to increase the recall for predicting creative pages (i.e., the consequences of not properly identifying, and then opening, creative pages are more serious than those of misidentifying other page types), we look at misclassification for this page type, as shown in Table 3. The finding suggests that most of the creative pages (431) are misclassified as "no content" for image pages, accounting for 21.46% of the total error. Similarly, for the pages misclassified as "factual", about 302 pages have images (15.04% of total error).

Table 3. Error analysis for misclassified creative predictions by the random forest model based on text features

Ground truth	Prediction	Page type	#error	%error
Creative	No content	Cover	245	12.20%
		Image	431	21.46%
		Text	142	7.07%
Creative	Factual	Cover	183	9.11%
		Image	302	15.04%
		Text	705	35.11%

Having determined that text features are insufficient to identify page-level content especially when that page includes images, we experimented with training an additional classification model using the page images themselves. For this purpose, we trained a YOLO-v3 object classification model [23] to distinguish between image and non-image pages. YOLO-v3 is a state-of-the-art, real-time object detection system that works quickly and accurately, and is substantially faster to train than previous image-detection algorithms.

First, we applied the human-created page labels from our training set to the YOLO-v3-detected bounding boxes on the page images, distinguishing those that are mostly text from those that are non-textual (or less-textual): image(s), whether a cover image, a music score, an illustration; or just blank pages. Next, we train the YOLO-v3 model on this image dataset. The trained model outputs the probability of each page type for every particular page, as shown in Fig. 3. The only caveat at present in this image detection model training is that we consider only generic labels for a page because we have too limited a number of volumes in the dataset for more granularity, whereas in a book, there might be many more fine-grained image classes such as author portrait, illustration, music score, advertisement, etc.

Fig. 3. Sample detections from the YOLO-v3 model (Sources: [4,6,9])

4   Results

4.1   Text and Image Features Ensemble

After we train the image prediction model, we apply that model to all the pages in our larger dataset, and gather the probabilities of each page's image classification type. Combining the text features we used in the previous analysis with these image classification probabilities, we now have a much richer representation of a page that takes into account both text and image features.

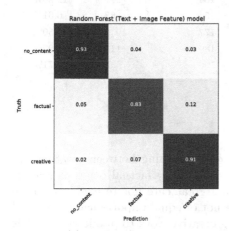

(a) confusion matrix

Page Type	Text			Text + Image		
	prec	rec	f1	prec	rec	f1
no content	0.85	0.91	0.88	0.92	0.93	0.93
factual	0.81	0.79	0.80	0.85	0.83	0.84
creative	0.89	0.87	0.88	0.90	0.91	0.90
accuracy			0.85			0.89

(b) metrics comparisson

Fig. 4. Results and comparison between random forest model for text feature only, and for combined text and image features

We then train the random forest prediction model on this combined feature set and compile the result. Figure 4 shows the confusion matrix and error analysis for this "ensemble features" model. Our finding suggests that the combined feature set improves our predictive model's accuracy from .85 to .89 on average, and with a .90 f1 score for creative content. As we can see in the figure, this method increases recall for creative content prediction (perhaps the most crucial measure of all) by 4% points, from 0.87 to 0.91. Table 4 shows the error analysis for this ensemble method, and the degree of improvement after applying image prediction to the model. Adding the image feature greatly improves the model's performance: we now have an additional 340 creative images "rescued" from the 733 previously misclassified pages when an image is present on the page. Furthermore, this model also improves the detection of creative content on the cover page by rescuing 203 pages from the 428 previously misclassified pages. However, this ensemble method did not improve the creative content prediction when the page mostly has text.

This result leads us to conclude that the strategy of using text and image features is a promising one for identifying page-level creative content, especially for cover pages and other pages with images.

Table 4. Error analysis for missclassified creative content predicted by the random forest model using combined text and image features with number and percentage of gain/improvement

Ground truth	Prediction	Page type	#error ($e1$) (text)	#error ($e2$) (text + image)	# gain $e_2 - e_1$	% gain
Creative	No content	Cover	245	48	197	9.81%
		Image	431	204	227	12.88%
		Text	142	54	88	6.61%
Creative	Factual	Cover	183	177	6	0.50%
		Image	302	189	113	11.22%
		Text	705	700	5	0.71%

4.2   Threshold Analysis

In a practical sense, our main purpose in distinguishing between creative and factual content is to allow the publication of as many factual pages as reasonably possible, while at the same time taking great care not to expose creative pages accidentally. But these two goals are not of equal importance: the second requires greater emphasis, because exposing creative work to public view entails a much greater risk than improperly concealing a factual page. Thus, we should maximize the recall of creative predictions, even if that comes at the expense of factual prediction recall.

To achieve this purpose, we conduct an error variance analysis of the latest model (the one trained on the combined text and image features). First, we use cross-validation to build models based on the training set and evaluate them over the validation set. From this analysis, we select the model that generalizes best on the cross-validated set. With this best-performing model in the cross-validation process, we examine the distributions of false negatives for creative content predictions. As we can see from Fig. 5, the probability of creative content with false negative predictions varies in the range of 0 to 0.5. Furthermore, the mean probability for false negative creative content predictions is 0.26. This is where we choose to set a threshold for detecting creative content: we choose this average error as the new threshold for creative content prediction. We evaluate our choice in the testing set, and with this method, we now achieve 96% recall for creative content prediction.

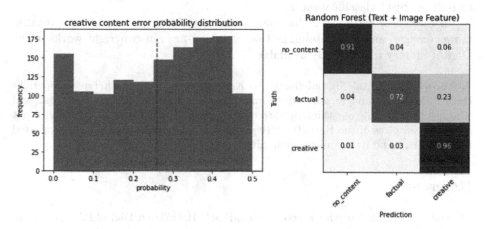

Fig. 5. Creative content error probability distributions, and a new confusion matrix after threshold adjustment

5 Conclusion

This paper presents empirical research on evaluating and tuning machine learning performance for the detection of "creative" and "factual" content at the page level, for a given range of pages tentatively considered to be front matter in HathiTrust Digital Library volumes. We start by evaluating various machine learning methods on statistical features using the HTRC Extracted Features dataset. Our findings suggest that the random forest model performs the best compared with three others models. However, concern still remains about the misclassification of "creative" pages that contain images and with little or no textual content. Thus, we trained an image object detection model using YOLO-v3 and combined this image model result with that used for text features. The latest approach shows that the combination of image and text features can improve the predictive model's accuracy compared to the model trained with only text features.

With these results for a labeled training set, there is more that we could do before applying our method to the entire 10.6 million copyright-protected volumes in the HathiTrust collection. We could apply our methods to a larger labeled dataset, assuming we have more labels, and evaluate the model's robustness. Another approach would be to use language models such as BERT [10] for classifying pages (though see above for the disadvantages of relying on language specificity). One challenge in implementing a model like this is that the full-text data from these particular volumes is also copyright protected; we would need to train and apply the models in a non-consumptive environment. To increase our bounding box label's precision in our image-based models, we could also prepare a new training set with more specific content-type labels. However, we would need to do this very carefully, and with a much more balanced dataset, in order to reduce object classification bias.

In any case, we believe that our work is well on its way toward making more content—and more useful, factual content—from in-copyright works in the Digital Library more openly available.

Acknowledgements. Special thanks to Kristina Eden Hall, HathiTrust Copyright Review Program Manager, who led the initial analyses on which this work is based, and who has helped guide our thinking throughout the project. This work was carried out under the auspices of the HathiTrust Research Center, which is generously supported by HathiTrust and its member community.

References

1. Catalog record: The wine marketing handbook. HathiTrust Digital Library, Example volume containing a mix of expressive and factual contents within front-matter pages. https://catalog.hathitrust.org/Record/005323091
2. Feist Pubs., Inc. v. Rural Tel. Svc. Co., Inc, 499 U.S. 340 (1991). Justia Law. https://supreme.justia.com/cases/federal/us/499/340/
3. Operationalizing "non-consumptive" fair use to revolutionize humanities research. HathiTrust Digital Library. https://www.hathitrust.org/blogs/perspectives-from-hathitrust/operationalizing-non-consumptive-fair-use-to-revolutionize
4. Cromos. Bogota: Grupo Titulos R.T.I. (1972)
5. Bottou, L.: Large-scale machine learning with stochastic gradient descent. In: Lechevallier, Y., Saporta, G. (eds.) Proceedings of COMPSTAT 2010, pp. 177–186. Springer, Heidelberg (2010). https://doi.org/10.1007/978-3-7908-2604-3_16
6. Britten, B.: Third suite for cello: op. 87. Faber u.a. (1976)
7. Capitanu, B., Underwood, T., Organisciak, P., Cole, T., Sarol, M.J., Downie, J.S.: The HathiTrust Research Center extracted feature dataset (1.0)[dataset]. HathiTrust Research Center (2016). https://doi.org/10.13012/J8X63JT3
8. Christenson, H.: Hathitrust. Libr. Resour. Tech. Serv. **55**(2), 93–102 (2011)
9. Derossi, P., Rovatti, P.A.: Fare la differenza. Triennale di Milano (1998)
10. Devlin, J., Chang, M.W., Lee, K., Toutanova, K.: Bert: pre-training of deep bidirectional transformers for language understanding. arXiv preprint arXiv:1810.04805 (2018)

11. El-Haj, M., Rayson, P., Alves, P., Herrero-Zorita, C., Young, S.: Multilingual financial narrative processing: analysing annual reports in English, Spanish And Portuguese. Multilingual Text Analysis: Challenges, Models, and Approaches, p. 441 (2019)
12. Girshick, R.: Fast R-CNN. In: Proceedings of the IEEE International Conference on Computer Vision, pp. 1440–1448 (2015)
13. HathiTrust: About our digital library: Statistics and visualizations. https://www.hathitrust.org/statistics_visualizations
14. HathiTrust Research Center: Initial findings regarding front matter identification in HathiTrust. https://github.com/htrc/ht-frontmatter-analysis
15. HathiTrust Research Center: HTRC extracted features dataset. https://analytics.hathitrust.org/datasets
16. He, K., Zhang, X., Ren, S., Sun, J.: Deep residual learning for image recognition. In: Proceedings of the IEEE Conference on Computer Vision and Pattern Recognition, pp. 770–778 (2016)
17. Lee, B.C.G., et al.: The newspaper navigator dataset: extracting and analyzing visual content from 16 million historic newspaper pages in chronicling America. arXiv preprint arXiv:2005.01583 (2020)
18. Liaw, A., Wiener, M., et al.: Classification and regression by randomforest. R News **2**(3), 18–22 (2002)
19. McConnaughey, L., Dai, J., Bamman, D.: The labeled segmentation of printed books. In: Proceedings of the 2017 Conference on Empirical Methods in Natural Language Processing, pp. 737–747 (2017)
20. Parulian, N.: Evaluating a machine learning approach to identifying expressive content at page level in HathiTrust. In: Digital Humanities 2020 (2020)
21. Parulian, N.: HT-frontmatter-analysis, December 2020. https://doi.org/10.6084/m9.figshare.13513167.v1
22. Platt, J., et al.: Probabilistic outputs for support vector machines and comparisons to regularized likelihood methods. Adv. Large Margin Classif. **10**(3), 61–74 (1999)
23. Redmon, J., Farhadi, A.: Yolov3: an incremental improvement. arXiv preprint arXiv:1804.02767 (2018)
24. Yu, H.F., Huang, F.L., Lin, C.J.: Dual coordinate descent methods for logistic regression and maximum entropy models. Mach. Learn. **85**(1–2), 41–75 (2011)

Semantics Expression of Peking Opera Painted Faces Based on Color Metrics

Guancan Yang[✉] [ID], Shuang Gao, Zeyu Feng, Lingling Wang, and Yidan Xu

School of Information Resource Management, Renmin University of China, Haidian District, Beijing, People's Republic of China
yanggc@ruc.edu.cn

Abstract. Color is an essential means for Peking Opera Painted Faces (POPF) to show their characters' emotional characteristics and image connotations. Peking opera Painted Faces' color selection has certain regularity and specific combination mode, reflecting the artistic connotation of Peking Opera Painted Faces.

Taking Peking Opera Painted Faces as the research object, the paper has constructed a color palette by extracting color information and conducts a quantitative analysis of color by clustering, and binning methods to explore the color combination rules of color semantics of single color and color combinations of Peking Opera Painted Faces, in the hope of contributing to the live transmission of traditional Chinese aesthetics.

Keywords: POPF · Intangible cultural heritage · Color semantics

1 Introduction

Peking Opera, as a branch of Chinese traditional cultures and arts, has a very distinct colorful facial makeup in the stage performance. As a stage performance art, the Peking Opera adopts multiple artistic techniques, such as singing, body movements, and facial painting, to highlight features like positions, characters, age, and actors' feelings. Painted face refers to the colorful facial makeup of an actor, generally speaking, the Painted face is usually reserved for the actors playing roles known as Jing (painted faces) and Chou (clowns), symbolizing semantics by cultural elements. The symbolic semantics of POPF is composed of cultural elements, such as the colors, the patterns, and the symbols.

There are quite a few face types in Peking Opera, and each with its own features. For example, "whole face" is the most basic and simple type, which uses one single color as the main color throughout the face. When the main color of its cheeks was retained, and the main color of the forehead was reduced to a narrow strip, making the main color of the face occupy six tenths of the face, it evolved into the "six-over-ten shaped pattern face". And when the eyebrows and nose were exaggerated, making the forehead and two cheeks present 3 obvious main color, it evolved into the three-block pattern face. Other face types such as the cross shaped pattern face also came into being step by step on this basic.

K. Toeppe et al. (Eds.): iConference 2021, LNCS 12645, pp. 490–501, 2021.
https://doi.org/10.1007/978-3-030-71292-1_38

A face painting can convey a lot of information to the audience to quickly recognize whether the actor's character is loyal or treachery, kind, or evil. Just like a mirror of the soul, painted faces are the creations of dramatic artists, based on their life experience and their analysis of the dramatic personae. The colors on the painted faces are a means to enrich the imagination further and exaggerate the complex characters in the repertoire. The various colors in the faces are given corresponding emotional colors, symbolizing a particular actor's personality, temperament, or role. With novel patterns, bright colors, standard or wry contours, and thick or thin lines, facial painting can arouse the audience's interest and add interest to Peking Opera performances.

Facial paintings are most fascinating and significant, for each type of face symbolizes the character's personality. Vividly painted faces enable audiences to see expressions even from a distance, a significant advantage in the days when dramatic performances were usually staged in the open air before large crowds. As shown in Table 1, the semantic features are mainly conveyed through two cultural elements: physical characteristics of the facial region such as eyebrows, eyes, nose, forehead, and mouth, and color characteristics such as red, orange, blue, white, black, purple, green, gold and silver.

Table 1. An example of POPF with symbolic semantics

Illustration	Cultural Elements	Description	Symbolic meanings
	Primary Color		Black symbolizes a character who is honest, genuine, and uninhibited.
	Secondary Color		The secondary color is used in conjunction with the primary color to make a face more colorful and the pattern more distinctive
Xian Mie, ZhaiYingHui	Type		colored three-tile face: the colored three-tile face was derived from the three-tile style of face-painting, A bold warrior or a hero.

The use of colors is not absolute but also has its flexibility. As shown in Table 1, a red face indicates uprightness and loyalty, a black face a rough and forthright character, blue face bravery and pride, white face treachery and cunning, and a face with a white patch a fawning and base character. To show kinship, father and son can have faces of the same color with similar patterns. The semantic meaning of single primary color obeys clear rules in traditional Peking Opera face painting. However, the semantic meanings presented by color combinations are rarely mentioned. There may be conflicts between the semantic features offered by color combinations and a single dominant color in exceptional cases (Table 2).

Table 2. Primary colors and characters of POPF

Primary colour	Symbol meaning language	Typical illustration
Red	Loyal, brave	
Blue	Calculating, unyielding	
Black	Upright, rude, outspoken	
White	Treacherous, wicked	
Green	Testy, bold, reckless	
Pink	Old, senile	
Purple	Calm, resolute, upright	
Yellow	Powerful, brutal, bold	

This paper's main objective was to reveal the semantic meanings of colors and color combinations in the context of Peking Opera Painted Faces. In traditional studies, scholars usually focus on the semantic meanings of the most dominant color in facial makeup. But what we are studying now is the semantic meanings of the color combination in Peking Opera Painted Faces. Therefore, on the one hand, we study the distribution characteristics of different colors in color combinations; on the other hand, we explore the semantic meanings corresponding to different color combinations to help us identify different Peking Opera Painted Faces. Semantic meanings can be effectively expressed through the colorful visual elements through POPF. Thus, understanding the color semantics of the POPF would contribute to the live transmission of traditional Chinese aesthetics.

2 Related Work

To better preserve and study Peking Opera facial makeup, experts and scholars began to digitize Peking Opera facial makeups. The digitalized technology of Peking Opera facial makeup pattern mainly uses digital modeling technology to build a vector pattern library, and vectored facial makeup can be designed through pattern combination [7]. Compared with the traditional imitation process of Peking Opera facial makeup, the creation process of this facial makeup image is visual and can be edited and modified at any time. On this basis, the facial makeup image and the texture of the paper are fused to form the paper-cut of Peking Opera facial makeup with real texture [8]. Recently, researchers have semantic analysis based on machine learning in Peking Opera facial makeup, mainly includes the scale according to the emotional adjectives Peking Opera facial makeup of image emotional semantic [10], using Pan Luofu theory of three-layer on the depth of the content of the image semantic annotation [11], facial makeup color and pattern design feature extracting, build facial makeup semantic word package [12]. These researches have realized the redesign of facial makeup based on facial makeup semantic word package, and the personalized drawing of facial makeup can be realized by mobile and web applications. In summary, our paper is the first to use data analysis to study color combinations of facial makeup and explore the relationship between different color combinations and emotional semantics.

3 Methodology

3.1 Data Collection

All the 397 Peking Opera Painted Face images we use originated from Peking Opera Faces by Menglin Zhao, covering 16 types and all the four characters of Peking Opera Faces. Yang, Zhang, Yu's research provides this article with detailed relative information. According to The History of Chinese Culture[1], they have labeled all the images with names, types, characters, painting skills, and shapes of eyebrows, eyes, forehead, and mouth. Their efforts on repeated individual tagging and validation contribute significantly to the data accuracy (Table 3).

---

[1] couldthephysical.blogspot.com.

Table 3. The number of POPF images statistics

Types of POPF	Counts	Types of POPF	Counts
Clown face	23	Fragmented pattern face	68
Colored three-tile face	41	Eunuch face	2
Colored ingot face	2	Wry face	6
Six-tenth face	16	Pictographic face	54
Three-tile face	94	Goblin face	5
Monk's face	18	The hero's face	1
Immortals face	8	Pattern ingot face	12
Cross-shaped pattern face	18	Entire face	28

of total proportion to the number of images that contain them.

This article extracts colors from these images, quantifying them and joining the color information with corresponding semantics, then trying to reveal the principles of colors and semantics by calculating the color similarity between various images and representing color palettes for different POPF types and characters (Fig. 1).

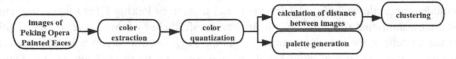

Fig. 1. Flow of experiments

Color Extraction. Since colors of images are identified by pixel, we need to assign the similar ones into several categories respectively to examine the overall color distribution. Histogram and k-means clustering are common approaches to cluster analysis. Briefly, histograms are generated by projecting each pixel as a colored point into 3D space, dividing each axis into two parts. Thus eight bins returned. K-means clustering, objective to minimize the distance from each cluster centers, is able to identify the most similar colors as several single clusters, whatever they are, thus minimizing the influence brought by color distortion of digital images. This article has tried the two methods above and compare their color extraction outcomes. Both of them generate the RGB model values of clustering centers with their percentage. (Shown in Fig. 2) The difference is that the histogram divides the color space in the same way. Thus the corresponding bars of different histograms can be compared intuitively. At the same time, the k-means clustering centers differ from each other broadly based on their original image, which shows the color distribution of each image directly, but those clusters are less suitable for comparisons among various images, as they are not designed to generate color distribution according to the same color criterion as histograms does. Hence the histograms will be used for comparison and quantitative calculating, and k-means clustering methods for palette generation to examine the overall color distribution.

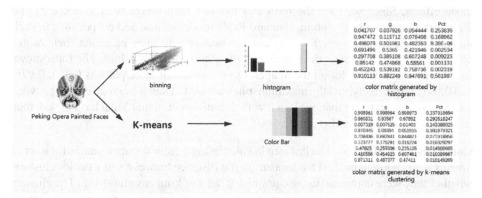

Fig. 2. The flow of data collection

As for the number of bins and k-means clustering centers, this article checked the most colorful image of about nine colors. Thus we decide the number of bins as eight and k-means clustering centers as nine to ensure no dominant color is left.

Palette Generation. Before palette designing, all the RGB model values of clustering centers are needed to be calibrated for two reasons. Firstly, due to many images being based on the scanned books, there will inevitably be color deviations. Secondly, not all of the RGB model values of k-means clustering centers are matched with Chinses traditional colors. Thus this article calibrates them according to a traditional Chinese color palette, which comes from the website https://colours.ichuantong.cn/, classifying 161 colors with their associated verbal names into nine categories: red, yellow, green, blue, pale, water, grey, black, and gold& silver, with 28, 28,32, 25, 6, 7, 14, 15 and 6 colors respectively. We design the algorithm to sum the absolute values of differences from RGB color model values between clustering centers and the standard colors on the classic palette. Then, we assign the least different one to each clustering center (Fig. 3).

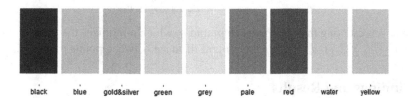

Fig. 3. Palette of traditional Chinese colors (Color figure online)

Background Elimination. On the one hand, the color deviations are caused by the early printing of books, and these color deviations have some impact on semantic analysis. All the JPG and PNG format images have white-like backgrounds, which should not have been included in the color extraction information. Thus, we set some rules to minimize those effects. Since we have the form that marked each image with nine colors and their verbal names, classification, standard RGB model values, and proportions in each image, we can identify which colors are the background ones based on their ratios, speculating upper and lower thresholds according to their RGB values. The form shows four background colors for all the images, the minimum of three paths is 0.949, 0.976, and 0.941, respectively, and the maximum ones are all 1. Then we extract colors between these two ones, and after that, we join it with the information that Yang has labeled, thus generate the raw data for this article.

Color Distance Metrics. The last step in calculating a color distance matrix for a set of images is to choose a method for measuring the distance between sets of color clusters, whether they were computed using color histograms or k-means clustering. The clusters summarize two important information about an object: the colors present in the image and the relative proportion of each color in the image. To measure the color similarity of two objects, a distance metric should take both features into account.

The earth mover'smover's distance (EMD) is a distance measure between two distributions or two signatures. It typically performs well because it accounts for all of the histograms' information and allows for partial matches in a quantitative, scalable way. It considers both spatial color information (where a cluster is in 3D color space) and size information (how large a cluster is, i.e., how much earth you have to shovel) [14]. In part, it implements the Hungarian algorithm to match up bins that are most similar in color *and* size, which tends to mitigate the effect of dividing pixels up into arbitrary ranges. Even if one color histogram has a large grey bin and no pixels in the black bin where another one has a large black bin and an empty grey one, the similarity of black and grey results in a lower transport cost than if the bins were treated as independent.

The calculating is generally as follows. Assume that a signature P with m clusters can be defined as $P = \{(p_1, \omega_{p1}), (p_2, \omega_{p2}) \cdots \cdots, (p_m, \omega_{pm})\}$, similarly another signature Q with n clusters as $Q = \{(q_1, \omega_{q1}), (q_2, \omega_{q2}) \cdots \cdots, (q_n, \omega_{qn})\}$. The EMD can be described as

$$EMD(P, Q) = \frac{\sum_{i=1}^{m}\sum_{j=1}^{n} f_{ij} d_{ij}}{\sum_{i=1}^{m}\sum_{j=i}^{n} f_{ij}}$$

where f_{ij} representing the flow between p_i and q_j which minimizes the overall cost. $min \sum_{i=1}^{m}\sum_{j=1}^{n} f_{ij} d_{ij}$, and d_{ij} the ground distance between points p_i and q_j.

4   Findings and Results

4.1   Overall Color Distribution

This article is based on covers 16 types of Peking Opera Painted Faces and all the four characters of Peking Opera. The numbers of each category are as follows. We sum up the proportion and frequency that each class has appeared in all the 397 images and calculate the ratio as a reference to judge whether a category usually plays dominant roles in a separate image. Among all the nine color classifications, the black, grey, red, and blue ones take the most proportions (shown as the most enormous bubbles of Fig. 4), then the yellow and gold & silver ones. Both the green and gold & silver colors may often play the leading part in a different picture due to their higher ratio of total proportion to the number of images that contain them.

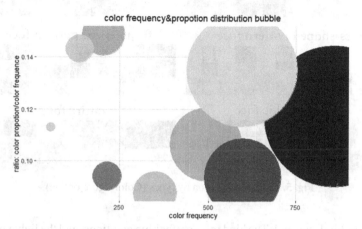

Fig. 4. Color distribution of a total of 397 images (Color figure online)

4.2 Color Distribution by Types

We calculate the total proportion of each color group by the type of Peking Opera Painted Faces. Pivot table was used to conduct addition and standardized operation, generating a 23 × 116 matrix (23 classes and 116 colors). Provided that not each type is enough to be regarded as statistic samples, we filter the types with less than 16 images, conducting statistics based on the other eight ones. Figure 5 shows the primary colors of each type.

To compare the color distribution of different images, we have binned the 3D colorspace into 8 (2 bins for each dimension) boxes to examine the distribution in each of them (usually representing colors that look alike). Then we compare the color bins of eight types with histograms.

4.3 Color Distribution by Characters

All the data processing operations are similar to the color statistics procedure group by types, except for the index, which has been replaced as characters. The following figures are based on the 4 × 116 (four characters and 116 colors) matrix that the former operation has generated. Figure 6 shows the color distribution of four characters: loyal,

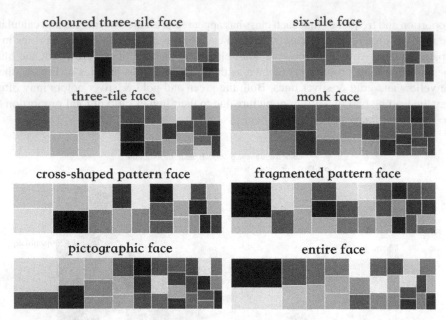

Fig. 5. Color distribution by types (Color figure online)

treacherous, kind, and evil. The kind roles prefer blue paintings, and the light yellow ones contribute a lot to the evil ones. The red-like colors take most proportions of the loyal ones, while the treacherous characters are usually presented with grey-like and pink-like colors. Interestingly, blue usually stands for bravery and pride in the traditional literature, and as the main color is the expression of Calculating, unyielding. However, we found that when used in combination with other colors, it can express another character, such as evil (Figs. 7 and 8).

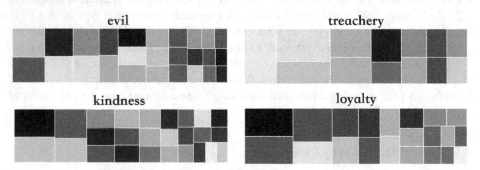

Fig. 6. Color distribution by characters (Color figure online)

4.4 Image Clustering

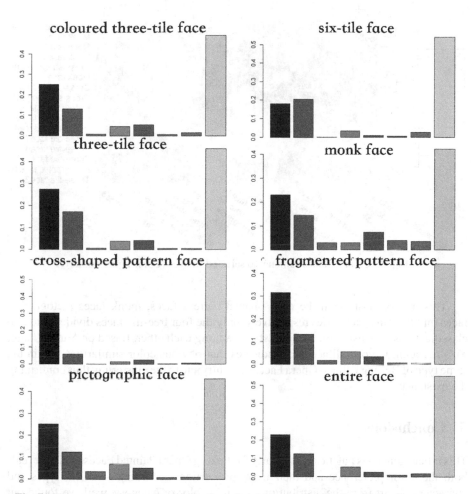

Fig. 7. Histograms of the color distribution of eight types after binning (Color figure online)

To compare the color distribution of different images, we have binned the 3D color space into 8 (2 bins for each dimension) boxes to examine the distribution in each of them (usually representing colors that look alike). Then we compare the color bins of eight types with histograms.

Since we have 397 images and it seems less intuitive to compare any two of them, we decided to use quantitative methods to calculate similarities between the sixteen different randomly selected images from 4 types, generating a basic clustering result to determine whether there are some principles. As for the method used for calculating the distance, we select the Earth Mover's Distance as it concerns both spatial color information and the size.

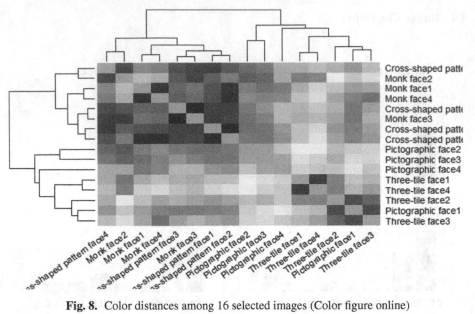

Cross-shaped patt(
Monk face2
Monk face1
Monk face4
Cross-shaped patt(
Monk face3
Cross-shaped patt(
Cross-shaped patt(
Pictographic face2
Pictographic face3
Pictographic face4
Three-tile face1
Three-tile face4
Three-tile face2
Pictographic face1
Three-tile face3

Fig. 8. Color distances among 16 selected images (Color figure online)

This matrix clusters all the cross-shaped pattern faces, monk faces pictographic faces into the same categories respectively, only the four tree-tile faces divided into two classifications, but also with not far distance among each other. Based on Yang, Zhang, Yu's research, the overall accuracy indicates that obvious color similarities within the same type of Beijing Painted Opera Faces do contribute to the clustering, thus confirming the existence.

5   Conclusions

This article generates palettes particularly for Peking Opera Painted Faces, which reveals both the color preference and their usual proportion, according to POPF types and characters. Apart from the distribution of single color or category, we have found out the color similarities within the same kind of Peking Painted Opera Faces and confirmed that quantitative methods.

A deep understanding of semantic color combinations is needed by both the reprocessing and reproducing of traditional culture. We hope this article contributes to this topic. There remain some issues that may decrease the accuracy of our basic color information. Firstly, the colors of digitalized images suffered from distortion in contrast to the original pictures, which slightly influenced the specific color names' judgment. Secondly, there might still some background colors remaining in the color extraction outcomes, which may be dealt with the algorithms that could better identify the outer edges of the painted faces.

References

1. Zhao, M.: Peking Opera. Beijing (1994). (in Chinese)
2. Yang, G., Zhang, H., Zhang, X., Yu, Y., Yang, J.: Digital inheritance of POPF based on image database and identification model. In: Digital Presentation and Preservation of Cultural and Scientific Heritage, DiPP 2019, pp. 315–322, Burgas (2019)
3. Lyn, B., Abhisekh, P., Maureen, S.: Affective color in visualization. In: Conference on Human Factors in Computing Systems, pp. 1364–1374. Association for Computing Machinery, New York (2017). https://doi.org/10.1145/3025453.3026041
4. Sharon, L., Julie, F., Chinmay, K., Maureen, S., Jeffrey, H.: Selecting semantically-resonant colors for data visualization. In: 15th Eurographics Conference on Visualization, pp.401–410. The Eurographs Association & John Wiley & Sons, Ltd., Chichester (2013). https://doi.org/10.1111/cgf.12127
5. Huang, D.Q.: Chinese Opera Masks. Beijing Arts and Crafts Publishing House, Beijing (2001). (in Chinese)
6. Luan, G.H.: Role Symbols: Chinese Opera Masks. Sanlian Bookstore, Beijing (2005).(in Chinese)
7. Cai, F.L.: Research on Digital Modeling and Rendering Technology of Peking Opera Facial Makeup, pp. 31–39. Zhejiang University, Hangzhou (2011). (in Chinese)
8. Xing, L.: Computer-aided Generation of Paper-cut of Peking Opera Facial Makeup. Liaoning Normal University, Dalian, pp. 31–40 (2017). (in Chinese)
9. Yang, L.Q.: Application of Beijing Opera Facial makeup Color in Design. Jiangxi Normal University, Nanchang (2012). (in Chinese)
10. Gao, J.Y.: Study on Personification of Peking Opera Facial Makeup, pp. 10–54. Zhejiang University, Hangzhou (2017). (in Chinese)
11. Lin, C.J. : A study of Chinese and Western Peking Opera facial makeup images: a case study of the current situation of middle school students' Facial makeup drawing. In: 3th Channel Science, pp. 161–164 (2012). (in Chinese)
12. Zhu, M.L., Wang, X.C.: Research on the digital application of Peking Opera facial makeup. In: 7th Art & Technology, pp. 164–138 (2016) (in Chinese)
13. Hannah, W., Mark, W.: Quantitative color profiling of digital 2 images with earth mover's distance using 3 the R package colordistance. PeerJ 7, e6398 (2019). https://doi.org/10.7717/peerj.6398
14. Hannah, W.: Color Distance Metrics. https://hiweller.github.io/colordistance/color-metrics.html
15. The history of Chinese culture. https://couldthephysical.blogspot.com/2020/07/according-to-history-of-chinese-culture.html

A Semantic Framework for Chinese Historical Events Based on Linked Data and Knowledge Graph

Hao Wang[1,2] ⓘ, Yueyan Li[1,2(✉)] ⓘ, and Sanhong Deng[1,2] ⓘ

[1] School of Information Management, Nanjing University, Nanjing 210023, China
dg1914005@smail.nju.edu.cn
[2] Jiangsu Key Laboratory of Data Engineering and Knowledge Service, Nanjing 210023, China

Abstract. In the era of big data, data redundancy has become an obstacle to deep reading. The objective of linked data as a new data organization model is to transform data into structured data following unified standards. The lack of Chinese conceptual terms has seriously hindered the semantization and standardization of Chinese domain ontology. Taking Chinese historical events as an example, ontology technology is used in this paper to standardize the definition of concepts and semantic relations in domain knowledge. Moreover, concepts from text resources are extracted through a deep learning algorithm Bi-LSTM-CRFs and combined with an external knowledge base to realize the fusion of related data within various data sets. Ultimately, the knowledge ontology of historical events is displayed in the way of a knowledge graph to further explore the practical application. The results show that the accuracy of the terms extraction of historical events is about 80% indicating the good recognition performance and portability of the model.

Keywords: Ontology · Linked data · Knowledge graph · Retrieval system

1 Introduction

"Open and share" is an eternal topic, and "linked data" is the foundation of "open data". Regardless of size, any information resource will lose its data value once it becomes a closed island. Linked data is a new way of data organization [1] that realizes the association between different data sets by various means, Moreover, through the Resource Description Framework (RDF), the structured data, unstructured data, and semi-structured data in the network are transformed into structured data with unified standards for human and machine understanding.

Humans cannot use computers to quickly obtain and discover accurate, comprehensive, integrated, and structured knowledge owing to the lack of high-quality linked data sets. Text data are the main network resources. Structured data are only a single linear organization of knowledge not able to reflect the multiple features of information resources and to meet the requirements of users' multi-dimensional knowledge retrieval. With the popularity of the ontology concept, the researchers agreed to transform unstructured data, semi-structured, and structured data into knowledge ontology. The purpose of

© Springer Nature Switzerland AG 2021
K. Toeppe et al. (Eds.): iConference 2021, LNCS 12645, pp. 502–513, 2021.
https://doi.org/10.1007/978-3-030-71292-1_39

an ontology is to provide a better comprehension of the multi relationship between information resources for the machine by standardizing the concept, attribute, and association relationship of a certain field [2].

Chinese historical events are a direct mapping of social, political, economic, and development in various dynasties. They fully demonstrate the trajectory of historical development and are an important channel to comprehend historical evolution. Historical events are mainly recorded in the form of unstructured text, for which there are no systematic structural arrangements and semantic association limiting utilization, innovation, and dissemination of historical event information. This study aims to realize the semantic association between Chinese historical events through computer technology.

To comprehensively understand, display, and discover new knowledge of Chinese historical events, this paper mainly addresses the following research questions:

RQ1: Construct historical event knowledge ontology models standardize and reveal the concepts, attributes, and associations of historical event knowledge.
RQ2: Determine which entities in the historical event ontology can be extracted by text mining? Which entities can be obtained from the external knowledge base, and how to integrate the two?
RQ3: How can one use the knowledge graphs to display the ontology of historical events?

2   Relevant Research

The most basic work of ontology learning is entity extraction. Named entity recognition method is an important solution for entity extraction [3]. Traditional machine learning approaches rely heavily on the corpus and have the problems of incomplete feature extraction, such as HMM [4], CRFs [5], and MEMM [6], In recent years, with the continuous in-depth research of deep neural networks, domestic scholars have utilized it to identify Chinese named entities or extract the relationship between entities, such as CNN [7], LSTM [8], and RNN [9]. However, these methods may not be able to take advantage of context information. Huang first attempted to integrate a Bi-LSTM with traditional CRFs in the task of entity extraction and constructed Bi-LSTM-CRF model composed of word embedding layer, context encoder layer, and decoder layer [10], which is also a popular neural network model in the field of entity extraction in recent years [11–13].

The domestic and abroad research on events mainly focuses on the extraction of entities and relationships of various types of events, such as financial [14, 15], emergencies [16], music [17], and historical [18, 19]. Its main purpose is to identify event elements based on pattern matching methods or based on machine learning methods, however, few scholars make knowledge representation of the extracted large-scale data. The main purpose of constructing the event semantic model is to facilitate the interoperability and interconnection of resources in various fields by standardizing the event components and the semantic structure of the related elements to support more intelligent applications. The event semantic representation model can be divided into two major parts. One is the event ontology model in the general field, such as Event Ontology [20], ABC [21], Event-Model-F [22], SEM [23] and the other one is the event ontology model in the professional field, such as NOEM, NIAO, CIDOC-CRM, and schema.org. NOEM is used to express event resources in the news field, NIAO is utilized to describe narrative images [24], CIDOC-CRM is an event-centered cultural heritage information ontology [25], and schema.org is used to standardize the definitions of literary events, including attributes such as participants, starting time, and location [26].

In general, the entity extraction technology provides technical support for the semantization of text knowledge. Ontology is the key technology to realize the semantic web by standardizing the extracted concepts and the relationship between concepts. Therefore, the computer can organize and interpret fine-grained knowledge in fine-granularity and provide decision-making guidance for human understanding and application of knowledge. In this paper, taking Chinese historical events as an example, it is tried to further study the knowledge organization and semantics of information resources such as text.

3 Method

3.1 Study Framework

The methodology utilized in this paper concentrates on developing a better knowledge ontology of using automated skills to realize knowledge standardization organization and avoiding the complexity of manually constructing ontology. The study framework is presented in Fig. 1.

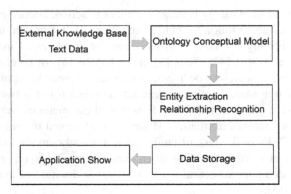

Fig. 1. Study framework

The model mainly includes four parts of collecting the related data, constructing the Ontology Conceptual model, extracting the relevant entities through machine learning and realizing knowledge ontology application display.

Ontology Model of Historical Events. To construct a general and extensible historical event knowledge ontology model, we first draw on the core classes and attributes of CIDOC-CRM and combine the user-defined classes and attributes. Then, we design concepts, attributes, and relational features in historical events based on extracted entities and the time concept relationship in the external knowledge base.

Historical events are the core of the historical events ontology, and person, time, and person are the main characteristics of historical events. Hence, the historical event ontology model mainly includes five parallel basic categories of *Event, Place, Person, Time*, and *Other*. "*Other*" is introduced to ensure the scalability of the historical event ontology model. The reuse criteria of the three entities including *Event, Place*, and *Person*, and their related attributes are derived from the Event, Place, and Person entities and attribute relationships in CIDOC-CRM respectively. Other entities and their attributes are user-defined.

Here, we conducted an in-depth analysis of various manifestations of the time. We further defined six time concepts, such as *Dynasty, Emperor, EmperorEra, Year, YearEra*, and *CommonEra*. The time entity (Time) is an abstract concept with no direct instance and contains all the concepts of time. The author establishes the hierarchical relationship between time based on the relationship of inclusion to further reveal the hierarchical relationship between time. *Dynasty* can be divided into two subclasses of *Emperor* and *Year. EmperorEra* is a subclass of *Emperor*, and *YearEra* is a subclass of *Year*.

Then, we defined nine object properties to describe the non-hierarchical relationship between all entities in historical events ontology, such as *hasParticipant, hasPlace, hasTime, hasEventOccured, hasEventHappened, hasEventParticipant, equals, includes* and *included. hasParticipant* is used to explain the participants in an event; *hasPlace* is utilized to describe the place of an event; *hasTime* is utilized to explain the relevant time in an event; *equals* is used to describe the corresponding relationship between times; *includes* is utilized to explain the containment relationship between times.

In this study, the reasoning rules are set up. There are some rules, including the inverse relationship, such as *hasTime* and *hasEventOccured, hasPlace* and *hasEventHappened, hasParticipant* and *hasEventParticipant*, and *includes* and *included*. Moreover, there is a transitive relationship, which *includes* and *equals* are transitive.

So far, the construction of the historical event ontology model is completed. The historical event ontology model is shown in Fig. 2.

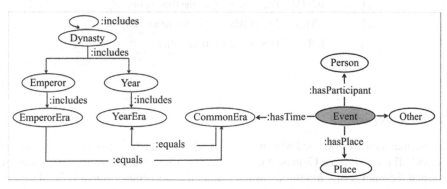

Fig. 2. The historical event ontology model

Bi-LSTM-CRFs Model. In the entity extraction part, in this study, deep neural networks (Bi-LSTM) are integrated with traditional machine learning methods (CRFs).

Moreover, the Bi-LSTM-CRFs method is used to extract event entities of historical texts to save contextual information and consider the effects of pre-labeling and post-labeling from the perspective of sentences. Before modeling, at first we must determine the labeling object. In general, there are two kinds of words and characters. In this study, the text is divided into word sequences. Characters other than entities are uniformly marked as "O". The role of the characters constituting the entity consists of two parts: first, the category of the entity, for which, this article mainly identifies four entities, event (EVE), person (PER), place (PLA), time (TIM). Second, the position of the character in the entity. "B" represents the beginning of the entity, "I" shows the middle character of the entity, and "E" represents the end of the entity. Hence, there are 13 kinds of character roles, as shown in Table 1.

Table 1. The role labeling method of the Bi-LSTM-CRFs model

Number	Role	Meaning
1	O	Non-entity characters
2	B-EVE	The beginning of the event entity
3	I-EVE	The middle part of the event entity
4	E-EVE	The end of the event entity
5	B-PER	The beginning of the person-name entity
6	I-PER	The middle part of the person-name entity
7	E-PER	The end of the person-name entity
8	B-PLA	The beginning of the place entity
9	I-PLA	The middle part of the place entity
10	E-PLA	The end of the place entity
11	B-TIM	The beginning of the time entity
12	I-TIM	The middle part of the time entity
13	E-TIM	The end of the time entity

3.2   Data Preparation

The original data are collected within four steps: first, collecting historical event names: to crawl all the names of Chinese historical events from pre-Qin to modern times, we searched the names of Chinese historical events listed in *Baidu Baike* [27], *Wikipedia* [28] and *History Dictionary* [29] with the term "Chinese historical events". By merging synonyms and removing duplicate event names in the above three parts, we get 1,584 historical event names. Second, crawling the first paragraph of the description of these events in *Baidu Baike*, where often contains time, location, and people of the event. Third, Collecting labeling corpus: some pages in *Baidu Baike* list the time, place, and people of events in the form of tables (some elements may be missing), we use it as a labeling corpus. Fourth, external knowledge base, to realize the deep correlation and expansion of the time dimension, we introduce external knowledge bases including the "List of the Sequence of Chinese Historical Dynasties and Their Corresponding Emperors" [30] and the "Comparison of the EmperorEra of CommonEra and the YearEra of CommonEra" [31].

We identify six sentence-breaking punctuation ("，", "．", "：", "！", "？", "；") to segment the text, and then the sentences are separated by spaces. In this paper, we use string matching to automatically filter phrases containing labeling corpus and use them as labeling corpus of events, people, time, and place, respectively.

4   Results and Discussion

4.1   Historical Event Entity Extraction Based on Bi-LSTM-CRFs Model

In this paper, the evaluation of the performance of the entity extraction is measured by three factors: Precision (P), Recall (R), and F-value (F1). We calculated the relatively good combination of parameter settings including the batch size of 20, the dropout probability of 0.5, the learning rate of 0.001, and the hidden layer nodes of 250 when using Bi-LSTM-CRFs to identify the event entities by setting different parameters. Then, we applied it to train the other three entities including the time entity, people entity, and place entity. The recognition results of the four entities are shown in Fig. 3.

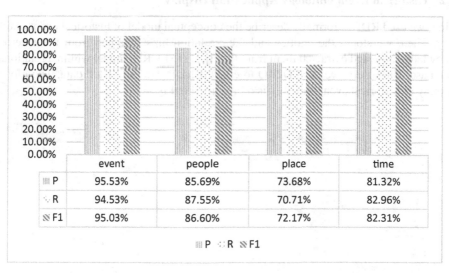

	event	people	place	time
▥ P	95.53%	85.69%	73.68%	81.32%
⋰ R	94.53%	87.55%	70.71%	82.96%
▨ F1	95.03%	86.60%	72.17%	82.31%

▥ P   ⋰ R   ▨ F1

Fig. 3. The different entities recognition results based on Bi-LSTM-CRFs

As shown in Fig. 3, the recognition effect of the event entity is significantly better compared to the other three entities. Mainly, the reason is that the composition of the event entity is relatively regular consisting of only Chinese characters, however, most of them contain words such as "battle", "campaign", and "of". In general, the model can make good use of the context features and the rules between character roles. Furthermore, event entity can be identified as more comprehensively and accurately. The recognition effect of the person entity is the second. This is mainly because the composition of ancient names is more complicated because of rare characters, as well as a non-Han person. However, the time entity is more special since it often contains numbers. Therefore, the recognition effect of time entities is better, however, its recognition effect is inferior to the former two. The recognition effect of the place entity is the worst due to its complicated composition method including the common expressions of place names (such as "province", "city", and "county", etc.) and the unconventional expressions (such as "Hexi Corridor" and "Today's Jinjiang estuary of Korea", etc.).

Based on the above analysis, the model integrates LSTM and CRFs. It has the advantages of learning the features of the corpus independently without expanding the features, hence, the model can well identify the event entity where P, R, and F1 are around 95%. Moreover, P, R, and F1 are around 80% for person entity, time entity, place entity. At the same time, it is found that the model can also identify numerous new events, hence, it can solve the problem of unregistered words. Consequently, the model has superior performance in terms of recognition.

So far, numerous scattered events, time, place, and person have been obtained, however, these entities are stored separately and cannot reflect their relationship well. The next section mainly discusses how to organize the extracted entities.

4.2 Historical Event Ontology Application Display

First, we used RDF to formally describe the conceptual model of historical event ontology. Then, we stored the entities and their relationships obtained from the external knowledge base and extracted them from the Bi-LSTM-CRFs model within a relational database. Ultimately, we used D2RQ to convert RDB data into RDF data. The global display of historical event ontology is represented in Fig. 4.

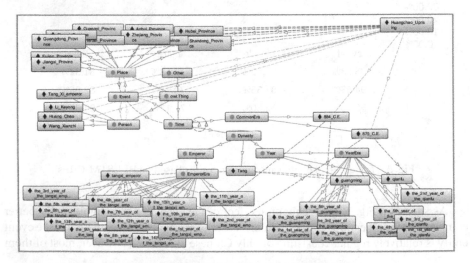

Fig. 4. The global display of historical event ontology

To enhance the practicability and operability of the historical event ontology model, we demonstrated the practical application of the historical event ontology through visualization. First, Apache jena and a third-party visualization plug-in Echarts [32] were used to display the knowledge graph of the retrieval results. Considering the event name "the Battle of Red Cliffs ", the historical event knowledge graph is represented in Fig. 5.

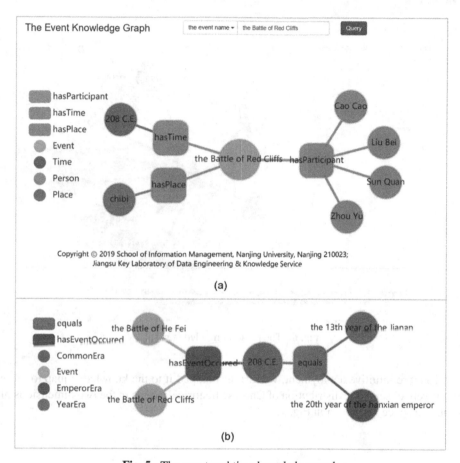

Fig. 5. The event and time knowledge graph

Based on Fig. 5(a), when the event name "the Battle of Red Cliffs" is entered, three properties of the event can be directly retrieved including :hasParticipant, :hasPlace, and :hasTime with multiple specific values. The time involved in the event include "208 C.E.". The participants are "Cao Cao", "Liu Bei", "Sun Quan" and "Zhou Yu". The place of the event include "chibi". Through the event knowledge graph, users can quickly comprehend the main constituent elements of an event and the relationship between the elements. Furthermore, the users can also click on any concept in the graph to further display the properties of the sub-concepts and their relationships, as shown in Fig. 5(b).

Furthermore, the historical event knowledge graph designed in this paper can also show deeper semantic relationships, for instance, between participants, as shown in Fig. 6.

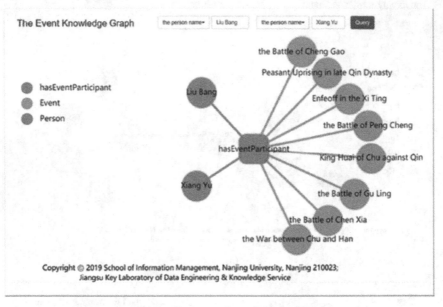

Fig. 6. The person knowledge graph

To more intuitive deployment, we further mapped it to the knowledge map to more intuitively observe the distribution of Chinese historical events in the two dimensions of time and space, as shown in Fig. 7.

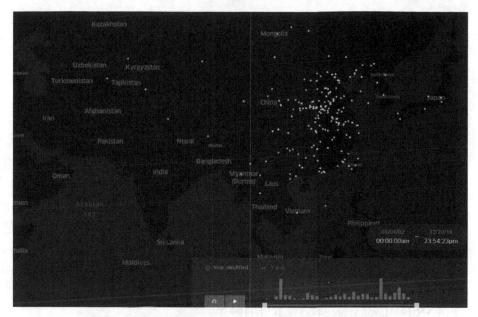

Fig. 7. The knowledge map display of Chinese historical events

5   Conclusions

With the development of the Semantic Web, data association technology aims to integrate various data sources. The research used entity extraction methods to mine the knowledge structure in text information resources, and integrated existing structured data avoiding a huge deal of repetitive work. This paper assists to promote the development of digital humanities research. Several future directions of this work include improving the conceptual model of historical event ontology, extracting more entities and relations through machine learning methods. At the practical application level, it can be applied to local historical events graph display, and it can also be used to realize knowledge mining based on event relationships, for example, discovering the growth trajectory of historical figures and their roles in historical changes by mining the activity trajectory of historical figures.

Acknowledgement. This work is an outcome of project "Research on Semantic Parsing and Humanities Computing of Chinese Intangible Cultural Heritage Text Driven by Linked Data" (No. 72074108) supported by National Natural Science Foundation of China and "The Semantic Analysis and Knowledge Graph Research of Local Chronicle Text Oriented to Humanistic Computing" (No. 14370113) supported by the Fundamental Research Funds for the Central Universities.

References

1. Speiser, S., Harth, A.: Integrating linked data and services with linked data services. In: Antoniou, G., et al. (eds.) ESWC 2011. LNCS, vol. 6643, pp. 170–184. Springer, Heidelberg (2011). https://doi.org/10.1007/978-3-642-21034-1_12

2. Studer, R., Benjamins, V.R., Fensel, D.: Knowledge engineering: principles and methods. Data Knowl. Eng. **25**(s1-2), 161–197 (1998)
3. Lample, G., Ballesteros, M., Subramanian, S., et al.: Neural architectures for named entity recognition. arXiv preprint arXiv:1603.01360 (2016)
4. Yu, S., Bai, S., Wu, P.: Description of the kent ridge digital labs system used for MUC-7. In: Proceedings of the 7th Message Understanding Conference, Fairfax, VA, p. 16 (1998)
5. McCallum, A., Li, W.: Early results for named entity recognition with conditional random fields, feature induction and web-enhanced lexicons. In: Proceedings of the 7th Conference on Natural Language Learning at HLT-NAACL, vol. 4, pp. 188–191. Association for Computational Linguistics, Stroudsburg (2003)
6. Borthwick, A., Sterling, J., Agichtein, E., et al.: NYU: description of the MENE named entity system as used in MUC-7. In: Proceedings of the 7th Message Understanding Conference, Fairfax, VA (1998)
7. Luong, M., Pham, H., Manning, CD.: Effective approaches to attention based neural machine translation. In: Proceedings of the 2015 Conference on Empirical Methods in Natural Language Processing, pp. 1414–1421 (2015)
8. Hochreiter, S., Schmidhuber, J.: Long short-term memory. Neural Comput. **9**(8), 1735–1780 (1997)
9. Goller, C., Kuchler, A.: Learning task-dependent distributed representations by backpropagation through structure. In: Proceedings of International Conference on Neural Networks (ICNN 1996), vol. 1, pp. 347–352. IEEE (1996)
10. Huang, Z., Wei, X., Kai, Y.: Bidirectional LSTM-CRF models for sequence tagging. Computer Science (2015)
11. Dong, C., Zhang, J., Zong, C., Hattori, M., Di, H.: Character-based LSTM-CRF with radical-level features for chinese named entity recognition. In: Lin, C.-Y., Xue, N., Zhao, D., Huang, X., Feng, Y. (eds.) ICCPOL/NLPCC-2016. LNCS (LNAI), vol. 10102, pp. 239–250. Springer, Cham (2016). https://doi.org/10.1007/978-3-319-50496-4_20
12. Ma, X., Hovy, E.: End-to-end sequence labeling via bi-directional LSTM-CNNs-CRF. In: Proceedings of the 54th Annual Meeting of the Association for Computational Linguistics, pp. 1064–1074 (2016)
13. Yang, F., Zhang, J., Liu, G., Zhou, J., Zhou, C., Sun, H.: Five-stroke based CNN-BiRNN-CRF network for chinese named entity recognition. In: Zhang, M., Ng, V., Zhao, D., Li, S., Zan, H. (eds.) NLPCC 2018. LNCS (LNAI), vol. 11108, pp. 184–195. Springer, Cham (2018). https://doi.org/10.1007/978-3-319-99495-6_16
14. Qiang, S., Luo, Y., Li, Y., et al.: Ontology reasoning for financial affairs with RBR and CBR. Data Anal. Knowl. Discov. **3**(08), 94–104 (2019)
15. Zou, X.: Research on financial event extraction technology based on deep learning. University of Electronic Science and Technology of China, Chengdu (2020)
16. Tang, M., Su, X., Wang, H.: A case study on emergency rapid response intelligence system–base on the public safety emergency. Inf. Sci. **37**(01), 105–111 (2019)
17. Song, F.: Research on typical event extraction technology in the field of music. Harbin Institute of Technology, Haerbin (2009)
18. Tang, H., Wang, H., Zhang, Z., et al.: Extracting names of historical events based on chinese character tags. Data Anal. Knowl. Discov. **2**(07), 89–100 (2018)
19. Wang, D., Gao, R., Shen, S., et al.: Research on automatic recognition of basic entity component of historic events for pre-qin classics. J. Natl. Libr. China **27**(01), 65–77 (2018)
20. Event Ontology. https://motools.sourceforge.net/event/event.html. Accessed 17 Oct 2018
21. Lagoze, C., Hunter, J.: The ABC ontology and model. In: Proceedings of the International Conference on Dublin Core and Metadata Applications, Tokyo, pp. 160–176. ACM, New York (2001)

22. Scherp, A., Franz, T., Saathoff, C., et al.: F-a model of events based on the foundational ontology dolce+DnS ultralight. In: Proceedings of the Fifth International Conference on Knowledge Capture, Redondo Beach, pp. 137–144. ACM, New York (2009)
23. Hage, W.V., Malaisé, V., Segers, R., et al.: The simple event model ontology. https://semant icweb.cs.vu.nl/2009/11/sem/. Accessed 25 Nov 2019
24. Xu, L., Wang, X.: Narrative image annotation ontology for semantic web. J. Libr. Sci. China **43**(5), 70–83 (2018)
25. What is the CIDOC CRM? https://www.cidoc-crm.org/. Accessed 26 Dec 2019
26. Event in Schema.org. https://schema.org.cn/Event. Accessed 26 Dec 2019
27. Baidu Baike Homepage. https://baike.baidu.com/. Accessed 25 Dec 2018
28. Wikipedia Homepage. https://www.wikipedia.org/. Accessed 25 Dec 2018
29. Zhu, Y.: History Dictionary. Academic Press, Beijing (2008)
30. List of the Sequence of Chinese Historical Dynasties and Their Corresponding Emperors. https://114.xixik.com/chaodai/#anchor1. Accessed 08 Oct 2019
31. Comparison of the EmperorEra of CommonEra and the YearEra of CommonEra. https://wenku.baidu.com/view/d85b2c745e0e7cd184254b35eefdc8d376ee14fc.html?from=search. Accessed 08 Oct 2019
32. Echarts Homepage. https://echarts.baidu.com/. Accessed 20 Dec 2019

Concept Identification of Directly and Indirectly Related Mentions Referring to Groups of Persons

Anastasia Zhukova[1]([✉]), Felix Hamborg[2,4], Karsten Donnay[3,4], and Bela Gipp[1,4]

[1] University of Wuppertal, Wuppertal, Germany
{zhukova,gipp}@uni-wuppertal.de
[2] University of Konstanz, Konstanz, Germany
felix.hamborg@uni-konstanz.de
[3] University of Zurich, Zurich, Switzerland
donnay@ipz.uzh.ch
[4] Heidelberg Academy of Sciences and Humanities, Heidelberg, Germany
https://dke.uni-wuppertal.de/en/

Abstract. Unsupervised concept identification through clustering, i.e., identification of semantically related words and phrases, is a common approach to identify contextual primitives employed in various use cases, e.g., text dimension reduction, i.e., replace words with the concepts to reduce the vocabulary size, summarization, and named entity resolution. We demonstrate the first results of an unsupervised approach for the identification of groups of persons as actors extracted from a set of related articles. Specifically, the approach clusters mentions of groups of persons that act as non-named entity actors in the texts, e.g., "migrant families" = "asylum-seekers." Compared to our baseline, the approach keeps the mentions of the geopolitical entities separated, e.g., "Iran leaders" ≠ "European leaders," and clusters (in)directly related mentions with diverse wording, e.g., "American officials" = "Trump Administration."

Keywords: News analysis · Coreference resolution · Media bias

1 Introduction

Methods for *concept identification* seek to identify words and phrases that refer to the same semantic concept. As such, concept identification is a crucial task employed in various use cases, such as information summarization, information extraction, named entity resolution, and coreference resolution. While in some domains, e.g., medicine, semantic (dis)similarities are clearly distinct, in others, e.g., the news domain, phrases referring to groups of persons are often *semantically highly related yet conceptually different*, e.g., "American officials" and "Israeli officials" have similar roles but act as different actors. Identification of conceptually fine-grained groups of persons is a challenging task due to two key issues: first, high semantic relatedness of mentions that yet perform conceptually different roles, e.g., "immigration lawyers" and "undocumented

© Springer Nature Switzerland AG 2021
K. Toeppe et al. (Eds.): iConference 2021, LNCS 12645, pp. 514–526, 2021.
https://doi.org/10.1007/978-3-030-71292-1_40

immigrants." Second, event-specific coreferential relations are often prone to high lexical diversity due to the word choice and labeling [7], e.g., "Dreamers" and "DACA recipients."

In this work, we propose an unsupervised concept identification approach that automatically extracts conceptually fine-grained clusters of related mentions referring to groups of people from a set of text documents. We narrow down our problem statement to news articles since word choice is especially subtle and rich in the news domain. The goal of our approach is to extract from news stories those group-actors that are the main content elements and yet missed by current coreference resolution and named entity recognition.

2 Related Work

Concept identification is a technique important across various use cases, e.g., for dimension reduction (cf. [4,9,10]), information extraction (cf. [8]), information summarization (cf. [2]), coreference resolution of the mentions referring to the same entities (cf. [19]), taxonomy construction (cf. [3]), and named entity or domain concept recognition (cf. [15,17]).

Scholars have proposed supervised tasks where a model is trained to identify domain-specific concepts, e.g., reactions to drugs [15,17], by automatically labeling phrases with their respective concepts, e.g., persons or other named entities. Most frequently, concept identification is an unsupervised task to explore the relations between the words or phrases contained in a text [8–10,15]. Unsupervised methods use clustering, e.g., K-means [9], which find patterns between the elements without prior knowledge. Such methods are typically integrated as preprocessing or intermediate steps so that their results can be used in downstream analysis steps. While less bound to the content of text datasets, clustering-based methods are more difficult to use because one has to find a clustering parameter configuration to yield suitable results for the dataset at hand.

3 Methodology

We propose an unsupervised clustering approach that identifies mentions *directly referring* to the same group of individuals in a given context, e.g., "asylum-seekers" and "Central American immigrants," and groups of individuals semantically related to countries or organizations as the representatives of both, i.e., *indirectly coreferential*, e.g., "White House officials" – "Trump administration." For the clustering itself, we employ the core principle of two clustering algorithms: 1) OPTICS clustering algorithm [1], i.e., we form clusters by decreasing cluster density; 2) hierarchical clustering (HC) [14], i.e., we use the weighted average linkage criterion to merge clusters.

3.1 Mention Extraction

A *mention* is a noun phrase (NP) automatically extracted from a parsed text, e.g., by CoreNLP [11]. We extract NPs not larger than 20 words. For each mention we assign a *representative phrase* (RP), i.e., a shortened version of the phrase that includes only the most frequent dependency parsing components of a NP: heads of NPs, compounds, and adjectival and noun modifiers. We use unique RPs as clustering units, i.e., we assume that within a narrow article-based context identical RPs of different mentions m_i share same meaning $rp_l = rp(m_i)$.

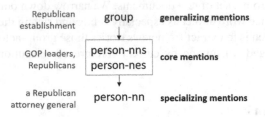

Fig. 1. Level of details among the mention types

To select mentions referring to groups of persons, we apply the entity type identification methodology proposed by Hamborg et al. [6] and keep all mentions of four entity types: (1) multiple persons NE ("person-nes"), e.g., "Republicans," (2) multiple persons non-NE ("person-nns"), e.g., "GOP leaders," (3) single person non-NE ("person-nn"), e.g., "a Republican attorney," and (4) group of people ("group"), e.g., "Republican establishment." Figure 1 depicts how these types form hypernym-hyponym relations. While "group" is the most general and aggregated type, "person-nn" is the type that has the largest level of details, i.e., the single instances of the groups. Due to the comparably balanced level of detail inherent to concepts of the types "person-nes" and "person-nns," we coin their mentions *core mentions*.

3.2 Pipeline

Our approach consists of six stages where the first identifies cluster cores and subsequent stages expand the clusters: (1) preprocessing, (2) identify cluster cores, (3) form cluster bodies, (4) add border mentions, (5) form non-core clusters, and (6) merge final clusters. Figure 2 depicts the principle of the approach.

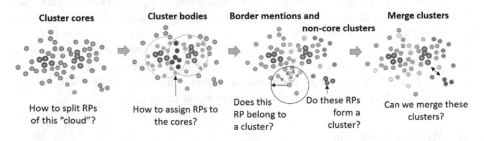

Fig. 2. Identification of mention clusters

3.3 Preprocessing

In early experiments, we observed that clustering the unweighted mean word vector representation of RPs, i.e., a mean vector of the vectorized phrases' words, yielded inefficient concept separation, e.g., phrases "American people" and "Mexican people" were clustered into one concept although they refer to different nations. On the contrary, two phrases could be coreferential but only in the narrow event-determined context, e.g., "young illegals" - "DACA recipients."

To improve the effectiveness of clustering, we apply modifications to the vector representation, i.e., (1) employ a weighting scheme of the named entity (NE) components of the RPs and (2) calculate more than one similarity matrix to introduce more than one level of similarity between RPs.

Word Vector Weighting. In the narrow article-specific context, word vector weighting [21] increases the semantic proximity in the vector space and facilitates the identification of the semantic relatedness and coreferential relations (cf. Fig. 3). We represent phrases as the mean of their weighted words' embedding, i.e.,

$$V(rp_i) = \sum_{\forall i \in |rp|} w_i \cdot v(i) \qquad (1)$$

where $v(i)$ is a vector representation of the i-th word and w_i is a weight assigned to this word. We use word2vec [13] as a word embedding model due to its ability to represent both single words and multi-word phrases, resulting in more precisely defined positions of phrases in the vector space.

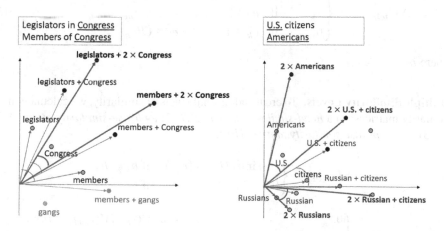

Fig. 3. The weighting of the NEs in phrases increases cosine similarity of related phrases and separates unrelated phrases

A vector representation $V(rp_k)$ depends on its relations to rp_l to which a similarity value is calculated. A weight w_i for a word v_i in (1) is selected as following:

$$w_i = \begin{cases} NG_{ne(rp_k),ne(rp_l)}, & \text{if } NG_{ne(rp_k),ne(rp_l)} > 0 \\ wt, & \text{if } ne(rp_k) \in NG \text{ and } ne(rp_l) = \emptyset \text{ or vice versa} \\ 1, & \text{else} \end{cases} \quad (2)$$

where $ne(rp_i)$ is an extracted NE from rp_i, e.g., $ne(\text{``Congress members''}) =$ "Congress" (if $ne_t \notin rp_k \Rightarrow ne(rp_k) = \emptyset$), NG is a *named entity (NE) grid*, i.e., a controlling matrix that allows or restricts similarity calculations between phrases that contain NEs, and $wt = 1.7$.

An NE-grid NG determines which types of mentions can be merged. For example, if $NG_{ne(rp_k),ne(rp_k)} = 0$, then the mentions of one geo-political entity (GPEs) are not compared to mentions of another GPEs, e.g., "French" $\neq$ "North Korea." If a value of a NG's cell $NG_{ne(rp_k),ne(rp_l)} > 0$ then NG favors to merge the corresponding RPs, e.g., "U.S." = "Americans."

The NE-grid is spanned across combined NE chains Ch of two types: country + nationality (Ch_{cn}) and organization + persons (Ch_{op}). To construct NE-chains, we use the relations between the terms in the semantic network ConceptNet [18]. We iterated over the extracted NEs and interlinked them if their corresponding ConceptNet terms have a "SimilarTo" relation. Afterward, we restore full connectivity between the sub-chains, i.e., the restored connectivity of the extracted "United States"-"U.S." and "U.S."-"American" chains yields a chain ch_a "United States"-"U.S."-"American." Based on the NE-chains, we constructed the NE-grid NG:

$$NG_{ne_k,ne_l} = \begin{cases} wt, & \text{if } ne_k \in ch_a \wedge ne_l \in ch_a \text{ where } ch_a \in Ch_m \\ 1, & \text{if } ne_k \in Ch_m \wedge ne_l \notin Ch_m \\ 0, & \text{if } ne_k \in Ch_m \wedge ne_l \in Ch_m \end{cases} \quad (3)$$

where $m = cn \vee op$.

Multiple Similarity Levels. To create additional levels of similarity, we calculate three similarity matrices: 1) a *head-similarity matrix* SH, 2) a *phrase-similarity matrix* SP, and 3) a *core-phrase similarity matrix* SPC:

$$SH_{h_i,h_j} = \begin{cases} \text{cossim}(v(h_i), v(h_j)) & \text{if } h_i \neq h_j \\ 0.5 & \text{if } h_i = h_j \end{cases} \quad (4)$$

$$SP(C)_{rp_i,rp_j} = \begin{cases} 0, & \text{if cossim}(V(rp_i), V(rp_j)) < thr_{sim_{rp}} \\ & \text{or } rp_i = rp_j \\ & \text{or } NG_{ne(rp_i),ne(rp_i)} = 0 \\ \text{cossim}(V(rp_i), V(rp_j)), & \text{else} \end{cases}$$

$$(5)$$

where $h_k = h(rp_i)$ is the head of a phrase, e.g., $h(\text{"Congress members"}) = \text{"members,"}$ $cossim$ is cosine similarity, $v(\cdot)/V(\cdot)$ is a vector representation of words or phrases, $thr_{sim_{rp}} = 0.4$ is a threshold for the minimum RP similarity, and SPC is a subset matrix of the SP with the RPs that are core-mentions.

The output of the preprocessing step consists of three similarity matrices (SH, SP, SPC) that represent similarity of RPs as to three levels and an NE-grid NG that determines restriction rules for operations between mentions.

3.4 Identification of the Cluster Cores

We start clustering with identification of the *cluster cores* (CC), i.e., cluster the core mentions' RPs (CRP) as the most distinctive among all RPs (see Sect. 3.1). Two core RPs crp_i and crp_j form a CC if they meet two requirements: (1) $SPC_{crp_i,crp_j} > 0$ and $SH_{crp_i,crp_j} > 0$, (2) crp_i and crp_j were similar to a sufficient number of other core RPs according to the *ratio matrix RM*. Following OPTIC's principle of creating more similarity levels compared to one similarity metric, we form a *ratio matrix RM* for the core RPs. Each element in RM shows a normalized count of the core RPs to which two RPs at a hand are similar to:

$$RM_{crp_i,crp_j} = \begin{cases} frac & \text{if frac} \geq OR_{thr} \wedge crp_i \neq crp_j \\ 0 & \text{else} \end{cases} \qquad (6)$$

where

$$frac = \frac{\sum(b(SPC_{crp_i,}) \wedge b(SPC_{crp_j,}))}{max(\sum b(SPC_{crp_i,}), \sum b(SPC_{crp_j}))} \qquad (7)$$

and $b(\cdot)$ is a binary representation of values in a vector (1 if a cell value is larger than 0, else 0); $OR_{thr} = 0.5 \leq \log_{5000}|RP| \leq 0.7$, i.e., the threshold is balanced based on the size of unique RPs: a larger number of RPs imposes more strict similarity requirements for the cluster cores.

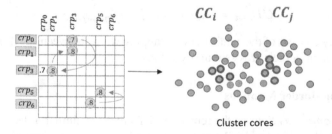

Cluster cores

Fig. 4. Identification of chains of related core representatives: this example yields two core clusters.

Finally, we iterate over the elements of RM and recursively collect chains of the interlinked CRPs, as shown in Fig. 4. A chain is considered complete once no other core RPs can be added to it.

3.5 Forming of Cluster Bodies

To further extend the clusters, we form *cluster bodies* CB by expanding the identified cored with the unclustered RPs (Fig. 5). First, we assign RPs to the cluster cores if a RP was similar to at least one of the core RPs and the merge is allowed by NG:

$$CB_i = \{rp \cup CC_i | \forall rp \in RP, \exists cc \in CC_i :$$
$$SP_{rp,cc} \geq 0.5 \text{ and } NG_{ne(rp),ne(\forall CC_i)} \neq 0\} \quad (8)$$

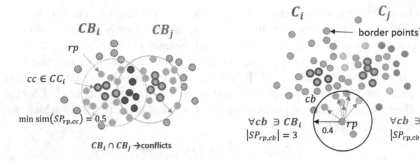

Fig. 5. Identification of cluster bodies   **Fig. 6.** Adding border mentions

Second, we intersect cluster bodies (CB) with each other to check if there were non-core RPs that belonged to both CBs. If so, we resolve the conflicting RPs by calculating a normalized similarity score between an $rp_{conf} \in CB_i \cap CB_j$ and non-conflicting RPs of each CB, and choosing a CB with the largest similarity score:

$$sim_{rp_{conf},CB_i} = \frac{1}{|CB_i|} \Big(\sum_{cb \in CB_i} |rp_{conf} \cap cb| + \sum_{cb \in CB_i} SP_{rp_{conf},cb} \Big) \quad (9)$$

$$CB_{best} = \text{argmax}_{i \in |CB|} \, sim_{rp_{conf},CB_i} \quad (10)$$

i.e., similarity consists of the number of overlapping words between an RP and clustered RPs and the sum of their cross-similarity values.

3.6 Adding Border Mentions

We define *border mentions* as the remaining RPs that arc similar at least to two body RPs (Fig. 6). We add a border RP rp to a cluster body CB_i and formed a cluster C_i if rp is similar to at least two RPs in CB_i and has the largest normalized similarity score to CB_i:

$$C_i = \{rp \cup CB_i | \forall rp \in RP :$$
$$|SP_{rp,\forall cb \in CB_i} > 0| \geq 2 \quad \wedge \quad NG_{ne(rp),ne(\forall cb \in CB_i)} \neq 0 \quad \wedge \quad (11)$$
$$max_{CB_i \in CB} \big(\frac{\sum_{cb \in CB_i} SP_{rp,cb}}{|\{\forall cb \in CB_i : SP_{rp,cb} > 0\}|} \big) \}$$

3.7 Form Non-core Clusters

Some unmerged RPs can form non-core clusters, i.e., they are similar to other RPs but do not meet requirements to become core points (see Fig. 2). We form a *non-core cluster* around a rp as:

$$nC_i = \{rp \bigcup_{rp_j \notin C} rp_j, \text{if } SP_{rp,rp_j} \geq 0.5\} \tag{12}$$

3.8 Merging Final Clusters

When all clusters are formed, the final step of the pipeline is to check if clusters can be further merged based on combined features of word count and word embeddings. We create an extended list of modifiers, i.e., all the previous (see Sect. 3.3) and also number and apposition modifiers. We compare the identified clusters according to a cosine similarity of the weighted vector representation using this extended list.

Each cluster C_i is, first, represented with the counted RPs' lowercased lemmas L_i. We treat clusters as documents and transformed the clusters into the TF-IDF representation [21]. Each cluster C_i is represented as a TF-IDF-weighted average word embedding representation of its lemmas:

$$VC(C_i) = \frac{\sum_{l \in L_i} t(l) \cdot v(l)}{|L_i|} \tag{13}$$

where $t(l)$ if a TF-IDF coefficient of a lemma l in a cluster C_i. We construct a cluster cross-similarity matrix SC, where each element is:

$$SC_{C_i,C_j} = \begin{cases} sim & \text{if } sim \geq 0.6 \wedge C_i \neq C_j \wedge \\ & \quad \forall l_k \in C_i, \forall l_l \in C_j : NG_{ne(l_k),ne(l_l)} \neq 0 \\ 0 & \text{else} \end{cases} \tag{14}$$

where $sim = \text{cossim}(VC(C_i), VC(C_j))$.

Following the principle from Fig. 4, we identify chains of clusters, i.e., the final clusters that contain related mentions.

4 Preliminary Evaluation and Discussion

As a preliminary evaluation, we extracted concepts of (in)directly related mentions from five sets of event-related news articles with the identical parameters and we qualitatively analyzed the results. We used NewsWCL50 (N) [6] and ECB+ (e) [5] as datasets that fulfill such criterion for the text collection.

Table 1 depicts examples of the identified concepts, i.e., clusters of the related mentions, from a subset of the events of each dataset. The column with concept names contains manually created labels that summarized automatically identified clusters of the related mentions. The column "Mentions" contains unique mentions of an identified clusters. Mentions are separated with the keywords that indicate the stages at which the mentions were clustered.

The analysis of the indirectly referring mentions to groups of people shows that the proposed clustering approach successfully separated mentions related to GPEs such as "Israeli officials" and "American officials." These mentions refer to different concepts but are quite similar due to the shared word "officials." The identified concepts from the event N9 ("American officials," "Iranian regime," "Israeli officials,", and "European leaders") show that the approach effectively separated mentions of multiple GPEs from the same text.

Clustering of directly referring mentions, e.g., from the "Central American migrants" concept from event N6, resolves mentions such as "Central American trans-gender women," "asylum-seekers," "caravan," and "undocumented immigrants." This demonstrates that the proposed approach successfully clustered mentions that are exposed to context-specific coreference relations, i.e., none of these mentions are common-known synonyms to each other. Moreover, the approach successfully separated the "Immigration lawyers" concept from the "Migrants" concept although the noun "immigration" is shared among the two, which makes these mentions semantically similar. On the contrary, the "Migrants" concept contains falsely clustered mentions that refer to the various supporters of the immigrant caravan. Separation of such mentions with semantically close yet conceptually different meanings remains the biggest challenge for the algorithm and requires improvements to the clustering approach.

To test, if a state-of-the art clustering algorithm achieved similar concepts, we reclustered the mentions from two exemplary chosen documents, N6 and N9 in Table 1, with hierarchical clustering (HC). Table 2 shows the results of HC with average linkage criterion, cosine distance (using a threshold 0.7) for both datasets[1]. Likewise in Table 1, we manually named the concepts which contained conceptually related mentions. While some of the mentions formed more narrowly and fine-grained defined concepts, HC also clustered conceptually different mentions and left approximately 25% of the input mentions unclustered ("NOT" clusters in Table 2).

The proposed clustering approach might be beneficial to cross-document coreference resolution (CDCR), i.e., resolution of the coreferential mentions of various entities across sets of related text documents. Such entity types as groups of people and mentions of the GPEs are some of the targets for CDCR. When implemented as a part of a CDCR model, our concept identification approach can have strong positive impact to the overall performance due the resolution of coreferential mentions of high lexical diversity. Such mentions are typically a subject of bias of word choice and labeling, i.e., contain biased wording that contains polarized connotation and typically is coreferential only in a narrow context of a reported event.

---

[1] The threshold was optimized per event as the one producing both the highest mean cross-phrase cosine similarity and clustering the most phrases.

Table 1. Results produced with the proposed concept identification approach. "N"/"e"+ID indicates a dataset and the internal ID of the events of each dataset.

eID	Concept name	Mentions
N1	Republican Congressional officials	CORE: House Republican committee chairmen, congressional committees, Republican chairmen, Republican Congressional intelligence officials, Congressional leadership BODY: House committees, congressional leaders, congressman BORDER: top aides, secretary, prudent law enforcement official, Leadership, chairmen, aides, his administration
	Lawmakers	CORE: Select lawmakers, lawmakers, Many Democrats, analysts BODY: Conservatives
	Mueller investigators	CORE: investigators, Mueller investigators BODY: Federal prosecutors
N3	Russian agents	CORE: Russian agents, Russian intelligence agents, Russians BORDER: voters, its agents, Russian officials
	U.S. intelligence	CORE: American public, intelligence committees, American people, Americans, U.S. intelligence community BORDER: people, public
N6	Migrants	CORE: Central American migrants, asylum-seekers, Similar migrant groups, Central Americans, gay migrants, American sponsors, Central American children, several American advocacy groups, Asylum-seeking immigrant, Central American transgender women, refugees, their case, undocumented immigrants, immigrant rights activists BODY: Asylum-seekers, individuals, queer, migrant families, legitimate asylum-seekers, Migrant caravan, migrants, individual BORDER: caravan main organizing group, past 24-h several groups, asylum seekers, families, his case, smugglers, immigration judges, particular group, caravan, sponsor, several groups, American sponsor, nonprofit group, children, Migrants, groups, protesters, his children, many migrants, group, their cases, her children, Immigrants, activists, their children, immigrants
	Immigration lawyers	CORE: volunteer lawyers, good attorneys, volunteer attorneys, immigration lawyers BODY: legal observers BORDER: attorney
	U.S. authorities	CORE: U.S. government officials, Trump administration, U.S. authorities, U.S. immigration officials, American border authorities BODY: Southwest border states, Other administration officials BORDER: officer, authorities, officials, U.S. immigration lawyers, asylum officer, inspectors, administration, lawyers, U.S. families, Attorneys, credible-fear officers, Lawyers, his family, your family, international residents, his administration
N9	American officials	CORE: Former intelligence officials, American officials, White House officials, outside experts, Officials BODY: Trump administration, intelligence community, officials BORDER: administration
	Iranian regime	CORE: brutal regime, Iran leaders, exhaustive regimes, inspectors, inspection regime, Iranian regime BORDER: regime
	Israeli officials	CORE: senior Israeli official, Israelis, Israeli networks, Israeli leader, Israeli officials
	European leaders	CORE: Europeans, European leaders
e41	South Sudanese refugee camp	CORE: Yida camp, camp, Enough Project sources, South Sudanese refugee camp, sources, Yida refugee camp BORDER: refugee camp
	South Sudan Liberation Army rebel group	CORE: armed dissident groups, South Sudan Liberation Army rebel group, pro-southern groups, activist group, backing rebel groups, armed groups, minority ethnic group, American activist BORDER: their groups, group
	Reuters correspondent	CORE: press conference, reporters, Reuters correspondent, November press conference BORDER: our correspondent

Table 2. Concepts identified by hierarchical clustering from the similar mentions of N6 and N9 in Table 1. The concepts are more narrowly defined or contain conceptually unrelated mentions. A lot of mentions compared to the proposed approach remain unclustered ("NOT" cluster).

eID	Concept name	Mentions
N6	cl_7	Central American migrants, Central American children, several American advocacy groups, past 24-h several groups, Other administration officials
	Migrants	Asylum-seekers, gay migrants, refugees, undocumented immigrants, Asylum-seekers, migrants, asylum seekers, smugglers, Migrants, Immigrants, immigrants
	Groups	Similar migrant groups, caravan main organizing group, several groups, groups, protesters, group, activists
	American sponsors	American sponsors, sponsor, American sponsor
	Immigration lawyers	Asylum-seeking immigrant, U.S. immigration lawyers, volunteer lawyers, volunteer attorneys, immigration lawyers
	Case	Their case, his case, their cases
	cl_20	Migrant families, families, children, his children, her children, their children, U.S. families, his family
	cl_0	Nonprofit group, many migrants, international residents
	U.S. authorities	U.S. government officials, U.S. authorities, American border authorities, authorities, officials, inspectors, legal observers
	Asylum officers	Officer, asylum officer, credible-fear officers
	Lawyers	lawyers, Attorneys, Lawyers, good attorneys, attorney
	NOT	Central Americans, Central American transgender women, immigrant rights activists, immigration judges, individuals, individual, queer, legitimate asylum-seekers, Migrant caravan, caravan, particular group, your family, Trump administration, U.S. immigration officials, Southwest border states, administration, his administration
N9	Officials	American officials, White House officials, outside experts, Officials, officials, Israeli officials
	Regime	Administration, brutal regime, exhaustive regimes, Iranian regime, regime
	Leaders	Iran leaders, Israeli leader, European leaders
	cl_4	Senior Israeli official, Israelis, Europeans
	NOT	Former intelligence officials, Trump administration, intelligence community, Israeli networks, inspectors, inspection regime

5   Conclusion and Future Work

We proposed a clustering approach to identify both direct mentions referring to groups of individuals and indirect person mentions related to the geo-political entity (GPEs) or organizations, i.e., job titles that represent these entities. In our evaluation, we found that terms such as "American officials" were resolved reliably as mentions related to GPEs or organizations. Moreover, the approach capably clustered mentions that lack NE-components while maintaining a fine-grained level of conceptualization among the clusters of these mentions. Further, the approach resolved mentions referring to groups of individuals that have highly-context dependent synonymous or coreferential relations, as apposed to universal synonyms. Thus, we think the approach is a robust solution to cross-document coreference resolution (CDCR), especially when employed in texts containing coreferential mentions with high lexical diversity.

As future work directions, we seek to test the proposed approach with other word vector models, e.g., fastText [12] and ELMo [16], or phrase vector models [20], pre-trained and fine-tuned on event-related news articles. We also seek to address current shortcomings, e.g., to resolve one-word mentions without modifiers, e.g., "officials," we plan to devise an additional word sense disambiguation step. Each particular occurrence of a one-word mention will be resolved based on the mention's the context. Lastly, we will perform a quantitative analysis of the approach applied to CDCR, i.e., tested on the state-of-the art manually annotated CDCR datasets.

References

1. Ankerst, M., Breunig, M.M., Kriegel, H.P., Sander, J.: Optics: ordering points to identify the clustering structure. In: Proceedings of the 1999 ACM SIGMOD International Conference on Management of Data, p. 49–60. SIGMOD, Association for Computing Machinery, New York, NY, USA (1999). https://doi.org/10.1145/304182.304187
2. Cambria, E., Poria, S., Hazarika, D., Kwok, K.: Senticnet 5: discovering conceptual primitives for sentiment analysis by means of context embeddings. In: Thirty-Second AAAI Conference on Artificial Intelligence (2018)
3. Cha, M., Gwon, Y., Kung, H.: Language modeling by clustering with word embeddings for text readability assessment. In: Proceedings of the 2017 ACM on Conference on Information and Knowledge Management, pp. 2003–2006 (2017)
4. Chen, N.C., Suh, J., Verwey, J., Ramos, G., Drucker, S., Simard, P.: Anchorviz: facilitating classifier error discovery through interactive semantic data exploration. In: 23rd International Conference on Intelligent User Interfaces, pp. 269–280 (2018)
5. Cybulska, A., Vossen, P.: Using a sledgehammer to crack a nut? lexical diversity and event coreference resolution. In: LREC, pp. 4545–4552 (2014)
6. Hamborg, F., Zhukova, A., Gipp, B.: Automated identification of media bias by word choice and labeling in news articles. In: Proceedings of the ACM/IEEE Joint Conference on Digital Libraries (JCDL), June (2019). https://doi.org/10.1109/JCDL.2019.00036
7. Hamborg, F., Zhukova, A., Gipp, B.: Illegal aliens or undocumented immigrants? Towards the automated identification of bias by word choice and labeling. In: Proceedings of the iConference 2019 (2019). https://doi.org/10.1007/978-3-030-15742-5_17
8. Han, X., et al.: Automatic spatially-aware fashion concept discovery. In: Proceedings of the IEEE International Conference on Computer Vision, pp. 1463–1471 (2017)

 9. Jia, C., Carson, M.B., Wang, X., Yu, J.: Concept decompositions for short text clustering by identifying word communities. Pattern Recognition **76**, 691–703 (2018). https://doi.org/10.1016/j.patcog.2017.09.045, http://www.sciencedirect.com/science/article/pii/S0031320317303953

10. Kim, H.K., Kim, H., Cho, S.: Bag-of-concepts: comprehending document representation through clustering words in distributed representation. Neurocomputing **266**, 336–352 (2017)

11. Manning, C.D., Surdeanu, M., Bauer, J., Finkel, J., Bethard, S.J., McClosky, D.: The Stanford CoreNLP natural language processing toolkit. In: Association for Computational Linguistics (ACL) System Demonstrations, pp. 55–60 (2014). http://www.aclweb.org/anthology/P/P14/P14-5010

12. Mikolov, T., Grave, E., Bojanowski, P., Puhrsch, C., Joulin, A.: Advances in pre-training distributed word representations. In: Proceedings of the International Conference on Language Resources and Evaluation (LREC 2018) (2018)

13. Mikolov, T., Sutskever, I., Chen, K., Corrado, G.S., Dean, J.: Distributed representations of words and phrases and their compositionality. In: Advances in Neural Information Processing Systems, pp. 3111–3119 (2013)

14. Murtagh, F., Contreras, P.: Algorithms for hierarchical clustering: an overview. Wiley Interdisciplinary Reviews: Data Mining and Knowledge Discovery **2**(1), 86–97 (2012)

15. Nikfarjam, A., Sarker, A., O'connor, K., Ginn, R., Gonzalez, G.: Pharmacovigilance from social media: mining adverse drug reaction mentions using sequence labeling with word embedding cluster features. J. Am. Med. Inform. Assoc. **22**(3), 671–681 (2015)

16. Peters, M.E., et al.: Deep contextualized word representations. In: Proceedings of NAACL-HLT, pp. 2227–2237 (2018)

17. Si, Y., Wang, J., Xu, H., Roberts, K.: Enhancing clinical concept extraction with contextual embeddings. J. Am. Med. Inform. Assoc. **26**(11), 1297–1304 (2019)

18. Speer, R., Chin, J., Havasi, C.: Conceptnet 5.5: an open multilingual graph of general knowledge. In: Thirty-First AAAI Conference on Artificial Intelligence (2017)

19. Subramanian, S., Roth, D.: Improving generalization in coreference resolution via adversarial training. In: Proceedings of the Eighth Joint Conference on Lexical and Computational Semantics (*SEM 2019), pp. 192–197. Association for Computational Linguistics, Minneapolis, Minnesota (Jun 2019). https://doi.org/10.18653/v1/S19-1021, https://www.aclweb.org/anthology/S19-1021

20. Wu, Y., Zhao, S., Li, W.: Phrase2vec: phrase embedding based on parsing. Inf. Sci. **517**, 100–127 (2020)

21. Zheng, G., Callan, J.: Learning to reweight terms with distributed representations. In: Proceedings of the 38th International ACM SIGIR Conference on Research and Development in Information Retrieval, pp. 575–584 (2015)

Education and Information Literacy

Promoting Diversity, Equity, and Inclusion in Library and Information Science through Community-Based Learning

Alex H. Poole[✉] (iD)

Department of Information Science, College of Computing & Informatics, Drexel University, Philadelphia, PA 19104, USA

Abstract. This paper contends that Community-Based Learning (CBL) promotes diversity, equity, and inclusion (DEI) in Library and Information Science and iSchool education. First, we set forth our methodological approach, which is a qualitative case study. Next, we review the literature on diversity, experiential learning, and Community-Based Learning (CBL). Third, we describe how one iSchool is implementing community-based learning in a novel way by embracing data science and design thinking in its pedagogical approach to a new three-course, twelve-credit post-Baccalaureate certificate. We discuss the institutional context for the certificate, the project partners, the twelve CBL Fellows, and the curriculum, which includes two new courses (Design Thinking for Digital Community Service and Data Analytics for Community-Based Data and Service) and a capstone. We conclude by offering directions for future research.

Keywords: Diversity · Pedagogy · Community-Based Learning

1 Introduction: An Opportunity for iSchool and LIS Education

In 2018, the Institute of Museum and Library Services (IMLS) characterized the lack of racial and ethnic diversity, equity, and inclusion (DEI) in Library and Information Science (LIS) education as an urgent problem [1]. In recommending that LIS programs engage in proactive recruitment and retention of people of color, IMLS advocated for the creation of national, cohort-based diversity scholarship programs and for targeted outreach to paraprofessionals.

Even as it underscored the need for demographic diversification, IMLS stressed libraries' position as locally embedded, public service-oriented community catalysts and assets [2]. LIS work, in other words, had shifted from collection-centric to user-centric [1]. IMLS therefore urged information professionals to propagate an expansive, holistic notion of community engagement. This engagement centers on developing and extending services to meet the information needs of underserved populations, including all ages, races and ethnicities, socioeconomic classes, geographic locations, and abilities [3].

To maximize engagement, IMLS identified five fundamental, outward-facing "community competencies" [1, p. 9]. They include understanding community engagement in

© Springer Nature Switzerland AG 2021
K. Toeppe et al. (Eds.): iConference 2021, LNCS 12645, pp. 529–540, 2021.
https://doi.org/10.1007/978-3-030-71292-1_41

the context of information services, developing user-centric leadership and management skills, honing critical thinking and problem-solving skills, and fostering communication and collaboration in culturally diverse environments. Only experiential learning in the community, not merely in a classroom setting, could inculcate such competencies [1].

Drexel University's Institute of Museum and Library Services (IMLS)-funded "Integrating Community-Based Learning into LIS Education" (2019–2022) project brings together the imperative for diversity and the imperative for community competencies. This paper argues that Community-Based Learning (CBL) promotes diversity, equity, and inclusion in iSchool as well as in Library and Information Science programs and pedagogy; it thereby increases the likelihood of a more demographically diverse future workforce.

First, we set forth our methodological approach. Second, we review the literature on diversity, experiential learning, and Community-Based Learning (CBL). Third, we delve into the case study. Finally, we offer lessons learned and directions for future research.

2 Methods

This paper reports on an exploratory qualitative case study situated in the interpretivist paradigm. The case study seeks a holistic, multi-faceted understanding of a contemporary, in-depth, and contextually situated phenomenon [4–6]. It centers on the work of one iSchool to promote demographic diversity, equity, and inclusion, particularly in terms of race and ethnicity, through a new three-course, twelve-credit post-Baccalaureate certificate.

This case study relies upon multiple sources of documentary evidence in service of trustworthiness [7]. Available, stable, and contextually grounded, documents may prove more accurate than self-reports and provide information not available through other data collection methods [8–10]. Documents in the study were procured through berrypicking: iterative and flexible searches involving a wide variety of techniques—footnote chasing, citation searching, journal run browsing, database searching and browsing (e.g. by subject, keyword, and author)—and a wide variety of sources [11]. Our analytical approach is inductive and grounded, as befits exploratory research [12].

3 Literature Review

3.1 Diversity, Equity, and Inclusion (DEI)

Racial and ethnic diversity, equity, and inclusion represents an urgent, longstanding, and obdurate challenge in the LIS profession and in its educational programs. Though LIS programs have adopted many ameliorative strategies, few seem to alter representation substantively and sustainably [13]. Scholars adduce demographic change (and parity) and social justice as key motivations for promoting diversity. First, demographic change is perhaps the most frequently noted justification in the scholarly literature for promoting diversity [13]. Jaeger and Hill summed up, "Until the composition of our field parallels the very diverse—and continually diversifying—composition of society as a whole , the information professions and institutions will not truly represent or be best positioned to be inclusive of and meet the needs of the many populations that comprise our diverse society" [14, p. 212].

The annual Association for Library and Information Science Education (ALISE) surveys of American Library Association-accredited North American programs provide the most comprehensive and reliable statistics on diversity.[1] Between 1980 and 2018, the aggregate LIS student population (as measured by degrees and certificates earned) diversified markedly, albeit unevenly (Table 1). Despite this demographic change, LIS has failed to keep pace with overall demographic changes in the U.S population, as a juxtaposition with 2010 statistics indicates (Table 2). This disjuncture remains particularly conspicuous among African Americans and Latinx people. "Integrating Community-Based Learning into LIS Education" helps to redress this demographic inequity.

In addition to demographic change, scholars invoke social justice as a reason for diversifying the profession. Social justice concerns such as civic engagement and participation, digital inclusion, social services, and community needs are the cynosure of the information professions' future [15].

Revolving around critical consciousness, reflexivity, and cultural competence, social justice seeks socially salubrious outcomes, viz. equity for oppressed, marginalized, or underrepresented groups [16–20]. As Cooke and her colleagues noted, "Integrating social justice across LIS education is vital for transforming LIS culture into social justice culture, a move that is a precondition for diversifying the profession and, in turn, better serving patron communities in service of a more just society" [21, p. 109]. Just such a commitment animates "Integrating Community-Based Learning into LIS Education." Experiential learning complements this social justice orientation.

3.2 Experiential Learning

John Dewey characterized fruitful education not only as fundamentally social, but as fundamentally experiential, grounded in the "intelligently directed development of possibilities inherent in ordinary experience" [22, p. 89]. While potentially more strenuous and difficult than traditional pedagogy, this democratic and humane approach involves interactive co-construction of meaning, a pedagogical space in which all contribute and all bear responsibility. What is more, an experiential learning strategy spurs lifelong learning. As Dewey concluded, "Education as growth or maturity should be an ever-present process" [22, p. 50].

David Kolb expanded upon Dewey [23]. He underscored experiential learning's processual, not outcome-based, nature. Learning is a continuous, holistic, adaptive process anchored in experience. The transformation of experience in its objective and in its subjective forms creates knowledge.

Experiential learning in the spirit of Kolb and Dewey dovetails with what Paulo Freire called problem-posing education [24]. Whereas traditional pedagogy relies on the "banking" approach, in which education mimics an act of depositing (students passively receive, memorize, and regurgitate content), problem-posing education embraces creative inquiry, stimulates authentic reflection, and enables action, transformation, and

---

[1] https://www.alise.org/statistical-report- [70, 71].

Table 1. LIS students (degrees and certificates)

	American Indian	Asian	African American	Hispanic	Hawaiian/Pacific Islander	White	International	2 or more	Unknown	Total
2018	18 (.30%)	156 (2.63%)	277 (4.66%)	372 (6.26%)	7 (.12%)	3,780 (63.61%)	309 (5.20%)	142 (2.39%)	881 (14.83%)	5,942
2010	38 (.53%)	252 (3.51%)[a]	313 (4.36%)	333 (4.63%)	N/A	5,032 (70.03%)	149 (2.07%)	N/A	1,068 (14.86%)	7,185
1980	10 (.21%)	118 (2.46%)	175 (3.64%)	66 (1.37%)	N/A	3,588 (74.69%)	N/A	N/A	N/A	4,804

[a]Category includes Asian and Pacific Islander.

Table 2. United States census

	American Indian	Asian/Pacific Islander	Black	Hispanic	White	Other	2 or more
2010	2,932,248 (.9%)	15,214,265 (4.9%)	38,929,319 (12.6%)	50,477,594 (16.3%)	223,553,265 (72.4%)	19,107,368 (6.2%)	9,009,073 (2.9%)
1980	1,420,400 (.6%)	3,500,439 (1.5%)	26,495,025 (11.7%)	14,608,673 (6.4%)	188,371,622 (83.1%)	6,758,319 (3.0%)	N/A

critical intervention. Freire insisted, "Education is...constantly remade in the praxis. In order to be, it must become" [24, p. 84]. This type of problem-based, experiential learning forms the backbone of Community-Based Learning.

3.3 Community-Based Learning (CBL)

LIS boasts a lengthy tradition of experiential learning, namely through service learning [25–46]. But although it promoted democratic citizenship, service learning remained circumscribed in its ability to immerse students in the community. It often relied on unidirectional learning, foregrounding rigid, programmatic student outcomes over learning for all stakeholders, including faculty and community members [47]. Service learning effectively presupposed that communities faced problems to which universities would minister. At worst, it smacked of missionary zeal, implying communities were dysfunctional, passive, and in need of uplift [48]. In other words, service learning potentially undercut the community's own agency and thus its capacity for reciprocal reflective action [47].

Etymologically, service harkens to *slave* By contrast, community engagement is rhetorically anodyne, harkening to *joint ownership*. Community engagement marries collaborative, participatory activities, community building, and reciprocal learning [48]. By promoting equality, equity, and social justice, community engagement fosters the knowledge and skills of democratic citizenship [49].

Grounded in reciprocal and reflective community engagement, Community-Based Learning (CBL) centers on collective stewardship of local places and spaces. It evokes *gemeinschaft*—organic community shored up by kinship and fellowship ties as well as by shared mores, customs, and history [50]. Prosaically, CBL highlights a commitment to working with the community, not in service to it. In short, students and community members co-articulate local needs, co-identify the causes and effects of local social problems, and co-create integrative practical strategies to tackle them [51, 52]. Augmenting the extant problem-solving capacity of community organizations, CBL promotes community resiliency and empowerment [53].

Expanding learning beyond the classroom, CBL embraces the ecosystems in which students are embedded; consequently, students see themselves as a vital and necessary part of their community [54, 55]. CBL amalgamates experiential, integrative learning, academic reflection, and intellectual mastery. It fosters political awareness and civil discourse, holistically engenders democratic, civic knowledge, skills, and values, and enjoins students to appreciate the relevance and urgency of a culturally competent, public-spirited, and critical social justice orientation [53, 55, 56].

By maximizing student engagement in civic, specifically local community involvement, CBL renders academic work more relevant—indeed, more meaningful—and thus spurs lifelong learning [49]. It helps cultivate student-citizens who take responsibility for their communities. Meanwhile, CBL focuses universities on current public issues, promoting mutually beneficial, respectful university-community relations. Given its payoffs for both campus and community collaborators, CBL encourages the formation of sustainable relationships [47, 49, 53–56]. Drexel University's Department of Information Science is conveying these benefits through a post-Baccalaureate Community-Based Learning (CBL) certificate.

4 "Integrating Community-Based Learning into LIS Education"

Drexel University's "Integrating Community-Based Learning into LIS Education" project takes root in the foundational principles, professional values and ethics, and socio-technical contexts of information work. It features twelve Fellows who will earn a post-Baccalaureate certificate by completing two CBL courses and a CBL capstone. Project partners include the Lindy Center for Civic Engagement, the Dornsife Center for Neighborhood Partnerships, and the Free Library of Philadelphia. In its conception, implementation, and execution, this project epitomizes community engagement, community competencies, and social justice work.

4.1 CBL Fellows

The project supports twelve CBL Fellows (six in 2020–2021, and six in 2021–2022). Foregrounding diversity, equity, and inclusion and seeking to help remedy the longstanding monochromaticity of LIS, the project concentrates on demographically underrepresented groups. Current Fellows (the first cohort) included three self-identified African Americans, one African American and Native American, one Central/South American, Caribbean/West Indian, and Puerto Rican, and one White. Five of six are paraprofessionals in local public library systems. To ensure equitable opportunity, Fellows receive full tuition support for the certificate. What is more, the certificate funnels into the College's ALA-accredited LIS major (part of the Master of Science in Information [MSI] degree). This offers Fellows an opportunity further to advance their careers.

Fellows engage in four complementary, overlapping activities. First, they identify and analyze the information needs of community partners; next they design and implement programs and services to meet those needs. Second, Fellows model core professional LIS values such as access, democracy, diversity, lifelong learning, the public good, professionalism, service, and social responsibility [57]. Third, they cultivate information literacy—creating, collecting, managing, synthesizing, and using information and data ethically—to support both individual and community needs [58]. Finally, Fellows engage in innovative research and leverage data to show the value of information organizations as community catalysts and by extension, to address broader community challenges related to poverty, public health, career development, demographic shifts, economic development, social and political engagement, and cultural heritage preservation.

The Fellows' certificate work turns on one data science CBL course (Data Analytics for Community-Based Data and Service), one design thinking CBL course (Design Thinking for Digital Community Service), and a ten-week, 120-h CBL capstone. Like the project overall, all three courses align with IMLS's priority of effectively embedding future information professionals in community organizations ranging from schools to faith-based or ethnic organizations, from media to restaurants, from businesses to non-profits [3, 59].

In their activities and assessments, these CBL courses embrace new approaches regarding course configuration (community hybrid and side-by-side), content (data science and design thinking), and partners (local businesses and non-profits as well as the Lindy Center, the Dornsife Center, and the Free Library).

4.2 Coursework

Data Analytics for Community-Based Data and Service. Community hybrid courses span the campus classroom and the community; they mandate a structured, for-credit extracurricular investment [51]. The community hybrid model aligns neatly with the field of data science, which is ever-more salient to LIS [60]. Resting upon computational thinking, the data science approach encourages students to understand the roles of big data and big data technology, the data lifecycle (namely, discover problems, solve problems, and communicate solutions), and the use of various tools to do so [61, 62].

In the three-credit community hybrid course "Data Analytics for Community-Based Data and Service," students explore urban civic engagement, democratic participation, and community change. The course intersperses classroom-based seminar style discussions and local community field work. Students not only assess the data and information needs of, but also design and develop sustainable data infrastructure with local small businesses or non-profit organizations.

Through this equitable, reciprocal, collaborative process involving readings, tools (e.g., R and Tableau), classroom-based reflective seminars, and community-based practice, students learn community information needs assessment, decision making, and information use, representation, and visualization. More specifically, they undertake critical real-world data analysis and assessment to learn the key phases and related challenges of domain-based data analytics. Further, they interact with and impact a range of audiences through democratic, participatory engagement, and thereby hone their oral and written communication skills. Finally, they leverage tools for loading, aggregating, analyzing, and visualizing project-based data. These activities prepare students to work as community-engaged and community-competent information professionals.

Design Thinking for Digital Community Service. In side-by-side courses, students and community members share their unique knowledge, experiences, and perspectives [51, 63]. The side-by-side model foregrounds respectful dialogue, collaboration, and experiential learning; it facilitates the co-creation of strategies to address social justice issues involving diversity, equity, and inclusion. The side-by-side approach dovetails with design thinking, which encourages creative, innovative, adaptable, transferrable, flexible, collaborative, empathetic, transparent, and strategic problem-solving [64–68].

A three-credit hour side-by-side course, "Design Thinking for Digital Community Service" provides an in-depth introduction to community information needs analysis. Divided between hybrid on-campus classroom discussion and work onsite at partnering public libraries, it involves course participants in civically-engaged, community-centric, problem-based active learning. Current MSI students and CBL Fellows collaboratively explore the major elements of design thinking, concentrating on digital information service design. They conduct a community information needs assessment ànd identify a significant community-based digital information service need. Subsequently, they co-develop a design thinking-based service to address the identified problem.

Capstone. Pursuant to her work in the Data Analytics and the Design Thinking courses, each Fellow completes a capstone (120 h over 10 weeks), which comprises a faculty-supervised, problem-based CBL project. As a culminating experience, the capstone enables the further refinement and application of data science, design thinking, and CBL skills to professional practice and the further nurturing of community relationships developed in course work.

Fellows relate theory to practice, and they integrate community-based learning with domain knowledge, with personal and professional reflection, and with creative problem-solving, written and oral communication, and research skills. In addition to pragmatic career planning and preparation, the capstone stimulates a sense of professional identity, encourages an identification with the profession's core values, and instills self-confidence and self-efficacy [69].

5 Conclusion

Drexel University's "Integrating Community-Based Learning into LIS Education" project breaks new ground in LIS and iSchool education. It will train two cohorts of demographically diverse, community-engaged, and community-competent information professionals. By generating a transferable pedagogical model, this project will both encourage and enable other iSchools and LIS programs nationally to implement similar learning programs.

Questions for future research as the project unfolds include three. First, how may we best measure or demonstrate the development of community competencies? Second, what types of community partners make for the most fruitful relationships? Third, how can the CBL model be made sustainable, embedded in the curriculum and not merely a one-off project?

Ultimately, the project will advance the urgent goals of social justice under the aegis of diversity, equity, and inclusion, and community engagement and competence in library and information science. The future viability of the information professions depends on this investment.

Acknowledgments. This project was made possible in part by the Institute of Museum and Library Services (RE-17-19-0006-19). I would like to thank Dr. Xia Lin (PI of this project), as well as my fellow co-PIs: Dr. Jane Greenberg, Dr. Denise Agosto, and Dr. Erjia Yan.

References

1. Sands, A.E., Toro, S., DeVoe, T., Fuller, S., Wolff-Eisenberg, C.: Positioning Library and Information Science Graduate Education for 21st Century Practice. Institute of Museum and Library Services, Washington, D.C. (2018). https://www.imls.gov/sites/default/files/publications/documents/imlspositioningreport.pdf
2. Norton, M.H., Dowdall, E.: Strengthening Networks, Sparking Change: Museums and Libraries as Community Catalysts. Institute of Museum and Library Services, Washington, D.C. (2017). https://www.imls.gov/sites/default/files/publications/documents/community-catalyst-report-january-2017.pdf
3. Hill, C., Proffitt, M., Streams, S.: IMLS Focus: Learning in Libraries. Institute of Museum and Library Services, Washington, D.C. (2015). https://www.imls.gov/sites/default/files/publications/documents/imlsfocuslearninginlibrariesfinalreport.pdf
4. Choemprayong, S., Wildemuth, B.: Case studies. In: Wildemuth, B. (ed.) Applications of Social Research Methods to Questions in Information and Library Science, pp. 51–61. Libraries Unlimited, Westport (2009)
5. Schwandt, T.A., Gates, E.F.: Case study methodology. In: Denzin, N.K., Lincoln, Y.S. (eds.) The SAGE Handbook of Qualitative Research, 5th edn., pp. 341–358. SAGE, Los Angeles (2018)
6. Yin, R.: Case Study Research: Design and Methods, 4th edn. SAGE, Los Angeles (2009)
7. Flick, U.: Triangulation. In: Denzin, N.K., Lincoln, Y.S. (eds.) The SAGE Handbook of Qualitative Research, 5th edn, pp. 444–461. SAGE, Los Angeles (2018)
8. Hodder, I.: The interpretation of documents and material culture. In: Lincoln, N.K. (ed.) Handbook of Qualitative Research, pp. 703–715. SAGE, Thousand Oaks (2000)
9. Lincoln, Y.S., Guba, E.G.: Naturalistic Inquiry. Sage Publications, Beverly Hills (1985)
10. Wildemuth, B.: Existing documents and artifacts as data. In: Wildemuth, B. (ed.) Applications of Social Research Methods to Questions in Information and Library Science, pp. 158–165. Libraries Unlimited, Westport (2009)
11. Bates, M.J.: The design of browsing and berrypicking techniques for the online search interface. Online Rev. 13(5), 407–424 (1989). https://doi.org/10.1108/eb024320
12. Bernard, H.R., Ryan, G.W.: Analyzing Qualitative Data: Systematic Approaches. SAGE, Los Angeles (2010)
13. Poole, A.H., Agosto, D., Greenberg, J., Lin, X., Yan, E.: Where Do We Stand? Diversity and Social Justice in North American Library and Information Science Education, vol. 62, no. 2 (in press)
14. Jaeger, P.T., Hill, R.F.: The long walk: diversity in information studies educational programs, professions, and institutions, pp. 209–215. In: Advances in Librarianship. Emerald Publishing Limited, Bingley (2017)
15. Jaeger, P.T., Shilton, K., Koepfler, J.: The rise of social justice as a guiding principle in library and information science research. Libr. Q. 86(1), 1–9 (2016). https://doi.org/10.1086/684142
16. Cooke, N.A., Sweeney, M.E.: Introduction. In: Cooke, N.A., Sweeney, M.E. (eds.) Teaching for Justice: Implementing Social Justice in the LIS Classroom, p. 15. Library Juice Press, Sacramento (2016)
17. Kumasi, K.D., Manlove, N.L.: Finding 'diversity levers' in the core library and information science curriculum: a social justice imperative. Libr. Trends 64(2), 415–443 (2015). https://doi.org/10.1353/lib.2015.0047
18. Mehra, B., Rioux, K.: Introduction. In: Mehra, B., Rioux, K. (eds.) Progressive Community Action: Critical Theory and Social Justice in Library and Information Science, p. 10. Library Juice Press, Sacramento (2016)

19. Rioux, K.: Metatheory in library and information science: a nascent social justice approach. J. Educ. Libr. Inf. Sci. **51**(1), 9–17 (2010)
20. Overall, P.M.: Cultural competence: a conceptual framework for library and information science professionals. Libr. Q. **79**(2), 175–204 (2009). https://doi.org/10.1086/597080
21. Cooke, N.A., Sweeney, M.E., Noble, S.U.: Social justice as topic and tool: an attempt to transform an LIS curriculum and culture. Libr. Q. **86**(1), 107–124 (2016). https://doi.org/10.1086/684147
22. Dewey, J.: Experience and Education. Collier Books, New York (1976)
23. Kolb, D.: Experiential Learning: Experience as the Source of Learning and Development, 2nd edn. Pearson Education Ltd, London (2014)
24. Freire, P.: Pedagogy of the Oppressed, 30th Anniversary edn. Continuum, New York (2000)
25. Albert, S.: Highlights of service learning experiences in selected LIS programs. In: Meyers, A., Jensen, K., Roy, L. (eds.) Service Learning: Linking Library Education and Practice, pp. 95–104. American Library Association, Chicago (2009)
26. Albertson, D., Whitaker, M.S., Perry, R.A.: Developing and organizing a community engagement project that provides technology literacy training to persons with intellectual disabilities. J. Educ. Libr. Inf. Sci. **52**(2), 142–151 (2011)
27. Albertson, D., Whitaker, M.S.: A service-learning framework to support an MLIS core curriculum. J. Educ. Libr. Inf. Sci. **52**(2), 152–163 (2011)
28. Ball, M.A.: Practicums and service learning in LIS education. J. Educ. Libr. Inf. Sci. **49**(1), 70–82 (2008)
29. Ball, M.A., Schilling, K.: Service learning, technology and LIS education. J. Educ. Libr. Inf. Sci. **47**(4), 277 (2006). https://doi.org/10.2307/40323821
30. Becker, N.J.: Service learning in the curriculum: preparing LIS students for the next millennium. J. Educ. Libr. Inf. Sci. **41**(4), 285–293 (2000)
31. Bloomquist, C.: Reflecting on reflection as a critical component in service learning. J. Educ. Libr. Inf. Sci. **56**(2), 169–172 (2015). https://doi.org/10.3138/jelis.56.2.169
32. Brannon, C.: Assessment in fieldwork courses: what are we rating? J. Educ. Libr. Inf. Sci. **55**(4), 274–302 (2014)
33. Bundy, M.L., Wasserman, P.: A departure in library education. J. Educ. Librariansh. **8**(2), 124 (1967). https://doi.org/10.2307/40322326
34. Caspe, M., Lopez, M.E.: Preparing the next generation of librarians for family and community engagement. J. Educ. Libr. Inf. Sci. **59**(4), 157–178 (2018). https://doi.org/10.3138/jelis.59.4.2018-0021
35. Chu, C.M.: Working from within: critical service learning as core learning in the MLIS curriculum. In: Meyers, A., Jensen, K., Roy, L. (eds.) Service Learning: Linking Library Education and Practice, pp. 105–123. American Library Association, Chicago (2009)
36. Coleman, J.G.: The role of the practicum in library schools. J. Educ. Libr. Inf. Sci. **30**(1), 19 (1989). https://doi.org/10.2307/40323496
37. Cooper, L.Z.: Student reflections on an LIS internship from a service learning perspective supporting multiple learning theories. J. Educ. Libr. Inf. Sci. **54**(4), 286–298 (2013)
38. Cuban, S., Hayes, E.: Perspectives of five library and information studies students involved in service learning at a community-based literacy program. J. Educ. Libr. Inf. Sci. **42**(2), 86 (2001). https://doi.org/10.2307/40324022
39. Hughes-Hassell, S., Vance, K.: Examining race, power, privilege, and equity in the youth services LIS classroom. In: Cooke, N.A., Sweeney, M.E. (eds.) Teaching for Justice: Implementing Social Justice in the LIS Classroom, pp. 103–137. Library Juice Press, Sacramento (2016)
40. Kimmel, S.C., Howard, J.K., Ruzzi, B.: Educating school library leaders for radical change through community service. J. Educ. Libr. Inf. Sci. **57**(2), 174–186 (2016). https://doi.org/10.3138/jelis.57.2.174

41. Oberg, D., Samek, T.: Humble empowerment: the LIS practicum. PNLA Q. **63**(3), 20–22 (1999)
42. O'Brien, H., Freund, L., Jantzi, L., Sinanan, S.: Investigating a peer-to-peer community service learning model for LIS education. J. Educ. Libr. Inf. Sci. **55**(4), 322–335 (2014)
43. Overall, P.M.: the effect of service learning on LIS students' understanding of diversity issues related to equity of access. J. Educ. Libr. Inf. Sci. **51**(4), 251–266 (2010)
44. Peterson, L.: A brief history of service learning in library and information science. In: Meyers, A., Jensen, K., Roy, L. (eds.) Service Learning: Linking Library Education and Practice, pp. 1–4. American Library Association, Chicago (2009)
45. Roy, L.: Service learning connecting diverse communities and LIS students and faculty. In: Meyers, A., Jensen, K., Roy, L. (eds.) Service Learning: Linking Library Education and Practice, pp. 73–82. American Library Association, Chicago (2009)
46. Roy, L.: Diversity in the classroom: incorporating service-learning experiences in the library and information science curriculum. J. Libr. Adm. **33**(3–4), 213–228 (2001). https://doi.org/10.1300/J111v33n03_04
47. Bishop, A., Bruce, B., Jeong, S.: Beyond service learning: toward community schools and reflective community learners. In: Meyers, A., Jensen, K., Roy, L. (eds.) Service Learning: Linking Library Education and Practice, pp. 16–31. American Library Association, Chicago (2009)
48. Mehra, B., Robinson, W.C.: The community engagement model in library and information science education: a case study of a collection development and management course. J. Educ. Libr. Inf. Sci. **50**(1), 15–38 (2009)
49. Melaville, A., Berg, A.C., Black, M.J.: Community-based learning: engaging students for success and citizenship. Partnerships/Community **40** (2006). https://digitalcommons.unomaha.edu/slcepartnerships/40
50. Tönnies, F.: Community and Civil Society. Cambridge University Press, Cambridge; New York (2001)
51. Lindy Center for Civic Engagement: Review of Community-Based Learning at Drexel University Provost Report, June 2018
52. Rickards, C.: Examining 21st century skill acquisition as a result of democratic engagement within a side-by-side community-based learning course. Ph.D., Drexel University, Philadelphia, PA (2015)
53. Ishisaka, H.A., Farwell, N., Sohng, S.S.L., Uehara, E.S.: Teaching notes: partnership for integrated community-based learning: a social work community-campus collaboration. J. Soc. Work Educ. **40**(2), 321–336 (2004). https://doi.org/10.1080/10437797.2004.10778496
54. Lowenstein, E., Martusewicz, R., Voelker, L.: Developing teachers' capacity for ecojustice education and community-based learning. Teach. Educ. Q. **37**(4), 99–118 (2010)
55. Wickersham, C., Westerberg, C., Jones, K., Cress, M.: Pivot points: direct measures of the content and process of community-based learning. Teach. Sociol. **44**(1), 17–27 (2016). https://doi.org/10.1177/0092055X15613786
56. Schamber, J., Mahoney, S.L.: The development of political awareness and social justice citizenship through community-based learning in a first-year general education seminar. J. Gen. Educ. **57**(2), 75–99 (2008). https://doi.org/10.1353/jge.0.0016
57. American Library Association: Core Values of Librarianship, 26 July 2006. https://www.ala.org/advocacy/intfreedom/corevalues
58. SCONUL Working Group on Information Literacy: The SCONUL Seven Pillars of Information Literacy, London, UK (2011). https://www.sconul.ac.uk/sites/default/files/documents/coremodel.pdf
59. Hill, C., Streams, S., Dooley, J., Morris, L.: IMLS Focus: Engaging Communities. Institute of Museum and Library Services, Washington, D.C. (2015)

60. Marchionini, G.: Information science roles in the emerging field of data science. J. Data Inf. Sci. **1**(2), 1–6 (2016). https://doi.org/10.20309/jdis.201609
61. Song, I.-Y., Zhu, Y.: Big data and data science: opportunities and challenges of ischools. J. Data Inf. Sci. **2**(3), 1–8 (2017). https://doi.org/10.1515/jdis-2017-0011
62. Song, I.-Y., Zhu, Y.: Big data and data science: what should we teach? Expert. Syst. **33**(4), 364–373 (2016). https://doi.org/10.1111/exsy.12130
63. Side-by-Side: Drexel University Lindy Center for Civic Engagement. https://drexel.edu/lindycenter/students/courses/community-based-learning/Side%20by%20Side/
64. Bell, S.: Design thinking. Am. Libr. **39**, 44–49 (2008)
65. Clarke, R.I.: What we mean when we say 'design': a field scan of coursework offerings on design topics in master's level library education. J. Educ. Libr. Inf. Sci. **61**(1), 2–4 (2020). https://doi.org/10.3138/jelis.61.1.2019-0037
66. Clarke, R.I.: Toward a design epistemology for librarianship. Libr. Q. **88**(1), 41–59 (2018). https://doi.org/10.1086/694872
67. Meier, J.J., Miller, R.K.: Turning the revolution into an evolution: the case for design thinking and rapid prototyping in libraries. CRLN **77**(6), 283–286 (2016). https://doi.org/10.5860/crln.77.6.9506
68. Bartlett, J.: Design thinking in libraries. Libr. Leadersh. Manag. **34**(4), 1–6 (2018)
69. McGuinness, C., Shankar, K.: Supporting reflection in the MLIS through a professionally-oriented capstone module. EFI **35**(2), 173–178 (2019). https://doi.org/10.3233/EFI-190256
70. Association of American Library Schools Library Education Statistical Report 1980. Association of American Library Schools (1980)
71. Wallace, D.P., Naidoo, J. (eds.): Library and Information Science Education Statistical Report 2010. Association for Library and Information Science Education (2010). https://ali.memberclicks.net/assets/documents/alise_statistical_report_2010.pdf

Embracing the Diversity: Teaching Recordkeeping Concepts to Students from Different Cultural and Linguistic Backgrounds

Viviane Frings-Hessami$^{(\boxtimes)}$

Monash University, Caulfield, VIC, Australia
`Viviane.Hessami@monash.edu`

Abstract. When teaching to students from diverse backgrounds, it is important to explain to them the meaning of the key concepts in the discipline and to discuss examples that they can easily relate to. The terms records and recordkeeping, which are key concepts in archival science, have their roots in national archival traditions and have specific meanings that may confuse students because these meanings are different from the ways the terms are commonly used in everyday language or in other English-speaking countries and because equivalent concepts may not exist in their first language. The linguistic misunderstandings that may ensue may then impact on the students' understanding of the whole course content, affecting their understanding of the role played by records in society and of the issues involved in their preservation. By discussing with the students the translations of these terms and simple examples in their cultural and linguistic contexts, we are embracing the diversity of students' backgrounds and experiences and engaging in a dialogue with them that enriches their experience and makes the course more relevant to them.

Keywords: Archival education · Cultural context · Languages · Translation · Records continuum · Personal recordkeeping · Digital preservation

1 Introduction

Understanding of a discipline is linked to an understanding of its key concepts. This is particularly true in archival science where the key concepts are rooted in national traditions. Eric Ketelaar wrote that "There are many ... terms in the professional archival terminology which are only understandable in another language when one knows and fully understands the professional, cultural, legal, historical, and sometimes political background of the term" [1]. In an article published in 1985, "Archives in the Tower of Babel", French archivist Michel Duchein asserted that because professional practices and methods vary from one country to another, translations of archival texts can only be approximative [2]. Ketelaar [1] argued that simple translations are not sufficient if a concept does not exist in another country and that the concept must be defined and

© Springer Nature Switzerland AG 2021
K. Toeppe et al. (Eds.): iConference 2021, LNCS 12645, pp. 541–550, 2021.
https://doi.org/10.1007/978-3-030-71292-1_42

explained in the technical language of that country. However, if students not only come from a different linguistic background, but also from a different discipline and are not familiar with the archival language of their own country, it becomes necessary to explain the terminology in simple non-technical terms that they can easily understand and relate to their personal experience.

In this paper, I discuss my experience teaching recordkeeping concepts in a multicultural and multidisciplinary environment in an Australian university. Developing materials to teach to students from different backgrounds made me realize how much the concepts that we use are rooted in a specific culture and, therefore, may not make much sense for people from other cultures, and led me to look for new ways to explain those concepts, to rethink the models that we use and to re-assess the course's priorities. I have been teaching at Monash University since 2015 and during that time we have experienced a dramatic shift in the student population enrolled in the postgraduate recordkeeping subjects. On the one hand, we have experienced a decline in the number of postgraduate students who enrolled with the intention of completing a specialization in archives and recordkeeping. On the other hand, a massive increase in the number of international students at the university led to an exponential increase in the number of students enrolling in the two recordkeeping subjects as electives, with the assumption that they were "easy" subjects. These students are studying various degrees in the Faculty of Information Technology, including Masters in Information Technology, Business Information Systems and Data Science, and in the Faculty of Business. The combination of these factors resulted in a shift from teaching to small classes of students (18 in the first semester of 2016), the majority of whom were intending to qualify as archivists and record managers, to very large classes of students (180 students in the first semester of 2019 and 142 in the first semester of 2020), most of whom had no previous understandings of records and archives and no intention of working in that area after graduating, with a very small minority of students still interested in working as information professionals. The vast majority of the students enrolled in one of these two subjects, the digital continuity subject taught every year in the first semester, are international students, mostly from China (68%), with a substantial group from India (17%), and a few from a variety of other countries, mostly in Asia (including Bangladesh, Vietnam, Thailand, and Saudi Arabia), and only 5% of Australian residents (based on Semester 1, 2019 enrolment data).

Therefore, we need to teach archival and digital preservation concepts to students who come from other disciplines and from other linguistic and cultural backgrounds. It is a challenge, but also an opportunity to try new ways of communicating content and raise awareness about recordkeeping and digital preservation issues among students who will go and work in other fields, particularly students who will work in information technology and will develop information systems that may contain records. The focus of the unit is on digital continuity, that is how we can make sure that the information we need will remain available for as long as we need it [3]. Most students come to the unit with no understanding of the fragility of digital information and many of them hold the misconception that digital records are more robust and last longer than paper records. A misunderstanding of the meaning of records may lead them to focus on data, rather than on the evidential characteristics of records and on recordkeeping processes, and to neglect the multiple interests that various stakeholders may have in those records and the issues associated with their long-term preservation.

The theory that underpins teaching of recordkeeping concepts in Australia (and that also influenced international records management standards) is the Continuum theory [4] and the model that is used as a framework for the subjects is the Records Continuum Model. The Records Continuum Model [5, 6] was developed as a teaching tool to represent the contexts of records creation, management and use over time and space. Its four dimensions, Create, Capture, Organize and Pluralize provide a way of mapping the creation of documents, their capture in recordkeeping systems, their organization into archives and their pluralization to meet the needs of various stakeholders. Contrary to the stages in the life cycle model, the dimensions are seen as happening simultaneously and enabling the representation of multiple perspectives of multiple actors [7].

The shift in the students' backgrounds and interests drove me to review the way I teach recordkeeping concepts to make them more relevant to the students' experiences. In this paper, I discuss how I explain the meaning of the key concepts and illustrate them through simple examples and how we engage in discussions with students from diverse backgrounds, thereby enriching their experience and the teaching material for the next cohort of students. The examples I use are grounded in a Records Continuum framework. However, many issues relating to language and terminology would also arise, albeit somewhat differently, if we used a life cycle framework.

2 Teaching Key Concepts

Records are defined in the International Records Management Standard ISO15489 as "information created, received and maintained as *evidence* and as an asset by an organization or person, in pursuit of legal obligations or in the *transaction* of business" [8]. However, many European archival traditions do not have a word equivalent to the English concept of "record". They use "archives" as a broader, more encompassing term and can have several translations for the word "record" depending on the context. For example, the French definition of archives is: "all the documents, whatever their date, their form and their material support, created or received by a natural or legal person, or by a department or agency, public or private, in the course of their activities" [9]. Archives are considered to be archives from the time they are created. There is no exact translation for the word "record". The translation used in the first edition of ISO 15489, adopted in 2001, "document d'archives", literally a document from the archives, is one of the most commonly used. However, the updated version of the standard adopted in 2016 used "document d'activité", literally "activity document" instead [10]. This translation was the subject of many controversies [11] and, in practice, is only used in official documents. The translation "documents d'archives" is still the most commonly used in the public sector where government institutions have long-standing archives and where public servants understand that the important documents that they create will one day get transferred to the archives. On the other hand, in the private sector, archives are perceived as old stuff and people prefer to refer to their records as "documents" or "records" using the English terminology. Archivists, for their part, prefer to make a distinction between the "archives courantes et intermediaires" (current and semi-current records) that are used to support current business needs and the "archives définitives" (permanent records) that are kept in archival repositories for their historical and cultural value. However, they find the concept of records being maintained as evidence problematic because this implies a selection among the documents created (since not all of them need to be kept as evidence), and this selection is done when the records are still in active use whereas in the French system, it is done when records no longer meet current business needs [12–14].

Similar translation issues occur in other European languages, including Dutch, German, Italian and Spanish. Other translation issues arise with Asian languages as I discovered in the process of teaching recordkeeping concepts to international students. The translation problems in some of the languages spoken by students have important implications for their understanding of the course material and therefore need to be discussed right from the start. Discussions with students have revealed that in several languages, the word "record" is used in English rather than vernacular terms that archivists may use, but that ordinary people are not familiar with. This is the case in Bangla, Urdu and several Indian and African languages, a legacy of British colonial influence in those countries. On the other hand, in Indonesian, like in Dutch, there is no word for record, but the words "dokumen" (document) and "arsip" (archives) are used. In other languages, the terms used by records managers and archivists may be different from the terms used by people who do not work in that field. Discussions with Chinese students also revealed that there was no agreement on how to translate the word "record" in Chinese. In Chinese, the common translation of record is *jì lù*, but that is not the term that records managers use, preferring *wén jiàn*, while *dàng'àn* is used for archives.

To further complicate the issue, the way the words "records" and "recordkeeping" are commonly used in Australia to encompass both records and archives is different from the way they are used in the rest of the English-speaking world. In Continuum theory, anything can be a record. The concept is not restricted to specific formats. It encompasses "oral and written records, literature, landscape, dance, art, the built environment, and artefacts" [15]. All records have the potential to become archives and should be viewed as such from the time of their creation. Recordkeeping encompasses both records management and archives management and all the processes from the setting up of recordkeeping systems to the design of access to archives to meet the needs of a variety of stakeholders throughout the lifespan of the records [16]. This is different from the life cycle perspective adopted in Europe and in North America, which is based on strict separations between current records and archives and between the roles played by records managers and archivists [17, 18]. The specific meaning of the term "recordkeeping" must therefore be clearly explained, and reiterated throughout the course, and it must be clearly distinguished from the spelling "record keeping" or "record-keeping", which are used in other English-speaking countries to refer to narrower understandings of the management of records to meet current business needs. It is a term that is difficult to translate in any language and is best kept in English to keep the specific connotations associated with it.

The word "continuum" also has a specific meaning in Continuum theory, which may cause confusion, but which may be less obvious to students and to researchers alike. The word implies a continuity, a sequence of actions that follow one another over time, as expressed in the Oxford Dictionary definition: "a continuous sequence in which adjacent elements are not perceptibly different from each other, but the extremes are quite distinct" [19]. Applied to the management of records and archives, it can mean that there is a continuity between records and archives, that records and archives are managed smoothly in an integrated way over time, without there being strict distinctions between different stages in their life cycle that correspond to different ways of managing them. This is how the Canadian archivist Jay Atherton, who was the first to talk of a continuum of records and archives, intended it [20]. Although different from the life cycle model, this interpretation of a continuum is a linear approach. However, in the Continuum theory developed in Australia and in the Records Continuum Model, the word "continuum" means something more than a smooth progression over time. The Records Continuum is not linear, it is multi-dimensional. The four dimensions are happening at the same time. Processes taking place in one dimension impact on what is happening in the other dimensions [21]. The use of the word continuum may therefore be confusing.

A comparison that I have found useful to explain the concept is that of a rainbow. The analogy with a rainbow helps to explain the smooth transition between dimensions and how they can blend into one another. A rainbow may be represented by seven curved lines of seven distinct colors, but the colors of a natural rainbow actually blend into each other. The colors are created by the refraction and dispersion of light and are blending into each other without clear separations between them. For example, green is not clearly distinct from blue and yellow, but is a mix of the two. The analogy also helps to explain the simultaneity of the four dimensions of the Records Continuum. In a drawing, the colored stripes are drawn one at a time, but the colors of the rainbow do not appear one after the other. One part of the rainbow may be clearer than another, but it is due to the position of the observer. The seven colors are present at the same time. Similarly, the four dimensions of the Records Continuum Model exist at the same time even if one (or several) of them may seem to be more prominent at a particular time or one (or several) of them may appear to be hidden for a while.

The recordkeeping terminology and its translation is discussed with students in the first week through a discussion of personal recordkeeping activities (which will be described in the next section), then again when explaining the Records Continuum Model, and later in the semester when we look at translations of the Universal Declaration on Archives, which has been translated into 42 languages [22], to reinforce students' understanding of the concepts. Experience has shown that a translation activity works best if it is combined with a discussion of examples of records and their evidential characteristics. If students are asked to think of translations of the word "record" in their language, they may come up with a translation that may or may not be equivalent to the meaning of records discussed in the course. However, if the discussion of translation is combined with a discussion of examples, students may come up with several translations, and the conversation can then progress to dissecting the meaning of each one and comparing them with the English concept, which can result in a better understanding of the concept and of cultural differences. We were fortunate in 2019 to be able to involve a visiting Chinese academic, Associate Professor Jian Chen from Shandong University, and a visiting Chinese PhD student in archival science, Wenting Lyu from Nanjing

University, who attended classes every week and with their experience of archival terminology and archival institutions in China helped build a bridge to Chinese students from other disciplinary backgrounds.

3 Personal Recordkeeping

Simple examples and personal recordkeeping examples are used in the course to illustrate the concepts taught. Students can easily relate personal recordkeeping examples to their personal experience and to their cultural background, which makes it easier for them to understand the concepts. Focusing on personal recordkeeping helps students who come from different backgrounds (culturally or professionally) to relate the material taught in the course with examples from their cultural background. Personal recordkeeping examples are discussed in the first tutorials. Students are asked to think of the roles that they play in society and of the records that they keep as part of those roles; then to pick one of these roles and think of the records that they keep as part of that role. They are asked to reflect on whether or not they can still access all the records that have been created in relation with that role or with an event and they are encouraged to reflect on how they could keep their records to ensure that the records remain available to them when they may want to access them in the future. When I did that activity with students face-to-face (before the COVID-19 pandemic forced us to online teaching), I made students pick a coin out of a bag and asked them to think of records associated with an event in their lives that occurred in the year the coin was minted, thereby encouraging them to think of older records, some of which may have been in analog formats. These activities are open-ended and allow students to reflect on records from their personal and cultural contexts that are important to them. They help them to understand the important role that some records play in their lives and the need to be proactive in preserving them. Many times, students have commented at the end of the activity that they would then go home and back up some important records.

A personal recordkeeping example, with a family photograph, is also used for teaching the Records Continuum Model. Since 2015, I have been using the example of a family photograph to teach the model and to discuss possible reuses of the photograph. Examples of the application of the Records Continuum Model, such as those described by McKemmish [15] and Reed [23], are useful for teaching purposes, but they may be perceived as too complex by students who are not familiar with the cultural contexts in which they are grounded. Using simple examples from everyday life and discussing the societal context of the creation and use of records [24, 25] can help make the model more accessible for students from non-English speaking backgrounds. In particular, the use of photographs can be very effective. Photographs are powerful teaching tools because they are easy to relate to and can provoke an emotive reaction. It is also easy to show that they can be meaningless without metadata, and thereby to illustrate the role played by metadata in capturing and preserving the evidential characteristics of records.

The photograph that I commonly use is an ordinary photograph of a family wedding. It was taken in 1996 with an analog camera. No names, place or date were written on the back of it, and I kept it in a plain envelope with other photographs of the wedding. We can assume that many photographs had been taken at that wedding and that some of these photographs were printed several times and distributed among friends and relatives. We can therefore discuss different uses for those photographs and different recordkeeping trails that they may have followed while being kept in different recordkeeping systems (frame, photo album, scrapbook, etc.). Over the years, students have suggested reuses such as being of interest to people who are collecting photographs about wedding fashion in the 1990s, hats or hairstyles, being used as an alibi for one of the people in the photograph, as well as being used in the lecture slides as an example to teach the Records Continuum Model. Many of those examples could not have been predicted when the photograph was taken. The discussion of reuses of photographs can also be combined with a discussion of the cultural factors that are reflected in photographs (e.g. setting, clothing) or that impact on the way photographs can be preserved and used over time (e.g. privacy concerns). This helps students to understand that each society has laws, regulations, customs and expectations that impact on the way records are created, managed and used in that society; and that what is consider an appropriate way, or the best way, to create, manage, preserve and use records is largely cultural and may vary over time and from one country to another [24]. Recordkeeping systems can take many different forms (from a simple box to an electronic records management system) that are influenced by the culture in which they are developed. The format of a photograph is the product of the technology used to produce it. Its content is impacted by the societal context in which it was taken and the socio-economic status of the people who figure in it. The fact that it exists is, in itself, a reflection of the value accorded to capturing pictures of some events in that society, the technology in existence and its affordability. Pictures may be kept for memory purposes or as evidence. In either case, they need to be captured and organized in a recordkeeping system and metadata added to them to locate them in their contexts, particularly if they are to be shared with people outside the immediate circle of family and friends, who may not be aware of that context. Steps need to be taken to preserve the photographs; these will be dependent on the technology available, the legislation in place and the social and cultural expectations, and they will require actions to be taken to ensure that the photographs will be preserved for as long as they may be needed [24].

4   Impact

Embracing the diversity in the students' backgrounds and languages and adjusting the course content to include discussion of linguistic differences and simple personal recordkeeping examples make the concepts taught easier for all students to understand and more relevant to their cultural contexts. A lack of material relevant to the personal, cultural and professional contexts of the students' may result in students dismissing the material taught to them as irrelevant to them (something they have to learn to graduate, but can quickly forget about if they do not plan to work as archivists or records managers), or as "Australian" theories and practices that are not relevant to their contexts. Moreover, a misunderstanding of the key concepts stemming from the students' inability to relate them to a familiar context is likely to result in a lack of understanding of important issues discussed in the course. For example, a confusion between record and data results in a lack of understanding of the processes that must be applied to preserve records as authentic evidence and of the characteristics that recordkeeping systems must have to preserve records. Coupled with a lack of understanding of the fragility of digital records, this may lead students to overlook the preemptive actions that should be taken to ensure that records will survive for as long as they will be needed. On the other hand, discussing translation and cultural issues can result in a better understanding of the key concepts, which will result in a better understanding of the key issues affecting the preservation of digital information and may get students interested in tackling some of those issues in their future professional lives.

In addition, teaching recordkeeping concepts to students who will not work as record-keeping professionals, but in IT jobs is an opportunity to address the communication problems that often hinder digital preservation projects [26] by sensitizing the students to recordkeeping issues and equipping them with an understanding of the terminology used by the recordkeeping professionals with whom they may one day collaborate to develop systems to preserve digital records.

5   Conclusion

Teaching to foreign students forces us to reflect on how to adjust our teaching practices to explain to people from diverse cultural and linguistic backgrounds recordkeeping concepts that may not have a direct equivalent in their languages and to develop examples that are culturally appropriate. Embracing the diversity and engaging in dialogues with the students improve their understanding of the concepts and issues and enriches the course material and the experience for all students. Students who will work as record-keeping professionals will gain an understanding of different archival traditions and will be better equipped to collaborate with colleagues from other cultural backgrounds, while those who will work in IT will be able to speak the same language as recordkeeping professionals and will be able to collaborate in designing systems that incorporate record-keeping functionalities to preserve records that meet the needs of various stakeholders in the short, medium and long terms.

References

1. Ketelaar, E.: The difference best postponed? Cultures and comparative archival science. Archivaria **44**, 142–148 (1997)
2. Duchein, M.: Les archives dans la Tour de Babel: Problems de terminologie archivistique internationale (Archives in the Tower of Babel: problems of international archival terminology). La Gazette des Arch. **129**, 103–113 (1985)
3. National Archives of Australia Digital Continuity 2020 Policy. https://www.naa.gov.au/information-management/information-management-policies/digital-continuity-2020-policy. Accessed 28 Sep 2020
4. McKemmish, S.: Recordkeeping in the continuum: an Australian tradition. In: Gilliland, A.J., McKemmish, S., Lau, A.J. (eds.) Research in the Archival Multiverse, pp. 122–160. Monash University Publishing, Clayton (2017)
5. Upward, F.: Structuring the records continuum part one: post custodial principles and properties. Arch. Manuscr. **24**(2), 268–285 (1996)

6. Upward, F.: Structuring the records continuum part two: structuration theory and recordkeeping. Arch. Manuscr. **25**(1), 10–35 (1997)

7. McKemmish, S., Upward, F.H., Reed, B.: Records continuum model. In: Bates, M.J., Niles-Maac, M. (eds.) Encyclopedia of Library and Information Sciences, 3rd edn., pp. 4447–4459. Taylor & Francis, New York (2010)

8. International Organization for Standardization: ISO 15489-1:2016(en) Information and documentation—Records management—Part 1: concepts and principles (2016). https://www.iso.org/obp/ui/en/#iso:std:iso:15489:-1:ed-2:v1:en

9. Loi n° 79-18 du 3 janvier 1979 sur les archives (Law No. 79-18 of 3 January 1979 on Archives), Article 1. https://www.legifrance.gouv.fr/affichTexte.do;jsessionid=3DA3918B1389C13FBFAC47442565E30A.tpdjo16v_3?cidTexte=JORFTEXT000000322519&dateTexte=19940228. Accessed 28 Sep 2020

10. International Organization for Standardization: ISO 15489-1:2016(fr) Information et documentation—Gestion des documents d'activité—Partie 1: Concepts et principes (2016). https://www.iso.org/obp/ui/fr/#iso:std:iso:15489:-1:ed-2:v1:fr

11. Chabin, M.A.: La norme ISO 15489 s'est-elle fait hara-kiri? (Did the ISO 15489 standard commit hara-kiri?), 13 March 2017. https://transarchivistique.fr/la-norme-iso-15489-sest-elle-fait-hara-kiri. Accessed 28 Sep 2020

12. Chabin, M.A.: Le records management (2012). https://www.arcateg.fr/wp-content/uploads/2017/03/MAC-Le-Records-management.-Concept-ct-usages-2012.pdf

13. de Boisdeffre, M.: The importance of records management in France. Rec. Manag J. **16**(2), 76–81 (2006)

14. Groupe métiers AAF-ADBS "Records Management": Comprendre et pratiquer le records management. Analyse de la norme ISO 15489 au regard des pratiques archivistiques françaises (Understanding and practicing records management. Analysis of the ISO 15489 standard in view of French archival practices). Documentaliste – Sciences de l' Information **42**(2), 106–116 (2005). https://www.cairn.info/revue-documentaliste-sciences-de-l-information-2005-2-page-106.htm?try_download=1

15. McKemmish, S.: Traces: document, record, archive, archives. In: McKemmish, S., Piggott, M., Reed, B., Upward, F. (eds.) Archives: Recordkeeping in Society, pp. 1–20. Centre for Information Studies, Charles Sturt University, Wagga Wagga (2005)

16. McKemmish, S.: Placing records continuum theory and practice. Arch. Sci. **1**(4), 333–359 (2001)

17. Williams, C.: Managing Archives: Foundations, Principles and Practice. Chandos, Oxford (2006)

18. Millar, L.A.: Archives Principles and Practices, 2nd edn. Facet Publishing, London (2017)

19. Continuum. https://www.lexico.com/definition/continuum. Accessed 28 Sep 2020

20. Atherton, J.: From life cycle to continuum: some thoughts on the records management – archives relationship. Archivaria **21**, 43–51 (1985)

21. Frings-Hessami, V.: The flexibility of the records continuum model: a response to Michael Karabinos' 'In the shadow of the continuum.' Arch. Sci. **20**(1), 51–64 (2020)

22. International Council on Archives: Universal Declaration on Archives. https://www.ica.org/en/universal-declaration-archives. Accessed 08 Jan 2021

23. Reed, B.: Reading the records continuum: interpretations and explorations. Arch. Manuscr. **33**(1), 18–43 (2005)

24. Frings-Hessami, V.: The societal embeddedness of records: teaching the meaning of the fourth dimension of the records continuum model in different cultural contexts. Arch. Sci. (2020). https://link.springer.com/article/10.1007/s10502-020-09349-6

25. Frings-Hessami, V.: La Perspective du Continuum des archives illustrée par l'exemple d'un document personnel (The perspective of the records continuum illustrated by the example of a personal record). Revue électronique suisse de science de l'information **19**, 149 (2018). https://www.ressi.ch/num19/article_149
26. Francis, P., Kong, A.: Making the strange familiar: bridging boundaries on database preservation projects. In: Coates, S., et al. (eds.) iPres 2014 Proceedings of the 11th International Conference on Digital Preservation, Melbourne, 6–10 October 2014, pp. 59–64 (2014). https://www.nla.gov.au/sites/default/files/ipres2014-proceedings-final.pdf

Exploring Interdisciplinary Data Science Education for Undergraduates: Preliminary Results

Fanjie Li[1] ⓘ, Zhiping Xiao[1] ⓘ, Jeremy Tzi Dong Ng[2] ⓘ, and Xiao Hu[2(✉)] ⓘ

[1] University of Hong Kong, Pokfulam Road, Hong Kong, Hong Kong S.A.R.
{fanjie,jakexiao}@connect.hku.hk
[2] University of Hong Kong Shenzhen Institute of Research and Innovation, Shenzhen, China
jntd@connect.hku.hk, xiaoxhu@hku.hk

Abstract. This paper reports a systematic literature review on undergraduate data science education followed by semi-structured interviews with two frontier data science educators. Through analyzing the hosting departments, design principles, curriculum objectives, and curriculum design of existing programs, our findings reveal that (1) the data science field is inherently interdisciplinary and requires joint collaborations between various departments. Multi-department administration was one of the solutions to offer interdisciplinary training, but some problems have also been identified in its practical implementation; (2) data science education should emphasize hands-on practice and experiential learning opportunities to prepare students for data analysis and problem-solving in real-world contexts; and (3) although the importance of comprehensive coverage of various disciplines in data science curricula is widely acknowledged, how to achieve an effective balance between various disciplines and how to effectively integrate domain knowledge into the curriculum still remain open questions. Findings of this study can provide insights for the design and development of emerging undergraduate data science programs.

Keywords: Data science education · Undergraduate · Interdisciplinarity · Curriculum design

1 Introduction

With the growing demand of data-savvy workforce in various sectors, data science programs designed for a variety of degree levels are on the rise. According to the statistics published by the Data Science Community, as of August 2020, 624 data science-related higher education programs have been implemented and delivered around the world [1]. Currently, data science education has been dominated by master-level programs (69%, 432 out of 624), while the bachelor's and PhD programs only count for 10% (N = 66) and 3.7% (N = 23) respectively [1].

Compared to master's program, the bachelor's program in data science is still in its emerging phase. Data science educators are still exploring effective solutions to designing curricula for undergraduate students, as their limited technical experience and prior

© Springer Nature Switzerland AG 2021
K. Toeppe et al. (Eds.): iConference 2021, LNCS 12645, pp. 551–561, 2021.
https://doi.org/10.1007/978-3-030-71292-1_43

background knowledge both pose more challenges and constraints on the curriculum structure. Hence, this study aims to probe existing literature on undergraduate-level data science programs and summarize their experience. Specifically, we are interested in the following research questions:

RQ1: How may the existing literature inform the curriculum design of emerging under-graduate data science programs, especially their practical insights on developing students' interdisciplinary learning experience?

RQ2: What are the challenges and opportunities in designing and implementing an interdisciplinary data science program for undergraduate students?

2 Methods

To answer these research questions, we conducted a systematic literature review and semi-structured interviews with some authors of the reviewed articles so as to further elicit their insights. This section outlines the search strategy, study selection procedure, and coding schema employed, as well as the subsequent interview with invited authors.

2.1 Search Strategy

To depict the current situation of undergraduate data science education, we searched and reviewed the literature indexed by the following databases: (1) Web of Science (WoS), (2) Scopus, and (3) ACM Digital Library (ACM DL), as these databases are representative of the fields closely related to the topic under discussion. Specifically, we chose WoS and Scopus because they broadly cover the computing, engineering, education, and social science fields [2], while another subject specific database (i.e., ACM DL) was selected given its focus on the scientific and educational computing literature.

To form the search query, we identified a set of keywords related to three facets: (1) data science, (2) education, and (3) undergraduate. Particularly, the third facet (i.e., under-graduate) was added because the curriculum design for undergraduate- and graduate-level program can differ significantly given their differences in program duration and student background. After including the alternative terms relevant to each facet, the final query was: ("data science" OR "big data") AND (education OR teaching OR learning OR curriculum OR curricula) AND (undergraduate OR bachelor). The query was applied to the title, abstract, and keyword fields. We did not restrict the publication timeframe but limited our search to English articles. Our literature search was performed in May 2020.

2.2 Study Selection and Citation Search

169 articles were obtained via this initial database searching. These articles then went through an iterative screening process where the inclusion and exclusion criteria were continuously refined. Table 1 summarized the final inclusion and exclusion criteria for study selection.

Table 1. Inclusion and exclusion criteria

Category	Inclusion and exclusion criteria
Study purpose	1. Included: Studies that focus on education, including program/course design, curriculum guideline, or pedagogical suggestions, etc. 2. Excluded: Studies that discuss programs in fields other than data science 3. Excluded: Studies that use data science methods for analyzing educational data (e.g., [3])
Target students	1. Included: The program mentioned should be designed for undergraduate students or be applicable to both undergraduate and graduate students 2. Excluded: Studies discussing programs designed for graduate students
Article type	1. Included: Full articles 2. Excluded: Articles with only an abstract or a brief introduction (e.g., posters)

During the study selection phase, we first assessed the relevance of the article based on its title and abstract. In case the information presented in the title or abstract is insufficient for reaching an inclusion decision, we read the full article to check whether the paper is aligned with our inclusion criteria. Out of the 169 articles obtained via database searching, 19 papers passed the study screening, while the other 150 papers failed to meet the inclusion criteria.

To complement the database searching results, we further performed citation searching for those 19 relevant papers, obtaining papers citing them which then went through the same study selection procedure. Only one new paper was identified as relevant, which resulted in 20 papers for our subsequent analysis.

2.3 Coding Schema

For the selected articles, a coding schema was designed based on iteratively reviewing the 20 studies. The coding schema covers (1) the basic information of the publication and the data science program being described, (2) program details, and (3) challenges and opportunities in program design and program development (see Table 2).

Table 2. Coding schema

Category	Codes	Description
Basic information	Year of publication	Year in which the article was published
	Country (program)	Country where the program was developed
Program details	Involved department(s)	Department(s) involved in the program

(continued)

Table 2. (*continued*)

Category	Codes	Description
	Design principles	Principles that guided the program design
	Learning outcomes	Expected learning outcomes of this program
	Courses	Courses included in the curriculum
	Course prerequisites	Prerequisites of courses in the program
Challenges & Opportunities	Challenges	Challenges in program design/development
	Opportunities	Opportunities in program design/development

2.4 Semi-structured Interviews

In addition to the document analysis of the literature, we further conducted semi-structured interviews with authors of these studies to elicit practical insights and suggestions from those frontier educators. An invitation email together with an informed consent form were sent to the corresponding author of each paper. Two of them have accepted our invitation and signed the consent form. A Zoom-based remote interview was conducted with each of them. Both of them have participated in the design of their corresponding programs.

The interview protocol contains questions on (1) interviewee's roles in the program (e.g., designer, director, regular teacher), (2) the courses they teach (e.g., a particular course, internship, capstone), (3) their opinions on designing an interdisciplinary data science program, (4) how their programs integrate domain knowledge and address the needs of interdisciplinary training in the curriculum design, (5) challenges and difficulties in curriculum design and program implementation, and (6) suggestions for other data science programs. The interviews lasted 20 min each and were audio-recorded and transcribed for further analysis.

3   Results and Discussions

3.1   Overview of Identified Publications and Programs

The papers obtained from this study were published between 2012 and 2020, and half of them (N = 10) were published in last three years (2018–2020). This suggests that undergraduate data science education is still in its emerging phase. A majority of these data science programs (85%, N = 17) were designed and delivered in the United States. 10% of programs (N = 2) were in China and the remaining one was in Australia.

3.2 Program and Curriculum Design

With our focus on how existing literature informs the curriculum design of emerging undergraduate data science programs, we further analyzed the following features of identified programs.

Hosting Department. The department in which the data science program was hosted varied from program to program. Particularly, 4 out of 20 (20%) programs were jointly offered by multiple departments [4–7], while the rest of them either did not provide relevant information in the publication (N = 5) or were hosted by departments from a single discipline (N = 11). For the programs jointly hosted by multi-departments, 2 out of 4 were resulted from collaborations between mathematics and computer science departments [5, 7]. Besides, one program [4] was offered by the departments of business and science. Another program [6] was brought about by a more interdisciplinary endeavor, which involved a committee of faculty representing ten disciplines. For the programs hosted in a single department, 3 out of 11 (27%) were offered by the computer science department [8–10], 3 (27%) by the mathematics or statistics department [11–13], 2 (18%) by departments in the field of information management [14, 15], while the rest of them were hosted by departments from other disciplines, including business (1) [16], journalism and communication (1) [17], and liberal arts (1) [18]. Such diversity in the hosting departments indicates the interdisciplinary nature of the data science field, which calls for collaborations between experts in different fields to offer interdisciplinary training to future data scientists.

Design Principles. Statements describing the design principles of the program (e.g., "the principles of this program are …", "this program is based on the rules of …") were identified in 80% of the articles (N = 16). Based on these statements, we plotted a word cloud diagram to extract and visualize the key principles that guided the program design (Fig. 1). As presented in Fig. 1, the frequently appearing principles mainly center around three aspects: (1) data at the core (or "center around data"), (2) opportunities for hands-on practice, and (3) disciplinary knowledge. Specifically, three articles explicitly highlighted the significance of data [11, 12, 19], with another two programs underscored that students should be trained with large and real-world datasets [13, 20]. Closely related to this principle, three programs further propounded that the curriculum should offer rich opportunities for hands-on practices with big data [9, 13, 14], which is in line with the pedagogical principle of experiential learning. Finally, we identified several design principles in relation to the coverage of disciplinary knowledge. For the breadth of disciplinary coverage, one article acknowledged that the curriculum design should reflect the interdisciplinary nature of the data science field [19]. As for the depth of disciplinary coverage, this article suggested that students should receive sufficient training in mathematical foundations as well as statistical and computational thinking, while other programs (e.g., [6, 13]) suggested that the curriculum should assume little prior background knowledge and avoid a high level of computer science and mathematics requirements. In line with this concern, [21] encouraged teaching with GUI-based analytics tools (e.g., RapidMiner) to reduce the programming requirement. Nonetheless, despite the ever-growing discussions on the breadth and depth of disciplinary coverage, how to achieve an effective balance of breadth (exposure to multiple disciplines) and depth (knowledge of pertinent disciplines) in the curriculum design still remain open questions. Last but not least, the importance of reaching an effective balance between disciplines has also been taken into consideration. For instance, [5] stressed that the program should provide balanced training in statistics and computer science.

Fig. 1. Word cloud generated from the program design principles

Learning Outcomes. The expected program learning outcomes often play an important role in shaping the program curriculum design. 16 articles (80%) explicitly described their curriculum objectives and expected learning outcomes. We plotted the frequent words using another word cloud diagram (Fig. 2). Being consistent with the visualization shown in Fig. 2, our coding also revealed that the expected learning outcomes of these data science programs were mainly fourfold: (1) Students are expected to acquire comprehensive knowledge about data science concepts, methods, and tools, especially developing familiarity with machine learning (e.g., predictive analytics) and essential statistical concepts and methods (e.g., probability, statistical inference); (2) Students should be able to flexibly apply and transfer their knowledge and skills for data analysis and problem solving in real-world contexts; (3) Students should be able to design and implement a standard data processing pipeline in a data-intensive application; (4) Students should be able to effectively communicate and present the data analysis outcomes using text, table, or other visualization techniques. These curriculum objectives generally aligned with the essential knowledge and skills throughout the data science life cycle [19]. Moreover, apart from the mathematical and computing knowledge, several programs (e.g., [6, 10, 20, 22, 23]) further included the domain expertise (e.g., business, political science) as part of their curriculum objectives.

Courses. Aligned with the aforementioned curriculum objectives, courses on statistics, machine learning, data analytics, programming, and data visualization were covered by most of the program curricula. Table 3 summarizes courses included in the reviewed programs. It is noteworthy that all of the 20 programs include courses on data mining, data analytics, or big data, confirming that it is the core knowledge and skillset of data science.

Fig. 2. Word cloud generated from the expected program learning outcomes

Besides mathematics and computing, more than half of the reviewed programs have also acknowledged the importance of communication and presentation skills, which hence offered training targeted at this competence (data visualization: N = 9, communication: N = 2). This echoes the findings of a recent study [24] that emphasized the importance of training data science students in communicating reproducible data analysis.

Courses on data curation and management are included in four programs, so are those on ethics and privacy. This indicates a misalignment with recent prevalent research on data governance, particularly on fairness, accountability, and transparency in data science [25]. Although these issues have been discussed in research, and in the context of data science education most recently [25], the actual inclusion of these into the curricula, especially on the undergraduate level has yet to be reflected in the literature. One program explicitly includes courses in application areas of data science such as sociology, economics, political science, and psychology [6]. Although it is well acknowledged that data science is an application-oriented field, most programs do not include courses in application areas.

Course Prerequisites. Though a few programs presented in the articles (20%, N = 4) contain courses with computer science or mathematics prerequisites, the majority of them (80%, N = 16) do not assume any prior experience or background knowledge. Among those programs with course prerequisites, several require programming experience in Python, Java, C++, or Linux environment (e.g., [9, 15]), while the others assume basic knowledge of mathematics and statistics (e.g., [11]). While this observation further reflects the significant role of mathematics and computer science in the data science curricula, it is also noteworthy that the majority of reviewed programs do not have course prerequisites. This might reflect the novice-friendly requirement for entering the data science field and its application-driven nature.

3.3 Challenges and Opportunities

Our document analysis of the literature and interviews with invited authors further revealed several challenges and opportunities in designing and implementing an interdisciplinary data science program.

Table 3. Overview of program curricula

Category	Course	Covered by # of programs
Mathematics	Statistics	9
	Calculus	5
	Linear algebra	2
	Probability theory	2
	Discrete structures	1
Computer science	Programming/computing	11
	Data structures & algorithms	6
	Machine learning/artificial intelligence	8
	Database management system/DB design	4
	Information system	3
	Introduction to software design	1
	Introduction to semantic technology	1
	Internet of Things	1
Data science	Introduction to data science	5
	Data analytics/big data/data mining	20
	Regression and forecasting models	1
	Business intelligence	1
	Data visualization	9
	Data curation	3
	Data manipulation	1
	Data organization & management	1
Others	Ethics and privacy	4
	Communication	2
	Asking interesting questions	1
	Quantitative decision making	1
	Management & organizational behaviour	1
	Project management	3
	Anthropology and sociology, biology, economics, philosophy, physics, political science, psychology	1

Challenges. 8 out of 20 articles discussed the challenges in program design and development, such as (1) students' difficulty in fulfilling mathematics and computer science course requirements, especially for those with no programming experience and those who studied liberal arts [4, 21], (2) limited faculty for course delivery and for maintaining active engagement with students considering the increasing class size [4], (3) challenges in designing experiential learning activities for international students due to the work visa problem [5], and (4) difficulties in covering relevant knowledge components within limited credit hours [17]. Besides, our interviews also revealed some problems encountered in multi-department administration: (1) It is hard to control how courses were set up in another department such as prerequisites (Interviewee #2); (2) Without a departmental home, students may not have an identity or community as a data science student. (Interviewee #1).

Opportunities. Despite the challenges mentioned above, there are also opportunities for the emerging undergraduate data science programs. Given the interdisciplinary nature of data science, the programs can be integrated with various social science (e.g., business) and liberal arts (e.g., journalism) majors. As pointed out by interviewee #1, it is flexible for each data science program to focus on strengths of their own institutions.

4 Conclusion and Future Work

To extract practical insights for the design and implementation of undergraduate data science programs and identify the challenges and opportunities in program design and development, we conducted a systematic literature review and performed semi-structured interviews with two frontier data science educators. Through analyzing the hosting departments, design principles, curriculum objectives, and curriculum design of the existing undergraduate data science programs, our findings reveal that (1) the data science field is inherently interdisciplinary and requires joint collaborations between various departments. Multi-department administration was one of the solutions to offer interdisciplinary training, but some problems has also been identified in its practical implementation (c.f. Sect. 3.3); (2) data science education should emphasize hands-on practices and experiential learning opportunities to prepare students for data analysis and problem-solving in real-world contexts; and (3) although the importance of comprehensive coverage of various disciplines in data science curricula is widely acknowledged, how to achieve an effective balance of breadth (exposure to multiple disciplines) and depth (knowledge of pertinent disciplines), especially the effective integration of domain knowledge, still remain open questions.

As a preliminary review of the status quo of undergraduate data science education, this study discussed the practical experience from existing literature and frontier educators, which may shed light on the design and development of emerging undergraduate data science programs. In future work we will continue interviewing more data science educators for an in-depth analysis of the curriculum, syllabus, and regulations.

Acknowledgments. This study is supported by a Teaching Development Grant sponsored by the University of Hong Kong and a grant (No. 61703357) by National Natural Science Foundation National Natural Science Foundation of China.

References

1. DataScienceCommunity. https://datascience.community/colleges. Accessed 15 Aug 2020
2. Mongeon, P., Paul-Hus, A.: The journal coverage of web of science and scopus: a comparative analysis. Scientometrics **106**(1), 213–228 (2015). https://doi.org/10.1007/s11192-015-1765-5
3. Belyakova, E.G., Zakharova, I.G.: Interaction of university students with educational content in the conditions of information educational environment. Educ. Sci. J. **21**(3), 77–105 (2019)
4. Rosenthal, S., Chung, T.: A data science major: building skills and confidence. In: Proceedings of the 51st ACM Technical Symposium on Computer Science Education, Portland, OR, USA, pp. 178–184. ACM (2020)
5. Adams, J.C.: Creating a balanced data science program. In: Proceedings of the 51st ACM Technical Symposium on Computer Science Education, Portland, OR, USA, pp. 185–191. ACM (2020)
6. Havill, J.: Embracing the liberal arts in an interdisciplinary data analytics program. In: Proceedings of the 50th ACM Technical Symposium on Computer Science Education, Minneapolis, MN, USA, pp. 9–14. ACM (2019)
7. Anderson, P., Bowring, J., McCauley, R., Pothering, G., Starr, C.: An undergraduate degree in data science: curriculum and a decade of implementation experience. In: Proceedings of the 45th ACM Technical Symposium on Computer Science Education, Atlanta, Georgia, USA, pp. 145–150. ACM (2014)
8. Carter, T., Hauselt, P., Martin, M., Thomas, M.: Building a big data research program at a small university. J. Comput. Sci. Coll. **28**(2), 95–102 (2012)
9. Eckroth, J.: A course on big data analytics. J. Parallel Distrib. Comput. **118**, 166–176 (2018)
10. Ramamurthy, B.: A practical and sustainable model for learning and teaching data science. In: Proceedings of the 47th ACM Technical Symposium on Computing Science Education, Memphis, TN, USA, pp. 169–174. ACM (2016)
11. Baumer, B.: A data science course for undergraduates: thinking with data. Am. Stat. **69**(4), 334–342 (2015)
12. Yan, D., Davis, G.E.: A first course in data science. J. Stat. Educ. **27**(2), 99–109 (2019)
13. Yavuz, F.G., Ward, M.D.: Fostering undergraduate data science. Am. Stat. **74**(1), 8–16 (2020)
14. Li, X., et al.: Curriculum reform in big data education at applied technical colleges and universities in China. IEEE Access **7**, 125511–125521 (2019)
15. Asamoah, D.A., Sharda, R., Hassan Zadeh, A., Kalgotra, P.: Preparing a data scientist: a pedagogic experience in designing a big data analytics course. Decis. Sci. J. Innov. Educ. **15**(2), 161–190 (2017)
16. Wymbs, C.: Managing the innovation process: infusing data analytics into the undergraduate business curriculum (lessons learned and next steps). J. Inf. Syst. Educ. **27**(1), 61 (2016)
17. Liao, H.T., Wang, Z., Wu, X.: Developing a minimum viable product for big data and AI education: action research based on a two-year reform of an undergraduate program of internet and new media. In: Proceedings of the 2019 4th International Conference on Big Data and Computing, Guangzhou, China, pp. 42–47. ACM (2019)
18. Mandel, T., Mache, J.: Developing a short undergraduate introduction to online machine learning. J. Comput. Sci. Coll. **32**(1), 144–150 (2016)
19. De Veaux, R.D., et al.: Curriculum guidelines for undergraduate programs in data science. Ann. Rev. Stat. Appl. **4**, 15–30 (2017)
20. Leman, S., House, L., Hoegh, A.: Developing a new interdisciplinary computational analytics undergraduate program: a qualitative-quantitative-qualitative approach. Am. Stat. **69**(4), 397–408 (2015)

21. Haynes, M., Groen, J., Sturzinger, E., Zhu, D., Shafer, J., McGee, T.: Integrating data science into a general education information technology course: an approach to developing data savvy undergraduates. In: Proceedings of the 20th Annual SIG Conference on Information Technology Education, Tacoma, WA, USA, pp. 183–188. ACM (2019)

22. Gupta, B., Goul, M., Dinter, B.: Business intelligence and big data in higher education: status of a multi-year model curriculum development effort for business school undergraduates, MS graduates, and MBAs. Commun. Assoc. Inf. Syst. **36**(1), 23 (2015)

23. Miah, S.J., Solomonides, I., Gammack, J.G.: A design-based research approach for developing data-focused business curricula. Educ. Inf. Technol. **25**(1), 553–581 (2020)

24. Yu, B., Hu, X.: Toward training and assessing reproducible data analysis in data science education. Data Intell. **1**(4), 381–392 (2019)

25. Bates, J., et al.: Integrating FATE/critical data studies into data science curricula: where are we going and how do we get there? In: Proceedings of the 2020 Conference on Fairness, Accountability, and Transparency, Barcelona, Spain, pp. 425–435. ACM (2020)

Pre-service Librarians' Perspective on the Role of Participatory Design in Libraries with Youth

Kung Jin Lee[⊠], Jin Ha Lee, and Jason C. Yip

University of Washington, Seattle, WA 98105, USA
{kjl26,jinhalee,jcyip}@uw.edu

Abstract. Participatory Design (PD) is a design methodology that incorporates the end users in the design process. An active area of research in PD focuses on designing new technology with children. As more libraries are offering different technologies to their patrons—especially to children—there is an increasing need to think about how to best incorporate such technologies into library services. Recent interest in the field has encouraged librarians to situate themselves as designers, and to find creative solutions to the problems that arise in library settings. However, design methods are not widely utilized in the field of library and information science. In this study, we have interviewed pre-service librarians and children participants who did participatory design in libraries within a service-learning course. These participatory design sessions focused on incorporating new technologies into library programming. Our study indicates that PD is a possible method for capturing the ethos of librarianship. Pre-service librarians found that PD allowed them to effectively enact values of service, such as democratic participation and creativity, while children valued being heard from adults in the library and helping their community.

Keywords: Informal learning · Participatory design · Youth program · Librarianship · Youth service

1 Introduction

An increasing number of libraries are now situating themselves as learning spaces and makerspaces, where patrons are provided opportunities to tinker with new technologies [29]. In these spaces, patrons have access to new technologies, such as virtual reality (VR), 3D printers and e-textiles [26, 28, 30]. These technologies allow people to connect with other adult mentors to learn. The public library space directly positions itself to address issues in equity by supporting marginalized communities who may not have access to technologies otherwise. Recent literature highlights the need for librarians to become designers in creating such democratic and collaborative learning spaces [3, 32].

In discussing how to be designers, prior research indicates that participatory design is one of the effective ways of designing digital learning spaces [31, 32]. Participatory design (PD) is a method wherein the end user is involved in the design process through democratic and collaborative means [13]. More recently PD has been adopted to include

© Springer Nature Switzerland AG 2021
K. Toeppe et al. (Eds.): iConference 2021, LNCS 12645, pp. 562–574, 2021.
https://doi.org/10.1007/978-3-030-71292-1_44

children in the design and development of digital learning spaces and technologies [10–12]. As opposed to the librarian solely designing the digital learning technologies curriculum, the librarian collaborates side-by-side with their patrons. In a recent study, Yip et al. [32] outlined the roles a librarian can play in partnership with youth by examining a case study of children designing with a single librarian. The study states how different roles librarians can inhabit in PD, including *designer with youth* and *supporter of youth* (such as being facilitators) [32]. However, we still have a limited understanding of how to best teach the method of PD to pre-service librarians.

Despite the active use of PD in libraries, pre-service librarians in library science programs are generally not well equipped to practice these design methods [4, 11, 15, 27]. Cross [8] states that design must be fostered through education and experience. Yet, there are currently few design opportunities for pre-service librarians in the Master of Library and Information Science (MLIS) program [5]. If we are able to understand how pre-service librarians experience, engage, and learn through design methods such as PD, we can better equip them for the changing field of Library and Information Science (LIS). As professionals they can practice such skills, even with the absence of university researchers.

To understand pre-service librarians' perspectives of PD, we conducted an exploratory study to develop digital activities for youth library programming. In this study, we developed a graduate-level class in which researchers, practitioners, and library patrons (children) collaborated together to engage in PD in libraries to build a set of guidelines for digital learning activities. The course was an *Academically Based Community Service* (ABCS) course, which is a form of service learning [20]. To investigate the perspective of the pre-service librarians as future librarians, we interviewed the MLIS students enrolled in the class whose career path was in librarianship. We also interviewed children participants. We aimed to answer the following research questions:

1. What perceptions do pre-service librarians have about their involvement in a participatory design team?
2. What values and challenges does engagement in participatory design bring to the learning environment in librarianship?
3. What is the experience of children engaged in participatory design in the library?

The article concludes with a theoretical contribution of how participatory design can be utilized as a form of pedagogy for librarianship, and how PD shapes identity for future librarians. We also offer practical suggestions by discussing future courses for pre-service librarians, which can better support their career in which they will technology-related service to the community.

2   Related Work

2.1   History of PD

Participatory design (PD) originated in Scandinavia during the 1950s. The core concept of this approach is to include the end user, who will use the technology and design it with designers. Floyd et al. [16] attributes the socio-cultural background of Scandinavia countries in their explanation as to why this approach originated from this specific region. Democratization is deeply committed and engrained in Scandinavian history. Norway and Sweden did not have a feudal system, which exemplified their goals of establishing an egalitarian society. Therefore, during the 1960s and 1970s when Scandinavian factory workers were threatened by new technology in the working environment, researchers worked with union members to find ways to include them in the design process [13]. During the mid-1980s, inspired by Scandinavian workers, the US also started to implement PD projects [13].

Both Ehn [14] and Floyd [16] discuss two values that guide PD: democracy and humanization. These two values can be distinguished from other approaches of system design. Within democracy, Ehn [14] discusses the importance of considering the conditions for proper legitimate user participation, which implies the creating of the design itself [14]. Similarly, Floyd [16] states, "the system should either reflect the interests of the systems owners, or as fairly as possible the interests of all those affected".

For humanization, Floyd [16] notes, "the system is primarily designed to compensate human weaknesses, or to support human strength". Similarly, Ehn [14] states, "the importance of making the participants' 'tacit knowledge' come into play in the design process". Ehn [14] and Floyd [16] both move beyond the approach of being techno-centered.

The guiding principle and the spirit of PD are still relevant today, especially where we see a growing number of new technologies. However, PD is often not inclusive to different demographic groups. As the public library is a democratic space, and librarians have long championed inclusion and access, we find opportunities of understanding how PD can be used in the public library space [21, 22]. In our study, the pre-service librarians worked closely with children to democratically create youth service programs for digital learning.

2.2 Participatory Design in Libraries

Most literature on PD in libraries focus on designing the physical space of the library [1, 17, 27]. For example, Brown-Sica et al. [1] used PD to identify new needs of the library patrons that differed from preconceptions people had in how library space is used. Some scholars have applied PD methods to design services for library patrons [11, 12, 18]. For instance, Druin et al. [11, 12] used PD to specifically understand children's needs as library patrons by working with them to design digital libraries for children. Marquez and Downey [24] also applied PD methods for service design to provide a satisfying user experience for the library patrons. The focus of these papers is twofold: the research either reflects on how PD is implemented in the space of the library with the patrons, or how including the patrons changes the design decisions being made. Though the majority emphasize the partnership being built during the design process, fewer papers examined the perspectives of librarians who participate in PD.

Design partnerships are an important component in PD. Yip et al. [31, 32] present four dimensions of PD partnership: 1) relationship building among the participants; 2) a concern on how designers and participants can co-facilitate the sessions; 3) how the participants and designers design-by-doing together; and 4) how idea elaboration occurs among everyone. In a co-design session, the dimensions of partnership are dynamic, and range from being balanced to unbalanced. "Unbalanced" moments refer to situations in co-design when either the children or adults are dominating in their contribution, which leads to unequal contribution. For example, in relationship building, "unbalanced" situations occur when adults are socially far from the children and "balance" occurs when closer adult-child relationships are established.

In a more recent study, Yip et al. [32] outlines, through a conceptual model for librarianship, how there is a difference between the traditional roles of being supporters of youth to being designers with youth. For instance, in a more traditional role, librarians are instructors whereas, as designers, they can co-facilitate and foster design relationships. The study argues that training librarians as design partners is about being able to shift between the two roles, rather than giving up their traditional role. This leads us to investigate how such skills can be taught in an MLIS course, and what support pre-service librarians may need in practicing such skills.

2.3 Librarians as Designers

Recently, some studies have argued that the field of LIS has been fundamentally aligned with design [3–5]. These studies point out that librarians have always engaged in design thinking methods and acted as designers, as they create new tools for information services. However, the literature also points out the absence of systematic education of design methods in librarianship.

In a 2020 study by Clarke et al., the authors use an online questionnaire to understand what design methods were being used in library practices, and where librarians gained such knowledge and skills [5]. The study reveals that commonly used design methods are interviews, surveys and observation to understand the user experience. The study also states how children's service and programming are an area where the librarians especially felt the need for design skills. On the questions of where the librarians were gaining such knowledge and skills, the study reveals that the librarians are self-taught or learned through informal sources like blogs. The article emphasizes the need for more courses to be developed, especially for librarians whose career trajectories are in youth and technology.

To understand what specific skill sets youth librarians need to develop, Subramaniam et al. (2018) conducted PD sessions with in-service youth librarians to outline skills to advance youth learning from disciplines outside of LIS [29]. The study coined the term *Youth eXperience (YX) librarian*, and the implications outline the knowledge and skills youth librarians must possess. The study reveals that librarians were in need of 1) training to keep abreast of current technology, and 2) skills to develop and sustain community partnerships. The study highlighted that the skills mentioned were those absent in the traditional librarianship curriculum. In our study, we aim to fill in this gap by reflecting on a class that emphasized such interpersonal skills through PD.

3   Research Method

3.1   Context

In this study, we interviewed pre-service librarians who were enrolled in a special topic course which was offered by the second author at the University of Washington titled

"Participatory Design in Libraries" in the Fall of 2017 and 2018. The goal of the PD sessions was to create a deeper understanding of how to integrate new technologies (e.g., Mario Maker, 3D printer and Arduino) in library programming. The partnering library was in the process of incorporating these technologies into their youth services. The pre-service librarians enrolled in the class had the chance to work with an urban public library in Columbia City in Seattle that serves a diverse community in terms of race, ethnicity, and socio-economic levels. As part of the class, the lead-instructor required the students to engage in the design sessions and to write a recommendation report to the library partner based on what students learned from the community. In a typical week, the students had one day in class to discuss theories through readings and one day in the library to work with the community. A total of 15 children (7 boys, 8 girls) who were ethnically diverse participated in the co-design group. The age of the children ranged from 7 to 11 years old (M = 8.6; SD = 1.2). Two professors and a teaching assistant also participated in the PD sessions.

3.2 Interview

We used a semi-structured interview protocol adapted from Merriam and Tisdell [25] to give flexibility for the participants to reflect on their experiences of the class. For pre-service librarians, we asked questions about their reasons for coming to the MLIS program, expectations of the class, engagement in participatory design sessions, reflections on the co-design sessions at the library, and their overall takeaways after completing the class. For the children's interview, we asked what they thought about designing with adults in the library, why they continued to come to the program, and their overall experience of designing in the library.

3.3 Participants

In this study, we interviewed a total of 17 pre-service librarians from the 2017 to 2018 cohort (14 women and three men; 11 first-year and six second-year students). Two were international pre-service librarians. All interviews were conducted in the following winter quarter of 2018 and 2019 to avoid any conflict of interest. For children, among the 15 children who participated, we were able to interview a total of seven children (ages = 7–11, 4 boys and 3 girls) who were all recruited by the librarian. The ethnicity of the children consisted of White, Black, Asian/White, Asian and Hispanic. All children and pre-service librarians signed either an assent or consent form as part of the study. Prior to engaging in the library design sessions, the researcher went over the assent forms with the children and caregiver. Pre-service librarians, prior to meeting the children, also reviewed ethics on working with minors with the researcher.

3.4 Procedure

The interviews were semi-structured and lasted an average of 34 min (SD = 13.8) for the pre-service librarians' interview. The pre-service librarians' interviews were held at meeting rooms at the University of Washington and through phone calls. For the pre-service librarians' interviews, participants did not receive compensation. For the children participants, we conducted the interviews in the library. The families received a 25-dollar gift card of their choice for their participation. The interviews were semi-structured and lasted an average of 12 min (SD = 1.3).

3.5 Data Analysis

We approached this analysis using a grounded approach [2]. We transcribed all interview data, and four researchers open coded all 24 interview responses with constant comparative analysis [25]. Each coder was in charge of open coding at least four interview transcripts. We developed a codebook through multiple discussions and by creating affinity diagrams of what has been seen in the interview data [19]. The codebook contained nine categories: 1) perceptions of participatory design; 2) limitation of PD in libraries; 3) relationship building; 4) challenges of PD; 5) designer identity; 6) structure of the class; 7) surprises in PD; 8) future confidence; and 9) lessons learned. Three members of the research team applied the coding scheme. We conducted an additional coding review to refine and clarify the codes. As a result, we removed the code *9) lessons learned* due to its overlap with other categories. We also merged *2) limitations of PD in libraries* and *4) challenges of PD* as both discussed the difficulties of executing PD in the library. The definitions of each category were also clarified during this process resulting in the final codebook (Table 1).

Table 1. Final codebook used for data analysis

Perceptions of PD	Perception and belief of PD as a method/technique used in the library
Limitation and challenges of PD in libraries	Possible and actual limitations/challenges raised by pre-service librarians while conducting PD in the library
Relationship building	Comments regarding the relationship built between the pre-service librarians and the community
Designer identity	Perception and belief of how pre-service librarians viewed themselves as a designer after the course
Structure of the class	Comments regarding the structure of class engaging in both theory and practice
Surprises in PD	Comments on what was unique or learnt through the process of engaging in PD with pre-service librarians and children
Future confidence	Comments regarding students confidence on conducting future sessions using PD as a method

4 Findings

First, we discuss how this course impacted pre-service librarians to reflect on the ways they thought about themselves, their work, and their relationship to design. Next, we discuss the concerns and limitations pre-service librarians felt with regards to conducting PD in a library setting. Lastly, we share the children's experiences of co-designing in the library with the pre-service librarians. All the names in the children's interviews are pseudonyms.

4.1 Perceptions of PD and the Confidence Level of Designer Identity

Pre-service librarians perceived PD as an effective way to do community engagement work. They mentioned that PD aligned with core values of librarianship, such as upholding democracy and participation. They thought PD should *"naturally become part of what librarians do in order to design or create and develop all the programming and resources and services."* (P2). Pre-service librarians pointed out that PD seems to be an efficient way to enact these values. P4 posed the rhetorical question, *"if you're designing something for someone like hey, why don't we involve them?"* Pre-service librarians also perceived that PD can create a more level playing field, which *"changes up the directional power structure"* (P11).

After participating in the course, pre-service librarians expressed mixed feelings about their identity as a designer. Some were able to conceive ways to utilize these skills in the future, whether leading PD activities themselves, or incorporating some of the ideas into workshops and discussions. However, some pre-service librarians still had doubts and concerns about doing PD in the library in their future work. In this particular class, recruiting children for the program was done by the local librarian who had a solid relationship with the community. The pre-service librarians reflected that, for this particular class, they were lucky to have an active librarian and people who were interested in the program. When it comes to building a community of interest around PD, some pre-service librarians worried about being able to replicate the same experience in the future. The findings suggest the importance of offering courses on topics like community outreach and engagement.

Some pre-service librarians also commented that their perception of their identity as designers depended on the context. They recognized that they certainly identify as designers in the class but not necessarily outside of the class. Some felt the need to become "more creative" or "have more design experience" in order to fully identify as designers. *"I don't go around saying I'm a designer but I like to think I'm a librarian who designs"* (P2) *"No. I, because when I was in the class, I always felt that I lacked some design thinking mind, because I couldn't come up with many ideas that are interesting or, say, creative. So, I think that's why I couldn't."* (P7). The following quotes demonstrate that pre-service librarians tended to hold certain expectations about being a designer, for example, that they need to be able to come up with interesting and creative ideas and be confident in their design skills rather than seeing the process of designing as a learning experience in and of itself. To help pre-service librarians identify as a designer, the quotes indicate the need for more opportunities to practice design methods in a positive and encouraging environment where even failure is perceived as a path to more successful designs.

4.2 Challenges and Limitations in Doing PD in the Libraries

Limitation: Practical. Though pre-service librarians found value in implementing PD in a library setting, they recognized that there were also limitations. They commented on the practical issues of doing PD in libraries without the class, such as lack of resources and librarian time. P5 states, *"I can see an organization not being willing to do it for the amount of time that it takes. I can definitely see that being a hard sell to devote that much time and energy into a program."* In our study, the ratio of the adult to child was one adult per two children. This was because the pre-service librarians enrolled in the class all participated in the library session. Therefore, the children were able to have attention from the different adults in the room who would work side-by-side and another adult who would act as a facilitator. However, the pre-service librarians questioned how this format would take place in the absence of the class. For instance, pre-service librarians questioned what it would look like if there were only one librarian to manage the co-design session.

Limitation: Conceptual. Aside from physical, financial, and resource limitations, pre-service librarians also recognized that practicing PD requires people to change their perceptions about how to solve problems. P12 noted, *"it's hard to conceptualize what [PD] is unless you've actually like seen it...I think like conveying that to a librarian or an educator or something that hasn't had any information about it before could be challenging."* Pre-service librarians feared that it may be difficult to justify this type of paradigm switch when high level managers do not fully understand the value of PD. As much as pre-service librarians perceived PD to be "flexible" and "adaptable" to incorporate different patrons' views, pre-service librarians also felt that PD was a concept still hard to grasp and communicate to the public.

Challenges of PD: Authority vs. Co-design Partners. Similar to prior studies, we also observed the tension between the pre-service librarians wanting to instruct as opposed to facilitating the session, which was more open-ended with a loose structure [6, 9, 33]. However, it was also dependent on the complexity of the technology. For instance, while pre-service librarians who worked with the video game *Super Mario Maker* did not mention the challenge of being co-design partners much, pre-service librarians who worked with 3D printers and Arduino had much more to say regarding the tension between being design partners and instructors. For instance, P1, who used 3D printers, stated *"the balance between learning the new technology and then designing, having the kids help design the program, right, and the balance between having a fun program and then having a program that produces an actually deliverable, I found a lot of struggle between getting the right balance in those two areas."*

For the pre-service librarians, there were challenges in co-designing new activities with children when there was only limited instruction given on how to use the technology to begin with. In our co-design session, we gave minimal instructions on Arduino and it was the first time that the majority of pre-service librarians used the technology. For instance, P14, who used Arduino, stated *"even though we got basic things, we didn't know how to go above and beyond and be curious about the things."* As both pre-service librarians and children had minimal knowledge of the technology, the majority of the time with the children was spent on figuring out how the technology worked. As a result, pre-service librarians noted that it did not feel like co-design. One pre-service librarian remarked *"I feel like we weren't co-designing. I felt like I was guiding them and teaching them a lot. I also think that was because we did Arduino. Also, since we were getting training on it and the children weren't, so there was some knowledge superiority going [on]."*

4.3 The Children's Experience Designing with Adults

The children enrolled in the PD program mainly participated because of the technology provided. For instance, when we asked the children why they continued to come to the design sessions, Rob (age $= 7$) stated, *"I like electronics a lot. It's like about technology."* Other children also discussed the opportunity to design stating *"Well, I like it because you get to, you're allowed to design stuff, and I get to know how to do different stuff."* (Sarah, age $= 9$). There were a handful of children who mentioned that they came to help other children. Jessy (age $= 9$), for instance, stated *"Well, we're helping the kids in the future to learn better."* However, even though we stated in our program we were designing for other children, it was difficult for many children to conceptualize designing for service as opposed to designing an artifact.

The children also talked about the different relationships with the adults in the design session. Some children viewed the adults as people similar to teachers *"They were kind of like teachers, but instead of teaching us to do stuff, they let us do stuff on our own kind of, which I liked, but they helped us when we needed help."* (Ally, age $= 10$), and also supporters of technology *"It's fun because they can give you ideas and tell you what you should do, kind of, and they help you."* (Liam, age $= 8$). Some children still viewed the adults as holding more of the traditional role of experts *"Well, they know much more than us"* (Tom, age $= 8$). The biggest difference between the participatory design sessions and other library programming or extracurricular activities was that the children noticed the number of adults present in the room *"There's like an equal number of grown-ups and kids. Because if it was [sic] kids... it'd kind of be boring, like really boring."* Rob (age $= 7$). The findings indicate how the children perceived the adults in the spectrum of both *supporters* and *design partners* [32]. They also indicated how the number of adults to children ratio influenced how the children designed with the adults. When there were approximately an equal number of both children and adults, the children felt more comfortable instead of one group outnumbering the other.

5 Discussion

Our findings show that the democratic nature of PD is well aligned with the values of librarianship and design. Pre-service librarians in the program worked closely with children in the design process for digital learning activities for future children at our partnering libraries. We attempted PD to support the use of design partnership in these settings [13, 32]. We were able to see that the pre-service librarians also had strong motivations to interact with children and the community they hope to serve in the future.

In this section, we extend our findings by providing suggestions for future directions to better support pre-service librarians so they can provide better technology-related services. Based on our interview data, we first identify the need for specific design-related courses for pre-service librarians. Additionally, we suggest ways of creating a more sustainable model for working with community partners. Finally, we discuss the opportunities and limitations of the term *design* in LIS.

5.1 Developing More Courses

Technology Related Courses. The findings showed that the selection of digital learning technology impacted the level of engagement. While prior literature indicated the growing number of new technologies in the library, our findings showed struggles of pre-service librarians balancing between learning new technology and co-designing with children [23]. One possible solution is to select a technology, which requires a lower barrier of entry, to co-design with children. Additionally, this can be addressed by choosing a technology children and adults are more familiar with. However, as there is also a need for pre-service librarians to keep up to date with current technologies, offering more technology-related courses could be useful. This is not necessarily because pre-service librarians can learn all the technologies they could use for youth programming, but because it will help them become more comfortable when they find themselves in situations where they have to quickly learn a new learning technology.

Community Engagement Related Courses. Despite the growing literature using PD as a method of design for systems, services, and space design for libraries, the pre-service librarians had to develop their understandings of the concept of PD [1, 17, 27]. From the pre-service librarian interviews, it became clear that the practical experience of PD in a real-life setting was immensely helpful for pre-service librarians to understand the concept beyond just reading the literature. The pre-service librarians found that the method of PD allowed them to get to know the patrons at a much deeper level, as they sensed the patrons opening up and being more transparent with their ideas once the trust was built and the relationship was solidified. As Yip et al. [31] discuss the relationship building spectrum of socially being far from the design partner to socially being close, we were able to see how pre-service librarians interacting with the patrons led to creating a more balanced design partnership by becoming closer to them.

5.2 Creating Partnership Within the Community

Our findings suggest how pre-service librarians perceived working as equal partners in PD to be a difficult model to replicate outside the classroom without support from external partners. One way to address this challenge is to involve volunteers from the community, who are already patrons in the library, for a more sustainable model. For example, as opposed to just the pre-service librarians working with children in the program, local teens can work side-by side with the children. Currently, our team is exploring ways the teens in the community can collaboratively develop a learning curriculum with children and librarians. So far, we can point to some successful and promising pilot cases in our library.

The methods in which different elements of PD sessions might be implemented (such as equal partnership, ideal size of the PD session) can vary. Some pre-service librarians viewed this flexibility as a potential obstacle to effectively communicating the idea and value of PD to people who are unfamiliar with this approach. Our findings suggest that while the course attempted to teach the students about the importance of working with the community, teaching how to effectively reach out and persuade various stakeholders was something that was missing in the class. For pre-service librarians to employ new approaches in programming, courses that specifically focus on communication and persuasion skills, as well as evaluation/assessment methods, can be useful. In addition to the challenges inherent in communicating the idea of PD, another barrier in widely adopting PD in libraries has to do with whether pre-service librarians themselves *identify* as designers.

5.3 Exposure for More Design

Regarding these issues of pre-service librarians' confidence, their designer identity, and their ability to communicate PD to other librarians, we believe it is crucial to expose pre-service librarians to more opportunities for design within the MLIS program [4, 5]. This will allow pre-service librarians to develop more confidence on their own abilities to design, communicate their design needs to other librarians, and lead PD activities as future librarians. From the interviews, it was apparent that pre-service librarians were fairly comfortable using the techniques learnt in class. However, when asked if they identify as designers, some were still hesitant, partially because of their perceived lack of their design abilities, but also due to the term "designer" still being perceived as more of an "artist" outside of the LIS context. This brings up a question about the usefulness of incorporating and applying the term "designer" in the LIS context. While we designed a course on PD and libraries, our intention was not to have every future librarian develop their own co-design team. Rather, we believe it is important to give librarians opportunities to work side-by-side with the community in a real-life setting.

6   Conclusion

This study explores pre-service librarian's perceptions of engaging in PD with children in the library within an MLIS course. Our study finds that pre-service librarians found value in interacting with patrons and collaboratively working with children in a partnership when confronted with a design challenge. While the class allowed the pre-service librarians to practice design methodologies, the pre-service librarians were not fully confident in their identities as designers. We believe this is natural, as the LIS field has situated itself as a social science for more than one hundred years and only recently, some started viewing the field with a design epistemology [3].

Findings of the study will help guide the future directions on creating curricula in the field of library and information science to allow pre-service librarians to practice design by engaging with projects where they work closely with libraries and with real problems. We argue that PD allows pre-service librarians to enact values of service, like democratic participation and creativity, through building strong design partnerships. If we believe that practicing design is an effective way for librarians in the ever-changing environment in the library, we need to provide them with opportunities to interact with the patrons, collaboratively work with patrons, and practice creating new solutions to the problems. Furthermore, we need to continue examining librarians' perspectives to understand whether such support increases the level of confidence in engaging in design.

References

1. Brown-Sica, M., Sobel, K., Rogers, E.: Participatory action research in learning commons design planning. New Libr. World **111**(7/8), 302–319 (2010)
2. Charmaz, K., Belgrave, L.: Qualitative interviewing and grounded theory analysis. SAGE Handb. Int. Res. Complex. Craft **2**, 347–365 (2012)
3. Clarke, R.I.: Toward a design epistemology for librarianship. Libr. Q. **88**(1), 41–59 (2018)
4. Clarke, R.I., Lee, J.H., Mayer, K.: Design topics in graduate library education: a preliminary investigation. In: Association for Library and Information Science Education Conference, Atlanta, Georgia, USA, 17–20 January 2017, Poster Session (2017)
5. Clarke, R.I., Amonkar, S., Rosenblad, A.: Design thinking and methods in library practice and graduate library education. J. Librariansh. Inf. Sci. **52**(3), 749–763 (2020)
6. Clegg, T., Gardner, C., Williams, O., Kolodner, J.: Promoting learning in informal learning environments. In: Proceedings of the 7th International Conference on Learning Sciences, Mahwah, NJ, pp. 92–98. International Society of the Learning Sciences (ICLS) (2006)
7. Clegg, T., Subramaniam, M.: Redefining mentorship in facilitating interest-driven learning in libraries. In: Reconceptualizing Libraries: Perspectives from the Information and Learning Sciences (2018)
8. Cross, N.: Expertise in design: an overview. Des. Stud. **25**, 427–441 (2004)
9. Davis, K., Subramaniam, M., Hoffman, K.M., Romeijn-Stout, E.L.: Technology use in rural and urban public libraries: implications for connected learning in youth programming. In: Proceedings of the Connected Learning Summit, Pittsburgh, PA, pp. 47–56. Carnegie Mellon ETC Press (2018)
10. Druin, A.: The role of children in the design of new technology. Behav. Inf. Technol. **21**(1), 1–25 (2002)
11. Druin, A.: What children can teach us: developing digital libraries for children with children. Libr. Q. **75**(1), 20–41 (2005)
12. Druin, A., et al.: Designing a digital library for young children. In: Proceedings of the 1st ACM/IEEE-CS Joint Conference on Digital Libraries, pp. 398–405. ACM, New York (2001)
13. Ehn, P.: Scandinavian design: on participation and skill. Participatory Design: Principles and Practices, pp. 41–77 (1993)
14. Ehn, P., Kyng, M.: The collective resource approach to systems design. Computers and Democracy, Avebury, Aldershot, pp. 17–58 (1987)
15. Ellis, R.D., Kurniawan, S.H.: Increasing the usability of online information for older users: a case study in participatory design. Int. J. Hum.-Comput. Interact. **12**(2), 263–276 (2000)
16. Floyd, C., Mehl, W.M., Resin, F.M., Schmidt, G., Wolf, G.: Out of Scandinavia: alternative approaches to software design and system development. Hum.-Comput. Interact. **4**(4), 253–350 (1989)

17. Foster, N.F., Gibbons, S.L. (eds.): Studying Students: The Undergraduate Research Project at the University of Rochester. Association of College and Research Libraries, Chicago (2007)
18. Foster, N.F., Dimmock, N., Bersani, A.: Participatory design of websites with web design workshops. Lib J. (2) (2008)
19. Harboe, G., Huang, E.M.: Real-world affinity diagramming practices: bridging the paper-digital gap. In: Proceedings of the 33rd Annual ACM Conference on Human Factors in Computing Systems, Seoul, pp. 95–104. ACM (2015)
20. Harkavy, I.: Back to the future: from service learning to strategic, academically-based community service. Metrop. Univ. Int. Forum **7**(1), 57–70 (1996)
21. Jaeger, P.T., Bertot, J.C., Subramaniam, M.: Preparing future librarians to effectively serve their communities. Libr. Q. **83**(3), 243–248 (2013)
22. Koh, K., Abbas, J.: Competencies for information professionals in learning labs and makerspaces. J. Educ. Libr. Inf. Sci. **56**(2), 114–129 (2015)
23. Lee, V.R., Phillips, A.L. (eds.): Reconceptualizing Libraries: Perspectives from the Information and Learning Sciences. Routledge, New York (2018)
24. Marquez, J., Downey, A.: Service design: an introduction to a holistic assessment methodology of library services. Weave: J. Libr. User Exp. **1**(2) (2015)
25. Merriam, S.B., Tisdell, E.J.: Qualitative Research: A Guide to Design and Implementation. Wiley, Hoboken (2015)
26. Moorefield-Lang, H.M.: Makers in the library: case studies of 3D printers and maker spaces in library settings. Library Hi Tech (2014)
27. Somerville, M.M., Brown-Sica, M.: Library space planning: a participatory action research approach. Electron. Libr. **29**(5), 669–681 (2011)
28. Spina, C., Lane, H.: E-textiles in Libraries: A Practical Guide for Librarians, (No. 69). Rowman & Littlefield Publishers, Lanham (2020)
29. Subramaniam, M., Scaff, L., Kawas, S., Hoffman, K.M., Davis, K.: Using technology to support equity and inclusion in youth library programming: current practices and future opportunities. Libr. Q. **88**(4), 315–331 (2018)
30. Oyelude, A.A.: Virtual reality (VR) and augmented reality (AR) in libraries and museums. Library Hi Tech News (2018)
31. Yip, J.C., et al.: Examining adult-child interactions in intergenerational participatory design. In: Proceedings of the 2017 CHI Conference on Human Factors in Computing Systems, Denver, CO, pp. 5742–5754. ACM (2017)
32. Yip, J.C., Lee, K.J., Lee, J.H.: Design partnerships for participatory librarianship: a conceptual model for understanding librarians co designing with digital youth. J. Am. Soc. Inf. Sci. **71**(10), 1242–1256 (2019)

A Pilot Ethnographic Study of Gamified English Learning Among Primary Four and Five Students in a Rural Chinese Primary School

Na Meng[1(✉)], Shum Yi Cameron Lee[2], and Samuel Kai Wah Chu[2]

[1] Jinling Institute of Technology, Nanjing, China
mengnacnnj@foxmail.com
[2] Faculty of Education, The University of Hong Kong, Hong Kong, China
{sycamlee,samchu}@hku.hk

Abstract. This pilot ethnographic study examines the feasibility of learning English with a gamified English e-learning platform among Primary Four (P4) and Primary Five (P5) students in a remote primary school in Henan, China. Forty-one students participated in a summer reading camp where the gamified platform in question was used. Results show that following 4 weeks of playing on the gamified platform, the majority of students developed substantial interest in reading more English books upon the fulfillment of their innate psychological needs for competence, relatedness and autonomy. The authors conclude that under a self-determination framework, the gamified platform has been effective in helping Chinese students in a rural community to learn English.

Keywords: Gamification · English reading literacy · Ethnographic study · Self-determination theory · Rural school

1 Introduction

English is a popular foreign language in China. Although many Chinese students learn English from as early as kindergarten [14], the education system can be a hurdle for those living in rural communities. The state's ringing document The English Curriculum Standards for Compulsory Education [8] prescribes that Primary Four (P4) and Five (P5) students should be able to understand short demands and orders in English, as well as read and understand simple stories and short essays with the help of visual aid like pictures. In rural communities however, that is simply unrealisable on P4 and P5 students. Gui and others in their 2019 survey found that over half of the survey participants who were English teachers in rural primary schools thought P4 and P5 students living in rural communities simply do not possess such a level of English ability that would allow them to meet state-envisaged standards [4]. Elsewhere, Qi's study [11] explained the incongruity between the state's expectations in English learning and students' actual English abilities by way of a qualitative study in which some students commented that their school, with its well-equipped facilities, had helped them learn English early on in

K. Toeppe et al. (Eds.): iConference 2021, LNCS 12645, pp. 575–586, 2021.
https://doi.org/10.1007/978-3-030-71292-1_45

their life, which enabled them to prepare well for the national college entrance examination and university, whereas some others from a lower socioeconomic background thought learning English only helped them insofar as their parents are appeased. Beset with this uneven distribution of resources accounting for a difference in perspectives, those lacking a means of access to a well-equipped learning environment inevitably fall behind the pack of others with relatively easier access. However, despite this hurdle, the growth by which educational technology developed in rural China in recent past [11] may work to level that playing field, a promising sign for rural students.

The notion that a proliferation of e-commerce can trickle down to education in rural parts of China is not as far-fetched as it sounds. In the 13th Five-Year Plan for Economic and Social Development in the People's Republic of China (2016–2020), one of the goals set by the state is that the poor of the nation can have access to the Internet, where teaching resources are increasingly stored and shared by means of cloud computing [5, 12]. The continuous efforts by the state and tech firms like Alibaba have borne tangible fruit: "The proportion of primary and secondary schools nationwide [including schools in rural and remote areas] connected to the network had exceeded 96%, helping to achieve education equalization and laying a solid foundation for network poverty alleviation" [6]. If such development continues unbridled, then it is likely that the goal of diminishing the education gap in China will further be realised at the most grassroots level, i.e. the village. On the other hand, what is most needed for China now is a creative (and practical) solution by which that goal can be crystallized. In this regard, the present study can be understood as that creative (and practical) agent of change, framed around the author's wish of encouraging rural Chinese students to learn English more by introducing a gamified platform to a rural primary school classroom.

The gamified platform concerned is named Reading Battle. With its game design principle, the platform has such game elements as leaderboard, e-badges, levels and a point system, all of which encourage players to keep track of their own progress. In the game, students must read the ebooks provided by external ebook systems, go back to the gamified platform, and solve the corresponding reading challenges. It has a total of 9,000 reading comprehension questions derived from close to 300 English books suitable for primary school students. The students under investigation in this study, comprising 18 boys and 23 girls (n = 41), were between 10 to 12-years old. They studied in P4 and P5 levels of SPDP, a village primary school in Henan, a Chinese province known for its agriculture. The students studying there are thus qualified as rural students, for whom owning a computer and having a language lesson delivered through a piece of educational technology were a luxury. It is on this note that Reading Battle, with its system design aimed to cater to children users, could help. The study itself took place between June 29 and July 26, 2020, during which the students were invited to read a number of English ebooks and complete the corresponding sets of reading challenges on Reading Battle. One of the authors was the voluntary summer English teacher during this time to gain a holistic understanding on the impact of the gamified platform on the students' English learning.

2 Research Questions

To examine the feasibility of learning English using a gamified platform, this study is framed around the main question of how Reading Battle motivated Chinese students in SPDP to learn English over the course of a summer reading camp. Pertaining to this question are three sub-questions modelled after the three pillars of self-determination theory:

1. How was the students' need for competence satisfied in the reading camp?
2. How was the students' need for relatedness satisfied in the reading camp?
3. How was the students' need for autonomy satisfied in the reading camp?

In relation to the main and sub-questions, we designed, implemented, and analysed the results derived from questionnaires, interviews, and participant observation. All data have been translated throughout this study (with the original wordings appended in Appendix 1).

3 Literature Review

In the current technology-driven culture (a term that appeared in Palmer's study [9]), adults are advised to take on a nuanced stance in structuring their children's life around technology [10]. Emerging from this cautious tone of a wider techno-averse tenor of the book is quite the reverse of those sentiments: when prudently applied, technology can and will put a child on a trajectory of success in life. In effect, what Plowman, Stephen and McPake [10] are actually promoting is a notable concept in the literature of adolescent education: the gamification of learning, or the application of game elements in an educational context with the goal of influencing learners' behaviour [3]. This study, in seeking to contribute to adolescent education, is derived from a theoretical presumption that reading, too, can be gamified and that a gamified platform can influence young learners of English to love reading and in doing so they put themselves on track to success.

Reading is an effective way of acquiring any language. The more one reads, the better it helps with the articulation of thoughts and ideas [7]. For Chinese youth, English literacy has a national importance attached, given that it is a mandatory school subject from Primary Three onwards in the state curriculum [8] and a popular foreign language subject on the National College Entrance Examination [1, 13]. As will be discussed in the following sections, how rural Chinese youths perceive and learn English in daily life will be understood with respect to their own learning goals, the school environment, and the gamified platform applied in this study.

Self-determination theory [2] is the study of human behavior that postulates if a person's three innate psychological needs—competence, relatedness and autonomy— are satisfied, that person will be motivated to strive to do better. Based on this theory, this study defines that: competence involves the reading skills picked up while using the gamified platform; relatedness refers to the relationships with parents and peers developed over the course of using the gamified platform; and autonomy can be said as the control over one's learning choices when using the gamified platform.

4   Methodology

In gamification literature, some studies with a quantitative design have largely overlooked the subjective experience of the users, which is critical in the overall assessment of the gamified platform, as any negative systemic issues hiding in plain sight can be brought up and patched. As such, the authors studied the students within the reading camp in the hopes of understanding their English learning in a day-to-day, informal setting. Towards this end, the study had three stages in its development (see Fig. 1).

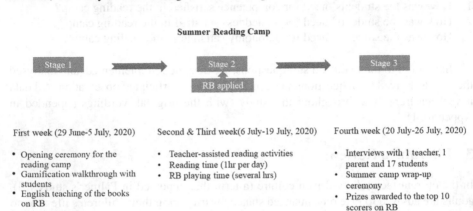

Summer Reading Camp

First week (29 June-5 July, 2020)	Second & Third week(6 July-19 July, 2020)	Fourth week (20 July-26 July, 2020)
• Opening ceremony for the reading camp • Gamification walkthrough with students • English teaching of the books on RB • Questionnaire survey	• Teacher-assisted reading activities • Reading time (1hr per day) • RB playing time (several hrs)	• Interviews with 1 teacher, 1 parent and 17 students • Summer camp wrap-up ceremony • Prizes awarded to the top 10 scorers on RB

Fig. 1. Overview of the study development

In the reading camp (as shown in Appendix 2), a typical day began with an hour of required silent reading time, followed by a free learning period where students could come and go to the computer lab on their own accord to use the gamified platform. The research team was stationed in the lab for the entire day and every day of the reading camp to help with any student who stayed in there. Given the opportunity to study the students closely inside the lab, participant observation took place on the spot.

4.1   Questionnaire

The pre-study questionnaire was a crucial instrument in helping the researchers to obtain behavioural data about the students, including their English level, their reading habits, and their perceptions towards English. It was distributed to students at the beginning of Stage 1 of the study design (Fig. 1). A total of 12 boys and 16 girls had completed the surveys. Results revealed that 88% of P4 and P5 students had no computer knowledge or any prior experience reading English on an electronic device. Most students had no idea what a website was, and only 6 students had come across an ebook, let alone read one on their own. Some computer knowledge was needed to read on the gamified platform, so some students were scared off due to a lack of it, such as S-LJH (each student in the study is assigned a pseudonym to ensure that their privacy is respected), while S-LXR and S-ZZY were not allowed to freely use any electronic device at home or elsewhere, since their parents imposed stern house rules restricting the use of electronics. To ensure that each student had access to the gamified platform, the research team had therefore arranged for the reading camp in the school's computer lab.

4.2 Interviews

At the end of the implementation, student and teacher interviews were conducted. The interviews were conducted at various places: in the classroom, at the teacher lounge, and in the computer lab to ensure that the interviewer could speak privately with individual interviewees one at a time. All of the interviews were video recorded and stored carefully for data protection and security.

4.3 Participant Observation

As the reading camp was held over the summer holiday of the school, all the English teachers had been on leave. In their stead, one of the authors had helped with the students, guiding them to use the computer in the school lab, monitoring much of the activities on the gamified platform, and ensuring a proper classroom decorum was adhered to inside the reading camp.

5 Results and Discussion

5.1 How was the Students' Need for Competence Satisfied in the Reading Camp?

Competence is the feeling that one is proficient in a certain task or skill. Based on the student questionnaires, eighty-eight percent of students believed that their vocabulary had expanded; that they became more competent in the English language; and that they had polished their own reading skills over the course of the camp.

Expanded Vocabulary Bank
Fifteen students commented that they had learned more English words, two of whom mentioned (Table 1):

Table 1. Comments

Comments
By using the gamified platform, I learned more English words (S-JGP)
I can understand new words, which I didn't know before (S-ZRZ)

More English Knowledge
Thirteen students remarked that they had acquired some reading skills while playing on the gamified platform (Table 2):

Table 2. Comments

Comments
Before gameplay:
Before I used the gamified platform, I would skip any new words when I read (S-LMY)
Before using the gamified platform, I did not know what to do with new words that I learned (S-LXR)
Before using the gamified platform, I would read books cursorily without fully comprehending the content (S-LBX)
After gameplay:
Now, I will seek help from teachers and classmates, and I will look up an English dictionary (S-LMY)
Now, I will try to guess a word by associating it with what I know, and understand its meaning from the context (S-LXR)
Now, I can understand the meaning of books well before answering questions on the gamified platform (S-LBX)

Improvised Reading Skills

Three came up with their own reading skills while tackling difficult reading problems (Table 3):

Table 3. Comments

Comments
When I saw new words, I would ask the teachers. If the teachers were not around, I would try to guess from the text's context on my own (S-JGP)
Now I think very carefully for the answer when questions get difficult (S-LZX)
Before using the gamified platform, I gave up pretty quickly when I found out there were so many questions on the exam. Now, after I used the gamified platform, the questions which were difficult for me seem to be easier (S-LZX)

5.2   How was the Students' Need for Relatedness Satisfied in the Reading Camp?

Relatedness is about the relationships fostered between one and one's immediate circle of attendants. In this study, the students became closer with their parents and peers in the computer lab over their reading journeys on the gamified platform.

More Time with Parents

Throughout the reading camp, students had more time with their parents at home where they read books together (Table 4):

Table 4. Comments

Comments
I like to have my parents join me when I read. I can now understand what my parents went through in raising me up; how they would feel when they care of me. I got this insight from a book I read on the gamified platform (S-LZX)
When I gave the wrong answers, my parents encouraged me and told me "It's okay to make mistakes, keep going!" (S-QSE)
While using the gamified platform, I like to have my parents with me because they can help me understand a word if I don't (S-YZY)

Connection and Constructive Competition with Peers

The gamified platform also seemed to drive connection between peers in the lab, as one student said (Table 5):

Table 5. Comment

Comment
In the past, if I came across English questions that bogged me down, I would never ask my classmates for help. But this has changed. Since I used the gamified platform, I was not too afraid of speaking up anymore because nobody in the class knew I would get a wrong answer. (S-ZW)

Other students felt the class had become competitive but in a way that fueled them to study together more (Table 6).

Table 6. Comment

Comment
I was not keen into reading before. But when I see the leaderboard, the thought that my classmates have all worked so hard is on my mind. If I do not study more, I will surely fall behind the rest of the class. (S-QSE)

5.3   How was the Students' Need for Autonomy Satisfied in the Reading Camp?

Autonomy refers to the feeling when one is in control of one's actions. Since the reading camp, students have been able to make their own individual calls on when to read, what genre to read, and how often to read.

When to Read

In the reading camp, many students became self-directed in their reading (Table 7):

Table 7. Comments

Comments
I seldom read in the past, let alone willing to read one. Now I read books out of my own accord (S-QSE)
I didn't take reading seriously. I used to hate reading. Now I want to read books. Not only do I not hate books, I also want to read them (S-ZW)
I used to feel intimidated when I saw a book. Now that I see a book, I want to pick it up and read aloud softly (S-ZW)

A quintessential example of behavioural change is S-ZW, who caught the attention of the teacher in the school. In the interview, the teacher (Teacher 1) elaborated (sic):

ZW was an under-motivated learner. He never paid attention in class and was never able to complete his English homework. I have always felt he was not too keen in learning at all. But since the reading camp, he seemed to have come to school with enthusiasm and used the computer more. All and all, he seemed to have changed his way of reading and learning.

Considering that S-ZW was a student with little to no motivation in learning, his changes have been transformative.

What Genre to Read

Whereas before the camp many students had never read an English book other than the state-prescribed textbooks (as affirmed in Qi's 2016 study), this study had introduced them to other genres unbeknownst to them (Table 8):

Table 8. Comments

Comments
Before using the gamified platform, I only read English textbooks, but now I read extracurricular English books, in addition to textbooks (S-YZY and S-QSE)
I never read a lot of books because my parents have never thought of getting books for me. Now I read all kinds of books, including folk tales, sciences, non-fiction or fairy tales. (S-LMY)

How Often to Read

Three students told the interviewer that they were now happy to read everyday (Table 9):

Table 9. Comments

Comments
I read books every day since I started using the gamified platform. I now find reading very interesting (S-CY)
(Since I used the gamified platform) I found reading quite meaningful and read every day (S-LMY)
Before using the gamified platform, I read books once a week. However, I read books every day now. Even if my parents do not buy me any books, I can read on the gamified platform (S-LXR)

6 Conclusion

This pilot ethnographic study has proven that Reading Battle was successfully run in a rural village in China. Based on the evidence gathered in participant observation and questionnaires, students were more motivated to learn English on the gamified platform than prior to the study. In Deci and Ryan's self-determination theory, the students, with their innate needs for competence, relatedness and autonomy fulfilled, can be said to have a strong tendency to outperform themselves in the reading camp. On a final note, the authors are optimistic that future gamification research in rural settings will be a worthwhile undertaking.

Acknowledgement. Our thanks go to SPDP who had welcomed us into Henan for this study.

Appendix 1: Students' Comments in the Original Chinese Wording (Listed in the Order of Appearance In Text)

See Appendix Tables 10, 11, 12.

Table 10. Competence

Students	Comments
(S-JGP)	使用阅读大挑战之后,让我们认识许多的英语单词,学会了以前不认识的英语单词。
(S-ZRZ)	认识了很多英语单词。
(S-LMY)	之前阅读的时候,有许多单词不会,然后就直接略过。
(S-LXR)	以前有很多单词不认识,就不管了。
(S-LBX)	以前,眼睛扫一眼就算了。
(S-LMY)	现在有不会的单词会问老师,也可以向旁边的同学问问,也可以自己查词典。
(S-LXR)	现在可以进行推测猜想。
(S-LBX)	现在,会先弄懂意思再去挑战做题。
(S-JGP)	不会的英语单词,问老师。老师不在身边,联系上下文自己猜。
(S-LZX)	遇到不会的题要多加思考,这样会找出更正确的答案。
(S-LZX)	以前,遇到一本书有很多题就会放弃。现在做了RB,觉得这些题变得特别简单。

Table 11. Relatedness

Students	Comments
(S-LZX)	我喜欢父母陪着我读书。我现在能理解父母。因为有一本书的内容让我体会到父母很辛苦。
(S-QSE)	我做错题的时候,他们会在旁边激励自己"错了没关系,继续"。
(S-YZY)	读书的时候,我喜欢父母的陪伴。因为有不会的单词的时候,他们可以给我解释。
(S-ZW)	以前遇到不会的题,不敢问同学。现在用了阅读大挑战,遇到不会的问同学,即使答错了,同学也不会笑你,因为同学们不知道是谁。
(S-QSE)	以前不重视阅读。因为从排行榜上看到其他同学那么努力的学习,如果我不学习,感觉太落后。

Table 12. Autonomy

Students	Comments
(S-QSE)	之前读的书特别少,而且不是很情愿读书。以前没有什么积极性,现在特别想读。
(S-ZW)	以前一点都不重视。以前看见书就觉得恶心,现在看见书,不但不觉得恶心还有点想读。
(S-ZW)	因为之前看到书就害怕,现在看到书,不会那么恐惧,就会拿起来看,然后小声的读。
(S-YZY, S-QSE)	以前都是课内的书,现在可以读课外的书。
(S-LMY)	因为之前都是不会去读那么多的书,爸爸妈妈也没有给我买。现在什么类型的书我都读,民间故事、科学类的、非小说类、童话故事什么都读。
(S-CY)	现在每天都读书,因为现在感觉读书非常有趣。
(S-LMY)	每天读的都很有意思。
(S-LXR)	以前一个星期读一次。现在每天都读。之前家长不是经常买书,现在可以在手机上读。

Appendix 2: Students Concentrated on Reading on the Gamified Learning Platform

See Appendix Figs. 2 and 3

Fig. 2. A silent reading period of the summer camp

Fig. 3. A different angle of the class during silent reading

References

1. Bianco, J., Orton, J., Gao, Y. (eds.): China and English: Globalisation and the Dilemmas of Identity. Multilingual Matters, Bristol, UK (2009)
2. Deci, E., Ryan, R.: A motivational approach to self: integration in personality. In: Dienstbier, R. (ed.) Nebraska Symposium on Motivation, Perspectives on Motivation, vol. 38, pp. 237–288. University of Nebraska Press, Lincoln (1991)
3. Deterding, S., Dixon, D., Khaled, R., Nacke, L.: From game design elements to gamefulness: defining gamification. In: Proceedings of the 15th International Academic MindTrek Conference: Envisioning Future Media Environments 2011, pp. 9–15. ACM, Tampere, Finland (2011)
4. Gui, M., He, Y., Shang, Y., Yu, Y.: Rural area primary school english teachers' perception of the english course standards for compulsory education农村小学英语教师对《课标》的认识. Basic Foreign Lang. Educ. **21**(2), 39–46 (2019)
5. Hong, Y.: China launches national cloud learning platform as teaching goes online amid epidemic. China Global Television Network, 21 February 2020. https://news.cgtn.com/news/2020-02-19/China-launches-national-cloud-learning-platform-for-online-education-Ods9XruOR2/index.html
6. Internet Network and Information Center: In: 45th Statistical Report on Internet Development, p. 17, April 2020. https://cnnic.com.cn/IDR/ReportDownloads/202008/P020200827549953874912.pdf
7. Krashen, S.D.: Free Voluntary Reading. Libraries Unlimited, Santa Barbara, CA (2011)
8. Ministry of Education, The People's Republic of China: Standard English Curriculum in Compulsory Education, 2011 (edn.) 义务教育英语课程标准(2011年版). Beijing Normal University Press, Beijing (2011)
9. Palmer, S.: Toxic Childhood: How the Modern World Is Damaging Our Children and What We Can Do About It. Orion, London, UK (2006)
10. Plowman, L., Stephen, C., McPake, J.: Growing Up With Technology: Young Children Learning in a Digital World. Routledge, New York, NY (2010)

11. Qi, G.Y.: The importance of English in primary school education in China: perceptions of students. Multiling. Educ. **6**(1), 1–18 (2016)
12. The 13th Five-Year Plan for Economic and Social Development of the People's Republic of China 2016-2020. Central Compilation & Translation Press, Beijing (n.d.)
13. Zhao, Y.: World Class Learners: Educating Creative and Entrepreneurial Students. Corwin Press, Thousand Oaks, CA (2012)
14. Zhou, W.: Children make early start at learning English. China Daily, 24 January 2019. https://www.chinadaily.com.cn/a/201901/24/WS5c48f51da3106c65c34e629f.html

Multidisciplinary Blockchain Research and Design: A Case Study in Moving from Theory to Pedagogy to Practice

Chelsea K. Palmer[1]([✉]) [iD], Chris Rowell[2], and Victoria L. Lemieux[1] [iD]

[1] School of Information, University of British Columbia, Vancouver, BC, Canada
chisel@student.ubc.ca, v.lemieux@ubc.ca
[2] Sauder School of Business, University of British Columbia, Vancouver, BC, Canada
christopher.rowell@sauder.ubc.ca

Abstract. The application of multidisciplinary theoretical models in an emerging field of study like blockchain can improve both collaborative learning and solution design, especially by creating a valuable shared language for colleagues from different disciplinary areas. This tripartite paper traces a journey from theory to practice by outlining the origin and development of the theoretical 'three layer trust model' for blockchain technologies, discussing the pedagogical utility of this model within a virtual education setting, and describing a student's application of the learned model in a technical blockchain product design setting. By providing a thorough grounding in the complex multidisciplinary balance involved in designing blockchain systems (and adding the autoethnographic reflections of participants in this multi-setting focal design application) the following paper supports the potential value of such theoretical models to establish shared language for complex concepts across disciplinary divides. Future research directions are suggested to establish greater validity for the concepts presented within this paper and dive deeper into the foundations of its many referenced disciplines.

Keywords: Multidisciplinary Design · Blockchain · Pedagogy

1 Introduction

The application of multidisciplinary theoretical models in an emerging field of study like blockchain can improve both collaborative learning and solution design, especially by creating a valuable shared language for colleagues from different disciplinary areas of expertise. While intentionally collaborative methods may not strictly be required in traditional pedagogy and design, they can be greatly beneficial for research, learning, and application in nascent technological domains, as we discuss in this paper. The context of this participatory research, focused on climate change solutions, demanded innovative ideation from all its collaborators. This tripartite paper first covers the origin and development of the theoretical three layer trust model for blockchain technologies, then discusses the pedagogical utility of this model within a virtual education setting, before

K. Toeppe et al. (Eds.): iConference 2021, LNCS 12645, pp. 587–602, 2021.
https://doi.org/10.1007/978-3-030-71292-1_46

describing the application of that learned model by one of the students in a technical blockchain product design setting.

The following paper begins with a literature review of terminology from the blockchain and distributed ledger field, and the concepts of social trust modeled therein. It will then shift to coverage of the established literature on multidisciplinary collaboration and tools to support it, as well as the broad range of design methodologies which lay the groundwork for our proposed approach. This will be followed by an overview of the background and context of the research described, as well as the specific methods used, and finally "Reflections on the Student Experience and Findings," which will switch briefly to a more personal narrative and reflection. Since this research was preliminary, its most significant contribution is as a qualitative account of the impact on teaching and design of collaboratively defined multidisciplinary tools like the three layer model we discuss. Overall, this contribution aims to highlight both strengths and areas of suggested improvement for the multidisciplinary model which we will describe in more depth below.

2 Background

Tricky problems and ethical conundrums in design are not a new topic in the realm of arts and material manufacture [1]. Similarly, multidisciplinarity - which we define for purposes of this paper as a process wherein people from different disciplines work together on a problem solution, each drawing on their disciplinary knowledge - has been well attended to in the networked learning space, as have critical design thinking and practice-focused design methodologies [2]. Additionally, critical perspectives on ethics and design are well established in the field of communications [3]. There is even an increasing adoption of ethics-centered approaches in science and technology design [4, 5]. Across all these approaches, a "design methodology" is any research approach which employs design frameworks or principles as one of its central elements.

In general, multidisciplinary frameworks and analyses prove useful in the study and design of complex computing systems in knowledge societies [6–8]. Additionally, multidisciplinarity is a recurring concern in novel technological education and networked learning [9–11]. Finally, multidisciplinarity arises as a core concern for iSchools in general, due to the tradition of the library and information sciences indexing all other disciplines at a meta-level [12]. Derry et al. establishes an early understanding that collaboration across disciplines involves unique elements of human cognition and communication [13]. Monk builds a parallel argument for the importance of developing shared language, and thus "common ground," in multidisciplinary undertakings [14]. Paletz presents a similar finding from multidisciplinary teams working with big data: effective communication starts with building shared mental models for the complex intersecting topics at hand [8]. Taken as a whole, this research drives home the potential value of explicitly collaborative methods for learning and design when focused on intrinsically multidisciplinary topics.

The following paper will present a design methodology which extends the Multidisciplinary Design Optimization [MDO] model [15]. Whereas MDO is often multidisciplinary across technical disciplines (e.g. building spacecraft, airplanes, self-driving vehicles), Lemieux and Feng's three layer model recognizes blockchains as fundamentally *socio-information-technical* systems revolving around social trust goals [16]. This distinction suggests that existing MDO frameworks are not fully suitable to blockchain design, thus Lemieux and Feng have further iterated on the specific requirements of blockchains and other distributed ledger technologies in this context [16]. The closest parallel research is Carroll and Bellotti's exploration of "the emerging design space of peer-to-peer currency," but even this work produced more broadly descriptive themes rather than a rigorous and potentially replicable, systems model [17].

3 Theory

3.1 Blockchain as a Multidisciplinary Design Space

While it is beyond the scope of the present paper to cover all facets of blockchain's multidisciplinarity, we will briefly establish preferred definitions for the terminology used herein. These preferred definitions are drawn from those established by International Organization for Standardization's [ISO] Standard 22739, which was formed with the input of over three hundred global experts collaborating across three years. Most crucially, ISO Standard 22739 establishes that *Distributed Ledger Technology* [DLT] utilizes shared ledgers which are coordinated and synchronized across a network via consensus mechanism, and that a *blockchain* is a specific type of distributed ledger data structure that appends data blocks which are confirmed as valid by the network consensus mechanism to a continuous, immutable chain [18]. These network effects are enabled by distributed computing systems, and often include an element of decentralization in control of the system. Both DLTs and their structural subset of blockchains rely on rigid standards of confirmation and validation to establish an on-chain norm for trust (which can be reliably verified by network participants) [19]. Despite the part-and-whole relationship established by the ISO standard, for simplicity in this paper we will simply refer to all types of distributed ledgers, including blockchains, by the term *blockchains*.

Multiple open access resources exist as foundational introductions to blockchain, distributed ledgers, and cryptoeconomics.[1] There are many volumes on the multidisciplinary concerns introduced by nascent blockchain technology. Some of these focus on the changes in law and regulations that may arise from decentralized protocols [23–25]. Other essays and texts cover the broader social, political, and economic implications of these tools and platforms [26–29]. Numerous papers cover technical aspects of DLT and blockchain design, including the common information architectures and consensus mechanisms utilized in these systems [19, 30–32].

Given the multidisciplinary focus of blockchain design efforts, one might expect that trade-offs among different design dimensions would be well-studied in the blockchain design field. So far, however, this is not the case. The most often cited design trade-off is "Buterin's Scalability Trilemma," which invokes the necessary compromises involved in balancing scalability, decentralization, and security in a "best of two" circumstance [30]. Additionally, these systems are further complicated by their reliance upon, and interoperation with, communities that are often contentious and non-homogeneous, in

---

[1] For further introductory reading on this topic see [20–22].

which unpredictable agents can disrupt the planned flow of ecosystem participation and governance [26].

Social trust can be taken as the idea that "one party to the relation believes the other party has incentive to act in his or her interest or to take his or her interest to heart" [33]. Numerous writers have associated blockchain technology with increased social trust of this kind [25, 33, 34]. At the technological level, one of the core driving factors behind this social trust association is these systems' incorporation of key-based cryptography and digital signatures from the cybersecurity field [35]. As the ISO standard vocabulary highlights, the critical quality of immutability in blockchain systems provides another foundation for a very specific sort of trust: network participants know that ledger records cannot be altered after they have been added to the chain of confirmed blocks [18].

In the ISO standard vocabulary, trust is itself defined as "the degree to which a user or other stakeholder has confidence that a product or system will behave as expected by that user or other stakeholder" [18]. ISO's more technical-focused definition of trust fits well with a focus on multidisciplinary systems. Taken together, these varied and granular definitions of trust within the blockchain context help illuminate its distinction from traditional notions of reputation-based interpersonal trust. Despite this attempted transition away from the importance of reputation, some research with cryptocurrency users suggests that elements of human and institutional trust are still widespread within these communities [36]. Beyond that, some authors seek to highlight that in a blockchain's technical information architecture is itself based upon trust between nodes [37].

3.2 Blockchain: The Three Layer Model as a Multidisciplinary Pedagogical and Design Framework

In this paper, our goal is to focus on how the three layer model provides a framework for generative conversations across and among epistemic communities for pedagogy and design. Lemieux and Feng's three layer trust model, which goes beyond fixed declarative definitions, was motivated by a desire to both broaden and deepen consideration of the necessary tradeoffs in blockchain solution design, which they argue will lead to better solutions with fewer unintended negative consequences [16]. By architecting space for generative discussions to arise around the complexity of multidisciplinary problems, the three layer trust model moves beyond the projection of rigid categorical definitions for specific material forms of "trust" seen in earlier research in the blockchain and cryptocurrency space [36, 38].

In 2018, the three layer trust model was born of the need to develop an appropriate framework for the problem-centered design of blockchains, in which the problems are themselves "wicked," multidimensional, and multidisciplinary [39]. Systems designed from a single point of view have often proved to have "blind" spots which render them ineffective, or even dangerous [40]. With this in mind, we aimed to design a framework which encouraged holistic problem analysis and afforded a common language, underpinned by a reasonably shared ontology and epistemic worldview [16]. The framework this produced was intended to enable meaningful engagement in the design process from graduate students in disciplines as diverse as engineering, business, and the arts. This three layer trust model establishes blockchain as an inherently multidisciplinary field of study, much in the same way that scholars are establishing artificial intelligence as multidisciplinary [41].

In 2019, a diverse group of blockchain scholars came together at the University of British Columbia to discuss Lemieux's original three layer model, especially the interactions among its three layers. This led to further theoretical refinements of the model. The primary change introduced at this stage arose from collaborators recognizing it more as a complex, dynamic systems model with four complex, interrelated sub-systems. In addition to refining the previous model, these ideas generated novel reflections on the capabilities and properties typically associated with blockchains (such as decentralization, security, governance, provenance and incentives) that were captured in an updated theoretical model disseminated to students in the Blockchain@UBC Summer Institute course. This new model conceived of the original three layers (the social, the informational and the technical) as sub-systems of blockchains as large complex, dynamic systems, and added a governance sub-system. The model also incorporated temporal and environmental interactions (see Appendix A).

4   Pedagogy

Over the past few years, there has been an increasingly visible output of research on blockchain in relationship to education and pedagogy. While many of these publications focus primarily on the use of blockchain technology as a supporting infrastructure to disrupt the creation, storage, and access of academic records and certifications, augment admissions processes, and enable new pedagogical approaches (e.g. [42–45]), a handful of papers provide valuable insights to the specific challenges of effectively weaving together the multidisciplinary threads of blockchain in teaching.

Blockchain's inherent conceptual novelty, stemming from its foundational and transformative nature [46], means that a fundamental shift in student mindset may be necessary to grasp its core tenets [47]. To address this, scholars have found active learning and gamification to be effective approaches for helping students explore and comprehend basic principles of blockchain, such as how data is structured and secured via cryptographic methods [47], and how the network can reach consensus on the state of the ledger [48]. Beyond basic principles, other scholars have argued that blockchain education should be applied to real-world business cases [49], emphasizing the entrepreneurial process and the co-creation of knowledge [50]. Together, prior research concludes that pedagogical approaches to blockchain education should be experiential, collaborative, and focused on real-world processes and outcomes which empower students' agentic behavior.

Our setting for multidisciplinary blockchain education was the 2020 Blockchain@UBC Summer Institute. This was the Institute's fourth overall iteration and the first time this was offered as a for-credit graduate-level course. In response to the COVID-19 pandemic, it was also the first delivery of this summer program in a fully virtual setting. The course was delivered over two full weeks of morning and afternoon sessions via online lectures facilitated by a primary instructor with guest speakers from industry and academia. Each session involved immersive case-based discussions and engagement in small virtual breakout groups.

The graduate students participating in this course came to the first session with various degrees of exposure to blockchain concepts, from absolute newcomers to relatively well-established industry participants, and from diverse disciplinary backgrounds (including Library and Archival Science, Electrical Engineering, Computer Science, Public Policy and Global Affairs, Psychology, Public Health, Occupational Therapy, and Business Administration). The course aimed to help this diverse cohort gain a holistic understanding of blockchain as a foundational technology and an appreciation of the different perspectives that contribute to blockchain use case design, analysis, and critique. A diversity of perspectives was emphasized as important for spurring innovation and creativity, and for helping to ensure that blockchain-based solutions not only create value, but also minimize social harm. In line with our inherently multidisciplinary goals, teaching combined systems-thinking and design-centric approaches anchored by the three layer trust model.

The course began by presenting the foundations of blockchain and distributed ledger technologies, including key definitions and core capabilities. Students were then introduced to the notion of blockchain use cases as complex systems, and to the three layer model of blockchain system design. During the first week of the Institute, students gained exposure to a range of use case applications across multiple industries, public sector domains, and social issues (including social media, finance, climate change, public procurement, healthcare, Indigenous data governance, and sports management). In the second week, the focus turned to more hands-on sessions that walked through how the three layer trust model is applied in existing blockchain systems to enable profoundly new capabilities (such as a self-sovereign digital identity for individuals).

At this point, students were also tasked with finding an academic article from their own discipline and communicating its core contribution(s) in a discussion post for a general audience by relating it to the three layer model and its practical implications. Students then reviewed and commented on one another's posts. The objective here was to sharpen students' ability to communicate the value of their own discipline in a multidisciplinary setting, deepen their appreciation for different perspectives, and facilitate a dialogue between these. The course concluded with a miniature virtual blockchain hackathon, where students worked in groups to design and present blockchain systems of their own that addressed issues related to the global pandemic. Groups were formed by the instructor to optimize their diversity with respect to academic discipline, gender identity, and cultural background.

Throughout the two weeks, the three layer model provided a common frame for examining blockchain use cases and designing new ones, which helped to ensure that multiple perspectives were effectively communicated and integrated in student collaboration and analysis. This grounding allowed students to gain an appreciation of the various disciplines involved in blockchain system design and governance, ensuring that multiple voices were heard in group collaborations.

5 Practice

Upon completion of the Summer Institute, one of the graduate students that attended the course proceeded to utilize the three layer trust model as a core project planning document in the discovery of scope and technical specifications for a blockchain solution prototype. In this section, we focus on an exemplar solution design (the focal solution design), which is explored in the format of an autoethnographic reflection from a graduate student who was first introduced to the three layer trust model within the pedagogical setting described above. This focal solution design setting aimed to deliver a Proof of Concept for the nonprofit Blockchain for Climate Foundation's mission to put the UNFCCC's Paris Agreement for carbon credit trading on a public blockchain ledger platform. Building upon Blockchain for Climate Foundation's long-standing warm relationships within the public Ethereum blockchain ecosystem, the graduate student employed a toolkit which combined the three layer trust model's framework with a "user stories"-driven Agile project management methodology, borrowed from the design practices of a local web development team [51]. This helped set the stage for a practical system prototype (which is presently being built by a blockchain developer), to model potential behavior for a fully featured platform fulfilling the United Nations' Paris Agreement carbon credit trading requirements.

On weekly check-in calls, and with asynchronous document collaboration in between, the small team brought together domain expertise from the carbon reduction industry, blockchain ethics, and user-centric design thinking to fully define and scope a prototype for implementation on an Ethereum blockchain test-net in Fall 2020. Along the way, the illuminating Question-Led Systems Three Layer Model Design Framework (Appendix A) consistently anchored the team's conversations around long-term social trust implications of many seemingly minute design choices for the prototype. At times, the team was thoroughly stumped by how to answer some of the higher-level questions from this framework. Inevitably, those questions that the team found hardest to answer served the most illuminating role in defining what still needed to be explored in the context of the proposed carbon credit trading use case.

6 Reflections on the Student Experience and Findings

My first exposure to the three layer model was through the Question-Led DLT Systems Design Framework in the context of an implementation of the first fully virtual Blockchain@UBC Summer Institute. This accelerated-pace course, which was offered through UBC's iSchool, took place just a few months after the COVID-19 lockdown. Many plans were in transition at that point, and many courses were understandably cancelled. I remember being quite happy to hear the Summer Institute was moving forward as planned for its fourth year. I had the pleasure of being present for the first two instances of this Summer Institute, and its corresponding Blockathon, as a community organizer in the blockchain space, and looked forward to experiencing it as a student for the first time.

The Question-Led DLT Systems Design Framework was presented to us early on to contextualize the projects and use cases we explored. Rather than being left to come up with discussion prompts on our own or sticking to the broader questions that might be provided by an instructor on the spot, we had a consistent anchoring document to refer to throughout all our group discussion sessions. It also proved to draw us together across disciplines, providing broader and deeper discussion points than we could have generated on our own. As the peers in my group came from outside my own graduate department in the iSchool, the shared language this model and its anchoring documents provided was supportive of much more productive collaboration than we might have achieved if we each tried to use mental models from our own preferred fields.

The one struggle we found with the model, and Question-Led Framework, was its sheer complexity and the many possible avenues available to converse upon. Especially in instances where we had a briefer period available to apply the framework to a given use case, the necessity to determine that pathway from first principles took up some time. Still, this was mostly a challenge of familiarity, because as our team became more accustomed to the full range of framing questions, we were better skilled at jumping directly into the relevant categories in analysis of any given blockchain system example. Any early stumbling blocks in our comprehension of the three layer model proved well worth the challenge, considering how useful this framework proved in the final deliverable for the course: our virtual implementation of a "Blockathon for Social Good" use case.

In this final group project, we worked with our established team to design a blockchain-based solution to any number of problems resulting from the actively unfolding COVID-19 pandemic. Our team chose to focus on supply chain coordination of vital consumer goods, which at that time were being stocked unreliably online and on grocery store shelves. Seeking to utilize already-existing government support for local-grown produce, we proposed the introduction of a verifiable and subsidized online platform for accessing food, toilet paper, and hand sanitizer at a time when these were difficult items for many to obtain. Our familiarity with the three layer trust model and its related concepts gave us excellent grounding to clearly define the system's goals, constraints, and capabilities in a tangible fashion. Perhaps the greatest value of our past use of the three layer model became clear as we constructed our final presentation on the project. At this point, our team realized we had started to unconsciously lean in the direction of automatically discussing the model's multiple complex axes[2] from the outset of any conversation about the system we were proposing.

Additionally, the paid summer collaboration I undertook with Blockchain for Climate Foundation, bolstered by an Innovator Skills Initiative Grant from New Ventures BC, was directly anchored in the Summer Institute course and its use of the three layer model. Although I had been operating as a de facto "blockchain professional" for a handful of years, primarily as a community educator on Bitcoin, I had not previously felt confident in my capacity to legitimately architect the technical requirements for a blockchain-based system. The hands-on curriculum design, driving us to collaboratively apply the three layer model's concepts to analyze multiple consecutive projects lent me greater confidence in the recurrent elements and building blocks of these systems. Most crucially, I was able to utilize the thorough Question-Led Framework to frame useful planning discussions about what might go wrong in engineering such a system. This meant these high-level concerns were discussed thoroughly in the technical specification discovery process, well before a single line of code was written.

---

[2] Representing social, informational, technical, and governance sub-systems, with the temporal and environmental axes in mind as well. See Appendix A for more details.

The public and permissionless blockchain our team focused on, Ethereum, is currently in the process of altering its foundational consensus mechanism [52]. This transition (from Proof-of-Work to Proof-of-Stake consensus) is intended to mitigate deleterious environmental effects of blockchain technology and support more effective scaling for widespread global use. The still-shifting timeline for this transition presented one of the significant challenges in the Blockchain for Climate Foundation's initial design decisions: should we build a full implementation based on the current Ethereum Proof-of-Work norms, or wait until the transition to ETH 2.0 became clearer? By utilizing the Question-led Framework to anchor our scope discussions, we could more clearly delineate necessary requirements for an immediate prototype in contrast to long-term design goals for the full system (these latter aspirations were recorded for later reference).

Finally, the more subtle gains from utilizing the three layer model and its foundational documents when planning an Ethereum system prototype were related to its efficacy as a lens on the previously "unknown unknowns." While some of the sections and topics validated system elements and choices that were already well-established,[3] others helped us understand the true breadth of possible ethical concerns in a multidisciplinary design setting. One powerful example related to framing questions on the temporal aspects of our blockchain system, leading us on long conversations about possible futures decades down the road. As so much of the climate change conversation is necessarily focused on immediate amelioration, it was refreshing to spend some time imagining post-crisis needs for a sustainable carbon credits trading system.

Additionally, the technical sub-system framing questions led us to explore ideas around interoperable trustless layers in the context of Internet of Things (IoT), which could be built in conjunction with this system for just such a long-term future. There is existing contemporary research on the concerns with interoperating blockchains with smart cyber-physical systems, especially those serving "safety-critical" purposes [37]. However, we are at such an early stage that implications for deeply layered interoperable systems between blockchains and IoT devices have not yet been fully explored, leaving rich possibilities for both liberation and exploitation of these powerful domains. These are just two examples of perhaps a dozen threads of dialogue shared by our small team of four collaborators during Summer 2020: the Question-Led Framework proved to be generative, associative, and intellectually expansive in the product design setting.

7 Conclusion

A unifying thread runs through the original genesis of the three layer model, its corresponding generative documents, and the research implementations described above: when dealing with complex systems, it is difficult to predict the crossover "knock on" effects of any given design decision. With the advent of multidisciplinary topics in advanced computing systems, the potential ripple effects begin to transcend even the complexity of yesteryear's most advanced chess games. As the systems we design together grow more complicated, elaborate, and interdependent, they are increasingly

---

[3] For example, our conscious decision to follow Privacy-by-Design principles whenever possible, a choice that was bolstered by informational sub-system questions from Appendix A.

embedded with power relations, social norms and social praxis woven together with specific materialized forms of human communication and novel technical configurations. This means it is crucial to engage in thorough dialogue on common ground before putting anything into action, which rings doubly true in systems employing immutable ledgers and programmatic (even self-executing and self-perpetuating) processes [35, 53].

This paper presents the three layer model as a useful tool for grounding blockchain research, education, and innovation. The three layer model was used to mobilize systems-thinking and design-centric pedagogical methods in a multidisciplinary graduate-level course to help students more deeply appreciate the importance of different perspectives, and practice communicating and integrating these in practical application. Case-based exercises, written assignments and discussions, and a virtual hackathon provided students opportunities to practice collaborating in multidisciplinary design, and the business benefits of this were realized in a student's practical application of the model in a real-world setting. Together, we illuminate how holistic, multidisciplinary frameworks can facilitate the conceptualization, communication, and application of nascent technologies by providing a common foundation for interpreting and integrating diverse perspectives. In this manner, we begin to establish collaborative pedagogical practices in which students from seemingly disparate disciplines and specializations come to understand the perspectives, theories, and methods which drive each other's fields.

The primary area for improvement in pedagogical application of the three layer model is in grounding its useful complexity with more approachable inroads for newcomers to this multidisciplinary field. While the Question-Led Framework provides a concrete and comprehensible one-pager, its content addresses high-level technical ideas across a broad set of disciplines. Even for this brief framing document, content accessibility might be improved by architecting a few suggested pathways to progress through the six major categories of questions. Another option would be providing some truncated versions of these documents for discussion prompt purposes, representing some of the primary questions in each of the major conceptual domains. This increased efficacy would be further bolstered by directly linking the ISO standard's blockchain terminology in support of the three layer model as early as possible in supporting documentation, to help anchor these concepts to concrete technical terms.

At their best, complex theoretical lenses like the three layer model and resulting Question-Led Framework (Appendix A) can serve to invite us to consider the potential "butterfly effect" of choices that seem innocuous to the designers and engineers who may be preoccupied inside their own filter-bubbles of enthusiasm. In the solution design setting, even when the small team reviewed evaluative questions which ultimately did not apply to the platform being built, the topics brought to the forefront proved valuable each time. Every iterative return to the deep concepts of the design decisions' long-term implications more fully rounded out the vision of the complex socio-informational-technical systems that this platform would inevitably interoperate with. In a nod to the classic concerns of Engineering, design teams invariably had a much stronger sense of what could potentially go wrong within the system.

We will conclude this paper by providing a few recommendations for future research directions, as well as parallel research that could more reproducibly establish the efficacy of multidisciplinary design frameworks in hands-on application by universities and startups alike. We envision a more controlled empirical experiment wherein groups are given the three layer model and others are given a less multidisciplinary design framework (essentially, A/B testing). It would be crucial to ensure diversity within the groups' population, to control for gender, disciplinary affiliation, economic status, and other such categories. Another research direction we envision to establish generalizability of the design framework's effectiveness involves testing it out for use in other multidisciplinary fields (such as AI).

Finally, we must highlight the inherent limitations of the research presented in this paper. As the research design was participatory, organic, and highly individualized, it cannot be validated or reproduced in the traditional sense. It primarily represents a reflection on the initial value observed in applying this multidisciplinary framework for both learning and professional practice. While we cannot declare the efficacy of applying this theoretical framework over any other pedagogical or design process approach, we hope to provide rich grounding for further reflective prototyping of thoughtful multidisciplinary lenses for reflection, discussion, and analysis. Ultimately, as existing design approaches in many cases appear to have yielded unintended consequences and poor societal outcomes, it is perhaps not a stretch to think an intentionally collaborative multidisciplinary approach would be embraced as a welcome alternative in the design of decentralized technology protocols and other emerging technologies.

Appendix A: Question-Led DLT System Design Framework

System Goal

- What is the stated purpose of the DLT system?
- How does the stated purpose support social trust?
- What problem(s) should this system solve?
- What use cases is the system designed to support?

System Constraints

- What behaviors must the system be designed not to tolerate?
- What is the system's space of permissible actions?

System Capabilities

- What capabilities must the system possess in order to achieve its goal within prescribed constraints?

Environment

- Is the environment in which the DLT system operates relatively homogeneous or is it more heterogenous?
- What assumptions about the environment does the DLT system make in its design/operation?

- What aspects of the environment does the system rely upon? At what points and for what purposes are these relied upon?
- How aligned with all aspects of the environment is the DLT system?
- What elements from the environment influence or constrain designers of the DLT system?
- What elements from the environment influence or constrain system actors or actants?

Social Sub-system

- Who are the social actors in the DLT? How are they identified/represented? How are their identities regulated?
- How does the DLT system empower or constrain their agency? What types of actions of social actors are forbidden, encouraged, or tolerated?
- Where is power located among social actors?
- What values are important to the social actors in this system?
- What expectations do we have of the behavior of the social actors?
- What actions will or might they take? How are these actions expected to impact upon others?
- When is the consent, permission, and authority of social actors needed, granted, or assumed?
- Will some social actors act on behalf of others? On what (moral, legal?) ground do they implement the will of others? Which others?
- How do social actors need to exercise (or do they exercise) discretion when conflict arises?

Informational Sub-system

- How does the ledger serve to support social trust in the context of the DLT system?
- What data is captured/flows through the system to support the system goal? What records are generated to support the system goal, either on ledger or off ledger?
- How are the data/records actants in the system identified and how are their identities regulated?
- What data and/or records must the system store? (What are the legal or regulatory obligations?)
- What data and/or records must not be stored in the system? (For purposes of privacy, financial risk management, or corporate policy.)
- Are there data and/or records that require special consideration? For example, are there data and/or records containing personally identifiable information that requires special treatment under law?
- Are there data and/or records that must not be kept indefinitely?
- Where are records stored? How are they propagated across networks? How are the intellectual components of the record assembled?

Technical Sub-system

- What are physical actants in the DLT system (e.g., sensors, vehicles)?

- How are the technical actants in the system identified and how are their identities regulated?
- How do the physical actants serve to support social trust in the context of the DLT system? What capabilities and properties do they require to support the system goal?
- What is the system architecture?
- What is the network architecture/topography?
- What social actors control the physical actants in the DLT system? How do these social actors empower or constrain the activity of physical actants?
- What level of authority/authorization do the physical actants have?

Governance Sub-system

- How much reliance will there be on internal or self-regulating governance versus external governance under normal operating conditions? Under abnormal operating conditions?
- How will consensus decisions be made among technical, informational, and social actants/actors?
- What incentives are or will need to be put in place so that the consensus mechanism operates in a manner that supports the goal of the system?
- How should decision management rights and decision control rights be allocated among various interacting components (where social, informational, or technical)?
- How will disagreement about those decisions be resolved?

Temporality

- What known future changes will the system have to be able to respond to?
- What mechanisms need to be put in place to assure the longevity of the system?
- Could future events bring about consequences where the platform ought to be completely replace or cease operation?
- How will the governance sub-system address actors/actants' changing relationships to the system over time?
- How will risk factors be addressed, including those that lie unknown in the future and that may present existential or systematic risk?
- How has/does power shift among social actors over time?

References

1. Fisher, T., Gamman, L. (eds.): Tricky Design: The Ethics of Things. Bloomsbury Visual Arts, London (2018)
2. Newton, C., Pak, B.: Virtuality and fostering critical design thinking: an exploration of the possibilities through critical theory, design practices and networked learning. In: Jandrić, P., Boras, D. (eds.) Critical Learning in Digital Networks, pp. 101–132. Springer International Publishing, Cham (2015). https://doi.org/10.1007/978-3-319-13752-0_6
3. Scherling, L., DeRosa, A.: Ethics in Design and Communication: Critical Perspectives. Bloomsbury Visual Arts, London (2020)

4. van den Hoven, J., Vermaas, P.E., van de Poel, I. (eds.): Handbook of Ethics, Values, and Technological Design. Springer Netherlands, Dordrecht (2015). https://doi.org/10.1007/978-94-007-6970-0

5. Vries, M.J., Cross, N., Grant, D.P. (eds.): Design Methodology and Relationships with Science. Springer Netherlands, Dordrecht (1993). https://doi.org/10.1007/978-94-015-8220-9

6. Bakry, S.H., Al-Ghamdi, A.: A framework for the knowledge society ecosystem: a tool for development. In: Lytras, M.D., et al. (eds.) The Open Knowledge Society: A Computer Science and Information Systems Manifesto, pp. 32–44. Springer-Verlag, Berlin (2008)

7. Muffatto, M.: Open Source: A Multidisciplinary Approach. Imperial College Press, London (2006)

8. Paletz, S.B.F.: Multidisciplinary teamwork and big data. In: Proceedings of the 2014 Workshop on Human Centered Big Data Research, pp. 32–35. ACM Press, Raleigh (2014). https://doi.org/10.1145/2609876.2609884

9. Adamczyk, P.D., Twidale, M.B.: Supporting multidisciplinary collaboration: requirements from novel HCI education. In: Proceedings of the SIGCHI Conference on Human Factors in Computing Systems, pp. 1073–1076 (2007). https://doi.org/10.1145/1240624.1240787

10. Jandrić, P.: The methodological challenge of networked learning: (Post)disciplinarity and critical emancipation. In: Ryberg, T., Sinclair, C., Bayne, S., de Laat, M. (eds.) Research, Boundaries, and Policy in Networked Learning, pp. 165–181. Springer, Heidelberg (2016). https://doi.org/10.1007/978-3-319-31130-2_10

11. Reich, R., Sahami, M., Weinstein, J.M., Cohen, H.: Teaching computer ethics: a deeply multidisciplinary approach. In: Proceedings of the 51st ACM Technical Symposium on Computer Science Education, pp. 296–302 (2020). https://doi.org/10.1145/3328778.3366951

12. Zuo, Z., Wang, X., Eichmann, D., Zhao, K.: Research collaborations in multidisciplinary institutions: a case study of iSchools. In: Proceedings of the 25th International Conference Companion on World Wide Web - WWW '16 Companion, pp. 443–448 (2016). https://doi.org/10.1145/2872518.2890522

13. Derry, S.J., Schunn, C.D., Gernsbacher, M.A. (eds.): Interdisciplinary Collaboration: An Emerging Cognitive Science. Lawrence Erlbaum Associates, Mahwah, N.J. (2005)

14. Monk, A.: Common ground in electronically mediated communication: Clark's theory of language use. In: Carroll, J.M. (ed.) HCI Models, Theories, and Frameworks: Toward a Multidisciplinary Science, pp. 265–289. Morgan Kaufmann Publishers, San Francisco (2003)

15. Alexandrov, N.M., Hussaini, M.Y. (eds.): Multidisciplinary design optimization: state of the art. In: Proceedings of the ICASE/NASA Langley Workshop on Multidisciplinary Design Optimization, Society for Industrial and Applied Mathematics, Hampton, V.A. (1997)

16. Lemieux, V.L., Feng, C.: Theorizing from multidisciplinary perspectives on the design of blockchain and distributed ledger systems (Part 2). In: Lemieux, V.L., Feng, C. (eds.) Building Decentralized Trust: Multidisciplinary Perspectives on the Design of Blockchains and Distributed Ledgers. Springer, Heidelberg (2020)

17. Carroll, J.M., Bellotti, V.: Creating value together: the emerging design space of peer-to-peer currency and exchange. In: Proceedings of the 18th ACM Conference on Computer Supported Cooperative Work & Social Computing, pp. 1500–1510 (2015). https://doi.org/10.1145/2675133.2675270

18. International Organization for Standardization: Blockchain and distributed ledger technologies – Vocabulary [ISO/FDIS Standard No. 22739] https://www.iso.org/standard/73771.html Accessed 18 Oct 2020

19. Butijn, B.-J., Tamburri, D.A., van den Heuvel, W.-J.: Blockchains: a systematic multivocal literature review. ACM Comput. Surv. 53(3), 1–37 (2020). https://doi.org/10.1145/3369052

20. Antonopoulos, A.: Mastering Bitcoin, 2nd edn. O'Reilly Media (2018). https://github.com/bitcoinbook/bitcoinbook Accessed 15 Sept 2020

21. Lemieux, V.L., Hofman, D., Batista, D., Joo, A.: Blockchain technology & recordkeeping. ARMA International Education Foundation (2019). http://armaedfoundation.org/wp-con tent/uploads/2019/06/AIEF-Research-Paper-Blockchain-Technology-Recordkeeping.pdf Accessed 15 Sept 2020

22. Nakamoto, S.: Bitcoin: a peer-to-peer electronic cash system (2008). https://bitcoin.org/bit coin.pdf Accessed 02 Oct 2020

23. Herian, R.: Regulating Blockchain: Critical Perspectives in Law and Technology. Routledge, London (2019)

24. Kianieff, M.: Blockchain Technology and the Law: Opportunities and Risks. Informa Law from Routledge, Abingdon (2019)

25. Werbach, K.: The Blockchain and the New Architecture of Trust. MIT Press, Boston (2018)

26. Cila, N., Ferri, G., de Waal, M., Gloerich, I., Karpinski, T.: The blockchain and the commons: dilemmas in the design of local platforms. In: Proceedings of the 2020 CHI Conference on Human Factors in Computing Systems, pp. 1–14 (2020). https://doi.org/10.1145/3313831. 3376660

27. Markey-Tower, B.: Anarchy, blockchain, and utopia: a theory of political socioeconomic systems organised using Blockchain. J Br. Blockchain Assoc. 1(1), 1–14 (2018)

28. Pschetz, L., et al.: Designing distributed ledger technologies for social change: the case of CariCrop. In: Proceedings of the 2020 CHI Conference on Human Factors in Computing Systems, pp. 1–12 (2020). https://doi.org/10.1145/3313831.3376364

29. Ragnedda, M., Destefanis, G. (eds.): Blockchain and Web 3.0: Social, Economic, and Technological Challenges. Routledge, New York (2019)

30. Altarawneh, A., Herschberg, T., Medury, S., Kandah, F., Skjellum, A.: Buterin's Scalability Trilemma viewed through a state-change-based classification for common consensus algo- rithms. In: 2020 10th Annual Computing and Communication Workshop and Conference (CCWC), pp. 727–736 (2020). https://doi.org/10.1109/CCWC47524.2020.9031204

31. Ølnes, S., Jansen, A.: Blockchain technology as infrastructure in public sector: an analytical framework. In: Proceedings of the 19th Annual International Conference on Digital Govern- ment Research Governance in the Data Age - DGO '18, pp. 1–10 (2018). https://doi.org/10. 1145/3209281.3209293

32. Porru, S., Pinna, A., Marchesi, M., Tonelli, R.: Blockchain-oriented software engineer- ing: challenges and new directions. In: 2017 IEEE/ACM 39th International Conference on Software Engineering Companion, pp. 169–171 (2017). https://doi.org/10.1109/ICSE-C.201 7.142

33. Cook, K.S., Hardin, S., Levi, M.: Cooperation Without Trust? p. 2. Russell Sage Foundation, New York (2005)

34. Casey, M.J., Vigna, P.: In blockchain we trust. MIT Technol. Rev. 121(3), 10–16 (2018)

35. Langer, A.M.: Blockchain analysis and design. In: Langer, A.M. (ed.) Analysis and Design of Next-Generation Software Architectures, pp. 149–164. Springer, Heidelberg (2020). https:// doi.org/10.1007/978-3-030-36899-9_7

36. Craggs, B., Rashid, A.: Trust beyond computation alone: human aspects of trust in blockchain technologies. In: 2019 IEEE/ACM 41st International Conference on Software Engineering: Software Engineering in Society, pp. 21–30 (2019). https://doi.org/10.1109/ICSE-SEIS.2019. 00011

37. Berger, C., Penzenstadler, B., Drögehorn, O.: On using blockchains for safety-critical systems. In: Proceedings of the 4th International Workshop on Software Engineering for Smart Cyber- Physical Systems, pp. 30–36 (2018). https://doi.org/10.1145/3196478.3196480

38. Sas, C., Khairuddin, I.E.: Exploring trust in Bitcoin technology: a framework for HCI research. In: Proceedings of the Annual Meeting of the Australian Special Interest Group for Computer Human Interaction, pp. 338–342 (2015). https://doi.org/10.1145/2838739.2838821

39. Lemieux, V.L., Bravo, M.: Introduction: theorizing from multidisciplinary perspectives on the design of blockchain and distributed ledger systems (Part 1). In: Lemieux, V., Feng, C. (eds.) Building Decentralized Trust: Multidisciplinary Perspectives on the Design of Blockchains and Distributed Ledgers. Springer, Heidelberg (2020). https://doi.org/10.1007/978-3-030-544 14-0_1

40. Kolko, J.: Wicked Problems: Problems Worth Solving [A handbook & call to action]. Ac4d, Austin (2012)

41. Dignum, V.: AI is multidisciplinary. AI Matters **5**(4), 18–21 (2020). https://doi.org/10.1145/3375637.3375644

42. Oyelere, S.S., et al.: Blockchain technology to support smart learning and inclusion: preservice teachers and software developers viewpoints. In: Rocha, Á., Adeli, H., Reis, L.P., Costanzo, S., Orovic, I., Moreira, F. (eds.) Trends and Innovations in Information Systems and Technologies, pp. 357–366. Springer International Publishing, Cham (2020). https://doi.org/10.1007/978-3-030-45697-9_35

43. Ciftci, G.T.: Change of the learning cycle after blockchain: chaining trust society. In: Sharma, R.C., Yildirim, H., Kurubacak, G. (eds.) Blockchain Technology Applications in Education, pp. 42–79. IGI Global (2020). https://doi.org/10.4018/978-1-5225-9478-9

44. Oyelere, S.S., et al.: Digital storytelling and blockchain as pedagogy and technology to support the development of an inclusive smart learning ecosystem. In: Rocha, Á., Adeli, H., Reis, L.P., Costanzo, S., Orovic, I., Moreira, F. (eds.) Trends and Innovations in Information Systems and Technologies, pp. 397–408. Springer International Publishing, Cham (2020). https://doi.org/10.1007/978-3-030-45697-9_39

45. Ralston, S.J.: Postdigital prospects for blockchain-disrupted higher education: beyond the theater, memes and marketing hype. Postdigit. Sci. Educ. **2**(2), 280–288 (2020). https://doi.org/10.1007/s42438-019-00091-6

46. Lakhani, K.R., Iansiti, M.: The truth about blockchain. Harvard Bus. Rev. **95**(1), 119–127 (2017)

47. Benson, K.C., Tran, B., Jonassen, L.: Pedagogy of blockchain: training college students on the basics of blockchain. Int. J. Eng. Res. Technol. **7**(5), 17–25 (2018). https://doi.org/10.17577/IJERTV7IS050022

48. Oktian, Y.E., Singgih, I.K., Ferdinand, F.N.: Serious game for blockchain education purposes (using Proof-of-Work consensus of Bitcoin). In: Proceedings of 2019 5th International Conference on New Media Studies (CONMEDIA 2019), pp. 177–183 (2019). https://doi.org/10.1109/conmedia46929.2019.8981820

49. Milovich Jr., M., Nicholson, J.A., Nicholson, D.B.: Applied learning of emerging technology: using business-relevant examples of blockchain. J. Inf. Syst. Educ. **31**(3), 187–195 (2020)

50. O'Dair, M., Beaven, Z.: Just go and do it: a blockchain technology "live project" for nascent music entrepreneurs. In: Smith, G.D., Dines, M., Parkinson, T. (eds.) Punk Pedagogies: Music, Culture and Learning, pp. 73–88. Taylor & Francis Group, Routledge (2018)

51. Van Oyen, C.: User stories. In: Countable Ops Manual (2020). https://countable-ops-manual.readthedocs.io/operations/USER_STORIES.html Accessed 15 Oct 2020

52. Ethereum Foundation: Ethereum 2.0 [Eth2] (2020). https://ethereum.org/en/eth2/ Accessed 19 Oct 2020

53. Wessling, F., Ehmke, C., Hesenius, M., Gruhn, V.: How much blockchain do you need?: Towards a concept for building hybrid DApp architectures. In: Proceedings of the 1st International Workshop on Emerging Trends in Software Engineering for Blockchain - WETSEB '18, pp. 44–47 (2018). https://doi.org/10.1145/3194113.3194121

How Asian Women's Intersecting Identities Impact Experiences in Introductory Computing Courses

Mina Tari[⊠], Vivian Hua, Lauren Ng, and Hala Annabi

ACCESS-IT Research Group, University of Washington, Seattle, WA 98105, USA
{minatari,vhua13,lng22,hpannabi}@uw.edu

Abstract. Asians are perceived as overrepresented in computing fields. However, understanding how intersecting identities complicates this view is essential. When considering gender, ethnicity, and socioeconomic class, it becomes clear Asians have varying experiences and representation within computing. Using critical race theory and feminist theory, our exploratory case study describes Asian women's perceptions of inclusionary and exclusionary factors in their introductory computing courses as well as their undergraduate teaching assistants (TAs). We found that intersecting identities and context of the university change the salience of race for Asian women. Additionally, undergraduate TAs are seen as more relatable because of near-peer status, and their personalities more impactful than any identity characteristic.

Keywords: Asian women · Introductory courses · Undergraduate teaching assistants · Critical race theory · Feminist theory

1 Importance of Asian Students' Intersecting Identities

In the U.S., diversity-focused computing research often considers Asians overrepresented. However, this perspective neglects multiplicity of Asian identities. First, the racial category "Asian" consists of over 67 ethnicities [1]. When statistics showing overrepresentation of Asians (e.g., in 2018, 15% in computing while only 5.4% in the U.S.) are broken down by ethnicity, it becomes clear there are severe disparities [1, 2]. Second, considering gender, it becomes clear that in computing, Asian *men* are seemingly overrepresented; in 2018, Asian women earned less than 3.5% of computing degrees, while Asian men earned over 10% [2]. Third, international Asian students make up the majority of international students in the U.S., yet also lack extensive descriptions of their experience [3]. In order to accurately reflect Asian students' experiences in education, especially in computing, considerable critical work is necessary.

Our research utilizes critical race and feminist theory to explore Asian women's experiences in introductory computing courses and determine their major factors of inclusion and exclusion. We also consider how intersecting identities (e.g., ethnicity, nationality, socioeconomic class) affects these perceptions. Additionally, we examine

© Springer Nature Switzerland AG 2021
K. Toeppe et al. (Eds.): iConference 2021, LNCS 12645, pp. 603–617, 2021.
https://doi.org/10.1007/978-3-030-71292-1_47

the role of undergraduate teaching assistants (TAs) and what aspects of their identity, if any, impact Asian women's experiences.

We conducted an exploratory case study between three computing departments at a public research university. Our findings indicate participants are not only impacted by content, instructors, and structure of computing programs, but the university's location and demographics. Asian women's intersecting identities mitigate many of these experiences. Additionally, personality traits of TAs are more impactful than any identity characteristics, though identity is not completely disregarded.

2   Related Work: Computing's Rocky History with Equity

Computing fails to attract marginalized identities because the field has been shaped to fit the interest, knowledge, and skills of privileged ones [4–7]. Because computing is perceived as successful, the majority of computing educators view little problem with instruction [8–10]. Unfortunately, the average dropout rate in computer science (CS) introductory courses range from 33–50% across institutions; students who pass still lack an understanding of basic topics [9]. Historical misconceptions of a "geek gene," "natural aptitude," and that computing is "harder to teach" avoids exploration of how and why computing pedagogy is exclusive to marginalized groups [8–13].

One such group is women of color, including Asian women. In computing-related education, women of color have been described as caught in a "double bind" [14, 15]. The assumptions have been that programs supporting women *or* minorities will in turn assist women of color [7, 15]. Unfortunately, history has shown programs serving women benefit *white* women, and programs serving minorities benefit minority *men* [7].

Additionally, due to enrollment limitations, computing fields have "weed-out" environments in overstuffed classrooms [16–18]. What little computing-related literature focused on women of color has found major exclusionary factors related to assuming an "objective meritocracy" for the "best and brightest" rather than acknowledgement of systemic bias [4, 7, 16, 18], isolating and competitive environments [4, 16, 19], content separated from real-world application [4, 7], and gaps in primary education [13, 16, 19]. Positively, the literature has found inclusionary factors related to collaborative environments [4, 7, 16, 18], undergraduate research opportunities [4, 17, 21], and mentorship roles, including teaching assistants [20, 22–25]. However, there is little exploration of how intersecting identities impact women of color's perceptions.

2.1   Revealing the Full Picture: Using Critical Race and Feminist Theory

In order to illuminate inclusionary and exclusionary factors Asian women perceive in computing education, we utilize critical race theory (CRT) and feminist theory. While computing is aware of their severe disparities [10, 12], their history of equity-focused research suffers from essentialism [26–28], lack of intersectionality [4, 7, 17], and deficiency-assimilation research [7, 18, 28]. Additionally, Western rhetorics of science and technological determinism have been used to shield computing from more structural-level critique, as problems are seen as rooted with "biased" people rather than "neutral" technology [6, 29–31]. Theoretical foundations like CRT and feminist theory are well-equipped to contextualize dynamics of inequity on multiple levels for students' experiences.

Combined, CRT and feminist theory emphasize the impossibility to focus on one identity factor as more important than others. Gender does not supersede race nor create a unifying experience, and vice-versa, as intersections change the entire experience [15, 32, 33]. In addition to understanding there are no universally valid, unbiased truths, CRT and feminist theory describe how inequitable structures are more difficult to perceive for those benefitting the most from them [6, 32, 33]. Therefore, those "lowest" in inequitable systems can see the full extent of their oppression, such as women of color [32, 33].

Furthermore, we incorporate the Individual Difference Theory of Gender and IT (IDTGIT), which draws on CRT and feminist theory to show how an individual-level, intersecting identities lead to differing perceptions of inequity. IDTGIT explores three constructs of individual differences related to perceptions of computing: (1) individual identity (e.g., personal demographics), (2) individual influence (e.g., personal characteristics), and (3) environmental influence (e.g., educational background, cultural attitudes) [34]. Therefore, our theoretical framework has a simultaneous understanding of systemic- and individual-level factors, best positioned to describe inclusionary and exclusionary factors in computing for marginalized identities such as Asian women.

2.2 Asian Women and Stereotypes

While there is a growing body of literature analyzing women of color's experiences in computing, as previously stated, Asian women are often overlooked due to their perceived overrepresentation. Literature also often conflates Asian and Pacific Islander experiences because of U.S. racial categorization, ignoring differences these groups face regarding imperialism, colonialism, and Indigeneity [35]. As part of CRT, we consider Asians' extensive immigration history in the U.S., and their stereotypes. First, how monolithic identity labels are used to portray a successful image for the whole group, avoiding analyzing disparities by intersecting factors [36–39]. Second, how that feeds into the model minority myth, dismissing other marginalized racial groups' claims of structural inequity, rooted in anti-blackness [40, 41].

We use CRT and feminist theory to understand how Asian women's experiences in computing differ based on ethnicity, nationality, and socioeconomic class, allowing for a more complex discussion on the feasibility of understanding marginalization. Furthermore, comparing findings to literature on women of color also illuminates a basis for affinity grouping and allyship in equitable work. In order to determine the most impactful inclusionary and exclusionary factors Asian women face in their introductory computing courses, and if this differs across intersecting identity characteristics, we must utilize CRT and feminist theory. Through such, we can develop solutions addressing the full extent of existent barriers, and move towards more equitable computing education from the perspective of those who need it most.

3   Methodology

We conducted an exploratory case study at a public research university in the Pacific Northwest (Yin). We used a single case design, with multiple embedded units of analysis with the university's three undergraduate computing programs: computer science (CS), information science (IS), and user-centered design and engineering (UCDE). These programs overlap in career outlooks, including software engineering, data science, information architecture, UX/UI design, and human-computer interaction research. Each program offers 1–2 introductory courses.

The case university is transitioning from a primarily second-year competitive major system to direct-to-major first-year admissions. CS and UCDE are almost completely direct-to-major, while IS is still competitive. This affects our participants, as most are first to third year students caught in the period between not directly admitted into a program but shut out from applying to computing majors.

We carried out 51 h-long, semi-structured interviews from self-identifying Asian women who had taken at least one introductory computing course. Interviews were conducted by a member of the research team, comprised of four women of color, three of Asian descent. The lead investigator was a PhD student who graduated from one of the university's computing departments, while two were undergraduates currently enrolled in the programs. The first set of interviews were held in a private room on campus, while the latter half were held on Zoom due to a shift to online courses in Winter 2020. Participants were recruited from course- and program-wide emails, in-person class visits, and social media posts on computing-related student organization pages, and were compensated $10.

Interviews discussed personal and family history, primary education experience, and computing course experience. Participants then described perceptions on their computing TAs and finally, impact of their identity characteristics. We audio recorded and transcribed interviews, analyzing using inductive and deductive techniques and Miles and Hubermann's [42] interactive model of content analysis and reached 82% inter-rater reliability.

4   Results

Our results revealed how intersecting identity characteristics impacted Asian women's experiences in computing courses. We first describe our participants' characteristics and how the intersections of such along with the university contexts impacted perceptions of ethnicity, gender, and nationality. Then, we discuss how participants perceived TA characteristics. Finally, we end with participants' descriptions of inclusionary and exclusionary factors. Please note that participants used 'female' and 'woman' interchangeably in response to questions on their gender, and we recognize it conflates sex and gender, though left quotes unedited to reflect participants' voices.

4.1   Our Participants

We collected demographic information that aligned with the individual identity and influence aspects of IDTGIT, including ethnicity, nationality, year in college, home language, major, and computing courses. Of 51 participants, we had 12 representative ethnicities with 22 East Asians (Chinese, Korean, Japanese, Taiwanese), 13 Southeast Asians (Filipino, Vietnamese, Malaysian, Burmese), and 11 South Asians (Indian, Nepalese). Four participants identified as bi- or multi-racial. Nine students chose not to disclose their eth-nicities. Seven participants were international students, while 44 were domestic. Eleven participants identified as first-generation students and 12 as first-generation citizens. Only 24/51 participants spoke English as their first language.

Thirty-five participants had taken introductory IS and/or CS, while about half (24/51) intended or were majoring in IS, and only 6 in CS or UCDE, with the rest split across social sciences, natural sciences, and humanities. The low enrollment of CS and UCDE may reflect the difficulties in the university's transitional period.

4.2 How Intersecting Identity Factors Impact Asian Women's Experiences in Computing

Broadly, our participants described how their experiences in introductory computing courses were shaped by their intersecting identities, in addition to the university's loca-tion and demographics. Participants indicated the high Asian population in the case city (in 2019, 15.1% compared to the nationwide 5.9%) and campus (24%) made their race less of a barrier. A persistent theme in participants' narratives was recognizing their minority status "in the real world," but not necessarily on campus. Thus, participants were more likely to describe gender as a salient barrier than race (33/51 compared to 12/51) in relation to computing classes. However, their experience of barriers differed by ethnicity, nationality, and socioeconomic class, as we will explain in this section.

Participants' Perceptions of Asians as Minorities. As stated above, the university's context affected participants' perceptions of race, and 16/51 of participants did not consider Asians as "traditional" minorities. Xinyi, domestic Chinese, describes: *Not really in [our state], because there's so many Asians here [...] 'cause when I was in high school, I feel like a minority.* Perceptions of minority status (or lack thereof) was often described in comparison to non-Asian racial minorities (e.g., Latinx or Black students) and the negative stereotypes attributed to them. Lihua, a domestic Chinese student, explains further:

> You never really look at an Asian and think, like, "oh, they're a gangster, they're poor and they're uneducated." Like, on the contrary, the stereotype is we're suc-cessful, we're smart, we make money. [...] Um, so I guess I don't perceive Asians as a minority in like, a bad way. As like, some people would perceive like African Americans and stuff [...] I don't feel ostracized for being Asian, but I kind of have to consider some things because I'm Asian.

For the 15/51 participants who saw Asians as minorities, this was impacted by their intersecting identities. First, regionality and ethnicity was important, because the high Asian percentage of students were mainly East and South Asians (specifically, Chinese, Indian, and Korean). Participants not from these regions pointed out how their attempts to describe their experience was shut down because of monolithic, overrepresented Asian stereotype.

Socioeconomic status impacted participants' experience in computing by affecting access to resources. In the case city, there are severe existing neighborhood class disparities, and Imen, a domestic Filipino student, describes how this intersects with her ethnicity:

> *My general experiences are different from the average Asian woman in [IS], just because a lot of the people I know very obviously come from high socioeconomic backgrounds [...] If you look at like immigration patterns, I think [Chinese] mostly immigrate here and do really well. But I know a lot of Filipinos move here and don't do super well. There's a lot of Filipinos in [city]. Most of them are in [this neighborhood], which is like a very low-income area and then all the Chinese are in [other neighborhood], just like a very high-income area.*

Participants also described how perceived overrepresentation of Asians in computing overlooks Asian women. Ling, a domestic Chinese first-generation student emphasizes gender:

> *I feel like yeah, we are still a minority, the model minority. But in STEM, I'd say like, Asians are overrepresented. But if you take into account gender, then yes the Asians and Pacific Islanders are extremely underrepresented and there aren't that many resources to help specifically with Asians because they just kind of assume oh Asians are overrepresented, but only the male aspect is and not the female aspect, like no one cares enough to target that.*

Five participants discussed how the model minority myth dismisses differences across ethnicity, regionality, or socioeconomic class, as well as adds pressure to educational choices for Asians. Additionally, 14/51 students discussed a monolithic view towards Asians, with similar consequences.

Influence of Family and Racial Stereotypes. Even when describing how their Asian racial identity is less salient on campus, participants made clear that they still faced stereotypes and microaggressions. First, the stereotypical "Asian immigrant dream" led participants to feel limited in career choices, and pressured from family. As family was the second most salient factor mentioned, (45/51), it cannot be overlooked. Participants with family members in computing often were motivated to explore the field, but could feel additional stress:

> *Aatiya, international Malaysian: I come from a family of engineers. So for me, it's kind of natural that I take IT [in school]. Expected, actually. My dad was saying "if you don't get top score in IT, you are a disgrace to my family. You're not my daughter, how could you?"*

Additionally, participants felt that the stereotype of Asians only being interested STEM and computing meant that faculty would not perceive them as having actual passion for the field, or need support in courses. Indeed, participants described having achievements dismissed by peers because of assumed inherent abilities in the field, as Lihua, domestic Chinese student, describes facing when accepted into CS:

I felt really terrible. I wanted to get in because I deserved it, because I belonged there. And I didn't want it to be written off because there's something that I couldn't control. I think it was just an insecurity that I wanted to get into CS [...] like I could succeed and not just because of my gender and race.

Participants also described balancing gender stereotypes, which was frustrating to deal with in addition to coursework.

Differences Between International and Domestic Participants. Nationality was another identity characteristic significantly affecting the experience of being an Asian woman in computing. International participants saw cultural values between the U.S. and Asian countries as the main difference between domestic and international Asian women. Guiying, international Chinese, additionally describes how language and cultural-specific knowledge makes boundary crossing more difficult:

People like to stay with people they identify with. And when I come to the school, I already observed this phenomenon. When people are from the same cultures and countries staying together, so I can't be the only one that's breaking [...] Sometimes as international students like, it could be the language when I feel I'm confident to speak out. [Sometimes it's] more culturally related to U.S., as examples to illustrate certain concepts. So when that brings up to me, I feel a bit disconnected. For example, like a professor say "have you watched this movie?" or "have you know this person from the U.S.?" I wouldn't be able to know.

Darsha, international Indian, describes how educational backgrounds with computing makes her "feel behind" compared to domestic Asians:

Usually Asians who are like, born in the U.S. or brought up here, have more exposure and opportunities starting from high school [...] For me it's difficult. In the first quarter at [university] was the first time I ever got expose to tech.

Socioeconomic factors also weigh heavily on international participants' experiences. International participants describe how it influenced career choices by perceiving a debt to their families, only exacerbated by the university's competitive major system:

Aatiya, international Malaysian: [Money] is why I'm working 20 h a week. That's my main stressor. And the reason why I'm so upset with like, not being able to apply [to majors] after my second year.

Ten of 44 domestic participants also saw cultural divides as the main difference. Additionally, domestic participants described how language barriers made it difficult to *"jump into conversations"* (Tala, domestic Filipino). Even for domestic participants who shared a language, they worried about proficiency with international students and even described feeling nervous about their *"fake Asian"* status (Lihua, domestic Chinese).

4.3 How TA Traits Impact Perceptions: Identity and Personality

In this section, we discuss what participants stated were the most beneficial traits of TAs, negative traits, and how undergraduate TAs are seen as more relatable.

Beneficial Traits of TAs. Thirty-six of 51 participants reported that TAs provide important encouragement in introductory computing courses. Eleven of 51 participants described TAs similar to them ethnically as more approachable. This was emphasized similarly across ethnic minority, women of color, or Asian TAs. Isha, first-generation domestic Indian, describes a sense of comfort with her woman of color TA, *"it's not gonna be weird like, I don't have to censor myself sometimes."* Amalia, domestic Filipino, preferred an Asian TA with a similar regional background, stating that *"there's like no cultural boundaries or so."*

Nine of 51 participants discussed TAs' gender as important, tied to perceptions of gender imbalance in computing, as Ling, first-generation domestic Chinese, explains: *I feel like female TAs are slightly more approachable, especially in the tech field just because females are still very underrepresented. But I don't know, male TA's can be really approachable too.* Five of 51 participants saw both gender and ethnicity as important. Other participants mentioned first-generation status, sexuality, and even educational background outside of computing were beneficial to hear.

However, our participants stated TAs' personality and teaching traits made them more approachable than any identity characteristics; 46/51 participants discussed at least one beneficial trait. The most reported traits were clear explanations of content (14/51), open availability and quick responsiveness (10/51), encouraging facilitation (9/51), positive personalities (9/51) and multiple forms of "teaching" (e.g., visual/kinesthetic examples, games) (7/51). Fundamentally, participants wanted TAs to signal a safe, open learning environment:

> *Oni, first-generation domestic Indian: This is not necessarily related to gender or anything but the way [my TA] explained to me was really patient and like, because I don't like feeling people are explaining to me because they think I'm dumb. I know that it's not an explicit thing, but like you know how you can feel that sometimes if [TAs] are going over something too fast and you don't want to be like, "oh, slow down," because you're already asked them for help?*

Additionally, participants felt their TA was more relatable when they shared personal stories:

> *Min, domestic Korean: [If TAs say] "Oh, when I was a freshman, I didn't under- stand how to do this," [students] might also relate. Trash[ing] on your own faults is something that's like, hard to do for a lot of people, but it's really helpful, espe- cially when everyone else is new to [the course] [...] It kind of opens the door for questions and then you don't feel like this TA knows everything, it's a good thing. [It's not] my question is stupid, right? It's more like, "oh, [the TA] was in my position, they would have had that same question."*

Participants appreciated simple actions, such as learning students' names or validating questions, as Shui, first-generation domestic, describes:

> *I like the whole after you answer a question you get some encouragement thing. Like, that's pretty validating. I have a professor this quarter who like, she's really nice and everything, but like after she calls on someone to talk, she doesn't really*

*acknowledge what they say and then she moves on to the next person. I feel like
that's a little bit like, "did I say something wrong" type situation? I like the whole,
like, "yeah," "good job," or like, "oh, that was close." [...] regardless if you did
get it right or wrong, it just feels like an accepted answer then.*

Dishearteningly, Shufen, a domestic biracial, describes the slight shock that she felt
when a TA made clear they were invested in her success as a student:

*Even though [TAs] are supposed to be teaching us, I always had this idea in mind
that they're just kind of doing it because they have to or something. So like, when
they actually try to look into me and help me out and stuff like that, I feel surprised,
which is... I don't know if that's a good thing or not.*

Unhelpful TA Traits. Participants also reported negative TA traits, all related to personality or teaching practices. Eighteen of 51 participants described aspects such as
poorly explaining concepts, being unresponsive through email, lacking uniform grading
policies, being awkward or unconfident, giving incorrect advice, and making constant
mistakes.

Do Undergraduate TAs Make a Difference? Roughly half (24/51) of participants
described their undergraduate TAs as more relatable, due to similar age, undergraduate
status, and course experience:

*Bo, domestic Asian: I really liked [my TA's] teaching style actually because she
was also an undergrad, she knows what we're going through. And she also took
the class, so she's like "oh I had trouble on this particular part. Do you guys need
help on that part?"*

Additionally, 7 participants described how undergraduate TAs were easier to approach than faculty, as Ly, a first-generation domestic Vietnamese states: *It felt more
comfortable rather than going up to our professor because he's taught this class a
million times. How could we ask stupid questions to [the instructor]?*
    Fourteen of 51 participants saw them in more mentor roles because of perceived
power differentials. Five participants saw them as instructors, because they lacked any
sort of rapport. Graduate TAs were seen less frequently as relatable (4/51), though
these participants stated a similar age was beneficial. This indicates near-peer status is
beneficial, even when not in the same program.

4.4 Factors that Enhance Inclusion in Computing Courses

The most reported inclusionary factor was collaboration with peers (44/51 participants). Participants described a wide variety of benefits. Most importantly, collaboration
mitigated isolation participants felt in their courses and university.
    Collaboration opportunities varied in participants' courses. In the introductory CS
series, collaboration is explicitly prohibited on assignments. IS and UCDE take the opposite approach, requiring collaboration on assignments and final projects. This greatly

impacted participants' perceptions. IS and UCDE were both described as more community oriented, welcoming, and collaborative. Other collaboration benefits included forming encouraging friendships and communities, as Ly, first-generation domestic Vietnamese, explains: *"I'm like, if [friend] thinks he can do CS then I can do it too. And then I also met people from UCDE who were doing CS like taking CS at the same time, as I was taking UCDE, they survived. And I was like okay I can do it."*

Thirty-seven participants described how investment in student resources, primarily student clubs, benefitted their computing experience. Many clubs were computing-affiliated (e.g., Women in IS), having open discussion around the many barriers students face with the competitive major process, and empowered students by meeting upper class Asian women and women of color. Other student resources included the Office of Minority and Diversity which had its own tutoring center and offered advising and professional development, a branch of Microsoft's Technology Education and Literacy in Schools program, and a state-run program to support low-income students into CS and engineering.

Thirty-six participants also described how holistic and creative course content was beneficial in their courses, because it allowed them to see more pathways in the majors. Creativity also allowed for participants to integrate their other interests with computing, while putting less pressure on finding a "correct" answer. This comes in tandem with hands-on work, as Guiying, international Chinese, states:

I like [my intro IS course] because it covers a lot of different topics [...] as an introductory course, it just help us go through like this extra step that we may have to face and gives us our options. So it's pretty inclusive and there's a lot of hands-on activities for us to really practice, instead of just being a lecture.

One new inclusionary factor participants discussed was the benefits of hearing more open discussions around diversity in their courses, and how that fostered a sense of inclusion, as Ruiling, domestic Chinese, explains:

I feel like at the beginning [of class], just acknowledging the kind of like, male-centered, white-centered environment that tech sometimes fosters, especially like tech companies, and explaining it to everyone in the class kind of... I think that set the tone for the course. [...] Because I could be like, oh okay so this professor at least recognizes there's a disparity [...] combined with the efforts of [professor] talking about diversity, it was not super intimidating compared to other classes.

A related inclusionary factor was participants' interest in their future work helping others, and working alongside people (7/51). This interest stemmed from multiple sources, including participants' upbringings and family background, personality traits, and interest in other fields (e.g., ethnic studies), alongside their socioeconomic status:

Imen, domestic Filipino: I want to work somewhere meaningful. The only thing I knew about tech was Microsoft and Google, you know, the big companies and they didn't seem very meaningful to me. And so I think that was a big like initial, probably a big barrier to a lot of people because you know like we don't really talk about how amazing tech is, all we know is the big tech companies [...] I should probably try to do something else, not just public health, you know? And like I also come from a low income family and so like what am I doing? Like should I be doing something that's going to pay more, so I can get back to my family?

4.5 Factors that Create Exclusion in Computing Courses

The most reported exclusionary factor in participants' introductory computing courses was an awareness of gender imbalance in the student body, instructors, and computing field. Thirty-three of 51 participants described gender disparities leading to several barriers, such as having ideas ignored in class discussions by other students, working harder to prove their competence, and assumptions they would only succeed in CS due to their gender. Aatiya, international Malaysian, explains being dismissed because of her gender, and overlooked for her friends who are men:

[Classmates who are men] assume I need help. Even though I'm doing better than them. And when they see me do better than them, even though I'm a girl, they're like, "oh, okay." And they'll be dismissive [...] It has been by first glance, because the way they interact with the guy next to them - who they also don't know, because he's my friend - they're more like "hey bro, how do you do [the problem]?"

This environment made participants feel more isolated, unmotivated, and even more unwilling to speak up. In response, participants would create spaces with other women, and seemed more open to connecting across race, as Tala states, *"I always identify with girls around me. Like yeah I don't really pay attention to what race they are. And so, it was nice having other girls in class."* This has made the IS and UCDE courses and majors more appealing, as they had more women in their programs.

The next two strongest barriers participants referenced related to competitive environments (32/51) and lack of collaboration (25/51). Both were fostered by the university's competitive major system. Participants were constantly faced impostor syndrome and comparisons to peers. Ironically, these participants felt they were the only ones who were struggling. In addition to feeling high pressure regarding grades (21/51), the environment discouraged students from even applying to computing majors, as Shui, first-generation domestic Indian, describes:

I don't know, it's just one of those things where I was just like, I know I'm not the smartest in [the CS course] and if they're only taking a handful... wouldn't it be the people who are at the top, you know? [...] that's the process I used to [not apply].

Additionally, mixed experience levels were frustrating, prevalent more in CS (as IS and UCDE were not taught in primary education). Repeatedly, students stated they would prefer a class solely for beginners, as students with experience made it known through "toxic" attitudes. Min, domestic Korean, describes socioeconomic class impacting experience in CS prior to university:

I feel that there's a correlation right with like, more wealthy [students] usually have a little more tech experience. Like they went to [wealthy neighborhood] high school and they all have really good [CS] programs because like Microsoft [supports them] and stuff like that. A lot of the lower income schools have like no coding classes, so the kids join [CS 1] and they have no experience [...]

Fast pacing (21/51) often came in tandem with the university's quarter system, making participants struggle to keep up with computing courses but even asking questions. Twenty-one participants discussed how large lecture classrooms exacerbated feeling like one of hundreds. This was mitigated by TA-led quiz sections, around 30 students. Upper class students reported that they enjoyed their much smaller higher-level courses as well.

Nine participants described having struggles with English throughout their education, with lasting effects into the university. Yun, international Chinese, describes how quiet international student stereotypes stems from not being able to articulate questions in another language:

It's easier for me [talking to Chinese students], because I can just speak Chinese and elaborate my questions more clearly. Sometimes when I went to like [CS TAs] or math study center, I'm a little bit afraid, because I don't know the professional like, some words for it, so I cannot say it clearly at all.

5   Discussion and Future Work

Our study revealed how intersectional identities impact Asian women's experiences in introductory computing courses. We found for our participants, the university's demographic context and students' identity intersections affected perceptions of inclusion and exclusion. Additionally, TAs' age and teaching/personal characteristics played a role in how our participants' perceived the TAs, and impact the TAs had on the participants' feelings of inclusion and exclusion in computing. Understanding how participants' individual-level experiences varies in relation to systemic-level biases illuminates the full extent of barriers in computing for Asian women. Additionally, we start to highlight similarities between Asian women's experiences and other women of color to further emphasize the levers of change to address systemic bias.

CRT and feminist theory were key in shaping our understanding. Participants led the conversations on barriers most impactful to them, while we contextualized these descriptions to historical contexts. This lens makes clear that intersecting identities cannot be delineated, but instead change the experience of viewing oneself as an Asian woman in computing, as is clear in CRT and feminist theory literature [6, 16, 26, 33]. Intersectionality then reveals the complexities of systemic bias and the varying impacts of exclusionary and exclusionary factors have on individuals.

Our study highlighted that ethnicity is important to consider because of varying Asian immigration histories and socioeconomic intersections, while nationality was important due to a misunderstanding that racial similarities surpass cultural boundaries [40, 41]. Asian women share the experience of identity-based barriers with other marginalized students in higher education, often invisible or dismissed by those in power [40, 41]. We affirm it would be impossible and irresponsible to claim to fully understand Asian women's experiences without adequate critical, intersectional approaches.

The most exclusive factors in introductory computing courses had to do with the environment being competitive and less developmental. Courses with mixed experience levels with computing only added to this exclusion. To address such environmental barriers one suggestion is for introductory courses be separated by previous skill level, having onramp experiences to provide leveling. Our participants' nationality and socioeconomic status played a large role in access to computing prior to university. Participants showed that even with these intersections, Asian women faced similar inclusionary factors (collaboration, mentorship) and exclusionary factors (competitive environments, isolation) to the literature on women of color's experiences in computing, such as competitive environments [4, 16, 17].

Of course, such environments stem from university structural issues. However, computing fields can use their proud clout and ability to combat it. Computing fields are aware of the many disparities they are causing and are motivated to address these disparities through a critical approach to understanding barriers and developing solutions [13]. Our work makes clear courses emphasizing collaboration, creativity, and open discussions around diversity can combat many of such exclusions. Furthermore, we found that Asian women benefited from minority-focused spaces, and should not be left out of this type of support.

Finally, our findings emphasize the key role TAs played in encouraging participants in their introductory computing courses. Undergraduate TAs were seen as more relatable, because of their near-peer status. Additionally, participants appreciated when TAs would share personal experiences with the course, especially prior struggles. While participants described how shared identity factors (e.g., race, ethnicity, and gender) can be beneficial, the most effective benefits stemmed from personality and teaching traits. Not surprisingly, many of these reported traits are well known, and are simple, such as remembering students' names, acknowledging and validating their questions, multiple forms of teaching and examples, and a general sense of care for students' success. Somehow, our participants have come to expect that systems of education care so little about them as individuals, they are surprised when given the most basic support. Future work will continue exploring Asian women's experiences on a larger scale, including multiple embedded case studies at several universities in different regional locations of the U.S. Considering how university location and contexts are key in understanding the salience of identity factors in Asian women's experiences.

In conclusion, understanding how intersectional identities affect perceptions is essential to begin developing meaningful solutions to entrenched systemic barriers to inclusion of Asian women [43]. Ignoring the interplay between individual-level identity and systemic-level barriers will only exacerbate inequities. Now more than ever, computing cannot turn away from the stark realities impacting their field, and higher education more broadly.

Acknowledgements. This work was partially funded by the NSF Graduate Research Fellowship Program. Additionally, we would like to thank Simran Bhatia for her consultation in the literature review and data analysis.

References

1. Pang, V.O., Han, P.P., Pang, J.M.: Asian American and Pacific Islander students: equity and the achievement gap. Educ. Res. **40**(8), 378–389 (2011)
2. U.S. Department of Education National Center for Education Statistics. Bachelor's degrees conferred by postsecondary institutions, by race/ethnicity and field of study: 2016–17 and 2017–18 (2018)
3. Lee, J.J.: Engaging international students. In: Student Engagement in Higher Education: Theoretical Perspectives and Practical Approaches for Diverse Populations. Routledge (2014)
4. Johnson, A.C.: Unintended consequences: how science professors discourage women of color. Sci. Educ. **91**(5), 805–821 (2007)
5. Fox, M.F., Johnson, D.G., Rosser, S.V.: Women, Gender, and Technology. University of Illinois Press, Urbana (2006)
6. Haraway, D.J., Wolfe, C.: A CYBORG MANIFESTO: science, technology, and socialist-feminism in the late twentieth century. In: Manifestly Haraway. University of Minnesota Press (2016)
7. Ong, M., Wright, C., Espinosa, L., Orfield, G.: Inside the double bind: a synthesis of empirical research on undergraduate and graduate women of color in science, technology, engineering, and mathematics. Harvard Educ. Rev. **81**(2), 172–209 (2011)
8. Wajcman, J.: TechnoFeminism. Polity Press, Cambridge (2004)
9. Robins, A.: Novice programmers and introductory programming. In: Fincher, S., Robins, A. (eds.) The Cambridge Handbook of Computing Education Research, Cambridge, United Kingdom (2019)
10. Blikstein, P., Moghadam, S.H.: Computing education literature review and voices from the field. In: Fincher, S., Robins, A. (eds.) The Cambridge Handbook of Computing Education Research, Cambridge, United Kingdom (2019)
11. Shepherd, K.: Higher education pedagogy. In: Fincher, S., Robins, A. (eds.) The Cambridge Handbook of Computing Education Research, Cambridge, United Kingdom (2019)
12. Lewis, C.M., Goode, J., Scott, A., Shah, N., Vakil, S.: Researching race in computer science education: demystifying key vocabulary and methods. In: Proceedings of the 51st ACM Technical Symposium on Computer Science Education, pp. 171–172 (2020)
13. Margolis, J.: Stuck in the Shallow End: Education, Race, and Computing. MIT Press, Cambridge (2008)
14. Malcom, L., Malcom, S.: The double bind: the next generation. Harvard Educ. Rev. **81**(2), 162–172 (2011)
15. Crenshaw, K.: Mapping the margins: intersectionality, identity politics, and violence against women of color. Stanford Law Rev. **43**(6), 1241 (1991)
16. Barker, L.J., Garvin-Doxas, K.: Making visible the behaviors that influence learning environment: a qualitative exploration of computer science classrooms. Comput. Sci. Educ. **14**(2), 119–145 (2004)
17. Espinosa, L.: Pipelines and pathways: women of color in undergraduate STEM majors and the college experiences that contribute to persistence. Harvard Educ. Rev. **81**(2), 209–241 (2011)
18. Sax, L.J., Blaney, J.M., Lehman, K.J., Rodriguez, S.L., George, K.L., Zavala, C.: Sense of belonging in computing: the role of introductory courses for women and underrepresented minority students. Soc. Sci. **7**(8), 122 (2018)
19. Goode, J.: If you build teachers, will students come? The role of teachers in broadening computer science learning for urban youth. J. Educ. Comput. Res. **36**(1), 65–88 (2007)
20. Barker, L.J., McDowell, C., Kalahar, K.: Exploring factors that influence computer science introductory course students to persist in the major. ACM SIGCSE Bull. **41**, 153–157 (2009)

21. Carpi, A., Ronan, D.M., Falconer, H.M., Lents, N.H.: Cultivating minority scientists: undergraduate research increases self-efficacy and career ambitions for underrepresented students in STEM: MENTORED UNDERGRADUATE RESEARCH AT A MSI. J. Res. Sci. Teach. **54**(2), 169–194 (2017)
22. Tari, M., Annabi, H.: Someone on my level: how women of color describe the role of teaching assistants in creating inclusive technology courses (2018)
23. Varma, R.: Making computer science minority-friendly. Commun. ACM **49**(2), 129–134 (2006)
24. Decker, A., Ventura, P., Egert, C.: Through the looking glass: reflections on using undergraduate teaching assistants in CS1. ACM SIGCSE Bull. **38**(1), 46–50 (2006)
25. Dickson, P.E., Dragon, T., Lee, A.: Using undergraduate teaching assistants in small classes. In: Proceedings of the 2017 ACM SIGCSE Technical Symposium on Computer Science Education - SIGCSE 2017, pp. 165–170 (2017)
26. Moraga, C., Anzaldua, G.: This Bridge Called My Back: Writings by Radical Women of Color, 2nd edn. Kitchen Table, New York (1983). 7. printing
27. Trauth, E.M.: The role of theory in gender and information systems research. Inf. Org. **23**(4), 277–293 (2013)
28. Kvasny, L.: Let the sisters speak: understanding information technology from the standpoint of the 'other'. ACM SIGMIS Database **37**(4), 13–25 (2006)
29. Harding, S.G.: The Postcolonial Science and Technology Studies Reader. Duke University Press, Durham N.C. (2011)
30. Hayles, K.: How We Became Posthuman: Virtual Bodies in Cybernetics, Literature, and Informatics. University of Chicago Press, Chicago (1999)
31. Tsosie, K., Claw, K.: Indigenizing science and reasserting indigeneity in research. Hum. Biol. **91**(3), 137–140 (2019)
32. Mohanty, C.T.: Under western eyes: feminist scholarship and colonial discourses (1991). https://doi.org/10.4324/9780203825235
33. Hooks, B.: Teaching Critical Thinking: Practical Wisdom. Routledge, New York (2010)
34. Trauth, F.M.: Odd girl out: an individual differences perspective on women in the IT profession. Inf. Technol. People **15**(2), 98–118 (2002)
35. Diaz, V.M.: "To 'P' or Not to 'P'" marking the territory between Pacific Islander and Asian American studies. J. Asian Am. Stud. **7**(3), 183–208 (2004)
36. Lei, J.L.: Teaching and learning with Asian American and Pacific Islander students. Race Ethn. Educ. **9**(1), 85–101 (2006)
37. Museus, S.D., Kiang, P.N.: Deconstructing the model minority myth and how it contributes to the invisible minority reality in higher education research. New Dir. Inst. Res. **142**, 5–15 (2009)
38. Poon, O., et al.: A critical review of the model minority myth in selected literature on Asian Americans and Pacific Islanders in higher education. Rev. Educ. Res. **86**(2), 469–502 (2016)
39. Suzuki, B.H.: Revisiting the model minority stereotype: implications for student affairs practice and higher education. New Dir. Student Serv. **2002**(97), 21–32 (2002)
40. Chen, G.A., Buell, J.Y.: Of models and myths: Asian(Americans) in STEM and the neoliberal racial project. Race Ethn. Educ. **21**, 1–19 (2017)
41. Iftikar, J.S., Museus, S.D.: On the utility of Asian critical (AsianCrit) theory in the field of education. Int. J. Qual. Stud. Educ. **31**(10), 935–949 (2018)
42. Miles, M., Huberman, M.: Qualitative Data Analysis: An Expanded Sourcebook, 2nd edn. Sage Publications, Thousand Oaks (1994)
43. Ogbonnaya-Ogburu, I.F., Smith, A.D.R., To, A., Toyama, K.: Critical race theory for HCI. In: Proceedings of the 2020 CHI Conference on Human Factors in Computing Systems, pp. 1–16 (2020)

Societal Information Cultures: Insights from the COVID-19 Pandemic

Gillian Oliver[1]([⊠]) [iD], Charles Jeurgens[2] [iD], Zhiying Lian[3] [iD],
Ragna Kemp Haraldsdottir[4] [iD], Fiorella Foscarini[5] [iD], and Ning Wang[3] [iD]

[1] Monash University, Melbourne, VIC 3145, Australia
`Gillian.Oliver@monash.edu`
[2] University of Amsterdam, 1012 XT Amsterdam, The Netherlands
[3] Renmin University of China, Beijing 100872, China
[4] University of Iceland, 102 Reykjavík, Iceland
[5] University of Toronto, Toronto, ON M5S 3G6, Canada

Abstract. National responses to the global COVID-19 pandemic provided the opportunity to gain insight into characteristics of societal information cultures. Experiences from four different countries (China, Australia, the Netherlands, and Iceland) were collected and analyzed from an information literacy perspective. Research was guided by Giddens' structuration theory.

Keywords: Societal information culture · Information literacy · Health literacy · Structuration modalities

1 Introduction

Data, and its interpretation as information, is at the heart of responses to the COVID-19 Pandemic. This unprecedented crisis has had a global impact and provides a unique opportunity to compare and contrast information related responses occurring almost simultaneously in different parts of the world. The purpose of our research was to investigate characteristics of societal information cultures (the values, attitudes and behaviours relating to information) through the lens of responses to the pandemic. We focus specifically on four very different countries, namely China, Australia, the Netherlands and Iceland, comparing their approaches to the dissemination of COVID-19 related data. We use a theoretical framework derived from Giddens' structuration theory to analyze societal information cultures, concentrating on information and health literacy perspectives.

The paper begins with a brief review of the literature relating to the critical nature of information in public health emergencies and then outlines our research design. This is followed by the findings for each country studied from the outbreak of the pandemic until 1st September 2020. The discussion section uses the framework to compare and contrast findings, and proposes an expansion of the theoretical framework. The conclusion indicates the further research streams that have emerged from this preliminary study.

K. Toeppe et al. (Eds.): iConference 2021, LNCS 12645, pp. 618–634, 2021.
https://doi.org/10.1007/978-3-030-71292-1_48

2   Information and Public Health Emergencies

This century's series of global public health emergencies (SARS, Ebola, H1N1, H7N9, MERS) has emphasized the critical role of real time and rapid information dissemination [1, 2]. Lessons learned from the 2003 SARS outbreak included the need for faster information exchange in the early phase of the outbreak, delays in sharing critical information with the World Health Organization (WHO) and possibilities of international players to hinder efforts to understand the cause and nature of the disease and to formulate the best strategy for containment [3, 4]. Governments may hesitate to report disease information because of possible political and economic repercussions [5].

Information has been identified as one of the four core elements of public health emergency legal preparedness together with laws, competencies, and coordination [6, 7], and the capabilities of information sharing and emergency warning as critical capabilities for public health preparedness [6, 8, 9]. Researchers have emphasized the need for empirical research to investigate what communication types are most effective for different demographics [10] and to develop emergency information strategies [11] that would enable regional public health agencies to release information with more autonomy [12, 13].

The WHO has developed global norms for sharing data and results during public health emergencies [15–18], with social media playing a key role in the dissemination of public health related information [19–21]. The negative role of social media in the public health emergencies [19, 22, 23] is a concern.

Lack of information literacy exposes citizens to risks and personal, social and physical harm [14]. The misinformation around the Covid-19 pandemic provides a vivid example of those risks. As the WHO Director General explained: "...we're not just fighting an epidemic; we're fighting an infodemic. Fake news spreads faster and more easily than this virus and is just as dangerous..."[1] Dis-, mis- and mal-information thrive in the online attention economy of sensational and click-bait content of social media sites underlining the need for people to have the skills to interpret and respond critically to information disseminated by digital media [14].

There is very little research investigating health related information at national level from an information culture perspective. The single study we identified focuses on China [24, 25]. This study motivated our adoption of the theoretical framework outlined in the next section. We did not identify any other relevant comparative studies.

Abilities to access health related information have been investigated by information literacy researchers [26, 27] and are clearly related to improved health literacy.

Health literacy has been defined as "the degree to which individuals can obtain, process, understand, and communicate about health-related information needed to make informed health decisions" [28] and encompasses a variety of skills [29], including the ability to use technology, to network and to interact with others socially [30]. More specifically, health information literacy may be described as "the set of abilities needed to: recognize a health information need; identify likely information sources and use them to retrieve relevant information; assess the quality of the information and its applicability

---

[1] https://www.who.int/dg/speeches/detail/munich-security-conference.

to a specific situation; and analyse, understand, and use the information to make good health decisions" [31].

Poor health literacy has been identified as a major but underestimated problem globally in the COVID-19 pandemic [32], exacerbating the risk of misinformation motivating resistance to public health measures. It is argued that "health literacy might help people to grasp the reasons behind the recommendations and reflect on outcomes of their various possible actions" [32].

3   Research Design

Our previous research [33] utilized a pyramid model of information cultures influenced by Gidden's theory of the recursiveness of agency and structure [34] which facilitated micro-level analysis. In this project, we shifted our focus to gain a macro, societal level view of complex and emerging information landscapes, motivating the need for a more expansive theoretical model. Accordingly, we adopted a framework which also drew from Giddens' structuration theory, with particular regard to the three modalities of structuration, i.e., interpretive schemes, resources, and norms. These modalities represent linkages between human action and social structure and have been conceptualized by Yingqin Zheng as the dimensions of societal information culture [24, 25]. This paper focuses primarily on the interpretive modality.

The interpretive modality is where participants make sense of, and communicate about, the information situations in which they are involved. Intrinsic to this is the existence of a knowledge base shared by all participants, thus Zheng equates this modality to information literacy, defined as "the capability of accessing, interpreting and using information" [24]. We have purposively included health literacy, as in this setting it appears to be inextricably intertwined with information literacy.

As all three modalities identified by Giddens contribute to the production and reproduction of information culture at a societal level, it is important to acknowledge that information literacy (i.e., the interpretive schemes constituting the first modality) depends on the "resources" available in a society, which Zheng equates to "information freedom" (second modality), and on the "formal and informal concepts and rules of behaviour", that is, the "information norms" governing information activities (third modality) [24].

Our objective in this research project was to compare the information activities related to the pandemic in different parts of the world, in order to examine how these activities shaped local societal information cultures, and what role has been played by information literacy and, more specifically, health literacy. The overarching research question was formulated as follows:

What differences in societal information cultures can be identified in China, Australia, the Netherlands and Iceland when examining the management of COVID-19 related information?

Supporting research questions that we used to guide our investigative activities in the four countries were:

- What COVID-19 related information/data is collected?
- What COVID-19 information/data is made available to citizens?
- How is information about COVID-19 communicated to citizens?

Each researcher developed an overview of the COVID-19 data in their own jurisdiction, based on analysis of government and specialist websites as well as media reports and discussion. This environmental scan took place in real time, i.e. as the crisis was unfolding, so there is extensive reliance on media reports as a source of data. Supplementary data is provided from a small-scale survey in China, and informal interviews in Australia. Zheng's model of the dimensions of societal information culture provided the framework to report findings relating to information and health literacy, and a basis for comparative analysis.

4 Findings

Findings from the four countries studied are reported below, in chronological order according to the timings of each outbreak of the coronavirus, thus beginning with China, followed by Australia, the Netherlands and then Iceland. A brief contextual summary is provided for each country, followed by specific observations relating to information and health literacy.

4.1 China

The news that COVID-19 can be transmitted from human to human was officially disclosed on 20 January 2020 and caused public panic in China. Local governments were required to make information on COVID-19 public in real time and with precision. The city of Wuhan was locked down on 23 January. Across the country, people were asked to stay at home as much as possible, wear masks and maintain one-metre distance from others when outside. When entering a neighborhood or some public spaces, people were also required to have their temperature taken and to show their Health Code[2]. The situation was under control by the end of March.

Information Literacy. Government statistics show that in March 2020 the number of Internet users in China had reached 0.904 billion, with 99.2% using instant messaging, 83% using search engines, and 80.9% accessing internet news sources.[3] This shows that at least half of the population of China has basic digital skills, but not all have the capabilities to acquire, understand and process health-related information and thus to make informed health decision. When the outbreak of COVID-19 first occurred, a lot of misinformation about it was transmitted through social media and various websites. For example, a lot of people falsely believed that the traditional Chinese medicines

---

[2] The health code is created on the basis of personal data and uses a colour code to demonstrate the status of people's health: green (healthy), yellow (in 7-day quarantine), red (in 14-day quarantine).

[3] The 45th China Statistical Report on Internet Development, available at http://www.cnnic.net.cn/hlwfzyj/hlwxzbg/hlwtjbg/202004/P020200428596599037028.pdf, accessed on July 25, 2020.

Banlangeng and *Shuanghuanglian* and garlic could control and cure COVID-19, so they rushed to pharmacies to buy them.[4] In 2019, the National Health Commission of China investigated the health literacy of 74,683 people aged between 15 and 69 from 31 provinces of China, concluding that a general level of health literacy belonged to 19.17% of the sampled population, which means that nearly 80 out of 100 individuals would lack health literacy. Levels of health literacy for rural residents, older citizens and residents in the Midwest of China were comparatively lower.[5]

From the start of the outbreak, people could access COVID-19 information from various channels: health commission websites (including those of the National Health Commission and local health commissions); local government apps, official WeChat accounts and press conferences; traditional mass media, including TV and radio; and other media including news apps, WeChat moments, microblogs, business websites. Some people would get information directly from their families and friends by word of mouth. Research identified as the top five channels used by the public to access scientific information about COVID-19, WeChat (66.66%), TV (65.83%), website (56.38%), news app (53.73%) and microblog (46.03%) [35]. Another study found that the most trusted information source was central official media, including CCTV (China Central TV) and People Daily Online, followed by information disclosed by non-government organizations, and finally the local news media and business websites. It is noteworthy that 61.3% of the 11,055 respondents questioned news sent by their acquaintances [36].

During the outbreak, the National Health Commission and local health commissions published daily statistics, identifying numbers of confirmed, recovered, deceased, severe, and imported from abroad cases, and provided scientific knowledge about COVID-19 via various media. Press conferences were held regularly to communicate updates and combat the spread of rumours; medical professionals were invited to attend the conferences to share scientific information on personal protection and control of the disease; news about COVID-19 was broadcast by national and local channels all day and night. Government and other media as well as business websites established anti-rumour platforms.[6] All such platforms enabled citizens to access information about COVID-19, and thus make informed health decisions. Current research reports that the majority of 5,982 respondents would not accept the following pieces of misinformation: "Chinese Academy of Science has invented the medicine to quickly cure COVID-19" (disbelieved by 75.7%); "COVID-19 is the biochemical weapon invented by foreign forces to target China" (disbelieved by (82.2%); and "COVID-19 can be transmitted from dogs and cats to human" (disbelieved by 68.8%) [37]. Wang et al.'s investigation found that 99.2% of the respondents to their survey believed that wearing masks outside and washing hands are necessary hygienic measures, and between 92.5% and 94% of the respondents actually did that [36].

---

[4] Can "Shuanghuanglian" "Banlangeng" control COVID-19? Medical experts: do not blindly believe in "magic medicine", available at https://kuaibao.qq.com/s/20200201A0JWZO00?refer=spider, access on August 24, 2020.

[5] The level of national health literacy rises to 19.17% in 2019, available at https://www.cn-health care.com/article/20200424/content-535201.html, accessed on August 28, 2020.

[6] Anti-rumour special column of the prevention and control of COVID-19, http://www.piyao.org. cn/2020yqpy/. See also, real-time anti-rumour on COVID-19, https://vp.fact.qq.com/home.

We conducted a survey on citizens' access to information on COVID-19 in China, via a questionnaire on the Wenjuanxing platform and distributed via WeChat on 29 August. A total of 142 people responded in two days. The survey found that the main business websites (e.g. Sohu and Sina, 66.9%), TV (55.63%), government WeChat official account (52.11%), WeChat comments (47.18%), and government websites (41.55%) were the top five ways to access information. Reasons given for these choices were: convenience (77.46%), authoritativeness (61.97%) and trustworthiness (52.82%). Over half of the participants (54.93%) questioned the authenticity of some information acquired from the above-mentioned channels, with 64.79% reporting that they confirmed authenticity by crosschecking with other information sources, tracing the information source (38.73%), and checking the information on anti-rumour platforms (30.99%). 99.3% of the participants stated that they wore a mask when going out, 96.48% washed hands frequently, 69.72% kept one-metre distance from others, 82.39% kept indoor ventilation, and 66.9% worked out frequently. Overall, our survey demonstrated that over half of the participants had adequate health literacy: they knew how to access information about COVID-19, and could make informed decisions about staying healthy. China has traditionally been regarded as an 'acquaintance society' [38], that is, a society where people tend to trust their acquaintances. Yet, many of the respondents of Wang et al.'s research questioned the accuracy of the information from their acquaintances during the outbreak [36].

Health literacy is influenced by a number of factors including age, gender, level of education, where people live [39] and social contexts. In our survey, 11 respondents (7.75%) reported eating garlic to stay healthy, and 5 (3.53%) said they took the traditional Chinese medicines *Banlangeng* and *Shuanghuanglian*. A survey of 5,632 primary and secondary school students in Beijing after the outbreak of COVID-19 found that 15% did not wash their hands frequently, and nearly 20% did not cover mouth and nose when sneezing and coughing [40].

4.2 Australia

The first confirmed case of COVID-19 in Australia was reported on 25 January 2020. Australia's governance model is based on the Westminster tradition with executive government, legislature and judiciary at national and state/territory level [41]. The initial response was coordinated at national level by the Commonwealth government and was heralded as being remarkably successful in comparison with other countries [42]. Unfortunately, this positive outcome reported in June 2020 no longer reflected the situation a few weeks later when Victoria, Australia's second most populated state, returned to strict lockdown measures when cases there rapidly exceeded the previously reported national statistics. As case numbers rose, indications were that this new wave of clusters could be linked to problems with staffing and security at hotels used as quarantine stations for returning travelers [43]. A distinction has been made between the first and second waves, with the former linked to returning travelers (wealthier individuals) from overseas, and the latter associated with community transmission in poorer communities [44]. At the time of writing, Melbourne, the capital city of Victoria, is experiencing a period of stringent stay-at-home restrictions which include the imposition of a nighttime curfew for the first time in the history of the city [45]. The findings reported below are centered on Victoria specifically because of its position as the hotspot of COVID-19 in Australasia and necessarily are heavily reliant on media commentary given the current and dynamic nature of the situation.

Information Literacy. Use of the Internet and engagement with social media are integral to the day to day lives of Australians[7]. In addition, Australia has a well-established reputation for global leadership of information literacy research and practice, with a well-established standards framework for embedding information literacy into curricula [46]. This suggests that the majority of the population are likely to have the skills needed to access and evaluate information about the pandemic, but one specific problem area has already emerged. Australia is a multi-cultural society, characterized by large communities of migrant populations ranging from refugees and asylum seekers to international students. For refugees, differing cultural norms, language barriers and lack of trust in officialdom all contribute to problems accessing health information [26]. The Australian Migrant and Refugee Women's Health Partnership highlights the main problems faced by these communities in accessing health related information, including low literacy and digital literacy, insufficient access to digital technologies, preference for in person communication, and limited understanding of what information can be trusted [47]. Similarly, older migrants have their own unique preferences and difficulties in accessing health related information [48].

There is a growing body of evidence that, despite official information being made available in a variety of languages, effective communication of pandemic policies and requirements has not taken place [49]. The Refugee Council of Australia has highlighted 'nonsensical' translations of official communications from Federal and Victorian governments, concluding that such errors will weaken trust in government sources [49]. We were able to conduct a preliminary investigation into this issue, thanks to one of our authors being an international student currently resident in Melbourne. In her experience, Chinese-language platforms, especially Chinese social media (WeChat public accounts, WeChat Moments, Weibo, etc.), are the main channels for obtaining information about the pandemic for Chinese students in Australia, despite the existence of various official multilingual forums.

Most of these WeChat public accounts do not have formal connections with Australian official institutions, and are likely to be established for commercial purposes, raising questions about the reliability of information provided. For example, after the initial apparent success of measures in controlling the virus, the Premier of Victoria announced the gradual easing of restrictions from 13 May. The potential for schools to change from online to on campus learning in the forthcoming semester was mentioned, which was communicated by one popular WeChat account targeted at Melbourne as "students are ready to return to school" without any reference to a specific time period.[8] The operator of this WeChat account is a media technology company from Beijing. It is a for-profit company, working with major Australian supermarkets to help them market their products. Promoting Australia as a safe environment to attract more international students is inherent to its business model.

---

[7] https://datareportal.com/reports/digital-2020-australia.

[8] https://mp.weixin.qq.com/s/BcopwfsRhuvtGGG8YU4trA.

WeChat public accounts may also produce or promote misinformation, exacerbating panic during the epidemic. For example, on 22 July, speaking to Australia's national broadcaster, epidemiologist Tony Blakely said Victoria risked spending months or even years isolated from other states. This was his expert opinion, but not a public statement issued by the government. However, some WeChat public accounts took his words out of context, claiming that "Victoria will be blocked for 2 years"[9]. Such expressions are very common, misinterpreting the government's policy intentions to varying degrees and causing concern among the Australian Chinese community. The extent to which Chinese communities in Australia have the ability to evaluate the accuracy of these statements is unknown, but it seems likely that few would consider going to official sources to confirm such statements.

4.3 Netherlands

On 27 February 2020, the first Dutch patient with COVID-19 infection was diagnosed in the Netherlands. One week later, the first COVID-19 tested patient died. The same day, inhabitants in the province Noord-Brabant were advised to limit social contacts and stay at home if they coughed, had a cold or fever. A week later this measure came into effect nationwide, accompanied by advice not to shake hands. On 15 March schools and childcare facilities, eating and drinking establishments and sports and fitness clubs were closed. In a live broadcast press conference in the evening of 23 March, the prime minister announced stricter measures: people should keep 1.5-m distance from each other, groups of more than two people in public spaces were prohibited, professional contacts were forbidden, shops should take measures to secure the 1.5-m policy. Fines were imposed if these measures were violated. The government appealed to everyone's responsibility to overcome this crisis and communicated these measures as a 'smart lockdown'. After 11 May restrictions were gradually lifted and measures adjusted according to the number of infections. To increase insight into the current situation, the Ministry of Public Health developed a 'Dashboard Coronavirus'[10] in which data about infections, hospitalization, and R-value are communicated among other things. In September, a test-version of an infection tracing app was made available in certain areas of the country. The total number of confirmed COVID-19 death cases between 27 February and 31 August was 3,419 male and 2,811 female; and in total 12,170 COVID-19 patients were hospitalized during the same period.[11]

Information Literacy. According to the Dutch National Bureau of Statistics (CBS), 97% of the residents of the Netherlands over the age of 12 have access to Internet facilities and 88% are online on a daily basis.[12] Compared to most European countries, the individual digital skills of Dutch citizens are considered high: 50% have above basic overall digital skills, 16% have low digital skills.[13] However, a general problem for

---

[9] https://mp.weixin.qq.com/s/s-cSu4_JYrwNqcyFp5gFEA.

[10] https://coronadashboard.rijksoverheid.nl.

[11] https://www.rivm.nl/coronavirus-covid-19/actueel; https://allecijfers.nl.

[12] https://www.cbs.nl/nl-nl/cijfers/detail/83429NED?dl=35852.

[13] https://is.gd/Ab9roR Digital skills are determined on the basis of results in four sub-areas: information, communication, computers/online services and software.

information consumers during the pandemic was the high degree of uncertainty about the reliability of the rapidly growing and ever-changing amount of COVID-19 related information that was released. Prime-minister Rutte emphasized the lack of knowledge about how best to tackle the crisis by saying: "with 50% of the knowledge, we have to make 100% of the decisions".[14] This means that insights are constantly adjusted, which might cause extra confusion for many people.

A 2018 survey showed that 9.5% of the Dutch population (1.5 million people) scored inadequate and 26.9% problematic in terms of health literacy [50]. Another survey, with a focus on the importance of the Internet as a crucial source for citizens to access information about COVID-19 developments, investigated how the Internet was used for purposes of searching and using information and communication in the Netherlands. The survey identified several groups of people as vulnerable, such as the elderly, lower educated, physically or mentally ill people, and people with low literacy skills, and concluded that these vulnerable groups are less likely to take advantage of the COVID-19 related information opportunities the Internet offers [51]. The way in which government agencies and the official health institutions make COVID-19 information available is by no means always understandable for these groups, and this results in alarming forms of digital information inequality. There have been non-governmental initiatives aiming to increase comprehensibility of COVID-19 related information. The *Reading and Writing Foundation* rewrites and reformats COVID-19 related press conferences and government information in simple language which is understandable by these vulnerable groups.[15] The *Pharos Foundation* translates COVID-19 related information in 13 languages to reduce information inequality for the many migrants in the Netherlands who do not have mastery of the Dutch language.[16]

Distinguishing the information sources people use is significant. The *National Institute for Public Health and Environmental Hygiene* (RIVM) is the official hub for collecting and disseminating COVID-19 related medical information. RIVM is a government agency which is independent in its research activities. It plays an important advisory role for policy- and decision-makers, and at the same time is the key-provider of COVID-19 information to the public. RIVM operates in a public health network in which doctors, general practitioners, medical laboratories and the Municipal Health Services (GGDs) cooperate and collect information about people who are tested positive for COVID-19.[17] The website of RIVM provides guidelines and large amounts of daily updated statistical information regarding the development of the virus, sometimes supplemented with explanation. Although this is probably the most accurate and detailed information hub about the pandemic, it is not always easy for citizens to interpret the data properly. This became painfully clear when the mortality rates from different data sources were compared. The Dutch National Bureau of Statistics keeps accurate mortality rates regardless of the cause of death and these figures show a big gap between the confirmed COVID-19

---

[14] Press conference prime-minister, 12 March https://www.youtube.com/watch?v=0iD1FN6I87Y.

[15] https://www.lezenenschrijven.nl/wat-wij-doen/corona-in-begrijpelijke-taal/.

[16] https://www.pharos.nl/coronavirus/. The government provides covid-19 information in English via https://www.government.nl/topics/coronavirus-covid-19.

[17] https://www.rivm.nl/documenten/epidemiologische-situatie-covid-19-in-nederland-23-maart-2020-0.

causes of death and the probable number of COVID-19 victims. For instance, between 30 March and 12 April, excess mortality was 3,793, meaning that 3,793 more people died than it could be expected based on the average mortality rates in the first ten weeks of 2020. In total, 2,178 deaths were registered as being infected with COVID-19 (based on confirmed testing), but it is more than probable that a significant part of the total excess mortalities is related to COVID-19, since by no means everyone has been tested because of limited test capacity.[18]

This complexity might be an important reason why these official health platforms are not the number one information source citizens use. Several surveys show that traditional media were the most popular sources of information on the pandemic [52, 53]. Of those surveyed in March, 76,8% used TV, 63% newspaper and mobile news applications, and 40% social media; only 39% used official health websites [53]. Traditional media agencies play a major role in the dissemination of accurate and understandable COVID-19 related information.

4.4 Iceland

Iceland is an island nation with only one major gateway into the country. It has around 364,000 inhabitants[19], one of the most sparsely populated countries in Europe. In January 2019, around 14,1% (50,272) of the inhabitants were immigrants.[20]

On 27 January a state of uncertainty was declared due to the COVID-19 outbreak. Two days later the Chief Epidemiologist advised against travelling to China and that arrivals from China should undertake a 14-day quarantine. On 3 February, Iceland identified several high-risk areas, including northern Italy and Tirol in Austria, earlier than other states.[21] At that point, the Directorate of Health and the Department of Civil Protection and Emergency Management revised the current pandemic preparedness response plan. They then initiated a nationwide surveillance program for COVID-19, including diagnostic testing which began on 31 January in close collaboration with the National University Hospital and deCODE genetics [54]. Initial testing was conducted on residents returning from high risk areas and contacts of confirmed cases. This was widened to include the general community who presented symptoms [55]. On 27 February, the first of what was to become daily press briefings, was held on national television, a national radio station and streamed on several local social media sites. These briefings were usually conducted by the Chief Epidemiologist, the Director of Health and the Chief Superintendent who informed the media and the public about the current situation of the pandemic and necessary measures, both globally and locally. After several daily briefings, it soon became clear that contact tracing was a community affair and this catch phrase became popular; "Follow Willow" [Hlýðum Víði] meaning that 'we do as Vidir says' (the Chief Superintendent). This catch phrase became a business idea as people started wearing T-shirts with the slogan.

---

[18] https://www.cbs.nl/nl-nl/nieuws/2020/16/sterfte-onder-bewoners-van-institutionele-huisho udens-bijna-verdubbeld/weekcijfers.

[19] https://hagstofa.is/utgafur/frettasafn/visindi-og-taekni/notkun-fyrirtaekja-a-samfelagsmidlum-i-evropu-2017/.

[20] https://www.statice.is/statistics/population/inhabitants/.

[21] https://www.covid.is/english.

The objective of the measures taken by the Icelandic authorities was to ensure that the necessary infrastructure, particularly the healthcare system, would be able to resist the strain of the pandemic (see footnote 21). The premise for these actions was a community-wide consensus to follow expert advice. "Civil protection is in our hands". The first COVID-19 infection in Iceland was confirmed on 28 February in a traveler returning from northern Italy. On 13 March, a ban on gatherings of more than 100 people was implemented, and a week later, all travel outside Iceland was designated as high risk. On 22 March, the regulation was updated so that a maximum of 20 people could gather simultaneously. Upper secondary schools and Universities were closed, and operations of Kindergartens and Primary schools were limited. Nursing homes were closed to visitors. Sports clubs, hair salons and similar establishments were closed. The first COVID-19 death was announced on 22 March, and the total number of deaths on 8 September was 10.

Starting on 13 March, Iceland has provided a COVID-19 dashboard for an overview of relevant data (see Fig. 1). The dashboard is the responsibility of the Directorate of Health and the Department of Civil Protection and Emergency Management. Approximately two weeks later, it was translated into 8 languages, including English, Polish, Lithuanian, Thai, and Arabic. Now it is possible to access the site in 11 languages.

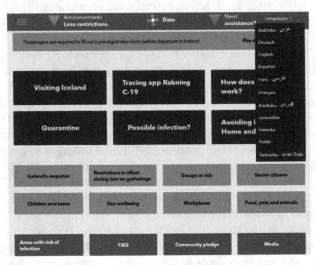

Fig. 1. Front page of Covid.is/English on 4 September 2020

The site is intended to be the centre for official health information related to Covid-19, including regular announcements, advice regarding isolation or quarantine, possible infection and statistical data.

The infection tracing app "Ranking C-19" became available on the App Store and Google Play on 2 April. People were encouraged through daily briefings by the Directory of Health to use the app. Only three weeks later, approximately 130,000 individuals in Iceland had started using it. The purpose of the app is to track those who are diagnosed with COVID-19. If registered in the app, people may be contacted by the Department of

Civil Protection and Emergency Management and asked to share their data. Individuals have a choice to agree to this by entering their national ID number into the app. If the individual agrees, the data is sent to the Contact Tracing Team who can use the location data to identify the individuals and places that have potentially been exposed to the virus.

Information Literacy. The Icelandic National Curriculum Guide outlines the frame and conditions for learning and teaching based on laws, regulations and international conventions. One of six fundamental pillars that form the curriculum is literacy [56]. Iceland is reported to have 99% of homes connected to the Internet [57]. With near omnipresent access, Icelanders are frequent Internet users.[22] Government departments support the COVID-19 dashboard by providing relevant information. Recent research from the Social Science Research Institute found that 97.5% of the respondents declared that they generally were "very or rather content" with the information provided to citizens about COVID-19 [58]. Respondents had considerable trust in the information provided by the Director of Health (very much 85.4%; rather good 13%), the Chief Epidemiologist (very much 87.9%; rather good 10.6%) and the Chief Superintendent (very much 81.8%; rather good 16.1%). In comparison, a total of 36.4% trusted the information provided by the government very much, 40.1% trusted information from the WHO very much, and 18.4% trusted information provided by the Media very much. A total of 9.2% had full trust in information provided by social media sites. Nearly half (47%) of respondents followed the briefings on national TV or radio three times or more per week.

The government set up a working group to focus on information disorders and COVID-19. The purpose of the group is to promote public health and health security by examining the extent of organized dissemination of dis- and misinformation about COVID-19 in Iceland. It is also to ensure access to educational material with reliable information about the pandemic and facilitate the distribution of correct information to the media and the general public.[23]

5 Analysis and Discussion

Despite some disparities in the initial reactions to the outbreak (partly a result of timing), what stands out when looking at the societal information cultures emerging from the cases examined is a certain uniformity. This may be surprising considering the very different histories and the current political, social, and economic circumstances of China, Australia, the Netherlands, and Iceland. All our case studies show a number of competing information sources – from traditional media and official websites to various social media platforms used by both the government and the general public – that complicate the information landscape in which we all try to navigate what we know, and what we do not yet know, about the pandemic. Extensive access to the Internet and widespread (digital) information literacy provide the basis on which governments try to build awareness and

---

[22] https://www.internetworldstats.com/stats4.htm.

[23] https://www.stjornarradid.is/verkefni/almannaoryggi/thjodaroryggisrad/vinnuhopur-um-upp lysingaoreidu-og-covid-19/ [In Icelandic] and partly on https://www.government.is/govern ment/covid-19/#measures.

consequent actions on the part of their citizens. Programs to increase health literacy of all strata of population, especially the more disadvantaged, appear to be in place in all countries examined. Yet, all suffer from the 'plague' of misinformation that the plethora of media outlets cannot but amplify.

The interpretive modality that was the main focus of this research project brought us to investigate how meaning-making is enacted socially when dealing with complex, ever-changing and potentially upsetting information, such as that related to a highly infectious novel global disease. The Chinese case study highlighted the effectiveness of government actions aiming at improving information literacy and fighting against "rumours" through the reinforcement of the normative framework (i.e., Giddens' third modality). With its efforts to broaden access to official health information through multiple translations, Australia tried to support its diverse population, thus emphasizing the facilitative or resource-based aspects of societal information culture (i.e., Giddens' second modality). The availability and transparency of information in society was also central to the Dutch case study, where, however, the understandability of official health information proved to be a major source of concern. In the Icelandic case, information norms, exemplified by the "expert advice" and the success of the contact tracing app, offered the insular community a good basis of trust in, and legitimization of, government's decisions, despite the lack of stable and unambiguous knowledge around the virus, its effects, and how humans can protect themselves against it.

One of the fundamental tenets of structuration theory is that structures are "inherently ambiguous, and subject to contested interpretation, application and use" [24]. As social science and humanities scholars of the 21st century, we all feel comfortable within this post-modern paradigm, and embrace plurality and fluidity in our critical approaches to information. However, when it comes to health, these very notions of ambiguity and contestation became problematic. We have been living in times of deep uncertainty for many years now; yet, the sense of fragility and disorientation that COVID-19 has thrown us in seems to have upset basic meaning-making mechanisms. Anecdotal evidence collected through this research (e.g., search for quick, home-made health remedies; preference for simple messages, even when unscientific; belief in charismatic leaders) shows attitudes towards information that might be labelled as 'irrational'. Is this a fourth modality, or dimension of structure, that should be considered when examining societal information cultures during a time of crisis?

6 Conclusion

Our limited study did not analyze important sources of information on the response to the pandemic, such as, parliamentary debates, and tools for the self-reporting of symptoms. These, together with investigations of how agencies explain the data they provide, the extent to which knowledge about collection and use of data is transferred internationally, demographic breakdowns of data about access to COVID-19 related information, and changes in the way health information is being communicated, are some of the areas we have identified for future research. From a more theoretical perspective, the suggestion that a fourth modality dealing with irrational information behaviour be added to the three identified by Giddens may be explored further.

References

1. Song, P., Karako, T.: COVID-19: Real-time dissemination of scientific information to fight a public health emergency of international concern. Biosci. Trends **14**(1), 1–2 (2020). https://doi.org/10.5582/bst.2020.01056

2. Moorthy, V., Restrepo, A., Preziosi, M., Swaminath, S.: Data sharing for novel coronavirus (COVID-19). Bull. World Health Organ. https://www.who.int/bulletin/volumes/98/3/20-251 561/en/. Accessed 15 Aug 2020

3. Oshitani, H.: Lessons learned from international responses to severe acute respiratory syndrome (SARS). Environ. Health Prev. Med. **10**(5), 251–254 (2005). https://doi.org/10.1007/BF02897698

4. Institute of Medicine (US) Forum on Microbial Threats, Knobler, S., Mahmoud, A., Lemon, S., Mack, A., Sivitz, L., Oberholtzer, K.: Learning from SARS: Preparing for the Next Disease Outbreak. National Academies Press (US), Washington, DC (2004)

5. Morse, S.S.: Global infectious disease surveillance and health intelligence. Health Aff. (Millwood) **26**(4), 1069–1077 (2007). https://doi.org/10.1377/hlthaff.26.4.1069

6. Olson, A.B., Ransom, M.M.: Legal preparedness for public health emergencies: a model for minimum competencies for mid-tier public health professionals. A Centre for Disease Control (2012). Ransom, M.M. (ed.), Associate Editor: Olson, A.B.

7. Rees, C.M., O'Brien, D., Briss, P.A., Miles, J., Namkung, P., Libbey, P.M.: Assessing information and best practices for public health emergency legal preparedness. J. Law Med. Ethics **36**(1), 42–46 (2008). DOI: 10.111/j.1748-720X.2008.00259.x

8. Nelson, C.D., Lurie, N., Wasserman, J., Zakowski, S.: Conceptualizing and defining public health emergency preparedness. Am. J. Public Health **97**(Suppl 1), S9–11 (2007). https://doi.org/10.2105/AJPH.2007.114496

9. Balajee, S., et al.: Sustainable model for public health emergency operations centers for global settings. Emerg. Infect. Dis. **23**(Suppl 1), S190 (2017). https://doi.org/10.3201/eid2313.170435

10. Savoia, E., Lin, L., Viswanath, K.: Communications in public health emergency preparedness: a systematic review of the literature biosecurity and bioterrorism. Biodefense Strategy Pract. Sci. **9**, 170–184 (2013). https://doi.org/10.1089/bsp.2013.003

11. Seyedin, S.H., Jamali, H.R.: Health information and communication system for emergency management in a developing country. Iran. J. Med. Syst. **35**(4), 591–597 (2011). https://doi.org/10.1007/s10916-009-9396-0

12. Glik, D.C.: Risk communication for public health emergencies. Annu. Rev. Public Health **28**, 33–54 (2007). https://doi.org/10.1146/annurev.publhealth.28.021406.144123

13. Cope, J.R., Frost, M., Richun, L., Xie, R.: Assessing knowledge and application of emergency risk communication principles among public health workers in China. Disaster Med. Public Health Preparedness **8**(3), 199–205 (2014). https://doi.org/10.1017/dmp.2014.29

14. Carmi, E., Yates, S.J., Lockley, E., Pawluczuk, A.: Data citizenship: rethinking data literacy in the age of disinformation, misinformation, and malinformation. Internet Policy Rev. **9**(2), 1–22 (2020). https://doi.org/10.14763/2020.2.1481

15. Wilson, K., Tigerstrom, B., McDougall, C.: Protecting global health security through the International Health Regulations: requirements and challenges. Can. Med. Assoc. J./Journal de l'Association medicale Canadienne **179**(1), 44–48 (2008). https://doi.org/10.1503/cmaj.080516

16. Dye, C., Bartolomeos, K., Moorthy, V., Kieny, M.P.: Data sharing in public health emergencies: a call to researchers. Bull. World Health Organ. **94**(3), 158 (2016). https://doi.org/10.2471/BLT.16.170860

17. Delaunay, S., Kahn, P., Tatay, M., Liu, J.: Knowledge sharing during public health emergencies: from global call to effective implementation. Bull. World Health Organ. **94**(4), 236–236A (2016). https://doi.org/10.2471/BLT.16.172650

18. Modjarrad, K., Moorthy, V.S., Millett, P., Gsell, P.S., Roth, C., Kieny, M.P.: Developing global norms for sharing data and results during public health emergencies. PLoS Med. **13**(1), e1001935 (2016). https://doi.org/10.1371/journal.pmed.1001935

19. Allington, D., Duffy, B., Wessely, S., Dhavan, N., Rubin, J.: Health-protective behavior, social media usage and conspiracy belief during the COVID-19 public health emergency. Psychol. Med., 1–7 (2020). https://doi.org/10.1017/s003329172000224x

20. Gu, H., et al.: Importance of internet surveillance in public health emergency control and prevention: evidence from a digital epidemiologic study during avian influenza a H7N9 outbreaks. J. Med. Internet Res. **16**(1), e20 (2020). https://doi.org/10.2196/jmir.2911

21. Simon, T., Goldberg, A., Adini, B.: Socializing in emergencies - a review of the use of social media in emergency situations. Int. J. Inf. Manage. **35**, 609–619 (2015). https://doi.org/10.1016/j.ijinfomgt.2015.07.001

22. Lin, L., Jung, M., McCloud, R.F., Viswanath, K.: Media use and communication inequalities in a public health emergency a case study of 2009–2010 pandemic influenza a virus subtype H1N1. Public Health Rep. **129** (6-suppl4), 49–60 (2014). https://doi.org/10.1177/003335491 41296s408

23. Hu, H., et al.: Information dissemination of public health emergency on social networks and intelligent computation. Comput. Intell. Neurosci. **2015** (2015). https://doi.org/10.1155/2015/181038

24. Zheng, Y.: Information culture and development: Chinese experience of E-Health. In: Proceedings of the 38th Annual Hawaii International Conference on System Sciences, Big Island, HI, USA, p. 153a (2005). https://doi.org/10.1109/hicss.2005.315

25. Heeks, R., Zheng, Y.: Conceptualising information culture in developing countries. IDPM Development Informatics Working Papers, No. 34. http://www.seed.manchester.ac.uk/sub jects/idpm/research/publications/wp/di/di-wp34/

26. Lloyd, A.: Building information resilience: how do resettling refugees connect with health information in regional landscapes—Implications for health literacy. Aust. Acad. Res. Libr. **45**(1), 48–66 (2014). https://doi.org/10.1080/00048623.2014.884916

27. Hicks, A., Lloyd, A.: It takes a community to build a framework: Information literacy within intercultural settings. J. Inf. Sci. **42**(3), 334–343 (2016). https://doi.org/10.1177/016555151 6630219

28. Berkman, N.D., Davis, T.C., McCormack, L.: Health literacy: what is it? J. Health Commun. **15**(S2), 9–19 (2010). https://doi.org/10.1080/10810730.2010.499985

29. Niemelä, R., Ek, S., Eriksson-Backa, K., Houtari, M.L.: A screening tool for assessing everyday health information literacy. Libri **62**, 125–134 (2012). https://doi.org/10.1515/libri-2012-0009

30. Berkman, N.D., et al.: Health literacy interventions and outcomes: an updated systematic review. Evid. Rep. Technol. Assess. (Full Rep.) **199**(1), 941 (2011)

31. Shipman, J.P., Kurtz-Rossi, S., Funk, C.J.: The health information literacy research project. J. Med. Libr. Assoc. JMLA **97**(4), 293–301 (2009). https://doi.org/10.3163/1536-5050.97.4.014

32. Paakkari, L., Okan, O.: COVID-19: health literacy is an underestimated problem. Lancet Public Health **5**(5), e249–e250 (2020). https://doi.org/10.1016/S2468-2667(20)30086-4

33. Foscarini, F., Jeurgens, C., Lian, Z., Oliver, G.: Continuities and discontinuities: using historical information culture for insight into the sustainability of innovations. In: Sundqvist, A., Berget, G., Nolin, J., Skjerdingstad, K.I. (eds.) iConference 2020. LNCS, vol. 12051, pp. 847–859. Springer, Cham (2020). https://doi.org/10.1007/978-3-030-43687-2_71

34. Giddens, A.: The Constitution of Society: Outline of the Theory of Structuration. University of California Press, California (1984)
35. Liu, S.T., et al.: Research on the ways of the public access to scientific knowledge on COVID-19 and the influence factors. Public Commun. Sci. Technol. (3), 4–8 (2020). https://doi.org/10.16607/j.cnki.1674-6708.2020.05.004
36. Wang, J., Gao, W.J., Chen, M.Q., Ying, X.P., Tan, X.Y., Liu, X.L.: Investigation report on the social psychology during the outbreak of COVID-19. Governance **2**, 55–64 (2020). https://doi.org/10.16619/j.cnki.cn10-1264/d.2020.z1.014
37. Zhao, J.X., Fu, C.Z., Meng, T.G.: Digital government application, information acquisition and government trust during sudden public crisis. J. Xi'an Jiaotong Univ. (Soc. Sci.) **40**(4), 12–22 (2020). https://doi.org/10.15896/j.xjtuskxb.202004002
38. Fei, X.T.: From the Soil: The Foundations of Chinese Society. People Press, Beijing (2008)
39. Yao, H.W., Shi, Q., Li, Y.H.: The current status of health literacy in China. Population Res. **40**(2), 88–97 (2016)
40. Xu, Y.: Nearly ten thousand of questionnaires show that the health literacy of primary and secondary school students in the first-tier city needs to be enhanced. Sch. Adm. **4**, 43–45 (2020)
41. Parliament of Australia: The Australian system of government. https://www.aph.gov.au/About_Parliament/House_of_Representatives/Powers_practice_and_procedure/00_-_Infosheets/Infosheet_20_-_The_Australian_system_of_government. Accessed 20 Aug 2020
42. Grattan Institute: Australia's COVID-19 response: the story so far. https://grattan.edu.au/news/australias-covid-19-response-the-story-so-far/. Accessed 20 Aug 2020
43. ABC News: Victorian hotel inquiry examines errors that could have caused 'every case' now in the state. https://www.abc.net.au/news/2020-07-20/victoria-coronavirus-hotel-quarantine-inquiry-day-1-in-melbourne/12471916. Accessed 20 Aug 2020
44. Taylor, J.: How a trust breakdown left Melbourne's minority communities hardest hit by Covid second wave. https://www.theguardian.com/australia-news/2020/aug/30/how-a-breakdown-of-trust-left-melbournes-ethnic-communities-hardest-hit-by-covid-second-wave?CMP=Share_iOSApp_Other. Accessed 21 Aug 2020
45. ABC News: As Melbourne moves to stage 4, how do its coronavirus restrictions compare to the world's toughest lockdowns? https://www.abc.net.au/news/2020-08-05/melbourne-stage-4-coronavirus-restrictions-vs-world/12518376. Accessed 21 Aug 2020
46. Bundy, A. (ed.): Australian and New Zealand Information Literacy Framework: Principles, Standards and Practice, 2nd edn. Australian and New Zealand Institute for Information Literacy, Adelaide (2004)
47. Migrant and Refugee Women's Health Partnership: enhancing health literacy strategies in the settlement of migrant and refugee women. https://culturaldiversityhealth.org.au/wp-content/uploads/2018/06/Enhancing-health-literacy-strategies-in-the-settlement-of-migrant-and-refugee-women-Feb-2018.pdf. Accessed 16 Aug 2020
48. Goodall, K., Ward, P., Newman, L.: Use of information and communication technology to provide health information: what do older migrants know, and what do they need to know? Qual. Prim. care **18**(1), 27–32 (2010)
49. Dalzell, S.: Government coronavirus messages left 'nonsensical' after being translated into other languages. https://www.abc.net.au/news/2020-08-13/coronavirus-messages-translated-to-nonsense-in-other-languages/12550520. Accessed 22 Aug 2020
50. Sørensen, K., Maindal, H.T., Heijmans, M., Rademakers, J.: Work in progress: a report on health literacy in Denmark and the Netherlands. Stud. Health Technol. Inform. **269**, 202–211 (2020). https://doi.org/10.3233/SHTI200033
51. Van Deursen, A.J.: Digital inequality during a pandemic: quantitative study of differences in COVID-19–related internet uses and outcomes among the general population. J. Med. Internet Res. **22**(8), e20073 (2020). https://doi.org/10.2196/20073

52. Te Poel, F., Linn, A., Baumgartner, S., Van Dijk, L., Smit, E.: Mediagebruik en infor-matiebehoeften van Nederlanders tijdens de Covid-19 crisis. Amsterdam Center for Health Communication. University of Amsterdam (2020)
53. Meier, K., Glatz, T., Guijt, M.C., Piccininni, M., van der Meulen, M., Atmar, K., et al.: Public perspectives on protective measures during the COVID-19 pandemic in the Netherlands, Germany and Italy: a survey study. PLoS One **15**(8), e0236917 (2020). https://doi.org/10. 1371/journal
54. Helgason, D., et al.: Beating the odds with systematic individualized care: nationwide prospec-tive follow-up of all patients with COVID-19 in Iceland. J. Intern. Med. (2020). https://doi. org/10.1111/joim.13135
55. Gudbjartsson, D.F., et al.: Spread of SARS-CoV-2 in the Icelandic population. New Engl. J. Med. **382**, 2302–2315 (2020). https://doi.org/10.1056/nejmoa2006100
56. Ministry of Education, Science and Culture: The Icelandic national curriculum guide for com-pulsory schools. https://www.stjornarradid.is/media/menntamalaraduneyti-media/media/rit ogskyrslur/adskr_grsk_ens_2012.pdf. Accessed 01 Sep 2020
57. Eurostat: Digital economy and society statistics – Households and individuals. European Commission. https://www.ec.europa.eu/eurostat/publications/all-publications. Accessed 02 Sep 2020
58. Social Science Research Institute. [Online panel survey on COVID-19: attitudes, conse-quences and concerns.] Unpublished raw data (2020)

Locating Embodied Forms of Urban Wayfinding: An Exploration

Rebecca Noone[✉]

University of Toronto, Toronto, Canada
rebecca.noone@utoronto.ca

Abstract. The following short paper looks at the embodied information practice of urban wayfinding in the context of pervasive locative media and mobile mapping technology. The author asks: what informational cues are encoded in the urban landscape and activated through embodied practices of wayfinding? To explore this question of street-level wayfinding, the author utilizes the exploratory method of arts-based research, focusing on the act of giving directions, both spoken and drawn, and developing the research in four unique cities: Amsterdam, London, New York, and Toronto. Analysis of the data uses visual grounded theory and situational analysis. Based on the findings, the author classifies three types of urban forms that helped guide navigation during these wayfinding encounters: pathways, transmitters, and markings. In unpacking the variants within these registers of spatial sense-making, the author identifies informational elements of the city present in its material and built environment but also in its social and tacit forms. The paper offers a framework to look at the multiplicities of information, structured and embodied, that guide wayfinding, situated beyond (but co-existent with) mobile mapping tools.

Keywords: Urban wayfinding · Embodied information practices · Arts-based methods

1 Introduction

The contemporary city is an information-rich environment where people, infrastructures, and technologies are intertwined. The city's informational configurations can be activated when navigating the city through decisions such as "taking a left" before the crosswalk or "turning right" at the park. Additionally, the city is entangled with personal shortcuts and "desire lines" that comprise local or individual navigation strategies [1]. The urban environment is layered with orientating cues and commands that animate the process of getting from A to B, cues and commands that are navigated through embodied information practices.

In the contemporary city, wayfinding is also informed by mobile mapping tools like Google Maps. The mobile map offers location awareness and real-time feedback providing a suite of information such as expected arrival times and anticipated areas of dely. The information practice of wayfinding in this regard is part of a broader technological

© Springer Nature Switzerland AG 2021
K. Toeppe et al. (Eds.): iConference 2021, LNCS 12645, pp. 635–644, 2021.
https://doi.org/10.1007/978-3-030-71292-1_49

shift towards "algorithmic culture" in which everyday wayfinding is activated by data-points to be computationally evaluated and shared [2]. However, informational networks have long been part of urban design, entangling information flows, social processes, and infrastructural arrangements [3, 4]. These urban forms are woven into the processes and practices of navigating the city. In previous papers, I have looked at the orientations towards the use of Google Maps [5]. In this paper I look at how the city activated as a site of information in the process of wayfinding beyond the digital map interface and the affordances of mobile mapping. As a starting point to this question, this paper looks at wayfinding in urban design and information science, and then connects these precedents to embodied information practice theory. These sensitizing literatures ground an exploratory and creative research project that looks at urban-wayfinding at street-level. This paper positions wayfinding as both a structured and an embodied information practice [6, 7] that is situated and sensed through the city's visible and invisible forms. The paper identifies forms and practices of wayfinding otherwise absented from computational mapping tools and establishes a preliminary framework by which to assesses the complexities of urban wayfinding as a type of information literacy [2].

2 Background

In the early 1960s, urban planner Kevin Lynch [8] popularized the term "wayfinding" as a specifically urban phenomenon. Lynch hypothesized that a person's ability to picture their city and visualize their movement through the city was a sign of successful urban planning. For Lynch, wayfinding is the act of reading and evaluating the environmental context, understanding the spatial characteristics of the setting, taking in the information displayed on signs, and assessing different options for moving through a space to a destination.

Wayfinding in information science research has applied urban design models of wayfinding to navigate the library's interior space [9–11]. Lauren Mandel [10, 11] has made significant contributions to wayfinding research in the context of the library to establish popular means by which patrons move through the library and the use of signage systems and spatial layout to find their way. Building out from Mandel's work, I look at wayfinding in relation to the dynamic environment of the city streets.

Urban wayfinding is an embodied information practice since information is negotiated through the body in relation to others and responsive to the affordances of the landscape and the tools at hand [12, 13]. Annemaree Lloyd's [4, 6, 14] framing of intuited and embodied information practices is an important sensitizing starting point for this research since it opens up the wayfinding experience to being directed beyond signage but also the tacit and affective elements of the urban experience that characterize urban life. Writing about mediated urban experiences, both Shannon Mattern [4] and Malcolm McCullough [15] situate attention within the city as responding to the "ambient" sensorial and informational infrastructures in the city that are both material and immaterial. Mattern labels these forms the city's "proto-algorithms" since they often predate or are absent from computational networking tools like mobile maps. Urban wayfinding is enacted by way of a city's design as well as sensed through embodied experience. How do we identify these informational cues as a way to shed light on wayfinding as an individual information practice?

3   Research Design

To focus my qualitative investigation of street-level wayfinding as an embodied information practice, I looked at how people give and share directions in the age of mobile maps. To be able to locate the moment that people give directions, I look to precedents in the arts [16] and social science research [8, 17] that have stopped passers-by on street corners and asked for direction. I characterize my use of these methods as arts-based [18, 19] since they incorporate modes of drawing and performance. Arts-based research is an experimental and processual approach to research that starts from a clearly established problem, weaving together theory and practice through an iterative process of generating and reflecting. Arts-based research is an emerging method in information science and a suitable means to explore sensorial and embodied information practices.

In the autumn of 2017 and the summer of 2018 I took to the streets of New York, London, Amsterdam, and Toronto, asking the city's inhabitants for directions. I selected these four cities for their majority English-speaking/English-conversant population and diverse street layouts. I walked through the central areas of these cities and approached passers-by for directions to nearby sites. I started by asking if they lived in the city as a means to ensure "local" population. I then requested they draw these directions with a piece of paper and a pen I had in tow. The act of asking for directions elicited multiple iterations of drawing of city streets and activated a look into spontaneous wayfinding strategies. The acts of sketching, diagraming, writing and illustrating – what I group together under the banner of "drawing" – mark an ineffable moment of situating, locating, and wayfinding. I did hundreds of times. In total I collected 220 drawings, 220 fieldnotes, and 20 interviews from all four cities combined. Each encounter was distinct.

Following collection, I used visual grounded theory [20] and situational analysis [21] to assess the data from the interdisciplinary theoretical perspectives of embodied information practices and urban studies. Findings show the complexity of wayfinding, negotiated through the tacit and material forms of technological interventions, urban configurations, and information affects. For this paper, I focus on the moment the city was used.

4   Findings: Wayfinding and the Informational City

When analyzing the empirical data, I noted when and how the city's forms and processes appeared in the directions and which ones made the city legible in the practice of giving directions. I observed three registers of city forms represented in the fieldnotes, drawings, and interview, which I labelled pathways, transmitters, and markings.

1. Pathways: the terrain on which routes are inscribed or performed:

    a. The pathways reflected in the built environment, such as streets, waterways, public squares
    b. The pathways reflected in the social space, such as the flows of people and the linguistic constructions of "going up" or "heading down"

2. Transmitters: the infrastructures (intended & relational) that guide movement:

   a. The transmitters rendered through formalized urban systems, such as public transit or public street maps and signage

   b. The transmitters rendered through informal public networks, such asking other people.

3. Markings: the discreet elements of the city that orient:

   a. The markings projected in a city's construction, such as landmarks

   b. The markings projected in the qualitative sense of place attached to sites

These registrars reflect a complex set of urban legibilities that bring together the intentionally designed, the ad-hoc, and the latent knowledges enacted during the wayfinding encounters across the four cities.

4.1 Pathways

Pathways are central to moving through the city [8]. Some pathways are material forms such as roadways, waterways, and public squares and some pathways are formed discursively and metaphorically through the patterns of directional commands and strategies that gave shape to "invisible" pathways of the city (see Fig. 1).

In North American cities, roadways were the most popular material pathway. The data reveals the dominance of streets and street names as a way to move around Toronto and New York, both grid-ironed cities. In both Toronto and New York 96% of encounters were oriented by a specific street name. By contrast, in London 47% of encounters made reference to specific street names and in Amsterdam only 33%. Instead in both cities, streets emerged as a relational, or qualitative experience. Rather than naming a street, a street might be referred to as the "busy street" as a way to differentiate it from another street.

Beyond the prescribed pathways of streets, waterways, and public squares, the data revealed attentions towards an ambient flow as a means to guide movement through the city. To code for this, I looked for the mention of "flow" "follow" and "along" in the dataset. My understanding of flow, as I saw it in the data, was a type of spontaneous or unplanned action: the unmanageable and the unpredictable types of flow that were assumed to exist when giving directions. Flow was based on following the movement of people, following the path of objects such as trams, or going along with an unfixed path. Discursive pathways were shaped through the language given to navigation either spoken or offered in text based commands. In some cases I was told to "go up" or "head down." In other cases, I was told to "go straight" when the route most definitely curved. Pathways shape how routes from A to B are experienced.

Attentions to the pathways and the ambient intelligences of the pathways vary across the four cities. In some encounters, pathways acted as guides, that mark the lines to walk along, where to turn, how far to go. Determining how to use a pathway was dependent upon the attention to the path as well as the ambient intelligences of how to pay attention

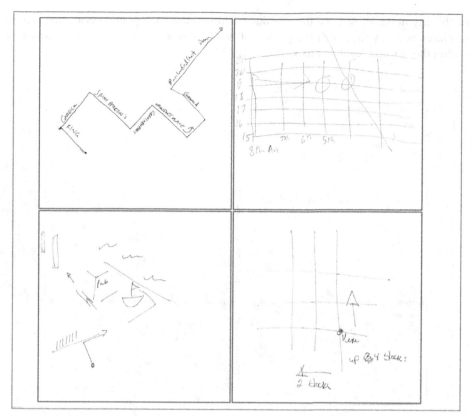

Fig. 1. Sample of directional drawings from the wayfinding encounter demonstrating pathways both material and tacit

to the path. These were not only discursive distinctions but a social and culturally-specific topography that generated a sense of city experience. The cultural specificity of pathways suggests divergence from the singular universalizing language of mobile digital maps such as Google Maps in its visual and textual descriptions of space.

4.2 Transmitters

The second register of the city is what I have called the transmitters (see Fig. 2). Transmitters are the infrastructures, intended and imagined, that guide movement through the city. The transmitters inform attentions as well as carry with them ambient intelligences of movement of how to get around a city. In the encounters, infrastructures were called upon to anchor the directions and activate a wayfinding strategy generating a legibility of space. Public transportation and its infrastructures, be that tram lines or subway maps, are more than simply means of transportation but are also forms that situate, spatialize, and orient through a city [17]. They are part of a strategy of moving through the city, providing a link from place to place but also engendering a specific type of information of the city in the knowledge they produce. These are the integrated networked infrastructures of a city that, with the growth of urban planning, forged a type of cohesion within the city and regulated its systems [22, 23].

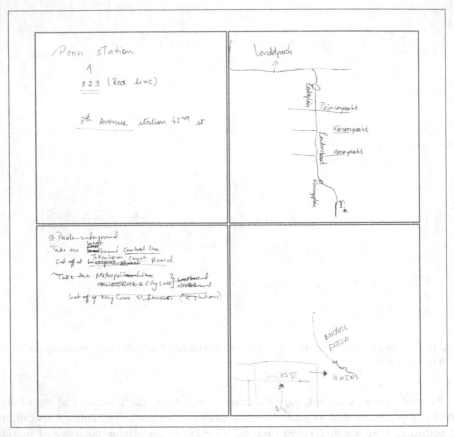

Fig. 2. Sample of directional drawing from the wayfinding encounter demonstrating transmitters, both material and tacit

Along with the formalized information transmitters of the city, informal and tacit information infrastructures became legible in these moments. The information infrastructures seemed to reference a type of ambient knowledge of being able to "ask someone else" once I was "closer" to my destination. Here informants would provide incomplete directions, often trailing off into uncertainty. It may be that they second-guessed the exact turn I was to make, or they were unsure of the length of a walk from an orientation point. As noted previously in this section, some informants would defer to the type of expertise of other people – often the transit workers, the taxi drivers, or even employees of a nearby coffee shop – as a strategy of wayfinding. The idea of the transmitter took on a mix of the informal and the assumptive – the assumption that people close to the site would know more about it; or, the assumption that those who were professionally suited to provide directions. How each type of transmitter functions is not so straightforward, or easily predicted. Rather, they overlap and intersect as built and ephemeral forms of sensemaking in the city.

4.3 Markings

Markings, the final register, were the discreet elements of the city that assumed the role of guiding points based on their presence and distinctiveness (see Fig. 3). Markings, in part, were the perceptible or orienting forms of the city. They both emerged from the built environment, such as notable tourist attractions and recognizable commercial sites, as well as extended to a broader definition, taking into account McCollough's [15] considerations of the ambient, as part of the "intrinsic (environmental) information" attached to the surroundings that is both specific and situated.

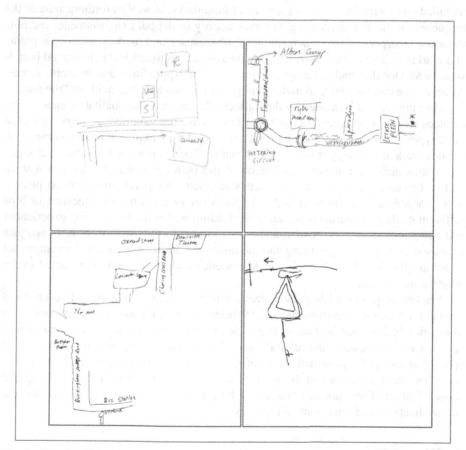

Fig. 3. Sample of directional drawing from the wayfinding encounter demonstrating markings, both material and tacit

Landmarks, according to Lynch, are the external reference points in wayfinding that are identified based on prominence in their spatial location, be that as a clear form, distinct from their surroundings [8]. In other words, they stand out from their context. What I found during my encounters was that landmarks and commercial sites often distinguished themselves from other forms of the built environment by way of architectural features or identifiable branding. Markings were also culturally specific references to a contextual and learned understanding of a city. Examples of distinctive landmarks are the CN Tower in Toronto, the Empire State Building in New York, the Weeping Tower in Amsterdam, or Big Ben in London. However, there were also the lesser known landmarks such as Paradiso concert venue in Amsterdam, the often-photographed Toronto sign outside of Toronto's city hall, the office tower of One Penn Place in New York, or the Savoy Hotel in London. There was of course overlap with the material forms of the built environment such as parks, squares, and bridges as function and landmark. I included sites such as Union Square in New York, Piccadilly Circus in London, Vondelpark in Amsterdam, or Nathan Phillip Square in Toronto in the category of landmark. I also included commercial sites in the category of landmarks, as well as further explored the frequency of the commercial site as a subcategory of the built environments and how these are incorporated into a perception of urban space and used as orientation points and markings. These sites emerged in the data set as multi-national commercial brands such as McDonalds, and its recognizable arches, the Apple Store and its iconic Apple. At times, the commercial landmarks were generic forms like "the mall" or "the pub."

Marking were also defined by their affects. These were the qualitative annotations of place tied up with perception and emotion. I have framed affective marking within three types of annotations: when informants asserted a qualitative annotation onto areas or sites, such as a "dodgy street," or "nice market," or a "favourite restaurant"; 2) when informants included a featural annotation of the built environment – such as a steep incline or many stairs; 3) when informants asserted a temporal annotation on place – such that a destination is perceived to be far away or close by. The question of how different qualitative markings socialize wayfinding within the intersecting experiences and constructions of race, gender, and class requires further investigation. In analysis I focused on the city's qualitative and the discursive forms used in the impromptu act of asking for directions that were made evident in what was said and enacted in the wayfinding moment.

Markings represented the personalized textures of the city, composed of material and immaterial forms of attentions that serve to orient, assure, and assert a punctuation or an affectation in the urban landscape. The choice of marking declared a personalization of space as well as speaks to the culturally specific landmarks – the particularized sense of space that disrupt the patterned senses of space – the scruffy triangles, the library with the lions, the long walks and the weaving fish hands that snake through an imagined sense of place. These are key markers of how to get from A to B based on discrete materializations and sensations of legibility.

5   Discussion

The three registers of pathways, transmitters, and markings and the multiple forms they take demonstrates how different types of attentions to space are activated through wayfinding. Through the registers of pathways, transmitters, and markings, this paper looks at how a city was made legible as a relation to situated actions of wayfinding. The forms that made the city legible were physical forms of the urban landscape but also ephemeral, affective, and, to return to Mattern, proto-algorithmic [4]. These modes of making one's way through a city are entangled in a city's material and social forms, encoded and decoded through the embodied information practice of wayfinding.

My study reflects the layers and gradations of material realities shaped by memory, attention and perception. Within the encounters, the ad hoc directions and spontaneous drawings represent more than a route but a sense of the city in which that moment reveals the urban contours that evade the digital map's algorithmic prediction. The study narrows in on wayfinding decisions that take place outside of negotiations with digital mapping interfaces but nevertheless occur contemporaneously to digital mapping tools. This framework offered by this paper helps information scholars and professionals better consider the manifold ways the city is operationalized at street level and provides a starting point to consider these practices in relation the information encoded within mobile digital maps. What forms of the city are absent in the mobile map's digital interface? Which embodied forms of wayfinding are indeterminate (and therefore cannot be operationalized) through the mobile map's data-driven infrastructures? Next steps of this research will be to assess the findings shared in this paper in relation to the "algorithmic culture" of digital maps and better understand what Lloyd calls "the epistemic views, practical usages and performative consequences" of algorithmic cultures in relation to "power, agency, reflexivity, and trust" [2].

References

1. Macfarlane, R.: The Old Ways a Journey on Foot. Penguin Press, New York (2012)
2. Lloyd, A.: Chasing Frankenstein's monster: Information literacy in the black box society. J. Documentation **75**(6), 1475–1485 (2019)
3. Barns, S.: Platform Urbanism: Negotiating Platform Ecosystems in Connected Cities. Springer, Singapore (2020)
4. Mattern, S.: Deep Mapping the Media City. University of Minnesota Press, Minnesota (2015)
5. Noone, R.: Navigating the Threshold of Information Spaces. In: Webb, J., Bedi, S. (eds.) Visualizing the Library: A Primer on Visual Research Methods in Library and Information Sciences, pp. 169–188. Facet Publishing, London (2020)
6. Lloyd, A.: Information literacy and literacies of information: a mid-range theory and model. J. Inf. Literacy **11**(1), 91–105 (2017)
7. Lloyd, A.: Researching fractured (information) landscapes: implications for library and information science researchers undertaking research with refugees and forced migration studies. J. Documentation **73**(1), 35–47 (2017)
8. Lynch, K.: The Image of the City. MIT Press, Cambridge (1960)
9. Björneborn, L.: Serendipity dimensions and users' information behaviour in the physical library interface. Inf. Res. **13**(4), 13–14 (2008)
10. Mandel, L.H.: Understanding and describing users' wayfinding behavior in public library facilities. J. Librarianship Inf. Sci. **50**(1), 23–33 (2018)
11. Mandel, L.H.: Finding their way: how public library users wayfind. Libr. Inf. Sci. Res. **35**(4), 264–271 (2013)
12. Savolainen, R.: Everyday life information seeking: approaching information seeking in the context of "way of life". Libr. Inf. Sci. Res. **17**(3), 259–294 (1995)

13. Lloyd, A., Olsson, M.: Being in place: embodied information practices. Inf. Res. (2017). http://informationr.net/ir/22-1/colis/colis1601.html
14. Lloyd, A.: Information literacy as a socially enacted practice. J. Documentation **68**(6), 772–783 (2012)
15. McCullough, M.: Ambient Commons: Attention in the Age of Embodied Information. MIT Press, Cambridge (2015)
16. Brouwn, S.: This Way Brouwn. [Collection of Drawings from Public Performances in Amsterdam]. MoMA, New York (1961)
17. Vertesi, J.: Mind the Gap: The London Underground Map and Users' Representations of Urban Space. Soc. Stud. Sci. **38**(1), 7 (2008)
18. Leavy, P.: Method Meets Art: Arts-Based Research Practice, 2nd edn. The Guilford Press, New York (2015)
19. Loveless, N.: How to Make Art at the End of the World: A Manifesto for Research-Creation. Duke University Press, Durham (2019)
20. Konecki, K. T.: Visual images and grounded theory methodology. In: Bryant, A., Charmaz, K. (eds.) The SAGE Handbook of Current Developments in Grounded Theory, pp. 352–373. SAGE Publications, Thousand Oaks (2019)
21. Clarke, A.E.: Situational Analysis: Grounded Theory After the Postmodern Turn. SAGE Publications, Thousand Oaks (2005)
22. Graham, S., Marvin, S.: Splintering Urbanism: Networked Infrastructures, Technological Mobilities and the Urban Condition. Routledge, New York (2001)
23. Thrift, N.J.: Spatial Formations. SAGE Publications, Thousand Oaks (1996)

Author Index

Aguirre, Alyssa I-47
Ahmed, Amira II-85
Ainiwaer, Abidan I-211
Albahlal, Bader I-421
Allen, Summer II-260
An, Xin I-199
Annabi, Hala I-603
Aritajati, Chulakorn I-248

Babu, Rakesh II-466
Bogers, Toine I-268
Brill, Rachel II-127
Bu, Yi I-137
Buchanan, George I-346
Burke, Jacob I-229

Caliandro, Alessandro I-396
Carbone, Kathy II-285
Carter, Daniel I-146, II-274
Challa, Bezawit II-319
Chen, Baitong I-137
Chen, Yi II-251, II-413
Chiu, Jeong-Yeou II-167
Choi, Kahyun I-68
Chu, Samuel Kai Wah I-575
Clarke, Cooper T. II-308
Copeland, Andrea II-441
Cummings, Brenna I-24

Dam, Tammy II-319
Deng, Sanhong I-502
Ding, Ying I-3, I-14, I-112, I-137, I-183
Dirks, Lisa G. II-394
Donnay, Karsten I-514, II-156
Douglas, Jennifer II-301
Duester, Emma II-327

Ebeid, Islam Akef I-112
Ekpenyong, Alasdair I-435

Fearn, Carolyn I-165
Feng, Zeyu I-490
Fenlon, Katrina II-308
Fergencs, Tamás I-328

Ferwerda, Bruce I-364
Fichman, Pnina II-127
Fleischmann, Kenneth R. I-24, II-384
Flynn, Olivia A. I-377
Foscarini, Fiorella I-618
Frings-Hessami, Viviane I-541
Fu, Yaming II-195

Gao, Shuang I-490
Garwood, Deborah A. II-348
Gilliland, Anne J. II-285
Gipp, Bela I-514, II-156, II-215
Gleason, Jacob I-313
Gorichanaz, Tim II-75
Graus, Mark P. I-364
Greenberg, Sherri I-24

Hamborg, Felix I-514, II-156, II-215
Han, Ruohua II-339
Handcock, Rebecca N. II-431
Hao, Liyuan I-199
Haraldsdottir, Ragna Kemp I-618
Hassan, Majdi I-112
He, Chaocheng I-190
He, Daqing I-47, I-446
He, Zhe II-18
Hilsabeck, Robin C. I-47
Ho, Tzu-Yi I-457
Hoffman, Kelly M. II-308
Holstrom, Chris II-404
Hong, Seoyeon I-287
Hosking, Richard II-431
Hu, Xiao I-551, II-493
Hua, Vivian I-603
Huang, Chun-Kai (Karl) II-431
Hussain, Shah II-99

Ishita, Emi II-475
Izumi, Hinako II-114

Jaiswal, Ajay I-183
Jeong, Eunmi (Ellie) II-361
Jeurgens, Charles I-618
Jiang, Tianji II-484

Jiang, Weiwei   I-3
Jiang, Yuwei   II-37
Johnson, Frances   II-85
Joho, Hideo   II-48

Kalantari, Niloofar   I-301
Kim, Soo Hyeon   II-441
Kitzie, Vanessa L.   II-3
Kodama, Mei   II-475
Koizumi, Masanori   II-458
Korsunska, Ania   II-374
Koya, Kushwanth   I-165
Kröber, Cindy   II-176

Langberg Schmidt, Amalie   I-268
Lee, Hyun Seung   II-466
Lee, Jin Ha   I-562
Lee, Kung Jin   I-562
Lee, Min Kyung   II-384
Lee, Myeong   II-319
Lee, Shum Yi Cameron   I-575
Lee, Tae Hee   II-466
Lemieux, Victoria L.   I-587
Lewis, Antonina   II-285
Li, Fanjie   I-551
Li, Jing   II-99
Li, Kai   I-446
Li, Lan   I-24
Li, Ling   I-199
Li, Linqi   II-484
Li, Si   II-251
Li, Xin   I-14
Li, Yueyan   I-502
Lian, Zhiying   I-618
Liang, Zhentao   I-97
Lin, Chang-Huei   II-167
Liu, Fei   I-97
Liu, Meijun   I-183
Liu, Ruilun   II-493
Lookingbill, Valerie   II-3
Lu, Kun   I-97
Lu, Yu   II-18
Lundquist, Nathaniel   I-313
Luo, Xiao   II-18
Luo, Zhimeng   I-47
Lv, Siyu   I-211

Ma, Feicheng   I-14
Ma, Linqing   II-339
Ma, Rongqian   I-446

Ma, Zexin   I-313
Ma, Ziqiao   II-37
Mahapasuthanon, Pattiya   I-301
Mahony, Simon   II-195
Mani, Nandita S.   I-124
Mao, Jin   I-97
Mariakakis, Alex   I-229
Markazi, Daniela M.   I-33, I-39
Matsubara, Masaki   II-114
McKay, Dana   I-346
McKemmish, Sue   II-285
McMenemy, David   II-207
Meier, Florian   I-268, I-328
Meng, Na   I-575
Min, Katherine   II-18
Ming, Junren   II-99
Montgomery, Lucy   II-431
Moore, Jenny C.   II-260
Morishima, Atsuyuki   II-114
Motti, Vivian Genaro   I-301
Murugadass, Abinav   I-377

Na, Jin-Cheon   I-411
Neylon, Cameron   II-431
Ng, Jeremy Tzi-Dong   I-551, II-493
Ng, Lauren   I-603
Noone, Rebecca   I-635

Oliver, Gillian   I-618
Ou, Guiyan   I-190
Ouaknine, Yohanan   II-66
Ozaygen, Alkim   II-431

Palmer, Chelsea K.   I-587
Parulian, Nikolaus Nova   I-478
Peterson, Mark Edwin   II-319
Poole, Alex H.   I-529, II-348

Qin, Kai   I-3

Rahmi, Rahmi   II-48
Rathnayake, Chamil   I-396
Rich, Kate   II-384
Robinson, Priscilla   II-319
Roelofs, Aniek   II-431
Rohman, Abdul   II-141
Rolan, Gregory   II-285
Romero-Masters, Philip   II-225
Roper, Jack   I-112

Rosson, Mary Beth   I-248
Rowell, Chris   I-587
Rudnitckaia, Lada   II-215
Ryu, Hyeyoung   I-287

Sanfilippo, Madelyn Rose   II-235
Sato, Itsumi   I-154
Seal, Abhik   I-112
Sebyakin, Andrey   I-78
Shang, Wenyi   I-469
Shaw, Miranda   II-308
Shenefiel, Chris   I-24
Shiroma, Kristina   II-384
Shiue, Hilary Szu Yin   II-308
Shvartzshnaider, Yan   II-235
Slota, Stephen C.   I-24
Soloviev, Vladimir   I-78
Spinde, Timo   II-215
Stratton, Caroline   II-274
Suzuki, Issei   II-458

Takaku, Masao   I-154
Tang, Jian   II-361
Tang, Xuli   I-14
Tari, Mina   I-603
Taylor, Medina   I-313
Tennis, Joseph T.   II-404
Thomas, Christy   II-260
Tomiura, Yoichi   II-475

Underwood, Ted   I-469

Vera, A. Nick   II-3
Verma, Nitin   I-24, II-384

Wagner, Travis L.   II-3
Walters, Kristin   I-33, I-39
Wang, Hao   I-502
Wang, Jun   I-457
Wang, Lin   II-37
Wang, Lingling   I-490

Wang, Ning   I-618
Wang, Shengang   II-413, II-466
Wang, Zhendong   I-47
Wanyan, Tingyi   I-112
Watanabe, Chiemi   II-114
Watanabe, Yukiko   II-475
Wilson, Katie   II-431
Wobbrock, Jacob O.   I-229
Worthey, Glen   I-478
Wu, Dan   I-211
Wu, Jiang   I-190
Wu, Jie   II-99

Xiao, Lianjie   I-3
Xiao, Lu   I-377
Xiao, Zhiping   I-551
Xie, Bo   I-47, II-384
Xie, Iris   II-466
Xu, Shuo   I-199
Xu, Yidan   I-490

Yan, Chengxi   I-457
Yang, Guancan   I-199, I-490
Yang, Li   I-411, II-413
Yip, Jason C.   I-562
Yu, Fei   I-124
Yu, Jianfei   I-411
Yu, Qi   I-137

Zhang, Chengzhi   I-411
Zhang, Chenyang   I-211
Zhang, Huiwen   I-346
Zhang, Mingrui "Ray"   I-229
Zhang, Ping   II-361
Zhang, Zhan   II-18
Zhao, He   II-99
Zhu, Xiaohua   II-260
Zhukova, Anastasia   I-514
Zolotaryuk, Anatoly   I-78
Zou, Ning   I-47
Zytko, Douglas   I-313